Ian Allan abc

# MILITARY AIRCRAFT MARKINGS 2000

Peter R. March &
Howard J. Curtis

# Contents

Introduction 5
Acknowledgements 6
Abbreviations 7
A Guide to the Location of Operational Bases in the UK 10
British Military Aircraft Serials 12
British Military Aircraft Markings 13
Civil Registered Aircraft in UK Military Service 101
RAF Maintenance/Support Command Cross Reference 105
RN Landing Platform and Shore Station code-letters 109
Ships' Numeric Code-Deck Letters Analysis 111
RN Code-Squadron-Base-Aircraft Cross-check 111
Historic Aircraft in Overseas Markings 112
Irish Military Aircraft Markings 128
Overseas Military Aircraft Markings 129
US Military Aircraft Markings 172
UK-based USAF/US Navy Aircraft 172
European-based USAF Aircraft 174
European-based US Navy/Army Aircraft 176
US-based USAF Aircraft 180
US based USN/USMC Aircraft 199
US based US Coast Guard Aircraft 202
US Government Aircraft 202
Military Aviation Sites on the Internet 203

*Photographs by Peter R. March (PRM) unless otherwise credited*

This twenty-first edition published 2000

ISBN 0 7110 2708 0



Published by Ian Allan Publishing

an imprint of Ian Allan Publishing Ltd,
Terminal House, Shepperton, Surrey TW17 8AS.

Printed by Ian Allan Printing Ltd,
Riverdene Business Park, Hersham, Surrey KT12 4RG

Code: 0003/F2

*Front cover:* Hawk T1A of No 100 Sqn based at RAF Leeming. *BAe*

*Back cover:* Sadly this Harrier GR7 was destroyed in a crash at Surfleet, Lincs, on 9 July 1999. *RAF*

# Introduction

This twenty-first annual edition of *abc Military Aircraft Markings*, jointly edited by Peter R. March and Howard J. Curtis, lists in alphabetical and numerical order all of the aircraft that carry a United Kingdom military serial, and **which are based, or might be seen, in the UK**. It also includes airworthy and current RAF/RN/Army aircraft that are based permanently or temporarily overseas. The term ***aircraft*** used here covers powered, manned aeroplanes, helicopters, airships and gliders. Included are all the current Royal Air Force, Royal Navy, Army Air Corps, Defence Procurement Agency, Defence Evaluation & Research Agency, manufacturers' test aircraft and civilian-owned aircraft with military markings.

Aircraft withdrawn from operational use but which are retained in the UK for ground training purposes or otherwise preserved by the Services and in the numerous museums and collections are listed. The serials of some incomplete aircraft have been included, such as the cockpit sections of machines displayed by the RAF, aircraft used by airfield fire sections and for service battle damage repair training (BDRT), together with significant parts of aircraft held by preservation groups and societies. Where only part of the aircraft fuselage remains the abbreviation <ff> for front fuselage/cockpit section or <rf> for rear fuselage is shown after the type. Many of these aircraft are allocated, and sometimes wear, a secondary identity, such as an RAF Logistics Command 'M' maintenance number. These numbers are listed against those aircraft to which they have been allocated.

A serial 'missing' is either because it was never issued as it formed part of a 'black-out block' (a practice that has now ceased) or because the aircraft is written off, scrapped, sold abroad or allocated an alternative marking. Aircraft used as targets on MoD ranges to which access is restricted, and un-manned target drones, are omitted, as are UK military aircraft that have been permanently grounded and are based overseas and unlikely to return to Britain.

In the main, the serials listed are those markings presently displayed on the aircraft. Where an aircraft carries a false serial it is quoted in *italic type*. Very often these serials are carried by replicas, that are denoted by <R> after the type. The manufacturer and aircraft type are given, together with recent alternative, previous, secondary or civil identity shown in round brackets. Complete records of multiple previous identities are only included where space permits. The operating unit and its based location, along with any known unit and base code markings in square brackets, are given as accurately as possible. The unit markings are normally carried boldly on the sides of the fuselage or on the aircraft's fin. In the case of RAF and AAC machines currently in service, they are usually one or two letters or numbers, while the RN continues to use a well-established system of three-figure codes between 000 and 999 together with a fin letter code denoting the aircraft's operational base. RN squadrons, units and bases are allocated blocks of numbers from which individual aircraft codes are issued. To help identification of RN bases and landing platforms on ships, a list of tail-letter codes with their appropriate name, helicopter code number, ship pennant number and type of vessel, is included; as is a helicopter code number/ships' tail-letter code grid cross-reference.

Codes change, for example when aircraft move between units, and therefore the markings currently painted on a particular aircraft might not be those shown in this edition because of subsequent events. The implementation of the Government's continuing civilian contractorisation and the reductions in service manpower, again account for many of the changes in this new edition. Aircraft currently under manufacture or not yet delivered to the Service, such as the new GKN-Westland WAH-64D Apaches at Yeovil and the C-130J Hercules temporarily stored at Cambridge, most of which carry civil registrations, are listed under their allocated RAF serial. Those airframes which may not appear in the next edition because of sale, accident, etc, have their fates, where known, given in italic type in the *locations* column.

The Irish Army Air Corps fleet is listed, together with the serials of other overseas air arms whose aircraft might be seen visiting the UK from time to time. The serial numbers are as usually presented on the individual machine or as they are normally identified. Where possible, the aircraft's base and operating unit have been shown.

USAF, US Army and US Navy aircraft based in the UK and in Western Europe, and types that regularly visit the UK from the USA, are each listed in separate sections by aircraft type. The serial number actually displayed on the aircraft is shown in full, with additional Fiscal Year (FY) or full serial information also provided. Where appropriate, details of the operating wing, squadron allocation and base are added. The USAF is, like the RAF, in a continuing period of change, resulting in the adoption of new unit titles, squadron and equipment changes and the closure of bases. Only details that concern changes effected by January 2000 are shown.

Veteran and vintage aircraft which carry overseas military markings but which are based in the UK have been separately listed showing their principal means of identification. This has been extended in this edition with the addition of warbirds based on mainland Europe that are likely to be seen visiting the UK. The growing list of aircraft in government or military service, often under contract to private operating companies, that carry civil registrations has again been included, but in this edition at the end of the respective country.

With the use of the Internet now very well established as a rich source of information, the new section that was first added to the 1999 edition, listing a selection of military aviation 'world wide web' sites, has been further expanded and up dated this year. Although only a few of these provide details of aircraft serials and markings, they do give interesting insights into air arms and their operating units, aircraft, museums and a broad range of associated topics.

Information shown is believed to be correct at 31 January 2000, and significant changes can be monitored through the monthly 'Military Markings' column in *Aircraft Illustrated* and for Internet up-dates the 'Airnet' column.

# Acknowledgements

The compilers again wish to thank the many people who have taken trouble to send comments, criticism and other useful information following the publication of the previous editions of *abc Military Aircraft Markings*. In particular the following:

Bill Allen, Alexis Antonakis, John Bennett, Wolfgang Birmes, Roy Blewett, Iwan Bogels, Marco Borst/P-3 Orion Research Group, Mick Boulanger, Damien Burke, John Caie, Graham Causer, Andy Dewey, Bob Dunn, Ben Dunnell, Ray Fitton, H D Flaxman, Wal Gandy, Graham Gaff, Howard Gent, Tom Gibbons, Malcolm Johnson, Thomas Kaminski, Bob Kent, Andy Lewis, Iain Logan, Malcolm Lowe, Andy March, Dan March, Bernard Martin, Jeff Middleton, David Moore, Ian Munro, Terry Nation, Keith Piggott, Clive Pattle, Hans Rollink, Mark Russell, Terry Senior, Tony Smith, Kev Storer, Michael Teiten, Mervyn Thomas, John Waller, Frank Weilbo and Mark Young, along with the Mil-Spotters Forum mailing list.

The compilation has relied heavily on the publications of the following aviation groups and societies: *Air-Britain News* (Air-Britain), *Airfield Review* (Airfield Research Group), *Air Link* (Lincolnshire Aviation Society), *BAC News* (Bristol Aero Collection), *British Aviation Review* (British Aviation Research Group), East London Aviation Society, Friends of Leeming Aviation Group, *Irish Air Letter*, *Military Aviation Review* (MAP), *Osprey* (Solent Aviation Society), *RAF News*, *Scramble* (Dutch Aviation Society), St Athan Aviation Group, *Stansted Aviation News* (Stansted Aviation Society), *SWAG MAG* (South West Aviation Group), *Ulster Air Mail* (Ulster Aviation Society) and *Update* (British Aviation Preservation Council), *Warbirds Worldwide* and the Wolverhampton Aviation Group.

**PRM & HJC** **January 2000**

Recently restored Bristol Bulldog K-2227 is in the RAF Museum. *PRM*

# Abbreviations

| | |
|---|---|
| **AAC** | Army Air Corps |
| **AACS** | Airborne Air Control Squadron |
| **AAS** | Aeromedical Airlift Squadron |
| **ABS** | Air Base Squadron |
| **ACC** | Air Combat Command |
| **ACCGS** | Air Cadets Central Gliding School |
| **ACCS** | Airborne Command and Control Squadron |
| **ACW** | Airborne Control Wing |
| **AD&StA** | Aberdeen, Dundee & St Andrews |
| **AEF** | Air Experience Flight |
| **AESS** | Air Engineering & Survival School |
| **AEW** | Airborne Early Warning |
| **AF** | Arméflyget (Army Air Battalion) |
| **AFB** | Air Force Base |
| **AFD** | Air Fleet Department |
| **AFRC** | Air Force Reserve Command |
| **AFSC** | Air Force Systems Command |
| **AFSK** | Armeflygskolan (Army Flying School) |
| **AFWF** | Advanced Fixed Wing Flight |
| **AG** | Airlift Group |
| **AGA** | Academia General del Aire (General Air Academy) |
| **AkG** | Aufklärüngsgeschwader (Reconnaissance Wing) |
| **AMC** | Air Mobility Command |
| **AMD-BA** | Avions Marcel Dassault-Breguet Aviation |
| **AMF** | Aircraft Maintenance Flight |
| **AMG** | Aircraft Maintenance Group |
| **AMIF** | Aircraft Maintenance Instruction Flight |
| **AMS** | Air Movements School |
| **AMW** | Air Mobility Wing |
| **ANG** | Air National Guard |
| **APS** | Aircraft Preservation Society |
| **ARS** | Air Refuelling Squadron |
| **ARW** | Air Refuelling Wing |
| **ARWS** | Advanced Rotary Wing Squadron |
| **AS** | Airlift Squadron/Air Squadron |
| **ASCW** | Airborne Surveillance Control Wing |
| **ASF** | Aircraft Servicing Flight |
| **AS&RU** | Aircraft Salvage and Repair Unit |
| **ATC** | Air Training Corps |
| **ATCC** | Air Traffic Control Centre |
| **Avn** | Aviation |
| **Avn Co** | Aviation Company |
| **AW** | Airlift Wing/Armstrong Whitworth Aircraft |
| **AWC** | Air Warfare Centre |
| **BAC** | British Aircraft Corporation |
| **BAe** | British Aerospace PLC |
| **BAPC** | British Aviation Preservation Council |
| **BATUS** | British Army Training Unit Suffield |
| **BBMF** | Battle of Britain Memorial Flight |
| **BDRF** | Battle Damage Repair Flight |
| **BDRT** | Battle Damage Repair Training |
| **Be** | Beech |
| **Bf** | Bayerische Flugzeugwerke |
| **BFWF** | Basic Fixed Wing Flight |
| **BG** | Bomber Group |
| **BGA** | British Gliding & Soaring Association |
| ***bk*** | black (squadron colours and markings) |
| ***bl*** | blue (squadron colours and markings) |
| **BNFL** | British Nuclear Fuels Ltd |
| **BnHATk** | Helicopter Attack Battalion |
| **BnHLn** | Liaison Battalion |
| **BP** | Boulton & Paul |
| ***br*** | brown (squadron colours and markings) |
| **BS** | Bomber Squadron |
| **B-V** | Boeing-Vertol |
| **BW** | Bomber Wing |
| **CAC** | Commonwealth Aircraft Corporation |
| **CAM** | College of Aviation Medicine |
| **CARG** | Cotswold Aircraft Restoration Group |
| **CASA** | Construcciones Aeronautics SA |
| **Cav** | Cavalry |
| **CC** | County Council |
| **CCF** | Combined Cadet Force/Canadian Car & Foundry Company |
| **CDE** | Chemical Defence Establishment |
| **CEAM** | Centre d'Expérimentation Aériennes Militaires (Military Air Experimental Centre) |
| **CEV** | Centre d'Essais en Vol (Flight Test Centre) |
| **CFS** | Central Flying School |
| **CGMF** | Central Glider Maintenance Flight |
| **CIFAS** | Centre d'Instruction des Forces Aériennes Stratégiques (Air Strategic Training Centre) |
| **CinC** | Commander in Chief |
| **CinCLANT** | Commander in Chief Atlantic |
| **CITac** | Centre d'Instruction Tactique (Tactical Training Centre) |
| **Co** | Company |
| **Comp** | Composite with |
| **CT** | College of Technology |
| **CTE** | Central Training Establishment |
| **CV** | Chance-Vought |
| **D-BA** | Daimler-Benz Aerospace |
| **D-BD** | Dassault-Breguet Dornier |
| **D&G** | Dumfries and Galloway |
| **DARA** | Defence Aviation Repair Agency |
| **DEODS** | Defence Explosives Ordnance Disposal School |
| **DERA** | Defence Evaluation and Research Agency |
| **Det** | Detachment |
| **DH** | de Havilland |
| **DHC** | de Havilland Canada |
| **DHFS** | Defence Helicopter Flying School |
| **dlt** | dopravni letka (Transport Squadron) |
| **DPA** | Defence Procurement Agency |
| **DTI** | Department of Trade and Industry |
| **EA** | Escadron Aérien (Air Squadron) |
| **EAC** | Ecole de l'Aviation de Chasse (Fighter Aviation School) |
| **EAP** | European Aircraft Project |
| **EAT** | Ecole de l'Aviation de Transport (Transport Aviation School) |
| **EC** | Escadre de Chasse (Fighter Wing) |
| **ECS** | Electronic Countermeasures Squadron |
| **EDA** | Escadre de Detection Aéroportée (Air Detection Wing) |
| **EdC** | Escadron de Convoyage |
| **EDCA** | Escadron de Détection et de Control Aéroportée (Airborne Detection & Control Sqn) |
| **EE** | English Electric/Escadrille Electronique |
| **EET** | Escadron Electronique Tactique (Tactical Electronics Flight) |
| **EH** | Escadron d'Helicoptères (Helicopter Flight) |
| **EHI** | European Helicopter Industries |
| **EL** | Escadre de Liaison (Liaison Wing) |
| **EMA** | East Midlands Airport |
| **EMVO** | Elementaire Militaire Vlieg Opleiding (Elementary Flying Training) |
| **ENOSA** | Ecole des Navigateurs Operationales Systemes d'Armees (Navigation School) |
| **EoN** | Elliot's of Newbury |
| **EPAA** | Ecole de Pilotage Elementaire de l'Armée de l'Air (Air Force Elementary Flying School) |
| **EPE** | Ecole de Pilotage Elementaire (Elementary Flying School) |
| **EPNER** | Ecole du Personnel Navigant d'Essais et de Reception |
| **EPTT** | Exhibition, Production & Transportation Team |
| **ER** | Escadre de Reconnaissance (Reconnaissance Wing) |

| | |
|---|---|
| **ERS** | Escadron de Reconnaissance Stratégique (Strategic Reconnaissance Squadron) |
| **ERV** | Escadre de Ravitaillement en Vol (Air Refuelling Wing) |
| **ES** | Escadrille de Servitude |
| **Esc** | Escuadron (Squadron) |
| **Esk** | Eskadrille (Squadron) |
| **Eslla** | Escuadrilla (Squadron) |
| **Esq** | Esquadra (Squadron) |
| **ET** | Escadre de Transport (Transport Squadron) |
| **ETE** | Escadron de Transport et Entrainment (Transport Training Squadron) |
| **ETEC** | Escadron de Transport d'Entrainement et de Calibration (Transport Training & Calibration Sqn) |
| **ETL** | Escadron de Transport Légère (Light Transport Squadron) |
| **ETO** | Escadron de Transition Operationnelle |
| **ETOM** | Escadron de Transport Outre Mer (Overseas Transport Squadron) |
| **ETPS** | Empire Test Pilots' School |
| **ETS** | Engineering Training School |
| **FAA** | Fleet Air Arm/Federal Aviation Administration |
| **FACF** | Forward Air Control Flight |
| **FBS** | Flugbereitschaftstaffel |
| **FBW** | Fly by wire |
| **FC** | Forskokcentralen (Flight Centre) |
| **FE** | Further Education |
| **FETC** | Fire and Emergency Training Centre |
| **ff** | Front fuselage |
| **FG** | Fighter Group |
| **FH** | Fairchild-Hiller |
| **FI** | Falkland Islands |
| **FlSt** | Flieger Staffel (Flight Squadron) |
| **Flt** | Flight |
| **FMA** | Fabrica Militar de Aviones |
| **FMT** | Flotila Militara de Transport (Transport Regiment) |
| **FMV** | Forsvarets Materielwerk |
| **FONA** | Flag Officer Naval Aviation |
| **FRADU** | Fleet Requirements and Air Direction Unit |
| **FRA** | FR Aviation |
| **FS** | Fighter Squadron |
| **FSAIU** | Flight Safety & Accident Investigation Unit |
| **FSCTE** | Fire Services Central Training Establishment |
| **FTS** | Flying Training School |
| **FTW** | Flying Training Wing |
| **Fw** | Focke Wulf |
| **FW** | Fighter Wing/Foster Wickner |
| **FWTS** | Fixed Wing Test Squadron |
| **FY** | Fiscal Year |
| **F3 OCU** | Tornado F3 Operational Conversion Unit |
| **GAL** | General Aircraft Ltd |
| **GAM** | Groupe Aerien Mixte (Composite Air Group) |
| ***gd*** | gold (squadron colours and markings) |
| **GD** | General Dynamics |
| **GHL** | Groupe d'Helicopteres Legeres (Light Helicopter Group) |
| **GI** | Ground Instruction/Groupement d'Instruction (Instructional Group) |
| **GKNW** | GKN Westland |
| ***gn*** | green (squadron colours and markings) |
| **GRD** | Gruppe fur Rustunggdienste (Group for Service Preparation) |
| **GT** | Grupo de Transporte (Transport Wing) |
| **GTT** | Grupo de Transporte de Tropos (Troop Carrier Wing) |
| ***gy*** | grey (squadron colours and markings) |
| **H&W** | Hereford and Worcester |
| **HAF** | Historic Aircraft Flight |
| **HC** | Helicopter Combat Support Squadron |
| **HF** | Historic Flying Ltd |
| **HFR** | Heeresfliegerregiment (Army Air Regiment) |
| **HFWS** | Heeresflieger Waffenschule (Army Air Weapons School) |
| **Hkp Div** | Helikopterdivisionen (Helicopter Division) |
| **HMA** | Helicopter Maritime Attack |
| **HMF** | Harrier Maintenance Flight/Helicopter Maintenance Flight |
| **HMS** | Her Majesty's Ship |
| **HOCU** | Harrier OCU |
| **HP** | Handley-Page |
| **HQ** | Headquarters |
| **HS** | Hawker Siddeley |
| **HSF** | Harrier Servicing Flight |
| **IAF** | Israeli Air Force |
| **INTA** | Instituto Nacional de Tecnica Aerospacial |
| **IOW** | Isle Of Wight |
| **IWM** | Imperial War Museum |
| **JATE** | Joint Air Transport Establishment |
| **JbG** | Jagdbombergeschwader (Fighter Bomber Wing) |
| **JFACSTU** | Joint Forward Air Control Students Training Unit |
| **JG** | Jagdgeschwader (Fighter Wing) |
| **Kridlo** | Wing |
| **Letka** | Squadron |
| **ltBVr** | letka Bitevnich Vrtulníkù (Attack Helicopter Squadron) |
| **LTG** | Lufttransportgeschwader (Air Transport Wing) |
| **LTV** | Ling-Temco-Vought |
| **LVG** | Luftwaffen Versorgungs Geschwader (Air Force Maintenance Wing)/Luft Verkehrs Gesellschaft |
| **LZO** | Letecky Zkusební Odbor (Aviation Test Department) |
| ***m*** | multi-coloured (squadron colours and markings) |
| **MAPK** | Mira Anachestisis Pantos Kerou (All Weather Interception Sqn) |
| **MARPAT** | Maritime Patrouillegroep (Maritime Patrol Group) |
| **MBB** | Messerschmitt Bolkow-Blohm |
| **MCAS** | Marine Corps Air Station |
| **McD** | McDonnell Douglas |
| **Med** | Medical |
| **MFG** | Marine Flieger Geschwader (Naval Air Wing) |
| **MH** | Max Holste |
| **MIB** | Military Intelligence Battalion |
| **MiG** | Mikoyan — Gurevich |
| **Mod** | Modified |
| **MR** | Maritime Reconnaissance |
| **MRF** | Meteorological Research Flight |
| **MS** | Morane-Saulnier |
| **MTM** | Mira Taktikis Metaforon (Tactical Transport Sqn) |
| **MU** | Maintenance Unit |
| **Mus'm** | Museum |
| **NA** | North American |
| **NACDS** | Naval Air Command Driving School |
| **NAEWF** | NATO Airborne Early Warning Force |
| **NAF** | Naval Air Facility |
| **NAS** | Naval Air Station |
| **NASU** | Naval Air Support Unit |
| **NATO** | North Atlantic Treaty Organisation |
| **NAWC** | Naval Air Warfare Center |
| **NAWC-AD** | Naval Air Warfare Center Aircraft Division |
| **NBC** | Nuclear, Biological and Chemical |
| **NE** | North-East |
| **NFATS** | Naval Force Aircraft Test Squadron |
| **NI** | Northern Ireland |
| **NMSU** | Nimrod Major Servicing Unit |
| **NYARC** | North Yorks Aircraft Restoration Centre |
| **OCU** | Operational Conversion Unit |
| **OEU** | Operation Evaluation Unit |
| **OFMC** | Old Flying Machine Company |

| | |
|---|---|
| *or* | orange (squadron colours and markings) |
| **OSAC** | Operational Support Airlift Command |
| **OVH Kmp** | Observations-Helicopter Kompagni |
| **PASF** | Puma Aircraft Servicing Flight |
| **PAT** | Priority Air Transport Detachment |
| **PBN** | Pilatus Britten-Norman |
| **PLM** | Pulk Lotnictwa Mysliwskiego (Fighter Regiment) |
| *pr* | purple (squadron colours and markings) |
| **PRU** | Photographic Reconnaissance Unit |
| **PVH Kmp** | Panservaerns-Helicopter Kompagni |
| **pzdlt** | prùzkumná dopravni letka (Reconnaissance & Transport Squadron) |
| *r* | red (squadron colours and markings) |
| **R** | Replica |
| **RAeS** | Royal Aeronautical Society |
| **RAF** | Royal Aircraft Factory/Royal Air Force |
| **RAFC** | Royal Air Force College |
| **RAFM** | Royal Air Force Museum |
| **RAFGSA** | Royal Air Force Gliding and Soaring Association |
| **RCAF** | Royal Canadian Air Force |
| **RE** | Royal Engineers |
| **Regt** | Regiment |
| **REME** | Royal Electrical & Mechanical Engineers |
| **rf** | Rear fuselage |
| **RJAF** | Royal Jordanian Air Force |
| **RM** | Royal Marines |
| **RMB** | Royal Marines Base |
| **RMC of S** | Royal Military College of Science |
| **RN** | Royal Navy |
| **RNAS** | Royal Naval Air Station |
| **RNAW** | Royal Naval Aircraft Workshop |
| **RNAY** | Royal Naval Aircraft Yard |
| **RNGSA** | Royal Navy Gliding and Soaring Association |
| **ROF** | Royal Ordnance Factory |
| **RQS** | Rescue Squadron |
| **R-R** | Rolls-Royce |
| **RS** | Reid & Sigrist/Reconnaissance Squadron |
| **RSV** | Reparto Sperimentale Volo (Experimental Flight School) |
| **RW** | Reconnaissance Wing |
| **SA** | Scottish Aviation |
| **Saab** | Svenska Aeroplan Aktieboleg |
| **SAH** | School of Air Handling |
| **SAL** | Scottish Aviation Limited |
| **SAOEU** | Strike/Attack Operational Evaluation Unit |
| **SAR** | Search and Rescue |
| **Saro** | Saunders-Roe |
| **SARTU** | Search and Rescue Training Unit |
| **SBoLK** | Stíhacie Bombardovacie Letecké Kridlo (Fighter Bomber Air Wing) |
| **SCW** | Strategic Communications Wing |
| **SEAE** | School of Electrical & Aeronautical Engineering |
| **SEPECAT** | Société Européenne de Production de l'avion Ecole de Combat et d'Appui Tactique |
| **SFDO** | School of Flight Deck Operations |
| **SHAPE** | Supreme Headquarters Allied Forces Europe |
| *si* | silver (squadron colours and markings) |
| **SIET** | Section d'Instruction et d'Etude du Tir |
| **SKTU** | Sea King Training Unit |
| **Skv** | Skvadron (Squadron) |
| **SLK** | Stíhacie Letecké Kridlo (Fighter Air Wing) |
| **slt** | stíhací letka (Fighter Squadron) |
| **SLV** | School Licht Vliegwezen (Flying School) |
| **Sm** | Smaldeel (Squadron) |
| **SNCAN** | Société Nationale de Constructions Aéronautiques du Nord |
| **SOES** | Station Operations & Engineering Squadron |
| **SOG** | Special Operations Group |
| **SOS** | Special Operations Squadron |
| **SoTT** | School of Technical Training |
| **SOW** | Special Operations Wing |
| **SPAD** | Société Pour les Apparells Deperdussin |
| **Sqn** | Squadron |
| **SSF** | Station Servicing Flight |
| **SWWAPS** | Second World War Aircraft Preservation Society |
| **TA** | Territorial Army |
| **TAP** | Transporten Avio Polk (Air Transport Regiment) |
| **T&EE** | Test & Evaluation Establishment |
| **TFC** | The Fighter Collection |
| **TGp** | Test Groep |
| **TIARA** | Tornado Integrated Avionics Research Aircraft |
| **tlt** | taktická letka (Tactical Squadron) |
| **TMF** | Tornado Maintenance Flight |
| **TMTS** | Trade Management Training School |
| **tpzlt** | taktická a prùzkumná letka (Tactical & Reconnaissance Squadron) |
| **TS** | Test Squadron |
| **TsAGI** | Tsentral'ny Aerogidrodinamicheski Instut (Central Aero & Hydrodynamics Institute) |
| **TsLw** | Technische Schule der Luftwaffe (Luftwaffe Technical School) |
| **TSW** | Tactical Supply Wing |
| **TW** | Test Wing |
| **UAS** | University Air Squadron |
| **Uberwg** | Uberwachunggeschwader (Surveillance Wing) |
| **UK** | United Kingdom |
| **UKAEA** | United Kingdom Atomic Energy Authority |
| **UNFICYP** | United Nations' Forces in Cyprus |
| **US** | United States |
| **USAF** | United States Air Force |
| **USAFE** | United States Air Forces in Europe |
| **USAREUR** | US Army Europe |
| **USCGS** | US Coast Guard Station |
| **USEUCOM** | United States European Command |
| **USMC** | United States Marine Corps |
| **USN** | United States Navy |
| **NWTSPM** | United States Navy Test Pilots School |
| **VAAC** | Vectored thrust Advanced Aircraft flight Control |
| **VFW** | Vereinigte Flugtechnische Werke |
| **VGS** | Volunteer Gliding School |
| **vlt** | vycviková letka (Training Squadron) |
| **VMGR** | Marine Aerial Refuelling/Transport Squadron |
| **VMGRT** | Marine Aerial Refuelling/Transport Training Squadron |
| **VQ** | Fleet Air Reconnaissance Squadron |
| **VR** | Fleet Logistic Support Squadron |
| **VS** | Vickers-Supermarine |
| **VSD** | Vegyes Szàllitorepülö Dandàr (Aircraft Transport Brigade) |
| **VSL** | Vycvikové Stredisko Letectva (Flying Training Centre) |
| *w* | white (squadron colours and markings) |
| **Wg** | Wing |
| **WLT** | Weapons Loading Training |
| **WRS** | Weather Reconnaissance Squadron |
| **WS** | Westland |
| **WTD** | Wehrtechnische Dienstelle (Technical Support Unit) |
| **WW2** | World War II |
| *y* | yellow (squadron colours and markings) |
| **zDL** | základna Dopravního Letectva (Air Transport Base) |
| **ZmDK** | Zmiesany Dopravny Kridlo (Mixed Transport Wing) |
| **zSL** | základna Skolního Letectva (Training Air Base) |
| **zTL** | základna Taktického Letectva (Tactical Air Base) |
| **zVrL** | základna Vrtulníkového Letectva (Helicopter Air Base) |

# A Guide to the Location of Operational Military Bases in the UK

This section is to assist the reader to locate the places in the United Kingdom where operational military aircraft are based. The term *aircraft* also includes helicopters and gliders.

The alphabetical order listing gives each location in relation to its county and to its nearest classified road(s) (*by* means adjoining; *of* means proximate to), together with its approximate direction and mileage from the centre of a nearby major town or city. Some civil airports are included where active military units are also based, but **excluded** are MoD sites with non-operational aircraft (eg *gate guardians*), the bases of privately-owned civil aircraft that wear military markings and museums.

| *User* | *Base name* | *County/Region* | *Location* | *Distance/direction from (town)* |
|---|---|---|---|---|
| DERA | Aberporth | Dyfed | N of A487 | 6m ENE of Cardigan |
| Army | Abingdon | Oxfordshire | W by B4017, W of A34 | 5m SSW of Oxford |
| RAF | Aldergrove/Belfast Airport | Co Antrim | W by A26 | 13m W of Belfast |
| RM | Arbroath | Angus | E of A933 | 2m NW of Arbroath |
| RAF/ Hunting | Barkston Heath | Lincolnshire | W by B6404, S of A153 | 5m NNE of Grantham |
| RAF | Benson | Oxfordshire | E by A423 | 1m NE of Wallingford |
| DERA/ RAF | Boscombe Down | Wiltshire | S by A303, W of A338 | 6m N of Salisbury |
| RAF | Boulmer | Northumberland | E of B1339 | 4m E of Alnwick |
| RAF | Brize Norton | Oxfordshire | W of A4095 | 5m SW of Witney |
| Marshall | Cambridge Airport/ Teversham | Cambridgeshire | S by A1303 | 2m E of Cambridge |
| RM/RAF | Chivenor | Devon | S of A361 | 4m WNW of Barnstaple |
| RAF | Church Fenton | Yorkshire North | S of B1223 | 7m WNW of Selby |
| RAF | Colerne | Wiltshire | S of A420, E of Fosse Way | 5m NE of Bath |
| RAF | Coltishall | Norfolk | W of B1150 | 9m NNE of Norwich |
| RAF | Coningsby | Lincolnshire | S of A153, W by B1192 | 10m NW of Boston |
| RAF | Cosford | Shropshire | W of A41, N of A464 | 9m WNW of Wolverhampton |
| RAF | Cottesmore | Leicestershire | W of A1, N of B668 | 9m NW of Stamford |
| RAF | Cranwell | Lincolnshire | N by A17, S by B1429 | 5m WNW of Sleaford |
| RN | Culdrose | Cornwall | E by A3083 | 1m SE of Helston |
| Army | Dishforth | Yorkshire North | E by A1 | 4m E of Ripon |
| USAF | Fairford | Gloucestershire | S of A417 | 9m ESE of Cirencester |
| RN | Fleetlands | Hampshire | E by A32 | 2m SE of Fareham |
| RAF | Glasgow Airport | Strathclyde | N by M8 jn 28 | 7m W of city |
| RAF | Halton | Buckinghamshire | N of A4011, S of B4544 | 4m ESE of Aylesbury |
| RAF | Henlow | Bedfordshire | E of A600, W of A6001 | 1m SW of Henlow |
| RAF | Honington | Suffolk | E of A134, W of A1088 | 6m S of Thetford |
| Army | Hullavington | Wiltshire | W of A429 | 1m N of M4 jn 17 |
| RAF | Kenley | Greater London | W of A22 | 1m W of Warlingham |
| RAF | Kinloss | Grampian | E of B9011, N of B9089 | 3m NE of Forres |
| RAF | Kirknewton | Lothian | E by B7031, N by A70 | 8m SW of Edinburgh |
| USAF | Lakenheath | Suffolk | W by A1065 | 8m W of Thetford |
| RAF | Leeming | Yorkshire North | E by A1 | 5m SW of Northallerton |
| RAF | Leuchars | Fife | E of A919 | 7m SE of Dundee |
| RAF | Linton-on-Ouse | Yorkshire North | E of B6265 | 10m NW of York |
| DERA | Llanbedr | Gwynedd | W of A496 | 7m NNW of Barmouth |
| RAF | Lossiemouth | Grampian | W of B9135, S of B9040 | 4m N of Elgin |
| RAF | Lyneham | Wiltshire | W of A3102, S of A420 | 10m WSW of Swindon |
| RAF | Marham | Norfolk | N by A1122 | 6m W of Swaffham |
| Army | Middle Wallop | Hampshire | S by A343 | 6m SW of Andover |
| USAF | Mildenhall | Suffolk | S by A1101 | 9m NNE of Newmarket |
| RAF | Newton | Nottinghamshire | N of A52, W of A46 | 7m E of Nottingham |
| RAF | Northolt | Greater London | N by A40 | 3m E of M40 jn 1 |
| RAF | Odiham | Hampshire | E of A32 | 2m S of M3 jn 5 |
| RN | Predannack | Cornwall | W by A3083 | 7m S of Helston |
| RN | Prestwick Airport | Strathclyde | E by A79 | 3m N of Ayr |
| RAF | St Athan | South Glamorgan | N of B4265 | 13m WSW of Cardiff |
| RAF | St Mawgan/Newquay | Cornwall | N of A3059 | 4m ENE of Newquay |
| RAF | Scampton | Lincolnshire | W by A15 | 6m N of Lincoln |
| RAF | Sealand | Flint | W by A550 | 6m WNW of Chester |
| RAF | Shawbury | Shropshire | W of B5063 | 7m NNE of Shrewsbury |
| RAF | Syerston | Nottinghamshire | W by A46 | 5m SW of Newark |

| *User* | *Base name* | *County/Region* | *Location* | *Distance/direction from (town)* |
|---|---|---|---|---|
| RAF | Ternhill | Shropshire | SW by A41 | 3m SW of Market Drayton |
| RAF/ Army | Topcliffe | Yorkshire North | E of A167, W of A168 | 3m SW of Thirsk |
| RAF | Valley | Gwynedd | S of A5 on Anglesey | 5m SE of Holyhead |
| RAF | Waddington | Lincolnshire | E by A607, W by A15 | 5m S of Lincoln |
| BAe | Warton | Lancashire | S by A584 | 8m SE of Blackpool |
| Army/ RAF | Wattisham | Suffolk | N of B1078 | 5m SSW of Stowmarket |
| DERA | West Freugh | Dumfries & Galloway | S by A757, W by A715 | 5m SE of Stranraer |
| RAF | Weston-on-the-Green | Oxfordshire | E by A43 | 9m N of Oxford |
| RAF | Wittering | Cambridgeshire | W by A1, N of A47 | 3m S of Stamford |
| RAF | Woodvale | Merseyside | W by A565 | 5m SSW of Southport |
| RAF | Wyton | Cambridgeshire | E of A141, N of B1090 | 3m NE of Huntingdon |
| WS | Yeovil | Somerset | N of A30, S of A3088 | 1m W of Yeovil |
| RN | Yeovilton | Somerset | S by B3151, S of A303 | 5m N of Yeovil |

C-130K Hercules C3 XV189 is scheduled to be replaced by a new C-130J Hercules C4. *PRM*

XZ111, a Jaguar GR1A operated by No 54 Squadron from RAF Coltishall. *PRM*

# British Military Aircraft Serials

The Committee of Imperial Defence through its Air Committee introduced a standardised system of numbering aircraft in November 1912. The Air Department of the Admiralty was allocated the first batch 1-200 and used these to cover aircraft already in use and those on order. The Army was issued with the next block from 201-800, which included the number 304 which was given to the Cody Biplane now preserved in the Science Museum. By the outbreak of World War 1 the Royal Navy was on its second batch of serials 801-1600 and this system continued with alternating allocations between the Army and Navy until 1916 when number 10000, a Royal Flying Corps BE2C, was reached.

It was decided not to continue with five digit numbers but instead to start again from 1, prefixing RFC aircraft with the letter A and RNAS aircraft with the prefix N. The RFC allocations commenced with A1 an FE2D and before the end of the year had reached A9999 an Armstrong Whitworth FK8. The next group commenced with B1 and continued in logical sequence through the C, D, E and F prefixes. G was used on a limited basis to identify captured German aircraft, while H was the last block of wartime-ordered aircraft. To avoid confusion I was not used, so the new postwar machines were allocated serials in the J range. A further minor change was made in the serial numbering system in August 1929 when it was decided to maintain four numerals after the prefix letter, thus omitting numbers 1 to 999. The new K series therefore commenced at K1000, which was allocated to an AW Atlas.

The Naval N prefix was not used in such a logical way. Blocks of numbers were allocated for specific types of aircraft such as seaplanes or flying-boats. By the late 1920s the sequence had largely been used up and a new series using the prefix S was commenced. In 1930 separate naval allocations were stopped and subsequent serials were issued in the 'military' range which had by this time reached the K series. A further change in the pattern of allocations came in the L range. Commencing with L7272 numbers were issued in blocks with smaller blocks of serials between not used. These were known as blackout blocks. As M had already been used as a suffix for Maintenance Command instructional airframes it was not used as a prefix. Although N had previously been used for naval aircraft it was used again for serials allocated from 1937.

With the build-up to World War 2 the rate of allocations quickly accelerated and the prefix R was being used when war was declared. The letters O and Q were not allotted, and nor was S which had been used up to S1865 for naval aircraft before integration into the RAF series. By 1940 the serial Z9999 had been reached, as part of a blackout block, with the letters U and Y not used to avoid confusion. The option to recommence serial allocation at A1000 was not taken up; instead it was decided to use an alphabetical two-letter prefix with three numerals running from 100 to 999. Thus AA100 was allocated to a Blenheim IV.

This two-letter, three-numeral serial system which started in 1940 continues today. The letters C, I, O, Q, U and Y were, with the exception of NC, not used. For various reasons the following letter combinations were not issued: DA, DB, DH, EA, GA to GZ, HA, HT, JE, JH, JJ, KR to KT, MR, NW, NZ, SA to SK, SV, TN, TR and VE. The first postwar serials issued were in the VP range while the end of the WZs had been reached by the Korean War. The current new issues are in the latter part of the ZJ range and there are now no blackout blocks of unallocated serials. This being so, and at the current rate of issue, the Z range will last for many years. Occasionally an 'out-of-sequence' serial is issued to a manufacturer's prototype or development aircraft viz ZK101 and ZT800.

**Note:** Whilst every effort has been made to ensure the accuracy of this publication, no part of the contents has been obtained from official sources. The compilers will be pleased to receive comments, corrections and further information for inclusion in subsequent editions of *Military Aircraft Markings* and the monthly up-date of additions and amendments that is published in *Aircraft Illustrated.* Please send your information to Military Aircraft Markings, PO Box 46, Westbury-on-Trym, Bristol BS9 1TF; fax to 0117 968 3928 or e-mail to HJCurtis@cwcom.net.

# British Military Aircraft Markings

A serial in *italics* denotes that it is not the genuine marking for that airframe.

| Serial | Type (other identity) [code] | Owner/operator, location or fate | Notes |
|---|---|---|---|
| *164* | Bleriot Type XI (BAPC 106/9209M) | RAF Museum, stored Wyton | |
| *168* | Sopwith Tabloid Scout <R> (G-BFDE) | RAF Museum, Hendon | |
| 304 | Cody Biplane (BAPC 62) | Science Museum, South Kensington | |
| *433* | Bleriot Type XXVII (BAPC 107/9202M) | RAF Museum, Hendon | |
| *687* | RAF BE2b <R> (BAPC 181) | RAF Museum, Hendon | |
| *1701* | RAF BE2c <R> (BAPC 117) | Privately owned, Orpington | |
| *2345* | Vickers FB5 Gunbus <R> (G-ATVP) | RAF Museum, Hendon | |
| 2699 | RAF BE2c | Imperial War Museum, Lambeth | |
| *2882* | Vickers FB5 Gunbus <R> (BAPC 234) | Barton Aviation Heritage Society, Barton | |
| *3066* | Caudron GIII (G-AETA/9203M) | RAF Museum, Hendon | |
| *5894* | DH2 <R> (G-BFVH) | Privately owned, Withybush | |
| *5964* | DH2 <R> (BAPC 112) | Museum of Army Flying, stored Middle Wallop | |
| *6232* | RAF BE2c <R> (BAPC 41) | Yorkshire Air Museum, stored Elvington | |
| 8359 | Short 184 <ff> | FAA Museum, RNAS Yeovilton | |
| A301 | Morane BB (frame) | RAF Museum, stored Wyton | |
| A1325 | RAF BE2e (G-BVGR) | Privately owned, Milden | |
| *A1742* | Bristol Scout D <R> (BAPC 38) | Privately owned, Solihull | |
| *A4850* | RAF SE5a <R> (BAPC 176) | Barton Aviation Heritage Society, Barton | |
| *A7317* | Sopwith Pup <R> (BAPC 179) | Midland Air Museum, Coventry | |
| *A8226* | Sopwith 1a Strutter <R> (G-BIDW) | RAF Museum, Hendon | |
| B1807 | Sopwith Pup (G-EAVX) [A7] | Privately owned, Keynsham, Avon | |
| *B2458* | Sopwith 1F.1 Camel <R> (G-BPOB/*F542*) [R] | Privately owned, Booker | |
| *B3459* | Nieuport Scout 17/23 <R> (G-BWMJ) [21] | Privately owned, Fairoaks | |
| *B6401* | Sopwith 1F.1 Camel <R> (G-AWYY/C1701) | FAA Museum, RNAS Yeovilton | |
| *B7270* | Sopwith 1F.1 Camel <R> (G-BFCZ) | Brooklands Museum, Weybridge | |
| *C1904* | RAF SE5a <R> (G-PFAP) [Z] | Privately owned, Syerston | |
| *C3011* | Phoenix Currie Super Wot (G-SWOT) [S] | The Real Aeroplane Company, Breighton | |
| C3988 | Sopwith 5F.1 Dolphin | RAF Museum, stored Wyton | |
| *C4451* | Avro 504J <R> (BAPC 210) | Southampton Hall of Aviation | |
| *C4918* | Bristol M1C <R> (G-BWJM) | The Shuttleworth Collection, Old Warden | |
| *C4940* | Bristol M1C <R> | | |
| *C4994* | Bristol M1C <R> (G-BLWM) | RAF Museum, Hendon | |
| *C9533* | RAF SE5a <R> (G-BUWE) [M] | Privately owned, DERA Boscombe Down | |
| *D276* | RAF SE5a <R> (BAPC 208) [A] | Prince's Mead Shopping Centre, Farnborough | |
| *D3419* | Sopwith 1F.1 Camel <R> (*F1921*/BAPC 59) | RAF Museum, Cosford | |
| D7560 | Avro 504K | Museum of Army Flying, Middle Wallop | |
| *D7889* | Bristol F2b Fighter (G-AANM/BAPC 166) | Privately owned, stored Sandown | |
| *D8084* | Bristol F2b Fighter (G-ACAA/F4516) [S] | The Fighter Collection, Duxford | |
| D8096 | Bristol F2b Fighter (G-AEPH) [D] | The Shuttleworth Collection, Old Warden | |
| *D8781* | Avro 504K <R> (G-ECKE) | Privately owned, Rougham | |
| *E373* | Avro 504K <R> (BAPC 178) | Privately owned, | |
| *E449* | Avro 504K (G-EBJE/9205M) | RAF Museum, Hendon | |
| *E2466* | Bristol F2b Fighter (BAPC 165) [I] | RAF Museum, Hendon | |
| E2581 | Bristol F2b Fighter [13] | Imperial War Museum, Duxford | |

| Notes | Serial | Type (other identity) [code] | Owner/operator, location or fate |
|---|---|---|---|
| | *F141* | RAF SE5a <R> (G-SEVA) [G] | Privately owned, DERA Boscombe Down |
| | *F235* | RAF SE5a <R> (G-BMDB) [B] | Privately owned, Boscombe Down |
| | F760 | SE5a Microlight <R> [A] | Privately owned, Redhill |
| | F904 | RAF SE5a (G-EBIA) | The Shuttleworth Collection, Old Warden |
| | F938 | RAF SE5a (G-EBIC/9208M) | RAF Museum, Hendon |
| | *F943* | RAF SE5a <R> (G-BIHF) [S] | Museum of Army Flying, Middle Wallop |
| | *F943* | RAF SE5a <R> (G-BKDT) | Yorkshire Air Museum, Elvington |
| | F1010 | Airco DH9A [C] | RAF Museum, Hendon |
| | F3556 | RAF RE8 | Imperial War Museum, Duxford |
| | *F4013* | Sopwith 1F.1 Camel <R> | Privately owned, Coventry |
| | *F5447* | RAF SE5a <R> (G-BKER) [N] | Privately owned, Cumbernauld |
| | *F5459* | RAF SE5a <R> (G-INNY) [Y] | Privately owned, Goodwood |
| | *F5475* | RAF SE5a <R> (BAPC 250) | Brooklands Museum, Weybridge |
| | F6314 | Sopwith 1F.1 Camel (9206M) [B] | RAF Museum, Hendon |
| | *F8010* | RAF SE5a <R> (G-BDWJ) [Z] | Privately owned, Graveley |
| | *F8614* | Vickers FB27A Vimy IV <R> (G-AWAU) | RAF Museum, Hendon |
| | | | |
| | *H1968* | Avro 504K <R> (BAPC 42) | Yorkshire Air Museum, stored Elvington |
| | H2311 | Avro 504K (G-ABAA) | Gr Manchester Mus of Science & Industry |
| | *H3426* | Hawker Hurricane <R> (BAPC 68) | Privately owned, |
| | H5199 | Avro 504K (BK892/3118M/ G-ACNB/G-ADEV) | The Shuttleworth Collection, Old Warden |
| | | | |
| | J7326 | DH53 Humming Bird (G-EBQP) | Privately owned, Audley End |
| | J8067 | Westland Pterodactyl 1a | Science Museum, South Kensington |
| | *J9941* | Hawker Hart 2 (G-ABMR) | RAF Museum, Hendon |
| | | | |
| | K1786 | Hawker Tomtit (G-AFTA) | The Shuttleworth Collection, Old Warden |
| | *K2050* | Isaacs Fury II (G-ASCM) | Privately owned, Brize Norton |
| | *K2059* | Isaacs Fury II (G-PFAR) | Privately owned, Dunkeswell |
| | *K2060* | Isaacs Fury II (G-BKZM) | Privately owned, Haverfordwest |
| | *K2075* | Isaacs Fury II (G-BEER) | Privately owned, Temple Bruer |
| | *K2227* | Bristol 105 Bulldog IIA (G-ABBB) | RAF Museum, Hendon |
| | *K2567* | DH82A Tiger Moth (DE306/ 7035M/G-MOTH) | Privately owned, Tadlow |
| | *K2572* | DH82A Tiger Moth (NM129/ G-AOZH) | Privately owned, Shoreham |
| | *K2572* | DH82A Tiger Moth <R> | The Aircraft Restoration Company, Duxford |
| | *K2587* | DH82A Tiger Moth <R> (G-BJAP) | Privately owned, Shobdon |
| | K3215 | Avro 621 Tutor (G-AHSA) | The Shuttleworth Collection, Old Warden |
| | K3661 | Hawker Nimrod II (G-BURZ) | Aero Vintage, St Leonards-on-Sea |
| | *K3731* | Isaacs Fury <R> (G-RODI) | Privately owned, Hailsham |
| | K4259 | DH82A Tiger Moth (G-ANMO) [71] | Privately owned, White Waltham |
| | K4972 | Hawker Hart Trainer IIA (1764M) | RAF Museum, Cosford |
| | *K5054* | Supermarine Spitfire <R> (BAPC 190/*EN398*) | Privately owned, Sevenoaks, Kent |
| | *K5054* | Supermarine Spitfire <R> (BAPC 214) | Privately owned, stored Sandown |
| | *K5054* | Supermarine Spitfire <R> (G-BRDV) | Front Line Aviation Museum, Sandown |
| | *K5054* | Supermarine Spitfire <R> | Kent Battle of Britain Museum, Hawkinge |
| | *K5414* | Hawker Hind (G-AENP/BAPC 78) [XV] | The Shuttleworth Collection, Old Warden |
| | K5600 | Hawker Audax I (2015M/G-BVVI) | Aero Vintage, St Leonards-on-Sea |
| | *K5673* | Hawker Fury I <R> (BAPC 249) | Brooklands Museum, Weybridge |
| | K6035 | Westland Wallace II (2361M) | RAF Museum, Hendon |
| | *K7271* | Hawker Fury II <R> (BAPC 148) | Privately owned, High Ercall |
| | K8042 | Gloster Gladiator II (8372M) | RAF Museum, Hendon |
| | K8203 | Hawker Demon I (G-BTVE/2292M) | Demon Displays, Hatch |
| | *K8203* | Isaacs Fury II (G-BWWN) [D] | Privately owned, Lower Upham |
| | *K9853* | VS300 Spitfire IA (AR213/G-AIST) [QV-H] | *Not painted as such* |
| | *K9926* | VS300 Spitfire I <R> (BAPC 217) [JH-C] | RAF Bentley Priory, on display |
| | K9942 | VS300 Spitfire I (8383M) [SD-V] | Medway Aircraft Preservation Society, Rochester |
| | *K9962* | VS300 Spitfire I <R> [JH-C] | Privately owned, Greenford, W London |
| | *L1070* | VS300 Spitfire I <R> (BAPC 227) [XT-A] | Edinburgh airport, on display |
| | L1592 | Hawker Hurricane I [KW-Z] | Science Museum, South Kensington |

| *Serial* | *Type (other identity) [code]* | *Owner/operator, location or fate* | *Notes* |
|---|---|---|---|
| *L1679* | Hawker Hurricane I <R> (BAPC 241) [JX-G] | Tangmere Military Aviation Museum | |
| *L1710* | Hawker Hurricane I <R> (BAPC 219) [AL-D] | RAF Biggin Hill, on display | |
| L2301 | VS Walrus I (G-AIZG) | FAA Museum, RNAS Yeovilton | |
| L2940 | Blackburn Skua I | FAA Museum, RNAS Yeovilton | |
| L5343 | Fairey Battle I [VO-S] | RAF Museum, Hendon | |
| *L6906* | Miles M14A Magister I (G-AKKY/ T9841/BAPC 44) | Museum of Berkshire Aviation, Woodley | |
| *L8756* | Bristol 149 Bolingbroke IVT (RCAF 10001) [XD-E] | RAF Museum, Hendon | |
| *L8841* | Bristol 149 Bolingbroke IVT (G-BPIV/*R3821*) [QY-C] | *Re-painted as R3821 (UX-N) Dec 1999* | |
| N248 | Supermarine S6A (*S1596*) | Southampton Hall of Aviation | |
| *N500* | Sopwith LC-1T Triplane <R> (G-PENY/G-BWRA) | Privately owned, Dunkeswell | |
| *N546* | Wright Quadruplane 1 <R> (BAPC 164) | Southampton Hall of Aviation | |
| N1671 | Boulton Paul P82 Defiant I (8370M) [EW-D] | RAF Museum, Hendon | |
| N1854 | Fairey Fulmar II (G-AIBE) | FAA Museum, RNAS Yeovilton | |
| *N2078* | Sopwith Baby (8214/8215) | FAA Museum, RNAS Yeovilton | |
| N2980 | Vickers Wellington IA [R] | Brooklands Museum, Weybridge | |
| *N3177* | RAF BE2e <R> | Barton Aviation Heritage Society, Barton | |
| *N3194* | VS300 Spitfire I <R> (BAPC 220) [GR-Z] | RAF Biggin Hill, on display | |
| *N3289* | VS300 Spitfire I <R> (BAPC 65) [DW-K] | Kent Battle of Britain Museum, Hawkinge | |
| *N3313* | VS300 Spitfire I <R> (*MH314*/ BAPC 69) [KL-B] | Kent Battle of Britain Museum, Hawkinge | |
| N3378 | Boulton Paul P82 Defiant I | Boulton Paul Association, Wolverhampton | |
| *N4389* | Fairey Albacore (N4172) [4M] | FAA Museum, RNAS Yeovilton | |
| N4877 | Avro 652A Anson I (G-AMDA) [VX-F] | Imperial War Museum, Duxford | |
| *N5182* | Sopwith Pup <R> (G-APUP/9213M) | RAF Museum, Hendon | |
| N5195 | Sopwith Pup (G-ABOX) | Museum of Army Flying, Middle Wallop | |
| *N5419* | Bristol Scout D <R> (N5419) | FAA Museum, RNAS Yeovilton | |
| *N5492* | Sopwith Triplane <R> (BAPC 111) | FAA Museum, RNAS Yeovilton | |
| N5628 | Gloster Gladiator II | RAF Museum, Hendon | |
| N5903 | Gloster Sea Gladiator II (*N2276*/ G-GLAD) [H] | The Fighter Collection, Duxford | |
| N5912 | Sopwith Triplane (8385M) | RAF Museum, Hendon | |
| *N6181* | Sopwith Pup (G-EBKY/N5180) | The Shuttleworth Collection, Old Warden | |
| *N6290* | Sopwith Triplane <R> (G-BOCK) | The Shuttleworth Collection, Old Warden | |
| *N6452* | Sopwith Pup <R> (G-BIAU) | FAA Museum, RNAS Yeovilton | |
| N6466 | DH82A Tiger Moth (G-ANKZ) | Privately owned, Sywell | |
| N6537 | DH82A Tiger Moth (G-AOHY) | AAC Historic Aircraft Flt, Middle Wallop | |
| N6720 | DH82A Tiger Moth (G-BYTN /7014M) [RUO-B] | Privately owned, Hatch | |
| N6797 | DH82A Tiger Moth (G-ANEH) | Privately owned, Goodwood | |
| N6812 | Sopwith 2F.1 Camel | Imperial War Museum, Lambeth | |
| N6847 | DH82A Tiger Moth (G-APAL) | Privately owned, Little Gransden | |
| N6965 | DH82A Tiger Moth (G-AJTW) [FL-J] (wreck) | Privately owned, Tibenham | |
| N6985 | DH82A Tiger Moth (G-AHMN) | AAC Historic Aircraft Flt, Middle Wallop | |
| N9191 | DH82A Tiger Moth (G-ALND) | Privately owned, Abergavenny | |
| N9192 | DH82A Tiger Moth (G-DHZF) [RCO-N] | Privately owned, Sywell | |
| N9389 | DH82A Tiger Moth (G-ANJA) | Privately owned, Seething | |
| N9899 | Supermarine Southampton I (fuselage) | RAF Museum, Hendon | |
| | | | |
| P1344 | HP52 Hampden I (9175M) [PL-K] | RAF Museum, stored Wyton | |
| P1344 | HP52 Hampden I <rf> (parts Hereford L6012) | RAF Museum, Hendon | |
| P2617 | Hawker Hurricane I (8373M) [AF-A] | RAF Museum, Hendon | |
| *P2793* | Hawker Hurricane I <R> (BAPC 236) [SD-M] | Eden Camp Theme Park, Malton, North Yorkshire | |
| P2902 | Hawker Hurricane I (G-ROBT) [DX-X] | Privately owned, Milden | |
| *P3059* | Hawker Hurricane I <R> (BAPC 64) [SD-N] | Kent Battle of Britain Museum, Hawkinge | |
| P3175 | Hawker Hurricane I (wreck) | RAF Museum, Hendon | |

| Notes | Serial | Type (other identity) [code] | Owner/operator, location or fate |
|---|---|---|---|
| | *P3208* | Hawker Hurricane I <R> (BAPC 63/*L1592*) [SD-T] | Kent Battle of Britain Museum, Hawkinge |
| | *P3386* | Hawker Hurricane I <R> (BAPC 218) [FT-A] | RAF Bentley Priory, on display |
| | *P3395* | Hawker Hurricane IV (KX829) [JX-B] | Birmingham Mus of Science & Industry, stored |
| | P3554 | Hawker Hurricane I (composite) | The Air Defence Collection, Salisbury |
| | P3717 | Hawker Hurricane I (composite) (DR348) | Privately owned, Hinckley, Leics |
| | *P4139* | Fairey Swordfish II (HS618) [5H] | FAA Museum, RNAS Yeovilton |
| | P6382 | Miles M14A Hawk Trainer 3 (G-AJRS) [C] | The Shuttleworth Collection, Old Warden |
| | P7350 | VS329 Spitfire IIA (G-AWIJ) [XT-D] | RAF BBMF, Coningsby |
| | P7540 | VS329 Spitfire IIA [DU-W] | Dumfries & Galloway Avn Mus, Dumfries |
| | *P8140* | VS329 Spitfire II <R> (*P9390*/ BAPC 71) [ZF-K] | Norfolk & Suffolk Avn Museum, Flixton |
| | *P8448* | VS329 Spitfire II <R> (BAPC 225) [UM-D] | RAF Cranwell, on display |
| | P9444 | VS300 Spitfire IA [RN-D] | Science Museum, South Kensington |
| | R1914 | Miles M14A Magister (G-AHUJ) | Privately owned, Strathallan |
| | *R3821* | Bristol 149 Bolingbroke IVT (G-BPIV/*Z5722*)/*L8841* [NU-X] | The Aircraft Restoration Company, Duxford |
| | R4907 | DH82A Tiger Moth II (G-ANCS) | *Repainted as G-ANCS by 1999* |
| | R4959 | DH82A Tiger Moth II (G-ARAZ) [59] | Privately owned, Temple Bruer |
| | *R5136* | DH82A Tiger Moth II (G-APAP) | *Repainted as G-APAP by 1999* |
| | R5172 | DH82A Tiger Moth II (G-AOIS) [FIJ-E] | Privately owned, Sherburn-in-Elmet |
| | R5250 | DH82A Tiger Moth II (G-AODT) | Privately owned, Tibenham |
| | R5868 | Avro 683 Lancaster I (7325M) [PO-S] | RAF Museum, Hendon |
| | *R6690* | VS300 Spitfire I <R> (BAPC 254) | Yorkshire Air Museum, Elvington |
| | R6915 | VS300 Spitfire I | Imperial War Museum, Lambeth |
| | R9125 | Westland Lysander III (8377M) [LX-L] | RAF Museum, Hendon |
| | R9371 | HP59 Halifax II <ff> | Cotswold Aircraft Rest'n Grp, Innsworth |
| | *S1287* | Fairey Flycatcher <R> (G-BEYB) | FAA Museum, RNAS Yeovilton |
| | *S1579* | Hawker Nimrod I <R> (G-BBVO) [571] | Privately owned, Basingstoke |
| | S1581 | Hawker Nimrod I (G-BWWK) | The Fighter Collection, Duxford |
| | S1595 | Supermarine S6B | Science Museum, South Kensington |
| | T5298 | Bristol 156 Beaufighter I (4552M) <ff> | Midland Air Museum, Coventry |
| | T5424 | DH82A Tiger Moth II (G-AJOA) | Privately owned, Chiseldon |
| | T5672 | DH82A Tiger Moth II (G-ALRI) | Privately owned, Chalmington |
| | T5854 | DH82A Tiger Moth II (G-ANKK) | Privately owned, Welshpool |
| | T5879 | DH82A Tiger Moth II (G-AXBW) [RUC-W] | Privately owned, Frensham |
| | T5968 | DH82A Tiger Moth II (G-ANNN) | *Repainted as G-ANNN by 1999* |
| | T6296 | DH82A Tiger Moth II (8387M) | RAF Museum, Hendon |
| | T6313 | DH82A Tiger Moth II (G-AHVU) | Privately owned, Liphook |
| | T6562 | DH82A Tiger Moth II (G-ANTE) | Privately owned, Sywelll |
| | T6818 | DH82A Tiger Moth II (G-ANKT) [91] | The Shuttleworth Collection, Old Warden |
| | T6953 | DH82A Tiger Moth II (G-ANNI) | Privately owned, Little Gransden |
| | *T6991* | DH82A Tiger Moth II (G-ANOR/ DE694) | Privately owned, Paddock Wood |
| | T7230 | DH82A Tiger Moth II (G-AFVE) | Privately owned, Boscombe Down |
| | T7281 | DH82A Tiger Moth II (G-ARTL) | Privately owned, Egton, nr Whitby |
| | T7404 | DH82A Tiger Moth II (G-ANMV) [04] | Privately owned, Booker |
| | T7793 | DH82A Tiger Moth II (G-ANKV) | Privately owned, Croydon, on display |
| | T7842 | DH82A Tiger Moth II (G-AMTF) | Privately owned, Boughton, Suffolk |
| | T7909 | DH82A Tiger Moth II (G-ANON) | Privately owned, Sherburn-in-Elmet |
| | *T7997* | DH82A Tiger Moth II (NL750/ G-AHUF) | Privately owned, Edburton |
| | T8191 | DH82A Tiger Moth II (G-BWMK) | Privately owned, Welshpool |
| | *T9707* | Miles M14A Magister I (G-AKKR/ 8378M/T9708) | Museum of Army Flying, Middle Wallop |
| | T9738 | Miles M14A Magister I (G-AKAT) | Privately owned, Breighton |

| *Serial* | *Type (other identity) [code]* | *Owner/operator, location or fate* | *Notes* |
|---|---|---|---|
| V1075 | Miles M14A Magister I (G-AKPF) | Privately owned, stored Sandown | |
| V3388 | Airspeed AS10 Oxford I (G-AHTW) | Imperial War Museum, Duxford | |
| *V6028* | Bristol 149 Bolingbroke IVT (G-MKIV) [GB-D] <rf> | The Aircraft Restoration Co, stored Duxford | |
| V7350 | Hawker Hurricane I (fuselage) | Brenzett Aeronautical Museum | |
| *V7467* | Hawker Hurricane I <R> (BAPC 223) [LE-D] | RAF Coltishall, on display | |
| *V7767* | Hawker Hurricane I <R> (BAPC 72) | Jet Age Museum, Staverton | |
| *V9441* | Westland Lysander IIIA (G-AZWT) [AR-A] | The Shuttleworth Collection, Old Warden | |
| *V9673* | Westland Lysander IIIA (V9300/ G-LIZY) [MA-J] | Imperial War Museum, Duxford | |
| *V9723* | Westland Lysander IIIA (*2442*/ OO-SOT) [MA-D] | SABENA Old Timers, Brussels, Belgium | |
| W1048 | HP59 Halifax II (8465M) [TL-S] | RAF Museum, Hendon | |
| *W2068* | Avro 652A Anson I (VH-ASM) [68] | RAF Museum, Hendon | |
| W2718 | VS Walrus I (G-RNLI) | Dick Melton Aviation, Great Yarmouth | |
| W4041 | Gloster E28/39 [G] | Science Museum, South Kensington | |
| W4050 | DH98 Mosquito | Mosquito Aircraft Museum, London Colney | |
| W5856 | Fairey Swordfish II (G-BMGC) [A2A] | RN Historic Flight, Yeovilton | |
| W9385 | DH87B Hornet Moth (G-ADND) [YG-L,3] | The Shuttleworth Collection, Old Warden | |
| X4590 | VS300 Spitfire I (8384M) [PR-F] | RAF Museum, Hendon | |
| X7688 | Bristol 156 Beaufighter I (3858M/ G-DINT) | Privately owned, Hatch | |
| Z2033 | Fairey Firefly I (G-ASTL) [275] | Imperial War Museum, Duxford | |
| Z2389 | Hawker Hurricane IIA | Brooklands Museum, Weybridge | |
| Z5207 | Hawker Hurricane IIB (G-BYDL) | Privately owned, Billingshurst | |
| *Z5252* | Hawker Hurricane IIB (G-BWHA/ Z5053) [GO-B] | Privately owned, Dursley, Glos | |
| Z7015 | Hawker Sea Hurricane IB (G-BKTH) [7-L] | The Shuttleworth Collection, Old Warden | |
| Z7197 | Percival P30 Proctor III (G-AKZN/8380M) | RAF Museum, Hendon | |
| *Z7258* | DH89A Dragon Rapide (NR786/ G-AHGD) | Privately owned, Membury (wreck) | |
| *Z7381* | Hawker Hurricane XIIA (G-HURI) [XR-T] | Historic Aircraft Collection, Audley End | |
| *AA550* | VS349 Spitfire VB <R> (BAPC 230/ *AA908*) [GE-P] | Eden Camp Theme Park, Malton, North Yorkshire | |
| AB130 | VS349 Spitfire VA (parts) | Privately owned, | |
| AB910 | VS349 Spitfire VB (G-AISU) [ZD-C] | RAF BBMF, Coningsby | |
| AD540 | VS349 Spitfire VB (wreck) | Dumfries & Galloway Avn Mus, Dumfries | |
| AE436 | HP52 Hampden I [PL-J] (parts) | Lincolnshire Avn Heritage Centre, E Kirkby | |
| AE977 | Hawker Sea Hurricane X (G-TWTD) | Hawker Restorations Ltd, Milden | |
| AL246 | Grumman Martlet I | FAA Museum, RNAS Yeovilton | |
| AM561 | Lockheed Hudson V (parts) | Cornwall Aero Park, Helston | |
| AP506 | Cierva C30A (G-ACWM) | The Helicopter Museum, Weston-super-Mare | |
| AP507 | Cierva C30A (G-ACWP) [KX-P] | Science Museum, South Kensington | |
| AR213 | VS300 Spitfire IA (G-AIST) [QV-H] | Privately owned, Booker | |
| AR501 | VS349 Spitfire LF VC (G-AWII) [NN-A] | The Shuttleworth Collection, Old Warden | |
| AR614 | VS349 Spitfire VC (5378M/ 7555M/G-BUWA) [DU-Z] | Privately owned, Earls Colne | |
| BB807 | DH82A Tiger Moth (G-ADWO) | Southampton Hall of Aviation | |
| *BE417* | Hawker Hurricane XIIB (G-HURR) [LK-A] | The Real Aeroplane Company, Breighton | |
| *BE421* | Hawker Hurricane IIC <R> (BAPC 205) [XP-G] | RAF Museum, Hendon | |
| BH328 | Hawker Hurricane IIb | Privately owned, Isle of Wight | |
| BL614 | VS349 Spitfire VB (4354M) [ZD-F] | RAF Museum, Hendon | |
| BL655 | VS349 Spitfire VB (wreck) | Lincolnshire Avn Heritage Centre, East Kirkby | |

| Notes | Serial | Type (other identity) [code] | Owner/operator, location or fate |
|---|---|---|---|
| | *BL924* | VS349 Spitfire VB <R> (BAPC 242) [AZ-G] | Tangmere Military Aviation Museum |
| | *BM361* | VS349 Spitfire VB <R> [XR-C] | RAF Lakenheath, on display |
| | BM597 | VS349 Spitfire LF VB (5718M/ G-MKVB) [JH-C] | Historic Aircraft Collection, Audley End |
| | *BN230* | Hawker Hurricane IIC (LF751/ 5466M) [FT-A] | RAF Manston, Memorial Pavilion |
| | *BR600* | VS361 Spitfire IX <R> (BAPC 222) [SH-V] | RAF Uxbridge, on display |
| | *BR600* | VS361 Spitfire IX <R> (BAPC 224) [JP-A] | *Sold to Canada* |
| | *BR600* | VS361 Spitfire IX <R> (fuselage) | Privately owned, Dunkeswell, derelict |
| | BW881 | Hawker Hurricane XIIA (G-KAMM) | Privately owned, Milden |
| | *CB733* | SA122 Bulldog (G-BCUV/G-112) | Privately owned, Old Sarum |
| | *DD931* | Bristol 152 Beaufort VIII (9131M) [L] | RAF Museum, Hendon |
| | DE208 | DH82A Tiger Moth II (G-AGYU) | Privately owned, Ronaldsway |
| | DE470 | DH82A Tiger Moth II (G-ANMY) | Privately owned, Oaksey Park, Wilts |
| | DE623 | DH82A Tiger Moth II (G-ANFI) | Privately owned, Cardiff |
| | DE673 | DH82A Tiger Moth II (6948M/ G-ADNZ) | Privately owned, Swanton Morley |
| | DE992 | DH82A Tiger Moth II (G-AXXV) | Privately owned, Upavon |
| | DF112 | DH82A Tiger Moth II (G-ANRM) | Privately owned, Clacton |
| | DF128 | DH82A Tiger Moth II (G-AOJJ) [RCO-U] | Privately owned, White Waltham |
| | DF155 | DH82A Tiger Moth II (G-ANFV) | Privately owned, Shempston Fm, Lossiemouth |
| | DF198 | DH82A Tiger Moth II (G-BBRB) | Privately owned, Biggin Hill |
| | DG202 | Gloster F9/40 (5758M) | RAF Museum, Cosford |
| | DG590 | Miles M2H Hawk Major (8379M/ G-ADMW) | RAF Museum, stored Wyton |
| | DP872 | Fairey Barracuda II (fuselage) | FAA Museum, stored Yeovilton |
| | DR613 | Foster-Wikner GM1 Wicko (G-AFJB) | Privately owned, Southampton |
| | DV372 | Avro 683 Lancaster I <ff> | Imperial War Museum, Lambeth |
| | EE416 | Gloster Meteor F3 <ff> | Martin Baker Aircraft, Chalgrove |
| | EE425 | Gloster Meteor F3 <ff> | Meteor Flight, Yatesbury |
| | EE531 | Gloster Meteor F4 (7090M) | Midland Air Museum, Coventry |
| | EE549 | Gloster Meteor F4 (7008M) [A] | Tangmere Military Aviation Museum |
| | EF545 | VS349 Spitfire VC <ff> | Privately owned, High Wycombe |
| | EJ693 | Hawker Tempest V (N7027E) [SA-J] | Privately owned, Booker |
| | EJ922 | Hawker Typhoon IB <ff> | RAF Manston History Museum |
| | EM720 | DH82A Tiger Moth II (G-AXAN) | Privately owned, Little Gransden |
| | EM727 | DH82A Tiger Moth II (G-AOXN) | Privately owned, Yeovil |
| | EN224 | VS366 Spitfire F XII (G-FXII) | Privately owned, Newport Pagnell |
| | *EN343* | VS365 Spitfire PR XI <R> (BAPC 226) | RAF Benson, on display |
| | *EN398* | VS361 Spitfire F IX <R> (BAPC 184) [WO-A] | Privately owned, North Weald |
| | EP120 | VS349 Spitfire LF VB (5377M/ 8070M/G-LFVB) [AE-A] | The Fighter Collection, Duxford |
| | EX976 | NA AT-6D Harvard III (FAP.1657) | FAA Museum, RNAS Yeovilton |
| | EZ259 | NA AT-6D Harvard III (G-BMJW) | Privately owned, Wakefield, West Yorkshire |
| | *FB226* | Bonsall Mustang <R> (G-BDWM) [MT-A] | Privately owned, Gamston |
| | FE695 | Noorduyn AT-16 Harvard IIB (G-BTXI) [94] | The Fighter Collection, Duxford |
| | FE905 | Noorduyn AT-16 Harvard IIB (LN-BNM) | RAF Museum, Hendon |
| | FE992 | Noorduyn AT-16 Harvard IIB (G-BDAM) [K-T] | Privately owned, Duxford |
| | FH153 | Noorduyn AT-16 Harvard IIB (G-BBHK) [GW-A] | Privately owned, stored Cardiff |
| | *FJ992* | Boeing-Stearman PT-17 Kaydet (*442*/G-BPTB) | Privately owned, Wevelgem, Belgium |
| | FM118 | Avro 683 Lancaster B X <ff> | Privately owned, Gosport, Hants |
| | *FR886* | Piper L-4J Cub (G-BDMS) | Privately owned, Old Sarum |

| Serial | Type (other identity) [code] | Owner/operator, location or fate | Notes |
|---|---|---|---|
| *FS628* | Fairchild Argus 2 (43-14601/ G-AIZE) | RAF Museum, Cosford | |
| FS668 | Noorduyn AT-16 Harvard IIB (PH-TBR) | Privately owned, The Netherlands | |
| FS890 | Noorduyn AT-16 Harvard IIB (7554M) | DPA, stored DERA Boscombe Down | |
| *FT323* | NA AT-6D Harvard III (FAP 1513) | Air Engineering Services, Swansea | |
| FT391 | Noorduyn AT-16 Harvard IIB (G-AZBN) | Privately owned, Shoreham | |
| *FX301* | NA AT-6D Harvard III (EX915/ G-JUDI) [FD-NQ] | Privately owned, Bryngwyn Bach, Clwyd | |
| *FX360* | Noorduyn AT-16 Harvard IIB (KF435) | Booker Aircraft Museum | |
| FX442 | Noorduyn AT-16 Harvard IIB [TO-M] | Privately owned, South Gorley, Hants | |
| *FX760* | Curtiss P-40N Kittyhawk IV (9150M) [GA-?] | RAF Museum, stored Wyton | |
| *HB275* | Beech C-45 Expeditor II (G-BKGM) | Privately owned, North Weald | |
| HB751 | Fairchild Argus III (G-BCBL) | Privately owned, Little Gransden | |
| *HD346* | NA B-25J Mitchell (44-29507/ N320SQ) [NO-V] | *Repainted as N5-149, 1999* | |
| HH379 | GAL48 Hotspur II (BAPC 261) | Museum of Army Flying, Middle Wallop | |
| HJ711 | DH98 Mosquito NF II [VI-C] | Night-Fighter Preservation Tm, Elvington | |
| HM354 | Percival P34 Proctor III (G-ANPP) | Privately owned, Stansted | |
| HM580 | Cierva C-30A (G-ACUU) | Imperial War Museum, Duxford | |
| HS503 | Fairey Swordfish IV (BAPC 108) | RAF Museum, stored Wyton | |
| JG891 | VS349 Spitfire LF VC (A58-178/ G-LFVC) | Historic Flying Ltd, Audley End | |
| *JR505* | Hawker Typhoon IB <ff> | Midland Air Museum, Coventry | |
| JV482 | Grumman Wildcat V | Ulster Aviation Society, Langford Lodge | |
| *JV579* | Grumman FM-2 Wildcat (N4845V/ G-RUMW) [F] | The Fighter Collection, Duxford | |
| KB889 | Avro 683 Lancaster B X (G-LANC) [NA-I] | Imperial War Museum, Duxford | |
| KB994 | Avro 683 Lancaster B X (G-BVBP) | Privately owned, Sandtoft | |
| *KD345* | Goodyear FG-1D Corsair (88297/ G-FGID) [130-A] | The Fighter Collection, Duxford | |
| KD431 | CV Corsair IV [E2-M] | FAA Museum, RNAS Yeovilton | |
| KE209 | Grumman Hellcat II | FAA Museum, RNAS Yeovilton | |
| *KE418* | Hawker Tempest <rf> | RAF Museum, stored Wyton | |
| KF183 | Noorduyn AT-16 Harvard IIB [3] | DPA/AFD, DERA Boscombe Down | |
| KF435 | Noorduyn AT-16 Harvard IIB <ff> | Privately owned, Swindon | |
| KF487 | Noorduyn AT-16 Harvard IIB | The Aircraft Restoration Co, Duxford, spares use | |
| KF488 | Noorduyn AT-16 Harvard IIB <ff> | Privately owned, Bournemouth | |
| KF532 | Noorduyn AT-16 Harvard IIB <ff> | Newark Air Museum, Winthorpe | |
| *KF584* | CCF T-6J Texan (*FT239*/G-BIWX/ G-RAIX) [RAI-X] | Privately owned, North Weald | |
| *KG374* | Douglas Dakota IV (KN645/8355M) [YS] | RAF Museum, Cosford | |
| *KJ351* | Airspeed AS58 Horsa II (TL659/BAPC 80) [23] | Museum of Army Flying, Middle Wallop | |
| KK995 | Sikorsky Hoverfly I [E] | RAF Museum, Hendon | |
| KL161 | NA B-25D Mitchell II (N88972/ G-BYDR) [VO-B] | The Fighter Collection, Duxford | |
| *KL216* | Republic P-47D Thunderbolt (45-49295/9212M) [RS-L] | RAF Museum, Cosford | |
| KN442 | Douglas Dakota C4 (G-AMPZ) | Atlantic Airlines, Coventry | |
| KN448 | Douglas Dakota C4 <ff> | Science Museum, South Kensington | |
| KN751 | Consolidated Liberator C VI (IAF HE807) [F] | RAF Museum, Cosford | |
| KP208 | Douglas Dakota IV [YS] | Airborne Forces Museum, Aldershot | |
| KZ191 | Hawker Hurricane IV (frame only) | Privately owned, North Weald | |
| *KZ321* | Hawker Hurricane IV (G-HURY) (frame only) | The Fighter Collection, stored Duxford | |
| LA198 | VS356 Spitfire F21 (7118M) [RAI-G] | Royal Scottish Mus'm of Flight, E Fortune | |
| LA226 | VS356 Spitfire F21 (7119M) | RAF Museum, stored Wyton | |
| LA255 | VS356 Spitfire F21 (6490M) [JX-U] | RAF No 1 Sqn, Wittering (preserved) | |

| *Notes* | *Serial* | *Type (other identity) [code]* | *Owner/operator, location or fate* |
|---|---|---|---|
| | LA546 | VS Seafire F46 | Charleston Aviation Services, Colchester |
| | LA564 | VS Seafire F46 | Privately owned, Newport Pagnell |
| | LB294 | Taylorcraft Plus D (G-AHWJ) | Museum of Army Flying, Whitchurch, Hants |
| | LB312 | Taylorcraft Plus D (*HH982*/ G-AHXE) | Privately owned, Old Sarum |
| | LB375 | Taylorcraft Plus D (G-AHGW) | Privately owned, Edge Hill |
| | LF363 | Hawker Hurricane IIC [SD-X] | RAF BBMF, Coningsby |
| | LF738 | Hawker Hurricane IIC (5405M) [UH-A] | RAF Museum, Cosford |
| | LF789 | DH82 Queen Bee (K3584/ BAPC 186) [R2-K] | Mosquito Aircraft Museum, London Colney |
| | LF858 | DH82 Queen Bee (G-BLUZ) | Privately owned, Rush Green |
| | LS326 | Fairey Swordfish II (G-AJVH) [L2] | RN Historic Flight, Yeovilton |
| | *LV907* | HP59 Halifax II (HR792) [NP-F] | Yorkshire Air Museum, Elvington |
| | LZ551 | DH100 Vampire | FAA Museum, RNAS Yeovilton |
| | LZ766 | Percival P34 Proctor III (G-ALCK) | Imperial War Museum, Duxford |
| | MA863 | VS349 Spitfire VC | Aero Vintage, St Leonards-on-Sea |
| | MF628 | Vickers Wellington T10 (9210M) | RAF Museum, Hendon |
| | MH434 | VS361 Spitfire LF IXB (G-ASJV) [PK-K] | The Old Flying Machine Company, Duxford |
| | *MH486* | VS361 Spitfire LF IX <R> (BAPC 206) [FF-A] | RAF Museum, Hendon |
| | *MH777* | VS361 Spitfire IX <R> (BAPC 221) [RF-N] | RAF Northolt, on display |
| | MJ147 | VS361 Spitfire LF IX | Privately owned, Kent |
| | MJ627 | VS509 Spitfire T9 (G-BMSB) [9G-P] | Privately owned, Coventry |
| | MJ730 | VS361 Spitfire HF IXE (G-HFIX) [GZ-?] | Privately owned, Staverton |
| | *MJ751* | VS361 Spitfire IX <R> (BAPC 209) [DU-V] | D-Day Museum, Shoreham Airport |
| | *MJ832* | VS361 Spitfire IX <R> (*L1096*/ BAPC 229) [DN-Y] | RAF Digby, on display |
| | *MK178* | VS361 Spitfire LF XVIE (TE311/ *X4474*/7241M) [LZ-V] | RAF EPTT, St Athan |
| | MK356 | VS361 Spitfire LF IXC (5690M) [2I-V] | RAF BBMF, Coningsby |
| | *MK356* | VS361 Spitfire LF IXC <R> [2I-V] | Kent Battle of Britain Museum, Hawkinge |
| | *MK673* | VS361 Spitfire LF XVIE (TB382/ *X4277*/7244M) [SK-E] | RAF EPTT, St Athan |
| | MK732 | VS361 Spitfire LF IXC (8633M/ G-HVDM/PH-OUQ) [OU-U] | Dutch Spitfire Flight, Lelystad, The Netherlands |
| | *MK805* | VS361 Spitfire LF IX <R> [SH-B] | Privately owned, Chiseldon |
| | MK912 | VS361 Spitfire LF IXE (G-BRRA) [MN-P] | Historic Flying Ltd, stored Audley End |
| | ML407 | VS509 Spitfire T9 (G-LFIX) [OU-V] | Privately owned, Duxford |
| | ML411 | VS361 Spitfire LF IXE | Privately owned, Kent |
| | ML417 | VS361 Spitfire LF IXE (G-BJSG) [2I-T] | The Old Flying Machine Company, Duxford |
| | ML427 | VS361 Spitfire IX (6457M) [ST-I] | Birmingham Mus of Science & Industry, stored |
| | ML796 | Short S25 Sunderland V | Imperial War Museum, Duxford |
| | ML824 | Short S25 Sunderland V [NS-Z] | RAF Museum, Hendon |
| | MN235 | Hawker Typhoon IB | RAF Museum, Hendon |
| | MP425 | Airspeed AS10 Oxford I (G-AITB) [G] | RAF Museum, Hendon |
| | MS902 | Miles M25 Martinet TT1 (TF-SHC) | Museum of Berkshire Aviation, Woodley |
| | MT197 | Auster IV (G-ANHS) | Privately owned, Spanhoe Lodge |
| | MT438 | Auster III (G-AREI) | Privately owned, Petersfield |
| | MT847 | VS379 Spitfire FR XIVE (6960M) [AX-H] | Gr Manchester Mus of Science & Industry |
| | *MT928* | VS359 Spitfire HF VIIIC (G-BKMI/ MV154)[ZX-M] | Privately owned, Filton |
| | MV262 | VS379 Spitfire FR XIV (G-CCVV) | Privately owned,Catfield |
| | MV293 | VS379 Spitfire FR XIV (G-SPIT) [OI-C] | The Fighter Collection, Duxford |
| | MW401 | Hawker Tempest II (IAF HA604/ G-PEST) | Privately owned, Hemswell, Lincs |
| | MW404 | Hawker Tempest II (IAF HA557) | Privately owned |
| | MW758 | Hawker Tempest II (IAF HA580) | Privately owned |
| | MW763 | Hawker Tempest II (IAF HA586/ G-TEMT) [HF-A] | Privately owned, Hemswell, Lincs |

| *Serial* | *Type (other identity) [code]* | *Owner/operator, location or fate* | *Notes* |
|---|---|---|---|
| MW810 | Hawker Tempest II (IAF HA591) | Privately owned, Hibaldstow, Lincs | |
| NF370 | Fairey Swordfish III | Imperial War Museum, Duxford | |
| NF389 | Fairey Swordfish III [D] | RN His Flt, BAE Systems Brough (rebuild) | |
| NJ673 | Auster 5D (G-AOCR) | Privately owned, Canterbury | |
| NJ695 | Auster 4 (G-AJXV) | Privately owned, Newark | |
| NJ703 | Auster 5 (G-AKPI) | Privately owned, Croft, Lincs | |
| *NJ719* | Auster 5 (TW385/G-ANFU) | Privately owned, Newcastle | |
| *NL750* | DH82A Tiger Moth II (T7997/ G-AOBH) | Privately owned, Thruxton | |
| NL772 | DH82A Tiger Moth II (G-BXMN) | Privately owned, Blackpool | |
| NL846 | DH82A Tiger Moth II (F-BGEQ) | Brooklands Museum, Weybridge | |
| NL985 | DH82A Tiger Moth I (7015M/ G-BWIK) | Privately owned, Sywell | |
| NM181 | DH82A Tiger Moth I (G-AZGZ) | Privately owned, Dunkeswell | |
| NP294 | Percival P31 Proctor IV [TB-M] | Lincolnshire Avn Heritage Centre, E Kirkby | |
| NP303 | Percival P31 Proctor IV (G-ANZJ) | Privately owned, Byfleet, Surrey | |
| NV778 | Hawker Tempest TT5 (8386M) | RAF Museum, stored Wyton | |
| NX534 | Auster III (G-BUDL) | Privately owned, Middle Wallop | |
| NX611 | Avro 683 Lancaster B VII (8375M/ G-ASXX) [DE-C,LE-C] | Lincolnshire Avn Heritage Centre, E Kirkby | |
| PA474 | Avro 683 Lancaster B I [QR-M] | RAF BBMF, Coningsby | |
| *PF179* | HS Gnat T1 (XR541/8602M) | Privately owned, Binbrook | |
| PK624 | VS356 Spitfire F22 (8072M) [RAU-T] | The Fighter Collection, Duxford | |
| PK664 | VS356 Spitfire F22 (7759M) [V6-B] | RAF Museum, stored Wyton | |
| PK683 | VS356 Spitfire F24 (7150M) | Southampton Hall of Aviation | |
| PK724 | VS356 Spitfire F24 (7288M) | RAF Museum, Hendon | |
| PL344 | VS361 Spitfire LF IXE (G-IXCC) [Y2-P] | Privately owned, Booker | |
| PL965 | VS365 Spitfire PR XI (G-MKXI) [R] | The Real Aeroplane Company, Breighton | |
| PM631 | VS390 Spitfire PR XIX [S] | RAF BBMF, Coningsby | |
| PM651 | VS390 Spitfire PR XIX (7758M) [X] | RAF Museum, stored Wyton | |
| PN323 | HP Halifax VII <ff> | Imperial War Museum, Lambeth | |
| PP566 | Fairey Firefly I (fuselage) | South Yorkshire Avn Museum, Firbeck | |
| PP972 | VS358 Seafire LF IIIC (G-BUAR) | Flying A Services, Earls Colne | |
| *PR536* | Hawker Tempest II (IAF HA457) [OQ-H] | RAF Museum, Hendon | |
| *PR772* | Hawker Fury FB10 (Iraqi AF 243/ G-BTTA) | *Repainted as VW238 by May 1999* | |
| PS853 | VS390 Spitfire PR XIX (G-MXIX/ G-RRGN) [C] | Rolls-Royce, Filton | |
| PS915 | VS390 Spitfire PR XIX (7548M/ 7711M) [UM-G] | RAF BBMF, Coningsby | |
| PT462 | VS509 Spitfire T9 (G-CTIX/ N462JC) [SW-A] | Privately owned, Caernarfon/Duxford | |
| PT879 | VS361 Spitfire LF IX (G-BYDE) | Privately owned, Isle of Wight | |
| PV202 | VS509 Spitfire T9 (G-TRIX) [5R-Q] | Privately owned, Goodwood | |
| PZ865 | Hawker Hurricane IIC (G-AMAU) [Q] | RAF BBMF, Coningsby | |
| RA848 | Slingsby Cadet TX1 | The Aeroplane Collection, stored Wigan | |
| RA854 | Slingsby Cadet TX1 | Privately owned, Wigan | |
| RA897 | Slingsby Cadet TX1 | Newark Air Museum store, Hucknall | |
| RD253 | Bristol 156 Beaufighter TF X (7931M) | RAF Museum, Hendon | |
| RF342 | Avro 694 Lincoln B II (G-29-1/ G-APRJ) | Privately owned, North Weald | |
| RF398 | Avro 694 Lincoln B II (8376M) | RAF Museum, Cosford | |
| *RG333* | Miles M38 Messenger IIA (G-AIEK) | Privately owned, Felton, Bristol | |
| RH377 | Miles M38 Messenger 4A (G-ALAH) | Privately owned, Stretton, Cheshire | |
| RH746 | Bristol 164 Brigand TF1 (fuselage) | North-East Aircraft Museum, stored Usworth | |
| RK858 | VS361 Spitfire LF IX | The Fighter Collection, Duxford | |
| RL962 | DH89A Dominie II (G-AHED) | RAF Museum, stored Wyton | |
| RM221 | Percival P31 Proctor IV (G-ANXR) | Privately owned, Biggin Hill | |
| RM689 | VS379 Spitfire F XIV (G-ALGT) (remains) | Rolls-Royce, Derby | |
| RM694 | VS379 Spitfire F XIV (6640M) | Privately owned, High Wycombe | |
| RM927 | VS379 Spitfire F XIV | Privately owned, High Wycombe | |
| *RN218* | Isaacs Spitfire <R> (G-BBJI) [N] | Privately owned, Langham | |
| RR232 | VS361 Spitfire HF IXC (G-BRSF) | Sussex Spraying Services, Lancing, W Sussex | |

| *Notes* | *Serial* | *Type (other identity) [code]* | *Owner/operator, location or fate* |
|---|---|---|---|
| | RT486 | Auster 5 (G-AJGJ) [PF-A] | Privately owned, Henstridge, Somerset |
| | RT520 | Auster 5 (G-ALYB) | South Yorkshire Avn Museum, Firbeck |
| | RT610 | Auster 5A-160 (G-AKWS) | Privately owned, Crowfield |
| | RW388 | VS361 Spitfire LF XVIE (6946M) [U4-U] | Stoke-on-Trent City Museum, Hanley |
| | RW393 | VS361 Spitfire LF XVIE (7293M) [XT-A] | RAF Museum, Cosford |
| | RX168 | VS358 Seafire L IIIC (IAC 157/ G-BWEM) | Privately owned, Bourne Park, Hants |
| | SL611 | VS361 Spitfire LF XVIE | Supermarine Aero Engineering, Stoke-on-Trent |
| | SL674 | VS361 Spitfire LF IX (8392M) [RAS-H] | RAF Museum, stored Wyton |
| | SM520 | VS361 Spitfire LF IX (G-BXHZ) | Privately owned, Oxford |
| | SM639 | VS361 Spitfire LF IX | Privately owned, Catfield |
| | SM832 | VS379 Spitfire F XIVE (G-WWII/ F-AZSJ) [YB-A] | Privately owned, Dijon, France |
| | SM845 | VS394 Spitfire FR XVIII (G-BUOS) | Privately owned, Audley End |
| | SX137 | VS384 Seafire F XVII | FAA Museum, RNAS Yeovilton |
| | SX300 | VS384 Seafire F XVII | Privately owned, Twyford, Bucks |
| | SX336 | VS384 Seafire F XVII (G-BRMG) | Privately owned, Twyford, Bucks |
| | TA122 | DH98 Mosquito FB VI [UP-G] | Mosquito Aircraft Museum, London Colney |
| | TA634 | DH98 Mosquito TT35 (G-AWJV) [8K-K] | Mosquito Aircraft Museum, London Colney |
| | TA639 | DH98 Mosquito TT35 (7806M) [AZ-E] | RAF Museum, Cosford |
| | TA719 | DH98 Mosquito TT35 (G-ASKC) [6T] | Imperial War Museum, Duxford |
| | TA805 | VS361 Spitfire HF IX (G-PMNF) | Privately owned, Sandown |
| | TB252 | VS361 Spitfire LF XVIE (G-XVIE) [GW-H] | Historic Flying Ltd, Audley End |
| | TB752 | VS361 Spitfire LF XVIE (8086M) [KH-Z] | RAF Manston, Memorial Pavilion |
| | TB885 | VS361 Spitfire LF XVIE (*R1247*) <ff> | Shoreham Aircraft Preservation Society |
| | TD248 | VS361 Spitfire LF XVIE (7246M/ G-OXVI) [D] | Privately owned, Antwerp, Belgium |
| | TD314 | VS361 Spitfire LF IX (*N601DA*) | Privately owned, Norwich |
| | TE184 | VS361 Spitfire LF XVIE (6850M/ G-MXVI) | *Repainted in US marks, 1999* |
| | TE462 | VS361 Spitfire LF XVIE (7243M) | Royal Scottish Mus'm of Flight, E Fortune |
| | TE517 | VS361 Spitfire LF XVIE (G-CCIX) | Privately owned, stored Booker |
| | TG263 | Saro SR A1 (G-12-1) [P] | Southampton Hall of Aviation |
| | TG511 | HP67 Hastings C1 (8554M) | RAF Museum, Cosford |
| | TG517 | HP67 Hastings T5 | Newark Air Museum, Winthorpe |
| | TG528 | HP67 Hastings C1A | Imperial War Museum, Duxford |
| | TJ118 | DH98 Mosquito TT35 <ff> | Mosquito Aircraft Museum, stored London Colney |
| | TJ138 | DH98 Mosquito B35 (7607M) [VO-L] | RAF Museum, Hendon |
| | *TJ324* | Auster 5 (G-APAH) | Privately owned, Cumbernauld |
| | TJ343 | Auster 5 (G-AJXC) | Privately owned, stored Hook |
| | *TJ398* | Auster AOP6 (BAPC 70) | Aircraft Pres'n Soc of Scotland, E Fortune |
| | TJ569 | Auster 5 (G-AKOW) | Museum of Army Flying, Middle Wallop |
| | TJ672 | Auster 5D (G-ANIJ) | Privately owned, Whitchurch, Hants |
| | *TJ704* | Beagle A61 Terrier 2 (VW993/ G-ASCD) [JA] | Yorkshire Air Museum, Elvington |
| | TJ707 | Auster 5 (frame) | South Yorkshire Avn Museum, Firbeck |
| | TK718 | GAL59 Hamilcar I | National Tank Museum, Bovington |
| | TK777 | GAL59 Hamilcar I (fuselage) | Museum of Army Flying, Middle Wallop |
| | TL615 | Airspeed AS58 Horsa II | Robertsbridge Aviation Society, Mayfield |
| | TS291 | Slingsby Cadet TX1 (BGA852) | Royal Scottish Mus'm of Flight, E Fortune |
| | TS423 | Douglas C-47A Dakota C3 (G-DAKS/N147DC) [A] | Privately owned, North Weald |
| | TS798 | Avro 685 York C1 (G-AGNV) | RAF Museum, Cosford |
| | TV959 | DH98 Mosquito T III [AF-V] | The Fighter Collection, stored Duxford |
| | *TV959* | DH98 Mosquito T III <R> | Privately owned, Heald Green, Cheshire |
| | TW439 | Auster 5 (G-ANRP) | The Real Aeroplane Company, Breighton |
| | TW448 | Auster 5 (G-ANLU) | Privately owned, Hedge End |
| | TW467 | Auster 5 (G-ANIE) [ROD-F] | Privately owned, Bassingbourn |
| | *TW511* | Auster 5 (G-APAF) | Privately owned, North Coates |

| *Serial* | *Type (other identity) [code]* | *Owner/operator, location or fate* | *Notes* |
|---|---|---|---|
| TW533 | Beagle A61 Terrier 2 (G-ASAX) | Privately owned, Netherley, Grampian | |
| TW536 | Auster AOP6 (7704M/G-BNGE) [TS-V] | Privately owned, Netheravon | |
| TW591 | Auster 6A (G-ARIH) [N] | Privately owned, Abbots Bromley | |
| TW641 | Beagle A61 Terrier 2 (G-ATDN) | Privately owned, Biggin Hill | |
| TW642 | Beagle A61 Terrier 1 (G-ARLO) | Privately owned, Chandlers Ford, Hants | |
| TX183 | Avro 652A Anson C19 (G-BSMF) | Privately owned, Arbroath | |
| TX213 | Avro 652A Anson C19 (G-AWRS) | North-East Aircraft Museum, Usworth | |
| TX214 | Avro 652A Anson C19 (7817M) | RAF Museum, Cosford | |
| TX226 | Avro 652A Anson C19 (7865M) | Air Atlantique Historic Flight, Coventry | |
| TX235 | Avro 652A Anson C19 | Caernarfon Air World | |
| | | | |
| VD165 | Slingsby T7 Kite (BGA 400) [F] | Privately owned, Dunstable | |
| VF301 | DH100 Vampire F1 (7060M) [RAL-G] | Midland Air Museum, Coventry | |
| VF512 | Auster 6A (G-ARRX) [PF-M] | Privately owned, White Waltham | |
| VF516 | Beagle A61 Terrier 2 (G-ASMZ) [T] | Privately owned, Bagby | |
| VF526 | Auster 6A (G-ARXU) [T] | Privately owned, Middle Wallop | |
| VF548 | Beagle A61 Terrier 1 (G-ASEG) | Privately owned, Dunkeswell | |
| VF611 | Beagle A61 Terrier 2 (G-ATBU) | Privately owned, Hucknall | |
| VH127 | Fairey Firefly TT4 [200/R] | FAA Museum, RNAS Yeovilton | |
| VL348 | Avro 652A Anson C19 (G-AVVO) | Newark Air Museum, Winthorpe | |
| VL349 | Avro 652A Anson C19 (G-AWSA) | Norfolk & Suffolk Avn Mus'm, Flixton | |
| VM325 | Avro 652A Anson C19 | Privately owned, Staverton | |
| VM360 | Avro 652A Anson C19 (G-APHV) | Royal Scottish Mus'm of Flight, E Fortune | |
| *VM791* | Slingsby Cadet TX3 (XA312/ 8876M) | RAF Manston History Museum | |
| VN148 | Grunau Baby IIb (BAPC 33/ BGA2400) | Privately owned, Dunstable | |
| VN485 | VS356 Spitfire F24 (7326M) | Imperial War Museum, Duxford | |
| *VN799* | EE Canberra T4 (WJ874) | RAF No 39(1 PRU) Sqn, Marham | |
| VP293 | Avro 696 Shackleton T4 [A] <ff> | Avro Aircraft Heritage Society, Coventry | |
| VP519 | Avro 652A Anson C19 (G-AVVR) <ff> | Privately owned, Wolverhampton | |
| VP952 | DH104 Devon C2 (8820M) | RAF Museum, Cosford | |
| VP955 | DH104 Devon C2 (G-DVON) | Privately owned, Little Staughton | |
| VP957 | DH104 Devon C2 (8822M) <ff> | No 1137 Sqn ATC, Belfast | |
| VP967 | DH104 Devon C2 (G-KOOL) | *Repainted as G-DOVE, 1999* | |
| VP975 | DH104 Devon C2 [M] | Science Museum, Wroughton | |
| VP978 | DH104 Devon C2 (8553M) | RAF Brize Norton, instructional use | |
| VP981 | DH104 Devon C2 (G-DHDV) | Air Atlantique Historic Flight, Coventry | |
| VR137 | Westland Wyvern TF1 | FAA Museum, stored RNAS Yeovilton | |
| VR192 | Pervical P40 Prentice T1 (G-APIT) | SWWAPS, Lasham | |
| VR249 | Percival P40 Prentice T1 (G-APIY) [FA-EL] | Newark Air Museum, Winthorpe | |
| VR259 | Percival P40 Prentice T1 (G-APJB) [M] | Air Atlantique Historic Flight, Coventry | |
| VR930 | Hawker Sea Fury FB11 (8382M) [110/O] | RN Historic Flight, Yeovilton | |
| VS356 | Percival P40 Prentice T1 (G-AOLU) | Privately owned, Montrose | |
| VS562 | Avro 652A Anson T21 (8012M) | Maes Artro Craft Village, Llanbedr | |
| VS610 | Percival P40 Prentice T1 (G-AOKL) [K-L] | The Shuttleworth Collection, stored Old Warden | |
| VS623 | Percival P40 Prentice T1 (G-AOKZ)[KQ-F] | Midland Air Museum, Coventry | |
| VT409 | Fairey Firefly AS5 <rf> | North-East Aircraft Museum, stored Usworth | |
| VT812 | DH100 Vampire F3 (7200M) [N] | RAF Museum, stored Wyton | |
| *VT871* | DH100 Vampire FB6 (J-1173/ *LZ551*/G-DHXX) | Source Classic Jet Flight, Bournemouth | |
| VT935 | Boulton Paul P111A (VT769) | Midland Air Museum, Coventry | |
| VT987 | Auster AOP6 (G-BKXP) | Aerobuild Ltd, Little Gransden, Cambs | |
| VV106 | Supermarine 510 (7175M) | FAA Museum, stored Wroughton | |
| VV217 | DH100 Vampire FB5 (7323M) | North-East Aircraft Museum, stored Usworth | |
| *VV612* | DH112 Venom FB50 (J-1523/ *WE402*/G-VENI) | Source Classic Jet Flight, Bournemouth | |
| VV901 | Avro 652A Anson T21 | Yorkshire Air Museum, Elvington | |
| *VW238* | Hawker Fury FB10 (Iraqi AF 243/ *PR772*/G-BTTA) [107/Q] | Old Flying Machine Company, Duxford | |
| VW453 | Gloster Meteor T7 (8703M) [Z] | RAF Innsworth, on display | |
| VW985 | Auster AOP6 (G-ASEF) | Privately owned, Upper Arncott, Oxon | |

| Notes | Serial | Type (other identity) [code] | Owner/operator, location or fate |
|---|---|---|---|
| | VX118 | Auster AOP6 (G-ASNB) | Vliegend Museum Seppe, The Netherlands |
| | *VX147* | Alon A2 Aircoupe (G-AVIL) | Privately owned, Monewdon |
| | VX185 | EE Canberra B(I)8 (7631M) <ff> | Royal Scottish Mus'm of Flight, E Fortune |
| | VX250 | DH103 Sea Hornet 21 [48] <rf> | Mosquito Aircraft Museum, London Colney |
| | VX272 | Hawker P.1052 (7174M) | FAA Museum, stored Wroughton |
| | VX275 | Slingsby T21B Sedbergh TX1 (8884M/BGA 572) | RAF Museum, stored Wyton |
| | VX461 | DH100 Vampire FB5 (7646M) | RAF Museum, stored Wyton |
| | VX573 | Vickers Valetta C2 (8389M) | RAF Museum, stored Cosford |
| | VX580 | Vickers Valetta C2 | Norfolk & Suffolk Avn Museum, Flixton |
| | VX595 | WS51 Dragonfly HR1 | FAA Museum, RNAS Yeovilton |
| | VX665 | Hawker Sea Fury FB11 <rf> | RN Historic Flight, at BAE SystemsBrough |
| | VX926 | Auster T7 (G-ASKJ) | Privately owned, Little Gransden |
| | VZ345 | Hawker Sea Fury T20S | RN Historic Flight, stored Yeovilton |
| | VZ467 | Gloster Meteor F8 (G-METE) [01] | Classic Jets Flying Museum, Kemble |
| | VZ477 | Gloster Meteor F8 (7741M) <ff> | Midland Air Museum, Coventry |
| | VZ608 | Gloster Meteor FR9 | Newark Air Museum, Winthorpe |
| | VZ634 | Gloster Meteor T7 (8657M) | Newark Air Museum, Winthorpe |
| | VZ638 | Gloster Meteor T7 (G-JETM) [HF] | Gatwick Aviation Museum, Charlwood, Surrey |
| | VZ728 | RS4 Desford Trainer (G-AGOS) | Snibston Discovery Park, stored Coalville |
| | VZ962 | WS51 Dragonfly HR1 [904] | The Helicopter Museum, Weston-super-Mare |
| | WA473 | VS Attacker F1 [102/J] | FAA Museum, RNAS Yeovilton |
| | WA576 | Bristol 171 Sycamore 3 (7900M/ G-ALSS) | Dumfries & Galloway Avn Mus, Dumfries |
| | WA577 | Bristol 171 Sycamore 3 (7718M/ G-ALST) | North-East Aircraft Museum, Usworth |
| | WA591 | Gloster Meteor T7 (7917M/ G-BWMF) [W] | Meteor Flight, Yatesbury |
| | WA630 | Gloster Meteor T7 [69] <ff> | Robertsbridge Aviation Society, Newhaven |
| | WA634 | Gloster Meteor T7/8 | RAF Museum, Cosford |
| | WA638 | Gloster Meteor T7(mod) | Martin Baker Aircraft, Chalgrove, spares use |
| | WA662 | Gloster Meteor T7 | South Yorkshire Avn Museum, Firbeck |
| | WA984 | Gloster Meteor F8 [A] | Tangmere Military Aviation Museum |
| | WB188 | Hawker Hunter F3 (7154M) | Tangmere Military Aviation Museum |
| | WB271 | Fairey Firefly AS5 [204/R] | RN Historic Flight, BAE SystemsDunsfold |
| | WB440 | Fairey Firefly AS6 <ff> | Privately owned, Newton-le-Willows |
| | WB491 | Avro 706 Ashton 2 (TS897/ G-AJJW) <ff> | Avro Aircraft Heritage Society, BAE SystemsWoodford |
| | WB556 | DHC1 Chipmunk T10 | RAFGSA, Bicester |
| | WB560 | DHC1 Chipmunk T10 | South Yorkshire Avn Museum, Firbeck |
| | WB565 | DHC1 Chipmunk T10 (G-PVET) [X] | Privately owned, Kemble |
| | WB569 | DHC1 Chipmunk T10 (G-BYSJ) [R] | Privately owned, Duxford |
| | WB584 | DHC1 Chipmunk T10 (7706M) <ff> | RAF Manston History Museum |
| | WB585 | DHC1 Chipmunk T10 (G-AOSY) [RCU-X] | Privately owned, Blackbushe |
| | WB588 | DHC1 Chipmunk T10 (G-AOTD) [D] | Privately owned, Biggin Hill |
| | WB615 | DHC1 Chipmunk T10 (G-BXIA) [E] | Privately owned, Blackpool |
| | WB624 | DHC1 Chipmunk T10 <ff> | Newark Air Museum, Winthorpe |
| | WB626 | DHC1 Chipmunk T10 <ff> | Privately owned, South Molton, Devon |
| | WB627 | DHC1 Chipmunk T10 (9248M) [N] | Dulwich College CCF |
| | WB645 | DHC1 Chipmunk T10 (8218M) | RAFGSA, Bicester, spares use |
| | WB652 | DHC1 Chipmunk T10 (G-CHPY) [V] | Privately owned, Cardiff |
| | WB654 | DHC1 Chipmunk T10 (G-BXGO) [U] | Privately owned, Booker |
| | WB657 | DHC1 Chipmunk T10 [908] | RN Historic Flight, Yeovilton |
| | WB660 | DHC1 Chipmunk T10 (G-ARMB) | Privately owned, Shipdham |
| | WB670 | DHC1 Chipmunk T10 (8361M) <ff> | Privately owned, Currie, Lothian |
| | WB671 | DHC1 Chipmunk T10 (G-BWTG) [910] | Privately owned, Epse, The Netherlands |
| | WB685 | DHC1 Chipmunk T10 (comp WP969/G-ATHC) | North-East Aircraft Museum, Usworth |
| | WB697 | DHC1 Chipmunk T10 (G-BXCT) [95] | Privately owned, Wickenby |
| | WB702 | DHC1 Chipmunk T10 (G-AOFE) | Privately owned, Goodwood |

| *Serial* | *Type (other identity) [code]* | *Owner/operator, location or fate* | *Notes* |
|---|---|---|---|
| WB703 | DHC1 Chipmunk T10 (G-ARMC) | Privately owned, White Waltham | |
| WB711 | DHC1 Chipmunk T10 (G-APPM) | Privately owned, Crowfield | |
| WB726 | DHC1 Chipmunk T10 (G-AOSK) [E] | Privately owned, Audley End | |
| WB733 | DHC1 Chipmunk T10 (comp WG422) | South Yorkshire Avn Museum, Firbeck | |
| WB758 | DHC1 Chipmunk T10 (7729M) [P] | Privately owned, Torbay | |
| WB763 | DHC1 Chipmunk T10 (G-BBMR) [14] | Privately owned, Camberley | |
| WB922 | Slingsby T21B Sedbergh TX1 (BGA 4366) | Privately owned, Kingston Deverill | |
| WB938 | Slingsby T21B Sedbergh TX1 | Privately owned, Halton | |
| WB943 | Slingsby T21B Sedbergh TX1 (BGA 2941) | Privately owned, Rufforth | |
| WB971 | Slingsby T21B Sedbergh TX1 (BGA 3324) | Privately owned, Tibenham | |
| WB975 | Slingsby T21B Sedbergh TX1 (BGA 3288) | Privately owned, Drumshade, Fife | |
| WB981 | Slingsby T21B Sedbergh TX1 (BGA 3238) | Privately owned, Aston Down | |
| WD286 | DHC1 Chipmunk T10 (G-BBND) [J] | Privately owned, Croydon, Cambs | |
| WD288 | DHC1 Chipmunk T10 (G-AOSO) [38] | Privately owned, Charlton Park, Wilts | |
| WD292 | DHC1 Chipmunk T10 (G-BCRX) | Privately owned, White Waltham | |
| WD293 | DHC1 Chipmunk T10 (7645M) <ff> | No 1367 Sqn ATC, Caerleon, Gwent | |
| WD305 | DHC1 Chipmunk T10 (G-ARGG) | Privately owned, Coventry | |
| WD310 | DHC1 Chipmunk T10 (G-BWUN) [B] | Privately owned, Ringmer, E Sussex | |
| WD318 | DHC1 Chipmunk T10 (8207M) <ff> | No 145 Sqn ATC, Timperley, Gr Manchester | |
| WD325 | DHC1 Chipmunk T10 [N] | AAC Historic Aircraft Flight, Middle Wallop | |
| WD331 | DHC1 Chipmunk T10 (G-BXDH) [J] | Privately owned, Kemble | |
| *WD355* | DHC1 Chipmunk T10 (WD335) <ff> | No 1955 Sqn ATC, Wells, Somerset | |
| WD356 | DHC1 Chipmunk T10 (7625M) | Privately owned, St Ives, Cambridgeshire | |
| WD363 | DHC1 Chipmunk T10 (G-BCIH) [5] | Privately owned, Andrewsfield | |
| WD370 | DHC1 Chipmunk T10 <ff> | Privately owned, Brighton | |
| WD373 | DHC1 Chipmunk T10 (G-BXDI) [12] | Privately owned, Perth | |
| WD377 | DHC1 Chipmunk T10 <ff> | RAF Millom Museum, Haverigg | |
| *WD379* | DHC1 Chipmunk T10 (WB696/ G-APLO) [K] | Privately owned, Jersey | |
| WD386 | DHC1 Chipmunk T10 (comp WD377) | Dumfries & Galloway Avn Mus, Dumfries | |
| WD390 | DHC1 Chipmunk T10 (G-BWNK) [68] | Privately owned, Breighton | |
| WD413 | Avro 652A Anson T21 (7881M/ G-BFIR/G-VROE) | Air Atlantique Historic Flight, Coventry | |
| WD646 | Gloster Meteor TT20 (8189M) [R] | RAF Manston History Museum | |
| WD686 | Gloster Meteor NF11 | Muckleburgh Collection, Weybourne | |
| WD790 | Gloster Meteor NF11 (8743M)<ff> | North-East Aircraft Museum, Usworth | |
| WD889 | Fairey Firefly AS5 <ff> | North-East Aircraft Museum, Usworth | |
| WD931 | EE Canberra B2 <ff> | RAF Museum, Cosford | |
| WD935 | EE Canberra B2 (8440M) <ff> | Privately owned, Bridgnorth | |
| WD954 | EE Canberra B2 <ff> | Privately owned, Romford, Essex | |
| WE113 | EE Canberra T4 <ff> | Privately owned, Woodhurst, Cambridgeshire | |
| WE122 | EE Canberra TT18 [845] <ff> | Blyth Valley Aviation Collection, Walpole, Suffolk | |
| WE139 | EE Canberra PR3 (8369M) | RAF Museum, Hendon | |
| WE168 | EE Canberra PR3 (8049M) <ff> | Privately owned, Colchester | |
| WE173 | EE Canberra PR3 (8740M) <ff> | Robertsbridge Aviation Society, Mayfield | |
| WE188 | EE Canberra T4 | Solway Aviation Society, Carlisle | |
| WE192 | EE Canberra T4 <ff> | Blyth Valley Aviation Collection, Walpole, Suffolk | |
| *WE275* | DH112 Venom FB50 (J-1601/ G-VIDI) | BAE SystemsHawarden, Fire Section | |
| *WE402* | DH112 Venom FB50 (J-1523/ G-VENI) | *Repainted as VV612, August 1999* | |
| WE569 | Auster T7 (G-ASAJ) | Privately owned, Sandy, Beds | |
| WE591 | Auster T7 (G-ASAK) [Y] | Privately owned, Biggin Hill | |
| WE600 | Auster T7 Antarctic (7602M) | RAF Museum, Cosford | |

| Notes | Serial | Type (other identity) [code] | Owner/operator, location or fate |
|---|---|---|---|
| | *WE724* | Hawker Sea Fury FB11 (VX653/ G-BUCM) [062] | The Fighter Collection, Duxford |
| | WE925 | Gloster Meteor F8 | Classic Jet Aircraft Group, Loughborough |
| | WE982 | Slingsby T30B Prefect TX1 (8781M) | RAF Museum, stored Cosford |
| | WE990 | Slingsby T30B Prefect TX1 (BGA 2583) | Privately owned, RAF Swanton Morley |
| | WF118 | Percival P57 Sea Prince T1 (G-DACA) | Gatwick Aviation Museum, Charlwood, Surrey |
| | WF122 | Percival P57 Sea Prince T1 [575/CU] | Flambards Village Theme Park, Helston |
| | WF128 | Percival P57 Sea Prince T1 (8611M) | Norfolk & Suffolk Avn Museum, Flixton |
| | WF137 | Percival P57 Sea Prince C1 | SWWAPS, Lasham |
| | WF145 | Hawker Sea Hawk F1 <ff> | Privately owned, Welshpool |
| | WF225 | Hawker Sea Hawk F1 [CU] | RNAS Culdrose, at main gate |
| | WF259 | Hawker Sea Hawk F2 [171/A] | Royal Scottish Mus'm of Flight,E Fortune |
| | WF369 | Vickers Varsity T1 [F] | Newark Air Museum, Winthorpe |
| | WF372 | Vickers Varsity T1 [A] | Brooklands Museum, Weybridge |
| | WF376 | Vickers Varsity T1 | Bristol Airport Fire Section |
| | WF408 | Vickers Varsity T1 (8395M) | Privately owned, East Grinstead |
| | WF410 | Vickers Varsity T1 [F] | Brunel Technical College, Lulsgate |
| | WF643 | Gloster Meteor F8 [X] | Norfolk & Suffolk Avn Museum, Flixton |
| | *WF714* | Gloster Meteor F8 (WK914) | Privately owned, stored Sandown |
| | WF784 | Gloster Meteor T7 (7895M) | Jet Age Museum, Staverton |
| | WF825 | Gloster Meteor T7 (8359M) [A] | Avon Air Museum, stored Malmesbury |
| | WF877 | Gloster Meteor T7 (G-BPOA) | Privately owned, Kemble |
| | WF911 | EE Canberra B2 <ff> | The Griffin Trust, Hooton Park, Cheshire |
| | WF922 | EE Canberra PR3 | Midland Air Museum, Coventry |
| | WG300 | DHC1 Chipmunk T10 <ff> | RAFGSA, Bicester |
| | WG303 | DHC1 Chipmunk T10 (8208M) <ff> | RAFGSA, Bicester |
| | WG307 | DHC1 Chipmunk T10 (G-BCYJ) | Privately owned, Shempston Fm, Lossiemouth |
| | WG308 | DHC1 Chipmunk T10 (G-BYHL) [71] | Privately owned, Gamston |
| | WG316 | DHC1 Chipmunk T10 (G-BCAH) | Privately owned, Shoreham |
| | WG321 | DHC1 Chipmunk T10 (G-DHCC) | Privately owned, Wevelgem, Belgium |
| | WG348 | DHC1 Chipmunk T10 (G-BBMV) | Privately owned, Croydon, Cambs |
| | WG350 | DHC1 Chipmunk T10 (G-BPAL) | Privately owned, Thruxton |
| | WG403 | DHC1 Chipmunk T10 [O] <ff> | *Scrapped* |
| | WG407 | DHC1 Chipmunk T10 (G-BWMX) | Privately owned, Spanhoe Lodge |
| | WG418 | DHC1 Chipmunk T10 (8209M/ G-ATDY) <ff> | No 1940 Sqn ATC, Levenshulme, Gr Manchester |
| | WG419 | DHC1 Chipmunk T10 (8206M) <ff> | No 1053 Sqn ATC, Armthorpe |
| | WG422 | DHC1 Chipmunk T10 (8394M/ G-BFAX) [116] | The Aircraft Restoration Co, Duxford |
| | WG432 | DHC1 Chipmunk T10 [L] | Museum of Army Flying, Middle Wallop |
| | WG465 | DHC1 Chipmunk T10 (G-BCEY) | Privately owned, White Waltham |
| | WG469 | DHC1 Chipmunk T10 (G-BWJY) [72] | Privately owned, Newtownards |
| | WG471 | DHC1 Chipmunk T10 (8210M) <ff> | No 301 Sqn ATC, Bury St Edmunds |
| | WG472 | DHC1 Chipmunk T10 (G-AOTY) | Privately owned, Netherthorpe |
| | WG477 | DHC1 Chipmunk T10 (8362M/ G-ATDP) <ff> | No 281 Sqn ATC, Birkdale, Merseyside |
| | WG482 | DHC1 Chipmunk T10 (VH-ZOT) [01] | Privately owned, Duxford |
| | *WG483* | DHC1 Chipmunk T10 (WG393/ VH-ZIT) | Privately owned, Duxford |
| | WG486 | DHC1 Chipmunk T10 | RAF BBMF, Coningsby |
| | WG511 | Avro 696 Shackleton T4 (fuselage) | Flambards Village Theme Park, Helston |
| | WG718 | WS51 Dragonfly HR3 [934] | Privately owned, Elvington |
| | WG719 | WS51 Dragonfly HR5 (G-BRMA) [902] | The Helicopter Museum, Weston-super-Mare |
| | WG724 | WS51 Dragonfly HR5 [932] | North-East Aircraft Museum, Usworth |
| | WG751 | WS51 Dragonfly HR5 | Chatham Historic Dockyard Trust |
| | *WG754* | WS51 Dragonfly HR3 (WG725/7703M) [912/CU] | Flambards Village Theme Park, Helston |
| | WG760 | EE P1A (7755M) | RAF Museum, Cosford |
| | WG763 | EE P1A (7816M) | Gr Manchester Mus of Science & Industry |
| | WG768 | Short SB5 (8005M) | RAF Museum, Cosford |
| | WG774 | BAC 221 | Science Museum, RNAS Yeovilton |

| Serial | Type (other identity) [code] | Owner/operator, location or fate | Notes |
|---|---|---|---|
| WG777 | Fairey FD2 (7986M) | RAF Museum, Cosford | |
| WG789 | EE Canberra B2/6 <ff> | Privately owned, Mendlesham, Suffolk | |
| | | | |
| WH132 | Gloster Meteor T7 (7906M) [J] | No 276 Sqn ATC, Chelmsford | |
| WH166 | Gloster Meteor T7 (8052M) [A] | Privately owned, Birlingham, Worcs | |
| WH291 | Gloster Meteor F8 | SWWAPS, Lasham | |
| WH301 | Gloster Meteor F8 (7930M) [T] | RAF Museum, Hendon | |
| WH364 | Gloster Meteor F8 (8169M) | Privately owned, Kemble | |
| WH453 | Gloster Meteor D16 [L] | DPA, stored DERA Llanbedr | |
| WH646 | EE Canberra T17A <ff> | Midland Air Museum, Coventry | |
| WH657 | EE Canberra B2 | Brenzett Aeronautical Museum | |
| WH665 | EE Canberra T17 (8763M) [J] | BAE SystemsFilton, Fire Section | |
| WH725 | EE Canberra B2 | Imperial War Museum, Duxford | |
| WH734 | EE Canberra B2(mod) | DPA, DERA Llanbedr | |
| WH739 | EE Canberra B2 <ff> | No 2475 Sqn ATC, Ammanford, Dyfed | |
| WH740 | EE Canberra T17 (8762M) [K] | East Midlands Airport Aeropark | |
| WH773 | EE Canberra PR7 (8696M) | Gatwick Aviation Museum, Charlwood, Surrey | |
| WH775 | EE Canberra PR7 (8128M/8868M) <ff> | Privately owned, Welshpool | |
| WH779 | EE Canberra PR7 [BP] | RAF, stored Marham | |
| WH780 | EE Canberra T22 <rf> | RAF St Athan, Fire Section | |
| WH791 | EE Canberra PR7 (8165M/ 8176M/8187M) | Newark Air Museum, Winthorpe | |
| WH796 | EE Canberra PR7 <ff> | Privately owned, Stock, Essex | |
| WH797 | EE Canberra T22 <rf> | RAF St Athan, Fire Section | |
| WH803 | EE Canberra T22 <ff> | Privately owned, Stock, Essex | |
| WH840 | EE Canberra T4 (8350M) <ff> | Privately owned, Flixton | |
| WH846 | EE Canberra T4 | Yorkshire Air Museum, Elvington | |
| WH849 | EE Canberra T4 | RAF No 39(1 PRU) Sqn, Marham | |
| WH850 | EE Canberra T4 <ff> | Barton Aviation Heritage Society, Barton | |
| WH854 | EE Canberra T4 <ff> | Martin Baker Aircraft, Chalgrove | |
| WH863 | EE Canberra T17 (8693M) [CP] <ff> | Newark Air Museum, Winthorpe | |
| WH876 | EE Canberra B2(mod) | DERA Aberporth, instructional use | |
| WH887 | EE Canberra TT18 [847] | DPA, stored DERA Llanbedr | |
| WH903 | EE Canberra B2 <ff> | Yorkshire Air Museum, Elvington | |
| WH903 | EE Canberra B2 (8584M) <ff> | Gatwick Aviation Museum, Charlwood, Surrey | |
| WH904 | EE Canberra T19 | Newark Air Museum, Winthorpe | |
| WH946 | EE Canberra B6(mod) (8185M)<ff> | Privately owned, Tetney, Grimsby | |
| WH953 | EE Canberra B6(mod) <ff> | Blyth Valley Aviation Collection, Walpole, Suffolk | |
| WH957 | EE Canberra E15 (8869M) <ff> | Lincolnshire Avn Heritage Centre, East Kirkby | |
| WH960 | EE Canberra B15 (8344M) <ff> | Privately owned, Hucknall | |
| WH964 | EE Canberra E15 (8870M) <ff> | Privately owned, Hants | |
| WH984 | EE Canberra B15 (8101M) <ff> | RAF Sealand | |
| WH991 | WS51 Dragonfly HR3 | Privately owned, Elvington | |
| | | | |
| *WJ231* | Hawker Sea Fury FB11 (WE726) [115/O] | FAA Museum, Yeovilton | |
| WJ358 | Auster AOP6 (G-ARYD) | Museum of Army Flying, stored Middle Wallop | |
| WJ565 | EE Canberra T17 (8871M) <ff> | Privately owned, Binbrook | |
| WJ567 | EE Canberra B2 <ff> | Privately owned, Houghton, Cambs | |
| WJ576 | EE Canberra T17 <ff> | Boulton Paul Association, Wolverhampton | |
| WJ581 | EE Canberra PR7 <ff> | Privately owned, Canterbury | |
| WJ603 | EE Canberra B2 (8664M) <ff> | Privately owned, Stock, Essex | |
| WJ630 | EE Canberra T17 [ED] | | |
| WJ633 | EE Canberra T17 [EF] <ff> | RAF Wyton | |
| WJ639 | EE Canberra TT18 [39] | North-East Aircraft Museum, Usworth | |
| WJ640 | EE Canberra B2 (8722M) <ff> | Pinewood Studios, Bucks | |
| WJ676 | EE Canberra B2 (7796M) <ff> | Privately owned, Heswall, Merseyside | |
| WJ677 | EE Canberra B2 <ff> | Privately owned, Redruth | |
| WJ680 | EE Canberra TT18 (G-BURM) [CT] | Canberra Flight, RAF Marham | |
| WJ717 | EE Canberra TT18 (9052M) <ff> | RAF St Athan, Fire Section | |
| WJ721 | EE Canberra TT18 [21] <ff> | Dundonald Aviation Centre, Strathclyde | |
| WJ731 | EE Canberra B2T [BK] <ff> | Privately owned, Beds | |
| WJ775 | EE Canberra B6 (8581M) [J] (fuselage) | Stanford Training Area, Bodney Camp, Norfolk | |
| WJ821 | EE Canberra PR7 (8668M) | Army, Bassingbourn, on display | |
| WJ863 | EE Canberra T4 <ff> | Cambridge Airport Fire Section | |
| WJ865 | EE Canberra T4 | Privately owned, Stamford, Lincs | |

| *Notes* | *Serial* | *Type (other identity) [code]* | *Owner/operator, location or fate* |
|---|---|---|---|
| | WJ866 | EE Canberra T4 [AV] | RAF, No 39 (1PRU) Sqn, Marham |
| | WJ872 | EE Canberra T4 (8492M) <ff> | No 327 Sqn ATC, Kilmarnock |
| | WJ874 | EE Canberra T4 [AS] | *Repainted as VN799, April 1999* |
| | WJ876 | EE Canberra T4 <ff> | |
| | WJ880 | EE Canberra T4 (8491M) <ff> | South Yorkshire Avn Museum, Firbeck |
| | WJ893 | Vickers Varsity T1 | DERA Aberporth Fire Section |
| | WJ903 | Vickers Varsity T1 <ff> | South Yorkshire Avn Museum, Firbeck |
| | WJ945 | Vickers Varsity T1 (G-BEDV) [21] | Imperial War Museum, Duxford |
| | WJ975 | EE Canberra T19 [S] | Bomber County Aviation Museum, Hemswell |
| | WJ992 | EE Canberra T4 | Bournemouth Int'l Airport, Fire Section |
| | WK102 | EE Canberra T17 (8780M) <ff> | Privately owned, Welshpool |
| | WK118 | EE Canberra TT18 <ff> | Privately owned, Worcester |
| | WK122 | EE Canberra TT18 [22] | Flambards Village Theme Park, Helston |
| | WK124 | EE Canberra TT18 (9093M) [CR] | MoD FSCTE, Manston |
| | WK126 | EE Canberra TT18 (N2138J) [843] | Jet Age Museum, Staverton |
| | WK127 | EE Canberra TT18 (8985M) <ff> | No 2484 Sqn ATC, Bassingbourn |
| | WK128 | EE Canberra B2 | DPA, DERA Llanbedr |
| | WK163 | EE Canberra B6(mod) (G-BVWC) | Classic Aviation Projects, Bruntingthorpe |
| | WK198 | VS Swift F4 (7428M) (fuselage) | North-East Aircraft Museum, Usworth |
| | WK275 | VS Swift F4 | Privately owned, Upper Hill, nr Leominster |
| | WK277 | VS Swift FR5 (7719M) [N] | Newark Air Museum, Winthorpe |
| | WK281 | VS Swift FR5 (7712M) [S] | Tangmere Military Aviation Museum |
| | WK511 | DHC1 Chipmunk T10 (G-BVBT) [905] | Kennet Aviation, Cranfield |
| | WK512 | DHC1 Chipmunk T10 (G-BXIM) [A] | Privately owned, Brize Norton |
| | WK517 | DHC1 Chipmunk T10 (G-ULAS) [84] | Privately owned, Booker |
| | WK518 | DHC1 Chipmunk T10 [K] | RAF BBMF, Coningsby |
| | WK522 | DHC1 Chipmunk T10 (G-BCOU) | Privately owned, High Easter |
| | WK549 | DHC1 Chipmunk T10 (G-BTWF) [Y] | Privately owned, Rufforth |
| | WK558 | DHC1 Chipmunk T10 (G-ARMG) | Privately owned, Wellesbourne Mountford |
| | WK570 | DHC1 Chipmunk T10 (8211M) <ff> | No 424 Sqn ATC, Southampton Hall of Aviation |
| | WK576 | DHC1 Chipmunk T10 (8357M) <ff> | No 1206 Sqn ATC, Lichfield |
| | WK584 | DHC1 Chipmunk T10 (7556M) <ff> | No 216 Sqn ATC, Bawtry |
| | WK585 | DHC1 Chipmunk T10 | RAF, stored Newton |
| | WK586 | DHC1 Chipmunk T10 (G-BXGX) [V] | Privately owned, Shoreham |
| | WK608 | DHC1 Chipmunk T10 [906] | RN Historic Flight, Yeovilton |
| | WK609 | DHC1 Chipmunk T10 (G-BXDN) [B] | Privately owned, Halton |
| | WK611 | DHC1 Chipmunk T10 (G-ARWB) | Privately owned, Thruxton |
| | WK613 | DHC1 Chipmunk T10 [P] | |
| | WK620 | DHC1 Chipmunk T10 [T] (fuselage) | Privately owned, Twyford, Bucks |
| | WK622 | DHC1 Chipmunk T10 (G-BCZH) | Privately owned, Horsford |
| | WK624 | DHC1 Chipmunk T10 (G-BWHI) | The Aircraft Restoration Co, Duxford |
| | WK626 | DHC1 Chipmunk T10 (8213M) <ff> | South Yorkshire Avn Museum, Firbeck |
| | WK628 | DHC1 Chipmunk T10 (G-BBMW) | Privately owned, Shoreham |
| | WK630 | DHC1 Chipmunk T10 (G-BXDG) [11] | Privately owned, Swanton Morley |
| | WK633 | DHC1 Chipmunk T10 (G-BXEC) [A] | Privately owned, Seething |
| | WK638 | DHC1 Chipmunk T10 (G-BWJZ) [83] | Privately owned, Breighton |
| | WK640 | DHC1 Chipmunk T10 (G-BWUV) [C] | Privately owned, Bagby |
| | WK642 | DHC1 Chipmunk T10 (G-BXDP) [94] | Privately owned, Eire |
| | WK654 | Gloster Meteor F8 (8092M) [X] | City of Norwich Aviation Museum |
| | WK800 | Gloster Meteor D16 [Z] | DPA, DERA Llanbedr |
| | *WK864* | Gloster Meteor F8 (WL168/7750M) [C] | Yorkshire Air Museum, Elvington |
| | WK935 | Gloster Meteor Prone Pilot (7869M) | RAF Museum, Cosford |
| | WK991 | Gloster Meteor F8 (7825M) | Imperial War Museum, Duxford |
| | WL131 | Gloster Meteor F8 (7751M) <ff> | South Yorkshire Avn Museum, Firbeck |
| | WL181 | Gloster Meteor F8 [X] | North-East Aircraft Museum, Usworth |
| | WL332 | Gloster Meteor T7 [888] | Privately owned, Long Marston |
| | WL345 | Gloster Meteor T7 | St Leonard's Motors, Hollington, E Sussex |
| | WL349 | Gloster Meteor T7 [Z] | On display, Staverton |
| | WL360 | Gloster Meteor T7 (7920M) [G] | Meteor Flight, Yatesbury |
| | WL375 | Gloster Meteor T7(mod) | Dumfries & Galloway Avn Mus, Dumfries |

| Serial | Type (other identity) [code] | Owner/operator, location or fate | Notes |
|---|---|---|---|
| WL405 | Gloster Meteor T7 | Martin Baker Aircraft, Chalgrove, spares use | |
| WL419 | Gloster Meteor T7 | Martin Baker Aircraft, Chalgrove | |
| WL505 | DH100 Vampire FB9 (7705M/ G-FBIX) | De Havilland Aviation, Swansea | |
| *WL505* | DH100 Vampire FB6 (J-1167/ *VZ304*/G-MKVI) | De Havilland Aviation, Swansea | |
| WL626 | Vickers Varsity T1 (G-BHDD) [P] | East Midlands Airport Aeropark | |
| WL627 | Vickers Varsity T1 (8488M) [D] <ff> | Privately owned, Preston, E Yorkshire | |
| WL679 | Vickers Varsity T1 (9155M) | RAF Museum, Cosford | |
| WL732 | BP P108 Sea Balliol T21 | RAF Museum, Cosford | |
| WL756 | Avro 696 Shackleton AEW2 (9101M) | *Scrapped at St Mawgan, April 1999* | |
| WL795 | Avro 696 Shackleton MR2C (8753M) [T] | RAF St Mawgan, on display | |
| WL798 | Avro 696 Shackleton MR2C (8114M) <ff> | Privately owned, Elgin | |
| *WL925* | Slingsby T31B Cadet TX3 (WV925) <ff> | RAF No 633 VGS, Cosford | |
| | | | |
| WM145 | AW Meteor NF11 <ff> | N Yorks Aircraft Recovery Centre, Chop Gate | |
| WM167 | AW Meteor NF11 (G-LOSM) | Privately owned, Bournemouth | |
| WM267 | Gloster Meteor NF11 <ff> | Blyth Valley Aviation Collection, Walpole, Suffolk | |
| WM292 | AW Meteor TT20 [841] | FAA Museum, stored RNAS Yeovilton | |
| *WM311* | AW Meteor TT20 (WM224/8177M) | Privately owned, North Weald | |
| WM366 | AW Meteor NF13 (4X-FNA) (comp VZ462) | SWWAPS, Lasham | |
| WM367 | AW Meteor NF13 <ff> | South Yorkshire Avn Museum, Firbeck | |
| WM571 | DH112 Sea Venom FAW21 [VL] | Southampton Hall of Aviation | |
| WM729 | DH113 Vampire NF10 [A] <ff> | Mosquito Aircraft Museum, Staverton | |
| WM913 | Hawker Sea Hawk FB5 (8162M) [456/J] | Newark Air Museum, Winthorpe | |
| WM961 | Hawker Sea Hawk FB5 [J] | Caernarfon Air World | |
| WM969 | Hawker Sea Hawk FB5 [10/Z] | Imperial War Museum, Duxford | |
| WM993 | Hawker Sea Hawk FB5 [034] | Privately owned, Peasedown St John, Avon | |
| | | | |
| *WN105* | Hawker Sea Hawk FB3 (WF299/ 8164M) | Privately owned, Birlingham, Worcs | |
| WN108 | Hawker Sea Hawk FB5 [033] | Ulster Aviation Society, Langford Lodge | |
| WN149 | BP P108 Balliol T2 | Boulton Paul Association, Wolverhampton | |
| WN411 | Fairey Gannet AS1 (fuselage) | Privately owned, Southampton | |
| WN493 | WS51 Dragonfly HR5 | FAA Museum, RNAS Yeovilton | |
| WN499 | WS51 Dragonfly HR5 [Y] | Caernarfon Air World | |
| WN516 | BP P108 Balliol T2 <ff> | North-East Aircraft Museum, Usworth | |
| WN534 | BP P108 Balliol T2 <ff> | Boulton Paul Association, Wolverhampton | |
| WN890 | Hawker Hunter F2 <ff> | South Yorkshire Avn Museum, Firbeck | |
| WN904 | Hawker Hunter F2 (7544M) [3] | RE 39 Regt, Waterbeach, on display | |
| WN907 | Hawker Hunter F2 (7416M) <ff> | Blyth Valley Aviation Collection, Walpole, Suffolk | |
| | | | |
| WP185 | Hawker Hunter F5 (7583M) | Privately owned, Great Dunmow, Essex | |
| WP190 | Hawker Hunter F5 (7582M/8473M/ *WP180*) [K] | Privately owned, Quedgeley, Glos. | |
| WP250 | DH113 Vampire NF10 <ff> | Privately owned, | |
| WP255 | DH113 Vampire NF10 <ff> | RAF Millom Museum, Haverigg | |
| WP270 | EoN Eton TX1 (8598M) | Gr Manchester Mus of Science & Industry, stored | |
| WP271 | EoN Eton TX1 | Privately owned, stored Keevil | |
| WP313 | Percival P57 Sea Prince T1 [568/CU] | FAA Museum, stored Wroughton | |
| WP314 | Percival P57 Sea Prince T1 (8634M) [573/CU] | Privately owned, Carlisle Airport | |
| WP321 | Percival P57 Sea Prince T1 (G-BRFC) [750/CU] | Privately owned, Bournemouth | |
| WP503 | WS51 Dragonfly HR3 [901] | Privately owned, Carnforth, Lancs | |
| WP515 | EE Canberra B2 <ff> | Privately owned, Welshpool | |
| WP772 | DHC1 Chipmunk T10 [Q] (wreck) | RAF Manston History Museum | |
| WP784 | DHC1 Chipmunk T10 <ff> | Privately owned, Long Marston | |
| WP788 | DHC1 Chipmunk T10 (G-BCHL) | Privately owned, Sleap | |
| WP790 | DHC1 Chipmunk T10 (G-BBNC) [T] | Mosquito Aircraft Museum, London Colney | |

| Notes | Serial | Type (other identity) [code] | Owner/operator, location or fate |
|---|---|---|---|
| | WP795 | DHC1 Chipmunk T10 (G-BVZZ) [901] | Privately owned, Lee-on-Solent |
| | WP800 | DHC1 Chipmunk T10 (G-BCXN) [2] | Privately owned, Halton |
| | WP803 | DHC1 Chipmunk T10 (G-HAPY) [G] | Privately owned, Booker |
| | WP805 | DHC1 Chipmunk T10 (G-MAJR) [D] | Privately owned, Fareham |
| | WP808 | DHC1 Chipmunk T10 (G-BDEU) | Privately owned, Binham |
| | WP809 | DHC1 Chipmunk T10 (G-BVTX) [78] | Privately owned, Husbands Bosworth |
| | WP833 | DHC1 Chipmunk T10 [H] | RAF, stored Newton |
| | WP839 | DHC1 Chipmunk T10 [A] | Privately owned, Thornton-Cleveleys, Lancs |
| | WP840 | DHC1 Chipmunk T10 (G-BXDM) [9] | Privately owned, Halton |
| | WP843 | DHC1 Chipmunk T10 (G-BDBP) [F] | Privately owned, Booker |
| | WP844 | DHC1 Chipmunk T10 (G-BWOX) [85] | Privately owned, Kings Coughton |
| | WP845 | DHC1 Chipmunk T10 <ff> | Privately owned, Leicestershire |
| | WP856 | DHC1 Chipmunk T10 (G-BVWP) [904] | Privately owned, Horsham |
| | WP857 | DHC1 Chipmunk T10 (G-BDRJ) [24] | Privately owned, Elstree |
| | WP859 | DHC1 Chipmunk T10 (G-BXCP) [E] | Privately owned, Eire |
| | WP860 | DHC1 Chipmunk T10 (G-BXDA) [6] | Privately owned, Cumbernauld |
| | WP863 | DHC1 Chipmunk T10 (8360M/ G-ATJI) <ff> | FR Aviation, Bournemouth |
| | WP864 | DHC1 Chipmunk T10 (8214M) <ff> | RAF, stored Newton |
| | WP871 | DHC1 Chipmunk T10 [W] | AAC, Middle Wallop, for display |
| | WP896 | DHC1 Chipmunk T10 (G-BWVY) [M] | Privately owned, London |
| | WP901 | DHC1 Chipmunk T10 (G-BWNT) [B] | Privately owned, East Midlands Airport |
| | WP903 | DHC1 Chipmunk T10 (G-BCGC) | Privately owned, Shoreham |
| | WP907 | DHC1 Chipmunk T10 <ff> (7970M) | Privately owned, Reading |
| | WP912 | DHC1 Chipmunk T10 (8467M) | RAF Museum, Cosford |
| | WP920 | DHC1 Chipmunk T10 (G-BXCR) [10] | *Sold as ZS-OMA, September 1999* |
| | WP921 | DHC1 Chipmunk T10 (G-ATJJ) <ff> | Privately owned, Brooklands |
| | WP925 | DHC1 Chipmunk T10 (G-BXHA) [C] | Privately owned, Camberley |
| | WP927 | DHC1 Chipmunk T10 (8216M/ G-ATJK) <ff> | No 247 Sqn ATC, Ashton-under-Lyne, Gr Manchester |
| | WP928 | DHC1 Chipmunk T10 (G-BXGM) [D] | Privately owned, Shoreham |
| | WP929 | DHC1 Chipmunk T10 (G-BXCV) [F] | Privately owned, Duxford |
| | WP930 | DHC1 Chipmunk T10 (G-BXHF) [J] | Privately owned, Redhill |
| | WP962 | DHC1 Chipmunk T10 [C] | RAF, stored Newton |
| | WP964 | DHC1 Chipmunk T10 [Y] | AAC Historic Aircraft Flight, Middle Wallop |
| | WP971 | DHC1 Chipmunk T10 (G-ATHD) | Privately owned, Denham |
| | WP972 | DHC1 Chipmunk T10 (8667M) <ff> | *Scrapped* |
| | *WP976* | DHC1 Chipmunk T10 (WP791/ G-APTS) | *Sold to Australia* |
| | WP978 | DHC1 Chipmunk T10 (7467M) <ff> | Privately owned, Bournemouth |
| | WP983 | DHC1 Chipmunk T10 (G-BXNN) [B] | Privately owned, London |
| | WP984 | DHC1 Chipmunk T10 (G-BWTO) [H] | Privately owned, Duxford |
| | *WR360* | DH112 Venom FB50 (J-1626/ G-DHSS) | Source Classic Jet Flight, Bournemouth |
| | *8R410* | DH112 Venom FB50 (J-1539/ G-DHUU/*WE410*) | Source Classic Jet Flight, Bournemouth |
| | *WR410* | DH112 Venom FB54 (J-1790/ G-BLKA) [N] | Source Classic Jet Flight, stored Bournemouth |
| | *WR421* | DH112 Venom FB50 (J-1611/ G-DHTT) | Source Classic Jet Flight, Bournemouth |
| | WR539 | DH112 Venom FB4 (8399M) [F] | Mosquito Aircraft Museum, Staverton |
| | WR960 | Avro 696 Shackleton AEW2 (8772M) | Gr Manchester Mus of Science & Industry |
| | WR963 | Avro 696 Shackleton AEW2 | Air Atlantique Historic Flight, Coventry |
| | WR971 | Avro 696 Shackleton MR3 (8119M) [Q] | Fenland & W Norfolk Aviation Museum, Wisbech |
| | WR974 | Avro 696 Shackleton MR3 (8117M) [K] | Gatwick Aviation Museum, Charlwood, Surrey |
| | WR977 | Avro 696 Shackleton MR3 (8186M) [B] | Newark Air Museum, Winthorpe |

| Serial | Type (other identity) [code] | Owner/operator, location or fate | Notes |
|---|---|---|---|
| WR982 | Avro 696 Shackleton MR3 (8106M) [J] | Gatwick Aviation Museum, Charlwood, Surrey | |
| WR985 | Avro 696 Shackleton MR3 (8103M) [H] | Privately owned, Long Marston | |
| WS103 | Gloster Meteor T7 [709/VL] | FAA Museum, stored Wroughton | |
| WS692 | Gloster Meteor NF12 (7605M) [C] | Newark Air Museum, Winthorpe | |
| WS726 | Gloster Meteor NF14 (7960M) [G] | No 1855 Sqn ATC, Royton, Gr Manchester | |
| WS739 | Gloster Meteor NF14 (7961M) | Newark Air Museum, Winthorpe | |
| WS760 | Gloster Meteor NF14 (7964M) | Meteor Flight, stored Yatesbury | |
| WS774 | Gloster Meteor NF14 (7959M) | Privately owned, Quedgeley, Glos | |
| WS776 | Gloster Meteor NF14 (7716M) [K] | Privately owned, Sandtoft | |
| WS788 | Gloster Meteor NF14 (7967M) [Z] | Yorkshire Air Museum, Elvington | |
| WS792 | Gloster Meteor NF14 (7965M) [K] | Brighouse Bay Caravan Park, Borgue, D&G | |
| WS807 | Gloster Meteor NF14 (7973M) [N] | Jet Age Museum, Staverton | |
| WS832 | Gloster Meteor NF14 [W] | Solway Aviation Society, Carlisle | |
| WS838 | Gloster Meteor NF14 | Midland Air Museum, Coventry | |
| WS843 | Gloster Meteor NF14 (7937M) [Y] | RAF Museum, Cosford | |
| *WT121* | Douglas Skyraider AEW1 (WT983) [415/CU] | FAA Museum, stored RNAS Yeovilton | |
| WT205 | EE Canberra B15 | No 2431 Sqn ATC, Eastwood, Essex | |
| WT308 | EE Canberra B(I)6 | RN, Predannack Fire School | |
| WT309 | EE Canberra B(I)6 <ff> | Privately owned, Farnborough | |
| WT333 | EE Canberra B6(mod) (G-BVXC) | Privately owned, Bruntingthorpe | |
| WT339 | EE Canberra B(I)8 (8198M) | RAF Barkston Heath Fire Section | |
| WT480 | EE Canberra T4 [AT] | RAF, stored Shawbury | |
| WT482 | EE Canberra T4 <ff> | Privately owned | |
| WT483 | EE Canberra T4 [83] | Privately owned, Long Marston | |
| WT486 | EE Canberra T4 (8102M) <ff> | Flight Experience Workshop, Belfast | |
| WT507 | EE Canberra PR7 (8131M/8548M) [44] <ff> | No 384 Sqn ATC, Mansfield | |
| WT509 | EE Canberra PR7 [BR] | RAF, stored Marham | |
| WT510 | EE Canberra T22 <ff> | Privately owned, Stock, Essex | |
| WT519 | EE Canberra PR7 [CH] | RAF Wyton, Fire Section | |
| WT520 | EE Canberra PR7 (8094M/8184M) <ff> | No 967 Sqn ATC, Warton | |
| WT525 | EE Canberra T22 <ff> | Privately owned, South Woodham Ferrers | |
| WT532 | EE Canberra PR7 (8728M/8890M) (fuselage) | Bournemouth Aviation Museum | |
| WT534 | EE Canberra PR7 (8549M) [43] <ff> | No 492 Sqn ATC, Shirley, W. Midlands | |
| WT536 | EE Canberra PR7 (8063M) <ff> | Privately owned, Portsmouth | |
| WT537 | EE Canberra PR7 | BAE SystemsSamlesbury, on display | |
| WT538 | EE Canberra PR7 [CJ] <ff> | RAF St Athan, Fire Section | |
| WT555 | Hawker Hunter F1 (7499M) | Vanguard Haulage, Greenford, London | |
| WT569 | Hawker Hunter F1 (7491M) | No 2117 Sqn ATC, Kenfig Hill, Mid-Glamorgan | |
| WT612 | Hawker Hunter F1 (7496M) | RAF Henlow on display | |
| WT619 | Hawker Hunter F1 (7525M) | Gr Manchester Mus of Science & Industry | |
| WT648 | Hawker Hunter F1 (7530M) <ff> | The Air Defence Collection, Salisbury | |
| WT651 | Hawker Hunter F1 [C] | Newark Air Museum, Winthorpe | |
| WT660 | Hawker Hunter F1 (7421M) [C] | Highland Aircraft Preservation Society, Inverness | |
| WT680 | Hawker Hunter F1 (7533M) [J] | No 1429 Sqn ATC, at DERA Aberporth | |
| WT684 | Hawker Hunter F1 (7422M) <ff> | South Yorkshire Avn Museum, Firbeck | |
| WT694 | Hawker Hunter F1 (7510M) | Caernarfon Air World | |
| WT711 | Hawker Hunter GA11 [833/DD] | Air Atlantique, Coventry | |
| *WT720* | Hawker Hunter F51 (RDAF E-408/8565M) [B] | RAF Sealand, on display | |
| WT722 | Hawker Hunter T8C (G-BWGN) [878/VL] | Classic Jet Aircraft Co, Exeter | |
| WT723 | Hawker Hunter PR11 (G-PRII) [866/VL,3] | Classic Jets, Brustem, Belgium | |
| WT744 | Hawker Hunter GA11 [868/VL] | South West Aviation Heritage, Eaglescott | |
| WT746 | Hawker Hunter F4 (7770M) [A] | Dumfries & Galloway Avn Mus, Dumfries | |
| WT799 | Hawker Hunter T8C [879] | Privately owned, North Weald | |
| WT804 | Hawker Hunter GA11 [831/DD] | FETC, Moreton-in-Marsh, Glos | |
| WT806 | Hawker Hunter GA11 | Privately owned, Sproughton | |
| WT859 | Supermarine 544 <ff> | Brooklands Museum, Weybridge | |
| WT867 | Slingsby T31B Cadet TX3 | Privately owned, Eaglescott | |

| Notes | Serial | Type (other identity) [code] | Owner/operator, location or fate |
|---|---|---|---|
| | WT898 | Slingsby T31B Cadet TX3 (BGA 3284/BGA 4412) | Privately owned, Rufforth |
| | WT899 | Slingsby T31B Cadet TX3 | Privately owned, Swindon |
| | WT902 | Slingsby T31B Cadet TX3 (BGA 3147) | Privately owned, Lleweni Parc, Clwyd |
| | WT905 | Slingsby T31B Cadet TX3 | Privately owned |
| | WT910 | Slingsby T31B Cadet TX3 (BGA 3953) | Privately owned, Challock |
| | WT933 | Bristol 171 Sycamore 3 (G-ALSW/7709M) | Newark Air Museum, Winthorpe |
| | | | |
| | WV106 | Douglas Skyraider AEW1 [427/C] | FAA Museum, at RNAS Culdrose |
| | WV198 | Sikorsky S55 Whirlwind HAR21 (G-BJWY) [K] | Solway Aviation Society, Carlisle |
| | WV256 | Hawker Hunter GA11 [862/VL] | RN, stored Shawbury |
| | WV276 | Hawker Hunter F4 (7847M) [D] | Privately owned, stored Sandown |
| | WV318 | Hawker Hunter T7B (G-FFOX) | Delta Jets, Kemble |
| | WV322 | Hawker Hunter T8C (9096M) [Y] | AMIF, RAFC Cranwell |
| | WV332 | Hawker Hunter F4 (7673M) <ff> | No 1254 Sqn ATC, Godalming |
| | WV372 | Hawker Hunter T7 (G-BXFI) [R] | Privately owned, Kemble |
| | WV381 | Hawker Hunter GA11 [732/VL] | UKAEA, Culham, Oxon |
| | WV382 | Hawker Hunter GA11 [830/VL] | Jet Avn Preservation Grp, Long Marston |
| | WV383 | Hawker Hunter T7 | DPA/AFD, DERA Boscombe Down |
| | WV396 | Hawker Hunter T8C (9249M) [91] | RAF Valley, at main gate |
| | WV483 | Percival P56 Provost T1 (7693M) [N-E] | Privately owned |
| | WV493 | Percival P56 Provost T1 (G-BDYG/7696M) [29] | Royal Scottish Mus'm of Flight, stored E Fortune |
| | WV499 | Percival P56 Provost T1 (7698M) [P-G] | Privately owned, Sandtoft |
| | WV562 | Percival P56 Provost T1 (7606M) [P-C] | RAF Museum, Cosford |
| | WV605 | Percival P56 Provost T1 [T-B] | Norfolk & Suffolk Avn Museum, Flixton |
| | WV606 | Percival P56 Provost T1 (7622M) [P-B] | Newark Air Museum, Winthorpe |
| | WV666 | Percival P56 Provost T1 (7925M/ G-BTDH) [O-D] | Privately owned, Shoreham |
| | WV679 | Percival P56 Provost T1 (7615M) [O-J] | Wellesbourne Wartime Museum |
| | WV703 | Percival P66 Pembroke C1 (8108M/*G-IIIM*) | Privately owned, Tattershall Thorpe |
| | WV705 | Percival P66 Pembroke C1 <ff> | Southampton Hall of Aviation, stored |
| | WV740 | Percival P66 Pembroke C1 (G-BNPH) | Privately owned, Jersey |
| | WV746 | Percival P66 Pembroke C1 (8938M) | RAF Museum, Cosford |
| | WV781 | Bristol 171 Sycamore HR12 (G-ALTD/7839M) | Caernarfon Air World |
| | WV783 | Bristol 171 Sycamore HR12 (G-ALSP/7841M) | RAF Museum, stored Wyton |
| | WV787 | EE Canberra B2/8 (8799M) | Newark Air Museum, Winthorpe |
| | WV795 | Hawker Sea Hawk FGA6 (8151M) | Kennet Aviation, Cranfield |
| | WV797 | Hawker Sea Hawk FGA6 (8155M) [491/J] | Midland Air Museum, Coventry |
| | WV798 | Hawker Sea Hawk FGA6 [026/CU] | SWWAPS, Lasham |
| | WV838 | Hawker Sea Hawk FGA4 | Phoenix Aviation Museum, Bruntingthorpe |
| | WV856 | Hawker Sea Hawk FGA6 [163] | FAA Museum, RNAS Yeovilton |
| | WV903 | Hawker Sea Hawk FGA4 (8153M) [128/C] | RN Historic Flight, stored Yeovilton |
| | *WV906* | Hawker Sea Hawk FGA6 (WV826) [182] | *To Malta, August 1999* |
| | WV908 | Hawker Sea Hawk FGA6 (8154M) [188/A] | RN Historic Flight, at BAE Systems, Dunsfold |
| | WV910 | Hawker Sea Hawk FGA6 <ff> | Boscombe Down Museum |
| | WV911 | Hawker Sea Hawk FGA4 [115/C] | BAe, Dunsfold |
| | | | |
| | WW138 | DH112 Sea Venom FAW22 [227/Z] | FAA Museum, RNAS Yeovilton |
| | WW145 | DH112 Sea Venom FAW22 [680/LM] | Royal Scottish Mus'm of Flight, E Fortune |
| | WW217 | DH112 Sea Venom FAW22 [351] | Newark Air Museum, Winthorpe |
| | WW388 | Percival P56 Provost T1 (7616M) [O-F] | Bomber County Aviation Museum, Hemswell |

| *Serial* | *Type (other identity) [code]* | *Owner/operator, location or fate* | *Notes* |
|---|---|---|---|
| WW421 | Percival P56 Provost T1 (7688M) [P-B] | Privately owned, Sandtoft | |
| WW442 | Percival P56 Provost T1 (7618M) [N] | Gatwick Aviation Museum, Charlwood, Surrey | |
| WW444 | Percival P56 Provost T1 [D] | Privately owned, Rugeley, Staffs | |
| WW447 | Percival P56 Provost T1 | Privately owned, Grazeley, Berks | |
| WW453 | Percival P56 Provost T1 (G-TMKI) [W-S] | Kennet Aviation, Cranfield | |
| WW654 | Hawker Hunter GA11 [834/DD] | Privately owned, Ford, W Sussex | |
| | | | |
| *WX643* | DHC1 Chipmunk T10 (8437M/ 8630M/WG362) [80] <ff> | RAF Newton, instructional use | |
| WX788 | DH112 Venom NF3 | Night-Fighter Preservation Team, Elvington | |
| WX853 | DH112 Venom NF3 (7443M) | Mosquito Aircraft Museum, London Colney | |
| WX905 | DH112 Venom NF3 (7458M) | Newark Air Museum, Winthorpe | |
| | | | |
| WZ425 | DH115 Vampire T11 | Privately owned, Birlingham, Worcs | |
| WZ450 | DH115 Vampire T11 <ff> | Lashenden Air Warfare Museum, Headcorn | |
| WZ458 | DH115 Vampire T11 (7728M) [31] <ff> | Blyth Valley Aviation Collection, Walpole, Suffolk | |
| WZ464 | DH115 Vampire T11 (N62430) [40] | Vintage Aircraft Team, Bruntingthorpe | |
| WZ507 | DH115 Vampire T11 (G-VTII) | De Havilland Aviation, Swansea | |
| WZ515 | DH115 Vampire T11 [60] | Solway Aviation Society, Carlisle | |
| WZ518 | DH115 Vampire T11 | North-East Aircraft Museum, Usworth | |
| WZ549 | DH115 Vampire T11 (8118M) [F] | Ulster Aviation Society, Langford Lodge | |
| WZ553 | DH115 Vampire T11 (G-DHYY) [40] | Source Classic Jet Flight, stored Bournemouth | |
| WZ557 | DH115 Vampire T11 | N Yorks Aircraft Recovery Centre, Chop Gate | |
| WZ581 | DH115 Vampire T11 <ff> | The Vampire Collection, Hemel Hempstead | |
| WZ584 | DH115 Vampire T11 [K] | Privately owned, Sandtoft | |
| WZ589 | DH115 Vampire T11 [19] | Lashenden Air Warfare Museum, Headcorn | |
| *WZ589* | DH115 Vampire T55 (U-1230/ G-DHZZ) | Source Classic Jet Flight, Bournemouth | |
| WZ590 | DH115 Vampire T11 [19] | Imperial War Museum, Duxford | |
| WZ608 | DH115 Vampire T11 [56] <ff> | Privately owned, | |
| WZ620 | DH115 Vampire T11 [68] | Avon Aviation Museum, Yatesbury | |
| WZ662 | Auster AOP9 (G-BKVK) | Privately owned, Middle Wallop | |
| WZ706 | Auster AOP9 (7851M/G-BURR) | Privately owned, Middle Wallop | |
| WZ711 | Auster AOP9/Beagle E3 (G-AVHT) | Privately owned, Middle Wallop | |
| WZ721 | Auster AOP9 | Museum of Army Flying, Middle Wallop | |
| WZ724 | Auster AOP9 (7432M) | AAC Middle Wallop, at main gate | |
| WZ729 | Auster AOP9 (G-BXON) | Privately owned, Newark-on-Trent | |
| WZ736 | Avro 707A (7868M) | Gr Manchester Mus of Science & Industry | |
| WZ744 | Avro 707C (7932M) | RAF Museum, Cosford | |
| WZ753 | Slingsby T38 Grasshopper TX1 | Southampton Hall of Aviation | |
| WZ767 | Slingsby T38 Grasshopper TX1 | North-East Aircraft Museum, stored Usworth | |
| WZ768 | Slingsby T38 Grasshopper TX1 (comp XK820) | Privately owned, Kirton-in-Lindsey, Lincs | |
| WZ769 | Slingsby T38 Grasshopper TX1 | Privately owned, stored Rufforth | |
| WZ772 | Slingsby T38 Grasshopper TX1 | Museum of Army Flying, Middle Wallop | |
| WZ779 | Slingsby T38 Grasshopper TX1 | Privately owned, Old Sarum | |
| WZ784 | Slingsby T38 Grasshopper TX1 | Privately owned, Thurrock College | |
| WZ791 | Slingsby T38 Grasshopper TX1 (8944M) | RAF Museum, Hendon | |
| WZ792 | Slingsby T38 Grasshopper TX1 | Privately owned, Sproughton | |
| WZ793 | Slingsby T38 Grasshopper TX1 | Whitgift School, Croydon | |
| WZ796 | Slingsby T38 Grasshopper TX1 | Privately owned, stored Nympsfield, Glos | |
| WZ816 | Slingsby T38 Grasshopper TX1 (BGA 3979) | Privately owned, stored Ashford, Kent | |
| WZ819 | Slingsby T38 Grasshopper TX1 (BGA 3498) | Privately owned, Halton | |
| WZ820 | Slingsby T38 Grasshopper TX1 | Shoreham Airport, on display | |
| WZ822 | Slingsby T38 Grasshopper TX1 | South Yorkshire Avn Museum, Firbeck | |
| WZ824 | Slingsby T38 Grasshopper TX1 | Privately owned, stored Strathaven, Strathclyde | |
| WZ825 | Slingsby T38 Grasshopper TX1 | RAF Museum, stored Cosford | |

| Notes | Serial | Type (other identity) [code] | Owner/operator, location or fate |
|---|---|---|---|
| | *WZ826* | Vickers Valiant B(K)1 (XD826/ 7872M) <ff> | Privately owned, Foulness |
| | WZ827 | Slingsby T38 Grasshopper TX1 | RAFGSA, stored Bicester |
| | WZ828 | Slingsby T38 Grasshopper TX1 (BGA 4421) | Privately owned, Bicester |
| | WZ829 | Slingsby T38 Grasshopper TX1 | RAFGSA, stored Bicester |
| | WZ831 | Slingsby T38 Grasshopper TX1 | Privately owned, stored Nympsfield, Glos |
| | WZ846 | DHC1 Chipmunk T10 (G-BCSC/ 8439M) <ff> | No 1404 Sqn ATC, Chatham |
| | WZ847 | DHC1 Chipmunk T10 (G-CPMK) [F] | Privately owned, Ashbourne |
| | WZ866 | DHC1 Chipmunk T10 (8217M/ G-ATEB) <ff> | South Yorkshire Avn Museum, Firbeck |
| | WZ868 | DHC1 Chipmunk T10 (G-BCIW) [H] | Privately owned, Sandtoft |
| | *WZ868* | DHC1 Chipmunk T10 (WG322/ G-ARMF) [H] | Privately owned, Twyford, Bucks |
| | WZ869 | DHC1 Chipmunk T10 (8019M) [R] <ff> | No 395 Sqn ATC, Handforth, Cheshire |
| | WZ872 | DHC1 Chipmunk T10 [E] | RAF, stored Newton |
| | WZ876 | DHC1 Chipmunk T10 (G-BBWN) <ff> | Privately owned, South Molton, Devon |
| | WZ879 | DHC1 Chipmunk T10 (G-BWUT) [73] | Aero Vintage, Rye |
| | WZ882 | DHC1 Chipmunk T10 (G-BXGP) [K] | Privately owned, Eaglescott |
| | | | |
| | XA109 | DH115 Sea Vampire T22 | Royal Scottish Mus'm of Flight, E Fortune |
| | XA127 | DH115 Sea Vampire T22 <ff> | FAA Museum, stored RNAS Yeovilton |
| | XA129 | DH115 Sea Vampire T22 | FAA Museum, stored Wroughton |
| | XA225 | Slingsby T38 Grasshopper TX1 | Churchers College, Petersfield, Hants |
| | XA230 | Slingsby T38 Grasshopper TX1 (BGA 4098) | Privately owned, Henlow |
| | XA231 | Slingsby T38 Grasshopper TX1 (8888M) | RAF Manston History Museum |
| | XA240 | Slingsby T38 Grasshopper TX1 (BGA 4556) | Privately owned, Keevil |
| | XA241 | Slingsby T38 Grasshopper TX1 | Shuttleworth Collection, Old Warden |
| | XA243 | Slingsby T38 Grasshopper TX1 (8886M) | Privately owned, Gransden Lodge, Cambs |
| | XA244 | Slingsby T38 Grasshopper TX1 | RAF, stored Cosford |
| | XA282 | Slingsby T31B Cadet TX3 | Caernarfon Air World |
| | XA286 | Slingsby T31B Cadet TX3 | Privately owned, stored Rufforth |
| | XA289 | Slingsby T31B Cadet TX3 | Privately owned, Eaglescott |
| | XA290 | Slingsby T31B Cadet TX3 | Privately owned, stored Rufforth |
| | XA293 | Slingsby T31B Cadet TX3 | Privately owned, Breighton |
| | XA302 | Slingsby T31B Cadet TX3 (BGA3786) | Privately owned, Syerston |
| | XA454 | Fairey Gannet COD4 | RNAS Yeovilton Fire Section |
| | XA459 | Fairey Gannet ECM6 [E] | Privately owned, Membury, Berks |
| | XA460 | Fairey Gannet ECM6 [768/BY] | Deeside College, Connah's Quay, Clwyd |
| | XA466 | Fairey Gannet COD4 [777/LM] | FAA Museum, stored Yeovilton |
| | XA508 | Fairey Gannet T2 [627/GN] | FAA Museum, at Midland Air Museum, Coventry |
| | XA564 | Gloster Javelin FAW1 (7464M) | RAF Museum, Cosford |
| | XA634 | Gloster Javelin FAW4 (7641M) | RAF Leeming, on display |
| | XA699 | Gloster Javelin FAW5 (7809M) | Midland Air Museum, Coventry |
| | XA847 | EE P1B (8371M) | Privately owned, Suffolk |
| | XA862 | WS55 Whirlwind HAR1 (G-AMJT) [9] | The Helicopter Museum, Weston-super-Mare |
| | XA864 | WS55 Whirlwind HAR1 | FAA Museum, stored Yeovilton |
| | XA868 | WS55 Whirlwind HAR1 | |
| | XA870 | WS55 Whirlwind HAR1 | Flambards Village Theme Park, Helston |
| | XA880 | DH104 Devon C2 (G-BVXR) | Privately owned, Staverton |
| | XA893 | Avro 698 Vulcan B1 (8591M) <ff> | RAF Museum, Cosford |
| | XA896 | Avro 698 Vulcan B1 <ff> | Privately owned, Reigate |
| | XA903 | Avro 698 Vulcan B1 <ff> | Privately owned, Wellesbourne Mountford |
| | XA917 | HP80 Victor B1 (7827M) <ff> | Privately owned, Guardbridge, Fife |
| | | | |
| | XB259 | Blackburn B101 Beverley C1 (G-AOAI) | Museum of Army Transport, Beverley |
| | XB261 | Blackburn B101 Beverley C1 <ff> | Duxford Aviation Society, Duxford |
| | XB446 | Grumman TBM-3 Avenger ECM6B | FAA Museum, Yeovilton |
| | XB480 | Hiller HT1 [537] | FAA Museum, stored Yeovilton |

| Serial | Type (other identity) [code] | Owner/operator, location or fate | Notes |
|---|---|---|---|
| XB812 | Canadair CL-13 Sabre F4 (9227M) [U] | RAF Museum, Hendon | |
| XD145 | Saro SR53 | RAF Museum, Cosford | |
| XD163 | WS55 Whirlwind HAR10 (8645M) [X] | The Helicopter Museum, Weston-super-Mare | |
| XD165 | WS55 Whirlwind HAR10 (8673M) [B] | AAC Wattisham, instructional use | |
| XD215 | VS Scimitar F1 <ff> | Privately owned, Cheltenham | |
| XD234 | VS Scimitar F1 [834] | *Scrapped* | |
| XD235 | VS Scimitar F1 <ff> | Privately owned, Welshpool | |
| XD317 | VS Scimitar F1 [112/R] | FAA Museum, RNAS Yeovilton | |
| XD332 | VS Scimitar F1 [194/C] | Southampton Hall of Aviation | |
| XD375 | DH115 Vampire T11 (7887M) [72] | Privately owned, Yorkshire | |
| XD377 | DH115 Vampire T11 (8203M) <ff> | South Yorkshire Avn Museum, Firbeck | |
| XD382 | DH115 Vampire T11 (8033M) | Anchor Surplus, Ripley, Derbys | |
| XD425 | DH115 Vampire T11 <ff> | RAF Millom Museum, Haverigg | |
| XD434 | DH115 Vampire T11 [25] | Fenland & W Norfolk Aviation Museum, Wisbech | |
| XD445 | DH115 Vampire T11 | Bomber County Aviation Museum, Hemswell | |
| XD447 | DH115 Vampire T11 [50] | Jet Avn Preservation Grp, Long Marston | |
| XD452 | DH115 Vampire T11 (7990M) [47] <ff> | Vampire Support Team, RAF Sealand | |
| XD459 | DH115 Vampire T11 [63] <ff> | Privately owned, Bruntingthorpe | |
| XD463 | DH115 Vampire T11 (8023M) | Privately owned, Nottingham | |
| XD506 | DH115 Vampire T11 (7983M) | Jet Age Museum, Staverton | |
| XD515 | DH115 Vampire T11 (7998M/*XM515*) | Privately owned, Rugeley, Staffs | |
| XD525 | DH115 Vampire T11 (7882M) <ff> | Campbell College CCF, Belfast | |
| XD528 | DH115 Vampire T11 (8159M) <ff> | Gamston Aerodrome Fire Section | |
| XD534 | DH115 Vampire T11 [41] | Military Aircraft Pres'n Grp, Barton | |
| XD535 | DH115 Vampire T11 <ff> | Barton Aviation Heritage Society, Barton | |
| XD536 | DH115 Vampire T11 (7734M) [H] | Alleyn's School CCF, Northolt | |
| XD542 | DH115 Vampire T11 (7604M) [28] | Montrose Air Station Museum | |
| XD547 | DH115 Vampire T11 [Z] (composite) | Dumfries & Galloway Avn Mus, Dumfries | |
| XD593 | DH115 Vampire T11 [50] | Newark Air Museum, Winthorpe | |
| XD595 | DH115 Vampire T11 <ff> | Privately owned, Glentham, Lincs | |
| XD596 | DH115 Vampire T11 (7939M) | Southampton Hall of Aviation | |
| XD599 | DH115 Vampire T11 <ff> | Privately owned, Welshpool | |
| XD602 | DH115 Vampire T11 (7737M) | Dundonald Aviation Centre, Strathclyde | |
| XD614 | DH115 Vampire T11 (8124M) <ff> | Privately owned, Southampton | |
| XD616 | DH115 Vampire T11 [56] | Mosquito Aircraft Museum, Staverton | |
| XD622 | DH115 Vampire T11 (8160M) | No 2214 Sqn ATC, Usworth | |
| XD624 | DH115 Vampire T11 [O] | Macclesfield Technical College | |
| XD626 | DH115 Vampire T11 [Q] | Midland Air Museum, Coventry | |
| XD674 | Hunting Jet Provost T1 (7570M) [T] | RAF Museum, Cosford | |
| *XD693* | Hunting Jet Provost T1 (XM129/G-AOBU) [Z-Q] | Kennet Aviation, Cranfield | |
| XD816 | Vickers Valiant B(K)1 <ff> | Brooklands Museum, Weybridge | |
| XD818 | Vickers Valiant B(K)1 (7894M) | RAF Museum, Hendon | |
| XD857 | Vickers Valiant B(K)1 <ff> | Privately owned, Foulness | |
| XD875 | Vickers Valiant B(K)1 <ff> | British Aviation Heritage, Bruntingthorpe | |
| XE317 | Bristol 171 Sycamore HR14 (G-AMWO) [S-N] | South Yorkshire Avn Museum, Firbeck | |
| XE327 | Hawker Sea Hawk FGA6 [644/LH] | Privately owned, Bruntingthorpe | |
| XE339 | Hawker Sea Hawk FGA6 (8156M) [149/E] | RN Historic Flight, stored Yeovilton | |
| XE340 | Hawker Sea Hawk FGA6 [131/Z] | FAA Museum, at Montrose Air Station Museum | |
| XE368 | Hawker Sea Hawk FGA6 [200/J] | Flambards Village Theme Park, Helston | |
| XE489 | Hawker Sea Hawk FGA6 (G-JETH) | Gatwick Aviation Museum, Charlwood, Surrey | |
| XE521 | Fairey Rotodyne Y (parts) | The Helicopter Museum, Weston-super-Mare | |
| XE584 | Hawker Hunter FGA9 <ff> | Privately owned, Woodford | |
| XE597 | Hawker Hunter FGA9 (8874M) <ff> | | |
| XE601 | Hawker Hunter FGA9 | Boscombe Down Museum | |
| XE606 | Hawker Hunter F6A (*XJ673*/8841M) | RAF Cottesmore | |
| XE624 | Hawker Hunter FGA9 (8875M) [G] | Army, Cawdor Barracks, Brawdy, on display | |

| Notes | Serial | Type (other identity) [code] | Owner/operator, location or fate |
|---|---|---|---|
| | XE627 | Hawker Hunter F6A [T] | Imperial War Museum, Duxford |
| | XE643 | Hawker Hunter FGA9 (8586M) <ff> | RAF EPTT, Aldergrove |
| | XE664 | Hawker Hunter F4 <ff> | Jet Age Museum, Staverton |
| | XE665 | Hawker Hunter T8C (G-BWGM) [876/VL] | Classic Jet Aircraft Co, Exeter |
| | XE668 | Hawker Hunter GA11 [832/DD] | RN, Predannack Fire School |
| | XE670 | Hawker Hunter F4 (7762M/8585M) <ff> | RAF Museum, Cosford |
| | XE685 | Hawker Hunter GA11 (G-GAII) [861/VL] | Privately owned, North Weald |
| | XE689 | Hawker Hunter GA11 (G-BWGK) [864/VL] | Privately owned, North Weald |
| | XE786 | Slingsby T31B Cadet TX3 | RAF, stored Arbroath |
| | XE793 | Slingsby T31B Cadet TX3 (8666M) | Privately owned |
| | XE796 | Slingsby T31B Cadet TX3 | Privately owned, stored North Weald |
| | XE799 | Slingsby T31B Cadet TX3 (8943M) [R] | RAFGSA, Syerston |
| | XE802 | Slingsby T31B Cadet TX3 | Privately owned, stored Cupar, Fife |
| | XE807 | Slingsby T31B Cadet TX3 (BGA3545) | Privately owned, Halesland |
| | XE849 | DH115 Vampire T11 (7928M) [V3] | Privately owned, Shobdon |
| | XE852 | DH115 Vampire T11 [H] | No 2247 Sqn ATC, Hawarden |
| | XE855 | DH115 Vampire T11 <ff> | Midland Air Museum, Coventry |
| | XE856 | DH115 Vampire T11 (G-DUSK) | Privately owned, Henlow |
| | XE864 | DH115 Vampire T11(comp XD435) <ff> | Privately owned, Welshpool |
| | XE872 | DH115 Vampire T11 [62] | Midland Air Museum, Coventry |
| | XE874 | DH115 Vampire T11 (8582M) [61] | Montrose Air Station Museum |
| | *XE897* | DH115 Vampire T11 (XD403) | Privately owned, Errol, Tayside |
| | *XE897* | DH115 Vampire T55 (U-1214/ G-DHVV) | Source Classic Jet Flight, Bournemouth |
| | XE920 | DH115 Vampire T11 (8196M/ G-VMPR) [A] | Vampire Support Team, Swansea |
| | XE921 | DH115 Vampire T11 [64] <ff> | Privately owned, Barton |
| | XE935 | DH115 Vampire T11 | South Yorkshire Avn Museum, Firbeck |
| | XE946 | DH115 Vampire T11 (7473M) <ff> | Privately owned, Heath Farm, North Rauceby, Lincs |
| | XE956 | DH115 Vampire T11 (G-OBLN) | De Havilland Aviation, Swansea |
| | XE979 | DH115 Vampire T11 [54] | Privately owned, Birlingham, Worcs |
| | XE982 | DH115 Vampire T11 (7564M) [01] | Privately owned, Dunkeswell |
| | XE985 | DH115 Vampire T11 (*WZ476*) | De Havilland Aviation, Swansea |
| | XE993 | DH115 Vampire T11 (8161M) | Privately owned, Cosford |
| | XE995 | DH115 Vampire T11 [53] | Privately owned, High Halden, Kent |
| | XE998 | DH115 Vampire T11 (*U-1215*) | Privately owned, Brooklands Museum, Weybridge |
| | XF113 | VS Swift F7 [19] <ff> | Boscombe Down Museum |
| | XF114 | VS Swift F7 (G-SWIF) | Privately owned, Scampton |
| | XF300 | Hawker Hunter GA11 [860/VL] | RN, stored Shawbury |
| | XF303 | Hawker Hunter F58A (J-4105/ G-BWOU) [105,A] | The Old Flying Machine Company, Scampton |
| | *XF314* | Hawker Hunter F51 (RDAF E-412) [N] | Privately owned, stored Sandown |
| | XF321 | Hawker Hunter T7 | Classic Jet Aircraft Co, Exeter (spares use) |
| | *XF324* | Hawker Hunter F51 (RDAF E-427) [D] | British Aviation Heritage, Bruntingthorpe |
| | XF357 | Hawker Hunter T8C (G-BWGL) | The Old Flying Machine Co, Duxford |
| | XF358 | Hawker Hunter T8C [870/VL] | DPA/AFD, DERA Boscombe Down |
| | XF368 | Hawker Hunter GA11 [863/VL] | RN, stored Shawbury |
| | XF375 | Hawker Hunter F6A (8736M/ G-BUEZ) [05] | The Old Flying Machine Co, Duxford |
| | XF382 | Hawker Hunter F6A [15] | Midland Air Museum, Coventry |
| | XF383 | Hawker Hunter F6 (8706M) <ff> | Privately owned, Kidlington |
| | XF509 | Hawker Hunter F6 (8708M) | Humbrol Paints, Marfleet, E Yorkshire |
| | XF515 | Hawker Hunter F6A (8830M/ G-KAXF) [R] | Kennet Aviation, Cranfield |
| | XF516 | Hawker Hunter F6A (8685M/ G-BVVC) [F] | Privately owned, Kemble |
| | *XF519* | Hawker Hunter FGA9 (8677M/ 8738M/9183M) (comp XJ695) [J] | MoD FSCTE, Manston |
| | XF522 | Hawker Hunter F6 <ff> | No 1365 Sqn ATC, Aylesbury |
| | XF526 | Hawker Hunter F6 (8679M) [78/E] | Privately owned, Birlingham, Worcs |

| *Serial* | *Type (other identity) [code]* | *Owner/operator, location or fate* | *Notes* |
|---|---|---|---|
| XF527 | Hawker Hunter F6 (8680M) | RAF Halton, on display | |
| XF545 | Percival P56 Provost T1 (7957M) [O-K] | Privately owned, Thatcham | |
| XF597 | Percival P56 Provost T1 (G-BKFW) [AH] | Privately owned, Thatcham | |
| XF603 | Percival P56 Provost T1 (G-KAPW) | Kennet Aviation, Cranfield | |
| XF690 | Percival P56 Provost T1 (8041M/ G-MOOS) | Kennet Aviation, Cranfield | |
| XF708 | Avro 716 Shackleton MR3 [203/C] | Imperial War Museum, Duxford | |
| XF785 | Bristol 173 (7648M/G-ALBN) | RAF Museum, stored Cosford | |
| XF836 | Percival P56 Provost T1 (8043M/ G-AWRY) [JG] | Privately owned, Thatcham | |
| XF844 | Percival P56 Provost T1 [70] | British Aviation Heritage, Bruntingthorpe | |
| XF877 | Percival P56 Provost T1 (G-AWVF) [JX] | Privately owned, Sandown | |
| XF926 | Bristol 188 (8368M) | RAF Museum, Cosford | |
| XF967 | Hawker Hunter T8C (9186M) [T] | AMIF, RAFC Cranwell | |
| XF994 | Hawker Hunter T8C [873/VL] | DPA/AFD, DERA Boscombe Down | |
| XF995 | Hawker Hunter T8B (9237M) [K] | AMIF, RAFC Cranwell | |
| XG154 | Hawker Hunter FGA9 (8863M) [54] | RAF Museum, Hendon | |
| XG160 | Hawker Hunter F6A (8831M/ G-BWAF) [U] | Royal Jordanian AF Historic Flt, stored Bournemouth | |
| XG164 | Hawker Hunter F6 (8681M) | RAF, stored Shawbury | |
| XG172 | Hawker Hunter F6A (8832M) [A] | Privately owned, North Weald | |
| *XG193* | Hawker Hunter FGA9 (XG297) (comp with WT741) | Bomber County Aviation Museum, Hemswell | |
| XG196 | Hawker Hunter F6A (8702M) [31] | Army, Mytchett, Surrey, on display | |
| XG209 | Hawker Hunter F6 (8709M) <ff> | Privately owned, Chelmsford | |
| XG210 | Hawker Hunter F6 | Privately owned, Beck Row, Suffolk | |
| XG225 | Hawker Hunter F6A (8713M) [S] | RAF Cosford on display | |
| XG226 | Hawker Hunter F6A (8800M) [28] <ff> | No 1242 Sqn ATC, Faversham, Kent | |
| XG252 | Hawker Hunter FGA9 (8840M) [U] | Privately owned, Bosbury, Hereford | |
| XG254 | Hawker Hunter FGA9 (8881M) | RAF Coltishall Fire Section | |
| XG274 | Hawker Hunter F6 (8710M) [71] | Privately owned, Sproughton | |
| XG290 | Hawker Hunter F6 (8711M)<ff> | Boscombe Down Museum | |
| XG297 | Hawker Hunter FGA9 <ff> | South Yorkshire Avn Museum, stored Firbeck | |
| XG325 | EE Lightning F1 <ff> | No 1476 Sqn ATC, Southend | |
| XG329 | EE Lightning F1 (8050M) | Privately owned, Flixton | |
| XG331 | EE Lightning F1 <ff> | Jet Age Museum, Staverton | |
| XG337 | EE Lightning F1 (8056M) [M] | RAF Museum, Cosford | |
| XG452 | Bristol 192 Belvedere HC1 (7997M/G-BRMB) | The Helicopter Museum, Weston-super-Mare | |
| XG454 | Bristol 192 Belvedere HC1 (8366M) | Gr Manchester Mus of Science & Industry | |
| XG462 | Bristol 192 Belvedere HC1 <ff> | The Helicopter Museum, stored Weston-super-Mare | |
| XG474 | Bristol 192 Belvedere HC1 (8367M) [O] | RAF Museum, Hendon | |
| XG496 | DH104 Devon C2 (G-ANDX) [K] | *Sold to Australia, 1999* | |
| XG502 | Bristol 171 Sycamore HR14 | Museum of Army Flying, Middle Wallop | |
| XG506 | Bristol 171 Sycamore HR14 (7852M) [S-P] | Bomber County Aviation Museum, Hemswell | |
| XG518 | Bristol 171 Sycamore HR14 (8009M) [S-E] | Norfolk & Suffolk Avn Museum, Flixton | |
| XG523 | Bristol 171 Sycamore HR14 <ff> [K] | Norfolk & Suffolk Avn Museum, Flixton | |
| XG540 | Bristol 171 Sycamore HR14 (7899M/8345M) [Y-S] | Botany Bay Village, Chorley, Lancs | |
| XG544 | Bristol 171 Sycamore HR14 | Privately owned, Tremar, Cornwall | |
| XG547 | Bristol 171 Sycamore HR14 (G-HAPR) [S-T] | The Helicopter Museum, Weston-super-Mare | |
| XG574 | WS55 Whirlwind HAR3 [752/PO] | FAA Museum, RNAS Yeovilton | |
| XG577 | WS55 Whirlwind HAR3 (9050M) | RAF Leconfield Crash Rescue Training | |
| XG588 | WS55 Whirlwind HAR3 (G-BAMH/ VR-BEP) | East Midlands Airport Aeropark | |
| XG594 | WS55 Whirlwind HAS7 [517/PO] | FAA Museum, at R. Scottish Mus'm of Flt, E Fortune | |
| XG596 | WS55 Whirlwind HAS7 [66] | THM/GKN Westland, Yeovil (under restoration) | |
| XG597 | WS55 Whirlwind HAS7 | Privately owned, Siddal, West Yorkshire | |
| XG613 | DH112 Sea Venom FAW21 | Imperial War Museum, Duxford | |
| XG629 | DH112 Sea Venom FAW22 <ff> | Privately owned, Stone, Staffs | |

| Notes | Serial | Type (other identity) [code] | Owner/operator, location or fate |
|---|---|---|---|
| | XG680 | DH112 Sea Venom FAW22 [438] | North-East Aircraft Museum, Usworth |
| | XG691 | DH112 Sea Venom FAW22 [93/J] | Jet Age Museum, Staverton |
| | XG692 | DH112 Sea Venom FAW22 [668/LM] | Privately owned, Baxterley, Warwickshire |
| | XG730 | DH112 Sea Venom FAW22 [499/A] | Mosquito Aircraft Museum, London Colney |
| | XG736 | DH112 Sea Venom FAW22 | Ulster Aviation Society, Newtownards |
| | XG737 | DH112 Sea Venom FAW22 [220/Z] | Jet Avn Preservation Grp, stored Long Marston |
| | XG743 | DH115 Sea Vampire T22 [597/LM] | Wymondham College, Norfolk |
| | XG766 | DH115 Sea Vampire T22 (N6-766/ G-SPDR) | De Havilland Aviation, Swansea |
| | *XG775* | DH115 Vampire T55 (U-1219/ G-DHWW) [VL] | Source Classic Jet Flight, Bournemouth |
| | XG797 | Fairey Gannet ECM6 [277] | Imperial War Museum, Duxford |
| | XG831 | Fairey Gannet ECM6 [396] | Flambards Village Theme Park, Helston |
| | XG882 | Fairey Gannet T5 (8754M) [771/LM] | Privately owned, Errol, Tayside |
| | XG883 | Fairey Gannet T5 [773/BY] | FAA Museum, at Museum of Berkshire Aviation, Woodley |
| | XG900 | Short SC1 | Science Museum, stored Wroughton |
| | XG905 | Short SC1 | Ulster Folk & Transpt Mus, Holywood, Co Down |
| | | | |
| | XH131 | EE Canberra PR9 [AA] | RAF No 39(1 PRU) Sqn, Marham |
| | XH132 | Short SC9 Canberra (8915M) <ff> | *Sold to Italy* |
| | XH134 | EE Canberra PR9 [AB] | RAF No 39(1 PRU) Sqn, Marham |
| | XH135 | EE Canberra PR9 [AC] | RAF No 39(1 PRU) Sqn, Marham |
| | XH136 | EE Canberra PR9 (8782M) <ff> | Phoenix Aviation, Bruntingthorpe |
| | XH165 | EE Canberra PR9 <ff> | Blyth Valley Aviation Collection, Walpole |
| | XH168 | EE Canberra PR9 [AD] | RAF No 39(1 PRU) Sqn, Marham |
| | XH169 | EE Canberra PR9 | RAF No 39(1 PRU) Sqn, Marham |
| | XH170 | EE Canberra PR9 (8739M) | RAF Wyton, on display |
| | XH171 | EE Canberra PR9 (8746M) [U] | RAF Museum, Cosford |
| | XH174 | EE Canberra PR9 <ff> | RAF, stored Shawbury |
| | XH175 | EE Canberra PR9 <ff> | Privately owned, Stock, Essex |
| | XH177 | EE Canberra PR9 <ff> | Privately owned, Stock, Essex |
| | XH278 | DH115 Vampire T11 (8595M/ 7866M) | Privately owned, Felton, Northumberland |
| | XH312 | DH115 Vampire T11 [18] | Privately owned, Dodleston, Cheshire |
| | XH313 | DH115 Vampire T11 [E] | Privately owned, Sandtoft |
| | XH318 | DH115 Vampire T11 (7761M) [64] | Privately owned, Southampton |
| | XH328 | DH115 Vampire T11 <ff> | Privately owned, stored Bournemouth |
| | XH330 | DH115 Vampire T11 [73] | Privately owned, Bridgnorth |
| | XH537 | Avro 698 Vulcan B2MRR (8749M) <ff> | Privately owned, Bruntingthorpe |
| | XH558 | Avro 698 Vulcan B2 (G-VLCN) | British Aviation Heritage, Bruntingthorpe |
| | XH560 | Avro 698 Vulcan K2 <ff> | Privately owned, Foulness |
| | XH563 | Avro 698 Vulcan B2MRR <ff> | Privately owned, Banchory, Fife |
| | XH568 | EE Canberra B6(mod) (G-BVIC) | Classic Aviation Projects, Bruntingthorpe |
| | XH584 | EE Canberra T4 (G-27-374) <ff> | South Yorkshire Avn Museum, Firbeck |
| | XH592 | HP80 Victor K1A (8429M) <ff> | Phoenix Aviation, Bruntingthorpe |
| | XH648 | HP80 Victor K1A | Imperial War Museum, Duxford |
| | XH669 | HP80 Victor K2 (9092M) <ff> | Privately owned, Foulness |
| | XH670 | HP80 Victor SR2 <ff> | Privately owned, Foulness |
| | XH672 | HP80 Victor K2 | RAF Museum, Cosford |
| | XH673 | HP80 Victor K2 (8911M) | RAF Marham, on display |
| | XH767 | Gloster Javelin FAW9 (7955M) [A] | City of Norwich Aviation Museum |
| | XH783 | Gloster Javelin FAW7 (7798M) <ff> | Privately owned, Catford |
| | XH837 | Gloster Javelin FAW7 (8032M) <ff> | Caernarfon Air World |
| | XH892 | Gloster Javelin FAW9 (7982M) [J] | Norfolk & Suffolk Avn Museum, Flixton |
| | XH897 | Gloster Javelin FAW9 | Imperial War Museum, Duxford |
| | XH903 | Gloster Javelin FAW9 (7938M) | Jet Age Museum, Staverton |
| | XH992 | Gloster Javelin FAW8 (7829M) [P] | Newark Air Museum, Winthorpe |
| | | | |
| | XJ314 | RR Thrust Measuring Rig | Science Museum, stored Wroughton |
| | XJ380 | Bristol 171 Sycamore HR14 (8628M) | Montrose Air Station Museum |
| | XJ389 | Fairey Jet Gyrodyne (XD759/ G-AJJP) | Museum of Berkshire Aviation, Woodley |
| | XJ409 | WS55 Whirlwind HAR10 (XD779) | Maes Artro Craft Village, Llanbedr |
| | XJ435 | WS55 Whirlwind HAR10 (8671M) [V] | RAF Manston History Museum, spares use |

| Serial | Type (other identity) [code] | Owner/operator, location or fate | Notes |
|---|---|---|---|
| XJ476 | DH110 Sea Vixen FAW1 <ff> | No 424 Sqn ATC, Southampton Hall of Avn | |
| XJ481 | DH110 Sea Vixen FAW1 [VL] | FAA Museum, at RNAY Fleetlands Museum | |
| XJ482 | DH110 Sea Vixen FAW1 [713/VL] | Norfolk & Suffolk Avn Museum, Flixton | |
| XJ488 | DH110 Sea Vixen FAW1 <ff> | Robertsbridge Aviation Society, Mayfield | |
| XJ494 | DH110 Sea Vixen FAW2 | Privately owned, Bruntingthorpe | |
| XJ560 | DH110 Sea Vixen FAW2 (8142M) [242] | Newark Air Museum, Winthorpe | |
| XJ565 | DH110 Sea Vixen FAW2 [127/E] | Mosquito Aircraft Museum, London Colney | |
| XJ571 | DH110 Sea Vixen FAW2 (8140M) [242/R] | Privately owned, Brooklands Museum, Weybridge | |
| XJ575 | DH110 Sea Vixen FAW2 <ff> [SAH-13] | Wellesbourne Wartime Museum | |
| XJ579 | DH110 Sea Vixen FAW2 <ff> | Midland Air Museum, Coventry | |
| XJ580 | DH110 Sea Vixen FAW2 [131/E] | Sea Vixen Society, Christchurch | |
| XJ607 | DH110 Sea Vixen FAW2 (8171M) <ff> | *Sold to Australia, 1997* | |
| XJ634 | Hawker Hunter F6A (8684M) [29] | *To Saudi Arabia, September 1999* | |
| XJ639 | Hawker Hunter F6A (8687M) [H] | Privately owned, Sproughton | |
| XJ676 | Hawker Hunter F6A (8844M) <ff> | Privately owned, Leavesden | |
| XJ714 | Hawker Hunter FR10 (comp XG226) | Jet Avn Preservation Grp, Long Marston | |
| XJ723 | WS55 Whirlwind HAR10 | Montrose Air Station Museum | |
| XJ726 | WS55 Whirlwind HAR10 | Caernarfon Air World | |
| XJ727 | WS55 Whirlwind HAR10 (8661M) [L] | RAF Manston History Museum | |
| XJ729 | WS55 Whirlwind HAR10 (8732M/ G-BVGE) | Privately owned, Ireland | |
| XJ758 | WS55 Whirlwind HAR10 (8464M) <ff> | Privately owned, Welshpool | |
| XJ763 | WS55 Whirlwind HAR10 (G-BKHA) [P] | *Sold to the USA, 1999,* | |
| *XJ771* | DH115 Vampire T55 (U-1215/ G-HELV) | Privately owned, Swansea | |
| XJ772 | DH115 Vampire T11 [H] | Mosquito Aircraft Museum, London Colney | |
| XJ823 | Avro 698 Vulcan B2A | Solway Aviation Society, Carlisle | |
| XJ824 | Avro 698 Vulcan B2A | Imperial War Museum, Duxford | |
| XJ917 | Bristol 171 Sycamore HR14 [H-S] | Bristol Aero Collection, stored Kemble | |
| XJ918 | Bristol 171 Sycamore HR14 (8190M) | RAF Museum, Cosford | |
| | | | |
| XK149 | Hawker Hunter F6A (8714M) [L] | Privately owned, Bruntingthorpe | |
| *XK378* | Auster AOP9 (TAD200/XS238) | Privately owned, Dale, Dyfed | |
| XK416 | Auster AOP9 (7855M/G-AYUA) | De Havilland Aviation, Swansea | |
| XK417 | Auster AOP9 (G-AVXY) | Privately owned, RAF Newton | |
| XK418 | Auster AOP9 (7976M) | SWWAPS, Lasham | |
| XK421 | Auster AOP9 (8365M) (frame) | South Yorkshire Avn Museum, Firbeck | |
| XK482 | Saro Skeeter AOP12 (7840M/ G-BJWC) [C] | Privately owned, Sywell | |
| XK488 | Blackburn NA39 Buccaneer S1 | FAA Museum, RNAS Yeovilton | |
| XK526 | Blackburn NA39 Buccaneer S2 (8648M) | RAF Honington, at main gate | |
| XK527 | Blackburn NA39 Buccaneer S2D (8818M) <ff> | Bournemouth Aviation Museum | |
| XK532 | Blackburn NA39 Buccaneer S1 (8867M) [632/LM] | The Fresson Trust, Inverness Airport | |
| XK533 | Blackburn NA39 Buccaneer S1 <ff> | Royal Scottish Mus'm of Flight, E Fortune | |
| XK590 | DH115 Vampire T11 [V] | Wellesbourne Wartime Museum | |
| XK623 | DH115 Vampire T11 (*G-VAMP*) [56] | Caernarfon Air World | |
| XK624 | DH115 Vampire T11 [32] | Norfolk & Suffolk Avn Museum, Flixton | |
| XK625 | DH115 Vampire T11 [12] | Brenzett Aeronautical Museum | |
| XK627 | DH115 Vampire T11 | Privately owned, Barton | |
| XK632 | DH115 Vampire T11 [67] | No 2370 Sqn ATC, Denham | |
| XK637 | DH115 Vampire T11 [56] | RAF Millom Museum, Haverigg | |
| XK655 | DH106 Comet C2(RC) (G-AMXA) <ff> | Gatwick Airport, on display (BOAC colours) | |
| XK659 | DH106 Comet C2(RC) (G-AMXC) <ff> | Privately owned, Elland, West Yorkshire | |
| XK695 | DH106 Comet C2(RC) (G-AMXH/ 9164M) <ff> | Mosquito Aircraft Museum, London Colney | |
| XK699 | DH106 Comet C2 (7971M) | RAF Lyneham on display | |

| Notes | Serial | Type (other identity) [code] | Owner/operator, location or fate |
|---|---|---|---|
| | XK724 | Folland Gnat F1 (7715M) | RAF Museum, Cosford |
| | XK740 | Folland Gnat F1 (8396M) | Southampton Hall of Aviation |
| | XK741 | Folland Gnat F1 (fuselage) | Midland Air Museum, Coventry |
| | XK776 | ML Utility 1 | Museum of Army Flying, Middle Wallop |
| | XK788 | Slingsby T38 Grasshopper TX1 | Privately owned, Sproughton |
| | XK789 | Slingsby T38 Grasshopper TX1 | Warwick School, Warwick |
| | XK790 | Slingsby T38 Grasshopper TX1 | Privately owned, stored Husbands Bosworth |
| | XK819 | Slingsby T38 Grasshopper TX1 | Privately owned, Selby |
| | XK822 | Slingsby T38 Grasshopper TX1 | Privately owned, Kenley |
| | XK895 | DH104 Sea Devon C20 (G-SDEV) [19/CU] | Privately owned, Shoreham |
| | XK896 | DH104 Sea Devon C20 (G-RNAS) (fuselage) | Privately owned, Filton (spares use) |
| | XK907 | WS55 Whirlwind HAS7 [U] | Midland Air Museum, Coventry |
| | XK911 | WS55 Whirlwind HAS7 [519/PO] | Privately owned, Derby |
| | XK936 | WS55 Whirlwind HAS7 [62] | Imperial War Museum, Duxford |
| | XK940 | WS55 Whirlwind HAS7 (G-AYXT) | Privately owned, Tibenham, Norfolk |
| | XK944 | WS55 Whirlwind HAS7 | No 617 Sqn ATC, Malpas, Cheshire |
| | XK987 | WS55 Whirlwind HAR10 (8393M) | *Scrapped at Swynnerton by 1998* |
| | XK988 | WS55 Whirlwind HAR10 [D] | AAC Middle Wallop Fire Section |
| | XL149 | Blackburn B101 Beverley C1 (7988M) <ff> | Newark Air Museum, Winthorpe |
| | XL160 | HP80 Victor K2 (8910M) <ff> | HP Victor Association, Walpole |
| | XL164 | HP80 Victor K2 (9215M) <ff> | Gatwick Aviation Museum, Charlwood, Surrey |
| | XL188 | HP80 Victor K2 (9100M) (fuselage) | RAF Kinloss Fire Section |
| | XL190 | HP80 Victor K2 (9216M) <ff> | RAF Manston History Museum |
| | XL231 | HP80 Victor K2 | Yorkshire Air Museum, Elvington |
| | XL318 | Avro 698 Vulcan B2 (8733M) | RAF Museum, Hendon |
| | XL319 | Avro 698 Vulcan B2 | North-East Aircraft Museum, Usworth |
| | XL360 | Avro 698 Vulcan B2A | Midland Air Museum, Coventry |
| | XL388 | Avro 698 Vulcan B2 <ff> | Blyth Valley Aviation Collection, Walpole |
| | XL391 | Avro 698 Vulcan B2 | Privately owned, Blackpool |
| | XL426 | Avro 698 Vulcan B2 (G-VJET) | Vulcan Restoration Trust, Southend |
| | XL445 | Avro 698 Vulcan K2 (8811M) <ff> | Blyth Valley Aviation Collection, Walpole |
| | XL449 | Fairey Gannet AEW3 <ff> | Privately owned, Booker |
| | XL472 | Fairey Gannet AEW3 [044/R] | Gatwick Aviation Museum, Charlwood, Surrey |
| | XL497 | Fairey Gannet AEW3 [041/R] | RN, Prestwick, on display |
| | XL500 | Fairey Gannet AEW3 [CU] | RNAS Culdrose |
| | XL502 | Fairey Gannet AEW3 (8610M/ G-BMYP) | Privately owned, Sandtoft |
| | XL503 | Fairey Gannet AEW3 [070/E] | FAA Museum, RNAS Yeovilton |
| | XL563 | Hawker Hunter T7 (9218M) | Privately owned, Bosbury, Hereford |
| | XL565 | Hawker Hunter T7 (parts of WT745) | Delta Jets, Kemble |
| | XL567 | Hawker Hunter T7 (8723M) [84] | Privately owned, Exeter |
| | XL568 | Hawker Hunter T7A (9224M) [C] | AMIF, RAFC Cranwell |
| | XL569 | Hawker Hunter T7 (8833M) [SC] | East Midlands Airport Aeropark |
| | *XL571* | Hawker Hunter T7 (XL572/ 8834M/G-HNTR) | Yorkshire Air Museum, Elvington |
| | XL572 | Hawker Hunter T7 (8834M/ G-HNTR) [83] | *Repainted as XL571 by March 1999* |
| | XL573 | Hawker Hunter T7 (G-BVGH) | Privately owned, North Weald |
| | XL577 | Hawker Hunter T7 (G-BXKF/ 8676M) [W] | Delta Jets, Kemble |
| | XL578 | Hawker Hunter T7 (fuselage) | Privately owned, Kemble |
| | XL580 | Hawker Hunter T8M [723] | FAA Museum, stored RNAS Yeovilton |
| | XL586 | Hawker Hunter T7 <rf> | Delta Jets, Kemble |
| | XL587 | Hawker Hunter T7 (8807M/ G-HPUX) [Z] | The Old Flying Machine Company, Duxford |
| | XL591 | Hawker Hunter T7 | Delta Jets, Kemble |
| | XL592 | Hawker Hunter T7 (8836M) [Y] | Classic Jet Aircraft Co, Exeter |
| | XL601 | Hawker Hunter T7 [874/VL] | Classic Jets, Brustem, Belgium |
| | XL602 | Hawker Hunter T8M (G-BWFT) | South West Aviation Heritage, Exeter |
| | XL603 | Hawker Hunter T8M [724] | Privately owned, Bruntingthorpe |
| | XL612 | Hawker Hunter T7 [2] | DPA/AFD/ETPS, DERA Boscombe Down |
| | XL613 | Hawker Hunter T7 (G-BVMB) | Classic Jet Aircraft Co, Exeter |
| | XL618 | Hawker Hunter T7 (8892M) [05] | Caernarfon Air World |
| | XL621 | Hawker Hunter T7 (G-BNCX) | Privately owned, Brooklands Museum |
| | XL623 | Hawker Hunter T7 (8770M) | The Planets Leisure Centre, Woking |
| | XL629 | EE Lightning T4 | DERA Boscombe Down, at main gate |

| Serial | Type (other identity) [code] | Owner/operator, location or fate | Notes |
|---|---|---|---|
| XL703 | SAL Pioneer CC1 (8034M) | RAF Museum, Cosford | |
| XL714 | DH82A Tiger Moth II (T6099/ G-AOGR) | Privately owned, Swanton Morley | |
| XL716 | DH82A Tiger Moth II (T7363/ G-AOIL) | Privately owned, Chandlers Ford | |
| XL735 | Saro Skeeter AOP12 | Privately owned, Tattershall Thorpe | |
| XL738 | Saro Skeeter AOP12 (7860M) | Privately owned, Ivybridge, Devon | |
| XL739 | Saro Skeeter AOP12 | AAC Wattisham, instructional use | |
| XL762 | Saro Skeeter AOP12 (8017M) | Royal Scottish Mus'm of Flight, E Fortune | |
| XL763 | Saro Skeeter AOP12 | Privately owned, Ivybridge, Devon | |
| XL764 | Saro Skeeter AOP12 (7940M) [J] | Newark Air Museum, Winthorpe | |
| XL765 | Saro Skeeter AOP12 | Privately owned, Clapham, Beds | |
| XL770 | Saro Skeeter AOP12 (8046M) | Southampton Hall of Aviation | |
| XL809 | Saro Skeeter AOP12 (G-BLIX) | Privately owned, Wilden, Beds | |
| XL811 | Saro Skeeter AOP12 | The Helicopter Museum, Weston-super-Mare | |
| XL812 | Saro Skeeter AOP12 (G-SARO) | Privately owned, Old Buckenham | |
| XL813 | Saro Skeeter AOP12 | Museum of Army Flying, Middle Wallop | |
| XL814 | Saro Skeeter AOP12 | AAC Historic Aircraft Flight, Middle Wallop | |
| XL824 | Bristol 171 Sycamore HR14 (8021M) | Gr Manchester Mus of Science & Industry | |
| XL829 | Bristol 171 Sycamore HR14 | Bristol Industrial Museum | |
| XL840 | WS55 Whirlwind HAS7 | Privately owned, Long Marston | |
| XL847 | WS55 Whirlwind HAS7 [83] | AAC Middle Wallop Fire Section | |
| XL853 | WS55 Whirlwind HAS7 [PO] | FAA Museum, RNAS Yeovilton | |
| XL875 | WS55 Whirlwind HAR9 | Perth Technical College | |
| XL929 | Percival P66 Pembroke C1 (G-BNPU) | D-Day Museum, Shoreham Airport | |
| XL954 | Percival P66 Pembroke C1 (9042M/N4234C/G-BXES) | Air Atlantique Historic Flight, Coventry | |
| XL993 | SAL Twin Pioneer CC1 (8388M) | RAF Museum, Cosford | |
| | | | |
| XM135 | BAC Lightning F1 [B] | Imperial War Museum, Duxford | |
| XM144 | BAC Lightning F1 (8417M) <ff> | South West Aviation Heritage, Eaglescott | |
| XM169 | BAC Lightning F1A (8422M) <ff> | N Yorks Aircraft Recovery Centre, Chop Gate | |
| XM172 | BAC Lightning F1A (8427M) | Wycombe Air Park, on display | |
| XM173 | BAC Lightning F1A (8414M) [A] | RAF Bentley Priory, at main gate | |
| XM191 | BAC Lightning F1A (7854M/8590M) <ff> | RAF EPTT, St Athan | |
| XM192 | BAC Lightning F1A (8413M) [K] | Bomber County Aviation Museum, Hemswell | |
| XM223 | DH104 Devon C2 (G-BWWC) [J] | Air Atlantique Historic Flight, Coventrya: | |
| XM279 | EE Canberra B(I)8 <ff> | Privately owned, Flixton | |
| XM300 | WS58 Wessex HAS1 | Welsh Industrial & Maritime Mus'm, stored Cardiff | |
| XM328 | WS58 Wessex HAS3 [653/PO] | SFDO, RNAS Culdrose | |
| XM330 | WS58 Wessex HAS1 | The Helicopter Museum, Weston-super-Mare | |
| XM349 | Hunting Jet Provost T3A (9046M) [T] | Global Aviation, Binbrook | |
| XM350 | Hunting Jet Provost T3A (9036M) | South Yorkshire Avn Museum, Firbeck | |
| XM351 | Hunting Jet Provost T3 (8078M) [Y] | RAF Museum, Cosford | |
| XM355 | Hunting Jet Provost T3 (8229M) [D] | Privately owned, Shobdon | |
| XM358 | Hunting Jet Provost T3A (8987M) [53] | Privately owned, Twyford, Bucks | |
| XM362 | Hunting Jet Provost T3 (8230M) | RAF No 1 SoTT, Cosford | |
| XM363 | Hunting Jet Provost T3 <ff> | RAF Cranwell | |
| XM365 | Hunting Jet Provost T3A (G-BXBH) [37] | Privately owned, Norwich | |
| XM369 | Hunting Jet Provost T3 (8084M) [C] | Privately owned, Portsmouth | |
| XM370 | Hunting Jet Provost T3A (G-BVSP) [10] | Privately owned, Norwich | |
| XM372 | Hunting Jet Provost T3A (8917M) [55] | RAF Linton-on-Ouse Fire Section | |
| XM375 | Hunting Jet Provost T3 (8231M) [B] | RAF Linton-on-Ouse Fire Section | |
| XM376 | Hunting Jet Provost T3A (G-BWDR) [27] | *Repainted as G-BWDR* | |
| XM378 | Hunting Jet Provost T3A (G-BWZE) [34] | Privately owned, Norwich | |
| XM379 | Hunting Jet Provost T3 | | |
| XM383 | Hunting Jet Provost T3A [90] | Newark Air Museum, Winthorpe | |

| Notes | Serial | Type (other identity) [code] | Owner/operator, location or fate |
|---|---|---|---|
| | XM401 | Hunting Jet Provost T3A [17] | |
| | XM402 | Hunting Jet Provost T3 (8055AM) [J] | Fenland & W Norfolk Aviation Museum, Wisbech |
| | XM403 | Hunting Jet Provost T3A (9048M) | |
| | XM404 | Hunting Jet Provost T3 (8055BM) | FETC, Moreton-in-Marsh, Glos |
| | XM405 | Hunting Jet Provost T3A (G-TORE) [42] | *Repainted as G-TORE* |
| | XM409 | Hunting Jet Provost T3 (8082M) <rf> | Air Scouts, Guernsey Airport |
| | XM410 | Hunting Jet Provost T3 (8054AM) [B] | RAF North Luffenham Training Area |
| | XM411 | Hunting Jet Provost T3 (8434M) <ff> | South Yorkshire Avn Museum, Firbeck |
| | XM412 | Hunting Jet Provost T3A (9011M) [41] | Privately owned, Sproughton |
| | XM414 | Hunting Jet Provost T3A (8996M) | Flight Experience Workshop, Belfast |
| | XM417 | Hunting Jet Provost T3 (8054BM) [D] <ff> | Privately owned, Hednesford, Staffs |
| | XM419 | Hunting Jet Provost T3A (8990M) [102] | DARA Training School, RAF St Athan |
| | XM425 | Hunting Jet Provost T3A (8995M) [88] | Privately owned, Longton, Staffs |
| | XM455 | Hunting Jet Provost T3A (8960M) [K] | *Sold as N455XM, August 1999* |
| | XM459 | Hunting Jet Provost T3A [F] | Global Aviation, Binbrook |
| | XM463 | Hunting Jet Provost T3A [38] (fuselage) | RAF Museum, Hendon |
| | XM468 | Hunting Jet Provost T3 (8081M) | Privately owned, Terrington St Clement |
| | XM470 | Hunting Jet Provost T3A (G-BWZZ) [12] | Privately owned, Humberside |
| | XM471 | Hunting Jet Provost T3A (8968M) [L,93] | *Sold as N471XN, July 1993* |
| | XM473 | Hunting Jet Provost T3A (8974M/ *G-TINY*) | Bedford College, instructional use |
| | XM474 | Hunting Jet Provost T3 (8121M) <ff> | South Yorkshire Avn Museum, Firbeck |
| | XM475 | Hunting Jet Provost T3A (9112M) [44] | MoD FSCTE, Manston |
| | XM478 | Hunting Jet Provost T3A (8983M/ G-BXDL) [33] | Transair(UK) Ltd, North Weald |
| | XM479 | Hunting Jet Provost T3A (G-BVEZ) [54] | Privately owned, Newcastle |
| | XM480 | Hunting Jet Provost T3 (8080M) | 4x4 Car Centre, Chesterfield |
| | XM496 | Bristol 253 Britannia C1 (EL-WXA) | Britannia Preservation Society, Kemble |
| | XM529 | Saro Skeeter AOP12 (7979M/ G-BDNS) | Privately owned, Handforth |
| | XM553 | Saro Skeeter AOP12 (G-AWSV) | Privately owned, Middle Wallop |
| | XM555 | Saro Skeeter AOP12 (8027M) | RAF Museum, Cosford |
| | XM561 | Saro Skeeter AOP12 (7980M) | South Yorkshire Avn Museum, Firbeck |
| | XM564 | Saro Skeeter AOP12 | National Tank Museum, Bovington |
| | XM569 | Avro 698 Vulcan B2 <ff> | Jet Age Museum, Staverton |
| | XM575 | Avro 698 Vulcan B2A (G-BLMC) | East Midlands Airport Aeropark |
| | XM594 | Avro 698 Vulcan B2 | Newark Air Museum, Winthorpe |
| | XM597 | Avro 698 Vulcan B2 | Royal Scottish Mus'm of Flight, E Fortune |
| | XM598 | Avro 698 Vulcan B2 (8778M) | RAF Museum, Cosford |
| | XM602 | Avro 698 Vulcan B2 (8771M) <ff> | Avro Aircraft Heritage Society, Woodford |
| | XM603 | Avro 698 Vulcan B2 | Avro Aircraft Heritage Society, Woodford |
| | XM607 | Avro 698 Vulcan B2 (8779M) | RAF Waddington, on display |
| | XM612 | Avro 698 Vulcan B2 | City of Norwich Aviation Museum |
| | XM652 | Avro 698 Vulcan B2 <ff> | Privately owned, Welshpool |
| | XM655 | Avro 698 Vulcan B2 (G-VULC) | Privately owned, Wellesbourne Mountford |
| | XM660 | WS55 Whirlwind HAS7 [78] | RAF Millom Museum, Haverigg |
| | XM685 | WS55 Whirlwind HAS7 (G-AYZJ) [513/PO] | Newark Air Museum, Winthorpe |
| | XM692 | HS Gnat T1 <ff> | Boscombe Down Museum |
| | XM693 | HS Gnat T1 (7891M) | BAE SystemsHamble, on display |
| | *XM693* | HS Gnat T1 (8618M/XP504/ G-TIMM) | Kennet Aviation, Cranfield |
| | XM697 | HS Gnat T1 (G-NAAT) | Privately owned, Dunsfold |
| | XM708 | HS Gnat T1 (8573M) | Privately owned, Kings Langley, Herts |
| | XM709 | HS Gnat T1 (8617M) [67] | Privately owned |
| | XM715 | HP80 Victor K2 | British Aviation Heritage, Bruntingthorpe |
| | XM717 | HP80 Victor K2 <ff> | RAF Museum, Hendon |

| *Serial* | *Type (other identity) [code]* | *Owner/operator, location or fate* | *Notes* |
|---|---|---|---|
| *XM819* | Lancashire EP9 Prospector (G-APXW) | Museum of Army Flying, Middle Wallop | |
| XM833 | WS58 Wessex HAS3 | SWWAPS, Lasham | |
| XM868 | WS58 Wessex HAS1 [517] | RN, Predannack Fire School | |
| XM870 | WS58 Wessex HAS3 [PO] | RN, Predannack Fire School | |
| XM874 | WS58 Wessex HAS1 [521/CU] | RN, Predannack Fire School | |
| XM927 | WS58 Wessex HAS3 (8814M) [660/PO] | RAF Shawbury Fire Section | |
| XN126 | WS55 Whirlwind HAR10 (8655M) [S] | Pinewood Studios, Elstree | |
| XN185 | Slingsby T21B Sedbergh TX1 (8942M/BGA 4077) | RAFGSA, Syerston | |
| XN187 | Slingsby T21B Sedbergh TX1 (BGA 3903) | Privately owned, Seighford | |
| XN198 | Slingsby T31B Cadet TX3 | Privately owned, Challock Lees | |
| XN238 | Slingsby T31B Cadet TX3 <ff> | South Yorkshire Avn Museum, Firbeck | |
| XN239 | Slingsby T31B Cadet TX3 (8889M) [G] | Imperial War Museum, Duxford | |
| XN243 | Slingsby T31B Cadet TX3 (BGA 3145) | Privately owned, Bicester | |
| XN246 | Slingsby T31B Cadet TX3 | Southampton Hall of Aviation | |
| XN258 | WS55 Whirlwind HAR9 [589/CU] | North-East Aircraft Museum, Usworth | |
| XN263 | WS55 Whirlwind HAS7 | Privately owned, Chichester | |
| *XN297* | WS55 Whirlwind HAR9 (XN311) [12] | Privately owned, Hull | |
| XN298 | WS55 Whirlwind HAR9 [810/LS] | International Fire Training Centre, Chorley | |
| XN299 | WS55 Whirlwind HAS7 [ZZ] | Tangmere Military Aviation Museum | |
| XN304 | WS55 Whirlwind HAS7 [64] | Norfolk & Suffolk Avn Museum, Flixton | |
| XN332 | Saro P531 (G-APNV) [759] | FAA Museum, stored Yeovilton | |
| XN334 | Saro P531 | FAA Museum, stored Wroughton | |
| XN341 | Saro Skeeter AOP12 (8022M) | Stondon Transport Mus & Garden Centre, Beds | |
| XN344 | Saro Skeeter AOP12 (8018M) | Science Museum, South Kensington | |
| XN351 | Saro Skeeter AOP12 (G-BKSC) | Privately owned, Ipswich | |
| XN380 | WS55 Whirlwind HAS7 | Lashenden Air Warfare Museum, Headcorn | |
| XN385 | WS55 Whirlwind HAS7 [T] | Botany Bay Village, Chorley, Lancs | |
| XN386 | WS55 Whirlwind HAR9 [435/ED] | South Yorkshire Avn Museum, Firbeck | |
| XN412 | Auster AOP9 | Cotswold Aircraft Rest'n Grp, Innsworth | |
| XN435 | Auster AOP9 (G-BGBU) | Privately owned, Egham | |
| XN437 | Auster AOP9 (G-AXWA) | Privately owned, North Weald | |
| XN441 | Auster AOP9 (G-BGKT) | Auster 9 Group, Melton Mowbray | |
| XN459 | Hunting Jet Provost T3A (G-BWOT) | Transair(UK) Ltd, North Weald | |
| XN462 | Hunting Jet Provost T3A [17] | FAA Museum, Yeovilton | |
| XN466 | Hunting Jet Provost T3A [29] <ff> | No 1005 Sqn ATC, Radcliffe, Gtr Manchester | |
| XN470 | Hunting Jet Provost T3A (G-BXBJ) [41] | *Sold to United Arab Emirates, Oct 1999* | |
| XN473 | Hunting Jet Provost T3A (8862M) [98] <ff> | | |
| XN492 | Hunting Jet Provost T3 (8079M) <ff> | South Yorkshire Avn Museum, Firbeck | |
| *XN493* | Hunting Jet Provost T3 (XN137) <ff> | Privately owned, Camberley | |
| XN494 | Hunting Jet Provost T3A (9012M) [43] | Crawley Technical College | |
| XN495 | Hunting Jet Provost T3A (8786M) [102] | RAF | |
| XN497 | Hunting Jet Provost T3A [52] | DARA, RAF St Athan | |
| XN498 | Hunting Jet Provost T3A (G-BWSH) [16] | *Repainted as G-BWSH* | |
| XN500 | Hunting Jet Provost T3A [48] | CSE Ltd, Oxford, ground instruction | |
| XN501 | Hunting Jet Provost T3A (8958M) [G] | Privately owned, Billockby, Norfolk | |
| XN503 | Hunting Jet Provost T3 <ff> | No 1284 Sqn ATC, Milford Haven | |
| XN505 | Hunting Jet Provost T3A [25] | Privately owned, Binbrook | |
| XN508 | Hunting Jet Provost T3A [47] | DARA, RAF St Athan | |
| XN510 | Hunting Jet Provost T3A (G-BXBI) [40] | Global Aviation, Binbrook | |
| XN511 | Hunting Jet Provost T3 (*XM426*) [64] <ff> | South Yorkshire Avn Museum, Firbeck | |

| Notes | Serial | Type (other identity) [code] | Owner/operator, location or fate |
|---|---|---|---|
| | XN549 | Hunting Jet Provost T3 (8235M) [32,P] | RAF Shawbury Fire Section |
| | XN551 | Hunting Jet Provost T3A (8984M) | DARA Training School, RAF St Athan |
| | XN554 | Hunting Jet Provost T3 (8436M) [K] | RAF North Luffenham Training Area |
| | XN573 | Hunting Jet Provost T3 [E] <ff> | Newark Air Museum, Winthorpe |
| | XN577 | Hunting Jet Provost T3A (8956M) [89,F] | Privately owned, Billockby, Norfolk |
| | XN579 | Hunting Jet Provost T3A (9137M) [14] | RAF North Luffenham Training Area |
| | XN582 | Hunting Jet Provost T3A (8957M) [95,H] | Arbury College, Cambridge |
| | XN584 | Hunting Jet Provost T3A (9014M) [E] | Phoenix Aviation, Bruntingthorpe |
| | XN586 | Hunting Jet Provost T3A (9039M) [91,S] | Brooklands Technical College |
| | XN589 | Hunting Jet Provost T3A (9143M) [46] | RAF Linton-on-Ouse, on display |
| | XN592 | Hunting Jet Provost T3 <ff> | No 1105 Sqn ATC, Winchester |
| | XN593 | Hunting Jet Provost T3A (8988M) [97,Q] | Privately owned, Billockby, Norfolk |
| | XN594 | Hunting Jet Provost T3 (8077M) [W] | *Sold to France, 1996* |
| | *XN594* | Hunting Jet Provost T3 (8234M/ XN458) | Privately owned, Ashington, W Sussex |
| | XN597 | Hunting Jet Provost T3 (7984M) [X] <ff> | RAF Millom Museum, Haverigg |
| | XN607 | Hunting Jet Provost T3 <ff> | N Yorks Aircraft Recovery Centre, Chop Gate |
| | XN629 | Hunting Jet Provost T3A (G-BVEG/G-KNOT) [49] | Transair (UK) Ltd, North Weald |
| | XN632 | Hunting Jet Provost T3 (8352M) | Privately owned, Birlingham, Worcs |
| | XN634 | Hunting Jet Provost T3A <ff> | Privately owned, Sproughton |
| | XN634 | Hunting Jet Provost T3A [53] <rf> | BAE SystemsWarton Fire Section |
| | XN636 | Hunting Jet Provost T3A (9045M) [15] | Privately owned |
| | XN637 | Hunting Jet Provost T3 (G-BKOU) [3] | Privately owned, North Weald |
| | XN647 | DH110 Sea Vixen FAW2 [707/VL] | Flambards Village Theme Park, Helston |
| | XN649 | DH110 Sea Vixen FAW2 [126] | DPA, stored DERA Farnborough |
| | XN650 | DH110 Sea Vixen FAW2 <ff> | Privately owned, Welshpool |
| | XN651 | DH110 Sea Vixen FAW2 <ff> | Communications & Electronics Museum, Bletchley Park |
| | XN657 | DH110 Sea Vixen D3 [TR-1] | Privately owned, Stock, Essex |
| | XN685 | DH110 Sea Vixen FAW2 (8173M) [03/VL] | Midland Air Museum, Coventry |
| | XN688 | DH110 Sea Vixen FAW2 (8141M) [511] | DERA Farnborough Fire Section |
| | XN691 | DH110 Sea Vixen FAW2 (8143M) [247/H] | Privately owned, North Weald |
| | XN696 | DH110 Sea Vixen FAW2 <ff> | Blyth Valley Aviation Collection, Walpole |
| | XN714 | Hunting H126 | RAF Museum, Cosford |
| | XN724 | EE Lightning F2A (8513M) [F] | Privately owned, Newcastle-upon-Tyne |
| | XN726 | EE Lightning F2A (8545M) <ff> | Privately owned, Foulness |
| | XN728 | EE Lightning F2A (8546M) [V] | Privately owned, Balderton, Notts |
| | XN734 | EE Lightning F3A (8346M/ G-BNCA) <ff> | Privately owned, Cranfield |
| | XN769 | EE Lightning F2 (8402M) <ff> | Privately owned, Sidcup, Kent |
| | XN776 | EE Lightning F2A (8535M) [C] | Royal Scottish Mus'm of Flight, E Fortune |
| | XN795 | EE Lightning F2A <ff> | Privately owned, Foulness |
| | XN817 | AW660 Argosy C1 | DERA West Freugh Fire Section |
| | XN819 | AW660 Argosy C1 (8205M) <ff> | Newark Air Museum, Winthorpe |
| | XN923 | HS Buccaneer S1 [13] | Gatwick Aviation Museum, Charlwood, Surrey |
| | XN928 | HS Buccaneer S1 (8179M) <ff> | RAF Manston History Museum |
| | XN929 | HS Buccaneer S1 (8051M) <ff> | Newark Air Museum, Winthorpe |
| | XN934 | HS Buccaneer S1 [631] (fuselage) | *Burnt at Predannack by Apr 1998* |
| | XN957 | HS Buccaneer S1 | FAA Museum, RNAS Yeovilton |
| | XN964 | HS Buccaneer S1 [613/LM] | Newark Air Museum, Winthorpe |
| | XN967 | HS Buccaneer S1 <ff> | Muckleburgh Collection, Weybourne, Norfolk |
| | *XN972* | HS Buccaneer S1 (8183M/XN962) <ff> | RAF Museum, Hendon |

| Serial | Type (other identity) [code] | Owner/operator, location or fate | Notes |
|---|---|---|---|
| XN974 | HS Buccaneer S2A | Yorkshire Air Museum, Elvington | |
| XN979 | HS Buccaneer S2 <ff> | | |
| XN983 | HS Buccaneer S2B <ff> | Privately owned, Terrington St Clement | |
| XP110 | WS58 Wessex HAS3 [55/FL] | RN AESS, *HMS Sultan*, Gosport, BDRT | |
| XP137 | WS58 Wessex HAS3 [711/DD] | SFDO, RNAS Culdrose | |
| XP142 | WS58 Wessex HAS3 | FAA Museum, stored Yeovilton | |
| XP150 | WS58 Wessex HAS3 [LS] | FETC, Moreton-in-Marsh, Glos | |
| XP157 | WS58 Wessex HAS1 [AN] | RNAS Yeovilton Fire Section | |
| XP159 | WS58 Wessex HAS1 (8877M) [047/R] | Privately owned, Brands Hatch | |
| XP160 | WS58 Wessex HAS1 | RN, Predannack Fire School | |
| XP165 | WS Scout AH1 | The Helicopter Museum, Weston-super-Mare | |
| XP166 | WS Scout AH1 (G-APVL) | Privately owned, East Dereham, Norfolk | |
| XP190 | WS Scout AH1 | South Yorkshire Avn Museum, Firbeck | |
| XP191 | WS Scout AH1 | Army, Bramley, Hants | |
| XP226 | Fairey Gannet AEW3 [073/E] | Newark Air Museum, Winthorpe | |
| XP241 | Auster AOP9 | Privately owned, Andrewsfield | |
| XP242 | Auster AOP9 (G-BUCI) | AAC Historic Aircraft Flight, Middle Wallop | |
| XP244 | Auster AOP9 (7864M/*M7922*) | Army SEAE, Arborfield | |
| *XP248* | Auster AOP9 (7863M/WZ679) | Privately owned, Sandy, Beds | |
| XP254 | Auster AOP11 (G-ASCC) | Privately owned, Tollerton | |
| XP279 | Auster AOP9 (G-BWKK) | Privately owned, Popham | |
| XP280 | Auster AOP9 | Snibston Discovery Park, Coalville | |
| XP281 | Auster AOP9 | Imperial War Museum, Duxford | |
| XP283 | Auster AOP9 (7859M) (frame) | Privately owned, Baxterley, Warwickshire | |
| XP299 | WS55 Whirlwind HAR10 (8726M) | RAF Museum, Cosford | |
| XP329 | WS55 Whirlwind HAR10 (8791M) [V] | Privately owned, Tattershall Thorpe | |
| XP344 | WS55 Whirlwind HAR10 (8764M) [H723] | RAF North Luffenham Training Area | |
| XP345 | WS55 Whirlwind HAR10 (8792M) [UN] | York Helicopter Preservation Group, Elvington | |
| XP346 | WS55 Whirlwind HAR10 (8793M) | Privately owned, Long Marston | |
| XP350 | WS55 Whirlwind HAR10 | Flambards Village Theme Park, Helston | |
| XP351 | WS55 Whirlwind HAR10 (8672M) [Z] | RAF Shawbury, on display | |
| XP353 | WS55 Whirlwind HAR10 (8720M) | Privately owned, Brands Hatch | |
| XP354 | WS55 Whirlwind HAR10 (8721M) | Privately owned, stored Cricklade, Wilts | |
| XP355 | WS55 Whirlwind HAR10 (8463M/G-BEBC) | City of Norwich Aviation Museum | |
| XP359 | WS55 Whirlwind HAR10 (8447M) | Dundonald Aviation Centre, Strathclyde | |
| XP360 | WS55 Whirlwind HAR10 [V] | Privately owned, Upper Hill, nr Leominster | |
| XP395 | WS55 Whirlwind HAR10 (8674M) [A] | Privately owned, Tattershall Thorpe | |
| XP398 | WS55 Whirlwind HAR10 (8794M) | Gatwick Aviation Museum, Charlwood, Surrey | |
| XP399 | WS55 Whirlwind HAR10 | Privately owned, Wickford, Essex | |
| XP404 | WS55 Whirlwind HAR10 (8682M) | The Helicopter Museum, Weston-super-Mare | |
| XP405 | WS55 Whirlwind HAR10 (8656M) [Y] | | |
| XP411 | AW660 Argosy C1 (8442M) [C] | RAF Museum, Cosford | |
| XP454 | Slingsby T38 Grasshopper TX1 | Wellingborough School, Wellingborough | |
| XP458 | Slingsby T38 Grasshopper TX1 | City of Norwich Aviation Museum | |
| XP488 | Slingsby T38 Grasshopper TX1 | Fenland & W Norfolk Aviation Museum, stored Wisbech | |
| XP493 | Slingsby T38 Grasshopper TX1 | Privately owned, stored Aston Down | |
| XP494 | Slingsby T38 Grasshopper TX1 | Privately owned, Rattlesden, Suffolk | |
| XP502 | HS Gnat T1 (8576M) | Privately owned, North Weald | |
| XP503 | HS Gnat T1 (8568M) [73] | Phoenix Aviation, Bruntingthorpe | |
| XP505 | HS Gnat T1 | Science Museum, Wroughton | |
| XP516 | HS Gnat T1 (8580M) [16] | DERA Structures Dept, Farnborough | |
| XP540 | HS Gnat T1 (8608M) [62] | Arbury College, Cambridge | |
| XP542 | HS Gnat T1 (8575M) [42] | R. Military College of Science, Shrivenham | |
| XP556 | Hunting Jet Provost T4 (9027M) [B] | RAF Cranwell Aviation Heritage Centre | |
| XP557 | Hunting Jet Provost T4 (8494M) [72] | Bomber County Aviation Museum, Hemswell | |
| XP558 | Hunting Jet Provost T4 (8627M) [20] | Privately owned, Norwich Airport | |
| XP563 | Hunting Jet Provost T4 (9028M) [C] | Privately owned, Bicester | |

| Notes | Serial | Type (other identity) [code] | Owner/operator, location or fate |
|---|---|---|---|
| | XP568 | Hunting Jet Provost T4 | Jet Avn Preservation Grp, Long Marston |
| | XP573 | Hunting Jet Provost T4 (8236M) [19] | Jersey Airport Fire Section |
| | XP585 | Hunting Jet Provost T4 (8407M) [24] | NE Wales Institute, Wrexham |
| | XP627 | Hunting Jet Provost T4 | North-East Aircraft Museum, Usworth |
| | XP629 | Hunting Jet Provost T4 (9026M) [P] | RAF North Luffenham Training Area |
| | XP638 | Hunting Jet Provost T4 (9034M) [A] | RAF Waddington, BDRT |
| | XP640 | Hunting Jet Provost T4 (8501M) [27] | Yorkshire Air Museum, Elvington |
| | XP642 | Hunting Jet Provost T4 (fuselage) | Privately owned, Luton |
| | XP672 | Hunting Jet Provost T4 (8458M/ G-RAFI) [03] | Privately owned, North Weald |
| | XP677 | Hunting Jet Provost T4 (8587M) <ff> | No 1343 Sqn ATC, East Grinstead |
| | XP680 | Hunting Jet Provost T4 (8460M) | FETC, Moreton-in-Marsh, Glos |
| | XP686 | Hunting Jet Provost T4 (8401M/ 8502M) [G] | RAF North Luffenham Training Area |
| | XP688 | Hunting Jet Provost T4 (9031M) [E] | Botany Bay Village, Chorley, Lancs |
| | XP701 | BAC Lightning F3 (8924M) <ff> | Robertsbridge Aviation Society, Mayfield |
| | XP703 | BAC Lightning F3 <ff> | Lightning Preservation Grp, RAF Coltishall |
| | XP706 | BAC Lightning F3 (8925M) | Lincs Lightning Pres'n Society, Hemswell |
| | XP745 | BAC Lightning F3 (8453M) <ff> | Greenford Haulage, West London |
| | XP772 | DHC2 Beaver AL1 (G-BUCJ) | AAC Historic Aircraft Flight, stored Duxford |
| | XP775 | DHC2 Beaver AL1 | Privately owned |
| | XP806 | DHC2 Beaver AL1 | Privately owned, Cumbernauld |
| | XP820 | DHC2 Beaver AL1 | AAC Historic Aircraft Flight, Middle Wallop |
| | XP821 | DHC2 Beaver AL1 [MCO] | Museum of Army Flying, Middle Wallop |
| | XP822 | DHC2 Beaver AL1 | Museum of Army Flying, Middle Wallop |
| | XP831 | Hawker P.1127 (8406M) | Science Museum, South Kensington |
| | XP841 | Handley-Page HP115 | FAA Museum, RNAS Yeovilton |
| | XP846 | WS Scout AH1 [B,H] (fuselage) | RE 39 Regt, Waterbeach, instructional use |
| | XP847 | WS Scout AH1 | Museum of Army Flying, Middle Wallop |
| | XP848 | WS Scout AH1 | AAC Arborfield, on display |
| | XP849 | WS Scout AH1 | Privately owned, East Dereham, Norfolk |
| | XP853 | WS Scout AH1 | Yeovil Naval College |
| | XP854 | WS Scout AH1 (7898M/TAD043) | AAC Wattisham, instructional use |
| | XP855 | WS Scout AH1 | Army SEAE, Arborfield |
| | XP856 | WS Scout AH1 | Army, Bramley, Hants |
| | XP883 | WS Scout AH1 | DERA Boscombe Down, Apprentice School |
| | XP884 | WS Scout AH1 | AAC Middle Wallop, instructional use |
| | XP885 | WS Scout AH1 | AAC Wattisham, instructional use |
| | XP886 | WS Scout AH1 | Yeovil College |
| | XP888 | WS Scout AH1 | Army SEAE, Arborfield |
| | XP890 | WS Scout AH1 [G] (fuselage) | Privately owned, Ipswich |
| | XP893 | WS Scout AH1 | AAC Middle Wallop, BDRT |
| | XP896 | WS Scout AH1 | *Crashed 20 November 1973* |
| | XP899 | WS Scout AH1 [D] | Army SEAE, Arborfield |
| | XP900 | WS Scout AH1 | AAC Wattisham, instructional use |
| | XP902 | WS Scout AH1 <ff> | South Yorkshire Avn Museum, Firbeck |
| | XP905 | WS Scout AH1 | Army SEAE, Arborfield |
| | XP907 | WS Scout AH1 (G-SROE) | Privately owned, Wattisham |
| | XP910 | WS Scout AH1 | Museum of Army Flying, Middle Wallop |
| | XP919 | DH110 Sea Vixen FAW2 (8163M) [706/VL] | Blyth Valley Aviation Collection, Walpole |
| | XP924 | DH110 Sea Vixen D3 (G-CVIX) | De Havilland Aviation, Swansea |
| | XP925 | DH110 Sea Vixen FAW2 [752] <ff> | No 1268 Sqn ATC, Haslemere, Surrey |
| | XP956 | DH110 Sea Vixen FAW2 | Privately owned |
| | XP980 | Hawker P.1127 | FAA Museum, RNAS Yeovilton |
| | XP984 | Hawker P.1127 | BAE SystemsDunsfold, at main gate |
| | | | |
| | XR220 | BAC TSR2 (7933M) | RAF Museum, Cosford |
| | XR222 | BAC TSR2 | Imperial War Museum, Duxford |
| | XR232 | Sud Alouette AH2 (F-WEIP) | Museum of Army Flying, Middle Wallop |
| | XR240 | Auster AOP9 (G-BDFH) | Privately owned, Booker |
| | XR241 | Auster AOP9 (G-AXRR) | The Aircraft Restoration Co, Duxford |
| | XR244 | Auster AOP9 | AAC Historic Aircraft Flight, Middle Wallop |
| | XR246 | Auster AOP9 (7862M/G-AZBU) | Auster 9 Group, RAF Newton |
| | XR267 | Auster AOP9 (G-BJXR) | Cotswold Aircraft Rest'n Grp, Innsworth |
| | XR271 | Auster AOP9 | Museum of Artillery, Woolwich |
| | XR371 | SC5 Belfast C1 | RAF Museum, Cosford |

| Serial | Type (other identity) [code] | Owner/operator, location or fate | Notes |
|---|---|---|---|
| XR379 | Sud Alouette AH2 | AAC Historic Aircraft Flight, Middle Wallop | |
| XR453 | WS55 Whirlwind HAR10 (8873M) [A] | RAF Odiham, on gate | |
| XR458 | WS55 Whirlwind HAR10 (8662M) [H] | Museum of Army Flying, Middle Wallop | |
| XR485 | WS55 Whirlwind HAR10 [Q] | Norfolk & Suffolk Avn Museum, Flixton | |
| XR486 | WS55 Whirlwind HCC12 (8727M/ G-RWWW) | Privately owned, Tibenham, Norfolk | |
| XR497 | WS58 Wessex HC2 [F] | RAF No 72 Sqn, Aldergrove | |
| XR498 | WS58 Wessex HC2 [X] | RAF No 72 Sqn, Aldergrove | |
| XR499 | WS58 Wessex HC2 [W] | RN AESS, *HMS Sultan*, Gosport | |
| XR501 | WS58 Wessex HC2 | RAF, stored Shawbury | |
| XR502 | WS58 Wessex HC2 [Z] | RAF, stored Shawbury | |
| XR503 | WS58 Wessex HC2 | RN AESS, *HMS Sultan*, Gosport | |
| XR504 | WS58 Wessex HC2 [*Joker*] | RAF No 84 Sqn, Akrotiri | |
| XR506 | WS58 Wessex HC2 [V] | RAF No 72 Sqn, Aldergrove | |
| XR507 | WS58 Wessex HC2 | RAF, stored Shawbury | |
| XR508 | WS58 Wessex HC2 [B] | RAF, stored RNAY Fleetlands | |
| XR511 | WS58 Wessex HC2 [L] | RAF No 72 Sqn, Aldergrove | |
| XR516 | WS58 Wessex HC2 [WB] | RN AESS, *HMS Sultan*, Gosport | |
| XR517 | WS58 Wessex HC2 [N] | Privately owned, Sproughton | |
| XR518 | WS58 Wessex HC2 [O] | RAF, stored RNAY Fleetlands | |
| XR520 | WS58 Wessex HC2 | RN AESS, *HMS Sultan*, Gosport | |
| XR523 | WS58 Wessex HC2 [M] | RAF, stored RNAY Fleetlands | |
| XR525 | WS58 Wessex HC2 [G] | RAF No 72 Sqn, Aldergrove | |
| XR526 | WS58 Wessex HC2 (8147M) | The Helicopter Museum, Weston-super-Mare | |
| XR528 | WS58 Wessex HC2 | RAF St Mawgan, instructional use | |
| XR529 | WS58 Wessex HC2 [E] | RAF No 72 Sqn, Aldergrove | |
| XR534 | HS Gnat T1 (8578M) [65] | Privately owned, Newark | |
| XR537 | HS Gnat T1 (8642M/G-NATY) [T] | Bournemouth Aviation Museum | |
| XR569 | HS Gnat T1 (8560M) [08] | Phoenix Aviation, Bruntingthorpe | |
| XR571 | HS Gnat T1 (8493M) | RAF *Red Arrows*, Cranwell, on display | |
| XR574 | HS Gnat T1 (8631M) [72] | RAF No 1 SoTT, Cosford | |
| XR588 | WS58 Wessex HC2 [*Hearts*] | RAF No 84 Sqn, Akrotiri | |
| XR595 | WS Scout AH1 (G-BWHU) [M] | Privately owned, Plymouth | |
| XR597 | WS Scout AH1 (fuselage) | Army, Wattisham, BDRT | |
| XR601 | WS Scout AH1 | Army SEAE, Arborfield | |
| *XR625* | WS Scout AH1 (XR633/*XR777*) | Privately owned, Sproughton | |
| XR627 | WS Scout AH1 [X] | AAC Wattisham, BDRT | |
| XR628 | WS Scout AH1 | Privately owned, Ipswich | |
| XR629 | WS Scout AH1 (fuselage) | Privately owned, Ipswich | |
| XR630 | WS Scout AH1 | AAC Middle Wallop, Fire Section | |
| XR635 | WS Scout AH1 | Army SEAE, Arborfield | |
| XR650 | Hunting Jet Provost T4 (8459M) [28] | Boscombe Down Museum | |
| XR654 | Hunting Jet Provost T4 <ff> | Privately owned, Barton | |
| XR658 | Hunting Jet Provost T4 (8192M) | Deeside College, Connah's Quay, Clwyd | |
| XR662 | Hunting Jet Provost T4 (8410M) [25] | Boulton Paul Association, Wolverhampton | |
| XR672 | Hunting Jet Provost T4 (8495M) [50] | RAF Halton, Fire Section | |
| XR673 | Hunting Jet Provost T4 (G-BXLO/9032M) [L] | Privately owned, North Weald | |
| XR681 | Hunting Jet Provost T4 (8588M) <ff> | No 1216 Sqn ATC, Newhaven, E Sussex | |
| XR700 | Hunting Jet Provost T4 (8589M) <ff> | RAF EPTT, Aldergrove | |
| XR713 | BAC Lightning F3 (8935M) [C] | RAF Leuchars, on display | |
| XR718 | BAC Lightning F6 (8932M) [DA] | Blyth Valley Aviation Collection, Walpole | |
| XR724 | BAC Lightning F6 (G-BTSY) | The Lightning Association, Binbrook | |
| XR725 | BAC Lightning F6 | Privately owned, Binbrook | |
| XR726 | BAC Lightning F6 <ff> | Privately owned, Harrogate | |
| XR728 | BAC Lightning F6 [JS] | Lightning Preservation Grp, Bruntingthorpe | |
| XR747 | BAC Lightning F6 <ff> | Lightning Flying Club, Plymouth | |
| XR749 | BAC Lightning F3 (8934M) [DA] | Tees-side Airport, on display | |
| XR751 | BAC Lightning F3 | Privately owned, Tremar, Cornwall | |
| XR753 | BAC Lightning F6 (8969M) [BP] | RAF Leeming on display | |
| XR754 | BAC Lightning F6 (8972M) <ff> | South Yorkshire Avn Museum, Firbeck | |
| XR755 | BAC Lightning F6 | Privately owned, Callington, Cornwall | |
| XR757 | BAC Lightning F6 <ff> | NATO Aircraft Museum, New Waltham, Humberside | |

| *Notes* | *Serial* | *Type (other identity) [code]* | *Owner/operator, location or fate* |
|---|---|---|---|
| | XR759 | BAC Lightning F6 <ff> | Privately owned, Haxey, Lincs |
| | XR770 | BAC Lightning F6 [AA] | NATO Aircraft Museum, New Waltham, Humberside |
| | XR771 | BAC Lightning F6 [BM] | Midland Air Museum, Coventry |
| | XR806 | BAC VC10 C1K | RAF Brize Norton Fire Section |
| | XR807 | BAC VC10 C1K | DARA, stored RAF St Athan |
| | XR808 | BAC VC10 C1K | RAF No 10 Sqn, Brize Norton |
| | XR810 | BAC VC10 C1K | RAF No 10 Sqn, Brize Norton |
| | *XR944* | Wallis WA116 (G-ATTB) | RAF Museum, Hendon |
| | XR954 | HS Gnat T1 (8570M) [30] | Privately owned, Bournemouth |
| | XR955 | HS Gnat T1 [SAH-2] | Privately owned, Leavesden |
| | XR977 | HS Gnat T1 (8640M) [3] | RAF Museum, Cosford |
| | XR985 | HS Gnat T1 (7886M) | Vintage Aircraft Team, Bruntingthorpe |
| | *XR991* | HS Gnat T1 (8624M/XS102/ G-MOUR) | Intrepid Aviation Co, North Weald |
| | *XR993* | HS Gnat T1 (8620M/XP534/ G-BVPP) | Kennet Aviation, Cranfield |
| | | | |
| | XS100 | HS Gnat T1 (8561M) [57] | Privately owned, Bournemouth |
| | XS101 | HS Gnat T1 (8638M) (G-GNAT) | Privately owned, Cranfield |
| | XS122 | WS58 Wessex HAS3 [655/PO] | RN AESS, *HMS Sultan*, Gosport |
| | XS128 | WS58 Wessex HAS1 [37] | RNAS Yeovilton Fire Section |
| | XS149 | WS58 Wessex HAS3 [661/GL] | The Helicopter Museum, Weston-super-Mare |
| | *XS165* | Hiller UH12E (G-ASAZ) [37] | Privately owned, North Weald |
| | XS176 | Hunting Jet Provost T4 (8514M) | Privately owned, Bruntingthorpe |
| | XS177 | Hunting Jet Provost T4 (9044M) [N] | RAF Valley Fire Section |
| | XS179 | Hunting Jet Provost T4 (8237M) [20] | University of Salford, Manchester |
| | XS180 | Hunting Jet Provost T4 (8238M) [21] | RAF St Athan (dismantled) |
| | XS181 | Hunting Jet Provost T4 (9033M) <ff> | Communications & Electronics Museum, Bletchley Park |
| | XS183 | Hunting Jet Provost T4 <ff> | Privately owned, Plymouth |
| | XS186 | Hunting Jet Provost T4 (8408M) [M] | RAF North Luffenham Training Area |
| | XS209 | Hunting Jet Provost T4 (8409M) [29] | Privately owned, Kemble |
| | XS215 | Hunting Jet Provost T4 (8507M) [17] | RAF Halton |
| | XS216 | Hunting Jet Provost T4 <ff> | No 2357 Sqn ATC, Goole |
| | XS217 | Hunting Jet Provost T4 (9029M) [O] | Privately owned, Bruntingthorpe |
| | XS218 | Hunting Jet Provost T4 (8508M) <ff> | No 447 Sqn ATC, Henley-on-Thames, Berks |
| | XS231 | BAC Jet Provost T5 (G-ATAJ) | Privately owned, Sproughton |
| | XS235 | DH106 Comet 4C | British Aviation Heritage, Bruntingthorpe |
| | XS416 | BAC Lightning T5 <ff> | NATO Aircraft Museum, New Waltham, Humberside |
| | XS417 | BAC Lightning T5 [DZ] | Newark Air Museum, Winthorpe |
| | XS420 | BAC Lightning T5 | Privately owned, Norfolk |
| | XS421 | BAC Lightning T5 <ff> | Privately owned, Foulness |
| | XS456 | BAC Lightning T5 [DX] | Privately owned, Wainfleet |
| | XS457 | BAC Lightning T5 <ff> | NATO Aircraft Museum, New Waltham, Humberside |
| | XS458 | BAC Lightning T5 | T5 Projects, Cranfield |
| | XS459 | BAC Lightning T5 [AW] | Fenland & W Norfolk Aviation Museum, Wisbech |
| | *XS463* | WS Wasp HAS1 (XT431) | The Helicopter Museum, Weston-super-Mare |
| | XS479 | WS58 Wessex HU5 (8819M) [XF] | Privately owned, Stock, Essex |
| | XS481 | WS58 Wessex HU5 | South Yorkshire Avn Museum, Firbeck |
| | XS482 | WS58 Wessex HU5 [A/D] | MoD FSCTE, Manston |
| | XS485 | WS58 Wessex HC5C (comp XR503) [*Hearts*] | RN AESS, *HMS Sultan*, Gosport |
| | XS486 | WS58 Wessex HU5 [524/CU,F] | RN Recruiting Team, Wroughton |
| | XS488 | WS58 Wessex HU5 (9056M) [XK] | AAC Wattisham, instructional use |
| | XS489 | WS58 Wessex HU5 [R] | RN AESS, *HMS Sultan*, Gosport |
| | XS491 | WS58 Wessex HU5 [XM] | South Yorkshire Avn Museum, Firbeck |
| | XS492 | WS58 Wessex HU5 [623] | RN, stored RNAY Fleetlands |
| | XS493 | WS58 Wessex HU5 | RN, stored RNAY Fleetlands |
| | XS496 | WS58 Wessex HU5 [625/PO] | RN AESS, *HMS Sultan*, Gosport |
| | XS498 | WS58 Wessex HC5C (comp XS677) [WK] | RN, Predannack Fire School |

| Serial | Type (other identity) [code] | Owner/operator, location or fate | Notes |
|---|---|---|---|
| XS507 | WS58 Wessex HU5 | RN AESS, *HMS Sultan*, Gosport | |
| XS508 | WS58 Wessex HU5 | FAA Museum, stored RNAS Yeovilton | |
| XS510 | WS58 Wessex HU5 [626/PO] | RN AESS, *HMS Sultan*, Gosport | |
| XS511 | WS58 Wessex HU5 [M] | RN AESS, *HMS Sultan*, Gosport | |
| XS513 | WS58 Wessex HU5 [419/CU] | RN AESS, *HMS Sultan*, Gosport | |
| XS514 | WS58 Wessex HU5 [L] | RN AESS, *HMS Sultan*, Gosport | |
| XS515 | WS58 Wessex HU5 [N] | RN AESS, *HMS Sultan*, Gosport | |
| XS516 | WS58 Wessex HU5 [Q] | RN, Predannack Fire School | |
| XS517 | WS58 Wessex HC5C (comp XS679) [*Diamonds*] | RN AESS, *HMS Sultan*, Gosport, BDRT | |
| XS520 | WS58 Wessex HU5 [F] | RN AESS, *HMS Sultan*, Gosport | |
| XS521 | WS58 Wessex HU5 | *Burnt at Saighton, 1998* | |
| XS522 | WS58 Wessex HU5 [ZL] | RN Predannack Fire School | |
| XS527 | WS Wasp HAS1 | FAA Museum, RNAS Yeovilton | |
| XS529 | WS Wasp HAS1 | RN, Predannack Fire School | |
| XS539 | WS Wasp HAS1 [435] | RNAY Fleetlands Apprentice School | |
| XS567 | WS Wasp HAS1 [434/E] | Imperial War Museum, Duxford | |
| XS568 | WS Wasp HAS1 [441] | RN AESS, *HMS Sultan*, Gosport | |
| XS569 | WS Wasp HAS1 | RNAY Fleetlands Apprentice School | |
| XS570 | WS Wasp HAS1 [445/P] | Warship Preservation Trust, Birkenhead | |
| XS572 | WS Wasp HAS1 (8845M) [414] | *Scrapped at Stafford by 1999* | |
| XS576 | DH110 Sea Vixen FAW2 [125/E] | Imperial War Museum, Duxford | |
| XS577 | DH110 Sea Vixen D3 <ff> | *Sold to Switzerland, 1999* | |
| XS587 | DH110 Sea Vixen FAW(TT)2 (8828M/G-VIXN) | Gatwick Aviation Museum, Charlwood, Surrey | |
| XS590 | DH110 Sea Vixen FAW2 [131/E] | FAA Museum, RNAS Yeovilton | |
| XS596 | HS Andover C1(PR) | DPA/AFD/*Open Skies*, DERA Boscombe Down | |
| XS598 | HS Andover C1 (fuselage) | FETC, Moreton-in-Marsh, Glos | |
| XS606 | HS Andover C1 | DPA/AFD/ETPS, DERA Boscombe Down | |
| XS639 | HS Andover E3A | RAF Museum, Cosford | |
| XS641 | HS Andover C1(PR) (9198M) [Z] | RAF No 1 SoTT, Cosford | |
| XS643 | HS Andover E3A | MoD FSCTE, Manston | |
| XS646 | HS Andover C1(mod) | DPA/AFD, DERA Boscombe Down | |
| XS652 | Slingsby T45 Swallow TX1 (BGA 1107) | Privately owned, Rufforth | |
| XS674 | WS58 Wessex HC2 [R] | Privately owned, Sproughton | |
| XS675 | WS58 Wessex HC2 [*Spades*] | RAF No 84 Sqn, Akrotiri | |
| XS677 | WS58 Wessex HC2 [WK] | RAF, stored Shawbury | |
| XS695 | HS Kestrel FGA1 | RAF Museum, stored Wyton | |
| XS709 | HS125 Dominie T1 [M] | RAF No 3 FTS/55(R) Sqn, Cranwell | |
| XS710 | HS125 Dominie T1 (9259M) [O] | RAF No 1 SoTT, Cosford | |
| XS711 | HS125 Dominie T1 [L] | RAF No 3 FTS/55(R) Sqn, Cranwell | |
| XS712 | HS125 Dominie T1 [A] | RAF No 3 FTS/55(R) Sqn, Cranwell | |
| XS713 | HS125 Dominie T1 [C] | RAF No 3 FTS/55(R) Sqn, Cranwell | |
| XS714 | HS125 Dominie T1 (9246M) [P] | MoD FSCTE, Manston | |
| XS726 | HS125 Dominie T1 [T] | RAF No 1 SoTT, Cosford | |
| XS727 | HS125 Dominie T1 [D] | RAF No 3 FTS/55(R) Sqn, Cranwell | |
| XS728 | HS125 Dominie T1 [E] | RAF No 3 FTS/55(R) Sqn, Cranwell | |
| XS729 | HS125 Dominie T1 [G] | RAF No 1 SoTT, Cosford | |
| XS730 | HS125 Dominie T1 [H] | RAF No 3 FTS/55(R) Sqn, Cranwell | |
| XS731 | HS125 Dominie T1 [J] | RAF No 3 FTS/55(R) Sqn, Cranwell | |
| XS732 | HS125 Dominie T1 [B] (fuselage) | DERA, Fort Halstead, Kent | |
| XS733 | HS125 Dominie T1 [Q] | RAF No 1 SoTT, Cosford | |
| XS734 | HS125 Dominie T1 (9260M) [N] | RAF No 1 SoTT, Cosford | |
| XS735 | HS125 Dominie T1 [R] | RAF Cranwell, instructional use | |
| XS736 | HS125 Dominie T1 [S] | RAF No 3 FTS/55(R) Sqn, Cranwell | |
| XS737 | HS125 Dominie T1 [K] | RAF No 3 FTS/55(R) Sqn, Cranwell | |
| XS738 | HS125 Dominie T1 [U] | RAF No 1 SoTT, Cosford | |
| XS739 | HS125 Dominie T1 [F] | RAF No 3 FTS/55(R) Sqn, Cranwell | |
| XS743 | Beagle B206Z Basset CC1 | DPA/AFD/ETPS, DERA Boscombe Down | |
| XS765 | Beagle B206Z Basset CC1 (G-BSET) | Privately owned, Cranfield | |
| XS770 | Beagle B206Z Basset CC1 (G-HRHI) | Privately owned, Cranfield | |
| XS790 | HS748 Andover CC2 <ff> | Boscombe Down Museum | |
| XS791 | HS748 Andover CC2 | Phoenix Aviation, Bruntingthorpe | |
| XS862 | WS58 Wessex HAS3 | Defence NBC Centre, Winterbourne Gunner | |
| XS863 | WS58 Wessex HAS1 | Imperial War Museum, Duxford | |
| XS866 | WS58 Wessex HAS1 [520/CU] | RN, Predannack Fire School | |
| XS868 | WS58 Wessex HAS1 | RN, Predannack Fire School | |
| XS870 | WS58 Wessex HAS1 [PO] | | |

| Notes | Serial | Type (other identity) [code] | Owner/operator, location or fate |
|---|---|---|---|
| | XS871 | WS58 Wessex HAS1 (8457M) [265] | Privately owned, Chippenham, Wilts |
| | XS872 | WS58 Wessex HAS1 [572/CU] | |
| | XS876 | WS58 Wessex HAS1 [523/PO] | SFDO, RNAS Culdrose |
| | XS881 | WS58 Wessex HAS1 | RN, Predannack Fire School |
| | XS885 | WS58 Wessex HAS1 [12/CU] | SFDO, RNAS Culdrose |
| | XS886 | WS58 Wessex HAS1 [527/CU] | Sea Scouts, Evesham, Worcs |
| | XS887 | WS58 Wessex HAS1 [403/FI] | Flambards Village Theme Park, Helston |
| | XS888 | WS58 Wessex HAS1 [521] | Guernsey Airport Fire Section |
| | XS897 | BAC Lightning F6 | South Yorkshire Avn Museum, Firbeck |
| | XS898 | BAC Lightning F6 <ff> | Privately owned, Lavendon, Bucks |
| | XS899 | BAC Lightning F6 <ff> | RAF Coltishall |
| | XS903 | BAC Lightning F6 [BA] | Yorkshire Air Museum, Elvington |
| | XS904 | BAC Lightning F6 [BQ] | Lightning Preservation Grp, Bruntingthorpe |
| | XS919 | BAC Lightning F6 | Wonderland Pleasure Park, Farnsfield, Notts |
| | XS922 | BAC Lightning F6 (8973M) <ff> | The Air Defence Collection, Salisbury |
| | XS923 | BAC Lightning F6 <ff> | Privately owned, Welshpool |
| | XS925 | BAC Lightning F6 (8961M) [BA] | RAF Museum, Hendon |
| | XS928 | BAC Lightning F6 [AD] | BAE SystemsWarton, at main gate |
| | XS932 | BAC Lightning F6 <ff> | D-Day Museum, Shoreham |
| | XS933 | BAC Lightning F6 <ff> | Privately owned, Terrington St Clement |
| | XS936 | BAC Lightning F6 | Castle Motors, Liskeard, Cornwall |
| | | | |
| | XT108 | Agusta-Bell 47G-3 Sioux AH1 [U] | Museum of Army Flying, Middle Wallop |
| | *XT123* | WS Sioux AH1 (XT827) [D] | AAC Middle Wallop, at main gate |
| | XT131 | Agusta-Bell 47G-3 Sioux AH1 [B] | AAC Historic Aircraft Flight, Middle Wallop |
| | XT133 | Agusta-Bell 47G-3 Sioux AH1 (7923M) | Royal Engineers' Museum, Chatham, stored |
| | XT140 | Agusta-Bell 47G-3 Sioux AH1 | Perth Technical College |
| | XT148 | Agusta-Bell 47G-3 Sioux AH1 | The Helicopter Museum, stored Weston-super-Mare |
| | XT150 | Agusta-Bell 47G-3 Sioux AH1 (7883M) [R] | AAC Netheravon, at main gate |
| | XT151 | WS Sioux AH1 [W] | Museum of Army Flying, stored Middle Wallop |
| | XT175 | WS Sioux AH1 (TAD175) | Privately owned, Oxford for ground instruction |
| | XT176 | WS Sioux AH1 [U] | FAA Museum, stored Yeovilton |
| | XT190 | WS Sioux AH1 | The Helicopter Museum, Weston-super-Mare |
| | XT200 | WS Sioux AH1 [F] | Newark Air Museum, Winthorpe |
| | XT223 | WS Sioux AH1 (G-BGZK/G-XTUN) | Privately owned, North Weald |
| | XT236 | WS Sioux AH1 (frame only) | North-East Aircraft Museum, stored Usworth |
| | XT242 | WS Sioux AH1 (composite) [12] | South Yorkshire Avn Museum, Firbeck |
| | XT255 | WS58 Wessex HAS3 (8751M) | |
| | XT257 | WS58 Wessex HAS3 (8719M) | Privately owned, East Grinstead |
| | XT277 | HS Buccaneer S2A (8853M) <ff> | Privately owned, Welshpool |
| | XT280 | HS Buccaneer S2A <ff> | Dundonald Aviation Centre, Strathclyde |
| | XT284 | HS Buccaneer S2A (8855M) <ff> | Privately owned, Stock, Essex |
| | XT288 | HS Buccaneer S2B (9134M) | Royal Scottish Museum of Flight, stored E Fortune |
| | XT420 | WS Wasp HAS1 [606] | Privately owned, East Dereham, Norfolk |
| | XT422 | WS Wasp HAS1 [324] | Privately owned, Burgess Hill |
| | XT427 | WS Wasp HAS1 [606] | FAA Museum, RNAS Yeovilton |
| | XT434 | WS Wasp HAS1 [455] | RNAY Fleetlands Apprentice School |
| | XT437 | WS Wasp HAS1 [423] | *Scrapped* |
| | XT439 | WS Wasp HAS1 [605] | Privately owned, King's Lynn |
| | XT443 | WS Wasp HAS1 [422/AU] | The Helicopter Museum, Weston-super-Mare |
| | XT453 | WS58 Wessex HU5 [A/B] | RN AESS, *HMS Sultan*, Gosport |
| | XT455 | WS58 Wessex HU5 [U] | RN AESS, *HMS Sultan*, Gosport |
| | XT456 | WS58 Wessex HU5 (8941M) [XZ] | RAF Aldergrove, BDRT |
| | XT458 | WS58 Wessex HU5 [622] | RN AESS, *HMS Sultan*, Gosport |
| | XT460 | WS58 Wessex HU5 | RN AESS, *HMS Sultan*, Gosport, BDRT |
| | XT463 | WS58 Wessex HC5C (comp XR508) [*Clubs*, PO] | RN, Predannack Fire School |
| | XT466 | WS58 Wessex HU5 (8921M) [XV] | RN AESS, *HMS Sultan*, Gosport |
| | XT467 | WS58 Wessex HU5 (8922M) [BF] | RAF Odiham Fire Section |
| | XT468 | WS58 Wessex HU5 (comp XT460) [628] | RN, Predannack Fire School |

| Serial | Type (other identity) [code] | Owner/operator, location or fate | Notes |
|---|---|---|---|
| XT469 | WS58 Wessex HU5 (8920M) | RAF No 16 MU, Stafford, ground instruction | |
| XT472 | WS58 Wessex HU5 [XC] | The Helicopter Museum, Weston-super-Mare | |
| XT474 | WS58 Wessex HU5 [820] | RN AESS, *HMS Sultan*, Gosport | |
| XT480 | WS58 Wessex HU5 [468/RG] | RNAY Fleetlands, on display | |
| XT482 | WS58 Wessex HU5 [ZM/VL] | FAA Museum, RNAS Yeovilton | |
| XT484 | WS58 Wessex HU5 [H] | RN AESS, *HMS Sultan*, Gosport | |
| XT485 | WS58 Wessex HU5 [621] | RN AESS, *HMS Sultan*, Gosport | |
| XT575 | Vickers Viscount 837 <ff> | Brooklands Museum, Weybridge | |
| XT595 | McD F-4K Phantom FG1 (8851M) <ff> | RAF EPTT, St Athan | |
| XT596 | McD F-4K Phantom FG1 | FAA Museum, RNAS Yeovilton | |
| XT597 | McD F-4K Phantom FG1 | Boscombe Down Museum | |
| XT601 | WS58 Wessex HC2 (9277M) (comp XS498) | RAF Odiham, BDRT | |
| XT602 | WS58 Wessex HC2 | RN AESS, *HMS Sultan*, Gosport, BDRT | |
| XT604 | WS58 Wessex HC2 | RAF, stored RNAY Fleetlands | |
| XT606 | WS58 Wessex HC2 [WL] | RAF, stored Shawbury | |
| XT607 | WS58 Wessex HC2 [P] | RAF, stored RNAY Fleetlands | |
| XT617 | WS Scout AH1 | AAC Wattisham, on display | |
| XT620 | WS Scout AH1 | AAC Dishforth Fire Section | |
| XT621 | WS Scout AH1 | R. Military College of Science, Shrivenham | |
| XT623 | WS Scout AH1 | Army SEAE, Arborfield | |
| XT626 | WS Scout AH1 [Q] | AAC Historic Aircraft Flt, Middle Wallop | |
| XT630 | WS Scout AH1 (G-BXRL) [X] | *Crashed 16 October 1999, Hartshill, near Nuneaton* | |
| XT631 | WS Scout AH1 [D] | Privately owned, Ipswich | |
| XT632 | WS Scout AH1 | Privately owned, Oaksey Park, Wilts | |
| XT633 | WS Scout AH1 | Army SEAE, Arborfield | |
| XT634 | WS Scout AH1 (G-BYRX) [T] | Privately owned, Thruxton | |
| XT638 | WS Scout AH1 [N] | AAC Middle Wallop, at gate | |
| XT640 | WS Scout AH1 | Army SEAE, Arborfield | |
| XT643 | WS Scout AH1 [Z] | Army, Thorpe Camp, East Wretham | |
| XT645 | WS Scout AH1 (fuselage) | Privately owned, Ipswich | |
| XT668 | WS58 Wessex HC2 [S] | RAF No 72 Sqn, Aldergrove | |
| XT670 | WS58 Wessex HC2 | RN AESS, *HMS Sultan*, Gosport, BDRT | |
| XT671 | WS58 Wessex HC2 (G-BYRC) [D] | Privately owned, Redhill | |
| XT672 | WS58 Wessex HC2 [WE] | RAF, stored Shawbury | |
| XT676 | WS58 Wessex HC2 [I] | RAF No 72 Sqn, Aldergrove | |
| XT677 | WS58 Wessex HC2 (8016M) | Privately owned, Stock, Essex | |
| XT680 | WS58 Wessex HC2 [*Diamonds*] | RAF No 84 Sqn, Akrotiri | |
| XT681 | WS58 Wessex HC2 [U] | RAF Benson, BDRT | |
| XT759 | WS58 Wessex HU5 [XY] | | |
| XT760 | WS58 Wessex HU5 (comp XT604) | *Sunk at Horsey Island* | |
| XT761 | WS58 Wessex HU5 | RN AESS, *HMS Sultan*, Gosport | |
| XT762 | WS58 Wessex HU5 | SFDO, RNAS Culdrose | |
| XT764 | WS58 Wessex HU5 [G] | RN AESS, *HMS Sultan*, Gosport | |
| XT765 | WS58 Wessex HU5 [J] | RN AESS, *HMS Sultan*, Gosport | |
| XT766 | WS58 Wessex HU5 (9054M) [822/CU] | RN AESS, *HMS Sultan*, Gosport, BDRT | |
| XT769 | WS58 Wessex HU5 [823] | FAA Museum, RNAS Yeovilton | |
| XT770 | WS58 Wessex HU5 (9055M) [P] | Privately owned, Shawell, Leics | |
| XT771 | WS58 Wessex HU5 [620/PO] | RN AESS, *HMS Sultan*, Gosport | |
| XT772 | WS58 Wessex HU5 (8805M) | SARTU RAF Valley, ground instruction | |
| XT773 | WS58 Wessex HU5 (9123M) [822/CU] | DARA, RAF St Athan, BDRT | |
| XT778 | WS Wasp HAS1 [430] | FAA Museum, stored Yeovilton | |
| XT780 | WS Wasp HAS1 [636] | RNAY Fleetlands Apprentice School | |
| XT781 | WS Wasp HAS1 (NZ3908/ G-KAWW) [423] | Kennet Aviation, Cranfield | |
| XT788 | WS Wasp HAS1 (G-BMIR) [316] (painted as XT78?) | Privately owned, Dunkeswell | |
| XT793 | WS Wasp HAS1 [456] | Privately owned, East Dereham, Norfolk | |
| XT803 | WS Sioux AH1 [Y] | Privately owned, Panshanger | |
| XT852 | McD YF-4M Phantom FGR2 | DERA West Freugh Fire Section | |
| XT863 | McD F-4K Phantom FG1 <ff> | Privately owned, Cowes, IOW | |
| XT864 | McD F-4K Phantom FG1 (8998M/ *XT684*) [BJ] | RAF Leuchars on display | |
| XT867 | McD F-4K Phantom FG1 (9064M) [BH] | RAF Leuchars BDRT | |
| XT891 | McD F-4M Phantom FGR2 (9136M) [Z] | RAF Coningsby, at main gate | |

| Notes | Serial | Type (other identity) [code] | Owner/operator, location or fate |
|---|---|---|---|
| | XT903 | McD F-4M Phantom FGR2 [X] | RAF Leuchars, BDRT |
| | XT905 | McD F-4M Phantom FGR2 [P] | RAF Coningsby, stored |
| | XT907 | McD F-4M Phantom FGR2 (9151M) [W] | DEODS, Chattenden, Kent |
| | XT914 | McD F-4M Phantom FGR2 | RAF Brampton, Cambs, on display |
| | XV101 | BAC VC10 C1K | RAF No 10 Sqn, Brize Norton |
| | XV102 | BAC VC10 C1K | RAF No 10 Sqn, Brize Norton |
| | XV103 | BAC VC10 C1K | RAF No 10 Sqn, Brize Norton |
| | XV104 | BAC VC10 C1K | RAF No 10 Sqn, Brize Norton |
| | XV105 | BAC VC10 C1K | RAF No 10 Sqn, Brize Norton |
| | XV106 | BAC VC10 C1K | RAF No 10 Sqn, Brize Norton |
| | XV107 | BAC VC10 C1K | RAF No 10 Sqn, Brize Norton |
| | XV108 | BAC VC10 C1K | RAF No 10 Sqn, Brize Norton |
| | XV109 | BAC VC10 C1K | RAF No 10 Sqn, Brize Norton |
| | XV118 | WS Scout AH1 (9141M) | RAF Air Movements School, Brize Norton |
| | XV121 | WS Scout AH1 (G-BYKJ) | Privately owned, Thruxton |
| | XV122 | WS Scout AH1 [D] | Royal Military College of Science, Shrivenham |
| | XV123 | WS Scout AH1 | The Helicopter Museum, Weston-super-Mare |
| | XV124 | WS Scout AH1 [W] | Army SEAE, Arborfield |
| | XV126 | WS Scout AH1 (G-SCTA) [X] | Privately owned, Thruxton |
| | XV127 | WS Scout AH1 | Museum of Army Flying, Middle Wallop |
| | XV130 | WS Scout AH1 (G-BWJW) [R] | Privately owned, Redhill |
| | XV131 | WS Scout AH1 [Y] | AAC 70 Aircraft Workshops, Middle Wallop, BDRT |
| | XV134 | WS Scout AH1 (G-BWLX) [P] | Privately owned, East Dereham, Norfolk |
| | XV136 | WS Scout AH1 [X] | AAC Netheravon, on display |
| | XV137 | WS Scout AH1 (G-CRUM) | Privately owned, Glenrothes |
| | XV138 | WS Scout AH1 | Privately owned, East Dereham |
| | XV139 | WS Scout AH1 | Yeovil College |
| | XV140 | WS Scout AH1 (G-KAXL) [K] | Kennet Aviation, Cranfield |
| | XV141 | WS Scout AH1 | REME Museum, Arborfield |
| | XV147 | HS Nimrod MR1(mod) (fuselage) | BAE Systems, Warton |
| | XV148 | HS Nimrod MR1(mod) <ff> | Privately owned, Guildford |
| | XV161 | HS Buccaneer S2B (9117M) <ff> | Privately owned, Birtley, Tyne & Wear |
| | XV165 | HS Buccaneer S2B <ff> | Jet Age Museum, Staverton |
| | XV168 | HS Buccaneer S2B | BAE SystemsBrough, on display |
| | XV176 | Lockheed C-130K Hercules C3 | RAF Lyneham Transport Wing |
| | XV177 | Lockheed C-130K Hercules C3 | RAF Lyneham Transport Wing |
| | XV178 | Lockheed C-130K Hercules C1 | RAF Lyneham Transport Wing |
| | XV179 | Lockheed C-130K Hercules C1 | RAF Lyneham Transport Wing |
| | XV181 | Lockheed C-130K Hercules C1 | RAF Lyneham Transport Wing |
| | XV182 | Lockheed C-130K Hercules C1 | RAF Lyneham Transport Wing |
| | XV183 | Lockheed C-130K Hercules C3 | RAF Lyneham Transport Wing |
| | XV184 | Lockheed C-130K Hercules C3 | RAF Lyneham Transport Wing |
| | XV185 | Lockheed C-130K Hercules C1 | RAF Lyneham Transport Wing |
| | XV186 | Lockheed C-130K Hercules C1 | RAF Lyneham Transport Wing |
| | XV187 | Lockheed C-130K Hercules C1 | RAF Lyneham Transport Wing |
| | XV188 | Lockheed C-130K Hercules C3 | RAF Lyneham Transport Wing |
| | XV189 | Lockheed C-130K Hercules C3 | RAF Lyneham Transport Wing |
| | XV190 | Lockheed C-130K Hercules C3 | RAF Lyneham Transport Wing |
| | XV191 | Lockheed C-130K Hercules C1 | RAF Lyneham Transport Wing |
| | XV192 | Lockheed C-130K Hercules C1 | RAF Lyneham Transport Wing |
| | XV195 | Lockheed C-130K Hercules C1 | RAF Lyneham Transport Wing |
| | XV196 | Lockheed C-130K Hercules C1 | RAF Lyneham Transport Wing |
| | XV197 | Lockheed C-130K Hercules C3 | RAF Lyneham Transport Wing |
| | XV199 | Lockheed C-130K Hercules C3 | RAF Lyneham Transport Wing |
| | XV200 | Lockheed C-130K Hercules C1 | RAF Lyneham Transport Wing |
| | XV201 | Lockheed C-130K Hercules C1K | RAF, stored Cambridge |
| | XV202 | Lockheed C-130K Hercules C3 | RAF Lyneham Transport Wing |
| | XV203 | Lockheed C-130K Hercules C1K | *Sold to Sri Lanka as CR-880, August 1999* |
| | XV205 | Lockheed C-130K Hercules C1 | RAF Lyneham Transport Wing |
| | XV206 | Lockheed C-130K Hercules C1 | RAF Lyneham Transport Wing |
| | XV207 | Lockheed C-130K Hercules C3 | LMASC/Marshall Aerospace, Cambridge |
| | XV208 | Lockheed C-130K Hercules W2 | DPA/MRF, DERA Boscombe Down |
| | XV209 | Lockheed C-130K Hercules C3 | RAF Lyneham Transport Wing |
| | XV210 | Lockheed C-130K Hercules C1 | RAF Lyneham Transport Wing |
| | XV211 | Lockheed C-130K Hercules C1 | RAF Lyneham Transport Wing |
| | XV212 | Lockheed C-130K Hercules C3 | RAF Lyneham Transport Wing |
| | XV213 | Lockheed C-130K Hercules C1K | *Sold to Sri Lanka as CR-881, August 1999* |
| | XV214 | Lockheed C-130K Hercules C3 | RAF Lyneham Transport Wing |

| Serial | Type (other identity) [code] | Owner/operator, location or fate | Notes |
|---|---|---|---|
| XV215 | Lockheed C-130K Hercules C1 | RAF Lyneham Transport Wing | |
| XV217 | Lockheed C-130K Hercules C3 | RAF Lyneham Transport Wing | |
| XV218 | Lockheed C-130K Hercules C1 | RAF No 1312 Flt, Mount Pleasant, FI | |
| XV219 | Lockheed C-130K Hercules C3 | RAF Lyneham Transport Wing | |
| XV220 | Lockheed C-130K Hercules C3 | RAF Lyneham Transport Wing | |
| XV221 | Lockheed C-130K Hercules C3 | RAF Lyneham Transport Wing | |
| XV222 | Lockheed C-130K Hercules C3 | RAF Lyneham Transport Wing | |
| XV223 | Lockheed C-130K Hercules C3 | RAF Lyneham Transport Wing | |
| XV226 | HS Nimrod MR2 | RAF Kinloss MR Wing | |
| XV227 | HS Nimrod MR2 | RAF Kinloss MR Wing | |
| XV228 | HS Nimrod MR2 | RAF Kinloss MR Wing | |
| XV229 | HS Nimrod MR2 | RAF Kinloss MR Wing | |
| XV230 | HS Nimrod MR2 | RAF Kinloss MR Wing | |
| XV231 | HS Nimrod MR2 | RAF Kinloss MR Wing | |
| XV232 | HS Nimrod MR2 | RAF Kinloss MR Wing | |
| XV233 | HS Nimrod MR2 | RAF No 42(R) Sqn, Kinloss | |
| XV234 | HS Nimrod MR2 | *To be converted to Nimrod MRA4 ZJ518* | |
| XV235 | HS Nimrod MR2 | RAF Kinloss MR Wing | |
| XV236 | HS Nimrod MR2 | RAF No 42(R) Sqn, Kinloss | |
| XV237 | HS Nimrod MR2 <ff> | Privately owned, St Austell | |
| *XV238* | HS Nimrod <R> (parts of G-ALYW) | RAF EPTT, St Athan | |
| XV240 | HS Nimrod MR2 [CXX] | RAF No 120 Sqn, Kinloss | |
| XV241 | HS Nimrod MR2 | RAF No 206 Sqn, Kinloss | |
| XV242 | HS Nimrod MR2 | *To be converted to Nimrod MRA4 ZJ517* | |
| XV243 | HS Nimrod MR2 | RAF No 120 Sqn, Kinloss | |
| XV244 | HS Nimrod MR2 | RAF Kinloss MR Wing | |
| XV245 | HS Nimrod MR2 | RAF No 201 Sqn, Kinloss | |
| XV246 | HS Nimrod MR2 | RAF Kinloss MR Wing | |
| XV247 | HS Nimrod MR2 | *To be converted to Nimrod MRA4 ZJ516* | |
| XV248 | HS Nimrod MR2 | RAF Kinloss MR Wing | |
| XV249 | HS Nimrod R1 | RAF No 51 Sqn, Waddington | |
| XV250 | HS Nimrod MR2 | RAF Kinloss MR Wing | |
| XV251 | HS Nimrod MR2 | *To be converted to Nimrod MRA4 ZJ514* | |
| XV252 | HS Nimrod MR2 | RAF No 201 Sqn, Kinloss | |
| XV253 | HS Nimrod MR2 (9118M) | RAF Kinloss, instructional use | |
| XV254 | HS Nimrod MR2 | RAF Kinloss MR Wing | |
| XV255 | HS Nimrod MR2 | RAF Kinloss MR Wing | |
| XV258 | HS Nimrod MR2 | *To be converted to Nimrod MRA4 ZJ515* | |
| XV259 | BAe Nimrod AEW3 <ff> | Privately owned, Carlisle | |
| XV260 | HS Nimrod MR2 [CXX] | RAF No 120 Sqn, Kinloss | |
| XV263 | BAe Nimrod AEW3P (8967M) <ff> | BAe, Warton, instructional use | |
| XV263 | BAE SystemsNimrod AEW3P (8967M) <rf> | FR Aviation, Bournemouth | |
| XV268 | DHC2 Beaver AL1 (G-BVER) | Privately owned | |
| XV277 | HS P.1127(RAF) | Privately owned, Sproughton | |
| XV279 | HS P.1127(RAF) (8566M) | RAF Harrier Maintenance School, Wittering | |
| XV280 | HS P.1127(RAF) <ff> | RNAS Yeovilton Fire Section | |
| XV290 | Lockheed C-130K Hercules C3 | RAF Lyneham Transport Wing | |
| XV291 | Lockheed C-130K Hercules C1 | RAF Lyneham Transport Wing | |
| XV292 | Lockheed C-130K Hercules C1 | RAF Lyneham Transport Wing | |
| XV293 | Lockheed C-130K Hercules C1 | RAF Lyneham Transport Wing | |
| XV294 | Lockheed C-130K Hercules C3 | RAF Lyneham Transport Wing | |
| XV295 | Lockheed C-130K Hercules C1 | RAF Lyneham Transport Wing | |
| XV296 | Lockheed C-130K Hercules C1K | RAF, stored Cambridge | |
| XV297 | Lockheed C-130K Hercules C1 | RAF Lyneham Transport Wing | |
| XV298 | Lockheed C-130K Hercules C1 | *Crashed 12 June 1999, Kukes, Albania* | |
| XV299 | Lockheed C-130K Hercules C3 | RAF Lyneham Transport Wing | |
| XV300 | Lockheed C-130K Hercules C1 | RAF Lyneham Transport Wing | |
| XV301 | Lockheed C-130K Hercules C3 | RAF Lyneham Transport Wing | |
| XV302 | Lockheed C-130K Hercules C3 | RAF Lyneham Transport Wing | |
| XV303 | Lockheed C-130K Hercules C3 | RAF Lyneham Transport Wing | |
| XV304 | Lockheed C-130K Hercules C3 | RAF Lyneham Transport Wing | |
| XV305 | Lockheed C-130K Hercules C3 | RAF Lyneham Transport Wing | |
| XV306 | Lockheed C-130K Hercules C1 | RAF Lyneham Transport Wing | |
| XV307 | Lockheed C-130K Hercules C3 | RAF Lyneham Transport Wing | |
| XV328 | BAC Lightning T5 <ff> | Phoenix Aviation, Bruntingthorpe | |
| XV332 | HS Buccaneer S2B (9232M) | RAF Marham Fire Section | |
| XV333 | HS Buccaneer S2B [234/H] | FAA Museum, RNAS Yeovilton | |
| XV337 | HS Buccaneer S2C (8852M) <ff> | Privately owned, Stock, Essex | |
| XV344 | HS Buccaneer S2C | DERA Farnborough, on display | |
| XV350 | HS Buccaneer S2B | East Midlands Airport Aeropark | |
| XV352 | HS Buccaneer S2B <ff> | RAF Manston History Museum | |

| Notes | Serial | Type (other identity) [code] | Owner/operator, location or fate |
|---|---|---|---|
| | XV353 | HS Buccaneer S2B (9144M) <ff> | Privately owned, |
| | XV359 | HS Buccaneer S2B [035/R] | RNAS Culdrose, on display |
| | XV361 | HS Buccaneer S2B | Ulster Aviation Society, Langford Lodge |
| | XV370 | Sikorsky SH-3D | RN AESS, *HMS Sultan*, Gosport |
| | XV371 | WS61 Sea King HAS1(DB) | RN AESS, *HMS Sultan*, Gosport |
| | XV372 | WS61 Sea King HAS1 | RAF St Mawgan, instructional use |
| | XV399 | McD F-4M Phantom FGR2 <ff> | Privately owned, Stock, Essex |
| | XV401 | McD F-4M Phantom FGR2 [I] | Boscombe Down Museum |
| | XV406 | McD F-4M Phantom FGR2 (9098M) [CK] | Solway Aviation Society, Carlisle Airport |
| | XV408 | McD F-4M Phantom FGR2 (9165M) [Z] | RAF Halton |
| | XV411 | McD F-4M Phantom FGR2 (9103M) [L] | MoD FSCTE, Manston |
| | XV415 | McD F-4M Phantom FGR2 (9163M) [E] | RAF Boulmer, on display |
| | XV420 | McD F-4M Phantom FGR2 (9247M) [BT] | RAF Neatishead, at main gate |
| | XV423 | McD F-4M Phantom FGR2 [Y] | RAF Leeming, BDRT |
| | XV424 | McD F-4M Phantom FGR2 (9152M) [I] | RAF Museum, Hendon |
| | XV426 | McD F-4M Phantom FGR2<ff> | Privately owned, RAF Coltishall |
| | XV435 | McD F-4M Phantom FGR2 [R] | DERA Llanbedr Fire Section |
| | XV460 | McD F-4M Phantom FGR2 [R] | RAF Coningsby, BDRT |
| | XV465 | McD F-4M Phantom FGR2 [S] | RAF Leeming, decoy |
| | XV467 | McD F-4M Phantom FGR2 (9158M) [F] | Benbecula Airport, on display |
| | XV468 | McD F-4M Phantom FGR2 (9159M) [H] | RAF Woodvale, on display |
| | XV474 | McD F-4M Phantom FGR2 [T] | The Old Flying Machine Company, Duxford |
| | XV490 | McD F-4M Phantom FGR2 <ff> | Privately owned, Nantwich |
| | XV497 | McD F-4M Phantom FGR2 | RAF Coningsby |
| | XV499 | McD F-4M Phantom FGR2 | RAF Leeming, WLT |
| | XV500 | McD F-4M Phantom FGR2 (9113M) | RAF St Athan, on display |
| | XV577 | McD F-4K Phantom FG1 (9065M) [AM] | RAF Leuchars, BDRT |
| | XV581 | McD F-4K Phantom FG1 (9070M) <ff> | No ?? Sqn ATC, Bridge of Don |
| | XV582 | McD F-4K Phantom FG1 (9066M) [M] | RAF Leuchars, on display |
| | XV586 | McD F-4K Phantom FG1 (9067M) [AJ] | RAF Leuchars, on display |
| | XV591 | McD F-4K Phantom FG1 <ff> | RAF Museum, Cosford |
| | XV625 | WS Wasp HAS1 [471] | RN AESS, *HMS Sultan*, Gosport |
| | XV629 | WS Wasp HAS1 | AAC Middle Wallop, BDRT |
| | XV631 | WS Wasp HAS1 (fuselage) | DERA Acoustics Dept, Farnborough |
| | XV642 | WS61 Sea King HAS2A | RN AESS, *HMS Sultan*, Gosport |
| | XV643 | WS61 Sea King HAS6 [703] | RN No 819 Sqn, Prestwick |
| | XV647 | WS61 Sea King HU5 [820/CU] | RN, stored RNAY Fleetlands |
| | XV648 | WS61 Sea King HU5 [708/PW] | RN No 819 Sqn, Prestwick |
| | XV649 | WS61 Sea King AEW2 [184/L] | RN No 849 Sqn, B Flt, Culdrose |
| | XV650 | WS61 Sea King AEW2 [185/L] | RN No 849 Sqn, B Flt, Culdrose |
| | XV651 | WS61 Sea King HU5 [599/CU] | DARA, RNAY Fleetlands |
| | XV653 | WS61 Sea King HAS6 [513/CU] | RN No 810 Sqn, Culdrose |
| | XV654 | WS61 Sea King HAS6 [705] (wreck) | RN AESS, *HMS Sultan*, Gosport |
| | XV655 | WS61 Sea King HAS6 [270/N] | RN No 814 Sqn, Culdrose |
| | XV656 | WS61 Sea King AEW2 [180/CU] | RN AMG, Culdrose |
| | XV659 | WS61 Sea King HAS6 [510/CU] | RN No 810 Sqn, Culdrose |
| | XV660 | WS61 Sea King HAS6 [269/N] | RN No 814 Sqn, Culdrose |
| | XV661 | WS61 Sea King HU5 [821] | RN No 771 Sqn, Culdrose |
| | XV663 | WS61 Sea King HAS6 [706/PW] | RN No 819 Sqn, Prestwick |
| | XV664 | WS61 Sea King AEW2 [186/N] | RN No 849 Sqn, A Flt, Culdrose |
| | XV665 | WS61 Sea King HAS6 [507/CU] | RN No 810 Sqn, Culdrose |
| | XV666 | WS61 Sea King HU5 [823/CU] | RN No 771 Sqn, Culdrose |
| | XV669 | WS61 Sea King HAS1 [10] | Privately owned, Gosport |
| | XV670 | WS61 Sea King HU5 [588] | DARA, RNAY Fleetlands |
| | XV671 | WS61 Sea King AEW2 [185/L] | RN AMG, Culdrose |
| | XV672 | WS61 Sea King AEW7 [182/L] | DPA/GKN Westland, Weston-super-Mare (conversion) |
| | XV673 | WS61 Sea King HU5 [597] | RN AESS, *HMS Sultan*, Gosport |
| | XV674 | WS61 Sea King HAS6 [705/PW] | RN AMG, Culdrose |

| Serial | Type (other identity) [code] | Owner/operator, location or fate | Notes |
|---|---|---|---|
| XV675 | WS61 Sea King HAS6 [701/PW] | RN No 819 Sqn, Prestwick | |
| XV676 | WS61 Sea King HAS6 [506] | RN No 810 Sqn, Culdrose | |
| XV677 | WS61 Sea King HAS6 [269] | RN AESS, *HMS Sultan*, Gosport | |
| XV696 | WS61 Sea King HAS6 [267/N] | RN No 814 Sqn, Culdrose | |
| XV697 | WS61 Sea King AEW2 [187/N] | RN No 849 Sqn, A Flt, Culdrose | |
| XV699 | WS61 Sea King HU5 [826/CU] | RN No 771 Sqn, Culdrose | |
| XV700 | WS61 Sea King HAS6 [005] | RN No 810 Sqn, Culdrose | |
| XV701 | WS61 Sea King HAS6 [268/N] | RN No 814 Sqn, Culdrose | |
| XV703 | WS61 Sea King HAS6 [706/PW] | RN No 819 Sqn, Prestwick | |
| XV704 | WS61 Sea King AEW2 [181/CU] | RN No 849 Sqn, HQ Flt, Culdrose | |
| XV705 | WS61 Sea King HU5 [821/CU] | RN, stored RNAY Fleetlands | |
| XV706 | WS61 Sea King HAS6 [011/L] | RN No 820 Sqn, Culdrose | |
| XV707 | WS61 Sea King AEW7 | DPA/GKN Westland, Weston-super-Mare (conversion) | |
| XV708 | WS61 Sea King HAS6 [501/CU] | RN No 810 Sqn, Culdrose | |
| XV709 | WS61 Sea King HAS6 [505/CU] | RN AESS, *HMS Sultan*, Gosport | |
| XV710 | WS61 Sea King HAS6 [269/N] | RN AESS, *HMS Sultan*, Gosport | |
| XV711 | WS61 Sea King HAS6 [515/CT] | RN No 810 Sqn, B Flt, Culdrose | |
| XV712 | WS61 Sea King HAS6 [266] | RN No 814 Sqn, Culdrose | |
| XV713 | WS61 Sea King HAS6 [018] | RN, stored RNAY Fleetlands | |
| XV714 | WS61 Sea King AEW2 [180] | RN No 849 Sqn, HQ Flt, Culdrose | |
| XV720 | WS58 Wessex HC2 | RN AESS, *HMS Sultan*, Gosport | |
| XV721 | WS58 Wessex HC2 [H] | RAF No 72 Sqn, Aldergrove | |
| XV722 | WS58 Wessex HC2 [WH] | RAF, stored Shawbury | |
| XV723 | WS58 Wessex HC2 [Q] | RAF No 72 Sqn, Aldergrove | |
| XV724 | WS58 Wessex HC2 | RAF, stored RNAY Fleetlands | |
| XV725 | WS58 Wessex HC2 [C] | RN AESS, *HMS Sultan*, Gosport | |
| XV726 | WS58 Wessex HC2 [J] | RAF No 72 Sqn, Aldergrove | |
| XV728 | WS58 Wessex HC2 [A] | Newark Air Museum, Winthorpe | |
| XV729 | WS58 Wessex HC2 | Privately owned, Redhill | |
| XV730 | WS58 Wessex HC2 [*Clubs*] | RAF No 84 Sqn, Akrotiri | |
| XV731 | WS58 Wessex HC2 [Y] | Privately owned, Redhill | |
| XV732 | WS58 Wessex HCC4 | RAF, stored Shawbury | |
| XV733 | WS58 Wessex HCC4 | RAF, stored Shawbury | |
| XV741 | HS Harrier GR3 [1,5] | SFDO, RNAS Culdrose | |
| XV744 | HS Harrier GR3 (9167M) [3K] | Royal Military College of Science, Shrivenham | |
| XV747 | HS Harrier GR3 (8979M) (fuselage) | No 1803 Sqn ATC, Hucknall | |
| XV748 | HS Harrier GR3 [3D] | Cranfield University | |
| XV751 | HS Harrier GR3 | Gatwick Aviation Museum, Charlwood, Surrey | |
| XV752 | HS Harrier GR3 (9078M) [B,HF] | RAF No 1 SoTT, Cosford | |
| XV753 | HS Harrier GR3 (9075M) [3F,4] | SFDO, RNAS Culdrose | |
| XV755 | HS Harrier GR3 [M] | RNAS Yeovilton Fire Section | |
| XV759 | HS Harrier GR3 [O] <ff> | Privately owned, South Molton, Devon | |
| XV779 | HS Harrier GR3 (8931M) [01,A] | RAF Wittering on display | |
| XV783 | HS Harrier GR3 [N] | SFDO, RNAS Culdrose | |
| XV784 | HS Harrier GR3 (8909M) <ff> | DERA Boscombe Down, GI use | |
| XV786 | HS Harrier GR3 <ff> | RNAS Culdrose, GI use | |
| XV786 | HS Harrier GR3 [S] <rf> | RN, Predannack Fire School | |
| XV798 | HS Harrier GR1(mod) | Bristol Aero Collection, stored Kemble | |
| XV804 | HS Harrier GR3 [O] | RAF North Luffenham Training Area | |
| XV808 | HS Harrier GR3 (9076M) [3J,6] | SFDO, RNAS Culdrose | |
| XV810 | HS Harrier GR3 (9038M) [K] | Privately owned, Bruntingthorpe | |
| XV814 | DH106 Comet 4 (G-APDF) <ff> | Privately owned, Chipping Campden | |
| XV863 | HS Buccaneer S2B (9115M/ 9139M/9145M) [S] | RAF Lossiemouth, on display | |
| XV864 | HS Buccaneer S2B (9234M) | MoD FSCTE, Manston | |
| XV865 | HS Buccaneer S2B (9226M) | Privately owned, Duxford | |
| XV867 | HS Buccaneer S2B <ff> | N Yorks Aircraft Recovery Centre, Chop Gate | |
| XW175 | HS Harrier T4(VAAC) | DPA/AFD, DERA Boscombe Down | |
| XW198 | WS Puma HC1 | RAF No 33 Sqn, Benson | |
| XW199 | WS Puma HC1 | RAF No 230 Sqn, Aldergrove | |
| XW200 | WS Puma HC1 | RAF No 33 Sqn, Benson | |
| XW201 | WS Puma HC1 | RAF No 33 Sqn, Benson | |
| XW202 | WS Puma HC1 | RAF No 33 Sqn, Benson | |
| XW204 | WS Puma HC1 | RAF No 72 Sqn, Aldergrove | |
| XW206 | WS Puma HC1 | RAF No 230 Sqn, Aldergrove | |
| XW207 | WS Puma HC1 | RAF No 33 Sqn, Benson | |
| XW208 | WS Puma HC1 | RAF No 33 Sqn, Benson | |
| XW209 | WS Puma HC1 | RAF No 72 Sqn, Aldergrove | |

| Notes | Serial | Type (other identity) [code] | Owner/operator, location or fate |
|---|---|---|---|
| | XW210 | WS Puma HC1 (comp XW215) | DPA/AFD, DERA Boscombe Down |
| | XW211 | WS Puma HC1 | RAF No 33 Sqn, Benson |
| | XW212 | WS Puma HC1 | RAF No 230 Sqn, Aldergrove |
| | XW213 | WS Puma HC1 | RAF No 230 Sqn, Aldergrove |
| | XW214 | WS Puma HC1 | RAF No 230 Sqn, Aldergrove |
| | XW216 | WS Puma HC1 [BY] | DPA/GKN Westland, Weston-super-Mare |
| | XW217 | WS Puma HC1 | RAF No 33 Sqn, Benson |
| | XW218 | WS Puma HC1 | RAF No 33 Sqn, Benson |
| | XW219 | WS Puma HC1 [AA] | RAF No 72 Sqn, Aldergrove |
| | XW220 | WS Puma HC1 | RAF No 230 Sqn, Aldergrove |
| | XW221 | WS Puma HC1 [AE] | RAF No 72 Sqn, Aldergrove |
| | XW222 | WS Puma HC1 | RAF No 230 Sqn, Aldergrove |
| | XW223 | WS Puma HC1 | RAF No 33 Sqn, Benson |
| | XW224 | WS Puma HC1 | RAF No 33 Sqn, Benson |
| | XW225 | WS Puma HC1 | |
| | XW226 | WS Puma HC1 | RAF No 33 Sqn, Benson |
| | XW227 | WS Puma HC1 | RAF No 230 Sqn, Aldergrove |
| | XW229 | WS Puma HC1 [AD] | RAF No 72 Sqn, Aldergrove |
| | XW231 | WS Puma HC1 | RAF No 230 Sqn, Aldergrove |
| | XW232 | WS Puma HC1 | RAF No 33 Sqn, Benson |
| | XW234 | WS Puma HC1 | RAF No 230 Sqn, Aldergrove |
| | XW235 | WS Puma HC1 | RAF No 33 Sqn, Benson |
| | XW236 | WS Puma HC1 [AB] | RAF No 72 Sqn, Aldergrove |
| | XW237 | WS Puma HC1 | RAF No 33 Sqn, Benson |
| | XW241 | Sud SA330E Puma | DERA Avionics & Sensors Dept, Farnborough |
| | XW264 | HS Harrier T2 <ff> | Jet Age Museum, Staverton |
| | XW265 | HS Harrier T4A [W] | RAF No 1 SoTT, Cosford |
| | XW266 | HS Harrier T4N | |
| | XW267 | HS Harrier T4 [SA] | Territorial Army, Chetwynd Barracks, Notts |
| | XW269 | HS Harrier T4 [BD] | RAF, stored DERA Boscombe Down |
| | XW270 | HS Harrier T4 (fuselage) | Phoenix Aviation, Bruntingthorpe |
| | XW271 | HS Harrier T4 [X,1] | SFDO, RNAS Culdrose |
| | XW272 | HS Harrier T4 (8783M) (fuselage) (comp XV281) | BAE SystemsDunsfold, Apprentice School |
| | XW276 | Aérospatiale SA341 Gazelle (F-ZWRI) | Newark Air Museum, Winthorpe |
| | XW281 | WS Scout AH1 (G-BYNZ) [U] | Privately owned, Thruxton |
| | XW283 | WS Scout AH1 [U] | RM, stored Yeovilton |
| | XW284 | WS Scout AH1 [A] (fuselage) | Privately owned, Ipswich |
| | XW289 | BAC Jet Provost T5A (G-BVXT/ G-JPVA) [73] | Kennet Aviation, Cranfield |
| | XW290 | BAC Jet Provost T5A (9199M) [41,MA] | RAF No 1 SoTT, Cosford |
| | XW291 | BAC Jet Provost T5 (G-BWOF) [N] | *Repainted as G-BWOF by August 1998* |
| | XW292 | BAC Jet Provost T5A (9128M) [32] | RAF No 1 SoTT, Cosford |
| | XW293 | BAC Jet Provost T5 (G-BWCS) [Z] | Privately owned, Sandtoft |
| | XW294 | BAC Jet Provost T5A (9129M) [45] | RAF No 1 SoTT, Cosford |
| | XW299 | BAC Jet Provost T5A (9146M) [60,MB] | RAF No 1 SoTT, Cosford |
| | XW301 | BAC Jet Provost T5A (9147M) [63,MC] | RAF No 1 SoTT, Cosford |
| | XW302 | BAC Jet Provost T5B (N166A/ G-BYED) | Privately owned, North Weald |
| | XW303 | BAC Jet Provost T5A (9119M) [127] | RAF No 1 SoTT, Cosford |
| | XW304 | BAC Jet Provost T5 (9172M) [MD] | RAF No 1 SoTT, Cosford |
| | XW309 | BAC Jet Provost T5 (9179M) [V,ME] | RAF No 1 SoTT, Cosford |
| | XW311 | BAC Jet Provost T5 (9180M) [W,MF] | RAF No 1 SoTT, Cosford |
| | XW312 | BAC Jet Provost T5A (9109M) [64] | RAF No 1 SoTT, Cosford |
| | XW315 | BAC Jet Provost T5A <ff> | Privately owned, Long Marston |
| | XW318 | BAC Jet Provost T5A (9190M) [78,MG] | RAF No 1 SoTT, Cosford |
| | XW320 | BAC Jet Provost T5A (9015M) [71] | RAF No 1 SoTT, Cosford |
| | XW321 | BAC Jet Provost T5A (9154M) [62,MH] | RAF No 1 SoTT, Cosford |
| | XW323 | BAC Jet Provost T5A (9166M) [86] | RAF Museum, Hendon |
| | XW324 | BAC Jet Provost T5 (G-BWSG) | Privately owned, North Weald |
| | XW325 | BAC Jet Provost T5B (G-BWGF) [E] | Privately owned, Woodford |
| | XW327 | BAC Jet Provost T5A (9130M) [62] | RAF No 1 SoTT, Cosford |

| Serial | Type (other identity) [code] | Owner/operator, location or fate | Notes |
|---|---|---|---|
| XW328 | BAC Jet Provost T5A (9177M) [75,MI] | RAF No 1 SoTT, Cosford | |
| XW330 | BAC Jet Provost T5A (9195M) [82,MJ] | RAF No 1 SoTT, Cosford | |
| XW333 | BAC Jet Provost T5A (G-BVTC) [12] | Global Aviation, Humberside | |
| XW335 | BAC Jet Provost T5A (9061M) [74] | RAF No 1 SoTT, Cosford | |
| XW351 | BAC Jet Provost T5A (9062M) [31] | RAF No 1 SoTT, Cosford | |
| XW353 | BAC Jet Provost T5A (9090M) [3] | RAF Cranwell, on display | |
| XW355 | BAC Jet Provost T5A (G-JPTV) [20] | *Repainted as G-JPTV, 1998* | |
| XW358 | BAC Jet Provost T5A (9181M) [59,MK] | RAF No 1 SoTT, Cosford | |
| XW360 | BAC Jet Provost T5A (9153M) [61,ML] | RAF No 1 SoTT, Cosford | |
| XW361 | BAC Jet Provost T5A (9192M) [81,MM] | RAF No 1 SoTT, Cosford | |
| XW363 | BAC Jet Provost T5A [36] | No ?? Sqn ATC, Blackburn | |
| XW364 | BAC Jet Provost T5A (9188M) [35,MN] | RAF No 1 SoTT, Cosford | |
| XW365 | BAC Jet Provost T5A (9018M) [73] | RAF No 1 SoTT, Cosford | |
| XW366 | BAC Jet Provost T5A (9097M) [75] | RAF No 1 SoTT, Cosford | |
| XW367 | BAC Jet Provost T5A (9193M) [64,MO] | RAF No 1 SoTT, Cosford | |
| XW370 | BAC Jet Provost T5A (9196M) [72,MP] | RAF No 1 SoTT, Cosford | |
| XW375 | BAC Jet Provost T5A (9149M) [52] | RAF No 1 SoTT, Cosford | |
| XW404 | BAC Jet Provost T5A (9049M) | DARA Training School, RAF St Athan | |
| XW405 | BAC Jet Provost T5A (9187M) [J,MQ] | RAF No 1 SoTT, Cosford | |
| XW409 | BAC Jet Provost T5A (9047M) | DARA Training School, RAF St Athan | |
| XW410 | BAC Jet Provost T5A (9125M) [80,MR] | RAF No 1 SoTT, Cosford | |
| XW413 | BAC Jet Provost T5A (9126M) [69] | RAF No 1 SoTT, Cosford | |
| XW416 | BAC Jet Provost T5A (9191M) [84,MS] | RAF No 1 SoTT, Cosford | |
| XW418 | BAC Jet Provost T5A (9173M) [MT] | RAF No 1 SoTT, Cosford | |
| XW419 | BAC Jet Provost T5A (9120M) [125] | RAF No 1 SoTT, Cosford | |
| XW420 | BAC Jet Provost T5A (9194M) [83,MU] | RAF No 1 SoTT, Cosford | |
| XW421 | BAC Jet Provost T5A (9111M) [60] | RAF No 1 SoTT, Cosford | |
| XW423 | BAC Jet Provost T5A (G-BWUW) [14] | Privately owned, Norwich | |
| XW425 | BAC Jet Provost T5A (9200M) [H,MV] | RAF No 1 SoTT, Cosford | |
| XW427 | BAC Jet Provost T5A (9124M) [67] | RAF No 1 SoTT, Cosford | |
| *XW428* | Hunting Jet Provost T4 (XR674/ G-TOMG/9030M) | *Crashed 1 August 1999, Woolaston, Glos* | |
| XW430 | BAC Jet Provost T5A (9176M) [77,MW] | RAF No 1 SoTT, Cosford | |
| XW432 | BAC Jet Provost T5A (9127M) [76,MX] | RAF No 1 SoTT, Cosford | |
| XW433 | BAC Jet Provost T5A (G-JPRO) [63] | Global Aviation, Humberside | |
| XW434 | BAC Jet Provost T5A (9091M) [78,MY] | RAF No 1 SoTT, Cosford | |
| XW436 | BAC Jet Provost T5A (9148M) [68] | RAF No 1 SoTT, Cosford | |
| XW527 | HS Buccaneer S2B <ff> | Privately owned, Wittering | |
| XW528 | HS Buccaneer S2B (8861M) [C] | RAF Coningsby Fire Section | |
| XW530 | HS Buccaneer S2B | Buccaneer Service Station, Elgin | |
| XW544 | HS Buccaneer S2B (8857M) [Y] | Privately owned, Shawbury | |
| XW547 | HS Buccaneer S2B (9095M/ 9169M) [R] | RAF Museum, Cosford | |
| XW549 | HS Buccaneer S2B (8860M) (fuselage) | RAF Kinloss, BDRT | |
| XW550 | HS Buccaneer S2B <ff> | Privately owned, West Horndon, Essex | |
| XW566 | SEPECAT Jaguar T2 | DERA Avionics & Sensors Dept, Farnborough | |
| XW612 | WS Scout AH1 (G-BXRR) [A] | *Repainted as G-BXRR by March 1999* | |
| XW613 | WS Scout AH1 (G-BXRS) [W] | Privately owned, Thruxton | |
| XW616 | WS Scout AH1 | AAC Dishforth, instructional use | |

| Notes | Serial | Type (other identity) [code] | Owner/operator, location or fate |
|---|---|---|---|
| | XW630 | HS Harrier GR3 | RN AESS, *HMS Sultan*, Gosport, on display |
| | XW635 | Beagle D5/180 (G-AWSW) | Privately owned, Spanhoe Lodge |
| | XW664 | HS Nimrod R1 | RAF No 51 Sqn, Waddington |
| | XW665 | HS Nimrod R1 | RAF No 51 Sqn, Waddington |
| | XW666 | HS Nimrod R1 <ff> | Jet Avn Preservation Grp, Long Marston |
| | XW750 | HS748 Series 107 | DPA/AFD, DERA Boscombe Down |
| | XW763 | HS Harrier GR3 (9002M/9041M) <ff> | Privately owned, Wigston, Leics |
| | XW768 | HS Harrier GR3 (9072M) [N] | RAF No 1 SoTT, Cosford |
| | XW784 | Mitchell-Procter Kittiwake I (G-BBRN) [VL] | Privately owned, Compton Abbas |
| | XW795 | WS Scout AH1 | Blessingbourne Museum, Fivemiletown, Co Tyrone, NI |
| | XW796 | WS Scout AH1 | AAC Wattisham, BDRT |
| | XW799 | WS Scout AH1 (G-BXSL) | Privately owned, Thruxton |
| | XW835 | WS Lynx | AAC Wattisham, instructional use |
| | XW837 | WS Lynx (fuselage) | RNAS Yeovilton Fire Section |
| | XW838 | WS Lynx (TAD 009) | Army SEAE, Arborfield |
| | XW839 | WS Lynx | The Helicopter Museum, Weston-super-Mare |
| | XW843 | WS Gazelle AH1 | *Scrapped, 1996* |
| | XW844 | WS Gazelle AH1 | AAC, stored RNAY Fleetlands |
| | XW845 | WS Gazelle HT2 [47/CU] | RN, stored Shawbury |
| | XW846 | WS Gazelle AH1 [M] | AAC No 671 Sqn/2 Regt, Middle Wallop |
| | XW847 | WS Gazelle AH1 | AAC No 665 Sqn/5 Regt, Aldergrove |
| | XW848 | WS Gazelle AH1 [D] | AAC No 671 Sqn/2 Regt, Middle Wallop |
| | XW849 | WS Gazelle AH1 [G] | RM No 847 Sqn, Yeovilton |
| | XW851 | WS Gazelle AH1 [H] | RM No 847 Sqn, Yeovilton |
| | XW852 | WS Gazelle HCC4 | RAF, stored RNAY Fleetlands |
| | XW853 | WS Gazelle HT2 [53/CU] | RN, stored Shawbury |
| | XW854 | WS Gazelle HT2 [46/CU] | RN, stored Shawbury |
| | XW855 | WS Gazelle HCC4 | RAF, stored RNAY Fleetlands |
| | XW856 | WS Gazelle HT2 [49/CU] | RN, stored Shawbury |
| | XW857 | WS Gazelle HT2 [55/CU] | RN, stored Shawbury |
| | XW858 | WS Gazelle HT3 [C] | RAF, stored Shawbury |
| | XW860 | WS Gazelle HT2 (TAD021) | Army SEAE, Arborfield |
| | XW861 | WS Gazelle HT2 [52/CU] | RN, stored Shawbury |
| | XW862 | WS Gazelle HT3 [D] | RAF, stored Shawbury |
| | XW863 | WS Gazelle HT2 (TAD022) [42/CU] | Army SEAE, Arborfield |
| | XW864 | WS Gazelle HT2 [54/CU] | RN, stored Shawbury |
| | XW865 | WS Gazelle AH1 [C] | AAC No 671 Sqn/2 Regt, Middle Wallop |
| | XW866 | WS Gazelle HT3 (G-BXTH) [E] | Flightline Ltd, Southend |
| | XW868 | WS Gazelle HT2 [50/CU] | RN, stored Shawbury |
| | XW870 | WS Gazelle HT3 [F] | RAF, stored Shawbury (damaged) |
| | XW871 | WS Gazelle HT2 [44/CU] | RN, stored Shawbury |
| | XW884 | WS Gazelle HT2 [41/CU] | RN, stored Shawbury |
| | XW885 | WS Gazelle AH1 | AAC, stored Shawbury |
| | XW887 | WS Gazelle HT2 [FL] | RN, stored Shawbury |
| | XW888 | WS Gazelle AH1 (TAD017) | Army SEAE, Arborfield |
| | XW889 | WS Gazelle AH1 (TAD018) | Army SEAE, Arborfield |
| | XW890 | WS Gazelle HT2 | RNAS Yeovilton, on display |
| | XW892 | WS Gazelle AH1 [C] | AAC, stored Shawbury |
| | XW893 | WS Gazelle AH1 <ff> | AAC, stored RNAY Fleetlands |
| | XW894 | WS Gazelle HT2 [37/CU] | RN, stored Shawbury |
| | XW895 | WS Gazelle HT2 (G-BXZD) [51/CU] | Privately owned, Culdrose |
| | XW897 | WS Gazelle AH1 [Y] | AAC No 658 Sqn/7 Regt, Netheravon |
| | XW898 | WS Gazelle HT3 [G] | RAF, stored Shawbury |
| | XW899 | WS Gazelle AH1 [Z] | AAC No 658 Sqn/7 Regt, Netheravon |
| | XW900 | WS Gazelle AH1 (TAD 900) | AAC Stockwell Hall, Middle Wallop, instructional use |
| | XW902 | WS Gazelle HT3 [H] | RAF, stored Shawbury |
| | XW903 | WS Gazelle AH1 | AAC, stored Shawbury |
| | XW904 | WS Gazelle AH1 [H] | AAC No 666(V) Sqn/7 Regt, Netheravon |
| | XW906 | WS Gazelle HT3 [J] | RAF, stored Shawbury |
| | XW907 | WS Gazelle HT2 [48/CU] | RN, stored Shawbury |
| | XW908 | WS Gazelle AH1 [A] | AAC No 666(V) Sqn/7 Regt, Netheravon |
| | XW909 | WS Gazelle AH1 | AAC No 656 Sqn/9 Regt, Dishforth |
| | XW910 | WS Gazelle HT3 (G-BXZE) [K] | Privately owned, Culdrose |
| | XW911 | WS Gazelle AH1 [H] | AAC, stored Shawbury |
| | XW912 | WS Gazelle AH1 (TAD019) | Army SEAE, Arborfield |
| | XW913 | WS Gazelle AH1 | AAC No 662 Sqn/3 Regt, Wattisham |

| Serial | Type (other identity) [code] | Owner/operator, location or fate | Notes |
|---|---|---|---|
| XW917 | HS Harrier GR3 (8975M) | RAF Cottesmore, at main gate | |
| XW919 | HS Harrier GR3 [W] | R. Military College of Science, Shrivenham | |
| XW922 | HS Harrier GR3 (8885M) | MoD FSCTE, Manston | |
| XW923 | HS Harrier GR3 (8724M) <ff> | RAF Wittering for rescue training | |
| XW924 | HS Harrier GR3 (9073M) [9] | RAF Cottesmore | |
| XW934 | HS Harrier T4 [Y] | DPA, DERA Farnborough | |
| XW986 | HS Buccaneer S2B | Delta Jets, Kemble | |
| | | | |
| XX105 | BAC 1-11/201AC (G-ASJD) | DPA/AFD, DERA Boscombe Down | |
| XX108 | SEPECAT Jaguar GR1A | DPA/AFD, DERA Boscombe Down | |
| XX109 | SEPECAT Jaguar GR1 (8918M) [US] | RAF Coltishall, ground instruction | |
| XX110 | SEPECAT Jaguar GR1 (8955M) [EP] | RAF No 1 SoTT, Cosford | |
| *XX110* | SEPECAT Jaguar GR1 <R> (BAPC 169) | RAF No 1 SoTT, Cosford | |
| XX112 | SEPECAT Jaguar GR3 [EA] | RAF No 6 Sqn, Coltishall | |
| XX115 | SEPECAT Jaguar GR1 (8821M) (fuselage) | RAF No 1 SoTT, Cosford | |
| XX116 | SEPECAT Jaguar GR3A | RAF AWC/SAOEU, DERA Boscombe Down | |
| XX117 | SEPECAT Jaguar GR3 [A] | RAF No 16(R) Sqn, Lossiemouth | |
| XX119 | SEPECAT Jaguar GR3A (8898M) [GD] | DARA, RAF St Athan (conversion) | |
| XX121 | SEPECAT Jaguar GR1 (92..M) [EQ] | Privately owned, Charlwood, Surrey | |
| XX139 | SEPECAT Jaguar T4 [T] | RAF No 16(R) Sqn, Lossiemouth | |
| XX140 | SEPECAT Jaguar T2 (9008M) [D,JJ] | Privately owned, Faygate, W Sussex | |
| XX141 | SEPECAT Jaguar T2A [T] | AMIF, RAFC Cranwell | |
| XX143 | SEPECAT Jaguar T2A [X] (wreck) | Privately owned, Charlwood, Surrey | |
| XX144 | SEPECAT Jaguar T2A [U] | RAF No 16(R) Sqn, Lossiemouth | |
| XX145 | SEPECAT Jaguar T2A | DPA/AFD/ETPS, DERA Boscombe Down | |
| XX146 | SEPECAT Jaguar T4 | RAF No 54 Sqn, Coltishall | |
| XX150 | SEPECAT Jaguar T4 [W] | RAF No 16(R) Sqn, Lossiemouth | |
| XX153 | WS Lynx AH1 | AAC Wattisham, instructional use | |
| XX154 | HS Hawk T1 | DPA, DERA Llanbedr | |
| XX156 | HS Hawk T1 | RAF No 4 FTS/19(R) Sqn, Valley | |
| XX157 | HS Hawk T1A | RN FRADU, Culdrose | |
| XX158 | HS Hawk T1A | RAF No 4 FTS/208(R) Sqn, Valley | |
| XX159 | HS Hawk T1A | RAF No 4 FTS/208(R) Sqn, Valley | |
| XX160 | HS Hawk T1 | DPA/BAE Systems, Warton | |
| XX161 | HS Hawk T1W | RAF No 4 FTS/208(R) Sqn, Valley | |
| XX162 | HS Hawk T1 | RAF CAM, DERA Boscombe Down | |
| XX163 | HS Hawk T1 (9243M) [PH] (wreck) | Phoenix Aviation, Bruntingthorpe | |
| XX165 | HS Hawk T1 | RAF No 4 FTS/208(R) Sqn, Valley | |
| XX167 | HS Hawk T1W | RAF No 4 FTS/208(R) Sqn, Valley | |
| XX168 | HS Hawk T1 | RAF No 4 FTS/208(R) Sqn, Valley | |
| XX169 | HS Hawk T1 | RAF No 4 FTS/208(R) Sqn, Valley | |
| XX170 | HS Hawk T1 | RAF No 4 FTS/208(R) Sqn, Valley | |
| XX171 | HS Hawk T1 | RN FRADU, Culdrose | |
| XX172 | HS Hawk T1 | RAF No 4 FTS/19(R) Sqn, Valley | |
| XX173 | HS Hawk T1 | DARA, RAF St Athan | |
| XX174 | HS Hawk T1 | RAF No 4 FTS/208(R) Sqn, Valley | |
| XX175 | HS Hawk T1 | RAF No 4 FTS/208(R) Sqn, Valley | |
| XX176 | HS Hawk T1W | DPA/BAE Systems, Warton | |
| XX177 | HS Hawk T1 | RAF No 4 FTS/208(R) Sqn, Valley | |
| XX178 | HS Hawk T1W | RAF No 4 FTS/208(R) Sqn, Valley | |
| XX179 | HS Hawk T1W | RAF No 4 FTS/208(R) Sqn, Valley | |
| XX181 | HS Hawk T1W | RAF No 4 FTS/208(R) Sqn, Valley | |
| XX183 | HS Hawk T1 | RAF No 4 FTS/208(R) Sqn, Valley | |
| XX184 | HS Hawk T1 | RAF No 4 FTS/19(R) Sqn, Valley | |
| XX185 | HS Hawk T1 | RAF No 4 FTS/208(R) Sqn, Valley | |
| XX187 | HS Hawk T1A | RN FRADU, Culdrose | |
| XX188 | HS Hawk T1A | RAF No 4 FTS/74(R) Sqn, Valley | |
| XX189 | HS Hawk T1A | RAF No 4 FTS/74(R) Sqn, Valley | |
| XX190 | HS Hawk T1A | RAF No 4 FTS/208(R) Sqn, Valley | |
| XX191 | HS Hawk T1A | RAF No 4 FTS/208(R) Sqn, Valley | |
| XX193 | HS Hawk T1A [CB] | *Crashed 22 October 1999, near Shap, Cumbria* | |
| XX194 | HS Hawk T1A [CO] | RAF No 100 Sqn/JFACSTU, Leeming | |
| XX195 | HS Hawk T1W | RAF No 4 FTS/208(R) Sqn, Valley | |
| XX196 | HS Hawk T1A | RAF No 4 FTS/74(R) Sqn, Valley | |

| Notes | Serial | Type (other identity) [code] | Owner/operator, location or fate |
|---|---|---|---|
| | XX198 | HS Hawk T1A | RAF No 4 FTS/208(R) Sqn, Valley |
| | XX199 | HS Hawk T1A | RAF No 4 FTS/74(R) Sqn, Valley |
| | XX200 | HS Hawk T1A [CF] | RAF No 100 Sqn, Leeming |
| | XX201 | HS Hawk T1A | RN FRADU, Culdrose |
| | XX202 | HS Hawk T1A | RAF No 4 FTS/19(R) Sqn, Valley |
| | XX203 | HS Hawk T1A | RAF No 4 FTS/74(R) Sqn, Valley |
| | XX204 | HS Hawk T1A | RAF No 4 FTS/208(R) Sqn, Valley |
| | XX205 | HS Hawk T1A | RN FRADU, Culdrose |
| | XX217 | HS Hawk T1A | RAF No 4 FTS/19(R) Sqn, Valley |
| | XX218 | HS Hawk T1A | RAF No 4 FTS/19(R) Sqn, Valley |
| | XX219 | HS Hawk T1A [CT] | RAF No 100 Sqn/JFACSTU, Leeming |
| | XX220 | HS Hawk T1A | RN FRADU, Culdrose |
| | XX221 | HS Hawk T1A | RAF No 4 FTS/74(R) Sqn, Valley |
| | XX222 | HS Hawk T1A [CA] | RAF No 100 Sqn, Leeming |
| | XX223 | HS Hawk T1 (fuselage) | Privately owned, Charlwood, Surrey |
| | XX224 | HS Hawk T1W | RAF No 4 FTS/208(R) Sqn, Valley |
| | XX225 | HS Hawk T1 | RAF No 4 FTS/208(R) Sqn, Valley |
| | XX226 | HS Hawk T1 [CR] | RAF No 100 Sqn, Leeming |
| | *XX226* | HS Hawk T1 <R> (*XX263*/ BAPC 152) | RAF EPTT, St Athan |
| | XX227 | HS Hawk T1A | RAF *Red Arrows*, Cranwell |
| | XX228 | HS Hawk T1A | RAF No 4 FTS/208(R) Sqn, Valley |
| | XX230 | HS Hawk T1A | RN FRADU, Culdrose |
| | XX231 | HS Hawk T1W | RAF No 4 FTS/74(R) Sqn, Valley |
| | XX232 | HS Hawk T1 | RAF No 4 FTS/19(R) Sqn, Valley |
| | XX233 | HS Hawk T1 | RAF *Red Arrows*, Cranwell |
| | XX234 | HS Hawk T1 | RAF No 4 FTS/208(R) Sqn, Valley |
| | XX235 | HS Hawk T1W | RAF No 4 FTS/19(R) Sqn, Valley |
| | XX236 | HS Hawk T1W | RAF No 4 FTS/19(R) Sqn, Valley |
| | XX237 | HS Hawk T1 | RAF *Red Arrows*, Cranwell |
| | XX238 | HS Hawk T1 | RAF No 4 FTS/208(R) Sqn, Valley |
| | XX239 | HS Hawk T1W | DARA, RAF St Athan |
| | XX240 | HS Hawk T1 | RAF No 4 FTS/208(R) Sqn, Valley |
| | XX242 | HS Hawk T1 | DARA, RAF St Athan |
| | XX244 | HS Hawk T1 | RAF No 4 FTS/208(R) Sqn, Valley |
| | XX245 | HS Hawk T1 | RAF No 4 FTS/208(R) Sqn, Valley |
| | XX246 | HS Hawk T1A | DPA/BAE Systems, Brough |
| | XX247 | HS Hawk T1A [CM] | RAF No 100 Sqn, Leeming |
| | XX248 | HS Hawk T1A [CJ] | RAF No 100 Sqn, Leeming |
| | XX249 | HS Hawk T1W | RAF No 4 FTS/208(R) Sqn, Valley |
| | XX250 | HS Hawk T1 | RAF No 4 FTS/208(R) Sqn, Valley |
| | XX252 | HS Hawk T1A (fuselage) | DERA Boscombe Down, structural testing |
| | XX253 | HS Hawk T1A | RAF *Red Arrows*, Cranwell |
| | *XX253* | HS Hawk T1 <R> (*XX297*/ BAPC 171) | RAF EPTT, St Athan |
| | XX254 | HS Hawk T1A | DPA/BAE Systems, Brough |
| | *XX254* | HS Hawk T1A <R> | Privately owned, Marlow, Bucks |
| | XX255 | HS Hawk T1A | RN FRADU, Culdrose |
| | XX256 | HS Hawk T1A | RAF No 4 FTS/74(R) Sqn, Valley |
| | XX258 | HS Hawk T1A | RAF No 4 FTS/74(R) Sqn, Valley |
| | XX260 | HS Hawk T1A | RAF *Red Arrows*, Cranwell |
| | XX261 | HS Hawk T1A | RAF No 4 FTS/208(R) Sqn, Valley |
| | XX263 | HS Hawk T1A | RN FRADU, Culdrose |
| | XX264 | HS Hawk T1A | RAF *Red Arrows*, Cranwell |
| | XX265 | HS Hawk T1A [CN] | RAF No 100 Sqn, Leeming |
| | XX266 | HS Hawk T1A | RAF *Red Arrows*, Cranwell |
| | XX278 | HS Hawk T1A [CC] | RAF No 100 Sqn, Leeming |
| | XX280 | HS Hawk T1A | RAF No 4 FTS/19 Sqn, Valley |
| | XX281 | HS Hawk T1A | RAF No 4 FTS/19(R) Sqn, Valley |
| | XX282 | HS Hawk T1A [CQ] | RAF No 100 Sqn, Leeming |
| | XX283 | HS Hawk T1W | RAF No 4 FTS/208(R) Sqn, Valley |
| | XX284 | HS Hawk T1A | RAF No 4 FTS/208(R) Sqn, Valley |
| | XX285 | HS Hawk T1A [CH] | RAF No 100 Sqn, Leeming |
| | XX286 | HS Hawk T1A | RN FRADU, Culdrose |
| | XX287 | HS Hawk T1A | RAF No 4 FTS/208(R) Sqn, Valley |
| | XX289 | HS Hawk T1A [CI] | RAF No 100 Sqn, Leeming |
| | XX290 | HS Hawk T1W | RAF No 4 FTS/208(R) Sqn, Valley |
| | XX292 | HS Hawk T1W | RAF *Red Arrows*, Cranwell |
| | XX294 | HS Hawk T1 | RAF *Red Arrows*, Cranwell |
| | XX295 | HS Hawk T1W [DA] | DPA/BAE Systems, Warton |
| | XX296 | HS Hawk T1 | RAF No 4 FTS/208(R) Sqn, Valley |
| | XX299 | HS Hawk T1W | RAF No 4 FTS/19(R) Sqn, Valley |
| | XX301 | HS Hawk T1A | RN FRADU, Culdrose |

| Serial | Type (other identity) [code] | Owner/operator, location or fate | Notes |
|---|---|---|---|
| XX303 | HS Hawk T1A | RAF No 4 FTS/74(R) Sqn, Valley | |
| XX304 | HS Hawk T1A (fuselage) | RAF, stored Shawbury | |
| XX306 | HS Hawk T1A | RAF *Red Arrows*, Cranwell | |
| XX307 | HS Hawk T1 | RAF *Red Arrows*, Cranwell | |
| XX308 | HS Hawk T1 | RAF *Red Arrows*, Cranwell | |
| XX309 | HS Hawk T1 | RAF No 4 FTS/19(R) Sqn, Valley | |
| XX310 | HS Hawk T1W | RAF No 4 FTS/208(R) Sqn, Valley | |
| XX311 | HS Hawk T1 | RN FRADU, Culdrose | |
| XX312 | HS Hawk T1W | RAF No 4 FTS/74(R) Sqn, Valley | |
| XX313 | HS Hawk T1W | RAF No 4 FTS/208(R) Sqn, Valley | |
| XX314 | HS Hawk T1W | RAF No 4 FTS/208(R) Sqn, Valley | |
| XX315 | HS Hawk T1A | RN FRADU, Culdrose | |
| XX316 | HS Hawk T1A | RAF No 4 FTS/74(R) Sqn, Valley | |
| XX317 | HS Hawk T1A | RAF No 4 FTS/74(R) Sqn, Valley | |
| XX318 | HS Hawk T1A | RAF No 4 FTS/74(R) Sqn, Valley | |
| XX319 | HS Hawk T1A | RAF No 100 Sqn, Leeming | |
| XX320 | HS Hawk T1A [CS] | RAF No 100 Sqn, Leeming | |
| XX321 | HS Hawk T1A [CG] | RAF No 100 Sqn, Leeming | |
| XX322 | HS Hawk T1A | RN FRADU, Culdrose | |
| XX323 | HS Hawk T1A | RAF No 4 FTS/74(R) Sqn, Valley | |
| XX324 | HS Hawk T1A | RAF No 4 FTS/19(R) Sqn, Valley | |
| XX325 | HS Hawk T1A [CE] | RAF No 100 Sqn, Leeming | |
| XX326 | HS Hawk T1A | DPA/BAE Systems, Brough (on rebuild) | |
| XX327 | HS Hawk T1 | RAF CAM, DERA Boscombe Down | |
| XX329 | HS Hawk T1A | RAF No 4 FTS/74(R) Sqn, Valley | |
| XX330 | HS Hawk T1A | RAF No 100 Sqn, Leeming | |
| XX331 | HS Hawk T1A [CK] | RAF No 100 Sqn, Leeming | |
| XX332 | HS Hawk T1A | RAF No 4 FTS/74(R) Sqn, Valley | |
| XX335 | HS Hawk T1A [CD] | RAF No 100 Sqn, Leeming | |
| XX337 | HS Hawk T1A | RN FRADU, Culdrose | |
| XX338 | HS Hawk T1W | RAF No 4 FTS/19(R) Sqn, Valley | |
| XX339 | HS Hawk T1A | RAF No 4 FTS/208(R) Sqn, Valley | |
| XX341 | HS Hawk T1 ASTRA [1] | DPA/AFD/ETPS, DERA Boscombe Down | |
| XX342 | HS Hawk T1 [2] | DPA/AFD/ETPS, DERA Boscombe Down | |
| XX343 | HS Hawk T1 [3] (wreck) | Boscombe Down Museum | |
| XX344 | HS Hawk T1 (8847M) (fuselage) | DERA Farnborough Fire Section | |
| XX345 | HS Hawk T1A | RAF No 4 FTS/74(R) Sqn, Valley | |
| XX346 | HS Hawk T1A | DPA/BAE Systems, Brough | |
| XX348 | HS Hawk T1A | RAF No 4 FTS/74(R) Sqn, Valley | |
| XX349 | HS Hawk T1W | RAF No 4 FTS/208(R) Sqn, Valley | |
| XX350 | HS Hawk T1A | RAF No 4 FTS/74(R) Sqn, Valley | |
| XX351 | HS Hawk T1A | DPA/BAE Systems, Warton | |
| XX352 | HS Hawk T1A [CP] | RAF No 100 Sqn/JFACSTU, Leeming | |
| XX370 | WS Gazelle AH1 | AAC No 665 Sqn/5 Regt, Aldergrove | |
| XX371 | WS Gazelle AH1 | AAC No 12 Flt, Brüggen | |
| XX372 | WS Gazelle AH1 | AAC No 657 Sqn/9 Regt, Dishforth | |
| XX375 | WS Gazelle AH1 | AAC No 663 Sqn/3 Regt, Wattlsham | |
| XX378 | WS Gazelle AH1 [Q] | AAC No 671 Sqn/2 Regt, Middle Wallop | |
| XX379 | WS Gazelle AH1 | AAC No 8 Flt, Middle Wallop | |
| XX380 | WS Gazelle AH1 [A] | RM No 847 Sqn, Yeovilton | |
| XX381 | WS Gazelle AH1 | AAC No 662 Sqn/3 Regt, Wattisham | |
| XX382 | WS Gazelle HT3 [M] | RAF, stored Shawbury | |
| XX383 | WS Gazelle AH1 [D] | AAC No 666(V) Sqn/7 Regt, Netheravon | |
| XX384 | WS Gazelle AH1 | AAC No 661 Sqn/1 Regt, Gütersloh | |
| XX385 | WS Gazelle AH1 | AAC No 663 Sqn/3 Regt, Wattisham | |
| XX386 | WS Gazelle AH1 | AAC No 12 Flt, Brüggen | |
| XX387 | WS Gazelle AH1 (TAD 014) | Army SEAE, Arborfield | |
| XX388 | WS Gazelle AH1 | AAC, stored Shawbury | |
| XX389 | WS Gazelle AH1 | AAC No 656 Sqn/9 Regt, Dishforth | |
| XX391 | WS Gazelle HT2 [56/CU] | RN, stored Shawbury | |
| XX392 | WS Gazelle AH1 | AAC No 3(V) Flt/7 Regt, Leuchars | |
| XX393 | WS Gazelle AH1 | AAC No 654 Sqn/4 Regt, Wattisham | |
| XX394 | WS Gazelle AH1 [X] | AAC No 654 Sqn/4 Regt, Wattisham | |
| XX396 | WS Gazelle HT3 (8718M) [N] | RAF EPTT, Henlow | |
| XX398 | WS Gazelle AH1 | AAC No 9 Regt, Dishforth | |
| XX399 | WS Gazelle AH1 | AAC No 656 Sqn/9 Regt, Dishforth | |
| XX403 | WS Gazelle AH1 | DARA, RNAY Fleetlands | |
| XX405 | WS Gazelle AH1 | AAC No 665 Sqn/5 Regt, Aldergrove | |
| XX406 | WS Gazelle HT3 [P] | RAF No 7 Sqn, Odiham | |
| XX409 | WS Gazelle AH1 [O] | AAC No 654 Sqn/4 Regt, Wattisham | |
| XX411 | WS Gazelle AH1 <rf> | FAA Museum, RNAS Yeovilton | |
| XX412 | WS Gazelle AH1 [B] | RM No 847 Sqn, Yeovilton | |
| XX413 | WS Gazelle AH1 [C] | RM, stored Shawbury | |

| Notes | Serial | Type (other identity) [code] | Owner/operator, location or fate |
|---|---|---|---|
| | XX414 | WS Gazelle AH1 | AAC No 651 Sqn/1 Regt, Gütersloh |
| | XX416 | WS Gazelle AH1 | AAC No 652 Sqn/1 Regt, Gütersloh |
| | XX417 | WS Gazelle AH1 | AAC No 667 Sqn/2 Regt, Middle Wallop |
| | XX418 | WS Gazelle AH1 | AAC, stored RNAY Fleetlands |
| | XX419 | WS Gazelle AH1 | DARA, RNAY Fleetlands |
| | XX431 | WS Gazelle HT2 [43/CU] | RN, stored Shawbury |
| | XX432 | WS Gazelle AH1 | AAC No 665 Sqn/5 Regt, Aldergrove |
| | XX433 | WS Gazelle AH1 [F] | AAC, stored Shawbury |
| | XX435 | WS Gazelle AH1 [W] | AAC No 1 Regt, Gütersloh |
| | XX436 | WS Gazelle HT2 [39/CU] | RN, stored Shawbury |
| | XX437 | WS Gazelle AH1 | AAC No 651 Sqn/1 Regt, Gütersloh |
| | XX438 | WS Gazelle AH1 | AAC No 657 Sqn/9 Regt, Dishforth |
| | XX439 | WS Gazelle AH1 | AAC No 652 Sqn/1 Regt, Gütersloh |
| | XX440 | WS Gazelle AH1 (G-BCHN) | RNAY Fleetlands Apprentice School |
| | XX441 | WS Gazelle HT2 [38/CU] | RN, stored Shawbury |
| | XX442 | WS Gazelle AH1 [E] | AAC No 666(V) Sqn/7 Regt, Netheravon |
| | XX443 | WS Gazelle AH1 [Y] | AAC Stockwell Hall, Middle Wallop, instructional use |
| | XX444 | WS Gazelle AH1 | AAC No 25 Flt, Belize |
| | XX445 | WS Gazelle AH1 [T] | AAC No 658 Sqn/7 Regt, Netheravon |
| | XX446 | WS Gazelle HT2 [57/CU] | RN, stored Shawbury |
| | XX447 | WS Gazelle AH1 [D1] | AAC No 671 Sqn/2 Regt, Middle Wallop |
| | XX448 | WS Gazelle AH1 | AAC No 664 Sqn/9 Regt, Dishforth |
| | XX449 | WS Gazelle AH1 | AAC No 664 Sqn/9 Regt, Dishforth |
| | XX450 | WS Gazelle AH1 [D] | RM No 847 Sqn, Yeovilton |
| | XX453 | WS Gazelle AH1 | AAC No 652 Sqn/1 Regt, Gütersloh |
| | XX454 | WS Gazelle AH1 (fuselage) | RAF Waddington, instructional use |
| | XX455 | WS Gazelle AH1 | AAC No 652 Sqn/1 Regt, Gütersloh |
| | XX456 | WS Gazelle AH1 | AAC No 3(V) Flt/7 Regt, Leuchars |
| | XX457 | WS Gazelle AH1 <ff> | Jet Avn Preservation Grp, Long Marston |
| | XX460 | WS Gazelle AH1 | AAC No 662 Sqn/3 Regt, Wattisham |
| | XX462 | WS Gazelle AH1 [W] | AAC No 658 Sqn/7 Regt, Netheravon |
| | XX467 | HS Hunter T66B/T7 (XL605/ G-TVII) [86] | Privately owned, Kemble |
| | XX469 | WS Lynx HAS2 (G-BNCL) | |
| | XX475 | HP137 Jetstream T2 (N1036S) | DPA, DERA West Freugh |
| | XX476 | HP137 Jetstream T2 (N1037S) [561/CU] | RN No 750 Sqn, Culdrose |
| | XX477 | HP137 Jetstream T1 (G-AXXS/ 8462M) <ff> | RAF Cranwell, instructional use |
| | XX478 | HP137 Jetstream T2 (G-AXXT) [564/CU] | RN No 750 Sqn, Culdrose |
| | XX479 | HP137 Jetstream T2 (G-AXUR) | RN, Predannack Fire School |
| | XX480 | HP137 Jetstream T2 (G-AXXU) [565/CU] | *Scrapped, 1999* |
| | XX481 | HP137 Jetstream T2 (G-AXUP) [560/CU] | RN, stored Culdrose |
| | XX482 | SA Jetstream T1 [J] | RAF No 3 FTS/45(R) Sqn, Cranwell |
| | XX483 | SA Jetstream T2 [562/CU] | *Scrapped, 1999* |
| | XX484 | SA Jetstream T2 [566/CU] | RN No 750 Sqn, Culdrose |
| | XX486 | SA Jetstream T2 [569/CU] | RN No 750 Sqn, Culdrose |
| | XX487 | SA Jetstream T2 [568/CU] | RN No 750 Sqn, Culdrose |
| | XX488 | SA Jetstream T2 [562/CU] | RN No 750 Sqn, Culdrose |
| | XX491 | SA Jetstream T1 [K] | RAF No 3 FTS/45(R) Sqn, Cranwell |
| | XX492 | SA Jetstream T1 [A] | RAF No 3 FTS/45(R) Sqn, Cranwell |
| | XX493 | SA Jetstream T1 [L] | RAF No 3 FTS/45(R) Sqn, Cranwell |
| | XX494 | SA Jetstream T1 [B] | RAF No 3 FTS/45(R) Sqn, Cranwell |
| | XX495 | SA Jetstream T1 [C] | RAF No 3 FTS/45(R) Sqn, Cranwell |
| | XX496 | SA Jetstream T1 [D] | RAF No 3 FTS/45(R) Sqn, Cranwell |
| | XX497 | SA Jetstream T1 [E] | RAF No 3 FTS/45(R) Sqn, Cranwell |
| | XX498 | SA Jetstream T1 [F] | RAF No 3 FTS/45(R) Sqn, Cranwell |
| | XX499 | SA Jetstream T1 [G] | RAF No 3 FTS/45(R) Sqn, Cranwell |
| | XX500 | SA Jetstream T1 [H] | RAF No 3 FTS/45(R) Sqn, Cranwell |
| | XX510 | WS Lynx HAS2 [69/LS] | SFDO, RNAS Culdrose |
| | XX513 | SA Bulldog T1 [10] | RAF CFS, Cranwell |
| | XX515 | SA Bulldog T1 [4] | RAF Manchester & Salford Universities AS/ No 10 AEF, Woodvale |
| | XX516 | SA Bulldog T1 | RAF Bristol UAS/No 3 AEF, Colerne |
| | XX518 | SA Bulldog T1 [S] | RAF Liverpool UAS, Woodvale |
| | XX519 | SA Bulldog T1 [14] | RAF, stored Newton |
| | XX520 | SA Bulldog T1 [A] | RAF, stored Newton |
| | XX521 | SA Bulldog T1 [G] | RAF University of Birmingham AS/ No 8 AEF, Cosford |

| Serial | Type (other identity) [code] | Owner/operator, location or fate | Notes |
|---|---|---|---|
| XX522 | SA Bulldog T1 [06] | RAF Aberdeen, Dundee & St Andrews UAS/No 12 AEF, Leuchars | |
| XX523 | SA Bulldog T1 [X] | RAF, stored Newton | |
| XX524 | SA Bulldog T1 [04] | RAF University of London AS/No 6 AEF, Benson | |
| XX525 | SA Bulldog T1 (*bl*) | RAF Universities of Glasgow & Strathclyde AS, Glasgow | |
| XX526 | SA Bulldog T1 [C] | RAF, Oxford UAS, Benson | |
| XX527 | SA Bulldog T1 [05] | RAF Aberdeen, Dundee & St Andrews UAS/No 12 AEF, Leuchars | |
| XX528 | SA Bulldog T1 [D] | RAF, stored Newton | |
| XX529 | SA Bulldog T1 [08] | RAF East Lowlands UAS, Leuchars | |
| *XX530* | SA Bulldog T1 (XX637/9197M) [F] | RAF EPTT, St Athan | |
| XX531 | SA Bulldog T1 [S,04] | RAF University of Wales AS, St Athan | |
| XX532 | SA Bulldog T1 [1] | RAF CFS, Cranwell | |
| XX533 | SA Bulldog T1 [U] | RAF Northumbrian Universities AS/No 11 AEF, Leeming | |
| XX534 | SA Bulldog T1 [B] | RAF University of Birmingham AS/No 8 AEF, Cosford | |
| XX535 | SA Bulldog T1 [S] | RAF East Midlands UAS/No 7 AEF, Newton | |
| XX536 | SA Bulldog T1 [6] | RAF Manchester & Salford Universities AS/No 10 AEF, Woodvale | |
| XX537 | SA Bulldog T1 [C] | RAF Yorkshire Universities AS/No 9 AEF, Church Fenton | |
| XX538 | SA Bulldog T1 [03] | RAF East Lowlands UAS, Leuchars | |
| XX539 | SA Bulldog T1 [L] | RAF Liverpool UAS, Woodvale | |
| XX540 | SA Bulldog T1 [15] | RAF CFS, Cranwell | |
| XX541 | SA Bulldog T1 [F] | RAF Bristol UAS/No 3 AEF, Colerne | |
| XX543 | SA Bulldog T1 [F] | RAF Yorkshire Universities AS/No 9 AEF, Church Fenton | |
| XX544 | SA Bulldog T1 [01] | RAF, stored Newton | |
| XX545 | SA Bulldog T1 [02] | RAF East Lowlands UAS, Leuchars, GI use | |
| XX546 | SA Bulldog T1 [03] | RAF Oxford UAS, Benson | |
| XX547 | SA Bulldog T1 [05] | RAF Oxford UAS, Benson | |
| XX548 | SA Bulldog T1 [06] | RAF, stored Newton | |
| XX549 | SA Bulldog T1 [6] | RAF Southampton UAS/No 2 AEF, DERA Boscombe Down | |
| XX550 | SA Bulldog T1 [Z] | RAF Northumbrian Universities AS/No 11 AEF, Leeming | |
| XX551 | SA Bulldog T1 [E] | RAF, stored Newton | |
| XX552 | SA Bulldog T1 [08] | RAF University of London AS/No 6 AEF, Benson | |
| XX553 | SA Bulldog T1 [07] | RAF University of London AS/No 6 AEF, Benson | |
| XX554 | SA Bulldog T1 [09] | RAF, stored Newton | |
| XX555 | SA Bulldog T1 [U] | RAF Liverpool UAS, Woodvale | |
| XX556 | SA Bulldog T1 [M] | RAF East Midlands UAS/No 7 AEF, Newton | |
| XX558 | SA Bulldog T1 [A] | RAF University of Birmingham AS/No 8 AEF, Cosford | |
| XX559 | SA Bulldog T1 | RAF Universities of Glasgow & Strathclyde AS, Glasgow | |
| XX560 | SA Bulldog T1 | RAF Universities of Glasgow & Strathclyde AS, Glasgow | |
| XX561 | SA Bulldog T1 [7] | RAF, stored Newton | |
| XX562 | SA Bulldog T1 [18] | RAF CFS, Cranwell | |
| XX611 | SA Bulldog T1 | RAF Universities of Glasgow & Strathclyde AS, Glasgow | |
| XX612 | SA Bulldog T1 [A,03] | RAF University of Wales AS, St Athan | |
| XX614 | SA Bulldog T1 [B] | RAF Oxford UAS, Benson | |
| XX615 | SA Bulldog T1 [2] | RAF Manchester & Salford Universities AS/No 10 AEF, Woodvale | |
| XX616 | SA Bulldog T1 | RAF, stored Newton | |
| XX617 | SA Bulldog T1 [2] | RAF CFS, Cranwell | |
| XX619 | SA Bulldog T1 [T] | RAF Northumbrian Universities AS/No 11 AEF, Leeming | |
| XX620 | SA Bulldog T1 [02] | RAF East Lowlands UAS, Leuchars | |
| XX621 | SA Bulldog T1 [G] | RAF Yorkshire Universities AS/No 9 AEF, Church Fenton | |
| XX622 | SA Bulldog T1 [B] | RAF Yorkshire Universities AS/No 9 AEF, Church Fenton | |

| Notes | Serial | Type (other identity) [code] | Owner/operator, location or fate |
|---|---|---|---|
| | XX623 | SA Bulldog T1 [M] | RAF, stored Newton |
| | XX624 | SA Bulldog T1 | RAF Bristol UAS/No 3 AEF, Colerne |
| | XX625 | SA Bulldog T1 [U,01] | RAF University of Wales AS, St Athan |
| | XX626 | SA Bulldog T1 [W,02] | RAF University of Wales AS, St Athan |
| | XX627 | SA Bulldog T1 [7] | RAF Southampton UAS/No 2 AEF, DERA Boscombe Down |
| | XX628 | SA Bulldog T1 [J] | RAF Bristol UAS/No 3 AEF, Colerne |
| | XX629 | SA Bulldog T1 [V] | RAF Liverpool UAS, Woodvale |
| | XX630 | SA Bulldog T1 [5] | RAF, stored Newton |
| | XX631 | SA Bulldog T1 [W] | RAF Northumbrian Universities AS/ No 11 AEF, Leeming |
| | XX632 | SA Bulldog T1 [A] | RAF Yorkshire Universities AS/No 9 AEF, Church Fenton |
| | XX633 | SA Bulldog T1 [X] | RAF Northumbrian Universities AS/ No 11 AEF, Leeming |
| | XX634 | SA Bulldog T1 [A] | RAF East Midlands UAS/No 7 AEF, Newton |
| | XX635 | SA Bulldog T1 (8767M) | DARA Training School, RAF St Athan |
| | XX636 | SA Bulldog T1 [Y] | RAF Northumbrian Universities AS/ No 11 AEF, Leeming |
| | XX638 | SA Bulldog T1 | RAF, stored Newtonl |
| | XX639 | SA Bulldog T1 [02] | RAF Oxford UAS, Benson |
| | XX640 | SA Bulldog T1 [K] | RAF Bristol UAS/No 3 AEF, Colerne |
| | XX653 | SA Bulldog T1 [E] | RAF, stored Newton |
| | XX654 | SA Bulldog T1 [3] | RAF CFS, Cranwell |
| | XX655 | SA Bulldog T1 [B] | RAF Bristol UAS/No 3 AEF, Colerne |
| | XX656 | SA Bulldog T1 [C] | RAF Bristol UAS/No 3 AEF, Colerne |
| | XX657 | SA Bulldog T1 [U] | RAF, stored Newton |
| | XX658 | SA Bulldog T1 [07] | RAF East Lowlands UAS, Leuchars |
| | XX659 | SA Bulldog T1 [E] | RAF Yorkshire Universities AS/No 9 AEF, Church Fenton |
| | XX661 | SA Bulldog T1 [6] | RAF CFS, Cranwell |
| | XX663 | SA Bulldog T1 [01] | RAF East Lowlands UAS, Leuchars |
| | XX664 | SA Bulldog T1 [04] | RAF East Lowlands UAS, Leuchars |
| | XX665 | SA Bulldog T1 | RAF, stored Newton |
| | XX666 | SA Bulldog T1 [08] | RAF, Leuchars (wreck) |
| | XX667 | SA Bulldog T1 [16] | RAF, stored Newton |
| | XX668 | SA Bulldog T1 [1] | RAF Manchester & Salford Universities AS/ No 10 AEF, Woodvale |
| | XX669 | SA Bulldog T1 (8997M) [B] | Privately owned, Cardiff |
| | XX670 | SA Bulldog T1 [C] | RAF University of Birmingham AS/ No 8 AEF, Cosford |
| | XX671 | SA Bulldog T1 [D] | RAF University of Birmingham AS/ No 8 AEF, Cosford |
| | XX672 | SA Bulldog T1 [E] | RAF University of Birmingham AS/ No 8 AEF, Cosford |
| | XX685 | SA Bulldog T1 [11] | RAF, stored Newton |
| | XX686 | SA Bulldog T1 [4] | RAF CFS, Cranwell |
| | XX687 | SA Bulldog T1 [13] | RAF CFS, Cranwell |
| | XX688 | SA Bulldog T1 [8] | RAF CFS, Cranwell |
| | XX689 | SA Bulldog T1 [D] | RAF Bristol UAS/No 3 AEF, Colerne |
| | XX690 | SA Bulldog T1 [A] | RAF Liverpool UAS, Woodvale |
| | XX691 | SA Bulldog T1 [10] | *Sold to Maltese Armed Forces* |
| | XX692 | SA Bulldog T1 [A] | *Sold to Maltese Armed Forces* |
| | XX693 | SA Bulldog T1 [07] | *Sold to Maltese Armed Forces* |
| | XX694 | SA Bulldog T1 [E] | RAF East Midlands UAS/No 7 AEF, Newton |
| | XX695 | SA Bulldog T1 [3] | RAF Manchester & Salford Universities AS/ No 10 AEF, Woodvale |
| | XX696 | SA Bulldog T1 [S] | *Sold to Maltese Armed Forces* |
| | XX697 | SA Bulldog T1 [H] | RAF Bristol UAS/No 3 AEF, Colerne |
| | XX698 | SA Bulldog T1 [9] | *Sold to Maltese Armed Forces* |
| | XX699 | SA Bulldog T1 [F] | RAF University of Birmingham AS/ No 8 AEF, Cosford |
| | XX700 | SA Bulldog T1 [17] | RAF, stored Newtonl |
| | XX701 | SA Bulldog T1 [2] | RAF Southampton UAS/No 2 AEF, DERA Boscombe Down |
| | XX702 | SA Bulldog T1 | RAF East Midlands UAS/No 7 AEF Newton |
| | XX704 | SA Bulldog T1 [U] | RAF East Midlands UAS/No 7 AEF, Newton |
| | XX705 | SA Bulldog T1 [5] | RAF Southampton UAS/No 2 AEF, DERA Boscombe Down |

| Serial | Type (other identity) [code] | Owner/operator, location or fate | Notes |
|---|---|---|---|
| XX706 | SA Bulldog T1 [1] | RAF Southampton UAS/No 2 AEF, DERA Boscombe Down | |
| XX707 | SA Bulldog T1 [4] | RAF Southampton UAS/No 2 AEF, DERA Boscombe Down | |
| XX708 | SA Bulldog T1 [3] | RAF Southampton UAS/No 2 AEF, DERA Boscombe Down | |
| XX709 | SA Bulldog T1 [E] | *Sold to Maltese Armed Forces* | |
| XX711 | SA Bulldog T1 [X] | RAF Liverpool UAS, Woodvale | |
| XX713 | SA Bulldog T1 [G] | RAF Bristol UAS/No 3 AEF, Colerne | |
| XX714 | SA Bulldog T1 [D] | *Sold to Maltese Armed Forces* | |
| XX720 | SEPECAT Jaguar GR3 [GB] | RAF No 54 Sqn, Coltishall | |
| XX722 | SEPECAT Jaguar GR1 [EF] | RAF, stored St Athan | |
| XX723 | SEPECAT Jaguar GR3A [GQ] | DARA, RAF St Athan (conversion) | |
| XX724 | SEPECAT Jaguar GR1A [GA] | RAF, stored Shawbury | |
| XX725 | SEPECAT Jaguar GR3A [GU] | DARA, RAF St Athan (conversion) | |
| *XX725* | SEPECAT Jaguar GR1 <R> (BAPC 150/*XX718*) [GU] | RAF EPTT, St Athan | |
| XX726 | SEPECAT Jaguar GR1 (8947M) [EB] | RAF No 1 SoTT, Cosford | |
| XX727 | SEPECAT Jaguar GR1 (8951M) [ER] | RAF No 1 SoTT, Cosford | |
| XX729 | SEPECAT Jaguar GR3 [EL] | RAF No 6 Sqn, Coltishall | |
| XX730 | SEPECAT Jaguar GR1 (8952M) [EC] | RAF No 1 SoTT, Cosford | |
| XX733 | SEPECAT Jaguar GR1B [ER] | RAF, stored Coltishall (wreck) | |
| XX736 | SEPECAT Jaguar GR1 (9110M) <ff> | BAE SystemsBrough | |
| XX737 | SEPECAT Jaguar GR3 [EE] | RAF AMF, Coltishall | |
| XX738 | SEPECAT Jaguar GR3 [GG] | DPA/AFD, DERA Boscombe Down | |
| XX739 | SEPECAT Jaguar GR1 (8902M) [I] | RAF No 1 SoTT, Cosford | |
| XX741 | SEPECAT Jaguar GR1A [04] | RAF, stored Shawbury | |
| XX743 | SEPECAT Jaguar GR1 (8949M) [EG] | RAF No 1 SoTT, Cosford | |
| XX744 | SEPECAT Jaguar GR1 | RAF Coltishall, instructional use | |
| XX745 | SEPECAT Jaguar GR1A [GV] | RAF No 54 Sqn, Coltishall | |
| XX746 | SEPECAT Jaguar GR1A (8895M) [09] | RAF No 1 SoTT, Cosford | |
| XX747 | SEPECAT Jaguar GR1 (8903M) | AMIF, RAFC Cranwell | |
| XX748 | SEPECAT Jaguar GR3 | RAF No 16(R) Sqn, Lossiemouth | |
| XX751 | SEPECAT Jaguar GR1 (8937M) [10] | RAF No 1 SoTT, Cosford | |
| XX752 | SEPECAT Jaguar GR1A [EQ] | RAF No 6 Sqn, Coltishall | |
| XX753 | SEPECAT Jaguar GR1 (9087M) <ff> | RAF EPTT, St Athan | |
| XX756 | SEPECAT Jaguar GR1 (8899M) [AM] | RAF No 1 SoTT, Cosford | |
| XX757 | SEPECAT Jaguar GR1 (8948M) [CU] | RAF No 1 SoTT, Cosford | |
| XX761 | SEPECAT Jaguar GR1 (8600M) <ff> | BAE SystemsWarton, instructional use | |
| XX763 | SEPECAT Jaguar GR1 (9009M) | DARA Training School, RAF St Athan | |
| XX764 | SEPECAT Jaguar GR1 (9010M) | DARA Training School, RAF St Athan | |
| XX765 | SEPECAT Jaguar ACT | RAF Museum, Cosford | |
| XX766 | SEPECAT Jaguar GR1A [EA] | RAF, stored St Athan | |
| XX767 | SEPECAT Jaguar GR3 [GE] | RAF No 54 Sqn, Coltishall | |
| XX818 | SEPECAT Jaguar GR1 (8945M) [DE] | RAF No 1 SoTT, Cosford | |
| XX819 | SEPECAT Jaguar GR1 (8923M) [CE] | RAF No 1 SoTT, Cosford | |
| XX821 | SEPECAT Jaguar GR1 (8896M) [P] | AMIF, RAFC Cranwell | |
| XX824 | SEPECAT Jaguar GR1 (9019M) [AD] | RAF No 1 SoTT, Cosford | |
| XX825 | SEPECAT Jaguar GR1 (9020M) [BN] | RAF No 1 SoTT, Cosford | |
| XX826 | SEPECAT Jaguar GR1 (9021M) [34,JH] | RAF No 1 SoTT, Cosford | |
| XX829 | SEPECAT Jaguar T2A [GZ] | RAF No 54 Sqn, Coltishall | |
| XX830 | SEPECAT Jaguar T2 | DPA/BAe, Warton | |
| XX832 | SEPECAT Jaguar T2A [EZ] | RAF No 6 Sqn, Coltishall | |
| XX833 | SEPECAT Jaguar T2B | RAF AWC/SAOEU, DERA Boscombe Down | |

| Notes | Serial | Type (other identity) [code] | Owner/operator, location or fate |
|---|---|---|---|
| | XX835 | SEPECAT Jaguar T4 [FY] | DARA, RAF St Athan (conversion) |
| | XX836 | SEPECAT Jaguar T2A [X] | DARA, RAF St Athan |
| | XX837 | SEPECAT Jaguar T2 (8978M) [Z] | RAF No 1 SoTT, Cosford |
| | XX838 | SEPECAT Jaguar T4 [R] | RAF No 16(R) Sqn, Lossiemouth |
| | XX839 | SEPECAT Jaguar T2A (9256M) | RAF, stored St Athan |
| | XX840 | SEPECAT Jaguar T4 [S] | RAF No 16(R) Sqn, Lossiemouth |
| | XX841 | SEPECAT Jaguar T2A [ES] | RAF, stored St Athan (damaged) |
| | XX842 | SEPECAT Jaguar T2B [X] | RAF No 16(R) Sqn, Lossiemouth |
| | XX845 | SEPECAT Jaguar T2A [ET] | RAF No 6 Sqn, Coltishall |
| | XX846 | SEPECAT Jaguar T4 [V] | DARA, RAF St Athan (conversion) |
| | XX847 | SEPECAT Jaguar T2A | RAF, stored St Athan |
| | XX885 | HS Buccaneer S2B (9225M) | RAF Lossiemouth, BDRT |
| | XX888 | HS Buccaneer S2B <ff> | Dundonald Aviation Centre, Strathclyde |
| | XX889 | HS Buccaneer S2B | Jet Age Museum, Staverton |
| | XX892 | HS Buccaneer S2B <ff> | Christies Garden Centre, Forres, Grampian |
| | XX893 | HS Buccaneer S2B <ff> | Privately owned, Birtley, Tyne & Wear |
| | XX894 | HS Buccaneer S2B [020/R] | Buccaneer Preservation Society, Kemble |
| | XX895 | HS Buccaneer S2B | The Planets Leisure Centre, Woking |
| | XX897 | HS Buccaneer S2B(mod) | Privately owned, Bournemouth |
| | XX899 | HS Buccaneer S2B <ff> | Midland Air Museum, Coventry |
| | XX900 | HS Buccaneer S2B | British Aviation Heritage, Bruntingthorpe |
| | XX901 | HS Buccaneer S2B | Yorkshire Air Museum, Elvington |
| | XX907 | WS Lynx AH1 | DERA Structures Dept, Farnborough |
| | XX910 | WS Lynx HAS2 | DERA Structures Dept, Farnborough |
| | XX914 | BAC VC10/1103 (8777M) <rf> | RAF AMS, Brize Norton |
| | XX919 | BAC 1-11/402AP (PI-C1121) | DPA/AFD, DERA Boscombe Down |
| | XX946 | Panavia Tornado (P02) (8883M) | RAF Museum, Hendon |
| | XX947 | Panavia Tornado (P03) (8797M) | DARA, RAF St Athan, BDRT |
| | XX948 | Panavia Tornado (P06) (8879M) [P] | RAF No 1 SoTT, Cosford |
| | XX955 | SEPECAT Jaguar GR1A [GK] | RAF, stored Shawbury |
| | XX956 | SEPECAT Jaguar GR1 (8950M) [BE] | RAF No 1 SoTT, Cosford |
| | XX958 | SEPECAT Jaguar GR1 (9022M) [BK,JG] | RAF No 1 SoTT, Cosford |
| | XX959 | SEPECAT Jaguar GR1 (8953M) [CJ] | RAF No 1 SoTT, Cosford |
| | XX962 | SEPECAT Jaguar GR1B [E] | AMIF, RAFC Cranwell |
| | XX965 | SEPECAT Jaguar GR1A [C] | AMIF, RAFC Cranwell |
| | XX966 | SEPECAT Jaguar GR1A (8904M) [EL] | RAF No 1 SoTT, Cosford |
| | XX967 | SEPECAT Jaguar GR1 (9006M) [AC,JD] | RAF No 1 SoTT, Cosford |
| | XX968 | SEPECAT Jaguar GR1 (9007M) [AJ,JE] | RAF No 1 SoTT, Cosford |
| | XX969 | SEPECAT Jaguar GR1A (8897M) [01] | RAF No 1 SoTT, Cosford |
| | XX970 | SEPECAT Jaguar GR3 [EH] | RAF No 6 Sqn, Coltishall |
| | XX974 | SEPECAT Jaguar GR3 [B] | RAF No 16(R) Sqn, Lossiemouth |
| | XX975 | SEPECAT Jaguar GR1 (8905M) [07] | RAF No 1 SoTT, Cosford |
| | XX976 | SEPECAT Jaguar GR1 (8906M) [BD] | RAF No 1 SoTT, Cosford |
| | XX977 | SEPECAT Jaguar GR1 (9132M) [DL,05] | DARA, RAF St Athan, BDRT |
| | XX979 | SEPECAT Jaguar GR1A | DARA, RAF St Athan |
| | XZ101 | SEPECAT Jaguar GR1A [D] | DARA, RAF St Athan |
| | XZ103 | SEPECAT Jaguar GR3 [FP] | RAF AMF, Coltishall (damaged) |
| | XZ104 | SEPECAT Jaguar GR3 [FM] | RAF No 41 Sqn, Coltishall |
| | XZ106 | SEPECAT Jaguar GR3 [FR] | RAF No 41 Sqn, Coltishall |
| | XZ107 | SEPECAT Jaguar GR3 [FH] | RAF No 41 Sqn, Coltishall |
| | XZ109 | SEPECAT Jaguar GR3 [EN] | RAF No 6 Sqn, Coltishall |
| | XZ111 | SEPECAT Jaguar GR1A [GO] | RAF No 54 Sqn, Coltishall |
| | XZ112 | SEPECAT Jaguar GR3A [GA] | DPA/AFD. DERA Boscombe Down |
| | XZ113 | SEPECAT Jaguar GR3 [FD] | RAF No 41 Sqn, Coltishall |
| | XZ114 | SEPECAT Jaguar GR1A [FB] | RAF, stored Shawbury |
| | XZ115 | SEPECAT Jaguar GR3 [FC] | RAF No 41 Sqn, Coltishall |
| | XZ117 | SEPECAT Jaguar GR3 [EP] | RAF No 6 Sqn, Coltishall |
| | XZ118 | SEPECAT Jaguar GR3 [FF] | RAF No 41 Sqn, Coltishall |
| | XZ119 | SEPECAT Jaguar GR1A [F] | AMIF, RAFC Cranwell |
| | XZ129 | HS Harrier GR3 [ETS] | RN ETS, Yeovilton |
| | XZ130 | HS Harrier GR3 (9079M) [A,HE] | RAF No 1 SoTT, Cosford |

| *Serial* | *Type (other identity) [code]* | *Owner/operator, location or fate* | *Notes* |
|---|---|---|---|
| XZ131 | HS Harrier GR3 (9174M) <ff> | No 2156 Sqn ATC, Brierley Hill, W Midlands | |
| XZ132 | HS Harrier GR3 (9168M) [C] | ATF, RAFC Cranwell | |
| XZ133 | HS Harrier GR3 [10] | Imperial War Museum, Duxford | |
| XZ135 | HS Harrier GR3 (8848M) <ff> | RAF EPTT, St Athan | |
| XZ138 | HS Harrier GR3 (9040M) <ff> | RAFC Cranwell, Trenchard Hall | |
| XZ145 | HS Harrier T4 [T] | SFDO, RNAS Culdrose | |
| XZ146 | HS Harrier T4 [S] | RAF North Luffenham Training Area | |
| XZ170 | WS Lynx AH9 | DPA/GKN Westland, Yeovil | |
| XZ171 | WS Lynx AH7 | AAC No 654 Sqn/4 Regt, Wattisham | |
| XZ172 | WS Lynx AH7 | AAC No 655 Sqn/5 Regt, Aldergrove | |
| XZ173 | WS Lynx AH7 | AAC No 1 Regt, Gütersloh | |
| XZ174 | WS Lynx AH7 | AAC No 655 Sqn/5 Regt, Aldergrove | |
| XZ175 | WS Lynx AH7 | AAC No 664 Sqn/9 Regt, Dishforth | |
| XZ176 | WS Lynx AH7 | AAC No 661 Sqn/1 Regt, Gütersloh | |
| XZ177 | WS Lynx AH7 | AAC No 654 Sqn/4 Regt, Wattisham | |
| XZ178 | WS Lynx AH7 | AAC No 1 Regt, Gütersloh | |
| XZ179 | WS Lynx AH7 | AAC No 652 Sqn/1 Regt, Gütersloh | |
| XZ180 | WS Lynx AH7 | RM No 847 Sqn, Yeovilton | |
| XZ181 | WS Lynx AH1 | DPA/GKN Westland, Yeovil | |
| XZ182 | WS Lynx AH7 [M] | DPA/GKN Westland, Weston-super-Mare (on repair) | |
| XZ183 | WS Lynx AH7 | AAC No 656 Sqn/9 Regt, Dishforth | |
| XZ184 | WS Lynx AH7 | AAC No 671 Sqn/2 Regt, Middle Wallop | |
| XZ185 | WS Lynx AH7 | AAC No 1 Regt, Gütersloh | |
| XZ186 | WS Lynx AH7 (wreckage) | DARA, RNAY Fleetlands | |
| XZ187 | WS Lynx AH7 | AAC No 667 Sqn/2 Regt, Middle Wallop | |
| XZ188 | WS Lynx AH7 | Army SEAE, Arborfield | |
| XZ190 | WS Lynx AH7 | AAC No 663 Sqn/3 Regt, Wattisham | |
| XZ191 | WS Lynx AH7 [X] | AAC, stored RNAY Fleetlands | |
| XZ192 | WS Lynx AH7 | DARA, RNAY Fleetlands (on rebuild) | |
| XZ193 | WS Lynx AH7 | DARA, RNAY Fleetlands | |
| XZ194 | WS Lynx AH7 | AAC No 664 Sqn/9 Regt, Dishforth | |
| XZ195 | WS Lynx AH7 | AAC No 655 Sqn/5 Regt, Aldergrove | |
| XZ196 | WS Lynx AH7 | AAC No 664 Sqn/9 Regt, Dishforth | |
| XZ197 | WS Lynx AH7 | AAC No 661 Sqn/1 Regt, Gütersloh | |
| XZ198 | WS Lynx AH7 | AAC No 663 Sqn/3 Regt, Wattisham | |
| XZ199 | WS Lynx AH7 | *Crashed 18 May 1999, Tilton on the Hill, Leics* | |
| XZ203 | WS Lynx AH7 [L] | AAC No 671 Sqn/2 Regt, Middle Wallop | |
| XZ205 | WS Lynx AH7 | AAC No 655 Sqn/5 Regt, Aldergrove | |
| XZ206 | WS Lynx AH7 | AAC No 25 Flt, Belize | |
| XZ207 | WS Lynx AH7 | AAC No 652 Sqn/1 Regt, Gütersloh | |
| XZ208 | WS Lynx AH7 | AAC No 9 Regt, Dishforth | |
| XZ209 | WS Lynx AH7 | AAC No 655 Sqn/5 Regt, Aldergrove | |
| XZ210 | WS Lynx AH7 | AAC No 1 Regt, Gütersloh | |
| XZ211 | WS Lynx AH7 | AAC No 656 Sqn/9 Regt, Dishforth | |
| XZ212 | WS Lynx AH7 | AAC No 656 Sqn/9 Regt, Dishforth | |
| XZ213 | WS Lynx AH1 (TAD 213) | RNAY Fleetlands Apprentice School | |
| XZ214 | WS Lynx AH7 | AAC No 657 Sqn/9 Regt, Dishforth | |
| XZ215 | WS Lynx AH7 [4] | AAC No 655 Sqn/5 Regt, Aldergrove | |
| XZ216 | WS Lynx AH7 | AAC No 1 Regt, Gütersloh | |
| XZ217 | WS Lynx AH7 | DARA, RNAY Fleetlands | |
| XZ218 | WS Lynx AH7 | AAC No 655 Sqn/5 Regt, Aldergrove | |
| XZ219 | WS Lynx AH7 | AAC No 9 Regt, Dishforth | |
| XZ220 | WS Lynx AH7 | AAC No 651 Sqn/1 Regt, Gütersloh | |
| XZ221 | WS Lynx AH7 | DARA, RNAY Fleetlands | |
| XZ222 | WS Lynx AH7 | AAC No 657 Sqn/9 Regt, Dishforth | |
| XZ228 | WS Lynx HAS3S [306] | RN No 815 Sqn, HQ Flt, Yeovilton | |
| XZ229 | WS Lynx HAS3S | RN No 815 Sqn, HQ Flt, Yeovilton | |
| XZ230 | WS Lynx HAS3S [302] | DARA, RNAY Fleetlands | |
| XZ232 | WS Lynx HAS3S [360/MC] | RN No 815 Sqn, *Manchester* Flt, Yeovilton | |
| XZ233 | WS Lynx HAS3(ICE) | RN No 702 Sqn, Yeovilton | |
| XZ234 | WS Lynx HAS3S [335/CF] | RN No 815 Sqn, *Cardiff* Flt, Yeovilton | |
| XZ235 | WS Lynx HAS3S [304] | RN No 815 Sqn, HQ Flt, Yeovilton | |
| XZ236 | WS Lynx HMA8 | DPA/AFD, DERA Boscombe Down | |
| XZ237 | WS Lynx HAS3S [630] | RN No 702 Sqn, Yeovilton | |
| XZ238 | WS Lynx HAS3S(ICE) [435/EE] | RN No 815 Sqn, *Endurance* Flt, Yeovilton | |
| XZ239 | WS Lynx HAS3S [345/NC] | RN No 815 Sqn, *Newcastle* Flt, Yeovilton | |
| XZ241 | WS Lynx HAS3S(ICE) [434/EE] | RN No 815 Sqn, *Endurance* Flt, Yeovilton | |
| XZ243 | WS Lynx HAS3 <ff> | SFDO, RNAS Culdrose | |
| XZ245 | WS Lynx HAS3S [332/LP] | RN No 815 Sqn, *Liverpool* Flt, Yeovilton | |
| XZ246 | WS Lynx HAS3S [635] | RN No 702 Sqn, Yeovilton | |

| Notes | Serial | Type (other identity) [code] | Owner/operator, location or fate |
|---|---|---|---|
| | XZ248 | WS Lynx HAS3S [634] | RN No 702 Sqn, Yeovilton |
| | XZ250 | WS Lynx HAS3S [631] | RN AMG, Yeovilton |
| | XZ252 | WS Lynx HAS3S | RN, stored RNAY Fleetlands |
| | XZ254 | WS Lynx HAS3S [355/SM] | RN No 815 Sqn, *Somerset* Flt, Yeovilton |
| | XZ255 | WS Lynx HMA8 [462/WM] | RN No 815 Sqn, *Westminster* Flt, Yeovilton |
| | XZ256 | WS Lynx HMA8 [352/SD] | RN No 815 Sqn, *Sheffield* Flt, Yeovilton |
| | XZ257 | WS Lynx HAS3S [644] | RN No 702 Sqn, Yeovilton |
| | XZ284 | HS Nimrod MR2 | RAF No 206 Sqn, Kinloss |
| | XZ286 | BAe Nimrod AEW3 <rf> | RAF Kinloss Fire Section |
| | XZ287 | BAe Nimrod AEW3 (9140M) (fuselage) | RAF TSW, Stafford |
| | XZ290 | WS Gazelle AH1 | AAC No 665 Sqn/5 Regt, Aldergrove |
| | XZ291 | WS Gazelle AH1 | AAC No 12 Flt, Brüggen |
| | XZ292 | WS Gazelle AH1 | AAC No 664 Sqn/9 Regt, Dishforth |
| | XZ294 | WS Gazelle AH1 [X] | AAC No 658 Sqn/7 Regt, Netheravon |
| | XZ295 | WS Gazelle AH1 | AAC No 12 Flt, Brüggen |
| | XZ296 | WS Gazelle AH1 | AAC No 669 Sqn/4 Regt, Wattisham |
| | XZ298 | WS Gazelle AH1 | AAC No 656 Sqn/9 Regt, Dishforth |
| | XZ299 | WS Gazelle AH1 | AAC No 665 Sqn/5 Regt, Aldergrove |
| | XZ300 | WS Gazelle AH1 [L] (wreck) | Army, Bramley, Hants |
| | XZ301 | WS Gazelle AH1 [U] | AAC No 654 Sqn/4 Regt, Wattisham |
| | XZ302 | WS Gazelle AH1 (fuselage) | AAC, stored RNAY Fleetlands |
| | XZ303 | WS Gazelle AH1 | AAC No 663 Sqn/3 Regt, Wattisham |
| | XZ304 | WS Gazelle AH1 | AAC No 6(V) Flt/7 Regt, Shawbury |
| | XZ305 | WS Gazelle AH1 (TAD020) | Army SEAE, Arborfield |
| | XZ307 | WS Gazelle AH1 | RNAY Fleetlands Apprentice School |
| | XZ308 | WS Gazelle AH1 [V] | AAC No 657 Sqn/9 Regt, Dishforth |
| | XZ309 | WS Gazelle AH1 | AAC No 6(V) Flt/7 Regt, Shawbury |
| | XZ311 | WS Gazelle AH1 | AAC No 6(V) Flt/7 Regt, Shawbury |
| | XZ312 | WS Gazelle AH1 | AAC No 664 Sqn/9 Regt, Dishforth |
| | XZ313 | WS Gazelle AH1 | AAC No 667 Sqn/2 Regt, Middle Wallop |
| | XZ314 | WS Gazelle AH1 | AAC No 8 Flt, Middle Wallop |
| | XZ315 | WS Gazelle AH1 | AAC No 665 Sqn/5 Regt, Aldergrove |
| | XZ316 | WS Gazelle AH1 [B] | AAC No 666(V) Sqn/7 Regt, Netheravon |
| | XZ317 | WS Gazelle AH1 [R] | AAC, stored Shawbury |
| | XZ318 | WS Gazelle AH1 | DPA/GKN Westland, Weston-super-Mare |
| | XZ320 | WS Gazelle AH1 | AAC No 654 Sqn/4 Regt, Wattisham |
| | XZ321 | WS Gazelle AH1 | AAC No 665 Sqn/5 Regt, Aldergrove |
| | XZ322 | WS Gazelle AH1 [N] | DARA, RAF St Athan, BDRT |
| | XZ323 | WS Gazelle AH1 | DARA, RNAY Fleetlands |
| | XZ324 | WS Gazelle AH1 | AAC No 3(V) Flt/7 Regt, Leuchars |
| | XZ325 | WS Gazelle AH1 [T] | Army SEAE, Arborfield |
| | XZ326 | WS Gazelle AH1 | AAC No 664 Sqn/9 Regt, Dishforth |
| | XZ327 | WS Gazelle AH1 | AAC No 656 Sqn/9 Regt, Dishforth |
| | XZ328 | WS Gazelle AH1 | AAC No 662 Sqn/3 Regt, Wattisham |
| | XZ329 | WS Gazelle AH1 [J] | AAC, stored Shawbury |
| | XZ330 | WS Gazelle AH1 [Y] | AAC No 671 Sqn/2 Regt, Middle Wallop |
| | XZ331 | WS Gazelle AH1 | AAC No 654 Sqn/4 Regt, Wattisham |
| | XZ332 | WS Gazelle AH1 [O] | Army SEAE, Arborfield |
| | XZ333 | WS Gazelle AH1 [A] | Army SEAE, Arborfield |
| | XZ334 | WS Gazelle AH1 [S] | AAC No 671 Sqn/2 Regt, Middle Wallop |
| | XZ335 | WS Gazelle AH1 | AAC No 6(V) Flt/7 Regt, Shawbury |
| | XZ337 | WS Gazelle AH1 | AAC No 662 Sqn/3 Regt, Wattisham |
| | XZ338 | WS Gazelle AH1 | AAC No 651 Sqn/1 Regt, Gütersloh |
| | XZ339 | WS Gazelle AH1 | AAC No 654 Sqn/4 Regt, Wattisham |
| | XZ340 | WS Gazelle AH1 [5A] | AAC No 29 Flt, BATUS, Suffield, Canada |
| | XZ341 | WS Gazelle AH1 | AAC No 3(V) Flt/7 Regt, Leuchars |
| | XZ342 | WS Gazelle AH1 | AAC, stored RNAY Fleetlands |
| | XZ343 | WS Gazelle AH1 | AAC No 661 Sqn/1 Regt, Gütersloh |
| | XZ344 | WS Gazelle AH1 | AAC No 657 Sqn/9 Regt, Dishforth |
| | XZ345 | WS Gazelle AH1 | AAC No 657 Sqn/9 Regt, Dishforth |
| | XZ346 | WS Gazelle AH1 | AAC No 665 Sqn/5 Regt, Aldergrove |
| | XZ347 | WS Gazelle AH1 | AAC No 662 Sqn/3 Regt, Wattisham |
| | XZ348 | WS Gazelle AH1 (wreck) | AAC, stored RNAY Fleetlands |
| | XZ349 | WS Gazelle AH1 [G1] | AAC No 671 Sqn/2 Regt, Middle Wallop |
| | XZ355 | SEPECAT Jaguar GR3A [FJ] | RAF No 41 Sqn, Coltishall |
| | XZ356 | SEPECAT Jaguar GR1A [EP] | RAF, stored Shawbury |
| | XZ357 | SEPECAT Jaguar GR3 [FK] | RAF No 41 Sqn, Coltishall |
| | XZ358 | SEPECAT Jaguar GR1A [L] | AMIF, RAFC Cranwell |
| | XZ360 | SEPECAT Jaguar GR3 [FN] | RAF No 41 Sqn, Coltishall |
| | XZ361 | SEPECAT Jaguar GR1A [FT] | RAF No 41 Sqn, Coltishall |
| | XZ363 | SEPECAT Jaguar GR3 [FO] | RAF No 41 Sqn, Coltishall |

| Serial | Type (other identity) [code] | Owner/operator, location or fate | Notes |
|---|---|---|---|
| *XZ363* | SEPECAT Jaguar GR1A <R> (*XX824*/BAPC 151) [A] | RAF EPTT, St Athan | |
| XZ364 | SEPECAT Jaguar GR3 [GJ] | RAF No 54 Sqn, Coltishall | |
| XZ366 | SEPECAT Jaguar GR3 [FS] | RAF No 41 Sqn, Coltishall | |
| XZ367 | SEPECAT Jaguar GR3A [GP] | DARA, RAF St Athan (conversion) | |
| XZ368 | SEPECAT Jaguar GR1 [8900M] [AG] | RAF No 1 SoTT, Cosford | |
| XZ369 | SEPECAT Jaguar GR3 [EF] | RAF No 6 Sqn, Coltishall | |
| XZ370 | SEPECAT Jaguar GR1 (9004M) [JB] | RAF No 1 SoTT, Cosford | |
| XZ371 | SEPECAT Jaguar GR1 (8907M) [AP] | RAF No 1 SoTT, Cosford | |
| XZ372 | SEPECAT Jaguar GR1A [ED] | RAF, stored St Athan | |
| XZ374 | SEPECAT Jaguar GR1 (9005M) [JC] | RAF No 1 SoTT, Cosford | |
| XZ375 | SEPECAT Jaguar GR1A (9255M) | RAF, stored St Athan | |
| XZ377 | SEPECAT Jaguar GR3 [EG] | RAF No 6 Sqn, Coltishall | |
| XZ378 | SEPECAT Jaguar GR1A [EP] | RAF, stored Shawbury | |
| XZ381 | SEPECAT Jaguar GR3 [D] | *Crashed 20 October 1999, Moray Firth* | |
| XZ382 | SEPECAT Jaguar GR1 (8908M) | Privately owned, Bruntingthorpe | |
| XZ383 | SEPECAT Jaguar GR1 (8901M) [AF] | RAF No 1 SoTT, Cosford | |
| XZ384 | SEPECAT Jaguar GR1 (8954M) [BC] | RAF No 1 SoTT, Cosford | |
| XZ385 | SEPECAT Jaguar GR1A [C] | RAF No 6 Sqn, Coltishall | |
| XZ389 | SEPECAT Jaguar GR1 (8946M) [BL] | RAF No 1 SoTT, Cosford | |
| XZ390 | SEPECAT Jaguar GR1A (9003M) [35,JA] | RAF No 1 SoTT, Cosford | |
| XZ391 | SEPECAT Jaguar GR3 [EB] | RAF No 6 Sqn, Coltishall | |
| XZ392 | SEPECAT Jaguar GR1A [GQ] | RAF, stored Shawbury | |
| XZ394 | SEPECAT Jaguar GR3 [GN] | RAF No 16(R) Sqn, Lossiemouth | |
| XZ396 | SEPECAT Jaguar GR1A [EM] | RAF No 6 Sqn, Coltishall | |
| XZ398 | SEPECAT Jaguar GR3 [FA] | RAF No 41 Sqn, Coltishall | |
| XZ399 | SEPECAT Jaguar GR3A [EJ] | DPA/AFD, DERA Boscombe Down | |
| XZ400 | SEPECAT Jaguar GR3 [GR] | RAF No 54 Sqn, Coltishall | |
| XZ431 | HS Buccaneer S2B (9233M) | RAF Marham Fire Section | |
| XZ439 | BAe Sea Harrier FA2 | DPA/BAe, Dunsfold | |
| XZ440 | BAe Sea Harrier FA2 [126] | RN, St Athan | |
| XZ445 | BAe Harrier T4A [721] (wreck) | *Scrapped* | |
| XZ455 | BAe Sea Harrier FA2 [001] (wreck) | *Scrapped* | |
| XZ457 | BAe Sea Harrier FA2 [714] (wreck) | *S crapped* | |
| XZ459 | BAe Sea Harrier FA2 [003/L] | RN, St Athan | |
| XZ492 | BAe Sea Harrier FA2 [127] (wreck) | *Scrapped* | |
| XZ493 | BAe Sea Harrier FRS1 (comp XV760) [126] | FAA Museum, at BAE SystemsDunsfold (restoration) | |
| XZ493 | BAe Sea Harrier FRS1 <ff> | RN Yeovilton, Fire Section | |
| XZ494 | BAe Sea Harrier FA2 [128] | RN No 800 Sqn, Yeovilton | |
| XZ497 | BAe Sea Harrier FA2 | RN, St Athan | |
| XZ499 | BAe Sea Harrier FA2 [123] | RN, St Athan | |
| XZ559 | Slingsby T61F Venture T2 (G-BUEK) | Privately owned, Tibenham | |
| XZ570 | WS61 Sea King HAS5(mod) | DPA/GKN Westland, Yeovil | |
| XZ571 | WS61 Sea King HAS6 [016/L] | RN No 820 Sqn, Culdrose | |
| XZ574 | WS61 Sea King HAS6 [015/L] | RN No 820 Sqn, Culdrose | |
| XZ575 | WS61 Sea King HU5 | DARA, RNAY Fleetlands (conversion) | |
| XZ576 | WS61 Sea King HAS6 | DPA/AFD, DERA Boscombe Down | |
| XZ578 | WS61 Sea King HU5 [708/PW] | RN AMG, Culdrose | |
| XZ579 | WS61 Sea King HAS6 [707/PW] | RN No 819 Sqn, Prestwick | |
| XZ580 | WS61 Sea King HAS6 [704/PW] | RN No 819 Sqn, Prestwick | |
| XZ581 | WS61 Sea King HAS6 | RN, stored RNAY Fleetlands | |
| XZ585 | WS61 Sea King HAR3 | RAF No 202 Sqn, E Flt, Leconfield | |
| XZ586 | WS61 Sea King HAR3 [S] | RAF No 78 Sqn, Mount Pleasant, FI | |
| XZ587 | WS61 Sea King HAR3 | RAF No 22 Sqn, C Flt, Valley | |
| XZ588 | WS61 Sea King HAR3 | RAF No 202 Sqn, E Flt, Leconfield | |
| XZ589 | WS61 Sea King HAR3 | RAF HMF, St Mawgan | |
| XZ590 | WS61 Sea King HAR3 | RAF Leconfield | |
| XZ591 | WS61 Sea King HAR3 [S] | DARA, RNAY Fleetlands | |
| XZ592 | WS61 Sea King HAR3 [S] | RAF HMF, St Mawgan | |
| XZ593 | WS61 Sea King HAR3 | RAF No 203(R) Sqn, St Mawgan | |
| XZ594 | WS61 Sea King HAR3 | RAF No 22 Sqn, C Flt, Valley | |
| XZ595 | WS61 Sea King HAR3 | RAF No 202 Sqn, D Flt, Lossiemouth | |
| XZ596 | WS61 Sea King HAR3 | RAF No 78 Sqn, Mount Pleasant, FI | |

| Notes | Serial | Type (other identity) [code] | Owner/operator, location or fate |
|---|---|---|---|
| | XZ597 | WS61 Sea King HAR3 | RAF No 202 Sqn, D Flt, Lossiemouth |
| | XZ598 | WS61 Sea King HAR3 | RAF No 202 Sqn, D Flt, Lossiemouth |
| | XZ599 | WS61 Sea King HAR3 [S] | RAF No 202 Sqn, A Flt, Boulmer |
| | XZ605 | WS Lynx AH7 [Y] | RM No 847 Sqn, Yeovilton |
| | XZ606 | WS Lynx AH7 | AAC No 667 Sqn/2 Regt, Middle Wallop |
| | XZ607 | WS Lynx AH7 | AAC No 9 Regt, Dishforth |
| | XZ608 | WS Lynx AH7 | AAC No 657 Sqn/9 Regt, Dishforth |
| | XZ609 | WS Lynx AH7 | AAC No 652 Sqn/1 Regt, Gütersloh |
| | XZ611 | WS Lynx AH7 | AAC No 661 Sqn/1 Regt, Gütersloh |
| | XZ612 | WS Lynx AH7 | RM No 847 Sqn, Yeovilton |
| | XZ613 | WS Lynx AH7 [F] | Army SEAE, Arborfield |
| | XZ614 | WS Lynx AH7 [X] | RM No 847 Sqn, Yeovilton |
| | XZ615 | WS Lynx AH7 | AAC No 655 Sqn/5 Regt, Aldergrove |
| | XZ616 | WS Lynx AH7 | AAC No 657 Sqn/9 Regt, Dishforth |
| | XZ617 | WS Lynx AH7 | AAC No 663 Sqn/3 Regt, Wattisham |
| | XZ630 | Panavia Tornado GR1 (8976M) | DARA, RAF St Athan, BDRT |
| | XZ631 | Panavia Tornado GR1 | DPA/BAe, Warton |
| | XZ641 | WS Lynx AH7 | AAC No 25 Flt, Belize |
| | XZ642 | WS Lynx AH7 | AAC No 663 Sqn/3 Regt, Wattisham |
| | XZ643 | WS Lynx AH7 | AAC No 654 Sqn/4 Regt, Wattisham |
| | XZ645 | WS Lynx AH7 | AAC No 9 Regt, Dishforth |
| | XZ646 | WS Lynx AH7 | AAC No 651 Sqn/1 Regt, Gütersloh |
| | XZ647 | WS Lynx AH7 | AAC No 655 Sqn/5 Regt, Aldergrove |
| | XZ648 | WS Lynx AH7 | AAC No 664 Sqn/9 Regt, Dishforth |
| | XZ649 | WS Lynx AH7 | AAC, stored RNAY Fleetlands |
| | XZ651 | WS Lynx AH7 | AAC No 657 Sqn/9 Regt, Dishforth |
| | XZ652 | WS Lynx AH7 [T] | AAC No 671 Sqn/2 Regt, Middle Wallop |
| | XZ653 | WS Lynx AH7 | AAC No 663 Sqn/3 Regt, Wattisham |
| | XZ654 | WS Lynx AH7 | AAC, stored RNAY Fleetlands |
| | XZ655 | WS Lynx AH7 | AAC No 655 Sqn/5 Regt, Aldergrove |
| | XZ661 | WS Lynx AH1 | AAC No 655 Sqn/5 Regt, Aldergrove |
| | XZ662 | WS Lynx AH7 | AAC No 655 Sqn/5 Regt, Aldergrove |
| | XZ663 | WS Lynx AH7 | AAC No 655 Sqn/5 Regt, Aldergrove |
| | XZ664 | WS Lynx AH7 | AAC No 663 Sqn/3 Regt, Wattisham |
| | XZ665 | WS Lynx AH7 | AAC, stored RNAY Fleetlands |
| | XZ666 | WS Lynx AH7 | Army SEAE, Arborfield |
| | XZ668 | WS Lynx AH7 [UN] (wreckage) | AAC Middle Wallop, instructional use |
| | XZ669 | WS Lynx AH7 | AAC No 663 Sqn/3 Regt, Wattisham |
| | XZ670 | WS Lynx AH7 | RM No 847 Sqn, Yeovilton |
| | XZ671 | WS Lynx AH7 <ff> | GKN Westland, Yeovil, instructional use |
| | XZ672 | WS Lynx AH7 | AAC No 655 Sqn/5 Regt, Aldergrove |
| | XZ673 | WS Lynx AH7 | AAC No 655 Sqn/5 Regt, Aldergrove |
| | XZ674 | WS Lynx AH7 | AAC No 656 Sqn/9 Regt, Dishforth |
| | XZ675 | WS Lynx AH7 [E] | AAC No 671 Sqn/2 Regt, Middle Wallop |
| | XZ676 | WS Lynx AH7 [N] | AAC No 671 Sqn/2 Regt, Middle Wallop |
| | XZ677 | WS Lynx AH7 | AAC, stored RNAY Fleetlands |
| | XZ678 | WS Lynx AH7 | AAC No 9 Regt, Dishforth |
| | XZ679 | WS Lynx AH7 | AAC No 1 Regt, Gütersloh |
| | XZ680 | WS Lynx AH7 | AAC No 656 Sqn/9 Regt, Dishforth |
| | XZ681 | WS Lynx AH1 | AAC Middle Wallop, BDRT |
| | XZ689 | WS Lynx HMA8 | RN No 702 Sqn, Yeovilton |
| | XZ690 | WS Lynx HMA8 [412/CW] | RN No 815 Sqn, *Cornwall* Flt, Yeovilton |
| | XZ691 | WS Lynx HMA8 | RN No 815 Sqn, HQ Flt, Yeovilton |
| | XZ692 | WS Lynx HMA8 [365/AY] | RN No 815 Sqn, *Argyll* Flt, Yeovilton |
| | XZ693 | WS Lynx HAS3S | RN AMG, Yeovilton |
| | XZ694 | WS Lynx HAS3S [420/EX] | RN No 815 Sqn, *Exeter* Flt, Yeovilton |
| | XZ695 | WS Lynx HMA8 | DARA, RNAY Fleetlands (conversion) |
| | XZ696 | WS Lynx HAS3S [363/MA] | RN No 815 Sqn, *Marlborough* Flt, Yeovilton |
| | XZ697 | WS Lynx HMA8 [308] | RN No 815 Sqn, HQ Flt, Yeovilton |
| | XZ698 | WS Lynx HMA8 [672] | RN No 702 Sqn, Yeovilton |
| | XZ699 | WS Lynx HAS3S [303] | RN AMG, Yeovilton |
| | XZ719 | WS Lynx HMA8 [644] | DARA, RNAY Fleetlands (conversion) |
| | XZ720 | WS Lynx HAS3S [411/EB] | RN No 815 Sqn, *Edinburgh* Flt, Yeovilton |
| | XZ721 | WS Lynx HMA8 [350/CL] | RN No 815 Sqn, *Cumberland* Flt, Yeovilton |
| | XZ722 | WS Lynx HMA8 [304] | RN No 815 Sqn, HQ Flt, Yeovilton |
| | XZ723 | WS Lynx HMA8 [404/IR] | RN No 815 Sqn, *Iron Duke* Flt, Yeovilton |
| | XZ724 | WS Lynx HAS3S [415/MM] | RN No 815 Sqn, *Monmouth* Flt, Yeovilton |
| | XZ725 | WS Lynx HMA8 [633] | DARA, RNAY Fleetlands (conversion) |
| | XZ726 | WS Lynx HMA8 | DARA, RNAY Fleetlands (conversion) |
| | XZ727 | WS Lynx HAS3S [303] | RN No 815 Sqn, HQ Flt, Yeovilton |
| | XZ728 | WS Lynx HMA8 [415/MM] | RN, stored RNAY Fleetlands |
| | XZ729 | WS Lynx HMA8 [632] | DARA, RNAY Fleetlands (conversion) |

| Serial | Type (other identity) [code] | Owner/operator, location or fate | Notes |
|---|---|---|---|
| XZ730 | WS Lynx HAS3CTS [302] | RN AMG,Yeovilton | |
| XZ731 | WS Lynx HMA8 [307] | RN No 815 Sqn, HQ Flt, Yeovilton | |
| XZ732 | WS Lynx HMA8 [318] | RN No 815 Sqn OEU, Yeovilton | |
| XZ733 | WS Lynx HAS3S [361/NF] | RN No 815 Sqn, *Norfolk* Flt, Yeovilton | |
| XZ735 | WS Lynx HAS3S [437/GT] | RN No 815 Sqn, *Grafton* Flt, Yeovilton | |
| XZ736 | WS Lynx HMA8 | DARA, RNAY Fleetlands (conversion) | |
| XZ920 | WS61 Sea King HU5 [822/CU] | RN, stored RNAY Fleetlands | |
| XZ921 | WS61 Sea King HAS6 [508] | RN No 810 Sqn, Culdrose | |
| XZ922 | WS61 Sea King HAS6 [503/CU] | RN AMG, Culdrose | |
| XZ930 | WS Gazelle HT3 [Q] | RAF, stored Shawbury | |
| XZ931 | WS Gazelle HT3 [R] | RAF, stored Shawbury | |
| XZ932 | WS Gazelle HT3 [S] | RAF, stored Shawbury | |
| XZ933 | WS Gazelle HT3 [T] | RAF, stored Shawbury | |
| XZ934 | WS Gazelle HT3 [U] | RAF, stored Shawbury | |
| XZ935 | WS Gazelle HCC4 | RAF, stored RNAY Fleetlands | |
| XZ936 | WS Gazelle HT2 [6] | DPA/AFD/ETPS, DERA Boscombe Down | |
| XZ937 | WS Gazelle HT2 [Y] | RAF, stored Shawbury | |
| XZ938 | WS Gazelle HT2 [45/CU] | RN, stored Shawbury | |
| XZ939 | WS Gazelle HT2 [9] | DPA/AFD/ETPS, DERA Boscombe Down | |
| XZ940 | WS Gazelle HT2 [O] | RAF, stored Shawbury | |
| XZ941 | WS Gazelle HT2 [B] | RAF, stored Shawbury | |
| XZ942 | WS Gazelle HT2 [42/CU] | RN, stored Shawbury | |
| XZ964 | BAe Harrier GR3 [D] | Royal Engineers Museum, Chatham | |
| XZ966 | BAe Harrier GR3 (9221M) [G] | MoD FSCTE, Manston | |
| XZ968 | BAe Harrier GR3 (9222M) [3G] | Muckleborough Collection, Weybourne | |
| XZ969 | BAe Harrier GR3 [D] | SFDO, RNAS Culdrose | |
| XZ971 | BAe Harrier GR3 (9219M) [G] | RAF, stored Shawbury | |
| XZ987 | BAe Harrier GR3 (9185M) [C] | RAF Stafford, at main gate | |
| XZ990 | BAe Harrier GR3 <ff> | No 1220 Sqn ATC, March, Cambs | |
| XZ990 | BAe Harrier GR3 <rf> | RAF Wittering, derelict | |
| XZ991 | BAe Harrier GR3 (9162M) [3A] | DARA, RAF St Athan, BDRT | |
| XZ993 | BAe Harrier GR3 (9240M) (fuselage) | DARA, RAF St Athan, BDRT | |
| XZ994 | BAe Harrier GR3 (9170M) [U] | RAF Air Movements School, Brize Norton | |
| XZ995 | BAe Harrier GR3 (9220M) [3G] | Shoreham Airport, on display | |
| XZ996 | BAe Harrier GR3 [2,3] | SFDO, RNAS Culdrose | |
| XZ997 | BAe Harrier GR3 (9122M) [V] | RAF Museum, Hendon | |
| | | | |
| ZA101 | BAe Hawk 100 (G-HAWK) | DPA/BAe, Warton | |
| ZA105 | WS61 Sea King HAR3 [S] | RAF HMF, St Mawgan | |
| ZA110 | BAe Jetstream T2 (F-BTMI) [563/CU] | RN, Culdrose (damaged) | |
| ZA111 | BAe Jetstream T2 (9Q-CTC) [565/CU] | RN No 750 Sqn, Culdrose | |
| ZA126 | WS61 Sea King HAS6 [504/CU] | RN No 810 Sqn, Culdrose | |
| ZA127 | WS61 Sea King HAS6 [509/CU] | RN No 810 Sqn, Culdrose | |
| ZA128 | WS61 Sea King HAS6 [010] | RN No 810 Sqn, Culdrose | |
| ZA129 | WS61 Sea King HAS6 [502/CU] | RN No 810 Sqn, Culdrose | |
| ZA130 | WS61 Sea King HU5 [587/CU] | DARA, RNAY Fleetlands | |
| ZA131 | WS61 Sea King HAS6 [271/N] | RN No 814 Sqn, Culdrose | |
| ZA133 | WS61 Sea King HAS6 [013/L] | RN No 820 Sqn, Culdrose | |
| ZA134 | WS61 Sea King HU5 [824/CU] | RN No 771 Sqn, Culdrose | |
| ZA135 | WS61 Sea King HAS6 [705/PW] | RN No 819 Sqn, Prestwick | |
| *ZA135* | WS61 Sea King HAS5 (XV657) [132] | RN ETS, Culdrose | |
| ZA136 | WS61 Sea King HAS6 [018/L] | DARA, RNAY Fleetlands (damaged) | |
| ZA137 | WS61 Sea King HU5 [820/CU] | RN No 771 Sqn, Culdrose | |
| ZA140 | BAe VC10 K2 (G-ARVL) [A] | RAF No 101 Sqn, Brize Norton | |
| ZA141 | BAe VC10 K2 (G-ARVG) [B] | RAF, stored St Athan | |
| ZA142 | BAe VC10 K2 (G-ARVI) [C] | RAF No 101 Sqn, Brize Norton | |
| ZA143 | BAe VC10 K2 (G-ARVK) [D] | RAF, reduced to spares, St Athan | |
| ZA144 | BAe VC10 K2 (G-ARVC) [E] | RAF No 101 Sqn, Brize Norton | |
| ZA147 | BAe VC10 K3 (5H-MMT) [F] | RAF No 101 Sqn, Brize Norton | |
| ZA148 | BAe VC10 K3 (5Y-ADA) [G] | RAF No 101 Sqn, Brize Norton | |
| ZA149 | BAe VC10 K3 (5X-UVJ) [H] | RAF No 101 Sqn, Brize Norton | |
| ZA150 | BAe VC10 K3 (5H-MOG) [J] | RAF No 101 Sqn, Brize Norton | |
| ZA166 | WS61 Sea King HU5 [511] | RN, AMG, Culdrose | |
| ZA167 | WS61 Sea King HU5 [822/CU] | RN No 771 Sqn, Culdrose | |
| ZA168 | WS61 Sea King HAS6 [512/CU] | RN AMG, Culdrose | |
| ZA169 | WS61 Sea King HAS6 [265/N] | DARA, RNAY Fleetlands | |
| ZA170 | WS61 Sea King HU5 | RN AESS, *HMS Sultan*, Gosport | |
| ZA175 | BAe Sea Harrier FA2 | RN No 801 Sqn, Yeovilton | |
| ZA176 | BAe Sea Harrier FA2 [122] | RN AMG, Yeovilton | |

| Notes | Serial | Type (other identity) [code] | Owner/operator, location or fate |
|---|---|---|---|
| | ZA195 | BAe Sea Harrier FA2 | DPA/BAE Systems, Dunsfold |
| | ZA250 | BAe Harrier T52 (G-VTOL) | Brooklands Museum, Weybridge |
| | ZA254 | Panavia Tornado F2 (fuselage) | RAF Coningsby, instructional use |
| | ZA267 | Panavia Tornado F2 | RAF Marham, instructional use |
| | ZA283 | Panavia Tornado F2 | DPA/AFD, DERA Boscombe Down |
| | ZA291 | WS61 Sea King HC4 [ZX] | RN No 848 Sqn, Yeovilton |
| | ZA292 | WS61 Sea King HC4 [ZR] | DPA/GKN Westland, Weston-super-Mare |
| | ZA293 | WS61 Sea King HC4 [ZO] | RN No 848 Sqn, Yeovilton |
| | ZA295 | WS61 Sea King HC4 [ZR] | RN No 848 Sqn, Yeovilton |
| | ZA296 | WS61 Sea King HC4 [VO] | RN No 846 Sqn, Yeovilton |
| | ZA297 | WS61 Sea King HC4 [C] | RN No 845 Sqn, Yeovilton |
| | ZA298 | WS61 Sea King HC4 [G] | RN No 845 Sqn, Yeovilton |
| | ZA299 | WS61 Sea King HC4 [ZT] | RN No 848 Sqn, Yeovilton |
| | ZA310 | WS61 Sea King HC4 [ZY] | RN No 848 Sqn, Yeovilton |
| | ZA312 | WS61 Sea King HC4 [ZS] | RN No 848 Sqn, Yeovilton |
| | ZA313 | WS61 Sea King HC4 [M] | RN No 845 Sqn, Yeovilton |
| | ZA314 | WS61 Sea King HC4 [F] | RN No 845 Sqn, Yeovilton |
| | ZA319 | Panavia Tornado GR1 [B-11] | RAF, stored St Athan |
| | ZA320 | Panavia Tornado GR1 [TAW] | RAF No 15(R) Sqn, Lossiemouth |
| | ZA321 | Panavia Tornado GR1 [TAB] | RAF No 15(R) Sqn, Lossiemouth |
| | ZA322 | Panavia Tornado GR1 [TAC] | RAF No 15(R) Sqn, Lossiemouth |
| | ZA323 | Panavia Tornado GR1 [TAZ] | RAF No 15(R) Sqn, Lossiemouth |
| | ZA324 | Panavia Tornado GR1 [TAY] | RAF No 15(R) Sqn, Lossiemouth |
| | ZA325 | Panavia Tornado GR1 [B-03] | RAF, stored St Athan |
| | ZA326 | Panavia Tornado GR1P | DPA/AFD, DERA Boscombe Down |
| | ZA327 | Panavia Tornado GR1 | DPA/BAe, Warton |
| | ZA328 | Panavia Tornado GR1 | DPA/BAe, Warton |
| | ZA352 | Panavia Tornado GR1 [B-04] | RAF, stored St Athan |
| | ZA353 | Panavia Tornado GR1 [B-53] | DPA/AFD, DERA Boscombe Down |
| | ZA354 | Panavia Tornado GR1 | DPA/BAe, Warton |
| | ZA355 | Panavia Tornado GR1 [TAA] | RAF No 15(R) Sqn, Lossiemouth |
| | ZA356 | Panavia Tornado GR1 [TP] | RAF No 15(R) Sqn, Lossiemouth |
| | ZA357 | Panavia Tornado GR1 [TS] | RAF No 15(R) Sqn, Lossiemouth |
| | ZA358 | Panavia Tornado GR1 | DPA/BAe, Warton |
| | ZA359 | Panavia Tornado GR1 | BAE SystemsWarton, Overseas Customer Training Centre |
| | ZA360 | Panavia Tornado GR1 [TC] | RAF No 15(R) Sqn, Lossiemouth |
| | ZA361 | Panavia Tornado GR1 [B-57] | RAF, stored St Athan |
| | ZA362 | Panavia Tornado GR1 [TR] | RAF No 15(R) Sqn, Lossiemouth |
| | ZA365 | Panavia Tornado GR4 [AJ-T] | DPA/BAe, Warton (conversion) |
| | ZA367 | Panavia Tornado GR1 [II] | RAF No 2 Sqn, Marham |
| | ZA369 | Panavia Tornado GR4A [U] | RAF No 13 Sqn, Marham |
| | ZA370 | Panavia Tornado GR1A [A] | RAF No 2 Sqn, Marham |
| | ZA371 | Panavia Tornado GR4A [C] | RAF No 13 Sqn, Marham |
| | ZA372 | Panavia Tornado GR1A [E] | RAF No 2 Sqn, Marham |
| | ZA373 | Panavia Tornado GR1A [H] | RAF No 2 Sqn, Marham |
| | ZA374 | Panavia Tornado GR1B [AJ-L] | RAF No 617 Sqn, Lossiemouth |
| | ZA375 | Panavia Tornado GR1B [AJ-W] | RAF No 617 Sqn, Lossiemouth |
| | ZA393 | Panavia Tornado GR1 [BE] | RAF No 14 Sqn, Brüggen |
| | ZA395 | Panavia Tornado GR1A [N] | RAF No 2 Sqn, Marham |
| | ZA398 | Panavia Tornado GR1A [S] | RAF No 2 Sqn, Marham |
| | ZA399 | Panavia Tornado GR1B [AJ-C] | RAF No 617 Sqn, Lossiemouth |
| | ZA400 | Panavia Tornado GR4A [T] | DPA/BAe, Warton (conversion) |
| | ZA401 | Panavia Tornado GR1A [R] | RAF No 2 Sqn, Marham |
| | ZA402 | Panavia Tornado GR1A | DPA/AFD, DERA Boscombe Down |
| | ZA404 | Panavia Tornado GR4A [P] | RAF No 13 Sqn, Marham |
| | ZA405 | Panavia Tornado GR1A [Y] | RAF No 2 Sqn, Marham |
| | ZA406 | Panavia Tornado GR1 [CI] | RAF No 14 Sqn, Brüggen |
| | ZA407 | Panavia Tornado GR1B [AJ-G] | RAF No 617 Sqn, Lossiemouth |
| | ZA409 | Panavia Tornado GR1B [FQ] | RAF No 12 Sqn, Lossiemouth |
| | ZA410 | Panavia Tornado GR1 | DPA/BAE Systems Warton |
| | ZA411 | Panavia Tornado GR1B [AJ-S] | RAF No 617 Sqn, Lossiemouth |
| | ZA412 | Panavia Tornado GR1 | RAF No 12 Sqn, Lossiemouth |
| | ZA446 | Panavia Tornado GR1B [U] | RAF AWC/SAOEU, DERA Boscombe Down |
| | ZA447 | Panavia Tornado GR1B [FA] | RAF No 12 Sqn, Lossiemouth |
| | ZA449 | Panavia Tornado GR1 [Q] | RAF No 2 Sqn, Marham |
| | ZA450 | Panavia Tornado GR1B [FB] | RAF No 12 Sqn, Lossiemouth |
| | ZA452 | Panavia Tornado GR1B [FC] | RAF No 15(R) Sqn, Lossiemouth |
| | ZA453 | Panavia Tornado GR1B [AJ-M] | RAF No 617 Sqn, Lossiemouth |
| | ZA455 | Panavia Tornado GR1B [TH] | RAF No 15(R) Sqn, Lossiemouth |
| | ZA456 | Panavia Tornado GR1B [AJ-Q] | RAF No 617 Sqn, Lossiemouth |

| Serial | Type (other identity) [code] | Owner/operator, location or fate | Notes |
|---|---|---|---|
| ZA457 | Panavia Tornado GR1B [AJ-J] | RAF No 617 Sqn, Lossiemouth | |
| ZA458 | Panavia Tornado GR4 | DPA/BAe, Warton (conversion) | |
| ZA459 | Panavia Tornado GR1B [AJ-B] | RAF No 617 Sqn, Lossiemouth | |
| ZA460 | Panavia Tornado GR1B [AJ-A] | RAFSt Athan | |
| ZA461 | Panavia Tornado GR1B [FD] | RAF No 12 Sqn, Lossiemouth | |
| ZA462 | Panavia Tornado GR1 [BV] | RAF No 14 Sqn, Brüggen | |
| ZA463 | Panavia Tornado GR1 [CR] | RAF No 12 Sqn, Lossiemouth | |
| ZA465 | Panavia Tornado GR1B [FF] | RAF No 12 Sqn, Lossiemouth | |
| ZA466 | Panavia Tornado GR1 <ff> | DARA, RAF St Athan, BDRT | |
| ZA469 | Panavia Tornado GR1B [AJ-O] | RAF, stored St Athan | |
| ZA470 | Panavia Tornado GR1 [BQ] | RAF No 14 Sqn, Brüggen | |
| ZA471 | Panavia Tornado GR1B [AJ-K] | RAF No 617 Sqn, Lossiemouth | |
| ZA472 | Panavia Tornado GR1 [CT] | RAF No 617 Sqn, Lossiemouth | |
| ZA473 | Panavia Tornado GR1B [FG] | RAF No 12 Sqn, Lossiemouth | |
| ZA474 | Panavia Tornado GR1B [AJ-F] | RAF No 617 Sqn, Lossiemouth | |
| ZA475 | Panavia Tornado GR1B [FH] | RAF No 12 Sqn, Lossiemouth | |
| ZA490 | Panavia Tornado GR1B [FJ] | RAF No 12 Sqn, Lossiemouth | |
| ZA491 | Panavia Tornado GR1B [FK] | RAF No 15(R) Sqn, Lossiemouth | |
| ZA492 | Panavia Tornado GR1B [TE] | RAF No 15(R) Sqn, Lossiemouth | |
| ZA541 | Panavia Tornado GR4 [DZ] | RAF No 31 Sqn, Brüggen | |
| ZA542 | Panavia Tornado GR4 [DM] | RAF No 31 Sqn, Brüggen | |
| ZA543 | Panavia Tornado GR4 | DPA/BAE Systems, Warton | |
| ZA544 | Panavia Tornado GR4 [VII] | RAF No 13 Sqn, Marham | |
| ZA546 | Panavia Tornado GR1 [W] | RAF No 13 Sqn, Marham | |
| ZA547 | Panavia Tornado GR4 [DC] | RAF No 31 Sqn, Brüggen | |
| ZA548 | Panavia Tornado GR4 [TQ] | RAF No 15 (R) Sqn, Lossiemouth | |
| ZA549 | Panavia Tornado GR4 [III] | RAF No 13 Sqn, Marham | |
| ZA550 | Panavia Tornado GR4 [DD] | RAF No 31 Sqn, Brüggen | |
| ZA551 | Panavia Tornado GR4 | DPA/BAE Systems, Warton | |
| ZA552 | Panavia Tornado GR4 [IV | RAF No 13 Sqn, Marham | |
| ZA553 | Panavia Tornado GR4 [DI] | RAF No 31 Sqn, Brüggen | |
| ZA554 | Panavia Tornado GR4 [DF] | RAF No 31 Sqn, Brüggen | |
| ZA556 | Panavia Tornado GR4 | DARA, RAF St Athan | |
| *ZA556* | Panavia Tornado GR1 <R> (*ZA368*/BAPC 155) [F] | RAF EPTT, St Athan | |
| ZA557 | Panavia Tornado GR4 [AC] | RAF No 9 Sqn, Brüggen | |
| ZA559 | Panavia Tornado GR4 [AD] | RAF No 9 Sqn, Brüggen | |
| ZA560 | Panavia Tornado GR4 [O] | RAF AWC/SAOEU, DERA Boscombe Down | |
| ZA562 | Panavia Tornado GR1 [TT] | RAF No 15(R) Sqn, Lossiemouth | |
| ZA563 | Panavia Tornado GR4 [AG] | RAF No 9 Sqn, Brüggen | |
| ZA564 | Panavia Tornado GR1 [CK] | RAF No 14 Sqn, Brüggen | |
| ZA585 | Panavia Tornado GR4 [AH] | RAF No 9 Sqn, Brüggen | |
| ZA587 | Panavia Tornado GR4 [F] | RAF No 15(R) Sqn, Lossiemouth | |
| ZA588 | Panavia Tornado GR1 [TM] | RAF No 15(R) Sqn, Lossiemouth | |
| ZA589 | Panavia Tornado GR4 [TE] | RAF, St Athan | |
| ZA590 | Panavia Tornado GR1 | RAF, stored St Athan | |
| ZA591 | Panavia Tornado GR4 [DJ] | RAF No 31 Sqn, Brüggen | |
| ZA592 | Panavia Tornado GR1 [C] | RAF No 2 Sqn, Marham | |
| ZA594 | Panavia Tornado GR4 [XIII] | RAF No 13 Sqn, Marham | |
| ZA595 | Panavia Tornado GR4 [VIII] | RAF No 13 Sqn, Marham | |
| ZA596 | Panavia Tornado GR4 | RAF No 14 Sqn, Brüggen | |
| ZA597 | Panavia Tornado GR1 [TA] | RAF No 15(R) Sqn, Lossiemouth | |
| ZA598 | Panavia Tornado GR4 [TN] | DPA/BAe, Warton (conversion) | |
| ZA599 | Panavia Tornado GR1 [TX] | RAF No 15(R) Sqn, Lossiemouth | |
| ZA600 | Panavia Tornado GR1 [TH] | RAF No 15(R) Sqn, Lossiemouth | |
| ZA601 | Panavia Tornado GR4 [TI] | DPA/BAe, Warton (conversion) | |
| ZA602 | Panavia Tornado GR4 [BY] | RAF No 14 Sqn, Brüggen | |
| ZA604 | Panavia Tornado GR1 [TY] | RAF No 15(R) Sqn, Lossiemouth | |
| ZA606 | Panavia Tornado GR4 | DPA/AFD, DERA Boscombe Down | |
| ZA607 | Panavia Tornado GR4 [AB] | RAF No 9 Sqn, Brüggen | |
| ZA608 | Panavia Tornado GR1 [TK] | RAF No 15(R) Sqn, Lossiemouth | |
| ZA609 | Panavia Tornado GR4 [Z] | DPA/BAe, Warton (conversion) | |
| ZA611 | Panavia Tornado GR1 [TG] | RAF No 15(R) Sqn, Lossiemouth | |
| ZA612 | Panavia Tornado GR4 [TZ] | DPA/BAE Systems, Warton (conversion) | |
| ZA613 | Panavia Tornado GR1 [TL] | RAF No 15(R) Sqn, Lossiemouth | |
| ZA614 | Panavia Tornado GR1 [TB] | RAF No 15(R) Sqn, Lossiemouth | |
| ZA634 | Slingsby T61F Venture T2 (G-BUHA) [C] | Privately owned, Rufforth | |
| ZA663 | Slingsby T61F Venture T2 (G-BUFP) | Privately owned, Currock Hill | |
| ZA670 | B-V Chinook HC2 (N37010) [BF] | RAF No 7 Sqn, Odiham | |
| ZA671 | B-V Chinook HC2 (N37011) | DARA, RNAY Fleetlands | |

| Notes | Serial | Type (other identity) [code] | Owner/operator, location or fate |
|---|---|---|---|
| | ZA673 | B-V Chinook HC2 (N37016)[NT] | RAF No 27 Sqn, Odiham |
| | ZA674 | B-V Chinook HC2 (N37019) [EF] | RAF No 18 Sqn, Odiham |
| | ZA675 | B-V Chinook HC2 (N37020) [EB] | RAF No 18 Sqn, Odiham |
| | ZA676 | B-V Chinook HC1 (N37021/9230M) [FG] (wreck) | MoD FSCTE, Manston |
| | ZA677 | B-V Chinook HC2 (N37022) [EG] | RAF No 7 Sqn, Odiham |
| | ZA678 | B-V Chinook HC1 (N37023/9229M) [EZ] (wreck) | RAF Odiham, BDRT |
| | ZA679 | B-V Chinook HC2 (N37025) [C] | RAF No 18 Sqn, Odiham |
| | ZA680 | B-V Chinook HC2 (N37026) [NX] | RAF No 27 Sqn, Odiham |
| | ZA681 | B-V Chinook HC2 (N37027) [ED] | RAF No 18 Sqn, Odiham |
| | ZA682 | B-V Chinook HC2 (N37029) [EW] | RAF No 7 Sqn, Odiham |
| | ZA683 | B-V Chinook HC2 (N37030) | RAF No 78 Sqn, Mount Pleasant, FI |
| | ZA684 | B-V Chinook HC2 (N37031) [EL] | DARA, RNAY Fleetlands |
| | ZA704 | B-V Chinook HC2 (N37033) [EJ] | *Crashed 25 Nov 1999, Seeb, Oman* |
| | ZA705 | B-V Chinook HC2 (N37035) [BE] | RAF No 18 Sqn, Odiham |
| | ZA707 | B-V Chinook HC2 (N37040) [EV] | RAF No 7 Sqn, Odiham |
| | ZA708 | B-V Chinook HC2 (N37042) [BC] | RAF No 18 Sqn, Odiham |
| | ZA709 | B-V Chinook HC2 (N37043) [EQ] | RAF No 18 Sqn, Odiham |
| | ZA710 | B-V Chinook HC2 (N37044) [EC] | RAF No 27 Sqn, Odiham |
| | ZA711 | B-V Chinook HC2 (N37046) [ET] | RAF No 7 Sqn, Odiham |
| | ZA712 | B-V Chinook HC2 (N37047) [ER] | RAF No 27 Sqn, Odiham |
| | ZA713 | B-V Chinook HC2 (N37048) [EM] | RAF No 78 Sqn, Mount Pleasant, FI |
| | ZA714 | B-V Chinook HC2 (N37051) | RAF No 27 Sqn, Odiham |
| | ZA717 | B-V Chinook HC1 (N37056/9238M) (wreck) | RAF Cranwell, BDRT |
| | ZA718 | B-V Chinook HC2 (N37058) | RAF No 18 Sqn, Odiham |
| | ZA720 | B-V Chinook HC2 (N37060) [EP] | RAF No 7 Sqn, Odiham |
| | ZA726 | WS Gazelle AH1 [F1] | AAC No 671 Sqn/2 Regt, Middle Wallop |
| | ZA728 | WS Gazelle AH1 | RM No 847 Sqn, Yeovilton |
| | ZA729 | WS Gazelle AH1 [V] | AAC, stored RNAY Fleetlands |
| | ZA730 | WS Gazelle AH1 | AAC, stored RNAY Fleetlands |
| | ZA731 | WS Gazelle AH1 [5C] | AAC No 29 Flt, BATUS, Suffield, Canada |
| | ZA733 | WS Gazelle AH1 | RNAY Fleetlands Apprentice School |
| | ZA734 | WS Gazelle AH1 | AAC No 25 Flt, Belize |
| | ZA735 | WS Gazelle AH1 | AAC No 25 Flt, Belize |
| | ZA736 | WS Gazelle AH1 | AAC No 29 Flt, BATUS, Suffield, Canada |
| | ZA737 | WS Gazelle AH1 | AAC No 1 Regt, Gütersloh |
| | ZA765 | WS Gazelle AH1 | *Scrapped at Fleetlands, 1999* |
| | ZA766 | WS Gazelle AH1 | AAC No 651 Sqn/1 Regt, Gütersloh |
| | ZA767 | WS Gazelle AH1 | *Crashed 11 September 1999, Belize* |
| | ZA768 | WS Gazelle AH1 [F] (wreck) | AAC, stored RNAY Fleetlands |
| | ZA769 | WS Gazelle AH1 [K] | Army SEAE, Arborfield |
| | ZA771 | WS Gazelle AH1 | AAC No 663 Sqn/3 Regt, Wattisham |
| | ZA772 | WS Gazelle AH1 | AAC No 665 Sqn/5 Regt, Aldergrove |
| | ZA773 | WS Gazelle AH1 [F] | AAC No 666(V) Sqn/7 Regt, Netheravon |
| | ZA774 | WS Gazelle AH1 | AAC No 665 Sqn/5 Regt, Aldergrove |
| | ZA775 | WS Gazelle AH1 | AAC No 665 Sqn/5 Regt, Aldergrove |
| | ZA776 | WS Gazelle AH1 [F] | RM No 847 Sqn, Yeovilton |
| | ZA777 | WS Gazelle AH1 [B] | AAC No 671 Sqn/2 Regt, Middle Wallop |
| | ZA802 | WS Gazelle HT3 [W] | RAF, stored Shawbury |
| | ZA803 | WS Gazelle HT3 [X] | RAF, stored Shawbury |
| | ZA804 | WS Gazelle HT3 [I] | RAF, stored Shawbury |
| | ZA934 | WS Puma HC1 [BZ] | RAF No 33 Sqn, Benson |
| | ZA935 | WS Puma HC1 | RAF No 230 Sqn, Aldergrove |
| | ZA936 | WS Puma HC1 | RAF No 33 Sqn, Benson |
| | ZA937 | WS Puma HC1 | RAF No 72 Sqn, Aldergrove |
| | ZA938 | WS Puma HC1 | RAF No 230 Sqn, Aldergrove |
| | ZA939 | WS Puma HC1 | RAF No 230 Sqn, Aldergrove |
| | ZA940 | WS Puma HC1 | RAF No 230 Sqn, Algergrove |
| | ZA947 | Douglas Dakota C3 [YS-H] | RAF BBMF, Coningsby |
| | | | |
| | ZB500 | WS Lynx 800 (G-LYNX/ZA500) | The Helicopter Museum, Weston-super-Mare |
| | ZB506 | WS61 Sea King Mk 4X | DPA/AFD, DERA Boscombe Down |
| | ZB507 | WS61 Sea King HC4 [ZN] | RN No 848 Sqn, Yeovilton |
| | ZB600 | BAe Harrier T4 | BAE SystemsDunsfold, for Indian Navy |
| | ZB601 | BAe Harrier T4 (fuselage) | BAE SystemsDunsfold |
| | ZB602 | BAe Harrier T4 | BAE SystemsDunsfold, for Indian Navy |
| | ZB603 | BAe Harrier T8 [722/VL] | DPA/BAe, Dunsfold (conversion) |
| | ZB604 | BAe Harrier T8 [722] | RN No 899 Sqn, Yeovilton |
| | ZB605 | BAe Harrier T8 [720/VL] | RN No 899 Sqn, Yeovilton |
| | ZB615 | SEPECAT Jaguar T2A | DPA/AFD, DERA Boscombe Down |

| Serial | Type (other identity) [code] | Owner/operator, location or fate | Notes |
|---|---|---|---|
| ZB625 | WS Gazelle HT3 [N] | DPA/AFD, DERA Boscombe Down | |
| ZB626 | WS Gazelle HT3 [L] | RAF, stored Shawbury | |
| ZB627 | WS Gazelle HT3 [A] | RAF, stored Shawbury | |
| ZB629 | WS Gazelle HCC4 | RAF, stored RNAY Fleetlands | |
| ZB646 | WS Gazelle HT2 [59/CU] | RN, stored Shawbury | |
| ZB647 | WS Gazelle HT2 [40/CU] | RN, stored Shawbury | |
| ZB648 | WS Gazelle HT2 <ff> | *Burnt at Predannack by July 1999* | |
| ZB649 | WS Gazelle HT2 [VL] | RN, stored Shawbury | |
| ZB665 | WS Gazelle AH1 | AAC No 665 Sqn/5 Regt, Aldergrove | |
| ZB666 | WS Gazelle AH1 | AAC No 664 Sqn/9 Regt, Dishforth | |
| ZB667 | WS Gazelle AH1 | DARA, RNAY Fleetlands | |
| ZB668 | WS Gazelle AH1 (TAD 015) | Army SEAE, Arborfield | |
| ZB669 | WS Gazelle AH1 | AAC No 654 Sqn/4 Regt, Wattisham | |
| ZB670 | WS Gazelle AH1 | AAC No 665 Sqn/5 Regt, Aldergrove | |
| ZB671 | WS Gazelle AH1 [5A] | AAC No 29 Flt, BATUS, Suffield, Canada | |
| ZB672 | WS Gazelle AH1 | DARA, RNAY Fleetlands | |
| ZB673 | WS Gazelle AH1 [P] | AAC No 671 Sqn/2 Regt, Middle Wallop | |
| ZB674 | WS Gazelle AH1 | AAC No 665 Sqn/5 Regt, Aldergrove | |
| ZB676 | WS Gazelle AH1 [C] | RM No 847 Sqn, Yeovilton | |
| ZB677 | WS Gazelle AH1 [3] | AAC No 29 Flt, BATUS, Suffield, Canada | |
| ZB678 | WS Gazelle AH1 | Army SEAE, Arborfield | |
| ZB679 | WS Gazelle AH1 | AAC No 16 Flt, Dhekelia, Cyprus | |
| ZB682 | WS Gazelle AH1 | AAC No 665 Sqn/5 Regt, Aldergrove | |
| ZB683 | WS Gazelle AH1 | AAC No 665 Sqn/5 Regt, Aldergrove | |
| ZB684 | WS Gazelle AH1 | AAC No 665 Sqn/5 Regt, Aldergrove | |
| ZB685 | WS Gazelle AH1 | AAC No 665 Sqn/5 Regt, Aldergrove | |
| ZB686 | WS Gazelle AH1 | AAC No 665 Sqn/5 Regt, Aldergrove | |
| ZB688 | WS Gazelle AH1 [H] | AAC No 671 Sqn/2 Regt, Middle Wallop | |
| ZB689 | WS Gazelle AH1 | AAC No 665 Sqn/5 Regt, Aldergrove | |
| ZB690 | WS Gazelle AH1 | AAC No 16 Flt, Dhekelia, Cyprus | |
| ZB691 | WS Gazelle AH1 | AAC No 9 Regt, Dishforth | |
| ZB692 | WS Gazelle AH1 | AAC No 9 Regt, Dishforth | |
| ZB693 | WS Gazelle AH1 | AAC No 29 Flt, BATUS, Suffield, Canada | |
| | | | |
| ZD230 | BAC Super VC10 K4 (G-ASGA) [K] | RAF No 101 Sqn, Brize Norton | |
| ZD234 | BAC Super VC10 (G-ASGF/8700M) | RAF Brize Norton, tanker simulator | |
| ZD235 | BAC Super VC10 K4 (G-ASGG) [L] | RAF No 101 Sqn, Brize Norton | |
| ZD239 | BAC Super VC10 (G-ASGK) | MoD FSCTE, Manston | |
| ZD240 | BAC Super VC10 K4 (G-ASGL) [M] | RAF No 101 Sqn, Brize Norton | |
| ZD241 | BAC Super VC10 K4 (G-ASGM) [N] | RAF No 101 Sqn, Brize Norton | |
| ZD242 | BAC Super VC10 K4 (G-ASGP) | RAF No 101 Sqn, Brize Norton | |
| ZD249 | WS Lynx HAS3S [642] | RN No 702 Sqn, Yeovilton | |
| ZD250 | WS Lynx HAS3S [302] | RN No 815 Sqn, HQ Flt, Yeovilton | |
| ZD251 | WS Lynx HAS3S [636] | RN No 702 Sqn, Yeovilton | |
| ZD252 | WS Lynx HMA8 [671] | RN No 702 Sqn, Yeovilton | |
| ZD253 | WS Lynx HAS3S [410/GC] | RN No 815 Sqn, *Gloucester* Flt, Yeovilton | |
| ZD254 | WS Lynx HAS3S | RN AMG, Yeovilton | |
| ZD255 | WS Lynx HAS3S [344/GW] | RN No 815 Sqn, *Glasgow* Flt, Yeovilton | |
| ZD257 | WS Lynx HMA8 [474/RM] | RN No 815 Sqn, *Richmond* Flt, Yeovilton | |
| ZD258 | WS Lynx HMA8 (*XZ258*) | RN No 702 Sqn, Yeovilton | |
| ZD259 | WS Lynx HMA8 [635] | DARA, RNAY Fleetlands (conversion) | |
| ZD260 | WS Lynx HMA8 [444/MR] | RN No 815 Sqn, *Montrose* Flt, Yeovilton | |
| ZD261 | WS Lynx HMA8 [319] | RN No 815 Sqn OEU, Yeovilton | |
| ZD262 | WS Lynx HMA8 [334/SN] | RN No 815 Sqn, *Southampton* Flt, Yeovilton | |
| ZD263 | WS Lynx HAS3S [306] | RN No 815 Sqn, HQ Flt, Yeovilton | |
| ZD264 | WS Lynx HAS3S [333/BM] | RN No 815 Sqn, Yeovilton | |
| ZD265 | WS Lynx HMA8 | RN AMG, Yeovilton | |
| ZD266 | WS Lynx HMA8 | DPA/GKN Westland, Yeovil | |
| ZD267 | WS Lynx HMA8 | DPA/GKN Westland, Yeovil | |
| ZD268 | WS Lynx HMA8 [670] | RN No 702 Sqn, Yeovilton | |
| ZD272 | WS Lynx AH7 [H] | AAC No 671 Sqn/2 Regt, Middle Wallop | |
| ZD273 | WS Lynx AH7 | AAC No 655 Sqn/5 Regt, Aldergrove | |
| ZD274 | WS Lynx AH7 | AAC No 664 Sqn/9 Regt, Dishforth | |
| ZD276 | WS Lynx AH7 [X] | DARA, RNAY Fleetlands | |
| ZD277 | WS Lynx AH7 | DARA, RNAY Fleetlands | |
| ZD278 | WS Lynx AH7 [A] | AAC No 671 Sqn/2 Regt, Middle Wallop | |
| ZD279 | WS Lynx AH7 | AAC No 655 Sqn/5 Regt, Aldergrove | |
| ZD280 | WS Lynx AH7 | AAC No 1 Regt, Gütersloh | |
| ZD281 | WS Lynx AH7 [K] | AAC No 671 Sqn/2 Regt, Middle Wallop | |
| ZD282 | WS Lynx AH7 [L] | RM No 847 Sqn, Yeovilton | |
| ZD283 | WS Lynx AH7 [P] | AAC No 671 Sqn/2 Regt, Middle Wallop | |
| ZD284 | WS Lynx AH7 [H] | AAC No 1 Regt, Gütersloh | |

| Notes | Serial | Type (other identity) [code] | Owner/operator, location or fate |
|---|---|---|---|
| | ZD285 | WS Lynx AH7 | DPA/AFD, DERA Boscombe Down |
| | ZD318 | BAe Harrier GR7 (fuselage) | DERA, Boscombe Down |
| | ZD319 | BAe Harrier GR7 | DPA/AFD, DERA Boscombe Down |
| | ZD320 | BAe Harrier GR7 | DPA/BAe, Dunsfold |
| | ZD321 | BAe Harrier GR7 [02] | RAF No 1 Sqn, Wittering |
| | ZD322 | BAe Harrier GR7 [03] | RAF No 4 Sqn, Cottesmore |
| | ZD323 | BAe Harrier GR7 [04] | RAF No 1 Sqn, Wittering |
| | ZD326 | BAe Harrier GR7 [07] | *Crashed 4 February 1999, Sonnsbeck, Germany* |
| | ZD327 | BAe Harrier GR7 [08] | RAF HOCU/No 20(R) Sqn, Wittering |
| | ZD328 | BAe Harrier GR7 [09] | RAF No 3 Sqn, Cottesmore |
| | ZD329 | BAe Harrier GR7 [10] | RAF No 3 Sqn, Cottesmore |
| | ZD330 | BAe Harrier GR7 [11] | RAF No 4 Sqn, Cottesmore |
| | ZD345 | BAe Harrier GR7 [12] | *Crashed 9 July 1999, Surfleet, Lincs* |
| | ZD346 | BAe Harrier GR7 [13] | RAF No 3 Sqn, Cottesmore |
| | ZD347 | BAe Harrier GR7 [14] | RAF HOCU/No 20(R) Sqn, Wittering |
| | ZD348 | BAe Harrier GR7 [15] | DARA, RAF St Athan |
| | ZD350 | BAe Harrier GR5 (9189M) <ff> | DARA, RAF St Athan, BDRT |
| | ZD351 | BAe Harrier GR7 (fuselage) | RAF, stored St Athan |
| | ZD352 | BAe Harrier GR7 [19] | RAF No 4 Sqn, Cottesmore |
| | ZD353 | BAe Harrier GR5 (fuselage) | BAE Systems Brough |
| | ZD354 | BAe Harrier GR7 [21] | RAF HOCU/No 20(R) Sqn, Wittering |
| | ZD375 | BAe Harrier GR7 [23] | RAF No 3 Sqn, Cottesmore |
| | ZD376 | BAe Harrier GR7 [24] | RAF No 1 Sqn, Wittering |
| | ZD378 | BAe Harrier GR7 [26] | RAF No 3 Sqn, Cottesmore |
| | ZD379 | BAe Harrier GR7 [27] | RAF No 3 Sqn, Cottesmore |
| | ZD380 | BAe Harrier GR7 [28] | RAF No 3 Sqn, Cottesmore |
| | ZD401 | BAe Harrier GR7 [30] | RAF No 4 Sqn, Cottesmore |
| | ZD402 | BAe Harrier GR7 [31] | RAF HOCU/No 20(R) Sqn, Wittering |
| | ZD403 | BAe Harrier GR7 [32] | RAF, stored St Athan |
| | ZD404 | BAe Harrier GR7 [33] | RAF HOCU/No 20(R) Sqn, Wittering |
| | ZD405 | BAe Harrier GR7 [34] | RAF AWC/SAOEU, DERA Boscombe Down |
| | ZD406 | BAe Harrier GR7 [35] | RAF HOCU/No 20(R) Sqn, Wittering |
| | ZD407 | BAe Harrier GR7 [36] | RAF HOCU/No 20(R) Sqn, Wittering |
| | ZD408 | BAe Harrier GR7 [37] | RAF No 4 Sqn, Cottesmore |
| | ZD409 | BAe Harrier GR7 [38] | RAF No 4 Sqn, Cottesmore |
| | ZD410 | BAe Harrier GR7 [39] | RAF No 3 Sqn, Cottesmore |
| | ZD411 | BAe Harrier GR7 [U] | RAF AWC/SAOEU, DERA Boscombe Down |
| | ZD412 | BAe Harrier GR5 (fuselage) | BAE SystemsBrough |
| | ZD431 | BAe Harrier GR7 [43] | RAF HOCU/No 20(R) Sqn, Wittering |
| | ZD433 | BAe Harrier GR7 [45] | RAF HOCU/No 20(R) Sqn, Wittering |
| | ZD435 | BAe Harrier GR7 [47] | RAF No 1 Sqn, Wittering |
| | ZD436 | BAe Harrier GR7 [48] | RAF No 3 Sqn, Cottesmore |
| | ZD437 | BAe Harrier GR7 [49] | RAF HOCU/No 20(R) Sqn, Wittering |
| | ZD438 | BAe Harrier GR7 [50] | RAF No 3 Sqn, Cottesmore |
| | ZD461 | BAe Harrier GR7 (fuselage) | RAF Wittering |
| | ZD462 | BAe Harrier GR7 [52] | DARA, RAF St Athan (damaged) |
| | ZD463 | BAe Harrier GR7 [53] | RAF HOCU/No 20(R) Sqn, Wittering |
| | ZD464 | BAe Harrier GR7 [54] | RAF No 1 Sqn, Wittering |
| | ZD465 | BAe Harrier GR7 [55] | RAF No 1 Sqn, Wittering |
| | ZD466 | BAe Harrier GR7 [56] | RAF HOCU/No 20(R) Sqn, Wittering |
| | ZD467 | BAe Harrier GR7 [57] | RAF No 1 Sqn, Wittering |
| | ZD468 | BAe Harrier GR7 [58] | RAF, stored St Athan |
| | ZD469 | BAe Harrier GR7 [59] | RAF No 4 Sqn, Cottesmore |
| | ZD470 | BAe Harrier GR7 [60] | RAF No 3 Sqn, Cottesmore |
| | ZD476 | WS61 Sea King HC4 [ZU] | RN No 848 Sqn, Yeovilton |
| | ZD477 | WS61 Sea King HC4 [H] | RN No 845 Sqn, Yeovilton |
| | ZD478 | WS61 Sea King HC4 [VG] | RN No 846 Sqn, Yeovilton |
| | ZD479 | WS61 Sea King HC4 [ZV] | RN No 848 Sqn, Yeovilton |
| | ZD480 | WS61 Sea King HC4 [E] | RN No 845 Sqn, Yeovilton |
| | ZD559 | WS Lynx AH5X | DPA/AFD, DERA Boscombe Down |
| | ZD560 | WS Lynx AH7 | DPA/AFD/ETPS, DERA Boscombe Down |
| | ZD565 | WS Lynx HMA8 [676] | RN No 702 Sqn, Yeovilton |
| | ZD566 | WS Lynx HMA8 [422/SU] | RN No 815 Sqn, *Sutherland* Flt, Yeovilton |
| | ZD574 | B-V Chinook HC2 (N37077) [EH] | RAF No 27 Sqn, Odiham |
| | ZD575 | B-V Chinook HC2 (N37078) [NZ] | RAF No 27 Sqn, Odiham |
| | ZD578 | BAe Sea Harrier FA2 [001/L] | RN No 801 Sqn, Yeovilton |
| | ZD579 | BAe Sea Harrier FA2 [003/L] | RN No 801 Sqn, Yeovilton |
| | ZD580 | BAe Sea Harrier FA2 | RN, stored St Athan |
| | ZD581 | BAe Sea Harrier FA2 | RN, stored St Athan |
| | ZD582 | BAe Sea Harrier FA2 [124] | RN No 800 Sqn, Yeovilton |

| Serial | Type (other identity) [code] | Owner/operator, location or fate | Notes |
|---|---|---|---|
| ZD607 | BAe Sea Harrier FA2 [125] | RN No 800 Sqn, Yeovilton | |
| ZD608 | BAe Sea Harrier FA2 | DARA, RAF St Athan | |
| ZD610 | BAe Sea Harrier FA2 [000] | RN No 801 Sqn, Yeovilton | |
| ZD611 | BAe Sea Harrier FA2 [710] | RN No 899 Sqn, Yeovilton | |
| ZD612 | BAe Sea Harrier FA2 [711] | RN No 899 Sqn, Yeovilton | |
| ZD613 | BAe Sea Harrier FA2 [002/L] | RN No 801 Sqn, Yeovilton | |
| ZD614 | BAe Sea Harrier FA2 [124] | RN AMG, Yeovilton | |
| ZD615 | BAe Sea Harrier FA2 [005/L] | RN No 801 Sqn, Yeovilton | |
| ZD620 | BAe 125 CC3 | RAF No 32(The Royal) Sqn, Northolt | |
| ZD621 | BAe 125 CC3 | RAF No 32(The Royal) Sqn, Northolt | |
| ZD625 | WS61 Sea King HC4 [VF] | RN No 846 Sqn, Yeovilton | |
| ZD626 | WS61 Sea King HC4 [ZZ] | RN No 848 Sqn, Yeovilton | |
| ZD627 | WS61 Sea King HC4 [VL] | RN No 846 Sqn, Yeovilton | |
| ZD630 | WS61 Sea King HAS6 [012/L] | RN No 820 Sqn, Culdrose | |
| ZD631 | WS61 Sea King HAS6 [66] (fuselage) | RN Predannack Fire School | |
| ZD633 | WS61 Sea King HAS6 [014/L] | RN No 820 Sqn, Culdrose | |
| ZD634 | WS61 Sea King HAS6 [503] | RN No 810 Sqn, Culdrose | |
| ZD636 | WS61 Sea King AEW2 [188/N] | RN No 849 Sqn, A Flt, Culdrose | |
| ZD637 | WS61 Sea King HAS6 [700/PW] | RN No 819 Sqn, Prestwick | |
| ZD657 | Schleicher ASW-19B Valiant TX1 [YW] | RAF No 662 VGS, Arbroath | |
| ZD658 | Schleicher ASW-19B Valiant TX1 [YX] | RAF No 631 VGS, Sealand | |
| ZD659 | Schleicher ASW-19B Valiant TX1 [YY] | RAF ACCGS, Syerston | |
| ZD660 | Schleicher ASW-19B Valiant TX1 [YZ] | RAF No 626 VGS, Predannack | |
| ZD667 | BAe Harrier GR3 (9201M) [3,2] | SFDO, RNAS Culdrose | |
| ZD668 | BAe Harrier GR3 [3E] | Phoenix Aviation, Bruntingthorpe | |
| ZD670 | BAe Harrier GR3 [3A] | The Trocadero, Leicester Square, London | |
| ZD703 | BAe 125 CC3 | RAF No 32(The Royal) Sqn, Northolt | |
| ZD704 | BAe 125 CC3 | RAF No 32(The Royal) Sqn, Northolt | |
| ZD707 | Panavia Tornado GR1 [BU] | RAF No 14 Sqn, Brüggen | |
| ZD708 | Panavia Tornado GR4 | DPA/BAE Systems, Warton | |
| ZD709 | Panavia Tornado GR4 [DG] | DPA/BAE Systems, Warton | |
| ZD710 | Panavia Tornado GR1 <ff> | Robertsbridge Aviation Society, Mayfield | |
| ZD711 | Panavia Tornado GR4 | RAF No 2 Sqn, Marham | |
| ZD712 | Panavia Tornado GR4 [BY] | DARA, RAF St Athan | |
| ZD713 | Panavia Tornado GR1 [TW] | RAF No 15(R) Sqn, Lossiemouth | |
| ZD714 | Panavia Tornado GR4 [DL] | RAF No 31 Sqn, Brüggen | |
| ZD715 | Panavia Tornado GR4 [JC] | DPA/BAe, Warton (conversion) | |
| ZD716 | Panavia Tornado GR1 [JM] | RAF, Brüggen | |
| ZD719 | Panavia Tornado GR1 [DE] | RAF No 14 Sqn, Brüggen | |
| ZD720 | Panavia Tornado GR4 | RAF, AMF Coningsby (damaged) | |
| ZD739 | Panavia Tornado GR1 [BI] | RAF No 14 Sqn, Brüggen | |
| ZD740 | Panavia Tornado GR4 [AF] | RAF No 9 Sqn, Brüggen | |
| ZD741 | Panavia Tornado GR4 [BZ] | RAF No 14 Sqn, Brüggen | |
| ZD742 | Panavia Tornado GR4 | DARA, RAF St Athan | |
| ZD743 | Panavia Tornado GR1 | RAF No 2 Sqn, Marham | |
| ZD744 | Panavia Tornado GR1 | RAF No 12 Sqn, Lossiemouth | |
| ZD745 | Panavia Tornado GR4 [DA] | RAF No 31 Sqn, Brüggen | |
| ZD746 | Panavia Tornado GR4 | DARA, RAF St Athan | |
| ZD747 | Panavia Tornado GR1 [AL] | RAF No 9 Sqn, Brüggen | |
| ZD748 | Panavia Tornado GR1 [AK] | RAF No 9 Sqn, Brüggen | |
| ZD749 | Panavia Tornado GR1 [BG] | RAF No 14 Sqn, Brüggen | |
| ZD788 | Panavia Tornado GR1 [BT] | RAF No 14 Sqn, Brüggen | |
| ZD789 | Panavia Tornado GR1 [AM] | RAF, stored St Athan (damaged) | |
| ZD790 | Panavia Tornado GR4 | DPA/BAe, Warton (conversion) | |
| ZD792 | Panavia Tornado GR4 [JG] | DARA, RAF St Athan | |
| ZD793 | Panavia Tornado GR1 [JH] | RAF No 17 Sqn, Brüggen | |
| ZD809 | Panavia Tornado GR1 [BA] | *Crashed 14 October 1999, near Belsay, Northumberland* | |
| ZD810 | Panavia Tornado GR1 [DB] | RAF No 31 Sqn, Brüggen | |
| ZD811 | Panavia Tornado GR4 [JJ] | DPA/BAE Systems, Warton (conversion) | |
| ZD812 | Panavia Tornado GR1 [BW] | RAF No 14 Sqn, Brüggen | |
| ZD842 | Panavia Tornado GR1 [DX] | RAF No 31 Sqn, Brüggen | |
| ZD843 | Panavia Tornado GR1 | RAF No 2 Sqn, Marham | |
| ZD844 | Panavia Tornado GR1 [DH] | RAF No 31 Sqn, Brüggen | |
| ZD847 | Panavia Tornado GR4 [AA] | RAF No 9 Sqn, Brüggen | |
| ZD848 | Panavia Tornado GR4 | DPA/BAE Systems, Warton(conversion) | |
| ZD849 | Panavia Tornado GR1 [CM] | RAF No 14 Sqn, Brüggen | |
| ZD850 | Panavia Tornado GR4 [DR] | DPA/BAE Systems, Warton (conversion) | |

| Notes | Serial | Type (other identity) [code] | Owner/operator, location or fate |
|---|---|---|---|
| | ZD851 | Panavia Tornado GR1 [BO] | RAF No 14 Sqn, Brüggen |
| | ZD890 | Panavia Tornado GR1 [AE] | RAF No 9 Sqn, Brüggen |
| | ZD892 | Panavia Tornado GR1 [BJ] | RAF No 617 Sqn, Lossiemouth |
| | ZD895 | Panavia Tornado GR1 [BF] | RAF No 12 Sqn, Lossiemouth |
| | ZD899 | Panavia Tornado F2 | DPA/BAE Systems, Warton (conversion) |
| | ZD900 | Panavia Tornado F2 (comp ZE343) | RAF, stored St Athan |
| | ZD901 | Panavia Tornado F2 (comp ZE154) | RAF, stored St Athan |
| | ZD902 | Panavia Tornado F2A(TIARA) | DPA/AFD, DERA Boscombe Down |
| | ZD903 | Panavia Tornado F2 (comp ZE728) | RAF, stored St Athan |
| | ZD904 | Panavia Tornado F2 (comp ZE759) | RAF, stored St Athan |
| | ZD905 | Panavia Tornado F2 (comp ZE258) | RAF, stored St Athan |
| | ZD906 | Panavia Tornado F2 (comp ZE294) | RAF, stored St Athan |
| | ZD932 | Panavia Tornado F2 (comp ZE255) | RAF, stored St Athan |
| | ZD933 | Panavia Tornado F2 (comp ZE729) | RAF, stored St Athan |
| | ZD934 | Panavia Tornado F2 (comp ZE786) <ff> | RAF, stored Shawbury |
| | ZD935 | Panavia Tornado F2 (comp ZE793) | RAF, stored St Athan |
| | ZD936 | Panavia Tornado F2 (comp ZE251) | RAF, stored St Athan |
| | ZD937 | Panavia Tornado F2 (comp ZE736) | DARA, RAF St Athan, BDRT |
| | ZD938 | Panavia Tornado F2 (comp ZE295) | RAF, stored St Athan |
| | ZD939 | Panavia Tornado F2 (comp ZE292) | RAF, stored St Athan |
| | ZD940 | Panavia Tornado F2 (comp ZE288) | RAF, stored St Athan |
| | ZD941 | Panavia Tornado F2 (comp ZE254) | RAF, stored St Athan |
| | ZD948 | Lockheed TriStar KC1 (G-BFCA) | RAF No 216 Sqn, Brize Norton |
| | ZD949 | Lockheed TriStar K1 (G-BFCB) | RAF No 216 Sqn, Brize Norton |
| | ZD950 | Lockheed TriStar KC1 (G-BFCC) | RAF No 216 Sqn, Brize Norton |
| | ZD951 | Lockheed TriStar K1 (G-BFCD) | RAF No 216 Sqn, Brize Norton |
| | ZD952 | Lockheed TriStar KC1 (G-BFCE) | RAF No 216 Sqn, Brize Norton |
| | ZD953 | Lockheed TriStar KC1 (G-BFCF) | RAF No 216 Sqn, Brize Norton |
| | ZD974 | Schempp-Hirth Kestrel TX1 [SY] | RAF ACCGS, Syerston |
| | ZD975 | Schempp-Hirth Kestrel TX1 [SZ] | RAF ACCGS, Syerston |
| | ZD980 | B-V Chinook HC2 (N37082) [EA] | RAF No 7 Sqn, Odiham |
| | ZD981 | B-V Chinook HC2 (N37083) [NV] | RAF No 27 Sqn, Odiham |
| | ZD982 | B-V Chinook HC2 (N37085) [EK] | RAF No 7 Sqn, Odiham |
| | ZD983 | B-V Chinook HC2 (N37086) [EI] | RAF No 18 Sqn, Odiham |
| | ZD984 | B-V Chinook HC2 (N37088) | DARA, RNAY Fleetlands |
| | ZD990 | BAe Harrier T8 [721/VL] | RN No 899 Sqn, Yeovilton |
| | ZD991 | BAe Harrier T8 (9228M) [722/VL] | DARA, RAF St Athan (on repair) |
| | ZD992 | BAe Harrier T8 [724/VL] | RN No 899 Sqn, Yeovilton |
| | ZD993 | BAe Harrier T8 [723/VL] | RN No 899 Sqn, Yeovilton |
| | ZD996 | Panavia Tornado GR1A [I] | RAF No 2 Sqn, Marham |
| | | | |
| | ZE116 | Panavia Tornado GR4A [X] | RAF No 13 Sqn, Marham |
| | ZE154 | Panavia Tornado F3 (comp ZD901) [AN] | RAF F3 OCU/No 56(R) Sqn, Coningsby |
| | ZE155 | Panavia Tornado F3 | DPA/BAe, Warton |
| | ZE156 | Panavia Tornado F3 [E] | RAF No 111 Sqn, Leuchars |
| | ZE157 | Panavia Tornado F3 [GK] | RAF No 43 Sqn, Leuchars |
| | ZE158 | Panavia Tornado F3 | RAF No 11 Sqn, Leeming |
| | ZE159 | Panavia Tornado F3 [R] | RAF No 111 Sqn, Leuchars |
| | ZE160 | Panavia Tornado F3 [DV] | RAF No 11 Sqn, Leeming |
| | ZE161 | Panavia Tornado F3 [DQ] | RAF No 11 Sqn, Leeming |
| | ZE162 | Panavia Tornado F3 [FK] | RAF No 25 Sqn, Leeming |
| | ZE163 | Panavia Tornado F3 (comp ZG753) | DARA, RAF St Athan |
| | ZE164 | Panavia Tornado F3 [DA] | RAF No 11 Sqn, Leeming |
| | ZE165 | Panavia Tornado F3 [Q] | RAF No 111 Sqn, Leuchars |
| | ZE168 | Panavia Tornado F3 [FN] | RAF No 25 Sqn, Leeming |
| | ZE199 | Panavia Tornado F3 [FL] | RAF No 25 Sqn, Leeming |
| | ZE200 | Panavia Tornado F3 [DB] | RAF No 11 Sqn, Leeming |
| | ZE201 | Panavia Tornado F3 [GA] | RAF No 43 Sqn, Leuchars |
| | ZE203 | Panavia Tornado F3 [FI] | RAF ASF, Leeming |
| | ZE204 | Panavia Tornado F3 [DD] | RAF No 11 Sqn, Leeming |
| | ZE206 | Panavia Tornado F3 | RAF No 25 Sqn, Leeming |
| | ZE207 | Panavia Tornado F3 [GC] | RAF No 43 Sqn, Leuchars |
| | ZE209 | Panavia Tornado F3 [CE] | RAF No 5 Sqn, Coningsby |
| | ZE210 | Panavia Tornado F3 (fuselage) | DARA, RAF St Athan (spares use) |
| | ZE250 | Panavia Tornado F3 [AM] | RAF F3 OCU/No 56(R) Sqn, Coningsby |
| | ZE251 | Panavia Tornado F3 (comp ZD936) [C] | RAF No 1435 Flt, Mount Pleasant, FI |
| | ZE253 | Panavia Tornado F3 [AC] | RAF F3 OCU/No 56(R) Sqn, Coningsby |
| | ZE254 | Panavia Tornado F3 (comp ZD941) | RAF No 5 Sqn, Coningsby |
| | ZE255 | Panavia Tornado F3 (comp ZD932) [AY] | RAF F3 OCU/No 56(R) Sqn, Coningsby |

| Serial | Type (other identity) [code] | Owner/operator, location or fate | Notes |
|---|---|---|---|
| ZE256 | Panavia Tornado F3 [AO] | RAF F3 OCU/No 56(R) Sqn, Coningsby | |
| ZE257 | Panavia Tornado F3 | RAF AWC/F3 OEU, Coningsby | |
| ZE258 | Panavia Tornado F3 (comp ZD905) [AQ] | RAF F3 OCU/No 56(R) Sqn, Coningsby | |
| ZE287 | Panavia Tornado F3 [AF] | RAF F3 OCU/No 56(R) Sqn, Coningsby | |
| ZE288 | Panavia Tornado F3 (comp ZD940) [AT] | RAF F3 OCU/No 56(R) Sqn, Coningsby | |
| ZE289 | Panavia Tornado F3 [C] | RAF F3 OCU/No 56(R) Sqn, Coningsby | |
| ZE290 | Panavia Tornado F3 [AG] | RAF F3 OCU/No 56(R) Sqn, Coningsby | |
| ZE291 | Panavia Tornado F3 [GQ] | RAF No 43 Sqn, Leuchars | |
| ZE292 | Panavia Tornado F3 (comp ZD939) [AZ] | RAF F3 OCU/No 56(R) Sqn, Coningsby | |
| ZE293 | Panavia Tornado F3 [HT] | DPA/AFD, DERA Boscombe Down | |
| ZE294 | Panavia Tornado F3 (comp ZD906) [AS] | RAF F3 OCU/No 56(R) Sqn, Coningsby | |
| ZE295 | Panavia Tornado F3 (comp ZD938) [AV] | RAF F3 OCU/No 56(R) Sqn, Coningsby | |
| ZE296 | Panavia Tornado F3 [AD] | RAF No 5 Sqn, Coningsby | |
| ZE338 | Panavia Tornado F3 [G] | RAF No 111 Sqn, Leuchars | |
| ZE339 | Panavia Tornado F3 [CK] | RAF No 5 Sqn, Coningsby | |
| ZE340 | Panavia Tornado F3 [AE] | RAF F3 OCU/No 56(R) Sqn, Coningsby | |
| ZE341 | Panavia Tornado F3 [J] | RAF No 111 Sqn, Leuchars | |
| ZE342 | Panavia Tornado F3 [W] | RAF No 111 Sqn, Leuchars | |
| ZE343 | Panavia Tornado F3 (comp ZD900) [AA] | RAF F3 OCU/No 56(R) Sqn, Coningsby | |
| ZE353 | McD F-4J(UK) Phantom (9083M) [E] | MoD FSCTE, Manston | |
| ZE354 | McD F-4J(UK) Phantom (9084M) [R] | RAF Coningsby Fire Section | |
| ZE356 | McD F-4J(UK) Phantom (9060M) [Q] | RAF Waddington, BDRT | |
| ZE360 | McD F-4J(UK) Phantom (9059M) [O] | MoD FSCTE, Manston | |
| ZE361 | McD F-4J(UK) Phantom (9057M) [P] | RAF Honington Fire Section | |
| ZE368 | WS61 Sea King HAR3 | RAF No 203(R) Sqn, St Mawgan | |
| ZE369 | WS61 Sea King HAR3 | RAF HMF, St Mawgan | |
| ZE370 | WS61 Sea King HAR3 | RAF No 202 Sqn, A Flt, Boulmer | |
| ZE375 | WS Lynx AH9 [2,9] | AAC No 659 Sqn/4 Regt, Wattisham | |
| ZE376 | WS Lynx AH9 | AAC No 659 Sqn/4 Regt, Wattisham | |
| ZE378 | WS Lynx AH7 | AAC No 654 Sqn/4 Regt, Wattisham | |
| ZE379 | WS Lynx AH7 | AAC No 657 Sqn/9 Regt, Dishforth | |
| ZE380 | WS Lynx AH9 [3] | DARA, RNAY Fleetlands | |
| ZE381 | WS Lynx AH7 | AAC No 655 Sqn/5 Regt, Aldergrove | |
| ZE382 | WS Lynx AH9 | DARA, RNAY Fleetlands | |
| ZE395 | BAe 125 CC3 | RAF No 32(The Royal) Sqn, Northolt | |
| ZE396 | BAe 125 CC3 | RAF No 32(The Royal) Sqn, Northolt | |
| ZE410 | Agusta A109A (AE-334) | AAC No 8 Flt, Netheravon | |
| ZE411 | Agusta A109A (AE-331) | AAC No 8 Flt, Netheravon | |
| ZE412 | Agusta A109A | AAC No 8 Flt, Netheravon | |
| ZE413 | Agusta A109A | AAC No 8 Flt, Netheravon | |
| ZE418 | WS61 Sea King AEW2 [182/CU] | RN No 849 Sqn, HQ Flt, Culdrose | |
| ZE420 | WS61 Sea King AEW2 [183/L] | RN No 849 Sqn, B Flt, Culdrose | |
| ZE422 | WS61 Sea King HAS6 [270/N] | RN AMG, Culdrose | |
| ZE425 | WS61 Sea King HC4 [J] | RN No 845 Sqn, Yeovilton | |
| ZE426 | WS61 Sea King HC4 [ZW] | RN No 848 Sqn, Yeovilton | |
| ZE427 | WS61 Sea King HC4 [B] | RN No 845 Sqn, Yeovilton | |
| ZE428 | WS61 Sea King HC4 [VK] | RN No 846 Sqn, Yeovilton | |
| ZE432 | BAC 1-11/479FU (DQ-FBV) | DPA/AFD/ETPS, DERA Boscombe Down | |
| ZE433 | BAC 1-11/479FU (DQ-FBQ) | DPA/GEC-Ferranti, Edinburgh | |
| ZE438 | BAe Jetstream T3 [76] | RN FONA/Heron Flight, Yeovilton | |
| ZE439 | BAe Jetstream T3 [77] | RN FONA/Heron Flight, Yeovilton | |
| ZE440 | BAe Jetstream T3 [78] | RN FONA/Heron Flight, Yeovilton | |
| ZE441 | BAe Jetstream T3 [79] | RN, stored Shawbury | |
| ZE449 | SA330L Puma HC1 (9017M/PA-12) | RAF Odiham | |
| ZE477 | WS Lynx 3 | The Helicopter Museum, Weston-super-Mare | |
| ZE495 | Grob G103 Viking T1 (BGA3000) [VA] | RAF No 622 VGS, Upavon | |
| ZE496 | Grob G103 Viking T1 (BGA3001) [VB] | RAF No 634 VGS, St Athan | |
| ZE498 | Grob G103 Viking T1 (BGA3003) [VC] | RAF No 614 VGS, Wethersfield | |

| Notes | Serial | Type (other identity) [code] | Owner/operator, location or fate |
|---|---|---|---|
| | ZE499 | Grob G103 Viking T1 (BGA3004) [VD] | RAF No 615 VGS, Kenley |
| | ZE501 | Grob G103 Viking T1 (BGA3006) [VE] | RAF No 636 VGS, Aberporth |
| | ZE502 | Grob G103 Viking T1 (BGA3007) [VF] | RAF No 614 VGS, Wethersfield |
| | ZE503 | Grob G103 Viking T1 (BGA3008) [VG] | RAF CGMF, Syerston |
| | ZE504 | Grob G103 Viking T1 (BGA3009) [VH] | RAF No 634 VGS, St Athan |
| | ZE520 | Grob G103 Viking T1 (BGA3010) [VJ] | RAF No 636 VGS, Aberporth |
| | ZE521 | Grob G103 Viking T1 (BGA3011) [VK] | RAF No 626 VGS, Predannack |
| | ZE522 | Grob G103 Viking T1 (BGA3012) [VL] | RAF No 634 VGS, St Athan |
| | ZE524 | Grob G103 Viking T1 (BGA3014) [VM] | RAF No 645 VGS, Catterick |
| | ZE526 | Grob G103 Viking T1 (BGA3016) [VN] | RAF No 636 VGS, Aberporth |
| | ZE527 | Grob G103 Viking T1 (BGA3017) [VP] | RAF CGMF, Syerston |
| | ZE528 | Grob G103 Viking T1 (BGA3018) [VQ] | RAF CGMF, Syerston |
| | ZE529 | Grob G103 Viking T1 (BGA3019) (comp ZE655) [VR] | RAF No 614 VGS, Wethersfield |
| | ZE530 | Grob G103 Viking T1 (BGA3020) [VS] | RAF No 611 VGS, Watton |
| | ZE531 | Grob G103 Viking T1 (BGA3021) [VT] | RAF No 615 VGS, Kenley |
| | ZE532 | Grob G103 Viking T1 (BGA3022) [VU] | RAF No 614 VGS, Wethersfield |
| | ZE533 | Grob G103 Viking T1 (BGA3023) [VV] | RAF No 622 VGS, Upavon |
| | ZE534 | Grob G103 Viking T1 (BGA3024) [VW] | RAF No 614 VGS, Wethersfield |
| | ZE550 | Grob G103 Viking T1 (BGA3025) [VX] | RAF ACCGS, Syerston |
| | ZE551 | Grob G103 Viking T1 (BGA3026) [VY] | RAF CGMF, Syerston |
| | ZE552 | Grob G103 Viking T1 (BGA3027) [VZ] | RAF No 661 VGS, Kirknewton |
| | ZE553 | Grob G103 Viking T1 (BGA3028) [WA] | RAF No 611 VGS, Watton |
| | ZE554 | Grob G103 Viking T1 (BGA3029) [WB] | RAF No 611 VGS, Watton |
| | ZE555 | Grob G103 Viking T1 (BGA3030) [WC] | RAF No 645 VGS, Catterick |
| | ZE556 | Grob G103 Viking T1 (BGA3031) [WD] | RAF No 662 VGS, Arbroath |
| | ZE557 | Grob G103 Viking T1 (BGA3032) [WE] | RAF No 622 VGS, Upavon |
| | ZE558 | Grob G103 Viking T1 (BGA3033) [WF] | RAF No 615 VGS, Kenley |
| | ZE559 | Grob G103 Viking T1 (BGA3034) [WG] | RAF No 631 VGS, Sealand |
| | ZE560 | Grob G103 Viking T1 (BGA3035) [WH] | RAF No 661 VGS, Kirknewton |
| | ZE561 | Grob G103 Viking T1 (BGA3036) [WJ] | RAF No 621 VGS, Hullavington |
| | ZE562 | Grob G103 Viking T1 (BGA3037) [WK] | RAF No 626 VGS, Predannack |
| | ZE563 | Grob G103 Viking T1 (BGA3038) [WL] | RAF No 631 VGS, Sealand |
| | ZE564 | Grob G103 Viking T1 (BGA3039) [WN] | RAF No 625 VGS, Hullavington |
| | ZE584 | Grob G103 Viking T1 (BGA3040) [WP] | RAF No 631 VGS, Sealand |
| | ZE585 | Grob G103 Viking T1 (BGA3041) [WQ] | RAF ACCGS, Syerston |
| | ZE586 | Grob G103 Viking T1 (BGA3042) [WR] | RAF No 631 VGS, Sealand |

| Serial | Type (other identity) [code] | Owner/operator, location or fate | Notes |
|---|---|---|---|
| ZE587 | Grob G103 Viking T1 (BGA3043) [WS] | RAF No 611 VGS, Watton | |
| ZE590 | Grob G103 Viking T1 (BGA3046) [WT] | RAF No 661 VGS, Kirknewton | |
| ZE591 | Grob G103 Viking T1 (BGA3047) [WU] | RAF No 631 VGS, Sealand | |
| ZE592 | Grob G103 Viking T1 (BGA3048) [WV] | RAF CGMF, Syerston (damaged) | |
| ZE593 | Grob G103 Viking T1 (BGA3049) [WW] | RAF No 621 VGS, Hullavington | |
| ZE594 | Grob G103 Viking T1 (BGA3050) [WX] | RAF No 615 VGS, Kenley | |
| ZE595 | Grob G103 Viking T1 (BGA3051) [WY] | RAF No 622 VGS, Upavon | |
| ZE600 | Grob G103 Viking T1 (BGA3052) [WZ] | RAF No 622 VGS, Upavon | |
| ZE601 | Grob G103 Viking T1 (BGA3053) [XA] | RAF No 611 VGS, Watton | |
| ZE602 | Grob G103 Viking T1 (BGA3054) [XB] | RAF No 645 VGS, Catterick | |
| ZE603 | Grob G103 Viking T1 (BGA3055) [XC] | RAF CGMF, Syerston | |
| ZE604 | Grob G103 Viking T1 (BGA3056) [XD] | RAF No 615 VGS, Kenley | |
| ZE605 | Grob G103 Viking T1 (BGA3057) [XE] | RAF CGMF, Syerston | |
| ZE606 | Grob G103 Viking T1 (BGA3058) [XF] | RAF No 625 VGS, Hullavington | |
| ZE607 | Grob G103 Viking T1 (BGA3059) [XG] | RAF No 625 VGS, Hullavington | |
| ZE608 | Grob G103 Viking T1 (BGA3060) [XH] | RAF No 621 VGS, Hullavington | |
| ZE609 | Grob G103 Viking T1 (BGA3061) [XJ] | RAF ACCGS, Syerston | |
| ZE610 | Grob G103 Viking T1 (BGA3062) [XK] | RAF No 626 VGS, Predannack | |
| ZE611 | Grob G103 Viking T1 (BGA3063) [XL] | RAF CGMF, Syerston (damaged) | |
| ZE613 | Grob G103 Viking T1 (BGA3065) [XM] | RAF No 625 VGS, Hullavington | |
| ZE614 | Grob G103 Viking T1 (BGA3066) [XN] | RAF No 631 VGS, Sealand | |
| ZE625 | Grob G103 Viking T1 (BGA3067) [XP] | RAF No 625 VGS, Hullavington | |
| ZE626 | Grob G103 Viking T1 (BGA3068) [XQ] | RAF No 626 VGS, Predannack | |
| ZE627 | Grob G103 Viking T1 (BGA3069) [XR] | RAF No 634 VGS, St Athan | |
| ZE628 | Grob G103 Viking T1 (BGA3070) [XS] | RAF ACCGS, Syerston | |
| ZE629 | Grob G103 Viking T1 (BGA3071) [XT] | RAF No 662 VGS, Arbroath | |
| ZE630 | Grob G103 Viking T1 (BGA3072) [XU] | RAF No 662 VGS, Arbroath | |
| ZE631 | Grob G103 Viking T1 (BGA3073) [XV] | RAF No 662 VGS, Arbroath | |
| ZE632 | Grob G103 Viking T1 (BGA3074) [XW] | RAF CGMF, Syerston (damaged) | |
| ZE633 | Grob G103 Viking T1 (BGA3075) [XX] | RAF No 614 VGS, Wethersfield | |
| ZE635 | Grob G103 Viking T1 (BGA3077) [XY] | RAF No 625 VGS, Hullavington | |
| ZE636 | Grob G103 Viking T1 (BGA3078) [XZ] | RAF CGMF, Syerston (damaged) | |
| ZE637 | Grob G103 Viking T1 (BGA3079) [YA] | RAF No 622 VGS, Upavon | |
| ZE650 | Grob G103 Viking T1 (BGA3080) [YB] | RAF ACCGS, Syerston | |
| ZE651 | Grob G103 Viking T1 (BGA3081) [YC] | RAF No 661 VGS, Kirknewton | |
| ZE652 | Grob G103 Viking T1 (BGA3082) [YD] | RAF CGMF, Syerston | |

| Notes | Serial | Type (other identity) [code] | Owner/operator, location or fate |
|---|---|---|---|
| | ZE653 | Grob G103 Viking T1 (BGA3083) [YE] | RAF No 661 VGS, Kirknewton |
| | ZE656 | Grob G103 Viking T1 (BGA3086) [YH] | RAF No 622 VGS, Upavon |
| | ZE657 | Grob G103 Viking T1 (BGA3087) [YJ] | RAF No 615 VGS, Kenley |
| | ZE658 | Grob G103 Viking T1 (BGA3088) [YK] | RAF No 621 VGS, Hullavington |
| | ZE659 | Grob G103 Viking T1 (BGA3089) [YL] | RAF No 636 VGS, Aberporth |
| | ZE677 | Grob G103 Viking T1 (BGA3090) | RAF, stored St Athan |
| | ZE678 | Grob G103 Viking T1 (BGA3091) [YN] | RAF No 621 VGS, Hullavington |
| | ZE679 | Grob G103 Viking T1 (BGA3092) [YP] | RAF No 622 VGS, Upavon |
| | ZE680 | Grob G103 Viking T1 (BGA3093) [YQ] | RAF CGMF, Syerston |
| | ZE681 | Grob G103 Viking T1 (BGA3094) [YR] | RAF No 615 VGS, Kenley |
| | ZE682 | Grob G103 Viking T1 (BGA3095) [YS] | RAF No 662 VGS, Arbroath |
| | ZE683 | Grob G103 Viking T1 (BGA3096) [YT] | RAF No 661 VGS, Kirknewton |
| | ZE684 | Grob G103 Viking T1 (BGA3097) [YU] | RAF No 621 VGS, Hullavington |
| | ZE685 | Grob G103 Viking T1 (BGA3098) [YV] | RAF CGMF, Syerston |
| | ZE686 | Grob G103 Viking T1 (BGA3099) | DPA/Slingsby Kirkbymoorside |
| | ZE690 | BAe Sea Harrier FA2 [123] | RN AMG, Yeovilton |
| | ZE691 | BAe Sea Harrier FA2 [710/VL] | RN, stored St Athan (damaged) |
| | ZE692 | BAe Sea Harrier FA2 [124] | DARA, RAF St Athan |
| | ZE693 | BAe Sea Harrier FA2 [127] | RN No 800 Sqn, Yeovilton |
| | ZE694 | BAe Sea Harrier FA2 [006/L] | RN No 801 Sqn, Yeovilton |
| | ZE695 | BAe Sea Harrier FA2 | RN, St Athan |
| | ZE696 | BAe Sea Harrier FA2 [715] | RN No 899 Sqn, Yeovilton |
| | ZE697 | BAe Sea Harrier FA2 [122] | RN No 800 Sqn, Yeovilton |
| | ZE698 | BAe Sea Harrier FA2 [127] | DARA, RAF St Athan |
| | ZE700 | BAe 146 CC2 (G-6-021) | RAF No 32(The Royal) Sqn, Northolt |
| | ZE701 | BAe 146 CC2 (G-6-029) | RAF No 32(The Royal) Sqn, Northolt |
| | ZE702 | BAe 146 CC2 (G-6-124) | RAF No 32(The Royal) Sqn, Northolt |
| | ZE704 | Lockheed TriStar C2 (N508PA) | RAF No 216 Sqn, Brize Norton |
| | ZE705 | Lockheed TriStar C2 (N509PA) | RAF No 216 Sqn, Brize Norton |
| | ZE706 | Lockheed TriStar C2A (N503PA) | RAF No 216 Sqn, Brize Norton |
| | ZE728 | Panavia Tornado F3 (comp ZD903) [AH] | RAF F3 OCU/No 56(R) Sqn, Coningsby |
| | ZE729 | Panavia Tornado F3 (comp ZD933) [CF] | RAF No 5 Sqn, Coningsby |
| | ZE731 | Panavia Tornado F3 [GF] | RAF No 43 Sqn, Leuchars |
| | ZE734 | Panavia Tornado F3 [GB] | RAF No 43 Sqn, Leuchars |
| | ZE735 | Panavia Tornado F3 [AL] | RAF F3 OCU/No 56(R) Sqn, Coningsby |
| | ZE736 | Panavia Tornado F3 (comp ZD937) [AX] | RAF F3 OCU/No 56(R) Sqn, Coningsby |
| | ZE737 | Panavia Tornado F3 [FF] | RAF No 25 Sqn, Leeming |
| | ZE755 | Panavia Tornado F3 [GJ] | RAF No 43 Sqn, Leuchars |
| | ZE756 | Panavia Tornado F3 | RAF AWC/F3 OEU, Coningsby |
| | ZE757 | Panavia Tornado F3 [AR] | RAF F3 OCU/No 56(R) Sqn, Coningsby |
| | ZE758 | Panavia Tornado F3 [GO] | RAF No 43 Sqn, Leuchars |
| | ZE763 | Panavia Tornado F3 [DG] | RAF No 11 Sqn, Leeming |
| | ZE764 | Panavia Tornado F3 [DH] | RAF No 11 Sqn, Leeming |
| | ZE785 | Panavia Tornado F3 [C] | RAF No 111 Sqn, Leuchars |
| | ZE786 | Panavia Tornado F3 (comp ZD934) [AN] | RAF F3 OCU/No 56(R) Sqn, Coningsby |
| | ZE788 | Panavia Tornado F3 | RAF No 5 Sqn,Coningsby |
| | ZE790 | Panavia Tornado F3 [GD] | RAF No 43 Sqn, Leuchars |
| | ZE791 | Panavia Tornado F3 [N] | RAF No 111 Sqn, Leuchars |
| | ZE793 | Panavia Tornado F3 (comp ZD935) [AI] | RAF F3 OCU/No 56(R) Sqn, Coningsby |
| | ZE794 | Panavia Tornado F3 [A] | RAF No 111 Sqn, Leuchars |
| | ZE808 | Panavia Tornado F3 [FA] | RAF No 25 Sqn, Leeming |
| | ZE810 | Panavia Tornado F3 [P] | RAF No 111 Sqn, Leuchars |
| | ZE812 | Panavia Tornado F3 [CW] | RAF No 5 Sqn, Coningsby |
| | ZE830 | Panavia Tornado F3 | *Crashed 17 November 1999, North Sea* |

| Serial | Type (other identity) [code] | Owner/operator, location or fate | Notes |
|---|---|---|---|
| ZE831 | Panavia Tornado F3 [GG] | RAF No 43 Sqn, Leuchars | |
| ZE834 | Panavia Tornado F3 [CX] | RAF No 5 Sqn, Coningsby | |
| ZE838 | Panavia Tornado F3 [GH] | RAF No 43 Sqn, Leuchars | |
| ZE839 | Panavia Tornado F3 [B] | RAF No 111 Sqn, Leuchars | |
| ZE887 | Panavia Tornado F3 [DJ] | RAF No 11 Sqn, Leeming | |
| ZE888 | Panavia Tornado F3 [T] | RAF No 111 Sqn, Leuchars | |
| ZE889 | Panavia Tornado F3 [H] | RAF No 1435 Flt, Mount Pleasant, FI | |
| ZE907 | Panavia Tornado F3 [GL] | RAF No 43 Sqn, Leuchars | |
| ZE908 | Panavia Tornado F3 [HV] | RAF No 25 Sqn, Leeming | |
| ZE934 | Panavia Tornado F3 [S] | RAF No 111 Sqn, Leuchars | |
| ZE936 | Panavia Tornado F3 [DL] | RAF No 11 Sqn, Leeming | |
| ZE941 | Panavia Tornado F3 [FE] | RAF No 25 Sqn, Leeming | |
| ZE942 | Panavia Tornado F3 | RAF AWC/F3 OEU, Coningsby | |
| ZE961 | Panavia Tornado F3 [FD] | RAF No 25 Sqn, Leeming | |
| ZE962 | Panavia Tornado F3 [FJ] | RAF No 25 Sqn, Leeming | |
| ZE963 | Panavia Tornado F3 [GE] | RAF No 43 Sqn, Leuchars | |
| ZE964 | Panavia Tornado F3 [GN] | RAF No 43 Sqn, Leuchars | |
| ZE965 | Panavia Tornado F3 [GM] | RAF No 43 Sqn, Leuchars | |
| ZE966 | Panavia Tornado F3 [DX] | RAF No 11 Sqn, Leeming | |
| ZE967 | Panavia Tornado F3 | RAF No 25 Sqn, Leeming | |
| ZE968 | Panavia Tornado F3 [DM] | RAF No 11 Sqn, Leeming | |
| ZE969 | Panavia Tornado F3 | RAF No 5 Sqn, Coningsby | |
| ZE982 | Panavia Tornado F3 | RAF AWC/F3 OEU, Coningsby | |
| ZE983 | Panavia Tornado F3 [DN] | RAF No 11 Sqn, Leeming | |
| | | | |
| ZF115 | WS61 Sea King HC4 | DPA/AFD, DERA Boscombe Down | |
| ZF116 | WS61 Sea King HC4 [P] | RN No 845 Sqn, Yeovilton | |
| ZF117 | WS61 Sea King HC4 [VQ] | RN No 846 Sqn, Yeovilton | |
| ZF118 | WS61 Sea King HC4 [VP] | RN No 846 Sqn, Yeovilton | |
| ZF119 | WS61 Sea King HC4 [VH] | RN No 846 Sqn, Yeovilton | |
| ZF120 | WS61 Sea King HC4 [K] | RN No 845 Sqn, Yeovilton | |
| ZF121 | WS61 Sea King HC4 [VJ] | DARA, RNAY Fleetlands | |
| ZF122 | WS61 Sea King HC4 [VU] | RN No 846 Sqn, Yeovilton | |
| ZF123 | WS61 Sea King HC4 [ZQ] | RN No 848 Sqn, Yeovilton | |
| ZF124 | WS61 Sea King HC4 [L] | RN No 845 Sqn, Yeovilton | |
| ZF130 | BAe 125-600B (G-BLUW) | DPA, stored BAE SystemsDunsfold | |
| ZF135 | Shorts Tucano T1 | RAF No 1 FTS, Linton-on-Ouse | |
| ZF136 | Shorts Tucano T1 | RAF No 1 FTS, Linton-on-Ouse | |
| ZF137 | Shorts Tucano T1 | RAF No 1 FTS, Linton-on-Ouse | |
| ZF138 | Shorts Tucano T1 | RAF No 1 FTS, Linton-on-Ouse | |
| ZF139 | Shorts Tucano T1 | RAF, stored Shawbury | |
| ZF140 | Shorts Tucano T1 | RAF No 1 FTS, Linton-on-Ouse | |
| ZF141 | Shorts Tucano T1 | RAF, stored Shawbury | |
| ZF142 | Shorts Tucano T1 | RAF No 1 FTS, Linton-on-Ouse | |
| ZF143 | Shorts Tucano T1 | RAF No 1 FTS, Linton-on-Ouse | |
| ZF144 | Shorts Tucano T1 | RAF No 1 FTS, Linton-on-Ouse | |
| ZF145 | Shorts Tucano T1 | RAF No 1 FTS, Linton-on-Ouse | |
| ZF160 | Shorts Tucano T1 | RAF No 1 FTS, Linton-on-Ouse | |
| ZF161 | Shorts Tucano T1 | RAF No 1 FTS, Linton-on-Ouse | |
| ZF162 | Shorts Tucano T1 | RAF No 1 FTS, Linton-on-Ouse | |
| ZF163 | Shorts Tucano T1 | RAF No 1 FTS, Linton-on-Ouse | |
| ZF164 | Shorts Tucano T1 | RAF, stored Shawbury | |
| ZF165 | Shorts Tucano T1 | RAF, stored Shawbury | |
| ZF166 | Shorts Tucano T1 | RAF No 1 FTS, Linton-on-Ouse | |
| ZF167 | Shorts Tucano T1 | RAF, stored Shawbury | |
| ZF168 | Shorts Tucano T1 | RAF No 1 FTS, Linton-on-Ouse | |
| ZF169 | Shorts Tucano T1 | RAF No 1 FTS, Linton-on-Ouse | |
| ZF170 | Shorts Tucano T1 | RAF No 1 FTS, Linton-on-Ouse | |
| ZF171 | Shorts Tucano T1 | RAF, stored Shawbury | |
| ZF172 | Shorts Tucano T1 | RAF, stored Shawbury | |
| ZF200 | Shorts Tucano T1 | RAF, stored Shawbury | |
| ZF201 | Shorts Tucano T1 | RAF, stored Shawbury | |
| ZF202 | Shorts Tucano T1 | RAF, stored Shawbury | |
| ZF203 | Shorts Tucano T1 | RAF No 1 FTS, Linton-on-Ouse | |
| ZF204 | Shorts Tucano T1 | RAF, stored Shawbury | |
| ZF205 | Shorts Tucano T1 | RAF, stored Shawbury | |
| ZF206 | Shorts Tucano T1 | RAF No 1 FTS, Linton-on-Ouse | |
| ZF207 | Shorts Tucano T1 | RAF No 1 FTS, Linton-on-Ouse | |
| ZF208 | Shorts Tucano T1 | RAF, stored Shawbury | |
| ZF209 | Shorts Tucano T1 | RAF, stored Shawbury | |
| ZF210 | Shorts Tucano T1 | RAF No 1 FTS, Linton-on-Ouse | |
| ZF211 | Shorts Tucano T1 | RAF No 1 FTS, Linton-on-Ouse | |
| ZF212 | Shorts Tucano T1 | RAF No 1 FTS, Linton-on-Ouse | |

| Notes | Serial | Type (other identity) [code] | Owner/operator, location or fate |
|---|---|---|---|
| | ZF238 | Shorts Tucano T1 | RAF No 1 FTS, Linton-on-Ouse |
| | ZF239 | Shorts Tucano T1 | RAF, stored Shawbury |
| | ZF240 | Shorts Tucano T1 | RAF, stored Shawbury |
| | ZF241 | Shorts Tucano T1 | RAF No 1 FTS, Linton-on-Ouse |
| | ZF242 | Shorts Tucano T1 | RAF No 1 FTS, Linton-on-Ouse |
| | ZF243 | Shorts Tucano T1 | RAF, stored Shawbury |
| | ZF244 | Shorts Tucano T1 | RAF, stored Shawbury |
| | ZF245 | Shorts Tucano T1 | RAF, stored Shawbury |
| | ZF263 | Shorts Tucano T1 | RAF No 1 FTS, Linton-on-Ouse |
| | ZF264 | Shorts Tucano T1 | RAF, stored Shawbury |
| | ZF265 | Shorts Tucano T1 | RAF, stored Shawbury |
| | ZF266 | Shorts Tucano T1 | RAF No 1 FTS, Linton-on-Ouse |
| | ZF267 | Shorts Tucano T1 | RAF, stored Shawbury |
| | ZF268 | Shorts Tucano T1 | RAF No 1 FTS, Linton-on-Ouse |
| | ZF269 | Shorts Tucano T1 | RAF, stored Shawbury |
| | ZF284 | Shorts Tucano T1 | RAF, stored Shawbury |
| | ZF285 | Shorts Tucano T1 | RAF, stored Shawbury |
| | ZF286 | Shorts Tucano T1 | RAF No 1 FTS, Linton-on-Ouse |
| | ZF287 | Shorts Tucano T1 | RAF, stored Shawbury |
| | ZF288 | Shorts Tucano T1 | RAF No 1 FTS, Linton-on-Ouse |
| | ZF289 | Shorts Tucano T1 | RAF, stored Shawbury |
| | ZF290 | Shorts Tucano T1 | RAF No 1 FTS, Linton-on-Ouse |
| | ZF291 | Shorts Tucano T1 | RAF, stored Shawbury |
| | ZF292 | Shorts Tucano T1 | RAF No 1 FTS, Linton-on-Ouse |
| | ZF293 | Shorts Tucano T1 | RAF No 1 FTS, Linton-on-Ouse |
| | ZF294 | Shorts Tucano T1 | RAF No 1 FTS, Linton-on-Ouse |
| | ZF295 | Shorts Tucano T1 | RAF No 1 FTS, Linton-on-Ouse |
| | ZF315 | Shorts Tucano T1 | RAF No 1 FTS, Linton-on-Ouse |
| | ZF317 | Shorts Tucano T1 | RAF, stored Shawbury |
| | ZF318 | Shorts Tucano T1 | RAF No 1 FTS, Linton-on-Ouse |
| | ZF319 | Shorts Tucano T1 | RAF No 1 FTS, Linton-on-Ouse |
| | ZF320 | Shorts Tucano T1 | RAF No 1 FTS, Linton-on-Ouse |
| | ZF338 | Shorts Tucano T1 | RAF, stored Shawbury |
| | ZF339 | Shorts Tucano T1 | RAF No 1 FTS, Linton-on-Ouse |
| | ZF340 | Shorts Tucano T1 | RAF, stored Shawbury |
| | ZF341 | Shorts Tucano T1 | RAF No 1 FTS, Linton-on-Ouse |
| | ZF342 | Shorts Tucano T1 | RAF No 1 FTS, Linton-on-Ouse |
| | ZF343 | Shorts Tucano T1 | RAF, stored Shawbury |
| | ZF344 | Shorts Tucano T1 | RAF, stored Shawbury |
| | ZF345 | Shorts Tucano T1 | RAF No 1 FTS, Linton-on-Ouse |
| | ZF346 | Shorts Tucano T1 | RAF No 1 FTS, Linton-on-Ouse |
| | ZF347 | Shorts Tucano T1 | RAF No 1 FTS, Linton-on-Ouse |
| | ZF348 | Shorts Tucano T1 | RAF No 1 FTS, Linton-on-Ouse |
| | ZF349 | Shorts Tucano T1 | RAF, stored Shawbury |
| | ZF350 | Shorts Tucano T1 | RAF No 1 FTS, Linton-on-Ouse |
| | ZF372 | Shorts Tucano T1 | RAF No 1 FTS, Linton-on-Ouse |
| | ZF373 | Shorts Tucano T1 | RAF, stored Shawbury |
| | ZF374 | Shorts Tucano T1 | RAF, stored Shawbury |
| | ZF375 | Shorts Tucano T1 | RAF No 1 FTS, Linton-on-Ouse |
| | ZF376 | Shorts Tucano T1 | RAF No 1 FTS, Linton-on-Ouse |
| | ZF377 | Shorts Tucano T1 | RAF, stored Shawbury |
| | ZF378 | Shorts Tucano T1 | RAF, stored Shawbury |
| | ZF379 | Shorts Tucano T1 | RAF No 1 FTS, Linton-on-Ouse |
| | ZF380 | Shorts Tucano T1 | RAF No 1 FTS, Linton-on-Ouse |
| | ZF405 | Shorts Tucano T1 | RAF No 1 FTS, Linton-on-Ouse |
| | ZF406 | Shorts Tucano T1 | RAF No 1 FTS, Linton-on-Ouse |
| | ZF407 | Shorts Tucano T1 | RAF, stored Shawbury |
| | ZF408 | Shorts Tucano T1 | RAF No 1 FTS, Linton-on-Ouse |
| | ZF409 | Shorts Tucano T1 | RAF, stored Shawbury |
| | ZF410 | Shorts Tucano T1 | RAF No 1 FTS, Linton-on-Ouse |
| | ZF411 | Shorts Tucano T1 | RAF, stored Shawbury |
| | ZF412 | Shorts Tucano T1 | RAF No 1 FTS, Linton-on-Ouse |
| | ZF413 | Shorts Tucano T1 | RAF No 1 FTS, Linton-on-Ouse |
| | ZF414 | Shorts Tucano T1 | RAF No 1 FTS, Linton-on-Ouse |
| | ZF415 | Shorts Tucano T1 | RAF, stored Shawbury |
| | ZF416 | Shorts Tucano T1 | RAF No 1 FTS, Linton-on-Ouse |
| | ZF417 | Shorts Tucano T1 | RAF No 1 FTS, Linton-on-Ouse |
| | ZF418 | Shorts Tucano T1 | RAF No 1 FTS, Linton-on-Ouse |
| | ZF445 | Shorts Tucano T1 | RAF No 1 FTS, Linton-on-Ouse |
| | ZF446 | Shorts Tucano T1 | RAF No 1 FTS, Linton-on-Ouse |
| | ZF447 | Shorts Tucano T1 | RAF No 1 FTS, Linton-on-Ouse |
| | ZF448 | Shorts Tucano T1 | RAF No 1 FTS, Linton-on-Ouse |
| | ZF449 | Shorts Tucano T1 | RAF No 1 FTS, Linton-on-Ouse |

| *Serial* | *Type (other identity) [code]* | *Owner/operator, location or fate* | *Notes* |
|---|---|---|---|
| ZF450 | Shorts Tucano T1 | RAF, stored Shawbury | |
| ZF483 | Shorts Tucano T1 | RAF No 1 FTS, Linton-on-Ouse | |
| ZF484 | Shorts Tucano T1 | RAF No 1 FTS, Linton-on-Ouse | |
| ZF485 | Shorts Tucano T1 (G-BULU) | RAF No 1 FTS, Linton-on-Ouse | |
| ZF486 | Shorts Tucano T1 | RAF No 1 FTS, Linton-on-Ouse | |
| ZF487 | Shorts Tucano T1 | RAF No 1 FTS, Linton-on-Ouse | |
| ZF488 | Shorts Tucano T1 | RAF No 1 FTS, Linton-on-Ouse | |
| ZF489 | Shorts Tucano T1 | RAF No 1 FTS, Linton-on-Ouse | |
| ZF490 | Shorts Tucano T1 | RAF No 1 FTS, Linton-on-Ouse | |
| ZF491 | Shorts Tucano T1 | RAF No 1 FTS, Linton-on-Ouse | |
| ZF492 | Shorts Tucano T1 | RAF No 1 FTS, Linton-on-Ouse | |
| ZF510 | Shorts Tucano T1 | DPA/AFD, DERA Boscombe Down | |
| ZF511 | Shorts Tucano T1 | DPA/AFD, DERA Boscombe Down | |
| ZF512 | Shorts Tucano T1 | RAF No 1 FTS, Linton-on-Ouse | |
| ZF513 | Shorts Tucano T1 | RAF No 1 FTS, Linton-on-Ouse | |
| ZF514 | Shorts Tucano T1 | RAF No 1 FTS, Linton-on-Ouse | |
| ZF515 | Shorts Tucano T1 | RAF No 1 FTS, Linton-on-Ouse | |
| ZF516 | Shorts Tucano T1 | RAF No 1 FTS, Linton-on-Ouse | |
| ZF534 | BAe EAP | Loughborough University | |
| ZF537 | WS Lynx AH9 | AAC No 659 Sqn/4 Regt, Wattisham | |
| ZF538 | WS Lynx AH9 | AAC No 653 Sqn/3 Regt, Wattisham | |
| ZF539 | WS Lynx AH9 | AAC No 653 Sqn/3 Regt, Wattisham | |
| ZF540 | WS Lynx AH9 | AAC No 653 Sqn/3 Regt, Wattisham | |
| ZF557 | WS Lynx HMA8 [407/YK] | RN No 815 Sqn, *York* Flt, Yeovilton | |
| ZF558 | WS Lynx HMA8 [348/CM] | RN No 815 Sqn, *Chatham* Flt, Yeovilton | |
| ZF560 | WS Lynx HMA8 [301] | RN No 815 Sqn, HQ Flt, Yeovilton | |
| ZF562 | WS Lynx HMA8 [336/CV] | RN No 815 Sqn, *Coventry* Flt, Yeovilton | |
| ZF563 | WS Lynx HMA8 [675] | RN No 702 Sqn, Yeovilton | |
| ZF573 | PBN 2T Islander CC2A (G-SRAY) | RAF Northolt Station Flight | |
| ZF578 | BAC Lightning F53 | Privately owned, Quedgeley, Glos | |
| ZF580 | BAC Lightning F53 | BAE SystemsSamlesbury, at main gate | |
| ZF582 | BAC Lightning F53 <ff> | Privately owned, Desborough, Northants | |
| ZF583 | BAC Lightning F53 | Solway Aviation Society, Carlisle | |
| ZF584 | BAC Lightning F53 | Ferranti Ltd, South Gyle, Edinburgh | |
| ZF587 | BAC Lightning F53 <ff> | Privately owned, Suffolk | |
| ZF588 | BAC Lightning F53 [L] | East Midlands Airport Aeropark | |
| ZF594 | BAC Lightning F53 | North-East Aircraft Museum, Usworth | |
| ZF595 | BAC Lightning T55 <ff> | Anglo-American Lightning Association, Bruntingthorpe | |
| ZF596 | BAC Lightning T55 <ff> | BAE SystemsNorth-West Heritage Group Warton | |
| ZF598 | BAC Lightning T55 | *Repainted as 55-713, 1999* | |
| ZF622 | Piper PA-31 Navajo Chieftain 350 (N35487) | DPA/AFD, DERA Boscombe Down | |
| ZF641 | EHI-101 [PP1] | SFDO, RNAS Culdrose | |
| ZF649 | EHI-101 Merlin [PP5] | DPA/GKN Westland, Yeovil | |
| *ZG101* | EHI-101 (mock-up) [GB] | GKN Westland/Agusta, Yeovil | |
| ZG471 | BAe Harrier GR7 [61] | RAF No 1 Sqn, Wittering | |
| ZG472 | BAe Harrier GR7 [62] | RAF No 1 Sqn, Wittering | |
| ZG474 | BAe Harrier GR7 [64] | RAF No 4 Sqn, Cottesmore | |
| ZG477 | BAe Harrier GR7 [67] | RAF No 3 Sqn, Cottesmore | |
| ZG478 | BAe Harrier GR7 [68] | RAF No 4 Sqn, Cottesmore | |
| ZG479 | BAe Harrier GR7 [69] | RAF HOCU/No 20(R) Sqn, Wittering | |
| ZG480 | BAe Harrier GR7 [70] | RAF No 1 Sqn, Wittering | |
| ZG500 | BAe Harrier GR7 [71] | RAF No 3 Sqn, Cottesmore | |
| ZG501 | BAe Harrier GR7 [E] | DPA/BAE Systems, Dunsfold | |
| ZG502 | BAe Harrier GR7 [73] | RAF No 1 Sqn, Wittering | |
| ZG503 | BAe Harrier GR7 [74] | RAF No 1 Sqn, Wittering | |
| ZG504 | BAe Harrier GR7 [75] | RAF No 4 Sqn, Cottesmore | |
| ZG505 | BAe Harrier GR7 [76] | RAF No 1 Sqn, Wittering | |
| ZG506 | BAe Harrier GR7 [77] | RAF No 3 Sqn, Cottesmore | |
| ZG507 | BAe Harrier GR7 [78] | RAF No 4 Sqn, Cottesmore | |
| ZG508 | BAe Harrier GR7 [79] | RAF No 1 Sqn, Wittering | |
| ZG509 | BAe Harrier GR7 [80] | RAF No 4 Sqn, Cottesmore | |
| ZG510 | BAe Harrier GR7 [81] | RAF No 4 Sqn, Cottesmore | |
| ZG511 | BAe Harrier GR7 [82] | RAF No 4 Sqn, Cottesmore | |
| ZG512 | BAe Harrier GR7 [83] | RAF HOCU/No 20(R) Sqn, Wittering | |
| ZG530 | BAe Harrier GR7 [84] | RAF No 4 Sqn, Cottesmore | |
| ZG531 | BAe Harrier GR7 [85] | RAF No 3 Sqn, Cottesmore | |
| ZG532 | BAe Harrier GR7 [86] | *Crashed 14 July 1999, Cornhill on Tweed* | |
| ZG705 | Panavia Tornado GR1A [J] | RAF No 13 Sqn, Marham | |

| Notes | Serial | Type (other identity) [code] | Owner/operator, location or fate |
|---|---|---|---|
| | ZG706 | Panavia Tornado GR1A [E] | RAF AWC/SAOEU, DERA Boscombe Down |
| | ZG707 | Panavia Tornado GR4A [B] | RAF No 13 Sqn, Marham |
| | ZG709 | Panavia Tornado GR4A [V] | RAF No 13 Sqn, Marham |
| | ZG710 | Panavia Tornado GR4A [D] | RAF No 13 Sqn, Marham |
| | ZG711 | Panavia Tornado GR4A [O] | DPA/BAE Systems, Warton (conversion) |
| | ZG712 | Panavia Tornado GR4A [F] | RAF No 13 Sqn, Marham |
| | ZG713 | Panavia Tornado GR4A [G] | DPA/BAE Systems, Warton (conversion) |
| | ZG714 | Panavia Tornado GR4A [Q] | DPA/BAe, Warton (conversion) |
| | ZG726 | Panavia Tornado GR4A [K] | RAF No 13 Sqn, Marham |
| | ZG727 | Panavia Tornado GR1A [L] | RAF No 13 Sqn, Marham |
| | ZG729 | Panavia Tornado GR4A [M] | DPA/BAe, Warton (conversion) |
| | ZG731 | Panavia Tornado F3 [BL] | DPA/BAe, Warton |
| | ZG750 | Panavia Tornado GR4 [DY] | RAF No 31 Sqn, Brüggen |
| | ZG751 | Panavia Tornado F3 [CO] | RAF No 5 Sqn, Coningsby |
| | ZG752 | Panavia Tornado GR1 [XI] | RAF No 13 Sqn, Marham |
| | ZG753 | Panavia Tornado F3 (fuselage) | RAF, stored St Athan |
| | ZG754 | Panavia Tornado GR1 [VI] | RAF No 13 Sqn, Marham |
| | ZG755 | Panavia Tornado F3 | RAF No 25 Sqn, Leeming |
| | ZG756 | Panavia Tornado GR1 [BX] | RAF No 14 Sqn, Brüggen |
| | ZG757 | Panavia Tornado F3 [U] | RAF No 111 Sqn, Leuchars |
| | ZG769 | Panavia Tornado GR1 [TN] | RAF No 15(R) Sqn, Lossiemouth |
| | ZG770 | Panavia Tornado F3 [CC] | RAF No 5 Sqn, Coningsby |
| | ZG771 | Panavia Tornado GR4 [AZ] | RAF No 9 Sqn, Brüggen |
| | ZG772 | Panavia Tornado F3 | RAF F3 OCU/No 56(R) Sqn, Coningsby |
| | ZG773 | Panavia Tornado GR4 | DPA/BAe, Warton |
| | ZG774 | Panavia Tornado F3 [D] | RAF No 1435 Flt, Mount Pleasant, FI |
| | ZG775 | Panavia Tornado GR4 [DN] | DPA/BAe, Warton (conversion) |
| | ZG776 | Panavia Tornado F3 [F] | RAF No 1435 Flt, Mount Pleasant, FI |
| | ZG777 | Panavia Tornado GR1 [BS] | RAF No 14 Sqn, Brüggen |
| | ZG778 | Panavia Tornado F3 | RAF No 5 Sqn, Coningsby |
| | ZG779 | Panavia Tornado GR1 [DK] | RAF No 31 Sqn, Brüggen |
| | ZG780 | Panavia Tornado F3 [GL] | RAF No 25 Sqn, Leeming |
| | ZG791 | Panavia Tornado GR4 [DC] | DPA/BAe, Warton (conversion) |
| | ZG792 | Panavia Tornado GR4 | DARA, St Athan |
| | ZG793 | Panavia Tornado F3 [CY] | RAF No 5 Sqn, Coningsby |
| | ZG794 | Panavia Tornado GR1 [BP] | RAF No 14 Sqn, Brüggen |
| | ZG795 | Panavia Tornado F3 [CB] | RAF No 5 Sqn, Coningsby |
| | ZG796 | Panavia Tornado F3 [D] | RAF No 5 Sqn, Coningsby |
| | ZG797 | Panavia Tornado F3 [GI] | RAF No 43 Sqn, Leuchars |
| | ZG798 | Panavia Tornado F3 [AP] | RAF F3 OCU/No 56(R) Sqn, Coningsby |
| | ZG799 | Panavia Tornado F3 [D] | RAF No 5 Sqn, Coningsby |
| | ZG816 | WS61 Sea King HAS6 [701/PW] | DPA/GKN Westland, Weston-super-Mare |
| | ZG817 | WS61 Sea King HAS6 [702/PW] | RN No 819 Sqn, Prestwick |
| | ZG818 | WS61 Sea King HAS6 | RN, stored RNAY Fleetlands |
| | ZG819 | WS61 Sea King HAS6 [265/N] | RN No 814 Sqn, Culdrose |
| | ZG820 | WS61 Sea King HC4 [A] | RN No 845 Sqn, Yeovilton |
| | ZG821 | WS61 Sea King HC4 [D] | RN No 845 Sqn, Yeovilton |
| | ZG822 | WS61 Sea King HC4 [VN] | RN No 846 Sqn, Yeovilton |
| | ZG844 | PBN 2T Islander AL1 (G-BLNE) | AAC AFWF, Middle Wallop |
| | ZG845 | PBN 2T Islander AL1 (G-BLNT) | AAC No 1 Flt, Aldergrove |
| | ZG846 | PBN 2T Islander AL1 (G-BLNU) | AAC AFWF, Middle Wallop |
| | ZG847 | PBN 2T Islander AL1 (G-BLNV) | AAC No 1 Flt, Aldergrove |
| | ZG848 | PBN 2T Islander AL1 (G-BLNY) | AAC No 1 Flt, Aldergrove |
| | ZG857 | BAe Harrier GR7 [89] | RAF No 4 Sqn, Cottesmore |
| | ZG858 | BAe Harrier GR7 [90] | RAF No 4 Sqn, Cottesmore |
| | ZG859 | BAe Harrier GR7 [91] | RAF No 4 Sqn, Cottesmore |
| | ZG860 | BAe Harrier GR7 [92] | RAF No 4 Sqn, Cottesmore |
| | ZG862 | BAe Harrier GR7 [94] | RAF No 1 Sqn, Wittering |
| | ZG875 | WS61 Sea King HAS6 [013/L] | RN FSAIU, Yeovilton (damaged) |
| | ZG879 | Powerchute Raider Mk 1 | DPA/Powerchute, Hereford |
| | ZG884 | WS Lynx AH9 | DPA/GKN Westland, Yeovil |
| | ZG885 | WS Lynx AH9 [7] | AAC No 653 Sqn/3 Regt, Wattisham |
| | ZG886 | WS Lynx AH9 | AAC No 653 Sqn/3 Regt, Wattisham |
| | ZG887 | WS Lynx AH9 | AAC No 653 Sqn/3 Regt, Wattisham |
| | ZG888 | WS Lynx AH9 | AAC No 653 Sqn/3 Regt, Wattisham |
| | ZG889 | WS Lynx AH9 | AAC No 653 Sqn/3 Regt, Wattisham |
| | ZG914 | WS Lynx AH9 | AAC No 653 Sqn/3 Regt, Wattisham |
| | ZG915 | WS Lynx AH9 [7] | DARA, RNAY Fleetlands |
| | ZG916 | WS Lynx AH9 [8] | DARA, RNAY Fleetlands |
| | ZG917 | WS Lynx AH9 [2,9] | AAC No 659 Sqn/4 Regt, Wattisham |
| | ZG918 | WS Lynx AH9 | AAC No 659 Sqn/4 Regt, Wattisham |
| | ZG919 | WS Lynx AH9 | AAC No 653 Sqn/3 Regt, Wattisham |

| *Serial* | *Type (other identity) [code]* | *Owner/operator, location or fate* | *Notes* |
|---|---|---|---|
| ZG920 | WS Lynx AH9 | AAC No 653 Sqn/3 Regt, Wattisham | |
| ZG921 | WS Lynx AH9 | AAC No 659 Sqn/4 Regt, Wattisham | |
| ZG922 | WS Lynx AH9 | DARA, RNAY Fleetlands | |
| ZG923 | WS Lynx AH9 | AAC No 653 Sqn/3 Regt, Wattisham | |
| ZG969 | Pilatus PC-9 (HB-HQE) | BAE SystemsWarton | |
| ZG989 | PBN 2T Islander ASTOR (G-DLRA) | DPA/PBN, Bembridge | |
| ZG993 | PBN 2T Islander AL1 (G-BOMD) | AAC No 1 Flight, Aldergrove | |
| ZG994 | PBN 2T Islander AL1 (G-BPLN) | *Crashed 30 June 1999, Lopcombe Corner, Wilts* | |
| | | | |
| ZH101 | Boeing E-3D Sentry AEW1 | RAF No 8 Sqn/No 23 Sqn, Waddington | |
| ZH102 | Boeing E-3D Sentry AEW1 | RAF No 8 Sqn/No 23 Sqn, Waddington | |
| ZH103 | Boeing E-3D Sentry AEW1 | RAF No 8 Sqn/No 23 Sqn, Waddington | |
| ZH104 | Boeing E-3D Sentry AEW1 | RAF No 8 Sqn/No 23 Sqn, Waddington | |
| ZH105 | Boeing E-3D Sentry AEW1 | RAF No 8 Sqn/No 23 Sqn, Waddington | |
| ZH106 | Boeing E-3D Sentry AEW1 | RAF No 8 Sqn/No 23 Sqn, Waddington | |
| ZH107 | Boeing E-3D Sentry AEW1 | RAF No 8 Sqn/No 23 Sqn, Waddington | |
| ZH115 | Grob G109B Vigilant T1 [TA] | RAF No 616 VGS, Henlow | |
| ZH116 | Grob G109B Vigilant T1 [TB] | RAF No 664 VGS, Belfast City Airport | |
| ZH117 | Grob G109B Vigilant T1 [TC] | RAF No 642 VGS, Linton-on-Ouse | |
| ZH118 | Grob G109B Vigilant T1 [TD] | RAF No 612 VGS, Abingdon | |
| ZH119 | Grob G109B Vigilant T1 [TE] | RAF No 632 VGS Ternhill | |
| ZH120 | Grob G109B Vigilant T1 [TF] | RAF No 663 VGS, Kinloss | |
| ZH121 | Grob G109B Vigilant T1 [TG] | RAF No 633 VGS, Cosford | |
| ZH122 | Grob G109B Vigilant T1 [TH] | RAF No 635 VGS, Samlesbury | |
| ZH123 | Grob G109B Vigilant T1 [TJ] | RAF ACCGS, Syerston | |
| ZH124 | Grob G109B Vigilant T1 [TK] | RAF No 642 VGS, Linton-on-Ouse | |
| ZH125 | Grob G109B Vigilant T1 [TL] | RAF No 633 VGS, Cosford | |
| ZH126 | Grob G109B Vigilant T1 [TM] | RAF No 637 VGS, Little Rissington | |
| ZH127 | Grob G109B Vigilant T1 [TN] | RAF No 642 VGS, Linton-on-Ouse | |
| ZH128 | Grob G109B Vigilant T1 [TP] | RAF No 624 VGS, Chivenor RMB | |
| ZH129 | Grob G109B Vigilant T1 [TQ] | RAF No 635 VGS, Samlesbury | |
| *ZH139* | BAe Harrier GR7 <R> (BAPC 191/ *ZD472*) | RAF EPTT, St Athan | |
| ZH141 | AS355F-1 Twin Squirrel HCC1 (G-OILX) | RAF No 32(The Royal) Sqn, Northolt | |
| ZH144 | Grob G109B Vigilant T1 [TR] | RAF No 616 VGS, Henlow | |
| ZH145 | Grob G109B Vigilant T1 [TS] | RAF ACCGS, Syerston | |
| ZH146 | Grob G109B Vigilant T1 [TT] | RAF CGMF, Syerston (damaged) | |
| ZH147 | Grob G109B Vigilant T1 [TU] | RAF No 632 VGS, Ternhill | |
| ZH148 | Grob G109B Vigilant T1 [TV] | RAF No 613 VGS, Halton | |
| ZH184 | Grob G109B Vigilant T1 [TW] | RAF No 612 VGS, Abingdon | |
| ZH185 | Grob G109B Vigilant T1 [TX] | RAF No 642 VGS, Linton-on-Ouse | |
| ZH186 | Grob G109B Vigilant T1 [TY] | RAF No 613 VGS, Halton | |
| ZH187 | Grob G109B Vigilant T1 [TZ] | RAF No 633 VGS, Cosford | |
| ZH188 | Grob G109B Vigilant T1 [UA] | RAF No 635 VGS, Samlesbury | |
| ZH189 | Grob G109B Vigilant T1 [UB] | RAF CGMF, Syserston | |
| ZH190 | Grob G109B Vigilant T1 [UC] | RAF CGMF, Syserston | |
| ZH191 | Grob G109B Vigilant T1 [UD] | RAF No 616 VGS, Henlow | |
| ZH192 | Grob G109B Vigilant T1 [UE] | RAF No 635 VGS, Samlesbury | |
| ZH193 | Grob G109B Vigilant T1 [UF] | RAF No 612 VGS, Abingdon | |
| ZH194 | Grob G109B Vigilant T1 [UG] | RAF No 624 VGS, Chivenor RMB | |
| ZH195 | Grob G109B Vigilant T1 [UH] | RAF ACCGS, Syerston | |
| ZH196 | Grob G109B Vigilant T1 [UJ] | RAF No 612 VGS, Abingdon | |
| ZH197 | Grob G109B Vigilant T1 [UK] | RAF No 633 VGS, Cosford | |
| ZH200 | BAe Hawk 200 | DPA, stored BAE SystemsWarton | |
| ZH205 | Grob G109B Vigilant T1 [UL] | RAF No 613 VGS, Halton | |
| ZH206 | Grob G109B Vigilant T1 [UM] | RAF No 633 VGS, Cosford | |
| ZH207 | Grob G109B Vigilant T1 [UN] | RAF No 632 VGS, Ternhill | |
| ZH208 | Grob G109B Vigilant T1 [UP] | RAF No 663 VGS, Kinloss | |
| ZH209 | Grob G109B Vigilant T1 [UQ] | RAF No 664 VGS, Belfast City Airport | |
| ZH211 | Grob G109B Vigilant T1 [UR] | RAF ACCGS, Syerston | |
| ZH247 | Grob G109B Vigilant T1 [US] | RAF ACCGS, Syerston | |
| ZH248 | Grob G109B Vigilant T1 [UT] | RAF ACCGS, Syerston | |
| ZH249 | Grob G109B Vigilant T1 [UU] | RAF CGMF, Syerston | |
| ZH257 | B-V CH-47C Chinook (AE-520/ 9217M) | AAC Wattisham, instructional use | |
| ZH263 | Grob G109B Vigilant T1 [UV] | RAF No 632 VGS, Ternhill | |
| ZH264 | Grob G109B Vigilant T1 [UW] | RAF No 616 VGS, Henlow | |
| ZH265 | Grob G109B Vigilant T1 [UX] | RAF No 663 VGS, Kinloss | |
| ZH266 | Grob G109B Vigilant T1 [UY] | RAF No 635 VGS, Samlesbury | |
| ZH267 | Grob G109B Vigilant T1 [UZ] | RAF No 637 VGS, Little Rissington | |
| ZH268 | Grob G109B Vigilant T1 [SA] | RAF No 613 VGS, Halton | |

| Notes | Serial | Type (other identity) [code] | Owner/operator, location or fate |
|---|---|---|---|
| | ZH269 | Grob G109B Vigilant T1 [SB] | RAF No 642 VGS, Linton-on-Ouse |
| | ZH270 | Grob G109B Vigilant T1 [SC] | RAF No 616 VGS, Henlow |
| | ZH271 | Grob G109B Vigilant T1 [SD] | RAF No 613 VGS, Halton |
| | ZH536 | PBN 2T Islander CC2 (G-BSAH) | RAF Northolt Station Flight |
| | ZH540 | WS61 Sea King HAR3A | RAF No 22 Sqn, B Flt, Wattisham |
| | ZH541 | WS61 Sea King HAR3A | RAF No 22 Sqn, A Flt, Chivenor RMB |
| | ZH542 | WS61 Sea King HAR3A | RAF No 22 Sqn, A Flt, Chivenor RMB |
| | ZH543 | WS61 Sea King HAR3A | RAF HMF, St Mawgan |
| | ZH544 | WS61 Sea King HAR3A | RAF No 22 Sqn, A Flt, Chivenor RMB |
| | ZH545 | WS61 Sea King HAR3A | RAF No 22 Sqn, B Flt, Wattisham |
| | ZH552 | Panavia Tornado F3 [CH] | RAF No 5 Sqn, Coninsgby |
| | ZH553 | Panavia Tornado F3 [AB] | RAF F3 OCU/No 56(R) Sqn, Coningsby |
| | ZH554 | Panavia Tornado F3 [AP] | RAF F3 OCU/No 56(R) Sqn, Coningsby |
| | ZH555 | Panavia Tornado F3 [CV] | RAF No 5 Sqn, Coningsby |
| | ZH556 | Panavia Tornado F3 [AK] | RAF F3 OCU/No 56(R) Sqn, Coningsby |
| | ZH557 | Panavia Tornado F3 [X] | RAF No 111 Sqn, Leuchars |
| | ZH559 | Panavia Tornado F3 [AJ] | RAF F3 OCU/No 56(R) Sqn, Coningsby |
| | ZH588 | Eurofighter Typhoon (DA2) | DPA/BAE Systems, Warton |
| | ZH590 | Eurofighter Typhoon (T) (DA4) | DPA/BAE Systems, Warton |
| | ZH653 | BAe Harrier T10 | DPA/BAE Systems, Dunsfold |
| | ZH654 | BAe Harrier T10 | DPA/BAE Systems, Dunsfold |
| | ZH655 | BAe Harrier T10 | RAF, stored St Athan (damaged) |
| | ZH656 | BAe Harrier T10 [104] | RAF No 3 Sqn, Cottesmore |
| | ZH657 | BAe Harrier T10 [XX] | RAF HOCU/No 20(R) Sqn, Wittering |
| | ZH658 | BAe Harrier T10 [106] | RAF HOCU/No 20(R) Sqn, Wittering |
| | ZH659 | BAe Harrier T10 [O] | RAF HOCU/No 20(R) Sqn, Wittering |
| | ZH660 | BAe Harrier T10 [P] | RAF No 1 Sqn, Wittering |
| | ZH661 | BAe Harrier T10 [Z] | RAF HOCU/No 20(R) Sqn, Wittering |
| | ZH662 | BAe Harrier T10 [R] | RAF HOCU/No 20(R) Sqn, Wittering |
| | ZH663 | BAe Harrier T10 [Q] | RAF HOCU/No 20(R) Sqn, Wittering |
| | ZH664 | BAe Harrier T10 [112] | RAF No 4 Sqn, Cottesmore |
| | ZH665 | BAe Harrier T10 [S] | RAF HOCU/No 20(R) Sqn, Wittering |
| | ZH762 | Westinghouse Skyship 500 (G-SKSC) | Westinghouse, stored Cardington |
| | ZH763 | BAC 1-11/539GL (G-BGKE) | DPA/AFD, DERA Boscombe Down |
| | ZH775 | B-V Chinook HC2 (N7424J) [NS] | RAF No 7 Sqn, Odiham |
| | ZH776 | B-V Chinook HC2 (N7424L) [ES] | RAF No 7 Sqn, Odiham |
| | ZH777 | B-V Chinook HC2 (N7424M) [NY] | RAF No 27 Sqn, Odiham |
| | ZH796 | BAe Sea Harrier FA2 [716/VL] | DARA, St Athan |
| | ZH797 | BAe Sea Harrier FA2 [714] | DPA/BAE Systems, Dunsfold |
| | ZH798 | BAe Sea Harrier FA2 [715] | RN No 899 Sqn, Yeovilton |
| | ZH799 | BAe Sea Harrier FA2 [730] | RN No 899 Sqn, Yeovilton |
| | ZH800 | BAe Sea Harrier FA2 [716] | RN No 899 Sqn, Yeovilton |
| | ZH801 | BAe Sea Harrier FA2 [731] | RN No 899 Sqn, Yeovilton |
| | ZH802 | BAe Sea Harrier FA2 [718] | RN No 899 Sqn, Yeovilton |
| | ZH803 | BAe Sea Harrier FA2 | DARA, St Athan |
| | ZH804 | BAe Sea Harrier FA2 | DARA, St Athan |
| | ZH805 | BAe Sea Harrier FA2 [715/VL] | DARA, St Athan |
| | ZH806 | BAe Sea Harrier FA2 [717] | RN No 899 Sqn, Yeovilton |
| | ZH807 | BAe Sea Harrier FA2 [719/VL] | RN No 899 Sqn, Yeovilton |
| | ZH808 | BAe Sea Harrier FA2 | RN AMG, Yeovilton |
| | ZH809 | BAe Sea Harrier FA2 [123] | RN No 800 Sqn, Yeovilton |
| | ZH810 | BAe Sea Harrier FA2 [004/L] | RN No 801 Sqn, Yeovilton |
| | ZH811 | BAe Sea Harrier FA2 [714] | RN No 899 Sqn, Yeovilton |
| | ZH812 | BAe Sea Harrier FA2 [006] | RN No 801 Sqn, Yeovilton |
| | ZH813 | BAe Sea Harrier FA2 | DPA/BAe, Dunsfold |
| | ZH814 | Bell 212 (G-BGMH) | AAC No 7 Flt, Brunei |
| | ZH815 | Bell 212 (G-BGCZ) | AAC No 7 Flt, Brunei |
| | ZH816 | Bell 212 (G-BGMG) | AAC No 7 Flt, Brunei |
| | ZH821 | EHI-101 Merlin HM1 | DPA/GKN Westland, Yeovil |
| | ZH822 | EHI-101 Merlin HM1 | DPA/GKN Westland, Yeovil |
| | ZH823 | EHI-101 Merlin HM1 | DPA/GKN Westland, Yeovil |
| | ZH824 | EHI-101 Merlin HM1 | DPA/AFD, DERA Boscombe Down |
| | ZH825 | EHI-101 Merlin HM1 | RN No 700M Sqn, Culdrose |
| | ZH826 | EHI-101 Merlin HM1 | RN No 700M Sqn, Culdrose |
| | ZH827 | EHI-101 Merlin HM1 | RN AMG, Culdrose |
| | ZH828 | EHI-101 Merlin HM1 [538/CU] | RN No 700M Sqn, Culdrose |
| | ZH829 | EHI-101 Merlin HM1 | DPA/GKN Westland, Yeovil |
| | ZH830 | EHI-101 Merlin HM1 | DPA/GKN Westland, Yeovil |
| | ZH831 | EHI-101 Merlin HM1 | RN No 700M Sqn, Culdrose |
| | ZH832 | EHI-101 Merlin HM1 | DPA/AFD, DERA Boscombe Down |
| | ZH833 | EHI-101 Merlin HM1 | RN No 824 Training Flt, Culdrose |
| | ZH834 | EHI-101 Merlin HM1 | DPA/GKN Westland, Yeovil |

| Serial | Type (other identity) [code] | Owner/operator, location or fate | Notes |
|---|---|---|---|
| ZH835 | EHI-101 Merlin HM1 [581/CU] | RN No 824 Training Flt, Culdrose | |
| ZH836 | EHI-101 Merlin HM1 | RN No 824 Training Flt, Culdrose | |
| ZH837 | EHI-101 Merlin HM1 | RN No 824 Training Flt, Culdrose | |
| ZH838 | EHI-101 Merlin HM1 | DPA/GKN Westland, Yeovil | |
| ZH839 | EHI-101 Merlin HM1 | DPA/GKN Westland, Yeovil, for RN | |
| ZH840 | EHI-101 Merlin HM1 | DPA/GKN Westland, Yeovil, for RN | |
| ZH841 | EHI-101 Merlin HM1 | DPA/GKN Westland, Yeovil, for RN | |
| ZH842 | EHI-101 Merlin HM1 | DPA/GKN Westland, Yeovil, for RN | |
| ZH843 | EHI-101 Merlin HM1 | GKN Westland, Yeovil, for RN | |
| ZH844 | EHI-101 Merlin HM1 | GKN Westland, Yeovil, for RN | |
| ZH845 | EHI-101 Merlin HM1 | GKN Westland, Yeovil, for RN | |
| ZH846 | EHI-101 Merlin HM1 | GKN Westland, Yeovil, for RN | |
| ZH847 | EHI-101 Merlin HM1 | GKN Westland, Yeovil, for RN | |
| ZH848 | EHI-101 Merlin HM1 | GKN Westland, Yeovil, for RN | |
| ZH849 | EHI-101 Merlin HM1 | GKN Westland, Yeovil, for RN | |
| ZH850 | EHI-101 Merlin HM1 | GKN Westland, Yeovil, for RN | |
| ZH851 | EHI-101 Merlin HM1 | GKN Westland, Yeovil, for RN | |
| ZH852 | EHI-101 Merlin HM1 | GKN Westland, Yeovil, for RN | |
| ZH853 | EHI-101 Merlin HM1 | GKN Westland, Yeovil, for RN | |
| ZH854 | EHI-101 Merlin HM1 | GKN Westland, Yeovil, for RN | |
| ZH855 | EHI-101 Merlin HM1 | GKN Westland, Yeovil, for RN | |
| ZH856 | EHI-101 Merlin HM1 | GKN Westland, Yeovil, for RN | |
| ZH857 | EHI-101 Merlin HM1 | GKN Westland, Yeovil, for RN | |
| ZH858 | EHI-101 Merlin HM1 | GKN Westland, Yeovil, for RN | |
| ZH859 | EHI-101 Merlin HM1 | GKN Westland, Yeovil, for RN | |
| ZH860 | EHI-101 Merlin HM1 | GKN Westland, Yeovil, for RN | |
| ZH861 | EHI-101 Merlin HM1 | GKN Westland, Yeovil, for RN | |
| ZH862 | EHI-101 Merlin HM1 | GKN Westland, Yeovil, for RN | |
| ZH863 | EHI-101 Merlin HM1 | GKN Westland, Yeovil, for RN | |
| ZH864 | EHI-101 Merlin HM1 | GKN Westland, Yeovil, for RN | |
| ZH865 | Lockheed C-130J-30 Hercules C4 (N130JA) | DPA/Lockheed-Martin, Marietta | |
| ZH866 | Lockheed C-130J-30 Hercules C4 (N130JE) | LMASC/Marshall Aerospace, Cambridge | |
| ZH867 | Lockheed C-130J-30 Hercules C4 (N130JJ) | LMASC/Marshall Aerospace, Cambridge | |
| ZH868 | Lockheed C-130J-30 Hercules C4 (N130JN) | Lockheed-Martin, Marietta | |
| ZH869 | Lockheed C-130J-30 Hercules C4 (N130JV) | LMASC/Marshall Aerospace, Cambridge | |
| ZH870 | Lockheed C-130J-30 Hercules C4 (*N73235*/N78235) | LMASC/Marshall Aerospace, Cambridge | |
| ZH871 | Lockheed C-130J-30 Hercules C4 (N73238) | DPA/AFD, DERA Boscombe Down | |
| ZH872 | Lockheed C-130J-30 Hercules C4 (N4249Y) | LMASC/Marshall Aerospace, Cambridge | |
| ZH873 | Lockheed C-130J-30 Hercules C4 (N4242N) | LMASC/Marshall Aerospace, Cambridge | |
| ZH874 | Lockheed C-130J-30 Hercules C4 (N41030) | LMASC/Marshall Aerospace, Cambridge | |
| ZH875 | Lockheed C-130J-30 Hercules C4 (N4099R) | RAF Lyneham Transport Wing | |
| ZH876 | Lockheed C-130J-30 Hercules C4 (N4080M) | RAF Lyneham Transport Wing | |
| ZH877 | Lockheed C-130J-30 Hercules C4 (N4081M) | RAF Lyneham Transport Wing | |
| ZH878 | Lockheed C-130J-30 Hercules C4 (N73232) | RAF Lyneham Transport Wing | |
| ZH879 | Lockheed C-130J-30 Hercules C4 (N4080M) | LMASC/Marshall Aerospace, Cambridge | |
| ZH880 | Lockheed C-130J Hercules C5 (N73238) | DPA/AFD, DERA Boscombe Down | |
| ZH881 | Lockheed C-130J Hercules C5 (N4081M) | LMASC/Marshall Aerospace, Cambridge | |
| ZH882 | Lockheed C-130J Hercules C5 (N4099R) | LMASC/Marshall Aerospace, Cambridge | |
| ZH883 | Lockheed C-130J Hercules C5 (N4242N) | LMASC/Marshall Aerospace, Cambridge | |
| ZH884 | Lockheed C-130J Hercules C5 (N4249Y) | LMASC/Marshall Aerospace, Cambridge | |
| ZH885 | Lockheed C-130J Hercules C5 (N41030) | LMASC/Marshall Aerospace, Cambridge | |

| Notes | Serial | Type (other identity) [code] | Owner/operator, location or fate |
|---|---|---|---|
| | ZH886 | Lockheed C-130J Hercules C5 (N73235) | LMASC/Marshall Aerospace, Cambridge |
| | ZH887 | Lockheed C-130J Hercules C5 (N4187W) | LMASC/Marshall Aerospace, Cambridge |
| | ZH888 | Lockheed C-130J Hercules C5 | Lockheed-Martin, for RAF |
| | ZH889 | Lockheed C-130J Hercules C5 | Lockheed-Martin, for RAF |
| | ZH890 | Grob G109B Vigilant T1 [SE] | RAF CGMF, Syerston |
| | ZH891 | B-V Chinook HC2A (N20075) | DPA/AFD, DERA Boscombe Down |
| | ZH892 | B-V Chinook HC2A (N2019V) | DPA/GKN Westland, Weston-super-Mare |
| | ZH893 | B-V Chinook HC2A (N2025L) | DPA/AFD, DERA Boscombe Down |
| | ZH894 | B-V Chinook HC2A (N2026E) | RAF No 27 Sqn, Odiham |
| | ZH895 | B-V Chinook HC2A (N2034K) | RAF No 7 Sqn, Odiham |
| | ZH896 | B-V Chinook HC2A (N2038G) | RAF No 18 Sqn, Odiham |
| | ZH897 | B-V Chinook HC3 (N2045G) | Boeing, Philadelphia, for RAF |
| | ZH898 | B-V Chinook HC3 (N2057Q) | Boeing, Philadelphia, for RAF |
| | ZH899 | B-V Chinook HC3 (N2057R) | Boeing, Philadelphia, for RAF |
| | ZH900 | B-V Chinook HC3 (N2060H) | Boeing, Philadelphia, for RAF |
| | ZH901 | B-V Chinook HC3 (N2060M) | Boeing, Philadelphia, for RAF |
| | ZH902 | B-V Chinook HC3 (N2064W) | Boeing, Philadelphia, for RAF |
| | ZH903 | B-V Chinook HC3 (N20671) | Boeing, Philadelphia, for RAF |
| | ZH904 | B-V Chinook HC3 (N2083K) | Boeing, Philadelphia, for RAF |
| | | | |
| | ZJ100 | BAe Hawk 102D | BAE SystemsWarton |
| | ZJ116 | EHI-101 (G-OIOI) (PP8) | DPA/GKN Westland, Yeovil |
| | ZJ117 | EHI-101 Merlin HC3 | DPA/GKN Westland, Yeovil |
| | ZJ118 | EHI-101 Merlin HC3 | DPA/GKN Westland, Yeovil |
| | ZJ119 | EHI-101 Merlin HC3 | DPA/GKN Westland, Yeovil |
| | ZJ120 | EHI-101 Merlin HC3 | GKN Westland, Yeovil, for RAF |
| | ZJ121 | EHI-101 Merlin HC3 | GKN Westland, Yeovil, for RAF |
| | ZJ122 | EHI-101 Merlin HC3 | GKN Westland, Yeovil, for RAF |
| | ZJ123 | EHI-101 Merlin HC3 | GKN Westland, Yeovil, for RAF |
| | ZJ124 | EHI-101 Merlin HC3 | GKN Westland, Yeovil, for RAF |
| | ZJ125 | EHI-101 Merlin HC3 | GKN Westland, Yeovil, for RAF |
| | ZJ126 | EHI-101 Merlin HC3 | GKN Westland, Yeovil, for RAF |
| | ZJ127 | EHI-101 Merlin HC3 | GKN Westland, Yeovil, for RAF |
| | ZJ128 | EHI-101 Merlin HC3 | GKN Westland, Yeovil, for RAF |
| | ZJ129 | EHI-101 Merlin HC3 | GKN Westland, Yeovil, for RAF |
| | ZJ130 | EHI-101 Merlin HC3 | GKN Westland, Yeovil, for RAF |
| | ZJ131 | EHI-101 Merlin HC3 | GKN Westland, Yeovil, for RAF |
| | ZJ132 | EHI-101 Merlin HC3 | GKN Westland, Yeovil, for RAF |
| | ZJ133 | EHI-101 Merlin HC3 | GKN Westland, Yeovil, for RAF |
| | ZJ134 | EHI-101 Merlin HC3 | GKN Westland, Yeovil, for RAF |
| | ZJ135 | EHI-101 Merlin HC3 | GKN Westland, Yeovil, for RAF |
| | ZJ136 | EHI-101 Merlin HC3 | GKN Westland, Yeovil, for RAF |
| | ZJ137 | EHI-101 Merlin HC3 | GKN Westland, Yeovil, for RAF |
| | ZJ138 | EHI-101 Merlin HC3 | GKN Westland, Yeovil, for RAF |
| | ZJ139 | AS355F-1 Twin Squirrel HCC1 (G-NUTZ) | RAF No 32(The Royal) Sqn, Northolt |
| | ZJ140 | AS355F-1 Twin Squirrel HCC1 (G-FFHI) | RAF No 32(The Royal) Sqn, Northolt |
| | ZJ164 | AS365N-2 Dauphin 2 (G-BTLC) | RN/Bond Helicopters, Plymouth |
| | ZJ165 | AS365N-2 Dauphin 2 (G-NTOO) | RN/Bond Helicopters, Plymouth |
| | ZJ166 | WS WAH-64D Apache AH1 (N9219G) | Boeing Helicopters, Mesa, for AAC |
| | ZJ167 | WS WAH-64D Apache AH1 (N3266B) | Boeing Helicopters, Mesa, for AAC |
| | ZJ168 | WS WAH-64D Apache AH1 (N3123T) | DPA/GKN Westland, Yeovil |
| | ZJ169 | WS WAH-64D Apache AH1 (N3114H) | Boeing Helicopters, Mesa, for AAC |
| | ZJ170 | WS WAH-64D Apache AH1 (N3065U) | Boeing Helicopters, Mesa, for AAC |
| | ZJ171 | WS WAH-64D Apache AH1 (N3266T) | DPA/GKN Westland, Yeovil |
| | ZJ172 | WS WAH-64D Apache AH1 | GKN Westland, for AAC |
| | ZJ173 | WS WAH-64D Apache AH1 | Boeing Helicopters, Mesa, for AAC |
| | ZJ174 | WS WAH-64D Apache AH1 | GKN Westland, for AAC |
| | ZJ175 | WS WAH-64D Apache AH1 | GKN Westland, for AAC |
| | ZJ176 | WS WAH-64D Apache AH1 | GKN Westland, for AAC |
| | ZJ177 | WS WAH-64D Apache AH1 | GKN Westland, for AAC |
| | ZJ178 | WS WAH-64D Apache AH1 | GKN Westland, for AAC |
| | ZJ179 | WS WAH-64D Apache AH1 | GKN Westland, for AAC |
| | ZJ180 | WS WAH-64D Apache AH1 | GKN Westland, for AAC |

| Serial | Type (other identity) [code] | Owner/operator, location or fate | Notes |
|---|---|---|---|
| ZJ181 | WS WAH-64D Apache AH1 | GKN Westland, for AAC | |
| ZJ182 | WS WAH-64D Apache AH1 | GKN Westland, for AAC | |
| ZJ183 | WS WAH-64D Apache AH1 | GKN Westland, for AAC | |
| ZJ184 | WS WAH-64D Apache AH1 | GKN Westland, for AAC | |
| ZJ185 | WS WAH-64D Apache AH1 | GKN Westland, for AAC | |
| ZJ186 | WS WAH-64D Apache AH1 | GKN Westland, for AAC | |
| ZJ187 | WS WAH-64D Apache AH1 | GKN Westland, for AAC | |
| ZJ188 | WS WAH-64D Apache AH1 | GKN Westland, for AAC | |
| ZJ189 | WS WAH-64D Apache AH1 | GKN Westland, for AAC | |
| ZJ190 | WS WAH-64D Apache AH1 | GKN Westland, for AAC | |
| ZJ191 | WS WAH-64D Apache AH1 | GKN Westland, for AAC | |
| ZJ192 | WS WAH-64D Apache AH1 | GKN Westland, for AAC | |
| ZJ193 | WS WAH-64D Apache AH1 | GKN Westland, for AAC | |
| ZJ194 | WS WAH-64D Apache AH1 | GKN Westland, for AAC | |
| ZJ195 | WS WAH-64D Apache AH1 | GKN Westland, for AAC | |
| ZJ196 | WS WAH-64D Apache AH1 | GKN Westland, for AAC | |
| ZJ197 | WS WAH-64D Apache AH1 | GKN Westland, for AAC | |
| ZJ198 | WS WAH-64D Apache AH1 | GKN Westland, for AAC | |
| ZJ199 | WS WAH-64D Apache AH1 | GKN Westland, for AAC | |
| ZJ200 | WS WAH-64D Apache AH1 | GKN Westland, for AAC | |
| ZJ201 | BAe Hawk 200RDA | *Crashed 6 June 1999, Bratislava, Slovak Republic* | |
| ZJ202 | WS WAH-64D Apache AH1 | GKN Westland, for AAC | |
| ZJ203 | WS WAH-64D Apache AH1 | GKN Westland, for AAC | |
| ZJ204 | WS WAH-64D Apache AH1 | GKN Westland, for AAC | |
| ZJ205 | WS WAH-64D Apache AH1 | GKN Westland, for AAC | |
| ZJ206 | WS WAH-64D Apache AH1 | GKN Westland, for AAC | |
| ZJ207 | WS WAH-64D Apache AH1 | GKN Westland, for AAC | |
| ZJ208 | WS WAH-64D Apache AH1 | GKN Westland, for AAC | |
| ZJ209 | WS WAH-64D Apache AH1 | GKN Westland, for AAC | |
| ZJ210 | WS WAH-64D Apache AH1 | GKN Westland, for AAC | |
| ZJ211 | WS WAH-64D Apache AH1 | GKN Westland, for AAC | |
| ZJ212 | WS WAH-64D Apache AH1 | GKN Westland, for AAC | |
| ZJ213 | WS WAH-64D Apache AH1 | GKN Westland, for AAC | |
| ZJ214 | WS WAH-64D Apache AH1 | GKN Westland, for AAC | |
| ZJ215 | WS WAH-64D Apache AH1 | GKN Westland, for AAC | |
| ZJ216 | WS WAH-64D Apache AH1 | GKN Westland, for AAC | |
| ZJ217 | WS WAH-64D Apache AH1 | GKN Westland, for AAC | |
| ZJ218 | WS WAH-64D Apache AH1 | GKN Westland, for AAC | |
| ZJ219 | WS WAH-64D Apache AH1 | GKN Westland, for AAC | |
| ZJ220 | WS WAH-64D Apache AH1 | GKN Westland, for AAC | |
| ZJ221 | WS WAH-64D Apache AH1 | GKN Westland, for AAC | |
| ZJ222 | WS WAH-64D Apache AH1 | GKN Westland, for AAC | |
| ZJ223 | WS WAH-64D Apache AH1 | GKN Westland, for AAC | |
| ZJ224 | WS WAH-64D Apache AH1 | GKN Westland, for AAC | |
| ZJ225 | WS WAH-64D Apache AH1 | GKN Westland, for AAC | |
| ZJ226 | WS WAH-64D Apache AH1 | GKN Westland, for AAC | |
| ZJ227 | WS WAH-64D Apache AH1 | GKN Westland, for AAC | |
| ZJ228 | WS WAH-64D Apache AH1 | GKN Westland, for AAC | |
| ZJ229 | WS WAH-64D Apache AH1 | GKN Westland, for AAC | |
| ZJ230 | WS WAH-64D Apache AH1 | GKN Westland, for AAC | |
| ZJ231 | WS WAH-64D Apache AH1 | GKN Westland, for AAC | |
| ZJ232 | WS WAH-64D Apache AH1 | GKN Westland, for AAC | |
| ZJ233 | WS WAH-64D Apache AH1 | GKN Westland, for AAC | |
| ZJ234 | Bell 412EP Griffin HT1 (C-FZLM/ G-BWZR) [S] | DHFS No 60(R) Sqn, RAF Shawbury | |
| ZJ235 | Bell 412EP Griffin HT1 (C-FZNF/ G-BXBF) [I] | DHFS No 60(R) Sqn, RAF Shawbury | |
| ZJ236 | Bell 412EP Griffin HT1 (C-FZLN/ G-BXBE) [X] | DHFS No 60(R) Sqn, RAF Shawbury | |
| ZJ237 | Bell 412EP Griffin HT1 (C-FZVV/ G-BXFF) [T] | DHFS No 60(R) Sqn, RAF Shawbury | |
| ZJ238 | Bell 412EP Griffin HT1 (C-FZXD/ G-BXFH) [Y] | DHFS No 60(R) Sqn, RAF Shawbury | |
| ZJ239 | Bell 412EP Griffin HT1 (C-GAFF/ G-BXHC) [R] | DHFS No 60(R) Sqn, RAF Shawbury | |
| ZJ240 | Bell 412EP Griffin HT1 (C-GAIE/ G-BXIR) [U] | DHFS No 60(R) Sqn/SARTU, RAF Valley | |
| ZJ241 | Bell 412EP Griffin HT1 (C-GAIG/ G-BXIS) [L] | DHFS No 60(R) Sqn/SARTU, RAF Valley | |
| ZJ242 | Bell 412EP Griffin HT1 (N2291Q/ G-BXDK) [E] | DHFS No 60(R) Sqn/SARTU, RAF Valley | |

| Notes | Serial | Type (other identity) [code] | Owner/operator, location or fate |
|---|---|---|---|
| | ZJ243 | AS350BA Squirrel HT2 (G-BWZS) | School of Army Aviation/No 670 Sqn, Middle Wallop |
| | ZJ244 | AS350BA Squirrel HT2 (G-BXMD) | School of Army Aviation/No 670 Sqn, Middle Wallop |
| | ZJ245 | AS350BA Squirrel HT2 (G-BXME) | School of Army Aviation/No 670 Sqn, Middle Wallop |
| | ZJ246 | AS350BA Squirrel HT2 (G-BXMJ) | School of Army Aviation/No 670 Sqn, Middle Wallop |
| | ZJ247 | AS350BA Squirrel HT2 (G-BXNB) | School of Army Aviation/No 670 Sqn, Middle Wallop |
| | ZJ248 | AS350BA Squirrel HT2 (G-BXNE) | School of Army Aviation/No 670 Sqn, Middle Wallop |
| | ZJ249 | AS350BA Squirrel HT2 (G-BXNJ) | School of Army Aviation/No 670 Sqn, Middle Wallop |
| | ZJ250 | AS350BA Squirrel HT2 (G-BXOG) | School of Army Aviation/No 670 Sqn, Middle Wallop |
| | ZJ251 | AS350BA Squirrel HT2 (G-BXNY) | School of Army Aviation/No 670 Sqn, Middle Wallop |
| | ZJ252 | AS350BA Squirrel HT2 (G-BXOK) | School of Army Aviation/No 670 Sqn, Middle Wallop |
| | ZJ253 | AS350BA Squirrel HT2 (G-BXPG) | School of Army Aviation/No 670 Sqn, Middle Wallop |
| | ZJ254 | AS350BA Squirrel HT2 (G-BXPJ) | School of Army Aviation/No 670 Sqn, Middle Wallop |
| | ZJ255 | AS350BB Squirrel HT1 (G-BXAG) | DHFS, RAF Shawbury |
| | ZJ256 | AS350BB Squirrel HT1 (G-BXCE) | DHFS, RAF Shawbury |
| | ZJ257 | AS350BB Squirrel HT1 (G-BXDJ) | DHFS, RAF Shawbury |
| | ZJ258 | AS350BB Squirrel HT1 (G-BXEO) | DHFS, RAF Shawbury |
| | ZJ259 | AS350BB Squirrel HT1 (G-BXFJ) | DHFS, RAF Shawbury |
| | ZJ260 | AS350BB Squirrel HT1 (G-BXGB) | DHFS, RAF Shawbury |
| | ZJ261 | AS350BB Squirrel HT1 (G-BXGJ) | DHFS, RAF Shawbury |
| | ZJ262 | AS350BB Squirrel HT1 (G-BXHB) | DHFS, RAF Shawbury |
| | ZJ263 | AS350BB Squirrel HT1 (G-BXHK) | DHFS, RAF Shawbury |
| | ZJ264 | AS350BB Squirrel HT1 (G-BXHW) | DHFS, RAF Shawbury |
| | ZJ265 | AS350BB Squirrel HT1 (G-BXHX) | DHFS, RAF Shawbury |
| | ZJ266 | AS350BB Squirrel HT1 (G-BXIL) | DHFS, RAF Shawbury |
| | ZJ267 | AS350BB Squirrel HT1 (G-BXIP) | DHFS, RAF Shawbury |
| | ZJ268 | AS350BB Squirrel HT1 (G-BXJE) | DHFS, RAF Shawbury |
| | ZJ269 | AS350BB Squirrel HT1 (G-BXJN) | DHFS, RAF Shawbury |
| | ZJ270 | AS350BB Squirrel HT1 (G-BXJR) | DHFS, RAF Shawbury |
| | ZJ271 | AS350BB Squirrel HT1 (G-BXKE) | DHFS, RAF Shawbury |
| | ZJ272 | AS350BB Squirrel HT1 (G-BXKN) | DHFS, RAF Shawbury |
| | ZJ273 | AS350BB Squirrel HT1 (G-BXKP) | DHFS, RAF Shawbury |
| | ZJ274 | AS350BB Squirrel HT1 (G-BXKR) | DHFS, RAF Shawbury |
| | ZJ275 | AS350BB Squirrel HT1 (G-BXLB) | DHFS, RAF Shawbury |
| | ZJ276 | AS350BB Squirrel HT1 (G-BXLE) | DHFS, RAF Shawbury |
| | ZJ277 | AS350BB Squirrel HT1 (G-BXLH) | DHFS, RAF Shawbury |
| | ZJ278 | AS350BB Squirrel HT1 (G-BXMB) | DHFS, RAF Shawbury |
| | ZJ279 | AS350BB Squirrel HT1 (G-BXMC) | DHFS, RAF Shawbury |
| | ZJ280 | AS350BB Squirrel HT1 (G-BXMI) | DHFS, RAF Shawbury |
| | ZJ300 | GEC Phoenix UAV | *For Army* |
| | ZJ327 to ZJ353 | GEC Phoenix UAV | *For Army* |
| | ZJ482 | GAF Jindivik 700 | *For DERA* |
| | ZJ483 | GAF Jindivik 700 | *For DERA* |
| | ZJ484 to ZJ495 | GAF Jindivik 800 | *For DERA* |
| | ZJ496 to ZJ513 | GAF Jindivik 900 | *For DERA* |
| | ZJ514 | BAe Nimrod MRA4 (XV251) [PA-4] | DPA/BAE Systems, Woodford (convn) |
| | ZJ515 | BAe Nimrod MRA4 (XV258) [PA-5] | DPA/BAE Systems, Woodford (convn) |
| | ZJ516 | BAe Nimrod MRA4 (XV247) [PA-1] | DPA/BAE Systems, Woodford (convn) |
| | ZJ517 | BAe Nimrod MRA4 (XV242) [PA-3] | DPA/BAE Systems, Woodford (convn) |
| | ZJ518 | BAe Nimrod MRA4 (XV234) [PA-2] | DPA/BAE Systems, Woodford (convn) |
| | ZJ519 | BAe Nimrod MRA4 | DPA/BAE Systems, for RAF |
| | ZJ520 | BAe Nimrod MRA4 | DPA/BAE Systems, for RAF |
| | ZJ521 | BAe Nimrod MRA4 | DPA/BAE Systems, for RAF |
| | ZJ522 | BAe Nimrod MRA4 | DPA/BAE Systems, for RAF |
| | ZJ523 | BAe Nimrod MRA4 | DPA/BAE Systems, for RAF |
| | ZJ524 | BAe Nimrod MRA4 | DPA/BAE Systems, for RAF |

| Serial | Type (other identity) [code] | Owner/operator, location or fate | Notes |
|---|---|---|---|
| ZJ525 | BAe Nimrod MRA4 | DPA/BAE Systems, for RAF | |
| ZJ526 | BAe Nimrod MRA4 | DPA/BAE Systems, for RAF | |
| ZJ527 | BAe Nimrod MRA4 | DPA/BAE Systems, for RAF | |
| ZJ528 | BAe Nimrod MRA4 | DPA/BAE Systems, for RAF | |
| ZJ529 | BAe Nimrod MRA4 | DPA/BAE Systems, for RAF | |
| ZJ530 | BAe Nimrod MRA4 | DPA/BAE Systems, for RAF | |
| ZJ531 | BAe Nimrod MRA4 | DPA/BAE Systems, for RAF | |
| ZJ532 | BAe Nimrod MRA4 | DPA/BAE Systems, for RAF | |
| ZJ533 | BAe Nimrod MRA4 | DPA/BAE Systems, for RAF | |
| ZJ534 | BAe Nimrod MRA4 | DPA/BAE Systems, for RAF | |
| ZJ535 | WS Super Lynx Mk 88A | GKN Westland, Yeovil, for German Navy as 83+20 | |
| ZJ536 | WS Super Lynx Mk 88A | GKN Westland, Yeovil, for German Navy as 83+21 | |
| ZJ537 | WS Super Lynx Mk 88A | GKN Westland, Yeovil, for German Navy as 83+22 | |
| ZJ538 | WS Super Lynx Mk 88A | GKN Westland, Yeovil, for German Navy as 83+23 | |
| ZJ539 | WS Super Lynx Mk 88A | GKN Westland, Yeovil, for German Navy as 83+24 | |
| ZJ540 | WS Super Lynx Mk 88A | GKN Westland, Yeovil, for German Navy as 83+25 | |
| ZJ541 | WS Super Lynx Mk 88A | GKN Westland, Yeovil, for German Navy as 83+26 | |
| ZJ542 | WS Super Lynx Mk 99 | *To S Korean Navy as 99-0721, 1 September 1999* | |
| ZJ543 | WS Super Lynx Mk 99 | GKN Westland, Yeovil, for S Korean Navy as 99-0722 | |
| ZJ544 | WS Super Lynx Mk 99 | GKN Westland, Yeovil, for S Korean Navy as 99-0723 | |
| ZJ545 | WS Super Lynx Mk 99 | GKN Westland, Yeovil, for S Korean Navy as 99-0725 | |
| ZJ546 | WS Super Lynx Mk 99 | GKN Westland, Yeovil, for S Korean Navy as 99-0726 | |
| ZJ547 | WS Super Lynx Mk 99 | GKN Westland, Yeovil, for S Korean Navy as 99-0727 | |
| ZJ548 | WS Super Lynx Mk 99 | GKN Westland, Yeovil, for S Korean Navy as 99-0728 | |
| ZJ549 | WS Super Lynx Mk 99 | GKN Westland, Yeovil, for S Korean Navy as 99-0729 | |
| ZJ555 | BAe Hawk 209 | *To Indonesian AF as TT-0217, 21 April 1999* | |
| ZJ556 | BAe Hawk 209 | *To Indonesian AF as TT-0218, 21 April 1999* | |
| ZJ557 | BAe Hawk 209 | *To Indonesian AF as TT-0219, 11 May 1999* | |
| ZJ558 | BAe Hawk 209 | *To Indonesian AF as TT-0220, 11 May 1999* | |
| ZJ559 | BAe Hawk 209 | *To Indonesian AF as TT-0221, 3 August 1999* | |
| ZJ560 | BAe Hawk 209 | *To Indonesian AF as TT-0222, 3 August 1999* | |
| ZJ561 | BAe Hawk 209 | *To Indonesian AF as TT-0223, 31 August 1999* | |
| ZJ562 | BAe Hawk 209 | *To Indonesian AF as TT-0224, 3 August 1999* | |
| ZJ563 | BAe Hawk 209 | *To Indonesian AF as TT-0225, 31 August 1999* | |
| ZJ564 | BAe Hawk 209 | *To Indonesian AF as TT-0226, 31 August 1999* | |
| ZJ565 | BAe Hawk 209 | BAE SystemsWarton, for Indonesian AF as TT-0227 | |
| ZJ566 | BAe Hawk 209 | BAE SystemsWarton, for Indonesian AF as TT-0228 | |
| ZJ567 | BAe Hawk 209 | BAE SystemsWarton, for Indonesian AF as TT-0229 | |
| ZJ568 | BAe Hawk 209 | BAE SystemsWarton, for Indonesian AF as TT-0230 | |
| ZJ569 | BAe Hawk 209 | BAE SystemsWarton, for Indonesian AF as TT-0231 | |
| ZJ570 | BAe Hawk 209 | BAE SystemsWarton, for Indonesian AF as TT-0232 | |

| Notes | Serial | Type (other identity) [code] | Owner/operator, location or fate |
|---|---|---|---|
| | ZJ580 to ZJ618 | Meteor Mirach 100-5 drone | *For RN* |
| | ZJ632 | BAe Hawk 127 | BAE Systems Warton, for R.Australian AF as A27-01 |
| | ZJ633 | BAe Hawk 127 | BAE Systems Warton, for R.Australian AF as A27-02 |
| | ZJ634 | BAe Hawk 127 | BAE Systems Warton, for R.Australian AF as A27-03 |
| | ZJ635 | AS355F-1 Twin Squirrel (G-NEXT) | DPA/AFD/ETPS, DERA Boscombe Down |
| | ZJ636 | BAe Hawk 127 | BAE Systems Warton, for R.Australian AF as A27-04 |
| | ZJ637 | BAe Hawk 127 | BAE Systems Warton, for R.Australian AF as A27-05 |
| | ZJ638 | BAe Hawk 127 | BAE Systems Warton, for R.Australian AF as A27-06 |
| | ZJ639 | BAe Hawk 127 | BAE Systems Warton, for R.Australian AF as A27-07 |
| | ZJ640 | BAe Hawk 127 | BAE Systems Warton, for R.Australian AF as A27-08 |
| | ZJ641 | BAe Hawk 127 | BAE Systems Warton, for R.Australian AF as A27-11 |
| | ZJ642 | BAe Hawk 127 | BAE Systems Warton, for R.Australian AF as A27-13 |
| | ZJ643 | BAe Hawk 127 | BAE Systems Warton, for R.Australian AF |
| | ZJ644 | BAe Hawk 127 | BAE Systems Warton, for R.Australian AF as A27-16 |
| | ZJ645 | D-BD Alpha Jet T1 | Dornier, for DERA |
| | ZJ646 | D-BD Alpha Jet T1 | Dornier, for DERA |
| | ZJ647 | D-BD Alpha Jet T1 | Dornier, for DERA |
| | ZJ648 | D-BD Alpha Jet T1 | Dornier, for DERA |
| | ZJ649 | D-BD Alpha Jet T1 | Dornier, for DERA |
| | ZJ650 | D-BD Alpha Jet T1 | Dornier, for DERA |
| | ZJ651 | D-BD Alpha Jet T1 | Dornier, for DERA |
| | ZJ652 | D-BD Alpha Jet T1 | Dornier, for DERA |
| | ZJ653 | D-BD Alpha Jet T1 | Dornier, for DERA |
| | ZJ654 | D-BD Alpha Jet T1 | Dornier, for DERA |
| | ZJ655 | D-BD Alpha Jet T1 | Dornier, for DERA |
| | ZJ656 | D-BD Alpha Jet T1 | Dornier, for DERA |
| | ZK101 | EHI-101 (I-HIOI) [PP7] | EH Industries, Montreal, Canada |
| | ZT800 | WS Super Lynx Mk 300 | DPA/GKN Westland, Yeovil |

Tornado GR1A in the distinctive markings of No 2 Squadron based at RAF Marham. *PRM*

Sea Harrier FA2 ZD610 with the markings and '000' code of 801 Naval Air Squadron. *PRM*

One of the new C-130J Hercules C3s (ZH869) newly delivered to the RAF at Lyneham. *PRM*

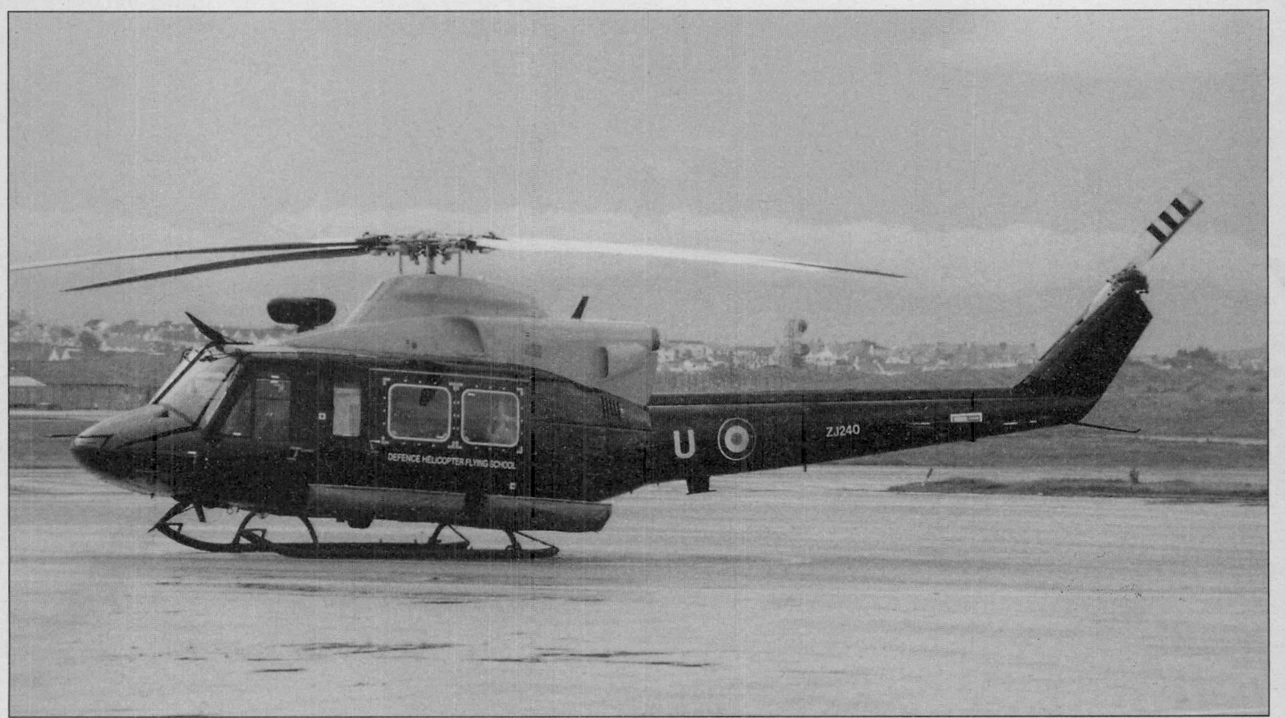


Based at RAF Valley with No 60(R) Squadron, this Griffin HT1 (ZJ240) is used by the Search & Rescue Training Unit. *Ken Storer*

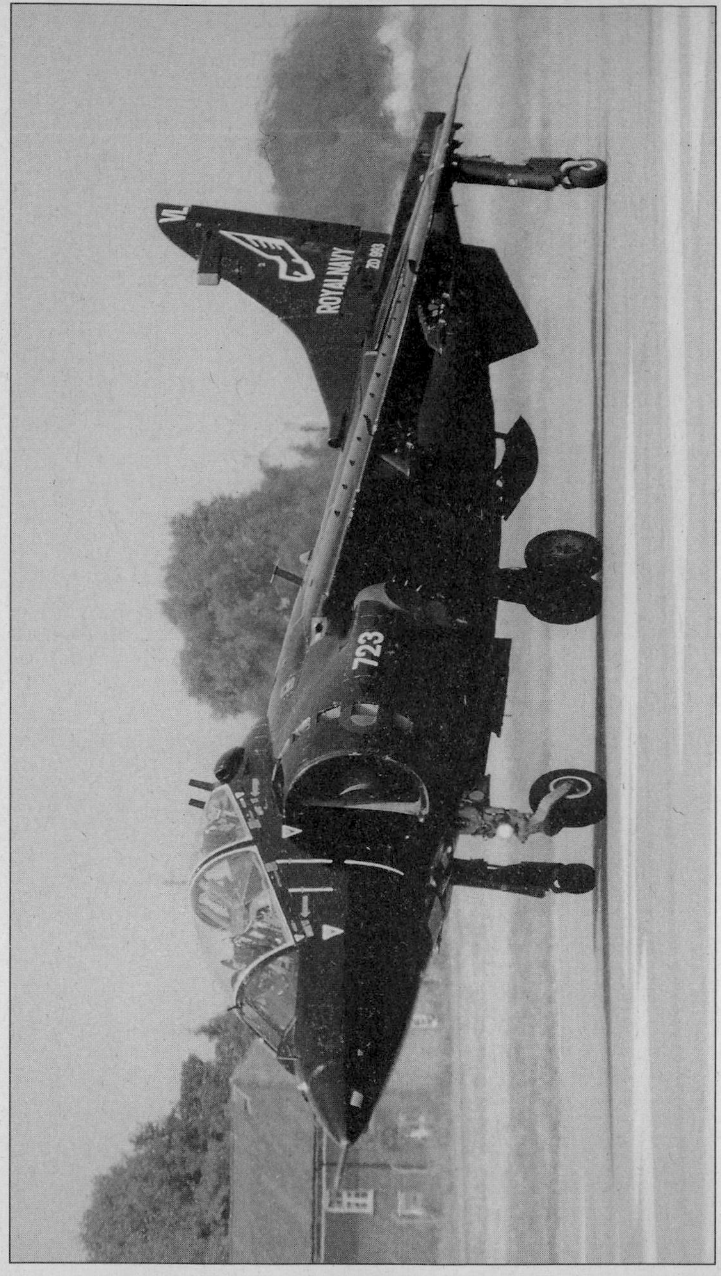

899 Naval Air Squadron operates this Harrier T8 (ZD993). *PRM*

WM167 is the only Meteor NF11 remaining airworthy in the UK. *PRM*

The Aircraft Restoration Company's Bristol Bolingbroke IVT L8841 flying with Shuttleworth's Westland Lysander IIIA V9441. *D. J. March*

# Civil Registered Aircraft in UK Military Service

| Serial | Type (other identity) [code] | Owner/operator, location or fate | Notes |
|---|---|---|---|
| G-BLVI | Slingsby T.67M Firefly 2 | Hunting Aircraft Ltd, Newton/Cranwell | |
| G-BNSO | Slingsby T.67M Firefly 2 | Hunting Aircraft Ltd/JEFTS, Barkston Heath | |
| G-BNSP | Slingsby T.67M Firefly 2 | Hunting Aircraft Ltd/CFS, Cranwell | |
| G-BNSR | Slingsby T.67M Firefly 2 | Hunting Aircraft Ltd/CFS, Cranwell | |
| G-BUUA | Slingsby T.67M Firefly 2 | Hunting Aircraft Ltd/JEFTS, Newton | |
| G-BUUB | Slingsby T.67M Firefly 2 | Hunting Aircraft Ltd/JEFTS, Newton | |
| G-BUUC | Slingsby T.67M Firefly 2 | Hunting Aircraft Ltd/JEFTS, Newton | |
| G-BUUD | Slingsby T.67M Firefly 2 | Hunting Aircraft Ltd/JEFTS, Newton | |
| G-BUUE | Slingsby T.67M Firefly 2 | Hunting Aircraft Ltd/JEFTS, Newton | |
| G-BUUF | Slingsby T.67M Firefly 2 | Hunting Aircraft Ltd/JEFTS, Newton | |
| G-BUUG | Slingsby T.67M Firefly 2 | Hunting Aircraft Ltd/JEFTS, Newton | |
| G-BUUI | Slingsby T.67M Firefly 2 | Hunting Aircraft Ltd/JEFTS, Newton | |
| G-BUUJ | Slingsby T.67M Firefly 2 | Hunting Aircraft Ltd/JEFTS, Newton | |
| G-BUUK | Slingsby T.67M Firefly 2 | Hunting Aircraft Ltd/JEFTS, Newton | |
| G-BUUL | Slingsby T.67M Firefly 2 | Hunting Aircraft Ltd/JEFTS, Barkston Heath | |
| G-BVHC | Grob G.115D-2 Heron | Shorts Bros/NFGF, Plymouth | |
| G-BVHD | Grob G.115D-2 Heron | Shorts Bros/NFGF, Plymouth | |
| G-BVHE | Grob G.115D-2 Heron | Shorts Bros/NFGF, Plymouth | |
| G-BVHF | Grob G.115D-2 Heron | Shorts Bros/NFGF, Plymouth | |
| G-BVHG | Grob G.115D-2 Heron | Shorts Bros/NFGF, Plymouth | |
| G-BWXA | Slingsby T.67M Firefly 260 | Hunting Aircraft Ltd/JEFTS, Barkston Heath | |
| G-BWXB | Slingsby T.67M Firefly 260 | Hunting Aircraft Ltd/JEFTS, Barkston Heath | |
| G-BWXC | Slingsby T.67M Firefly 260 | Hunting Aircraft Ltd/JEFTS, Barkston Heath | |
| G-BWXD | Slingsby T.67M Firefly 260 | Hunting Aircraft Ltd/JEFTS, Barkston Heath | |
| G-BWXE | Slingsby T.67M Firefly 260 | Hunting Aircraft Ltd/JEFTS, Barkston Heath | |
| G-BWXF | Slingsby T.67M Firefly 260 | Hunting Aircraft Ltd/JEFTS, Barkston Heath | |
| G-BWXG | Slingsby T.67M Firefly 260 | Hunting Aircraft Ltd/JEFTS, Barkston Heath | |
| G-BWXH | Slingsby T.67M Firefly 260 | Hunting Aircraft Ltd/JEFTS, Barkston Heath | |
| G-BWXI | Slingsby T.67M Firefly 260 | Hunting Aircraft Ltd/JEFTS, Barkston Heath | |
| G-BWXJ | Slingsby T.67M Firefly 260 | Hunting Aircraft Ltd/JEFTS, Barkston Heath | |
| G-BWXK | Slingsby T.67M Firefly 260 | Hunting Aircraft Ltd/JEFTS, Barkston Heath | |
| G-BWXL | Slingsby T.67M Firefly 260 | Hunting Aircraft Ltd/JEFTS, Barkston Heath | |
| G-BWXM | Slingsby T.67M Firefly 260 | Hunting Aircraft Ltd/JEFTS, Barkston Heath | |
| G-BWXN | Slingsby T.67M Firefly 260 | Hunting Aircraft Ltd/JEFTS, Barkston Heath | |
| G-BWXO | Slingsby T.67M Firefly 260 | Hunting Aircraft Ltd/JEFTS, Barkston Heath | |
| G-BWXP | Slingsby T.67M Firefly 260 | Hunting Aircraft Ltd/JEFTS, Barkston Heath | |
| G-BWXR | Slingsby T.67M Firefly 260 | Hunting Aircraft Ltd/JEFTS, Barkston Heath | |
| G-BWXS | Slingsby T.67M Firefly 260 [6] | Hunting Aircraft Ltd/JEFTS, Barkston Heath | |
| G-BWXT | Slingsby T.67M Firefly 260 | Hunting Aircraft Ltd/JEFTS, Barkston Heath | |
| G-BWXU | Slingsby T.67M Firefly 260 | Hunting Aircraft Ltd/JEFTS, Barkston Heath | |
| G-BWXV | Slingsby T.67M Firefly 260 | Hunting Aircraft Ltd/JEFTS, Barkston Heath | |
| G-BWXW | Slingsby T.67M Firefly 260 | Hunting Aircraft Ltd/JEFTS, Barkston Heath | |
| G-BWXX | Slingsby T.67M Firefly 260 | Hunting Aircraft Ltd/JEFTS, | |

| Notes | Serial | Type (other identity) [code] | Owner/operator, location or fate |
|---|---|---|---|
| | | | Barkston Heath |
| | G-BWXY | Slingsby T.67M Firefly 260 | Hunting Aircraft Ltd/JEFTS, Barkston Heath |
| | G-BWXZ | Slingsby T.67M Firefly 260 | Hunting Aircraft Ltd/JEFTS, Barkston Heath |
| | G-BYUA | Grob G.115E Tutor | Bombardier/Cambridge UAS/No 5 AEF, Wyton |
| | G-BYUB | Grob G.115E Tutor | Bombardier/CFS, Cranwell |
| | G-BYUC | Grob G.115E Tutor | Bombardier/CFS, Cranwell |
| | G-BYUD | Grob G.115E Tutor | Bombardier/CFS, Cranwell |
| | G-BYUE | Grob G.115E Tutor | Bombardier/Cambridge UAS/No 5 AEF, Wyton |
| | G-BYUF | Grob G.115E Tutor | Bombardier/CFS, Cranwell |
| | G-BYUG | Grob G.115E Tutor | Bombardier/CFS, Cranwell |
| | G-BYUH | Grob G.115E Tutor | Bombardier/CFS, Cranwell |
| | G-BYUI | Grob G.115E Tutor | Bombardier/Cambridge UAS/No 5 AEF, Wyton |
| | G-BYUJ | Grob G.115E Tutor | Bombardier/Cambridge UAS/No 5 AEF, Wyton |
| | G-BYUK | Grob G.115E Tutor | Bombardier/CFS, Cranwell |
| | G-BYUL | Grob G.115E Tutor | Bombardier/Cambridge UAS/No 5 AEF, Wyton |
| | G-BYUM | Grob G.115E Tutor | Bombardier/CFS, Cranwell |
| | G-BYUN | Grob G.115E Tutor | Bombardier/CFS, Cranwell |
| | G-BYUO | Grob G.115E Tutor | Bombardier/CFS, Cranwell |
| | G-BYUP | Grob G.115E Tutor | Bombardier/CFS, Cranwell |
| | G-BYUR | Grob G.115E Tutor | Bombardier/CFS, Cranwell |
| | G-BYUS | Grob G.115E Tutor | Grob/Bombardier for RAF |
| | G-BYUT | Grob G.115E Tutor | Grob/Bombardier for RAF |
| | G-BYUU | Grob G.115E Tutor | Grob/Bombardier for RAF |
| | G-BYUV | Grob G.115E Tutor | Grob/Bombardier for RAF |
| | G-BYUW | Grob G.115E Tutor | Grob/Bombardier for RAF |
| | G-BYUX | Grob G.115E Tutor | Grob/Bombardier for RAF |
| | G-BYUY | Grob G.115E Tutor | Grob/Bombardier for RAF |
| | G-BYUZ | Grob G.115E Tutor | Grob/Bombardier for RAF |
| | G-BYVA | Grob G.115E Tutor | Grob/Bombardier for RAF |
| | G-BYVB | Grob G.115E Tutor | Grob/Bombardier for RAF |
| | G-BYVC | Grob G.115E Tutor | Grob/Bombardier for RAF |
| | G-BYVD | Grob G.115E Tutor | Grob/Bombardier for RAF |
| | G-BYVE | Grob G.115E Tutor | Grob/Bombardier for RAF |
| | G-BYVF | Grob G.115E Tutor | Grob/Bombardier for RAF |
| | G-BYVG | Grob G.115E Tutor | Grob/Bombardier for RAF |
| | G-BYVH | Grob G.115E Tutor | Grob/Bombardier for RAF |
| | G-BYVI | Grob G.115E Tutor | Grob/Bombardier for RAF |
| | G-BYVJ | Grob G.115E Tutor | Grob/Bombardier for RAF |
| | G-BYVK | Grob G.115E Tutor | Grob/Bombardier for RAF |
| | G-BYVL | Grob G.115E Tutor | Grob/Bombardier for RAF |
| | G-BYVM | Grob G.115E Tutor | Grob/Bombardier for RAF |
| | G-BYVN | Grob G.115E Tutor | Grob/Bombardier for RAF |
| | G-BYVO | Grob G.115E Tutor | Grob/Bombardier for RAF |
| | G-BYVP | Grob G.115E Tutor | Grob/Bombardier for RAF |
| | G-BYVR | Grob G.115E Tutor | Grob/Bombardier for RAF |
| | G-BYVS | Grob G.115E Tutor | Grob/Bombardier for RAF |
| | G-BYVT | Grob G.115E Tutor | Grob/Bombardier for RAF |
| | G-BYVU | Grob G.115E Tutor | Grob/Bombardier for RAF |
| | G-BYVV | Grob G.115E Tutor | Grob/Bombardier for RAF |
| | G-BYVW | Grob G.115E Tutor | Grob/Bombardier for RAF |
| | G-BYVX | Grob G.115E Tutor | Grob/Bombardier for RAF |
| | G-BYVY | Grob G.115E Tutor | Grob/Bombardier for RAF |
| | G-BYVZ | Grob G.115E Tutor | Grob/Bombardier for RAF |
| | G-BYWA | Grob G.115E Tutor | Grob/Bombardier for RAF |
| | G-BYWB | Grob G.115E Tutor | Grob/Bombardier for RAF |
| | G-BYWC | Grob G.115E Tutor | Grob/Bombardier for RAF |
| | G-BYWD | Grob G.115E Tutor | Grob/Bombardier for RAF |
| | G-BYWE | Grob G.115E Tutor | Grob/Bombardier for RAF |
| | G-BYWF | Grob G.115E Tutor | Grob/Bombardier for RAF |
| | G-BYWG | Grob G.115E Tutor | Grob/Bombardier for RAF |
| | G-BYWH | Grob G.115E Tutor | Grob/Bombardier for RAF |
| | G-BYWI | Grob G.115E Tutor | Grob/Bombardier for RAF |
| | G-BYWJ | Grob G.115E Tutor | Grob/Bombardier for RAF |
| | G-BYWK | Grob G.115E Tutor | Grob/Bombardier for RAF |
| | G-BYWL | Grob G.115E Tutor | Grob/Bombardier for RAF |
| | G-BYWM | Grob G.115E Tutor | Grob/Bombardier for RAF |

| Serial | Type (other identity) [code] | Owner/operator, location or fate | Notes |
|---|---|---|---|
| G-BYWN | Grob G.115E Tutor | Grob/Bombardier for RAF | |
| G-BYWO | Grob G.115E Tutor | Grob/Bombardier for RAF | |
| G-BYWP | Grob G.115E Tutor | Grob/Bombardier for RAF | |
| G-BYWR | Grob G.115E Tutor | Grob/Bombardier for RAF | |
| G-BYWS | Grob G.115E Tutor | Grob/Bombardier for RAF | |
| G-BYWT | Grob G.115E Tutor | Grob/Bombardier for RAF | |
| G-BYWU | Grob G.115E Tutor | Grob/Bombardier for RAF | |
| G-BYWV | Grob G.115E Tutor | Grob/Bombardier for RAF | |
| G-BYWW | Grob G.115E Tutor | Grob/Bombardier for RAF | |
| G-BYWX | Grob G.115E Tutor | Grob/Bombardier for RAF | |
| G-BYWY | Grob G.115E Tutor | Grob/Bombardier for RAF | |
| G-BYWZ | Grob G.115E Tutor | Grob/Bombardier for RAF | |
| G-BYXA | Grob G.115E Tutor | Grob/Bombardier for RAF | |
| G-BYXB | Grob G.115E Tutor | Grob/Bombardier for RAF | |
| G-BYXC | Grob G.115E Tutor | Grob/Bombardier for RAF | |
| G-BYXD | Grob G.115E Tutor | Grob/Bombardier for RAF | |
| G-BYXE | Grob G.115E Tutor | Grob/Bombardier for RAF | |
| G-BYXF | Grob G.115E Tutor | Grob/Bombardier for RAF | |
| G-BYXG | Grob G.115E Tutor | Grob/Bombardier for RAF | |
| G-BYXH | Grob G.115E Tutor | Grob/Bombardier for RAF | |
| G-BYXI | Grob G.115E Tutor | Grob/Bombardier for RAF | |
| G-BYXJ | Grob G.115E Tutor | Grob/Bombardier for RAF | |
| G-BYXK | Grob G.115E Tutor | Grob/Bombardier for RAF | |
| G-BYXL | Grob G.115E Tutor | Grob/Bombardier for RAF | |
| G-BYXM | Grob G.115E Tutor | Grob/Bombardier for RAF | |
| G-BYXN | Grob G.115E Tutor | Grob/Bombardier for RAF | |
| G-BYXO | Grob G.115E Tutor | Grob/Bombardier for RAF | |
| G-BYXP | Grob G.115E Tutor | Grob/Bombardier for RAF | |
| G-BYXR | Grob G.115E Tutor | Grob/Bombardier for RAF | |
| G-BYXS | Grob G.115E Tutor | Grob/Bombardier for RAF | |
| G-BYXT | Grob G.115E Tutor | Grob/Bombardier for RAF | |
| G-BYXX | Grob G.115E Tutor | Grob/Bombardier for RAF | |
| G-BYXY | Grob G.115E Tutor | Grob/Bombardier for RAF | |
| G-BYXZ | Grob G.115E Tutor | Grob/Bombardier for RAF | |
| G-BYYA | Grob G.115E Tutor | Grob/Bombardier for RAF | |
| G-BYYB | Grob G.115E Tutor | Grob/Bombardier for RAF | |
| G-FFRA | Dassault Falcon 20DC (N902FR) | FR Aviation, Tees-side | |
| G-FRAD | Dassault Falcon 20E (G-BCYF) | FR Aviation, Bournemouth | |
| G-FRAE | Dassault Falcon 20E (N910FR) | FR Aviation, Bournemouth | |
| G-FRAF | Dassault Falcon 20E (N911FR) | FR Aviation, Bournemouth | |
| G-FRAH | Dassault Falcon 20DC (N900FR) | FR Aviation, Tees-side | |
| G-FRAI | Dassault Falcon 20E (N901FR) | FR Aviation, Tees-side | |
| G-FRAJ | Dassault Falcon 20E (N903FR) | FR Aviation, Tees-side | |
| G-FRAL | Dassault Falcon 20DC (N904FR) | FR Aviation, Tees-side | |
| G-FRAM | Dassault Falcon 20DC (N907FR) | FR Aviation, Bournemouth | |
| G-FRAO | Dassault Falcon 20DC (N906FR) | FR Aviation, Bournemouth | |
| G-FRAP | Dassault Falcon 20DC (N908FR) | FR Aviation, Bournemouth | |
| G-FRAR | Dassault Falcon 20DC (N909FR) | FR Aviation, Bournemouth | |
| G-FRAS | Dassault Falcon 20C (117501) | FR Aviation, Tees-side | |
| G-FRAT | Dassault Falcon 20C (117502) | FR Aviation, Tees-side | |
| G-FRAU | Dassault Falcon 20C (117504) | FR Aviation, Tees-side | |
| G-FRAW | Dassault Falcon 20ECM (117507) | FR Aviation, Tees-side | |
| G-FRBA | Dassault Falcon 20C | FR Aviation, Bournemouth | |
| G-HONG | Slingsby T.67M Firefly 2 | Hunting Aircraft Ltd/JEFTS, Newton | |
| G-KONG | Slingsby T.67M Firefly 2 | Hunting Aircraft Ltd/JEFTS, Newton | |
| G-XXEA | Sikorsky S-76C+ | Air Hanson/The Royal Flight, Blackbushe | |

Chipmunk T10 G-BBND carries its former RAF serial and Cambridge UAS markings. *Daniel March*

# RAF Maintenance Command/ Support Command/Logistics Command 'M' number Cross-reference

1764M/K4972
2015M/K5600
2292M/K8203
2361M/K6035
3118M/H5199/(BK892)
3858M/X7688
4354M/BL614
4552M/T5298
5377M/EP120
5378M/AR614
5405M/LF738
5466M/*BN230*/(LF751)
5690M/MK356
5718M/BM597
5758M/DG202
6457M/ML427
6490M/LA255
6640M/RM694
6850M/TE184
6946M/RW388
6948M/DE673
6960M/MT847
7008M/EE549
7014M/N6720
7015M/NL985
7035M/*K2567*/(DE306)
7060M/VF301
7090M/EE531
7118M/LA198
7119M/LA226
7150M/PK683
7154M/WB188
7174M/VX272
7175M/VV106
7200M/VT812
7241M/*MK178*(TE311)
7243M/TE462
7244M/*MK673*(TB382)
7246M/TD248
7256M/TB752
7257M/TB252
7279M/TB752
7281M/TB252
7288M/PK724
7293M/RW393
7323M/VV217
7325M/R5868
7326M/VN485
7362M/475081/(VP546)
7416M/WN907
7421M/WT660
7422M/WT684
7428M/WK198
7432M/WZ724
7438M/*18671*/(WP905)
7443M/WX853
7458M/WX905
7464M/XA564
7467M/WP978
7470M/XA553
7473M/XE946
7491M/WT569
7496M/WT612
7499M/WT555
7510M/WT694
7525M/WT619
7530M/WT648
7532M/WT651
7533M/WT680
7544M/WN904
7548M/PS915
7554M/FS890
7555M/AR614
7556M/WK584
7564M/XE982
7570M/XD674
7582M/WP190
7583M/WP185
7602M/WE600
7605M/WS692
7606M/WV562
7607M/TJ138
7615M/WV679
7616M/WW388
7618M/WW442
7622M/WV606
7625M/WD356
7631M/VX185
7641M/XA634
7645M/WD293
7646M/VX461
7648M/XF785
7673M/WV332
7688M/WW421
7693M/WV483
7696M/WV493
7698M/WV499
7703M/WG725
7704M/TW536
7705M/WL505
7706M/WB584
7709M/WT933
7711M/PS915
7712M/WK281
7715M/XK724
7716M/WS776
7718M/WA577
7719M/WK277
7728M/WZ458
7729M/WB758
7734M/XD536
7737M/XD602
7741M/VZ477
7750M/*WK864*/(WL168)
7751M/WL131
7755M/WG760
7758M/PM651
7759M/PK664
7761M/XH318
7762M/XE670
7764M/XH318
7770M/WT746
7793M/XG523
7796M/WJ676
7798M/XH783
7806M/TA639
7809M/XA699
7816M/WG763
7817M/TX214
7825M/WK991
7827M/XA917
7829M/XH992
7839M/WV781
7840M/XK482
7841M/WV783
7851M/WZ706
7852M/XG506
7854M/XM191
7855M/XK416
7859M/XP283
7860M/XL738
7862M/XR246
7863M/*XP248*
7864M/XP244
7865M/TX226
7866M/XH278
7868M/WZ736
7869M/WK935
7872M/*WZ826*/(XD826)
7881M/WD413
7882M/XD525
7883M/XT150
7886M/XR985
7887M/XD375
7891M/XM693
7894M/XD818
7895M/WF784
7898M/XP854
7899M/XG540
7900M/WA576
7906M/WH132
7917M/WA591
7920M/WL360
7923M/XT133
7925M/WV666
7928M/XE849
7930M/WH301
7931M/RD253
7932M/WZ744
7933M/XR220
7937M/WS843
7938M/XH903
7939M/XD596
7940M/XL764
7955M/XH767
7957M/XF545
7959M/WS774
7960M/WS726
7961M/WS739
7964M/WS760
7965M/WS792
7967M/WS788
7970M/WP907
7971M/XK699
7973M/WS807
7976M/XK418
7979M/XM529
7980M/XM561
7982M/XH892
7983M/XD506
7984M/XN597
7986M/WG777
7988M/XL149
7990M/XD452
7997M/XG452
7998M/*XM515*/(XD515)
8005M/WG768
8009M/XG518
8010M/XG547
8012M/VS562
8016M/XT677
8017M/XL762
8018M/XN344
8019M/WZ869
8021M/XL824
8022M/XN341
8023M/XD463
8027M/XM555
8032M/XH837
8033M/XD382
8034M/XL703
8041M/XF690
8043M/XF836
8046M/XL770
8049M/WE168
8050M/XG329
8051M/XN929
8052M/WH166
8054AM/XM410
8054BM/XM417
8055AM/XM402
8055BM/XM404
8056M/XG337
8057M/XR243
8063M/WT536
8070M/EP120
8072M/PK624
8073M/TB252
8078M/XM351
8079M/XN492
8080M/XM480
8081M/XM468
8082M/XM409
8086M/TB752
8092M/WK654
8094M/WT520
8101M/WH984
8102M/WT486
8103M/WR985
8106M/WR982
8108M/WV703
8114M/WL798
8117M/WR974
8118M/WZ549
8119M/WR971
8121M/XM474
8124M/XD614
8128M/WH775
8131M/WT507
8140M/XJ571
8141M/XN688
8142M/XJ560
8143M/XN691
8147M/XR526
8151M/WV795
8153M/WV903
8154M/WV908
8155M/WV797
8156M/XE339
8158M/XE369
8159M/XD528
8160M/XD622
8161M/XE993
8162M/WM913

# RAF Maintenance Cross-reference

8163M/XP919
8164M/*WN105*/(WF299)
8165M/WH791
8169M/WH364
8173M/XN685
8176M/WH791
8177M/*WM311*/(WM224)
8179M/XN928
8183M/*XN972*/(XN962)
8184M/WT520
8185M/WH946
8186M/WR977
8187M/WH791
8189M/WD646
8190M/XJ918
8192M/XR658
8196M/XE920
8198M/WT339
8203M/XD377
8205M/XN819
8206M/WG419
8207M/WD318
8208M/WG303
8209M/WG418
8210M/WG471
8211M/WK570
8213M/WK626
8214M/WP864
8216M/WP927
8217M/WZ866
8218M/WB645
8229M/XM355
8230M/XM362
8231M/XM375
8234M/XN458
8235M/XN549
8236M/XP573
8237M/XS179
8238M/XS180
8344M/WH960
8345M/XG540
8350M/WH840
8352M/XN632
8355M/*KG374*/(KN645)
8357M/WK576
8359M/WF825
8360M/WP863
8361M/WB670
8362M/WG477
8364M/WG464
8365M/XK421
8366M/XG454
8367M/XG474
8368M/XF926
8369M/WE139
8370M/N1671
8371M/XA847
8372M/K8042
8373M/P2617
8375M/NX611
8376M/RF398
8377M/R9125
8378M/*T9707*
8379M/DG590
8380M/Z7197
8382M/VR930
8383M/K9942
8384M/X4590
8385M/N5912
8386M/NV778
8387M/T6296
8388M/XL993
8389M/VX573
8392M/SL674
8394M/WG422
8395M/WF408
8396M/XK740
8399M/WR539
8401M/XP686
8402M/XN769
8406M/XP831
8407M/XP585
8408M/XS186
8409M/XS209
8410M/XR662
8413M/XM192
8414M/XM173
8417M/XM144
8422M/XM169
8427M/XM172
8429M/XH592
8434M/XM411
8436M/XN554
8437M/*WX643*/(WG362)
8439M/WZ846
8440M/WD935
8442M/XP411
8447M/XP359
8453M/XP745
8457M/XS871
8458M/XP672
8459M/XR650
8460M/XP680
8462M/XX477
8463M/XP355
8464M/XJ758
8465M/W1048
8466M/L-866
8467M/WP912
8468M/MM5701/(BT474)
8470M/584219
8471M/701152
8472M/120227/(VN679)
8473M/WP190
8474M/494083
8475M/360043/(PJ876)
8476M/24
8477M/4101/(DG200)
8478M/10639
8479M/730301
8481M/191614
8482M/112372/(VK893)
8483M/420430
8484M/5439
8485M/997
8486M/BAPC 99
8487M/J-1172
8488M/WL627
8491M/WJ880
8492M/WJ872
8493M/XR571
8494M/XP557
8495M/XR672
8501M/XP640
8502M/XP686
8507M/XS215
8508M/XS218
8509M/XT141
8513M/XN724
8514M/XS176
8535M/XN776
8538M/XN781
8545M/XN726
8546M/XN728
8548M/WT507
8549M/WT534
8554M/TG511
8560M/XR569
8561M/XS100
8565M/*WT720*/(E-408)
8566M/XV279
8568M/XP503
8570M/XR954
8573M/XM708
8575M/XP542
8576M/XP502
8578M/XR534
8581M/WJ775
8582M/XE874
8583M/BAPC 94
8584M/WH903
8585M/XE670
8586M/XE643
8587M/XP677
8588M/XR681
8589M/XR700
8590M/XM191
8591M/XA813
8595M/XH278
8598M/WP270
8600M/XX761
8602M/*PF179*/(XR541)
8606M/XP530
8608M/XP540
8610M/XL502
8611M/WF128
8617M/XM709
8618M/*XM693*/(XP504)
8620M/XP534
8624M/*XR991*/(XS102)
8627M/XP558
8628M/XJ380
8630M/*WX643*/(WG362)
8631M/XR574
8633M/MK732
8634M/WP314
8638M/XS101
8640M/XR977
8642M/XR537
8645M/XD163
8648M/XK526
8653M/XS120
8655M/XN126
8656M/XP405
8657M/VZ634
8661M/XJ727
8662M/XR458
8664M/WJ603
8666M/XE793
8668M/WJ821
8671M/XJ435
8672M/XP351
8673M/XD165
8674M/XP395
8676M/XL577
8677M/*XF519*/(XJ695)
8679M/XF526
8680M/XF527
8681M/XG164
8682M/XP404
8685M/XF516
8687M/XJ639
8693M/WH863
8696M/WH773
8700M/ZD234
8702M/XG196
8703M/VW453
8706M/XF383
8708M/XF509
8709M/XG209
8710M/XG274
8711M/XG290
8713M/XG225
8714M/XK149
8718M/XX396
8719M/XT257
8720M/XP353
8721M/XP354
8722M/WJ640
8723M/XL567
8724M/XW923
8726M/XP299
8727M/XR486
8728M/WT532
8729M/WJ815
8732M/XJ729
8733M/XL318
8736M/XF375
8738M/*XF519*/(XJ695)
8739M/XH170
8740M/WE173
8741M/XW329
8743M/WD790
8746M/XH171
8749M/XH537
8751M/XT255
8753M/WL795
8762M/WH740
8763M/WH665
8764M/XP344
8767M/XX635
8768M/A-522
8769M/A-528
8770M/XL623
8771M/XM602
8772M/WR960
8777M/XX914
8778M/XM598
8779M/XM607
8780M/WK102
8781M/WE982
8782M/XH136
8783M/XW272
8785M/XS642
8786M/XN495
8791M/XP329
8792M/XP345
8793M/XP346
8794M/XP398
8796M/XK943
8797M/XX947
8799M/WV787
8800M/XG226
8805M/XT772
8807M/XL587
8810M/XJ825
8814M/XM927
8818M/XK527
8819M/XS479
8820M/VP952
8821M/XX115
8822M/VP957
8828M/XS587
8830M/XF515
8831M/XG160
8832M/XG172
8833M/XL569
8834M/*XL571*
8836M/XL592
8838M/*34037*/(429356)
8839M/*69*/(XG194)
8840M/XG252
8841M/XE606
8844M/XJ676
8847M/XX344
8848M/XZ135

8851M/XT595
8852M/XV337
8853M/XT277
8855M/XT284
8857M/XW544
8860M/XW549
8861M/XW528
8862M/XN473
8863M/XG154
8867M/XK532
8868M/WH775
8869M/WH957
8870M/WH964
8871M/WJ565
8873M/XR453
8874M/XE597
8875M/XE624
8876M/*VM791*/(XA312)
8877M/XP159
8879M/XX948
8880M/XF435
8881M/XG254
8883M/XX946
8884M/VX275
8885M/XW922
8886M/XA243
8888M/XA231
8889M/XN239
8890M/WT532
8892M/XL618
8895M/XX746
8896M/XX821
8897M/XX969
8898M/XX119
8899M/XX756
8900M/XZ368
8901M/XZ383
8902M/XX739
8903M/XX747
8904M/XX966
8905M/XX975
8906M/XX976
8907M/XZ371
8908M/XZ382
8909M/XV784
8910M/XL160
8911M/XH673
8917M/XM372
8918M/XX109
8920M/XT469
8921M/XT466
8922M/XT467
8923M/XX819
8924M/XP701
8925M/XP706
8931M/XV779
8932M/XR718
8934M/XR749
8935M/XR713
8937M/XX751
8938M/WV746
8941M/XT456
8942M/XN185
8943M/XE799
8944M/WZ791
8945M/XX818
8946M/XZ389
8947M/XX726
8948M/XX757
8949M/XX743
8950M/XX956
8951M/XX727
8952M/XX730
8953M/XX959
8954M/XZ384
8955M/XX110
8956M/XN577
8957M/XN582
8958M/XN501
8961M/XS925
8967M/XV263
8969M/XR753
8972M/XR754
8973M/XS922
8974M/XM473
8975M/XW917
8976M/XZ630
8978M/XX837
8979M/XV747
8983M/XM478
8984M/XN551
8985M/WK127
8986M/XV261
8987M/XM358
8988M/XN593
8990M/XM419
8995M/XM425
8996M/XM414
8997M/XX669
8998M/XT864
9002M/XW763
9003M/XZ390
9004M/XZ370
9005M/XZ374
9006M/XX967
9007M/XX968
9008M/XX140
9009M/XX763
9010M/XX764
9011M/XM412
9012M/XN494
9014M/XN584
9015M/XW320
9017M/ZE449
9018M/XW365
9019M/XX824
9020M/XX825
9021M/XX826
9022M/XX958
9026M/XP629
9027M/XP556
9028M/XP563
9029M/XS217
9030M/XR674
9031M/XP688
9032M/XR673
9033M/XS181
9034M/XP638
9036M/XM350
9038M/XV810
9039M/XN586
9040M/XZ138
9041M/XW763
9042M/XL954
9044M/XS177
9045M/XN636
9046M/XM349
9047M/XW409
9048M/XM403
9049M/XW404
9050M/XG577
9052M/WJ717
9054M/XT766
9055M/XT770
9056M/XS488
9057M/ZE361
9059M/ZE360
9060M/ZE356
9061M/XW335
9062M/XW351
9064M/XT867
9065M/XV577
9066M/XV582
9067M/XV586
9070M/XV581
9072M/XW768
9073M/XW924
9075M/XV753
9076M/XV808
9078M/XV752
9079M/XZ130
9083M/ZE353
9084M/ZE354
9087M/XX753
9090M/XW353
9091M/XW434
9092M/XH669
9093M/WK124
9095M/XW547
9096M/WV322
9097M/XW366
9098M/XV406
9100M/XL188
9103M/XV411
9109M/XW312
9110M/XX736
9111M/XW421
9112M/XM475
9113M/XV500
9115M/XV863
9117M/XV161
9118M/XV253
9119M/XW303
9120M/XW419
9122M/XZ997
9123M/XT773
9124M/XW427
9125M/XW410
9126M/XW413
9127M/XW432
9128M/XW292
9129M/XW294
9130M/XW327
9131M/*DD931*
9132M/XX977
9133M/*413573*
9134M/XT288
9136M/XT891
9137M/XN579
9139M/XV863
9140M/XZ287
9141M/XV118
9143M/XN589
9144M/XV353
9145M/XV863
9146M/XW299
9147M/XW301
9148M/XW436
9149M/XW375
9150M/*FX760*
9151M/XT907
9152M/XV424
9153M/XW360
9154M/XW321
9155M/WL679
9158M/XV467
9159M/XV468
9162M/XZ991
9163M/XV415
9165M/XV408
9166M/XW323
9167M/XV744
9168M/XZ132
9169M/XW547
9170M/XZ994
9172M/XW304
9173M/XW418
9174M/XZ131
9175M/P1344
9176M/XW430
9177M/XW328
9179M/XW309
9180M/XW311
9181M/XW358
9183M/*XF519*/(XJ695)
9185M/XZ987
9186M/XF967
9187M/XW405
9188M/XW364
9189M/ZD350
9190M/XW318
9191M/XW416
9192M/XW361
9193M/XW367
9194M/XW420
9195M/XW330
9196M/XW370
9197M/*XX530*/(XX637)
9198M/XS641
9199M/XW290
9200M/XW425
9201M/ZD667
9202M/*433*
9203M/*3066*
9205M/*E449*
9206M/F6314
9207M/8417/18
9208M/F938
9209M/164
9210M/MF628
9211M/733682
9212M/*KL216*/(45-49295)
9213M/N5182
9215M/XL164
9216M/XL190
9217M/ZH257
9218M/XL563
9219M/XZ971
9220M/XZ995
9221M/XZ966
9222M/XZ968
9224M/XL568
9225M/XX885
9226M/XV865
9227M/XB812
9228M/ZD991
9229M/ZA678
9230M/ZA676
9231M
9232M/XV332
9233M/XZ431
9234M/XV864
9236M
9237M/XF995
9238M/ZA717
9239M/7198/18
9241M
9242M
9243M/XX163
9244M
9245M
9246M/XS714
9247M/XV420
9248M/WB627
9249M/WV396

9250M/162068
9251M
9252M
9253M
9254M
9255M/XZ375
9256M/XX839
9257M
9258M
9259M/XS710
9260M/XS734
9261M
9262M
9263M
9264M
9265M
9266M
9267M
9268M
9269M
9270M
9271M
9272M
9273M
9274M
9275M
9276M
9277M/XT601
9278M
9279M
9280M

With smoke stained tail, from its reverse thrust RB199s, Tornado F3 ZE757 is flown by No 56 (R) Squadron. *PRM*

Tiger Moth K4259 is privately owned and based at White Waltham. *PRM*

# RN Landing Platform and Shore Station Code-letters

| Code | Deck Letters | Vessel Name & Pennant No | Vessel Type & Unit |
|---|---|---|---|
| — | AS | RFA *Argus* (A135) | Aviation Training ship |
| 365/6 | AY | HMS *Argyll* (F231) | Type 23 (815 Sqn) |
| 328/9 | BA | HMS *Brave* (F94) | Type 22 (815 Sqn) |
| — | BD | RFA *Sir Bedivere* (L3004) | Landing ship |
| — | BV | RFA *Black Rover* (A273) | Fleet tanker |
| 335 | CF | HMS *Cardiff* (D108) | Type 42 (815 Sqn) |
| 350/1 | CL | HMS *Cumberland* (F85) | Type 22 (815 Sqn) |
| - | CM | HMS *Chatham* (F87) | Type 22 |
| 515 | CT | HMS *Campbeltown* (F86) | Type 22 (810 Sqn) |
| — | CU | RNAS Culdrose (HMS *Seahawk*) | — |
| 336/7 | CV | HMS *Coventry* (F98) | Type 22 (815 Sqn) |
| 412/3 | CW | HMS *Cornwall* (F99) | Type 22 (815 Sqn) |
| — | DC | HMS *Dumbarton Castle* (P265) | Fishery protection |
| — | DG | RFA *Diligence* (A132) | Maintenance |
| 411 | EB | HMS *Edinburgh* (D97) | Type 42 (815 Sqn) |
| 434/5 | EE | HMS *Endurance* (A171) | Ice Patrol (815 Sqn) |
| 420 | EX | HMS *Exeter* (D89) | Type 42 (815 Sqn) |
| — | FA | RFA *Fort Austin* (A386) | Support ship |
| — | FR | RFA *Fort Rosalie* (A385) | Support ship |
| — | FL | RNAY Fleetlands | — |
| — | FS | HMS *Fearless* (L10) | Assault |
| 410 | GC | HMS *Gloucester* (D96) | Type 42 (815 Sqn) |
| — | GD | RFA *Sir Galahad* (L3005) | Landing ship |
| — | GR | RFA *Sir Geraint* (L3027) | Landing ship |
| 437 | GT | HMS *Grafton* (F80) | Type 23 (815 Sqn) |
| — | GV | RFA *Gold Rover* (A271) | Fleet tanker |
| 344 | GW | HMS *Glasgow* (D88) | Type 42 (815 Sqn) |
| — | GY | RFA *Grey Rover* (A269) | Fleet tanker |
| — | HR | HMS *Herald* (H138) | Survey ship |
| — | ID | HMS *Intrepid* (L11) | Assault |
| 404 | IR | HMS *Iron Duke* (F234) | Type 23 (815 Sqn) |
| — | L | HMS *Illustrious* (R06) | Carrier |
| 457 | LA | HMS *Lancaster* (F229) | Type 23 (815 Sqn) |
| — | LC | HMS *Leeds Castle* (P258) | Fishery protection |
| 332 | LP | HMS *Liverpool* (D92) | Type 42 (815 Sqn) |
| 363/4 | MA | HMS *Marlborough* (F233) | Type 23 (815 Sqn) |
| 360 | MC | HMS *Manchester* (D95) | Type 42 (815 Sqn) |
| 415 | MM | HMS *Monmouth* (F235) | Type 23 (815 Sqn) |
| 444 | MR | HMS *Montrose* (F236) | Type 23 (815 Sqn) |
| — | N | HMS *Invincible* (R05) | Carrier |
| 345 | NC | HMS *Newcastle* (D87) | Type 42 (815 Sqn) |
| 361/2 | NF | HMS *Norfolk* (F230) | Type 23 (815 Sqn) |
| 372 | NL | HMS *Northumberland* (F238) | Type 23 (815 Sqn) |
| 417 | NM | HMS *Nottingham* (D91) | Type 42 (815 Sqn) |
| — | O | HMS *Ocean* (L12) | Helicopter carrier |
| — | ON | RFA *Olna* (A123) | Fleet tanker |
| — | OW | RFA *Olwen* (A122) | Fleet tanker |
| — | PO | RNAS Portland (HMS *Osprey*) | — |
| — | PV | RFA *Sir Percivale* (L3036) | Landing ship |
| — | PW | Prestwick Airport (HMS *Gannet*) | — |
| — | R | HMS *Ark Royal* (R07) | Carrier |
| 474 | RM | HMS *Richmond* (F239) | Type 23 (815 Sqn) |
| 352/3 | SD | HMS *Sheffield* (F96) | Type 22 (815 Sqn) |
| 355 | SM | HMS *Somerset* (F82) | Type 23 (815 Sqn) |
| 334 | SN | HMS *Southampton* (D90) | Type 42 (815 Sqn) |
| 422 | SU | HMS *Sutherland* (F81) | Type 23 (815 Sqn) |
| — | TM | RFA *Sir Tristram* (L3505) | Landing ship |
| — | VL | RNAS Yeovilton (HMS *Heron*) | — |
| 462 | WM | HMS *Westminster* (F237) | Type 23 (815 Sqn) |
| 407 | YK | HMS *York* (D98) | Type 42 (815 Sqn) |
| — | — | HMS *Albion* (L14) | Assault |
| — | — | HMS *Bulwark* (*L15*) | Assault |
| — | — | RFA *Fort Victoria* (A387) | Auxiliary Oiler |

## RN Landing Platforms

| Code | Deck Letters | Vessel Name & Pennant No | Vessel Type & Unit |
|---|---|---|---|
| — | — | RFA *Fort George* (A388) | Auxiliary Oiler |
| — | — | HMS *Kent* (F78) | Type 23 |
| — | — | HMS *Portland* (F79) | Type 23 |
| — | — | HMS *St Albans* (F83) | Type 23 |
| — | — | RFA *Wave Knight* (A389) | Auxiliary Oiler |
| — | — | RFA *Wave Ruler (A390)* | Fleet tanker |

This Hurricane replica *BE421* is displayed outside of the RAF Museum at Hendon. *PRM*

Operated by Air Atlantique Historic Flight, this Percival Prentice (VR259) is based at Coventry. *PRM*

# Ships' Numeric Code – Deck Letters Analysis

| | 0 | 1 | 2 | 3 | 4 | 5 | 6 | 7 | 8 | 9 |
|---|---|---|---|---|---|---|---|---|---|---|
| 32 | | | | | | | | | BA | BA |
| 33 | | | LP | | SN | CF | CV | CV | | |
| 34 | | | | | GW | NC | | | | |
| 35 | CL | CL | SD | SD | | SM | | | | |
| 36 | MC | NF | NF | MA | MA | AY | AY | | | |
| 37 | | | NL | | | | | | | |
| 40 | | | | | IR | | | YK | | |
| 41 | GC | EB | CW | CW | | MM | | NM | | |
| 42 | EX | | SU | | | | | | | |
| 43 | | | | | EE | EE | | GT | | |
| 44 | | | | | MR | | | | | |
| 45 | | | | | | | | LA | | |
| 46 | | | WM | | | | | | | |
| 47 | | | | | RM | | | | | |

# RN Code – Squadron – Base – Aircraft Cross-check

| *Deck/Base Code Numbers* | *Letters* | *Unit* | *Location* | *Aircraft Type(s)* |
|---|---|---|---|---|
| 000 — 006 | L | 801 Sqn | Yeovilton | Sea Harrier FA2 |
| 010 — 020 | L | 820 Sqn | Culdrose | Sea King HAS6 |
| 122 — 129 | N | 800 Sqn | Yeovilton | Sea Harrier FA2 |
| 180 — 182 | CU | 849 Sqn HQ Flt | Culdrose | Sea King AEW2 |
| 183 — 185 | L | 849 Sqn B Flt | Culdrose | Sea King AEW2 |
| 186 — 188 | R | 849 Sqn A Flt | Culdrose | Sea King AEW2 |
| 264 — 274 | N | 814 Sqn | Culdrose | Sea King HAS6 |
| 300 — 308 | PO | 815 Sqn | Yeovilton | Lynx HAS3/HMA8 |
| 318 — 319 | PO | 815 Sqn OEU | Yeovilton | Lynx HMA8 |
| 328 — 479 | * | 815 Sqn | Yeovilton | Lynx HAS3/HMA8 |
| 500 — 515 | CT/CU/CW | 810 Sqn | Culdrose | Sea King HAS6 |
| 535 — 541 | CU | 700M Sqn | Culdrose | Merlin HM1 |
| 560 — 573 | CU | 750 Sqn | Culdrose | Jetstream T2 |
| 576 — 579 | - | FONA | Yeovilton | Jetstream T3 |
| 580 — 585 | CU | 824 Training Flight | Culdrose | Merlin HM1 |
| 630 — 648 | PO | 702 Sqn | Yeovilton | Lynx HAS3 |
| 670 — 676 | PO | 702 Sqn | Yeovilton | Lynx HMA8 |
| 700 — 709 | PW | 819 Sqn | Prestwick | Sea King HAS6 |
| 710 — 719 | VL | 899 Sqn | Yeovilton | Sea Harrier FA2 |
| 720 — 724 | VL | 899 Sqn | Yeovilton | Harrier T8 |
| 730 — 731 | VL | 899 Sqn | Yeovilton | Sea Harrier FA2 |
| 820 — 827 | CU | 771 Sqn | Culdrose | Sea King HU5 |

*See foregoing separate ships' Deck Letters Analysis

Note that only the 'last two' digits of the Code are worn by some aircraft types.

# Historic Aircraft in Overseas Markings

Some *historic, classic and warbird* aircraft carry the markings of overseas air arms and can be seen in the UK, mainly preserved in museums and collections or taking part in air shows.

| *Notes* | *Serial* | *Type (other identity)* | *Owner/operator, location* |
|---|---|---|---|
| | **ARGENTINA** | | |
| | 0729 | Beech T-34C Turbo Mentor | FAA Museum, stored Wroughton |
| | 0767 | Aermacchi MB339AA | Rolls-Royce Heritage Trust, Filton |
| | A-515 | FMA IA58 Pucara (ZD485) | RAF Museum, Cosford |
| | A-517 | FMA IA58 Pucara (G-BLRP) | Privately owned, Channel Islands |
| | A-522 | FMA IA58 Pucara (8768M) | FAA Museum, at NE Aircraft Museum, Usworth |
| | A-528 | FMA IA58 Pucara (8769M) | Norfolk & Suffolk Avn Museum, Flixton |
| | A-533 | FMA IA58 Pucara (ZD486) <ff> | Boscombe Down Museum |
| | A-549 | FMA IA58 Pucara (ZD487) | Imperial War Museum, Duxford |
| | AE-409 | Bell UH-1H Iroquois [656] | Museum of Army Flying, Middle Wallop |
| | AE-422 | Bell UH-1H Iroquois | FAA Museum, RNAS Yeovilton |
| | **AUSTRALIA** | | |
| | A2-4 | Supermarine Seagull V (VH-ALB) | RAF Museum, Hendon |
| | A16-199 | Lockheed Hudson IIIA (G-BEOX) [SF-R] | RAF Museum, Hendon |
| | A17-48 | DH82A Tiger Moth (G-BPHR) | Privately owned, Swindon |
| | *A19-144* | Bristol 156 Beaufighter XIc (JM135/A8-324) | The Fighter Collection, Duxford |
| | A92-480 | GAF Jindivik 4A | DERA Llanbedr, on display |
| | A92-664 | GAF Jindivik 4A | Maes Artro Craft Village, Llanbedr |
| | A92-708 | GAF Jindivik 4A | Bristol Aero Collection, stored Kemble |
| | WH588 | Hawker Sea Fury FB11 (N588/G-EEMV) [114/NW] | Privately owned, Sywell |
| | **BELGIUM** | | |
| | FT-36 | Lockheed T-33A | Dumfries & Galloway Avn Mus, Dumfries |
| | *H-50* | Noorduyn AT-16 Harvard IIB (OO-DAF) | Privately owned, Brasschaat, Belgium |
| | HD-75 | Hanriot HD1 (G-AFDX) | RAF Museum, Hendon |
| | IF-68 | Hawker Hunter F6 <ff> | Privately owned, Welshpool |
| | K-16 | Douglas C-53D Skytrooper (OT-CWG/N49G) | Air Dakota, Brussels, Belgium |
| | L-44 | Piper L-18C Super Cub (OO-SPQ) | Privately owned, Belgium |
| | L-57 | Piper L-18C Super Cub (OO-GDH) | Privately owned, Belgium |
| | *SG-3* | VS379 Spitfire FR XIV (RN201/SG-31/G-BSKP) | Privately owned, Catfield |
| | V-18 | Stampe SV-4B (OO-GWD) | Antwerp Stampe Centre, Antwerp-Deurne, Belgium |
| | V-29 | Stampe SV-4B (OO-GWB) | Antwerp Stampe Centre, Antwerp-Deurne, Belgium |
| | **BOTSWANA** | | |
| | OJ1 | BAC Strikemaster 83 (ZG805/G-BXFU) | Global Aviation, Humberside |
| | OJ4 | BAC Strikemaster 87 (G-AYHR/G-UNNY) [Z2] | The Aircraft Restoration Company, Duxford |
| | OJ7 | BAC Strikemaster 83 (ZG809/G-BXFX) | Global Aviation, Humberside |
| | OJ8 | BAC Strikemaster 83 (ZG811/G-BXFV) | Global Aviation, Humberside |
| | OJ10 | BAC Strikemaster 87 (G-BXFS) | Privately owned, North Weald |
| | **BRAZIL** | | |
| | 1317 | Embraer T-27 Tucano | Shorts, Belfast (engine test bed) |
| | **BURKINA FASO** | | |
| | BF-8431 | SIAI-Marchetti SF.260 (F-GOBF) [31] | Privately owned, Elstree |
| | **CANADA** | | |
| | 622 | Piasecki HUP-3 Retriever (51-16622/N6699D) | The Helicopter Museum, Weston-super-Mare |
| | 920 | VS Stranraer (CF-BXO) [Q-N] | RAF Museum, Hendon |

| *Serial* | *Type (other identity)* | *Owner/operator, location* | *Notes* |
|---|---|---|---|
| 3349 | NA64 Yale (N55904) | ducAir, Lelystad, The Netherlands | |
| 5450 | Hawker Hurricane XII (G-TDTW) | Hawker Restorations Ltd, Milden | |
| 9059 | Bristol 149 Bolingbroke IVT | Privately owned, Portsmouth | |
| *9754* | Consolidated PBY-5A Catalina (VP-BPS) [P] | Privately owned, Lasham | |
| 9893 | Bristol 149 Bolingbroke IVT | Imperial War Museum store, Duxford | |
| 9940 | Bristol 149 Bolingbroke IVT | Royal Scottish Mus'm of Flight, E Fortune | |
| 15195 | Fairchild PT-19A Cornell | RAF Museum, stored Wyton | |
| *16693* | Auster J/1N Alpha (G-BLPG) [693] | Privately owned, Headcorn | |
| *18013* | DHC1 Chipmunk 22 (G-TRIC) [013] | Privately owned, North Weald | |
| 18393 | Avro Canada CF-100 Canuck IVB (G-BCYK) | Imperial War Museum, Duxford | |
| *18671* | DHC1 Chipmunk 22 (WP905/ 7438M/G-BNZC) [671] | Privately owned, Wombleton | |
| *20310* | CCF T-6J Harvard IV (G-BSBG) [310] | Privately owned, Liverpool | |
| 21417 | Canadair CT-133 Silver Star | Yorkshire Air Museum, Elvington | |
| 23140 | Canadair CL-13 Sabre [AX] (fuselage) | Midland Air Museum, Coventry | |
| 23380 | Canadair CL-13 Sabre <rf> | RAF Millom Museum, Haverigg | |
| *FJ777* | Boeing-Stearman PT-13D Kaydet (42-17786/G-BRTK) | Privately owned, Swanton Morley | |

**CHINA**

| | | | |
|---|---|---|---|
| 828 | Lavochkin La-9 (G-BWUD) | The Old Flying Machine Company, Duxford | |
| 1532008 | Nanchang CJ-6A Chujiao (G-BVFX) [08] | Privately owned, Breighton | |
| 2232028 | Nanchang CJ-6A Chujiao (G-BVVF) [69] | Privately owned, Bishop Auckland | |
| 2632016 | Nanchang CJ-6A Chujiao (G-BXZB) (also wears *2632019*) | Privately owned, Sandtoft | |

**CZECH REPUBLIC**

| | | | |
|---|---|---|---|
| 3677 | Letov S-102 (MiG-15) (613677) | Royal Scottish Museum of Flight, E Fortune | |
| 3794 | Letov S-102 (MiG-15) (623794) | Imperial War Museum, stored Duxford | |
| 9147 | Mil Mi-4 | The Helicopter Museum, Weston-super-Mare | |

**DENMARK**

| | | | |
|---|---|---|---|
| A-011 | SAAB A-35XD Draken | NATO Aircraft Museum, New Waltham, Humberside | |
| AR-107 | SAAB S-35XD Draken | Newark Air Museum, Winthorpe | |
| E-402 | Hawker Hunter F51 | Privately owned, Kemble | |
| E-409 | Hawker Hunter F51 (*XF383*) | City of Norwich Aviation Museum | |
| E-419 | Hawker Hunter F51 | North-East Aircraft Museum, Usworth | |
| E-420 | Hawker Hunter F51 (G-9-442) | Privately owned, Walton-on-Thames | |
| E-421 | Hawker Hunter F51 | Brooklands Museum, Weybridge | |
| E-423 | Hawker Hunter F51 (G-9-444) | SWWAPS, Lasham | |
| E-424 | Hawker Hunter F51 (G-9-445) | South Yorkshire Avn Museum, Firbeck | |
| E-425 | Hawker Hunter F51 | Midland Air Museum, Coventry | |
| E-430 | Hawker Hunter F51 | Gatwick Aviation Museum, Charlwood, Surrey | |
| ET-272 | Hawker Hunter T7 <ff> | Privately owned, North Weald | |
| ET-273 | Hawker Hunter T7 <ff> | South Yorkshire Avn Museum, Firbeck | |
| K-682 | Douglas C-47A Skytrain (OY-BPB) | Foreningen For Flyvende Mus, Vaerløse, Denmark | |
| L-866 | Consolidated PBY-6A Catalina (8466M) | RAF Museum, Cosford | |
| R-756 | Lockheed F-104G Starfighter | Midland Air Museum, Coventry | |
| S-881 | Sikorsky S-55C | The Helicopter Museum, Weston-super-Mare | |
| S-882 | Sikorsky S-55C | The Helicopter Museum, Weston-super-Mare | |
| S-886 | Sikorsky S-55C | The Helicopter Museum, Weston-super-Mare | |
| S-887 | Sikorsky S-55C | The Helicopter Museum, Weston-super-Mare | |

**EGYPT**

| | | | |
|---|---|---|---|
| 0446 | Mikoyan MiG-21UM <ff> | Thameside Aviation Museum, Tilbury | |
| 2684 | Mikoyan MiG-19 <ff> | | |
| 7907 | Sukhoi Su-7 <ff> | Robertsbridge Aviation Society, Mayfield | |

| Notes | Serial | Type (other identity) | Owner/operator, location |
|---|---|---|---|
| | **FINLAND** | | |
| | VI-3 | Valtion Viima 2 (OO-EBL) | Privately owned, Wevelghem, Belgium |
| | **FRANCE** | | |
| | 3 | Mudry/CAARP CAP-10B (G-BXRA) | Privately owned, Sedlescombe, Sussex |
| | *06* | Dewoitine D27 (290/F-AZJD) | The Old Flying Machine Company, Duxford |
| | 20 | MH1521C1 Broussard (G-BWGG) [315-SQ] | Privately owned, Rednal |
| | 37 | Nord 3400 (G-ZARA) [MAB] | Privately owned, Boston |
| | 57 | Dassault Mystère IVA [8-MT] | Imperial War Museum, Duxford |
| | 68 | Nord 3400 [MHA] | Privately owned, Coventry |
| | 70 | Dassault Mystère IVA | Midland Air Museum, Coventry |
| | 78 | Nord 3202 (G-BIZK) | Privately owned, Swanton Morley |
| | 79 | Dassault Mystère IVA [8-NB] | Norfolk & Suffolk Avn Museum, Flixton |
| | 83 | Dassault Mystère IVA [8-MS] | Newark Air Museum, Winthorpe |
| | 84 | Dassault Mystère IVA [8-NF] | Lashenden Air Warfare Museum, Headcorn |
| | 85 | Dassault Mystère IVA [8-MV] | British Aviation Heritage, Bruntingthorpe |
| | 100 | Mudry/CAARP CAP-10B (G-BXRB) | Privately owned, Sedlescombe, Sussex |
| | 101 | Dassault Mystère IVA [8-MN] | Bomber County Aviation Museum, Hemswell |
| | 105 | Nord N2501F Noratlas (F-AZVM) [62-SI] | Le Noratlas de Provence, Aix-les-Milles, France |
| | FR108 | SO1221 Djinn [CDL] | The Helicopter Museum, Weston-super-Mare |
| | 120 | SNCAN Stampe SV4C (G-AZGC) | Privately owned, Reading |
| | 121 | Dassault Mystère IVA | City of Norwich Aviation Museum |
| | 134 | Mudry/CAARP CAP-10B (G-BXRC) | Privately owned, Sedlescombe, Sussex |
| | 135 | Mudry/CAARP CAP-10B (G-BXFE) | Privately owned, Sedlescombe, Sussex |
| | 143 | Morane-Saulnier MS733 Alcyon (G-MSAL) | The Squadron, North Weald |
| | FR145 | SO1221 Djinn [CDL] | Privately owned, Luton |
| | 146 | Dassault Mystère IVA [8-MC] | North-East Aircraft Museum, Usworth |
| | 185 | MH1521M Broussard (G-BWLR) | Privately owned, Longhope |
| | 282 | Dassault MD311 Flamant (F-AZFX) [316-KY] | Memorial Flt Association, la Ferté-Alais, France |
| | 316 | MH1521M Broussard (F-GGKR) [315-SN] | The Old Flying Machine Company, Duxford |
| | 318 | Dassault Mystère IVA [8-NY] | Dumfries & Galloway Avn Mus, Dumfries |
| | 319 | Dassault Mystère IVA [8-ND] | Rebel Air Museum, Andrewsfield |
| | 348 | SO4050 Vautour IIN (F-AZHP) | Privately owned, Bretigny, France |
| | 396 | Stampe SV4A (G-BWRE) | Privately owned, stored Sandown |
| | 538 | Dassault Mirage IIIE [3-QH] | Yorkshire Air Museum, Elvington |
| | *1197* | Bleriot XI <R> (G-BPVE) | Bianchi Avn Film Services, Booker |
| | 17473 | Lockheed T-33A | Midland Air Museum, Coventry |
| | 42157 | NA F-100D Super Sabre [11-ML] | North-East Aviation Museum, Usworth |
| | 42204 | NA F-100D Super Sabre [11-MQ] | |
| | 63938 | NA F-100F Super Sabre [11-MU] | Lashenden Air Warfare Museum, Headcorn |
| | 125716 | Douglas AD-4N Skyraider (F-AZFN) [22-DG] | Privately owned, Etampes, France |
| | 126965 | Douglas AD-4NA Skyraider (OO-FOR) | Privately owned, Braaschaat, Belgium |
| | 517545 | NA T-28S Fennec (N14113) [CD-113] | The Aircraft Restoration Company, Duxford |
| | 517692 | NA T-28S Fennec (F-AZFV/ G-TROY) [142] | The Old Flying Machine Company, Duxford |
| | 18-1528 | PA-18 Cub 95 (F-MBCH) | Privately owned, stored Southampton |
| | *56-5395* | Piper L-18C Super Cub (52-2436/ G-CUBJ) [CDG] | Privately owned, Oaksey Park |
| | *C850* | Salmson 2A2 <R> | Barton Aviation Heritage Society, Barton |
| | *MS824* | Morane-Saulnier Type N <R> (G-AWBU) | Privately owned, Booker |
| | **GERMANY** | | |
| | - | Fieseler Fi103R-IV (V-1) (BAPC 91) | Lashenden Air Warfare Museum, Headcorn |
| | - | Focke-Achgelis Fa330A-1 (8469M) | RAF Museum, Cosford |
| | - | Fokker Dr1 Dreidekker <R> (BAPC 88) | FAA Museum, RNAS Yeovilton |

| *Serial* | *Type (other identity)* | *Owner/operator, location* | *Notes* |
|---|---|---|---|
| *2* | Messerschmitt Bf109G-10 (151591/D-HDME) | Privately owned, Mannheim, Germany | |
| *3* | SNCAN 1101 Noralpha (G-BAYV) | Barton Aviation Heritage Society, Barton | |
| 6 | Messerschmitt Bf109G-2/Trop (10639/8478M/G-USTV) | RAF/Imperial War Museum, Duxford | |
| *7* | Klemm Kl35D (G-BWRD) | *Returned to Germany 1999* | |
| *8* | Focke Wulf Fw190 <R> (G-WULF) | The Real Aeroplane Company, Breighton | |
| *10* | Nord 1002 (G-ETME) | Privately owned, Duxford | |
| *14* | Fiat G46-3B (G-BBII) | Privately owned, stored Staverton | |
| *14* | Messerschmitt Bf109 <R> (BAPC 67) | Kent Battle of Britain Museum, Hawkinge | |
| *14* | Pilatus P-2 (G-BJAX) | Privately owned, stored Duxford | |
| *14* | SNCAN 1101 Noralpha (G-BSMD) | Privately owned, North Weald | |
| *152/17* | Fokker Dr1 Dreidekker <R> (G-ATJM) | Privately owned, North Weald | |
| 210/16 | Fokker EIII (BAPC 56) | Science Museum, South Kensington | |
| *422/15* | Fokker EIII <R> (G-AVJO) | Privately owned, Booker | |
| *425/17* | Fokker Dr1 Dreidekker <R> (BAPC 133) | Kent Battle of Britain Museum, Hawkinge | |
| *425/17* | Fokker Dr1 Dreidekker <R> (G-BWRJ) | *Returned to Germany 1999* | |
| *450/17* | Fokker Dr1 Dreidekker <R> (G-BVGZ) | Museum of Army Flying, Middle Wallop | |
| *626/8* | Fokker DVII <R> (N6268) | Blue Max Movie Aircraft Museum, Booker | |
| 959 | Mikoyan MiG-21SPS | The Old Flying Machine Company, Duxford | |
| 1190 | Messerschmitt Bf109E-3 [4] | Imperial War Museum, Duxford | |
| 1227 | Focke-Wulf Fw190A-5 (G-FOKW) [DG+HO] | Privately owned, Milden | |
| 1342 | Messerschmitt Bf109E-3 (G-BYDS) | Privately owned, Milden | |
| *1480* | Messerschmitt Bf109 <R> (BAPC 66) [6] | Kent Battle of Britain Museum, Hawkinge | |
| 2100 | Focke-Wulf Fw189A-1 [V7+1H] | Privately owned, Sandtoft | |
| 4101 | Messerschmitt Bf109E-3 (DG200/8477M) [12] | RAF Museum, Hendon | |
| *6357* | Messerschmitt Bf109 <R> (BAPC 74) [6] | Kent Battle of Britain Museum, Hawkinge | |
| 7198/18 | LVG CVI (G-AANJ/9239M) | The Air Historical Branch, at RAF Museum, Hendon | |
| 8147 | Messerschmitt Bf109F-4 | Charleston Aviation Services, Colchester | |
| 8417/18 | Fokker DVII (9207M) | RAF Museum, Hendon | |
| 12802 | Antonov An-2T (D-FOFM) | Privately owned, Lahr, Germany | |
| 100143 | Focke-Achgelis Fa330A-1 | Imperial War Museum, Duxford | |
| 100502 | Focke-Achgelis Fa330A-1 | The Real Aeroplane Company, Breighton | |
| 100509 | Focke-Achgelis Fa330A-1 | Science Museum, stored Wroughton | |
| 100545 | Focke-Achgelis Fa330A-1 | Fleet Air Arm Museum stored, Wroughton | |
| 100549 | Focke-Achgelis Fa330A-1 | Lashenden Air Warfare Museum, Headcorn | |
| 112372 | Messerschmitt Me262A-2a (AM.51/VK893/8482M) [9K+XK] | RAF Museum, Cosford | |
| 120227 | Heinkel He162A-2 Salamander (VH513/8472M) [2] | RAF Museum, Hendon | |
| 120235 | Heinkel He162A-1 Salamander (AM.68) | Imperial War Museum, Lambeth | |
| 191316 | Messerschmitt Me163B Komet | Science Museum, South Kensington | |
| 191614 | Messerschmitt Me163B Komet (8481M) | RAF Museum, Cosford | |
| 191659 | Messerschmitt Me163B Komet (8480M) [15] | Royal Scottish Mus'm of Flight, E Fortune | |
| 191660 | Messerschmitt Me163B Komet (AM.214) [3] | Imperial War Museum, Duxford | |
| 280020 | Flettner Fl282/B-V20 Kolibri (frame only) | Midland Air Museum, Coventry | |
| 360043 | Junkers Ju88R-1 (PJ876/8475M) [D5+EV] | RAF Museum, Hendon | |
| 420430 | Messerschmitt Me410A-1/U2 (AM.72/8483M) [3U+CC] | RAF Museum, Cosford | |
| 475081 | Fieseler Fi156C-7 Storch (VP546/AM.101/7362M)[GM+AK] | RAF Museum, Cosford | |

| Notes | Serial | Type (other identity) | Owner/operator, location |
|---|---|---|---|
| | 494083 | Junkers Ju87D-3 (8474M) [RI+JK] | RAF Museum, Hendon |
| | 584219 | Focke Wulf Fw190F-8/U1 (AM.29/8470M) [38] | RAF Museum, Hendon |
| | 701152 | Heinkel He111H-23 (8471M) [NT+SL] | RAF Museum, Hendon |
| | 730301 | Messerschmitt Bf110G-4 (AM.34/8479M) [D5+RL] | RAF Museum, Hendon |
| | 733682 | Focke Wulf Fw190A-8/R7 (AM.75/9211M) | Imperial War Museum, Lambeth |
| | *1Z-NK* | Amiot AAC1/Ju52 (Port.AF 6316) | Imperial War Museum, Duxford |
| | *2+1* | Focke Wulf Fw190 <R> (G-SYFW) [7334] | Privately owned, Guernsey, CI |
| | *4+1* | Focke Wulf Fw190 <R> (G-BSLX) | Privately owned, Riseley |
| | *6J+PR* | CASA 2.111D (G-AWHB) | Privately owned, North Weald |
| | 20+48 | Mikoyan MiG-23BN [702] | DERA, Farnborough |
| | 22+35 | Lockheed F-104G Starfighter | SWWAPS, Lasham |
| | 22+57 | Lockheed F-104G Starfighter | NATO Aircraft Museum, New Waltham, Humberside |
| | 96+21 | Mil Mi-24D (406) | Imperial War Museum, Duxford |
| | 96+26 | Mil Mi-24D (429) | The Helicopter Museum, Weston-super-Mare |
| | 97+04 | Putzer Elster B (G-APVF) | Privately owned, Tadlow |
| | 98+14 | Sukhoi Su-22M-4 | The Old Flying Machine Company, stored Scampton |
| | 99+24 | NA OV-10B Bronco (F-AZKM) | Privately owned, Montelimar, France |
| | *AM+YA* | Zlin Z381 Bestmann (G-AMYA) | Privately owned, Wombleton, N Yorks |
| | *BU+CC* | CASA 1.131E Jungmann (G-BUCC) | Privately owned, Goodwood |
| | *BU+CK* | CASA 1.131E Jungmann (G-BUCK) | Privately owned, White Waltham |
| | *CC+43* | Pilatus P-2 (G-CJCI) | Privately owned, Norwich |
| | *CF+HF* | Morane-Saulnier MS502 (EI-AUY) | Imperial War Museum, Duxford |
| | *D5397/17* | Albatros DVA <R> (G-BFXL) | FAA Museum, RNAS Yeovilton |
| | *FI+S* | Morane-Saulnier MS505 (G-BIRW) | Royal Scottish Mus'm of Flight, E Fortune |
| | *FM+BB* | Messerschmitt Bf109G-6 (D-FMBB) | Daimler-Benz Aerospace, Manching, Germany |
| | *JA+120* | Canadair CL-13 Sabre 4 (MM19607) | Privately owned |
| | *LG+01* | Bücker Bü133C Jungmeister (G-AYSJ) | The Fighter Collection, Duxford |
| | *LG+03* | Bücker Bü133C Jungmeister (G-AEZX) | Privately owned, Milden |
| | *NJ+C11* | Nord 1002 (G-ATBG) | Privately owned, Sutton Bridge |
| | *S4+A07* | CASA 1.131E Jungmann (G-BWHP) | Privately owned, Yarcombe |
| | *S5+B06* | CASA 1.131E Jungmann 2000 (G-BSFB) | Privately owned, Stretton |
| | *TA+RC* | Morane-Saulnier MS505 (G-BPHZ) | The Aircraft Restoration Co, Duxford |
| | *TQ+BJ* | Focke-Wulf Fw44 Stieglitz (LV-ZAU) | Privately owned, Booker |

**GHANA**

| Notes | Serial | Type (other identity) | Owner/operator, location |
|---|---|---|---|
| | G-102 | SA122 Bulldog | Privately owned, Bourne Park, Hants |
| | G-107 | SA122 Bulldog (G-BCUO) | Privately owned, Henstridge |
| | G-108 | SA122 Bulldog (G-BCUP) | Privately owned, Bourne Park, Hants |

**GREECE**

| Notes | Serial | Type (other identity) | Owner/operator, location |
|---|---|---|---|
| | 51-6171 | NA F-86D Sabre | North-East Aircraft Museum, Usworth |
| | 52-6541 | Republic F-84F Thunderflash [541] | North-East Aircraft Museum, Usworth |

**HONG KONG**

| Notes | Serial | Type (other identity) | Owner/operator, location |
|---|---|---|---|
| | HKG-5 | SA128 Bulldog (G-BULL) | Privately owned, Slinfold |

**HUNGARY**

| Notes | Serial | Type (other identity) | Owner/operator, location |
|---|---|---|---|
| | 501 | Mikoyan MiG-21PF | Imperial War Museum, Duxford |

**INDIA**

| Notes | Serial | Type (other identity) | Owner/operator, location |
|---|---|---|---|
| | Q497 | EE Canberra T4 (fuselage) | BAE Systems Warton Fire Service |

**INDONESIA**

| Notes | Serial | Type (other identity) | Owner/operator, location |
|---|---|---|---|
| | LL-5306 | BAe Hawk T53 | BAE Systems Dunsfold |
| | LL-5313 | BAe Hawk T53 | BAE Systems Dunsfold |
| | LL-5315 | BAe Hawk T53 | BAE Systems Dunsfold |

| Serial | Type (other identity) | Owner/operator, location | Notes |
|---|---|---|---|
| LL-5317 | BAe Hawk T53 | BAE Systems Dunsfold | |
| LL-5319 | BAe Hawk T53 | BAE Systems Dunsfold | |
| LL-5320 | BAe Hawk T53 | BAE Systems Dunsfold | |
| **IRAQ** | | | |
| 333 | DH115 Vampire T55 <ff> | Military Aircraft Pres'n Grp, Barton | |
| **ISRAEL** | | | |
| 41 | NA P-51D Mustang (G-LYNE) | Privately owned, Tees-side | |
| **ITALY** | | | |
| MM5701 | Fiat CR42 (BT474/8468M) [13-95] | RAF Museum, Hendon | |
| MM53211 | Fiat G46-4 (BAPC 79) [ZI-4] | The Aircraft Restoration Co, stored Duxford | |
| MM53432 | NA T-6D Texan [RM-11] | Privately owned, South Wales | |
| MM53692 | CCF T-6G Texan | RAeS Medway Branch, Rochester | |
| MM53774 | Fiat G59-4B (I-MRSV) [181] | Privately owned, Parma, Italy | |
| MM54099 | NA T-6G Texan (G-BRBC) [RR-56] | Privately owned, Chigwell | |
| MM54-2372 | Piper L-21B Super Cub | Privately owned, Kesgrave, Suffolk | |
| *W7* | Avia FL3 (G-AGFT) | Privately owned, Leicester | |
| **JAPAN** | | | |
| - | Yokosuka MXY 7 Ohka II (BAPC 159) | Defence School, Chattenden | |
| 24 | Kawasaki Ki100-1B (8476M/BAPC 83) | RAF Museum, Cosford | |
| 3685 | Mitsubishi A6M3-2 Zero | Imperial War Museum, Duxford | |
| 5439 | Mitsubishi Ki46-III (8484M/ BAPC 84) | RAF Museum, Cosford | |
| 15-1585 | Yokosuka MXY 7 Ohka II (BAPC 58) | Science Museum, at FAA Museum, RNAS Yeovilton | |
| 997 | Yokosuka MXY 7 Ohka II (8485M/BAPC 98) | Gr Manchester Mus of Science & Industry | |
| I-13 | Yokosuka MXY 7 Ohka II (8486M/BAPC 99) | RAF Museum, Cosford | |
| **NETHERLANDS** | | | |
| 204 | Lockheed SP-2H Neptune [V] | RAF Museum, Cosford | |
| *361* | Hawker Fury FB10 (N36SF) | Privately owned, Kemble | |
| *A-12* | DH82A Tiger Moth (PH-TYG) | Privately owned, Gilze-Rijen, The Netherlands | |
| B-64 | Noorduyn AT-16 Harvard IIB (PH-LSK) | Privately owned, Gilze-Rijen, The Netherlands | |
| B-71 | Noorduyn AT-16 Harvard IIB (PH-MLM) | Privately owned, Gilze-Rijen, The Netherlands | |
| B-118 | Noorduyn AT-16 Harvard IIB (PH-IIB) | Privately owned, Gilze-Rijen, The Netherlands | |
| E-14 | Fokker S-11 Instructor (PH-AFS) | Privately owned, Lelystad, The Netherlands | |
| E-15 | Fokker S-11 Instructor (G-BIYU) | Privately owned, White Waltham | |
| E-18 | Fokker S-11 Instructor (PH-HTC) | Dukes of Brabant AF, Eindhoven, The Netherlands | |
| E-20 | Fokker S-11 Instructor (PH-GRB) | Privately owned, Gilze-Rijen, The Netherlands | |
| E-27 | Fokker S-11 Instructor (PH-HOL) | Privately owned, Lelystad, The Netherlands | |
| E-31 | Fokker S-11 Instructor (G-BEPV) | Privately owned, Elstree | |
| E-32 | Fokker S-11 Instructor (PH-HOI) | Privately owned, Gilze-Rijen, The Netherlands | |
| E-36 | Fokker S-11 Instructor (PH-ACG) | Privately owned, Lelystad, The Netherlands | |
| E-39 | Fokker S-11 Instructor (PH-HOG) | Privately owned, Lelystad, The Netherlands | |
| *G-29* | Beech D18S (N5369X) | Dutch Dakota Assn, Schiphol, The Netherlands | |
| N-202 | Hawker Hunter F6 [10] <ff> | Privately owned, Eaglescott | |
| N-250 | Hawker Hunter F6 (G-9-185) <ff> | Imperial War Museum, Duxford | |
| N-268 | Hawker Hunter FGA78 (Qatar QA-10) | Yorkshire Air Museum, Elvington | |
| N-315 | Hawker Hunter T7 | Jet Avn Preservation Grp, Long Marston | |
| *N5-149* | NA B-25J Mitchell (44-29507/ *HD346*/PH-XXV) [232511] | Dukes of Brabant AF, Eindhoven, The Netherlands | |
| R-109 | Piper L-21B Super Cub (54-2337/ PH-GAZ) | Privately owned, Gilze-Rijen, The Netherlands | |

| Notes | Serial | Type (other identity) | Owner/operator, location |
|---|---|---|---|
| | R-122 | Piper L-21B Super Cub (54-2412/ PH-PPW) | Privately owned, Gilze-Rijen, The Netherlands |
| | R-137 | Piper L-21B Super Cub (54-2427/ PH-PSC) | Privately owned, Gilze-Rijen, The Netherlands |
| | R-151 | Piper L-21B Super Cub (54-2441/ G-BIYR) | Privately owned, Dunkeswell |
| | R-163 | Piper L-21B Super Cub (54-2453/ G-BIRH) | Privately owned, Lee-on-Solent |
| | R-167 | Piper L-21B Super Cub (54-2457/ G-LION) | Privately owned, Turweston, Bucks |
| | R-177 | Piper L-21B Super Cub (54-2467/ PH-KNR) | Privately owned, Gilze-Rijen, The Netherlands |
| | R-181 | Piper L-21B Super Cub (54-2471/ PH-GAU) | Privately owned, Gilze-Rijen, The Netherlands |
| | *R-345* | Piper J-3C Cub (PH-UCS) | Privately owned, The Netherlands |
| | S-9 | DHC2 L-20A Beaver (G-BUVF/ PH-DHC) | KLu Historic Flt, Gilze-Rijen, The Netherlands |
| | *Y-74* | Consolidated PBY-5A Catalina (PH-PBY/C-FHHR) | Cat Air, Lelystad, The Netherlands |
| | **NEW ZEALAND** | | |
| | NZ3009 | Curtiss P-40E Kittyhawk (ZK-RMH) | The Old Flying Machine Company, Duxford |
| | NZ3905 | WS Wasp HAS1 (XT487) | GKN Westland, Weston-super-Mare |
| | NZ3907 | WS Wasp HAS1 (XT435/G-RIMM) | Privately owned, Cranfield |
| | NZ3909 | WS Wasp HAS1 (XT782) | Kennet Aviation, Cranfield, spares use |
| | NZ5648 | Goodyear FG-1D Corsair (NX55JP/G-BXUL) [648] | The Old Flying Machine Company, Duxford |
| | *NZ6361* | BAC Strikemaster 87 (OJ5/G-BXFP) | Privately owned, North Weald |
| | **NORTH KOREA** | | |
| | - | WSK Lim-2 (MiG-15) (G-BMZF) | FAA Museum, RNAS Yeovilton |
| | 1211 | WSK Lim-5 (MiG-17F) (G-BWUF) | The Old Flying Machine Company, Duxford |
| | **NORWAY** | | |
| | *423/427* | Gloster Gladiator I (L8032/ G-AMRK/*N2308*) | The Shuttleworth Collection, Old Warden |
| | 848 | Piper L-18C Super Cub (LN-ACL) [FA-N] | Privately owned, Norway |
| | 56321 | SAAB S91B Safir (G-BKPY) [U-AB] | Newark Air Museum, Winthorpe |
| | **POLAND** | | |
| | 05 | WSK SM-2 (Mi-2) (1005) | The Helicopter Museum, Weston-super-Mare |
| | 07 | WSK SM-1 (Mi-1) (2007) | The Helicopter Museum, Weston-super-Mare |
| | 309 | WSK SBLim-2A (MiG-15UTI) <ff> | Royal Scottish Museum of Flight, E Fortune |
| | 408 | WSK-PZL Mielec TS-11 Iskra (1H-0408) | The Old Flying Machine Company, Scampton |
| | 1018 | WSK-PZL Mielec TS-11 Iskra (1H-1018) | British Aviation Heritage, Bruntingthorpe |
| | 1120 | WSK Lim-2 (MiG-15bis) | RAF Museum, Hendon |
| | 09008 | WSK SBLim-2A (MiG-15UTI) | Privately owned, Sproughton |
| | **PORTUGAL** | | |
| | 1366 | OGMA/DHC1 Chipmunk T20 (CS-DAO) | Privately owned, stored Beds |
| | 1367 | OGMA/DHC1 Chipmunk T20 | Privately owned, stored Beds |
| | 1372 | OGMA/DHC1 Chipmunk T20 (HB-TUM) | Privately owned, Switzerland |
| | *1377* | DHC1 Chipmunk 22 (G-BARS) | Privately owned, Yeovilton |
| | 1741 | CCF Harvard IV (G-HRVD) | Air Atlantique Historic Flight, Coventry |
| | 1747 | CCF T-6J Harvard IV (*20385*/ G-BGPB) | The Aircraft Restoration Co, Duxford |
| | **QATAR** | | |
| | QA12 | Hawker Hunter FGA78 <ff> | The Planets Leisure Centre, Woking |
| | QP30 | WS Lynx Mk 28 (G-BFDV/TD 013) | Army SEAE, Arborfield |
| | QP31 | WS Lynx Mk 28 | RNAY Fleetlands Apprentice School |
| | QP32 | WS Lynx Mk 28 (TAD 016) | AAC Stockwell Hall, Middle Wallop |

| Serial | Type (other identity) | Owner/operator, location | Notes |
|---|---|---|---|
| **RUSSIA & FORMER SOVIET UNION** | | | |
| – | Mil Mi-24V (35324248 10853) | Privately owned, Hawarden | |
| 2 | Yakovlev Yak-52 (9311708/ G-YAKS) | Privately owned, North Weald | |
| 03 | Mil Mi-24D (3532461715415) | Privately owned, Hawarden | |
| 04 | Mikoyan MiG-23ML (024003607) | Privately owned, Hawarden | |
| 04 | Yakovlev Yak-52 (9211612/ RA-22521) | Privately owned, Wellesbourne Mountford | |
| 05 | Yakovlev Yak-50 (832507/YL-CBH) | Privately owned, Strathallan | |
| 06 | Mil Mi-24D (3532464505029) | Privately owned, Hawarden | |
| *07* | Yakovlev Yak-18M (G-BMJY) | Privately owned, North Weald | |
| 09 | Yakovlev Yak-52 (9411809/ G-BVMU) | Privately owned, Sandy, Beds | |
| 11 | SPP Yak C-11 (F-AZPM) | Privately owned, North Weald | |
| 12 | Let L-29 Delfin (194555/ES-YLM/ G-DELF) | Privately owned, Manston | |
| 15 | Yakovlev Yak-52 (844605/ G-BVVW) | Privately owned, Sudbury, Suffolk | |
| 15 | Yakovlev Yak-52 (866915/LY-ABQ) | Privately owned, Leicester | |
| 18 | Let L-29S Delfin (591771/YL-PAF) | Privately owned, Hawarden | |
| 19 | Yakovlev Yak-52 (811202/YL-CBI) | Privately owned, Cumbernauld | |
| 20 | Aero L-39C Albatros (931520/ ES-ZLA) | Privately owned, Gamston | |
| 20 | Lavochkin La-11 | The Fighter Collection, Duxford | |
| 20 | Yakovlev Yak-52 (790404/YL-CBJ) | Privately owned, Strathallan | |
| 23 | Mikoyan MiG-27D (83712515040) | Privately owned, Hawarden | |
| *26* | Yakovlev Yak-52 (9111306/ G-BVXK) | Privately owned, White Waltham | |
| *27* | SPP Yak C-11 (G-OYAK) | Privately owned, North Weald | |
| 27 | Yakovlev Yak-52 (9111307/ G-YAKX) | Privately owned, Old Sarum | |
| 31 | Yakovlev Yak-52 (9111311/ RA-02209) | Privately owned, Rendcomb | |
| 35 | Sukhoi Su-17M-3 (25102) | Privately owned, Hawarden | |
| *36* | SPP C-11 (G-KYAK) | Privately owned, North Weald | |
| *36* | SPP Yak C-11 (G-IYAK) | Privately owned, Earls Colne | |
| 40 | Yakovlev Yak-55M (920506/ RA-01333/G-YAKM) | Privately owned, | |
| 42 | Yakovlev Yak-52 (833901/ LY-AMU) | Privately owned, North Weald | |
| 46 | Yakovlev Yak-52 (9111413/ RA-44413) | Privately owned, White Waltham | |
| 48 | Yakovlev Yak-52 (RA-44514) | Privately owned, White Waltham | |
| 49 | Yakovlev Yak-55M (880606/ RA-44526) | Privately owned, White Waltham | |
| 50 | Mikoyan MiG-23MF (023003508) | Privately owned, Hawarden | |
| 50 | Yakovlev Yak-50 (812003/ G-BWJT) | Privately owned, Little Gransden | |
| *50* | Yakovlev Yak-50 (822305/ G-BXNO) | Privately owned, Denham | |
| 51 | Curtiss P-40E Warhawk (41-13570) | Privately owned, stored Sandown | |
| 51 | Let L-29S Delfin (491273/YL-PAG) | Privately owned, Hawarden | |
| 51 | Yakovlev Yak-50 (812004/ G-BWYK) | Privately owned, Little Gransden | |
| 52 | Yakovlev Yak-52 (877610/ G-BVVA) | Privately owned, Redhill | |
| 52 | Yakovlev Yak-52 (878202/ G-BWVR) | Privately owned, Sherburn | |
| *52* | Yakovlev Yak-52 (888802/ G-BXID) | Privately owned, Wellesbourne Mountford | |
| *52* | Yakovlev Yak-52 (800708/ LY-AMP) | Privately owned, Breighton | |
| 54 | Sukhoi Su-17M (69004) | Privately owned, Hawarden | |
| 55 | Yakovlev Yak-52 (9111505/ G-BVOK) | Intrepid Aviation, North Weald | |
| 56 | Yakovlev Yak-52 (811504/ LY-AKW) | Privately owned, Hawarden | |
| 56 | Yakovlev Yak-52 (9111506/ RA-44516) | Privately owned, White Waltham | |
| 64 | Let L-29 Delfin (394912/ES-YLO/ G-MAYA) | Privately owned, Lydd | |
| *69* | Hawker Hunter FGA9 (8839M/ XG194) | RAF North Luffenham Training Area | |
| *69* | Yakovlev Yak-50 (801810/G-BTZB) | Privately owned, Audley End | |

| Notes | Serial | Type (other identity) | Owner/operator, location |
|---|---|---|---|
| | 69 | Yakovlev Yak-52 (855509/LY-ALS) | Privately owned, North Weald |
| | 71 | Mikoyan MiG-27K (61912507006) | Privately owned, Hawarden |
| | *72* | Yakovlev Yak-52 (9111608/ G-BXAV) | Privately owned, North Weald |
| | 74 | Yakovlev Yak-52 (877404/LY-AOK) | Privately owned, Tollerton |
| | 84 | Aero L-39 Albatros | Privately owned, North Weald |
| | 96 | Yakovlev Yak-55 (901103/ RA-44525) | Privately owned, White Waltham |
| | 100 | Yakovlev Yak-52 (866904/G-YAKI) | Privately owned, Popham |
| | 107 | Yakovlev Yak-50 (822210/LY-AGG) | Privately owned, Old Sarum |
| | *111* | Aero L-39ZO Albatros (*28+02*/ G-OTAF) | The Old Flying Machine Company, Duxford |
| | 112 | Yakovlev Yak-52 (822610/LY-AFB) | Privately owned, Little Gransden |
| | 139 | Yakovlev Yak-52 (833810/ G-BWOD) | Privately owned, Sywell |
| | *503* | Mikoyan MiG-21SMT (G-BRAM) | Bournemouth Aviation Museum |
| | 1342 | Yakovlev Yak-1 (G-BTZD) | Privately owned, Milden |
| | *6247* | WSK SBLim-2A (MiG-15UTI) (622047/G-OMIG) | The Old Flying Machine Company, Duxford |
| | 899404 | Yakovlev Yak-52 (G-CCCP) | Privately owned, Little Gransden |
| | *1-12* | Yakovlev Yak-52 (9011013/ RA-02293) | Privately owned, Halfpenny Green |
| | **SAUDI ARABIA** | | |
| | 405 | Agusta-Bell AB.212 | Privately owned, Margate |
| | 420 | Agusta-Bell AB.212 | Privately owned, Margate |
| | 55-713 | BAC Lightning T55 (ZF598) | Midland Air Museum, Coventry |
| | **SINGAPORE** | | |
| | 311 | BAC Strikemaster 84 (N2146S/ G-SARK) | Classic Jets Flying Museum, Biggin Hill |
| | **SLOVAKIA** | | |
| | 7708 | Mikoyan MiG-21MF | RAF Benevolent Fund, DERA Boscombe Down |
| | **SOUTH AFRICA** | | |
| | 92 | Westland Wasp HAS1 (G-BYCX) | Privately owned, Thruxton |
| | 6130 | Lockheed Ventura II (AJ469) | RAF Museum, Cosford |
| | **SOUTH VIETNAM** | | |
| | *24550* | Cessna L-19E Bird Dog (G-PDOG) [GP] | Privately owned, Lincs |
| | **SPAIN** | | |
| | *B.2I-27* | CASA 2.111B (He111H-16) (B.2I-103) | The Old Flying Machine Company, Duxford |
| | C.4E-88 | Messerschmitt Bf109E | Privately owned, Hungerford |
| | C.4K-102 | Hispano HA 1.112M1L Buchon (G-BWUE) | The Real Aeroplane Company, Sandown (restoration) |
| | E.1-9 | CASA 1.133L Jungmeister (G-BVXJ) | The Real Aeroplane Company, Breighton |
| | E.3B-143 | CASA 1.131E Jungmann (G-JUNG) | Privately owned, White Waltham |
| | E.3B-153 | CASA 1.131E Jungmann (G-BPTS) [781-75] | The Old Flying Machine Company, Duxford |
| | E.3B-350 | CASA 1.131E Jungmann (G-BHPL) [05-97] | Privately owned, Kemble |
| | (E.3B-369) | CASA 1.131E Jungmann (G-BPDM) [781-32] | Privately owned, Chilbolton |
| | E.3B-521 | CASA 1.131E Jungmann [781-3] | RAF Museum Store, Cardington |
| | *EM-01* | DH60G Moth (G-AAOR) | Privately owned, Rendcomb |
| | ES.1-16 | CASA 1.133L Jungmeister | Privately owned, Stretton, Cheshire |
| | **SWEDEN** | | |
| | *081* | CFM 01 Tummelisa <R> (SE-XIL) | Privately owned, Karlstad, Sweden |
| | 05108 | DH60 Moth | Privately owned, Langham |
| | 17239 | SAAB B-17A (SE-BYH) [7-J] | Flygvapenmuseum, Linköping, Sweden |
| | *28693* | DH100 Vampire FB6 (J-1184/ SE-DXY) [9-G] | Scandinavian Historic Flight, Oslo, Norway |
| | 29640 | SAAB J-29F [20-08] | Midland Air Museum, Coventry |
| | 29670 | SAAB J-29F (SE-DXB) [10-R] | Flygvapenmuseum/F10 Wing, Angelholm, Sweden |
| | 32028 | SAAB 32A Lansen (G-BMSG) | Privately owned, Cranfield |

| Serial | Type (other identity) | Owner/operator, location | Notes |
|---|---|---|---|
| *34668* | Hawker Hunter F58 (J-4089/ SE-DXA) [9-G] | Scandinavian Historic Flight, Oslo, Norway | |
| 35075 | SAAB J-35J Draken [40] | Imperial War Museum, Duxford | |
| A14 | Thulin A/Bleriot XI (SE-XMC) | Privately owned, Karlstad, Sweden | |
| *N3-615* | NA P-51D Mustang (26158/ SE-BKG) | Privately owned, Hässlo, Sweden | |

**SWITZERLAND**

| Serial | Type (other identity) | Owner/operator, location | Notes |
|---|---|---|---|
| *A-10* | CASA 1.131E Jungmann (G-BECW) | Privately owned, Denham | |
| *A-57* | CASA 1.131E Jungmann (G-BECT) | Privately owned, Shoreham | |
| A-701 | Junkers Ju52/3m (HB-HOS) | Ju-Air, Dubendorf, Switzerland | |
| A-702 | Junkers Ju52/3m (HB-HOT) | Ju-Air, Dubendorf, Switzerland | |
| A-703 | Junkers Ju52/3m (HB-HOP) | Ju-Air, Dubendorf, Switzerland | |
| A-806 | Pilatus P3-03 (G-BTLL) | Privately owned, stored Headcorn | |
| C-552 | EKW C-3605 (/G-DORN) | Privately owned, North Weald | |
| C-558 | EKW C-3605 | Privately owned, Catfield | |
| J-1008 | DH100 Vampire FB6 | Mosquito Aircraft Museum, London Colney | |
| J-1149 | DH100 Vampire FB6 (G-SWIS) | Privately owned, Bournemouth | |
| J-1172 | DH100 Vampire FB6 (8487M) | RAF Museum Restoration Centre, Cardington | |
| J-1573 | DH112 Venom FB50 (G-VICI) | Source Classic Jet Flight, Bournemouth | |
| J-1605 | DH112 Venom FB50 (G-BLID) | Gatwick Aviation Museum, Charlwood, Surrey | |
| J-1614 | DH112 Venom FB50 (G-VENM) | Kennet Aviation, Cranfield | |
| J-1629 | DH112 Venom FB50 | Source Classic Jet Flight, Bournemouth | |
| J-1632 | DH112 Venom FB50 (G-VNOM) | Kennet Aviation, Cranfield | |
| J-1649 | DH112 Venom FB50 | Source Classic Jet Flight, Bournemouth | |
| J-1704 | DH112 Venom FB54 | RAF Museum, Cosford | |
| J-1712 | DH112 Venom FB54 | Botany Bay Village, Chroley, Lancs | |
| J-1758 | DH112 Venom FB54 (N203DM) | Privately owned, North Weald | |
| J-4021 | Hawker Hunter F58 (G-BWIU) | Historic Flying Ltd/OFMC, Scampton | |
| J-4031 | Hawker Hunter F58 (G-BWFR) | The Old Flying Machine Company, Scampton | |
| J-4058 | Hawker Hunter F58 (G-BWFS) | The Old Flying Machine Company, Scampton | |
| J-4066 | Hawker Hunter F58 (G-BXNZ) | The Old Flying Machine Company, Scampton | |
| J-4072 | Hawker Hunter F58 | Privately owned, Scampton | |
| J-4081 | Hawker Hunter F58 (G-BWKB) | The Old Flying Machine Company, Scampton | |
| J-4083 | Hawker Hunter F58 (G-EGHH) | Privately owned, Bournemouth | |
| J-4090 | Hawker Hunter F58 (G-SIAL) | The Old Flying Machine Company, Scampton | |
| J-4091 | Hawker Hunter F58 | British Aviation Heritage, Bruntingthorpe | |
| J-4105 | Hawker Hunter F58A (G-BWOU) | The Old Flying Machine Co, Scampton | |
| U-80 | Bücker Bü133D Jungmeister (G-BUKK) | Privately owned, White Waltham | |
| U-95 | Bücker Bü133C Jungmeister (G-BVGP) | Privately owned, Rednal, Shropshire | |
| U-99 | Bücker Bü133C Jungmeister (G-AXMT) | Privately owned, Breighton | |
| U-110 | Pilatus P-2 (G-PTWO) | Privately owned, Earls Colne | |
| U-142 | Pilatus P-2 (G-BONE) | Privately owned, Cheltenham | |
| U-1234 | DH115 Vampire T55 (G-DHAV) | De Havilland Aviation, Swansea | |
| V-54 | SE3130 Alouette II (G-BVSD) | Privately owned, Staverton | |

**USA**

| Serial | Type (other identity) | Owner/operator, location | Notes |
|---|---|---|---|
| - | Bell UH-1H Iroquois (Arg. AE-406) | Privately owned, Greenford, W London | |
| - | Noorduyn AT-16 Harvard IIB (KLu B-168) | American Air Museum, Duxford | |
| *1* | Spad XIII <R> (G-BFYO/*S3398*) | American Air Museum, Duxford | |
| *2* | Boeing-Stearman N2S-5 Kaydet (G-AZLE) | Privately owned, Tongham | |
| *5* | Boeing P-26A Peashooter <R> (G-BEEW) | Privately owned, Barton | |
| *14* | Boeing-Stearman A75N-1 Kaydet (G-ISDN) | Privately owned, Rendcomb | |
| *23* | Fairchild PT-23 (N49272) | Privately owned, Halfpenny Green | |
| *26* | Boeing-Stearman A75N-1 Kaydet (G-BAVO) | Privately owned, Old Buckenham | |
| *27* | NA SNJ-7 Texan (90678/G-BRVG) | Intrepid Aviation, North Weald | |

| Notes | Serial | Type (other identity) | Owner/operator, location |
|---|---|---|---|
| | *33-K* | PA-18 Super Cub 95 (51-15541/ G-BJLH) | Privately owned, Felthorpe |
| | *43* | Noorduyn AT-16 Harvard IIB (43-13064/G-AZSC) [SC] | Privately owned, Duxford |
| | *44* | Boeing-Stearman D75N-1 Kaydet (42-15852/G-RJAH) | Privately owned, Rendcomb |
| | *44* | Piper L-21B Super Cub (54-2405/ G-BWHH) | Privately owned, Felthorpe |
| | *49* | Curtiss P-40M Kittyhawk (43-5802/ G-KITT/*P8196*) | The Fighter Collection, Duxford |
| | *57* | WS55 Whirlwind HAS7 (XG592) | *Task Force* Adventure Park, Cowbridge, S Glam |
| | *85* | WAR P-47 Thunderbolt <R> (G-BTBI) | Privately owned, Carlisle |
| | *112* | Boeing-Stearman PT-13D Kaydet (42-17397/G-BSWC) | Privately owned, Old Sarum |
| | *118* | Boeing-Stearman PT-13A Kaydet (38-470/G-BSDS) | Privately owned, Swanton Morley |
| | *208* | Boeing-Stearman N2S-5 Kaydet (42-17223/N75664) | Privately owned, Spanhoe Lodge, Northants |
| | 243 | Boeing-Stearman A75N-1 Kaydet (41-25243/G-BUKE) | Privately owned, Goodwood |
| | *295* | Ryan PT-22 Recruit (41-20806/ N56028) | Privately owned, Oaksey Park, Wilts |
| | *379* | Boeing-Stearman PT-13D Kaydet (42-14865/G-ILLE) | Privately owned, Compton Abbas |
| | *441* | Boeing-Stearman N2S-4 Kaydet (30010/G-BTFG) | Privately owned, Bryngwyn Bach, Clwyd |
| | *540* | Piper L-4H Grasshopper (43-29877/G-BCNX) | Privately owned, Monewden |
| | *628* | Beech D17S (44-67761/N18V) | Privately owned, stored North Weald |
| | *744* | Boeing-Stearman A75N-1 Kaydet (42-16532/OO-USN) | Privately owned, Wevelghem, Belgium |
| | *796* | Boeing-Stearman PT-13D Kaydet (N43SV) | Privately owned, Rendcomb |
| | *854* | Ryan PT-22 Recruit (42-17378/ G-BTBH) | Privately owned, Wellesbourne Mountford |
| | *855* | Ryan PT-22 Recruit (41-15510/ N56421) | Privately owned, Halfpenny Green |
| | *897* | Aeronca 11AC Chief (G-BJEV) [E] | Privately owned, English Bicknor, Glos |
| | *1164* | Beech D18S (G-BKGL) | The Aircraft Restoration Co, Duxford |
| | *1180* | Boeing-Stearman N2S-3 Kaydet (3403/G-BRSK) | Privately owned, Tibenham |
| | 2525 | Curtiss JN-4D Jenny (N2525/ G-ECAB) | Aerosuperbatics, Rendcomb |
| | *2807* | NA T-6G Texan (49-3072/ G-BHTH) [V-103] | Northbrook College, Shoreham |
| | *5547* | Lockheed T-33A (51-9036) | Newark Air Museum, Winthorpe |
| | 6136 | Boeing-Stearman A75N-1 Kaydet (42-16136/G-BRUJ) [205] | Privately owned, Liverpool |
| | *6771* | Republic F-84F Thunderstreak (BAF FU-6) | RAF Manston History Museum |
| | 07539 | Boeing-Stearman N2S-3 Kaydet (N63590) [143] | Privately owned, Tibenham |
| | 7797 | Aeronca L-16A (47-0797/G-BFAF) | Privately owned, Finmere |
| | 8178 | NA F-86A Sabre (48-0178/ G-SABR) [FU-178] | Golden Apple Operations/OFMC, Duxford |
| | 8242 | NA F-86A Sabre (48-0242) [FU-242] | American Air Museum, Duxford |
| | *01532* | Northrop F-5E Tiger II <R> | RAF Alconbury on display |
| | 14286 | Lockheed T-33A (51-4286) | American Air Museum, Duxford |
| | O-14419 | Lockheed T-33A (51-4419) | Midland Air Museum, Coventry |
| | *14863* | NA AT-6D Harvard III (41-33908/ G-BGOR) | Privately owned, Goudhurst, Kent |
| | 15154 | Bell OH-58A Kiowa (70-15154) | R. Military College of Science, Shrivenham |
| | 16445 | Bell AH-1F Hueycobra (69-16445) | R. Military College of Science, Shrivenham |
| | 16506 | Hughes OH-6A Cayuse (67-16506) | The Helicopter Museum, Weston-super-Mare |
| | 16579 | Bell UH-1H Iroquois (66-16579) | The Helicopter Museum, Weston-super-Mare |
| | 16718 | Lockheed T-33A (51-6718) | City of Norwich Aviation Museum |

| *Serial* | *Type (other identity)* | *Owner/operator, location* | *Notes* |
|---|---|---|---|
| 18263 | Boeing-Stearman PT-17 Kaydet (41-8263/N38940) [822] | Privately owned, Tibenham | |
| 19252 | Lockheed T-33A (51-9252) | Tangmere Military Aviation Museum | |
| *20249* | Noorduyn AT-16 Harvard IIB (PH-KLU) [XS-249] | Privately owned, Lelystad, The Netherlands | |
| 21605 | Bell UH-1H Iroquois (72-21605) | American Air Museum, Duxford | |
| *21714* | Grumman F8F-2P Bearcat (121714/G-RUMM) [201-B] | The Fighter Collection, Duxford | |
| *24518* | Kaman HH-43F Huskie (62-4535) | Midland Air Museum, Coventry | |
| *28521* | CCF Harvard IV (G-TVIJ) [TA-521] | Privately owned, Woodchurch, Kent | |
| 30861 | NA TB-25J Mitchell (44-30861/ N9089Z) | Privately owned, North Weald | |
| 31145 | Piper L-4B Grasshopper (43-1145/ G-BBLH) [26-G] | Privately owned, Biggin Hill | |
| 31171 | NA B-25J Mitchell (44-31171/ N7614C) | American Air Museum, Duxford | |
| 31952 | Aeronca O-58B Defender (G-BRPR) | Privately owned, Earls Colne | |
| *34037* | NA TB-25N Mitchell (44-29366/ N9115Z/8838M) | RAF Museum, Hendon | |
| 37414 | McD F-4C Phantom (63-7414) | Midland Air Museum, Coventry | |
| 37699 | McD F-4C Phantom (63-7699) | Midland Air Museum, Coventry | |
| *38674* | Thomas-Morse S4 Scout <R> (G-MTKM) | Privately owned, Rugby | |
| *39624* | Wag Aero Sport Trainer (G-BVMH) [39-D] | Privately owned, Lincoln | |
| *40467* | Grumman F6F-5K Hellcat (80141/ G-BTCC) [19] | The Fighter Collection, Duxford | |
| *41386* | Thomas-Morse S4 Scout <R> (G-MJTD) | Privately owned, Hitchin | |
| 42163 | NA F-100D Super Sabre (54-2163) [HE] | Dumfries & Galloway Avn Mus, Dumfries | |
| 42165 | NA F-100D Super Sabre (54-2165) [VM] | American Air Museum, Duxford | |
| 42174 | NA F-100D Super Sabre (54-2174) [UH] | Midland Air Museum, Coventry | |
| 42196 | NA F-100D Super Sabre (54-2196) [LT] | Norfolk & Suffolk Avn Museum, Flixton | |
| *43578* | Boeing-Stearman N2S-3 Kaydet (N1364V) [578] | Privately owned, North Weald | |
| *46214* | Grumman TBM-3E Avenger (69327/CF-KCG) [X-3] | American Air Museum, Duxford | |
| 46867 | Grumman FM-2 Wildcat (N909WJ) | Flying A Services, North Weald | |
| 48846 | Boeing B-17E Fortress (44-8846/ F-AZDX) [DS-M] | Assoc Fortresse Toujours Volant, Rouen, France | |
| 53319 | Grumman TBM-3R Avenger (G-BTDP) [319-RB] | Privately owned, North Weald | |
| *54137* | CCF Harvard IV (MM54137/ G-CTKL) [69] | Privately owned, North Weald | |
| 54433 | Lockheed T-33A (55-4433) | Norfolk & Suffolk Avn Museum, Flixton | |
| 54439 | Lockheed T-33A (55-4439) | North-East Aircraft Museum, Usworth | |
| 58811 | NA B-25J Mitchell (45-8811/ F-AZID) [HD] | Privately owned, Athens, Greece | |
| 60312 | McD F-101F Voodoo (56-0312) | Midland Air Museum, Coventry | |
| 60689 | Boeing B-52D Stratofortress (56-0689) | American Air Museum, Duxford | |
| *63000* | NA F-100D Super Sabre (54-2212) [FW-000] | USAF Croughton, Oxon, at gate | |
| *63319* | NA F-100D Super Sabre (54-2269) [FW-319] | RAF Lakenheath, on display | |
| *63428* | Republic F-105G Thunderchief (62-4428) | USAF Croughton, Oxon, at gate | |
| 66692 | Lockheed U-2CT (56-6692) | American Air Museum, Duxford | |
| 70270 | McD F-101B Voodoo (57-270) (fuselage) | Midland Air Museum, Coventry | |
| 79863 | Grumman F6F-5K Hellcat (N79863) | Flying A Services, North Weald | |
| 80425 | Grumman F7F-3P Tigercat (N7235C/G-RUMT) [WT-14] | The Fighter Collection, Duxford | |
| 82062 | DHC U-6A Beaver (58-2062) | Midland Air Museum, Coventry | |
| 85869 | Grumman TBM-3E Avenger (F-AZJA) [401-AK] | Privately owned, Etampes, France | |
| *91007* | Lockheed T-33A (51-8566/ G-NASA) [TR-007] | De Havilland Aviation, Swansea | |

| Notes | Serial | Type (other identity) | Owner/operator, location |
|---|---|---|---|
| | *93542* | CCF Harvard IV (G-BRLV) [LTA-542] | Privately owned, North Weald |
| | 96995 | CV F4U-4 Corsair (OE-EAS) [BR-37] | Tyrolean Jet Services, Innsbruck, Austria |
| | 97264 | CV F4U-4 Corsair (F-AZVJ) [403] | Flying Legend, Dijon, France |
| | *111836* | NA AT-6C Harvard IIA (41-33262/ G-TSIX) [JZ-6] | The Real Aeroplane Company, Breighton |
| | 111989 | Cessna L-19A Bird Dog (51-11989/ N33600) | Museum of Army Flying, Middle Wallop |
| | 115042 | NA T-6G Texan (51-15042/ G-BGHU) [TA-042] | Privately owned, Headcorn |
| | 115302 | Piper L-18C Super Cub (51-15302/ G-BJTP) [TP] | Privately owned, Bidford |
| | 115684 | Piper L-21A Super Cub (51-15684/ G-BKVM) [DC] | Privately owned, Woodhall Spa |
| | *122351* | Beech C-45G (51-11665/G-BKRG) | Privately owned, Bruntingthorpe |
| | 124143 | Douglas AD-4NA Skyraider (F-AZDP) [205-RM] | Amicale J-B Salis, la Ferté-Alais, France |
| | *124485* | Boeing B-17G Fortress (44-85784/ G-BEDF) [DF-A] | B-17 Preservation Ltd, Duxford |
| | 124724 | CV F4U-5NL Corsair (F-AZEG) [22] | Amicale J-B Salis, la Ferté-Alais, France |
| | 126922 | Douglas AD-4NA Skyraider (G-RAID) [402-AK] | The Fighter Collection, Duxford |
| | 126956 | Douglas AD-4NA Skyraider (F-AZDQ) [3-RM] | Aéro Retro, St Rambert d'Albon, France |
| | 127002 | Douglas AD-4NA Skyraider (F-AZHK) [618-G] | Privately owned, le Castellet, France |
| | 138179 | NA T-28A Trojan (OE-ESA) [BA] | Tyrolean Jet Services, Innsbruck, Austria |
| | 140547 | NA T-28C Trojan (N2800Q) | Privately owned |
| | 146289 | NA T-28C Trojan (N99153) [2W] | Norfolk & Suffolk Aviation Museum, Flixton |
| | *150225* | WS58 Wessex 60 (G-AWOX) [123] | Privately owned, Lulsgate |
| | *151632* | NA TB-25N Mitchell (44-30925/ G-BWGR) | Privately owned, North Weald |
| | 153008 | McD F-4N Phantom | RAF Alconbury, BDRT |
| | 155529 | McD F-4S Phantom (ZE359) [AJ-114] | American Air Museum, Duxford |
| | 155848 | McD F-4S Phantom [WT-11] | Royal Scottish Mus'm of Flight, E Fortune |
| | 159233 | HS AV-8A Harrier [CG-33] | FAA Museum, RNAS Yeovilton |
| | 160810 | Bell AH-1T Sea Cobra <ff> | GEC, Rochester |
| | 162068 | McD AV-8B Harrier II (9250M) (fuselage) | RAF Wittering, BDRT |
| | 162071 | McD AV-8B Harrier II (fuselage) | Rolls-Royce, Filton |
| | *211072* | Boeing-Stearman PT-17 Kaydet (N50755) | Privately owned, Swanton Morley |
| | *217786* | Boeing-Stearman PT-17 Kaydet (41-8169/CF-EQS) [25] | American Air Museum, Duxford |
| | 219993 | Bell P-39Q Airacobra (42-19993/N139DP) | The Fighter Collection |
| | *226413* | Republic P-47D Thunderbolt (45-49192/N47DD) [ZU-N] | American Air Museum, Duxford |
| | *226671* | Republic P-47M Thunderbolt (G-THUN) [LH-X,MX-X] | The Fighter Collection, Duxford |
| | *231983* | Boeing B-17G Fortress (44-83735/ F-BDRS) [IY-G] | American Air Museum, Duxford |
| | 234539 | Fairchild PT-19B Cornell (42-34539/N50429) [63] | Privately owned, Dunkeswell |
| | *237123* | Waco CG-4A Hadrian (BAPC 157) (fuselage) | Yorkshire Air Museum, Elvington |
| | 238410 | Piper L-4A Grasshopper (42-38410/G-BHPK) [44-A] | Privately owned, Tibenham |
| | *243809* | Waco CG-4A Hadrian (BAPC 185) | Museum of Army Flying, Middle Wallop |
| | 252983 | Schweizer TG-3A (42-52983/ N66630) | American Air Museum, Duxford |
| | 269097 | Bell P-63A Kingcobra (42-69097/ G-BTWR) | The Fighter Collection, Duxford |
| | *290321* | Douglas C-53C Skytrooper (43-2022/N32MS) | Bevrijdende Vleugels, Eindhoven, The Netherlands |
| | 314887 | Fairchild Argus III (43-14887/ G-AJPI) | Privately owned, Swanton Morley |

| *Serial* | *Type (other identity)* | *Owner/operator, location* | *Notes* |
|---|---|---|---|
| 315211 | Douglas C-47A (43-15211/ N1944A) [J8-Z] | Privately owned, Booker | |
| 315509 | Douglas C-47A (43-15509/ G-BHUB) [W7-S] | American Air Museum, Duxford | |
| 329405 | Piper L-4H Grasshopper (43-29405/G-BCOB) [23-A] | Privately owned, South Walsham | |
| *329417* | Piper L-4A Grasshopper (42-38400/G-BDHK) | Privately owned, Coleford | |
| 329471 | Piper L-4H Grasshopper (43-29471/G-BGXA) [44-F] | Privately owned, Martley, Worcs | |
| 329601 | Piper L-4H Grasshopper (43-29601/G-AXHR) [44-D] | Privately owned, Nayland | |
| 329854 | Piper L-4H Grasshopper (43-29854/G-BMKC) [44-R] | Privately owned, St Just | |
| 329934 | Piper L-4H Grasshopper (43-29934/G-BCPH) [72-B] | Privately owned, White Waltham | |
| 330238 | Piper L-4H Grasshopper (43-30238/G-LIVH) [24-A] | Privately owned, Barton | |
| 330485 | Piper L-4H Grasshopper (43-30485/G-AJES) [44-C] | Privately owned, Saltash | |
| *343251* | Boeing-Stearman N2S-5 Kaydet (43517/G-NZSS) [27] | Privately owned, Swanton Morley | |
| *413573* | NA P-51D Mustang (44-73415/ 9133M/N6526D) [B6-V] | RAF Museum, Hendon | |
| *414151* | NA P-51D Mustang (44-73140/ NL314BG) [HO-M] | Flying A Services, North Weald | |
| 434602 | Douglas A-26B Invader (44-34602/N167B) [S] | Scandinavian Historic Flight, Oslo, Norway | |
| 435710 | Douglas A-26C Invader (44-35710/N7705C) | Historic Invader Avn, Schiphol, The Netherlands | |
| *436021* | Piper J-3C Cub 65 (G-BWEZ) | Privately owned, Cumbernauld | |
| *442268* | Noorduyn AT-16 Harvard IIB (KF568/LN-TEX) [TA-268] | Scandinavian Historic Flight, Oslo, Norway | |
| 454467 | Piper L-4J Grasshopper (45-4467/ G-BILI) [44-J] | Privately owned, White Waltham | |
| 454537 | Piper L-4J Grasshopper (45-4537/ G-BFDL) [04-J] | Privately owned, Pontefract | |
| 461748 | Boeing B-29A Superfortress (44-61748/G-BHDK) [Y] | American Air Museum, Duxford | |
| *463209* | NA P-51D Mustang <R> (BAPC 255) [WZ-S] | American Air Museum, Duxford | |
| *463221* | NA P-51D Mustang (44-73149/ G-BTCD) [E2-Z] | The Old Flying Machine Company, Duxford | |
| 472035 | NA P-51D Mustang (44-72035/ F-AZMU) | Aéro Retro, St Rambert d'Albon, France | |
| 472216 | NA P-51D Mustang (44-72216/ G-BIXL) [AJ-L] | Privately owned, North Weald | |
| *472218* | CAC-18 Mustang 22 (A68-192/ G-HAEC) [WZ-I] | Privately owned, Woodchurch, Kent | |
| *472258* | NA P-51D Mustang (44-73979) [WZ-I] | Imperial War Museum, Lambeth | |
| 472773 | NA P-51D Mustang (44-72773/ G-SUSY) [QP-M] | Privately owned, Sywell | |
| 473877 | NA P-51D Mustang (44-73877/ N167F) [E2-D] | Scandinavian Historic Flight, Oslo, Norway | |
| *474008* | NA P-51D Mustang (44-73339/ G-SIRR) [VF-R] | Intrepid Aviation, North Weald | |
| 474425 | NA P-51D Mustang (44-74425/ NL11T) [OC-G] | Dutch Mustang Flt, Lelystad, The Netherlands | |
| *474832* | NA P-51D Mustang (44-74506/ F-AZJJ) [GA-N] | Air B Aviation, Marmaz, France | |
| 474923 | NA P-51D Mustang (44-74923/ N6395) | Privately owned, Lelystad, The Netherlands | |
| 479744 | Piper L-4H Grasshopper (44-79744/G-BGPD) [49-M] | Privately owned, Marsh, Bucks | |
| 479766 | Piper L-4H Grasshopper (44-79766/G-BKHG) [63-D] | Privately owned, Goldcliff, Gwent | |
| 480015 | Piper L-4H Grasshopper (44-80015/G-AKIB) [44-M] | Privately owned, Bodmin | |
| 480133 | Piper L-4J Grasshopper (44-80133/G-BDCD) [44-B] | Privately owned, Slinfold | |
| 480321 | Piper L-4J Grasshopper (44-80321/G-FRAN) [44-H] | Privately owned, Rayne, Essex | |

| *Notes* | *Serial* | *Type (other identity)* | *Owner/operator, location* |
|---|---|---|---|
| | 480480 | Piper L-4J Grasshopper (44-80480/G-BECN) [44-E] | Privately owned, Kersey, Suffolk |
| | 480551 | Piper L-4J Grasshopper (44-80551/LN-KLT) [43-S] | Scandinavian Historic Flight, Oslo, Norway |
| | 480636 | Piper L-4J Grasshopper (44-80636/G-AXHP) [58-A] | Privately owned, Southend |
| | 480752 | Piper L-4J Grasshopper (44-80752/G-BCXJ) [39-E] | Privately owned, Old Sarum |
| | 483868 | Boeing B-17G Fortress (44-83868/N5237V) [A-N] | RAF Museum, Hendon |
| | 486893 | NA B-25J Mitchell (N6123C) | Tyrolean Jet Services, Innsbruck, Austria |
| | 493209 | NA T-6G Texan (49-3209/ G-DDMV/*41*) | Privately owned, Sywell |
| | 511701A | Beech C-45H (51-11701/G-BSZC) [AF258] | Privately owned, Bryngwyn Bach |
| | *607327* | PA-18 Super Cub 95 (G-ARAO) [09-L] | Privately owned, Denham |
| | *2106449* | NA P-51C Mustang (43-25147/ N51PR/G-PSIC) [HO-W] | The Fighter Collection, Duxford |
| | *2-134* | NA T-6G Texan (114700) | Privately owned, North Weald |
| | 3-1923 | Aeronca O-58B Defender (43-1923/G-BRHP) | Privately owned, Chiseldon |
| | *18-2001* | Piper L-18C Super Cub (52-2401/ G-BIZV) | Privately owned, Oxenhope |
| | 39-139 | Beech YC-43 Traveler (N295BS) | Dukes of Brabant AF, Eindhoven, The Netherlands |
| | 40-1766 | Boeing-Stearman PT-17 Kaydet | Privately owned, Swanton Morley |
| | 41-33275 | NA AT-6C Texan (G-BICE) [CE] | Privately owned, Ipswich |
| | 42-12417 | NA AT-16 Harvard IIB | Thameside Aviation Museum, East Tilbury |
| | 42-40557 | Consolidated B-24D Liberator <ff> | American Air Museum, Duxford |
| | 42-58678 | Taylorcraft DF-65 (G-BRIY) [IY] | Privately owned, North Weald |
| | *42-78044* | Aeronca 11AC Chief (G-BRXL) | Privately owned, High Cross, Herts |
| | 42-84555 | NA AT-6D Harvard III (FAP.1662/ G-ELMH) [EP-H] | Privately owned, Hardwick, Norfolk |
| | 42-93510 | Douglas C-47A Skytrain [CM] <ff> | Privately owned, Kew |
| | 42-100611 | Douglas C-47A Skytrain (6W-SAF) [4U] <ff> | Museum of Berkshire Aviation, Woodley |
| | 43-9628 | Douglas A-20G Havoc <ff> | Privately owned, Hinckley, Leics |
| | 44-14291 | NA P-51D Mustang | Classic Warbirds, Norwich |
| | 44-14574 | NA P-51D Mustang (fuselage) | East Essex Aviation Museum, Clacton |
| | 44-51228 | Consolidated B-24M Liberator [RE-N] | American Air Museum, Duxford |
| | 44-79609 | Piper L-4H Grasshopper (G-BHXY) [PR] | Privately owned, Bodmin |
| | 44-80594 | Piper L-4J Grasshopper (G-BEDJ) | Privately owned, White Waltham |
| | 51-14526 | NA T-6G Texan (G-BRWB) | Monafield Ltd, Audley End |
| | 51-15227 | NA T-6G Texan (G-BKRA) [10] | Privately owned, Shoreham |
| | *51-15673* | Piper L-18C Super Cub (53-4781/ G-CUBI) | Privately owned, Felixkirk |
| | 52-8543 | CCF T-6J Harvard IV (G-BUKY) [66] | Privately owned, Breighton |
| | 54-223 | NA F-100D Super Sabre (54-2223) | Newark Air Museum, Winthorpe |
| | 54-2447 | Piper L-21B Super Cub (G-SCUB) | Privately owned, Anwick |
| | 54-2474 | Piper L-21B Super Cub (G-PCUB) | Privately owned, Headcorn |
| | *54-21261* | Lockheed T-33A-N Silver Star (N33VC/G-TBRD) | Golden Apple Operations/OFMC, Duxford |
| | 64-17657 | Douglas A-26A Invader (N99218) <ff> | Tower Museum, Ludham, Norfolk |
| | *65-777* | McD F-4C Phantom (63-7419) [LN] | RAF Lakenheath, on display |
| | 67-120 | GD F-111E Aardvark [UH] | American Air Museum, Duxford |
| | 68-0060 | GD F-111E Aardvark <ff> | Dumfries & Galloway Avn Mus, Dumfries |
| | 72-1447 | GD F-111F Aardvark <ff> | American Air Museum, Duxford |
| | *72-448* | GD F-111E Aardvark (68-0011) [LN] | RAF Lakenheath, on display |
| | 77-259 | Fairchild A-10A Thunderbolt [AR] | American Air Museum, Duxford |
| | 80-219 | Fairchild GA-10A Thunderbolt [AR] | RAF Alconbury, on display |
| | *92-048* | McD F-15A Eagle (74-0131) [LN] | RAF Lakenheath, on display |
| | *146-11042* | Wolf WII <R> (G-BMZX) [7] | Privately owned, Haverfordwest |
| | *146-11083* | Wolf WII <R> (G-BNAI) [5] | Privately owned, Haverfordwest |
| | *H-57* | Piper L-4A Grasshopper (42-36375/G-AKAZ) | Privately owned, Duxford |

| Serial | Type (other identity) | Owner/operator, location | Notes |
|---|---|---|---|
| *I-492* | Ryan PT-22 Recruit (41-15236/G-BPUD) | Privately owned, Swanton Morley | |
| **YUGOSLAVIA** | | | |
| 23170 | Soko G-2A Galeb (YU-YAB) | Privately owned, Biggin Hill | |
| 30140 | Soko P-2 Kraguj (G-RADA) [140] | Privately owned, Biggin Hill | |
| 30146 | Soko P-2 Kraguj (G-BSXD) [146] | Privately owned, Elstree | |
| 30149 | Soko P-2 Kraguj (G-SOKO) [149] | Privately owned, Liverpool | |
| 30151 | Soko P-2 Kraguj [151] | Privately owned, Bournemouth | |
| 51182 | UTVA-66 (YU-DMN) | Privately owned, Biggin Hill | |
| 51183 | UTVA-66 (YU-DMT) | Privately owned, Biggin Hill | |

The OFMC's FG-1D Corsair is painted in RNZAF colours as NZ5648. *PRM*

The Fighter Collection's AD-4NA Skyraider 126922. *Daniel March*

# Irish Military Aircraft Markings

| Notes | Serial | Type (other identity) | Owner/operator, location |
|---|---|---|---|
| | 34 | Miles M14A Magister (N5392) | IAC Engineering Wing stored, Baldonnel |
| | 141 | Avro 652A Anson C19 | IAC Engineering Wing stored, Baldonnel |
| | 164 | DHC1 Chipmunk T20 | IAC Engineering Wing stored, Baldonnel |
| | 168 | DHC1 Chipmunk T20 | IAC No 2 Support Wing, Gormanston |
| | 172 | DHC1 Chipmunk T20 | IAC Training Wing stored, Gormanston |
| | *176* | DH104 Dove 4 (VP-YKF) | Privately owned, |
| | 177 | Percival P56 Provost T51 (G-BLIW) | Privately owned, Shoreham |
| | 183 | Percival P56 Provost T51 | IAC Engineering Wing stored, Baldonnel |
| | 184 | Percival P56 Provost T51 | South East Aviation Enthusiasts, Waterford |
| | 187 | DH115 Vampire T55 | Av'n Society of Ireland, stored, Waterford |
| | 189 | Percival P56 Provost T51 (comp XF846) | IAC Baldonnel Fire Section |
| | 191 | DH115 Vampire T55 | IAC Museum, Baldonnel |
| | 192 | DH115 Vampire T55 | South East Aviation Enthusiasts, Waterford |
| | 193 | DH115 Vampire T55 <ff> | IAC Baldonnel Fire Section |
| | 195 | Sud SA316 Alouette III | IAC No 3 Support Wing, Baldonnel |
| | 196 | Sud SA316 Alouette III | IAC No 3 Support Wing, Baldonnel |
| | 197 | Sud SA316 Alouette III | IAC No 3 Support Wing, Baldonnel |
| | 198 | DH115 Vampire T11 (XE977) | IAC Engineering Wing stored, Baldonnel |
| | 199 | DHC1 Chipmunk T22 | IAC Training Wing store, Gormanston (spares) |
| | 202 | Sud SA316 Alouette III | IAC No 3 Support Wing, Baldonnel (under repair) |
| | 203 | Reims-Cessna FR172H | IAC No 2 Support Wing, Gormanston |
| | 205 | Reims-Cessna FR172H | IAC No 2 Support Wing, Gormanston |
| | 206 | Reims-Cessna FR172H | IAC No 2 Support Wing, Gormanston |
| | 207 | Reims-Cessna FR172H | IAC Engineering Wing, Baldonnel, instructional use |
| | 208 | Reims-Cessna FR172H | IAC No 2 Support Wing, Gormanston |
| | 209 | Reims-Cessna FR172H | IAC No 2 Support Wing, Gormanston, wfu |
| | 210 | Reims-Cessna FR172H | IAC No 2 Support Wing, Gormanston |
| | 211 | Sud SA316 Alouette III | IAC No 3 Support Wing, Baldonnel |
| | 212 | Sud SA316 Alouette III | IAC No 3 Support Wing, Baldonnel |
| | 213 | Sud SA316 Alouette III | IAC No 3 Support Wing, Baldonnel |
| | 214 | Sud SA316 Alouette III | IAC No 3 Support Wing, Baldonnel |
| | 215 | Fouga CM170 Super Magister | IAC, stored Baldonnel |
| | 216 | Fouga CM170 Super Magister | IAC Engineering Wing, Baldonnel |
| | 217 | Fouga CM170 Super Magister | IAC, stored Baldonnel |
| | 218 | Fouga CM170 Super Magister | IAC, stored Baldonnel |
| | 219 | Fouga CM170 Super Magister | IAC, stored Baldonnel |
| | 220 | Fouga CM170 Super Magister | IAC, stored Baldonnel |
| | 222 | SIAI SF-260WE Warrior | IAC Training Wing, Baldonnel |
| | 225 | SIAI SF-260WE Warrior | IAC Training Wing, Baldonnel |
| | 226 | SIAI SF-260WE Warrior | IAC Training Wing, Baldonnel |
| | 227 | SIAI SF-260WE Warrior | IAC Training Wing, Baldonnel |
| | 229 | SIAI SF-260WE Warrior | IAC Training Wing, Baldonnel |
| | 230 | SIAI SF-260WE Warrior | IAC Training Wing, Baldonnel |
| | 231 | SIAI SF-260WE Warrior | IAC Training Wing, Baldonnel |
| | 237 | Aérospatiale SA342L Gazelle | IAC No 3 Support Wing, Baldonnel |
| | 240 | Beech Super King Air 200MR | IAC No 1 Support Wing, Baldonnel |
| | 241 | Aérospatiale SA342L Gazelle | IAC No 3 Support Wing, Baldonnel |
| | 243 | Reims-Cessna FR172K | IAC No 2 Support Wing, Gormanston |
| | 244 | Aérospatiale SA365F Dauphin II | IAC No 3 Support Wing, Baldonnel |
| | 245 | Aérospatiale SA365F Dauphin II | IAC No 3 Support Wing, Baldonnel |
| | 246 | Aérospatiale SA365F Dauphin II | IAC No 3 Support Wing, Baldonnel |
| | 247 | Aérospatiale SA365F Dauphin II | IAC No 3 Support Wing, Baldonnel |
| | 251 | Grumman G1159C Gulfstream IV | IAC No 1 Support Wing, Baldonnel |
| | 252 | Airtech CN.235 MPA Persuader | IAC No 1 Support Wing, Baldonnel |
| | 253 | Airtech CN.235 MPA Persuader | IAC No 1 Support Wing, Baldonnel |
| | 254 | PBN-2T Defender 4000 (G-BWPN) | Garda Air Support Unit, Baldonnel |
| | 255 | AS355N Twin Squirrel (G-BXEV) | Garda Air Support Unit, Baldonnel |

# Overseas Military Aircraft Markings

Aircraft included in this section are a selection of those likely to be seen visiting UK civil and military airfields on transport flights, exchange visits, exercises and for air shows. It is not a comprehensive list of *all* aircraft operated by the air arms concerned.

**ALGERIA**
**Force Aérienne Algérienne/ Al Quwwat al Jawwiya al Jaza'eriya**

**Lockheed C-130H Hercules**
4911 (7T-WHT)
4912 (7T-WHS)
4913 (7T-WHY)
4914 (7T-WHZ)
4924 (7T-WHR)
4926 (7T-WHQ)
4928 (7T-WHJ)
4930 (7T-WHI)
4934 (7T-WHF)
4935 (7T-WHE)

**Lockheed C-130H-30 Hercules**
4984 (7T-WHN)
4987 (7T-WHO)
4989 (7T-WHL)
4997 (7T-WHA)
5224 (7T-WHB)
(7T-WHM)
(7T-WHP)

**Algerian Govt**

**Dassault Falcon 900**
Ministry of Defence, Boufarik
7T-VPA (81)
7T-VPB (82)

**Grumman G.1159A Gulfstream III/ G.1159C Gulfstream IVSP**
Ministry of Defence, Boufarik
7T-VPR (1288) Gulfstream IVSP
7T-VPS (1291) Gulfstream IVSP
7T-VRD (399) Gulfstream III

**AUSTRALIA**
**Royal Australian Air Force**

**Boeing 707-338C/368C***
33 Sqn, Amberley
A20-261*
A20-623
A20-624
A20-627
A20-629

**Lockheed C-130H Hercules**
36 Sqn, Richmond, NSW
A97-001
A97-002
A97-003
A97-004
A97-005
A97-006
A97-007
A97-008
A97-009
A97-010
A97-011
A97-012

**Lockheed C-130E Hercules**
37 Sqn, Richmond, NSW
A97-159
A97-160
A97-167
A97-168
A97-171
A97-172
A97-177
A97-178
A97-180
A97-181
A97-189
A97-190

**Lockheed C-130J-30 Hercules**
37 Sqn, Richmond, NSW
A97-440
A97-441
A97-442
A97-447
A97-448
A97-449
A97-450
A97-464
A97-465
A97-466
A97-467
A97-468

**Lockheed P-3C Orion**
10/11 Sqns, Maritime Patrol Group, Edinburgh, NSW

| | |
|---|---|
| A9-656 | 10 Sqn |
| A9-657 | 11 Sqn |
| A9-658 | 10 Sqn |
| A9-659 | 11 Sqn |
| A9-660 | 11 Sqn |
| A9-661 | 10 Sqn |
| A9-662 | 11 Sqn |
| A9-663 | 11 Sqn |
| A9-664 | 11 Sqn |
| A9-665 | 10 Sqn |
| A9-751 | 11 Sqn |
| A9-752 | 10 Sqn |
| A9-753 | 10 Sqn |
| A9-755 | 11 Sqn |
| A9-756 | 11 Sqn |
| A9-757 | 10 Sqn |
| A9-758 | 10 Sqn |
| A9-759 | 10 Sqn |
| A9-760 | 10 Sqn |

**AUSTRIA**
**Öesterreichische Luftstreitkräfte**

**SAAB 35ÖE Draken**
Fliegerregiment II
1 Staffel/Uberwg, Zeltweg;
2 Staffel/Uberwg, Graz

| | | |
|---|---|---|
| 01 | (351401) | 1 Staffel |
| 02 | (351402) | 1 Staffel |
| 03 | (351403) | 1 Staffel |
| 04 | (351404) | 1 Staffel |
| 05 | (351405) | 1 Staffel |
| 06 | (351406) | 1 Staffel |
| 07 | (351407) | 1 Staffel |
| 08 | (351408) | 1 Staffel |
| 09 | (351409) | 1 Staffel |
| 10 | (351410) | 1 Staffel |
| 11 | (351411) | 1 Staffel |
| 12 | (351412) | 1 Staffel |
| 13 | (351413) | 2 Staffel |
| 14 | (351414) | 2 Staffel |
| 15 | (351415) | 2 Staffel |
| 16 | (351416) | 2 Staffel |
| 18 | (351418) | 2 Staffel |
| 19 | (351419) | 2 Staffel |
| 20 | (351420) | 2 Staffel |
| 21 | (351421) | 2 Staffel |
| 22 | (351422) | 2 Staffel |
| 23 | (351423) | 2 Staffel |
| 24 | (351424) | 2 Staffel |

**SAAB 105ÖE**
Fliegerregiment III
1 Staffel/JbG, Linz

**(yellow)**

| | |
|---|---|
| B | (105402) |
| D | (105404) |
| E | (105405) |
| F | (105406) |
| G | (105407) |
| I | (105409) |
| J | (105410) |

**(green)**

| | |
|---|---|
| A | (105411) |
| B | (105412) |
| D | (105414) |
| GF-16 | (105416) |
| G | (105417) |

**(red)**

| | |
|---|---|
| B | (105422) |
| C | (105423) |
| D | (105424) |
| E | (105425) |
| F | (105426) |
| G | (105427) |
| H | (105428) |
| I | (105429) |
| J | (105430) |

**(blue)**

| | |
|---|---|
| A | (105431) |
| B | (105432) |

C (105433)
D (105434)
E (105435)
F (105436)
G (105437)
I (105439)
J (105440)

**Short SC7 Skyvan 3M**
Fliegerregiment I
Flachenstaffel, Tulln
5S-TA
5S-TB

**BAHRAIN**
**Boeing 727-2M7**
Govt of Bahrain
A9C-BA

**Boeing 747SP-21**
Bahrain Amiri Flt
A9C-HHH

**Grumman G.1159 Gulfstream IITT/ G.1159C Gulfstream IV**
Govt of Bahrain
A9C-BAH Gulfstream IV
A9C-BG Gulfstream IITT

**BELGIUM**
**Force Aérienne Belge/ Belgische Luchtmacht**
**D-BD Alpha Jet E**
7/11 Smaldeel (1 Wg), Bevekom
AT-01
AT-02
AT-03
AT-05
AT-06
AT-08
AT-10
AT-11
AT-12
AT-13
AT-14
AT-15
AT-17
AT-18
AT-19
AT-20
AT-21
AT-22
AT-23
AT-24
AT-25
AT-26
AT-27
AT-28
AT-29
AT-30
AT-31
AT-32
AT-33

**Airbus A.310-322**
21 Smaldeel (15 Wg), Melsbroek
CA-01
CA-02

**Dassault Falcon 900B**
21 Smaldeel (15 Wg), Melsbroek
CD-01

**Swearingen Merlin IIIA**
21 Smaldeel (15 Wg), Melsbroek
CF-01
CF-02
CF-04
CF-05
CF-06

**Lockheed C-130H Hercules**
20 Smaldeel (15 Wg), Melsbroek
CH-01
CH-02
CH-03
CH-04
CH-05
CH-07
CH-08
CH-09
CH-10
CH-11
CH-12

**Dassault Falcon 20E**
21 Smaldeel (15 Wg), Melsbroek
CM-01
CM-02

**Hawker-Siddeley HS748 Srs 2A**
21 Smaldeel (15 Wg), Melsbroek
CS-01
CS-02
CS-03

**General Dynamics F-16**
(MLU aircraft are marked with a *)
1,2,350 Smaldeel (2 Wg), Florennes [FS];
23,31,349 Smaldeel, OCU (10 Wg), Kleine-Brogel [BL]

| | | |
|---|---|---|
| FA-27 | F-16A | 2 Wg |
| FA-46 | F-16A | 2 Wg |
| FA-47 | F-16A | 2 Wg |
| FA-48 | F-16A* | 2 Wg |
| FA-49 | F-16A(R) | 10 Wg |
| FA-50 | F-16A | 2 Wg |
| FA-53 | F-16A(R) | 10 Wg |
| FA-55 | F-16A | 2 Wg |
| FA-56 | F-16A* | 10 Wg |
| FA-57 | F-16A* | 10 Wg |
| FA-58 | F-16A | 10 Wg |
| FA-60 | F-16A* | 10 Wg |
| FA-61 | F-16A | 2 Wg |
| FA-65 | F-16A | 23 Sm |
| FA-66 | F-16A | 10 Wg |
| FA-67 | F-16A | 31 Sm |
| FA-68 | F-16A | 2 Sm |
| FA-69 | F-16A | 31 Sm |
| FA-70 | F-16A | 10 Wg |
| FA-71 | F-16A | 31 Sm |
| FA-72 | F-16A | 2 Wg |
| FA-73 | F-16A | 10 Wg |
| FA-74 | F-16A* | 10 Wg |
| FA-75 | F-16A* | 10 Wg |
| FA-76 | F-16A* | 10 Wg |
| FA-77 | F-16A* | 10 Wg |
| FA-78 | F-16A* | 10 Wg |
| FA-81 | F-16A | 10 Wg |
| FA-82 | F-16A(R)* | 10 Wg |
| FA-83 | F-16A* | 10 Wg |
| FA-84 | F-16A | 10 Wg |
| FA-86 | F-16A* | 10 Wg |
| FA-87 | F-16A | 2 Wg |
| FA-88 | F-16A | 2 Wg |
| FA-89 | F-16A | 10 Wg |
| FA-90 | F-16A | 31 Sm |
| FA-91 | F-16A | 10 Wg |
| FA-92 | F-16A(R) | 10 Wg |
| FA-93 | F-16A* | 10 Wg |
| FA-94 | F-16A(R) | 2 Wg |
| FA-95 | F-16A | 10 Wg |
| FA-96 | F-16A | 10 Wg |
| FA-97 | F-16A* | 10 Wg |
| FA-98 | F-16A* | 10 Wg |
| FA-99 | F-16A* | 10 Wg |
| FA-100 | F-16A* | 10 Wg |
| FA-101 | F-16A* | 10Wg |
| FA-102 | F-16A* | 10 Wg |
| FA-103 | F-16A | 349 Sm |
| FA-104 | F-16A* | 10 Wg |
| FA-106 | F-16A | 2 Wg |
| FA-107 | F-16A | 2 Wg |
| FA-108 | F-16A* | 10 Wg |
| FA-109 | F-16A | 2 Wg |
| FA-110 | F-16A | 2 Wg |
| FA-111 | F-16A | 10 Wg |
| FA-112 | F-16A* | 10 Wg |
| FA-114 | F-16A | 10 Wg |
| FA-115 | F-16A* | 350 Sm |
| FA-116 | F-16A | 10 Wg |
| FA-117 | F-16A | 2 Wg |
| FA-118 | F-16A | 2 Sm |
| FA-119 | F-16A | 2 Wg |
| FA-120 | F-16A* | 10 Wg |
| FA-121 | F-16A | 1 Sm |
| FA-122 | F-16A* | 10 Sm |
| FA-123 | F-16A | 2 Wg |
| FA-124 | F-16A | 10 Wg |
| FA-125 | F-16A | 1 Sm |
| FA-126 | F-16A* | 10 Wg |
| FA-127 | F-16A | 2 Wg |
| FA-128 | F-16A | 2 Wg |
| FA-129 | F-16A | 2 Wg |
| FA-130 | F-16A | 2 Wg |
| FA-131 | F-16A(R) | 2 Wg |
| FA-132 | F-16A | 2 Wg |
| FA-133 | F-16A | 2 Wg |
| FA-134 | F-16A | 2 Wg |
| FA-135 | F-16A | 10 Wg |
| FA-136 | F-16A | 10 Wg |
| FB-01 | F-16B | 2 Wg |
| FB-02 | F-16B | OCU |
| FB-04 | F-16B* | OCU |
| FB-05 | F-16B | 2 Wg |
| FB-07 | F-16B | OCU |
| FB-08 | F-16B | OCU |
| FB-09 | F-16B | OCU |
| FB-10 | F-16B | 10 Wg |
| FB-12 | F-16B | OCU |
| FB-14 | F-16B* | 10 Wg |
| FB-15 | F-16B* | OCU |
| FB-17 | F-16B* | OCU |
| FB-18 | F-16B | OCU |
| FB-19 | F-16B | 10 Wg |
| FB-20 | F-16B | 2 Wg |
| FB-21 | F-16B* | 10 Wg |
| FB-22 | F-16B* | OCU |
| FB-23 | F-16B | 10 Wg |

FB-24 F-16B OCU

**Fouga CM170 Magister**
Fouga Flight/7 Smaldeel (1Wg), Bevekom
MT-04
MT-13
MT-14
MT-26
MT-34
MT-35
MT-36
MT-40
MT-44
MT-48

**Westland Sea King Mk48/48A***
40 Smaldeel, Koksijde
RS-01
RS-02
RS-03*
RS-04
RS-05

**SIAI Marchetti SF260MB/SF260D***
Ecole de Pilotage Elementaire (5 Sm/1 Wg), Bevekom
ST-02
ST-03
ST-04
ST-06
ST-12
ST-15
ST-16
ST-17
ST-18
ST-19
ST-20
ST-21
ST-22
ST-23
ST-24
ST-25
ST-26
ST-27
ST-31
ST-32
ST-34
ST-35
ST-36
ST-40*
ST-41*
ST-42*
ST-43*
ST-44*
ST-45*
ST-46*
ST-47*
ST-48*

**Aviation Légère de la Force Terrestre/ Belgische Landmacht**
**Sud SA318C/SE3130* Alouette II**
16 BnHLn, Bierset;
SLV, Brasschaat
A-22* 16 BnHLn
A-37* 16 BnHLn
A-40 SLV
A-41 SLV
A-42 16 BnHLn
A-43 16 BnHLn
A-44 SLV
A-46 16 BnHLn
A-47 16 BnHLn
A-49 16 BnHLn
A-50 16 BnHLn
A-53 16 BnHLn
A-54 SLV
A-55 SLV
A-57 SLV
A-59 16 BnHLn
A-61 SLV
A-62 16 BnHLn
A-64 SLV
A-65 SLV
A-66 SLV
A-68 16 BnHLn
A-69 16 BnHLn
A-70 SLV
A-72 SLV
A-73 16 BnHLn
A-74 SLV
A-75 16 BnHLn
A-77 16 BnHLn
A-78 16 BnHLn
A-79 SLV
A-80 16 BnHLn
A-81 16 BnHLn

**Britten-Norman BN-2A/BN-2B-21* Islander**
16 BnHLn, Bierset;
SLV, Brasschaat
B-01 LA SLV
B-02* LB SLV
B-03* LC 16 BnHLn
B-04* LD SLV
B-07* LG 16 BnHLn
B-08* LH 16 BnHLn
B-09* LI 16 BnHLn
B-10* LJ 16 BnHLn
B-11* LK 16 BnHLn
B-12 LL SLV

**Agusta A109HA/HO***
17 BnHATk, Bierset;
18 BnHATk, Bierset;
SLV, Brasschaat
H-01* SLV
H-02* SLV
H-03* SLV
H-04* 17 BnHATk
H-05* 17 BnHATk
H-06* 17 BnHATk
H-07* 17 BnHATk
H-08* 18 BnHATk
H-09* 18 BnHATk
H-10* 18 BnHATk
H-11* SLV
H-12* SLV
H-13* SLV
H-14* SLV
H-15* SLV
H-16* 18 BnHATk
H-17* 17 BnHATk
H-18* 18 BnHATk
H-19 17 BnHATk
H-20 18 BnHATk
H-21 18 BnHATk
H-22 17 BnHATk
H-23 18 BnHATk
H-24 17 BnHATk
H-25 18 BnHATk
H-26 18 BnHATk
H-27 18 BnHATk
H-28 18 BnHATk
H-29 18 BnHATk
H-30 18 BnHATk
H-31 18 BnHATk
H-32 18 BnHATk
H-33 18 BnHATk
H-34 17 BnHATk
H-35 18 BnHATk
H-36 17 BnHATk
H-37 17 BnHATk
H-38 17 BnHATk
H-39 18 BnHATk
H-40 18 BnHATk
H-41 17 BnHATk
H-42 17 BnHATk
H-43 17 BnHATk
H-44 17 BnHATk
H-45 17 BnHATk
H-46 17 BnHATk

**Force Navale Belge/Belgische Zeemacht**
**Sud SA316B Alouette III**
Koksijde Heli Flight
M-1 (OT-ZPA)
M-2 (OT-ZPB)
M-3 (OT-ZPC)

**Gendarmerie/Rijkswacht**
**Britten-Norman PBN-2T Islander**
Luchsteundetachment, Melsbroek
G-05 (OT-GLA)

**Cessna 182 Skylane**
Luchsteundetachment, Melsbroek
G-01 C.182Q
G-03 C.182R
G-04 C.182R

**MDH MD.900 Explorer**
Luchsteundetachment, Melsbroek
G-10
G-11

**Sud Alouette II**
Luchsteundetachment, Melsbroek
G-90
G-93
G-94

**BOTSWANA**
**Botswana Defence Force**
**Grumman G.1159C Gulfstream IV**
OK-1

**Lockheed C-130B Hercules**
OM-1
OM-2

**BRAZIL**
**Força Aérea Brasileira**
**Boeing KC-137**
2° GT 2° Esq, Galeão
2401
2402

2403
2404

**Lockheed C-130E Hercules**
1° GT, 1° Esq, Galeão;
1° GTT, 1° Esq, Afonsos

| | | |
|---|---|---|
| 2451 | C-130E | 1° GTT |
| 2453 | C-130E | 1° GTT |
| 2454 | C-130E | 1° GTT |
| 2455 | C-130E | 1° GTT |
| 2456 | C-130E | 1° GTT |
| 2458 | SC-130E | 1° GT |
| 2459 | SC-130E | 1° GT |
| 2461 | KC-130H | 1° GT |
| 2462 | KC-130H | 1° GT |
| 2463 | C-130H | 1° GT |
| 2464 | C-130H | 1° GT |
| 2465 | C-130H | 1° GT |
| 2467 | C-130H | 1° GT |

## BRUNEI

**Airbus A.340**
Brunei Govt, Bandar Seri Bergawan

| | |
|---|---|
| V8-AM1 | A.340-211 |
| V8-BKH | A.340-212 |
| V8-JBB | A.340-213 |

**Boeing 747-430**
Brunei Govt, Bandar Seri Bergawan
V8-AL1

**Boeing 767-27GER**
Brunei Govt, Bandar Seri Bergawan
V8-MJB

**Gulfstream V**
Brunei Govt, Bandar Seri Bergawan
V8-007

## BULGARIA

**Bulgarsky Voenno-Vazdushni Sily**

**Antonov An-30**
16 TAP, Sofia/Dobroslavtzi
055

**Bulgarian Govt**

**Dassault Falcon 50**
Bulgarian Govt, Sofia
LZ-011

**Tupolev Tu-154M**
Bulgarian Govt, Sofia
LZ-BTQ

## BURKINA FASO

**Boeing 727-14**
Govt of Burkina Faso, Ouagadougou
XT-BBE

## CAMEROON

**Grumman G.1159A Gulfstream III**
Govt of Cameroon, Yaounde
TJ-AAW

## CANADA

**Canadian Forces**

**Lockheed CC-130 Hercules**
**CC-130E/CC-130E(SAR)***
402 Sqn, Winnipeg (17 Wing);
413 Sqn, Greenwood (SAR) (14 Wing);
424 Sqn, Trenton (SAR) (8 Wing);
426 Sqn, Trenton (8 Wing);
429 Sqn, Trenton (8 Wing);
435 Sqn, Winnipeg (17 Wing);
436 Sqn, Trenton (8 Wing)

| | |
|---|---|
| 130305* | 8 Wing |
| 130306* | 14 Wing |
| 130307 | 8 Wing |
| 130308* | 8 Wing |
| 130310* | 14 Wing |
| 130311* | 14 Wing |
| 130313 | 8 Wing |
| 130314* | 14 Wing |
| 130315* | 14 Wing |
| 130316 | 8 Wing |
| 130317 | 8 Wing |
| 130319 | 8 Wing |
| 130320 | 8 Wing |
| 130323 | 8 Wing |
| 130324* | 8 Wing |
| 130325 | 8 Wing |
| 130326 | 8 Wing |
| 130327 | 8 Wing |
| 130328 | 8 Wing |

**CC-130H/CC-130H(T)***

| | |
|---|---|
| 130332 | 17 Wing |
| 130333 | 17 Wing |
| 130334 | 8 Wing |
| 130335 | 8 Wing |
| 130336 | 17 Wing |
| 130337 | 17 Wing |
| 130338* | 17 Wing |
| 130339* | 8 Wing |
| 130340* | 17 Wing |
| 130341* | 17 Wing |
| 130342* | 17 Wing |

**CC-130H-30**

| | |
|---|---|
| 130343 | 8 Wing |
| 130344 | 17 Wing |

**Lockheed CP-140 Aurora/ CP-140A Arcturus***
404/405/415 Sqns, Greenwood (14 Wing);
407 Sqn, Comox (19 Wing)

| | | |
|---|---|---|
| 140101 | | 14 Wing |
| 140102 | | 14 Wing |
| 140103 | | 407 Sqn |
| 140104 | | 407 Sqn |
| 140105 | [LQ-Y] | 14 Wing |
| 140106 | | 14 Wing |
| 140107 | | 407 Sqn |
| 140108 | | 14 Wing |
| 140109 | | 14 Wing |
| 140110 | | 14 Wing |
| 140111 | | 14 Wing |
| 140112 | | 407 Sqn |
| 140113 | | 14 Wing |
| 140114 | [GX-N] | 14 Wing |
| 140115 | | 14 Wing |
| 140116 | | 14 Wing |
| 140117 | | 14 Wing |
| 140118 | | 407 Sqn |
| 140119* | | 14 Wing |
| 140120* | | 14 Wing |
| 140121* | | 14 Wing |

**De Havilland Canada CC-142**
402 Sqn, Winnipeg (17 Wing)

| | |
|---|---|
| 142801 | CC-142 |
| 142802 | CC-142 |
| 142803 | CT-142 |
| 142804 | CT-142 |
| 142805 | CT-142 |
| 142806 | CT-142 |

**Canadair CC-144/CE-144 Challenger**
412 Sqn, Trenton (8 Wing);
434 Sqn, Greenwood (14 Wing)

| | | |
|---|---|---|
| 144601 | CC-144A | 434 Sqn |
| 144602 | CC-144A | 434 Sqn |
| 144603 | CE-144A | 434 Sqn |
| 144604 | CC-144A | 434 Sqn |
| 144606 | CE-144A | 434 Sqn |
| 144607 | CE-144A | 434 Sqn |
| 144608 | CE-144A | 434 Sqn |
| 144609 | CE-144A | 434 Sqn |
| 144611 | CE-144A | 434 Sqn |
| 144614 | CC-144B | 412 Sqn |
| 144615 | CC-144B | 412 Sqn |
| 144616 | CC-144B | 412 Sqn |

**Airbus CC-150 Polaris (A310-304)**
437 Sqn, Trenton (8 Wing)

| | |
|---|---|
| 15001 | 216 |
| 15002 | 212 |
| 15003 | 202 |
| 15004 | 205 |
| 15005 | 201 |

## CHILE

**Fuerza Aérea de Chile**

**Boeing 707**
Grupo 10, Santiago

| | |
|---|---|
| 901 | 707-321B |
| 902 | 707-351C |
| 903 | 707-330B |
| 904 | 707-358C |

**Extra EA-300**
*Los Halcones*

| | |
|---|---|
| 021 | [6] |
| 022 | [7] |
| 024 | [2] |
| 025 | [3] |
| 027 | [4] |
| 028 | [5] |
| 029 | [1] |

**Grumman G.1159A Gulfstream III**
911

**Lockheed C-130B/C-130H Hercules**
Grupo 10, Santiago

| | |
|---|---|
| 993 | C-130B |
| 994 | C-130H |
| 995 | C-130H |
| 996 | C-130H |
| 998 | C-130B |

**CROATIA**

**Canadair CL.601 Challenger**
Croatian Govt, Zagreb
9A-CRO
9A-CRT

**CZECH REPUBLIC**
**Ceske Vojenske Letectvo**

**Aero L-39/L-59 Albatros**
42 slt/4 zTL, Cáslav;
321 tpzlt & 322 tlt/32 zTL, Náměšt;
341 vlt/34 zSL, Pardubice;
LZ0, Praha/Kbely
0001 L-39MS LZO
0004 L-39MS LZO
0005 L-39MS LZO
0103 L-39C 341 vlt/34 zSL
0105 L-39C 341 vlt/34 zSL
0106 L-39C 341 vlt/34 zSL
0107 L-39C 341 vlt/34 zSL
0108 L-39C 341 vlt/34 zSL
0113 L-39C 341 vlt/34 ZSL
0115 L-39C 341 vlt/34 ZSL
0440 L-39C 341 vlt/34 zSL
0441 L-39C 341 vlt/34 zSL
0444 L-39C 341 vlt/34 zSL
0445 L-39C 341 vlt/34 zSL
0448 L-39C 341 vlt/34 zSL
2341 L-39ZA 42 slt/4 zTL
2344 L-39ZA 42 slt/4 zTL
2347 L-39ZA 42 slt/4 zTL
2350 L-39ZA 42 slt/4 zTL
2415 L-39ZA 42 slt/4 zTL
2418 L-39ZA 42 slt/4 zTL
2421 L-39ZA 42 slt/4 zTL
2424 L-39ZA 32 zTL
2427 L-39ZA 42 slt/4 zTL
2430 L-39ZA 42 slt/4 zTL
2433 L-39ZA 42 slt/4 zTL
2436 L-39ZA 42 slt/4 zTL
3903 L-39ZA 32 zTL
4605 L-39C 341 vlt/34 ZSL
4606 L-39C 341 vlt/34 ZSL
5013 L-39ZA 32 zTL
5015 L-39ZA 32 zTL
5017 L-39ZA 32 zTL
5019 L-39ZA 32 zTL

**Aero L-159 ALCA/L-159T***
LZO, Praha/Kbely
5831*
5832

**Antonov An-24V**
1 dlt/6 zDL, Praha/Kbely
7109
7110

**Antonov An-26/An-26Z-1M***
1 dlt/6 zDL, Praha/Kbely
2408
2409
2507
3209*
4201

**Antonov An-30FG**
344 pzdlt/34 zSL, Pardubice
1107

**Canadair CL.601-3A Challenger**
1 dlt/6 zDL, Praha/Kbely
5105

**Let 410 Turbolet**
1 dlt/6 zDL, Praha/Kbely;
344 pzdlt/34 zSL, Pardubice
0503 L-410MA 344 pzdlt/34 zSL
0712 L-410UVP-S 344 pzdlt/34 zSL
0731 L-410UVP 1 dlt/6 zDL
0926 L-410UVP-T 1 dlt/6 zDL [4]
0928 L-410UVP-T 1 dlt/6 zDL
0929 L-410UVP-T 1 dlt/6 zDL [2]
1132 L-410UVP-T 1 dlt/6 zDL [3]
1134 L-410UVP 1 dlt/6 zDL
1504 L-410UVP 1 dlt/6 zDL
1523 L-410FG 344 pzdlt/34 zSL
1525 L-410FG 344 pzdlt/34 zSL
1526 L-410FG 344 pzdlt/34 zSL
2312 L-410UVP-E 1 dlt/6 zDL
2601 L-410UVP-E 1 dlt/6 zDL
2602 L-410UVP-E 1 dlt/6 zDL
2710 L-410UVP-E 1 dlt/6 zDL

**Let 610M**
1 dlt/6 zDL, Praha/Kbely;
LZO, Praha/Kbely
0003 1 dlt/6 zDL
0005 LZO

**Mikoyan MiG-21MF/MiG-21UM***
42 slt/4 zTL, Cáslav;
LZO, Ceske Budejovice
2205 42 slt/4 zTL
2500 42 slt/4 zTL
2614 42 slt/4 zTL
3186* 42 slt/4 zTL
3746* 42 slt/4 zTL
4017 42 slt/4 zTL
4127 42 slt/4 zTL
4175 42 slt/4 zTL
4307 LZO
5031* 42 slt/4 zTL
5201 42 slt/4 zTL
5203 LZO
5210 42 slt/4 zTL
5212 42 slt/4 zTL
5213 42 slt/4 zTL
5214 42 slt/4 zTL
5301 42 slt/4 zTL
5302 42 slt/4 zTL
5303 42 slt/4 zTL
5304 42 slt/4 zTL
5305 42 slt/4 zTL
5508 42 slt/4 zTL
5512 42 slt/4 zTL
5581 42 slt/4 zTL
5603 42 slt/4 zTL
7701 42 slt/4 zTL
7802 42 slt/4 zTL
9011* 42 slt/4 zTL
9332* 42 slt/4 zTL
9333* 42 slt/4 zTL
9341* 42 slt/4 zTL
9399* 42 slt/4 zTL
9410 42 slt/4 zTL
9414 42 slt/4 zTL
9707 42 slt/4 zTL
9711 42 slt/4 zTL
9801 42 slt/4 zTL
9802 LZO
9804 42 slt/4 zTL
9805 42 slt/4 zTL

**Mikoyan MiG-23ML/ MiG-23UB***
41 slt/4 zTL, Cáslav
2402
2406
2409
2410
2422
2423
2425
3303
3304
3307
4641
4645
4850
4855
4860
8107*
8109*
8327*

**Mil Mi-24**
331 ltBVr/33 zVrL, P_erov
0103 Mi-24D
0140 Mi-24D
0142 Mi-24D
0146 Mi-24D
0151 Mi-24D
0214 Mi-24D
0216 Mi-24D
0217 Mi-24D
0218 Mi-24D
0219 Mi-24D
0220 Mi-24D
0701 Mi-24V1
0702 Mi-24V1
0703 Mi-24V1
0705 Mi-24V1
0709 Mi-24V1
0710 Mi-24V1
0788 Mi-24V1
0789 Mi-24V1
0790 Mi-24V1
0812 Mi-24V1
0815 Mi-24V1
0816 Mi-24V1
0834 Mi-24V2
0835 Mi-24V2
0836 Mi-24V2
0837 Mi-24V2
0838 Mi-24V2
0839 Mi-24V2
4010 Mi-24D
4011 Mi-24D

6050 Mi-24DU

**Sukhoi Su-22M-4K/Su-22UM-3K***
321 tpzlt/32 zTL, Náměšt

| | | |
|---|---|---|
| 2217 | | |
| 2218 | | |
| 2619 | 34 | NA-2D |
| 2620 | 35 | NA-2D |
| 2701 | 36 | |
| 3313 | 24 | NA-2A |
| 3314 | 23 | |
| 3315 | 39 | NA-2B |
| 3402 | 05 | |
| 3403 | 08 | NA-1B |
| 3404 | 09 | |
| 3405 | | |
| 3406 | 12 | |
| 3407 | 10 | |
| 3701 | 02 | NA-1A |
| 3703 | 43 | NA-1D |
| 3704 | 44 | NA-1D |
| 3705 | 51 | |
| 3706 | 52 | NA-1E |
| 3802 | 26 | NA-2B |
| 3803 | 27 | NA-2B |
| 4005 | 30 | NA-2C |
| 4006 | 31 | NA-2C |
| 4007 | 32 | NA-2C |
| 4008 | 29 | NA-2B |
| 4010 | 28 | NA-2B |
| 4011 | 22 | NA-2A |
| 4208 | 53 | NA-1E |
| 4209 | 54 | NA-1E |
| 6602 | 55 | * |
| 7103 | 03 | NA-1A* |
| 7104 | 40 | NA-2C* |
| 7309 | 41 | NA-2D* |
| 7310 | 25 | NA-2A* |

**Sukhoi Su-25K/Su-25UBK***
322 tlt/32 zTL, Náměšt
1002
1004
1005
3348*
5003
5006
5007
5008
5039
5040
6019
6020
8076
8077
8078
8079
8080
8081
9013
9014
9093
9094
9098
9099

**Tupolev Tu-154**
1 dlt/6 zDL, Praha/Kbely
0601 Tu-154B-2
1016 Tu-154M

**Yakovlev Yak-40**
1 dlt/6 zDL, Praha/Kbely
0260 Yak-40
1257 Yak-40K

## DENMARK
### Flyvevåbnet

**Lockheed C-130H Hercules**
Eskadrille 721, Vaerløse
B-678
B-679
B-680

**Canadair CL.604 Challenger**
Eskadrille 721, Vaerløse
C-066
C-080

**General Dynamics F-16**
Eskadrille 723, Aalborg;
Eskadrille 726, Aalborg;
Eskadrille 727, Skrydstrup;
Eskadrille 730, Skrydstrup;
LMTAS, Fort Worth

| | | |
|---|---|---|
| E-004 | F-16A* | Esk 726 |
| E-005 | F-16A | Esk 730 |
| E-006 | F-16A | Esk 726 |
| E-007 | F-16A | Esk 726 |
| E-008 | F-16A* | Esk 723 |
| E-011 | F-16A | |
| E-016 | F-16A | Esk 726 |
| E-017 | F-16A | Esk 726 |
| E-018 | F-16A | Esk 726 |
| E-024 | F-16A | Esk 723 |
| E-070 | F-16A | |
| E-074 | F-16A | Esk 730 |
| E-075 | F-16A | Esk 723 |
| E-107 | F-16A | Esk 730 |
| E-174 | F-16A | Esk 727 |
| E-176 | F-16A | Esk 726 |
| E-177 | F-16A* | Esk 723 |
| E-178 | F-16A | Esk 723 |
| E-180 | F-16A | Esk 723 |
| E-181 | F-16A | Esk 723 |
| E-182 | F-16A | Esk 730 |
| E-183 | F-16A | Esk 730 |
| E-184 | F-16A | Esk 727 |
| E-187 | F-16A | Esk 727 |
| E-188 | F-16A | Esk 723 |
| E-189 | F-16A | Esk 723 |
| E-190 | F-16A* | Esk 723 |
| E-191 | F-16A | Esk 730 |
| E-192 | F-16A | Esk 730 |
| E-193 | F-16A | Esk 726 |
| E-194 | F-16A | Esk 723 |
| E-195 | F-16A | Esk 723 |
| E-196 | F-16A | Esk 723 |
| E-197 | F-16A | Esk 727 |
| E-198 | F-16A | Esk 730 |
| E-199 | F-16A | Esk 727 |
| E-200 | F-16A | Esk 723 |
| E-202 | F-16A | Esk 730 |
| E-203 | F-16A | Esk 723 |
| E-596 | F-16A* | Esk 723 |
| E-597 | F-16A* | Esk 723 |
| E-598 | F-16A* | Esk 730 |
| E-599 | F-16A* | Esk 730 |
| E-600 | F-16A* | Esk 723 |
| E-601 | F-16A | Esk 727 |
| E-602 | F-16A | Esk 730 |
| E-603 | F-16A | Esk 726 |
| E-604 | F-16A* | Esk 723 |
| E-605 | F-16A* | Esk 723 |
| E-606 | F-16A* | Esk 723 |
| E-607 | F-16A | Esk 730 |
| E-608 | F-16A* | Esk 723 |
| E-609 | F-16A* | Esk 727 |
| E-610 | F-16A* | Esk 727 |
| E-611 | F-16A | Esk 727 |
| ET-022 | F-16B | Esk 727 |
| ET-197 | F-16B | Esk 726 |
| ET-198 | F-16B | Esk 726 |
| ET-199 | F-16B | Esk 726 |
| ET-204 | F-16B* | LMTAS |
| ET-206 | F-16B | Esk 730 |
| ET-207 | F-16B* | Esk 723 |
| ET-208 | F-16B | Esk 730 |
| ET-210 | F-16B | Esk 727 |
| ET-612 | F-16B* | Esk 723 |
| ET-613 | F-16B* | Esk 723 |
| ET-614 | F-16B* | Esk 723 |
| ET-615 | F-16B | Esk 727 |
| ET-626 | F-16B | Esk 727 |

**Grumman G.1159A Gulfstream III**
Eskadrille 721, Vaerløse
F-249
F-313

**SAAB T-17 Supporter**
Eskadrille 721, Vaerløse;
Flyveskolen, Karup (FLSK)

| | |
|---|---|
| T-401 | FLSK |
| T-402 | FLSK |
| T-403 | FLSK |
| T-404 | FLSK |
| T-405 | FLSK |
| T-407 | Esk 721 |
| T-408 | FLSK |
| T-409 | FLSK |
| T-410 | FLSK |
| T-411 | FLSK |
| T-412 | FLSK |
| T-413 | FLSK |
| T-414 | FLSK |
| T-415 | FLSK |
| T-417 | FLSK |
| T-418 | Esk 721 |
| T-419 | FLSK |
| T-420 | Esk 721 |
| T-421 | FLSK |
| T-423 | FLSK |
| T-425 | FLSK |
| T-426 | FLSK |
| T-427 | FLSK |
| T-428 | FLSK |
| T-429 | FLSK |
| T-430 | FLSK |
| T-431 | Esk 721 |
| T-432 | FLSK |

**Sikorsky S-61A Sea King**
Eskadrille 722, Vaerløse
Detachments at:
Aalborg, Ronne, Skrydstrup
U-240
U-275
U-276
U-277
U-278
U-279
U-280
U-481

**Søvaernets Flyvetjaeneste (Navy)**

**Westland Lynx Mk 80/90***
Eskadrille 722, Vaerløse
S-134
S-142
S-175
S-181
S-191
S-249*
S-256*

**Haerens Flyvetjaeneste (Army)**

**Hughes 500M**
OVH Kmp, Vandel;
PVH Kmp, Vandel
H-201
H-202
H-203
H-205
H-206
H-207
H-209
H-211
H-213
H-244
H-245
H-246

**Aérospatiale AS.550C-2 Fennec**
PVH Kmp, Vandel
P-090
P-234
P-254
P-275
P-276
P-287
P-288
P-319
P-320
P-339
P-352
P-369

**ECUADOR**
**Fuerza Aérea Ecuatoriana**

**Lockheed C-130H/L.100-30* Hercules**
Ala de Transporte 11, Quito
FAE-892
FAE-893*

**EGYPT**
**Al Quwwat al-Jawwiya ilMisriya**

**Lockheed C-130H/ C-130H-30* Hercules**
16 Sqn, Cairo West
1271/SU-BAB
1272/SU-BAC
1273/SU-BAD
1274/SU-BAE
1275/SU-BAF
1277/SU-BAI
1278/SU-BAJ
1279/SU-BAK
1280/SU-BAL
1281/SU-BAM
1282/SU-BAN
1283/SU-BAP
1284/SU-BAQ
1285/SU-BAR
1286/SU-BAS
1287/SU-BAT
1288/SU-BAU
1289/SU-BAV
1290/SU-BAW
1291/SU-BAX
1292/SU-BAY
1293/SU-BKS*
1294/SU-BKT*
1295/SU-BKU*

**Egyptian Govt**

**Airbus A.340-211**
Egyptian Govt, Cairo
SU-GGG

**Boeing 707-366C**
Egyptian Govt, Cairo
SU-AXJ

**Grumman G.1159A Gulfstream III/ G.1159C Gulfstream IV**
Egyptian Air Force/Govt, Cairo

| | |
|---|---|
| SU-BGM | Gulfstream IV |
| SU-BGU | Gulfstream III |
| SU-BGV | Gulfstream III |
| SU-BNC | Gulfstream IV |
| SU-BND | Gulfstream IV |

**FINLAND**
**Suomen Ilmavoimat**

**Fokker F.27 Friendship**
Tukilentolaivue, Jyväskylä/Tikkakoski

| | |
|---|---|
| FF-1 | F.27-100 |
| FF-2 | F.27-100 |
| FF-3 | F.27-400M |

**FRANCE**
**Armée de l'Air**

**Aérospatiale SN601 Corvette**
CEV, Bretigny

| | |
|---|---|
| 1 | MV |
| 2 | MW |
| 10 | MX |

**Aérospatiale TB-30 Epsilon**
**Cartouche Dorée*,
(EPAA 00.315) Cognac;
EPAA 00.315, Cognac;
SOCATA, Tarbes

| | | |
|---|---|---|
| 1 | 315-UA | |
| 2 | 315-UB | |
| 3 | FZ | SOCATA |
| 4 | 315-UC | |
| 5 | 315-UD | |
| 6 | 315-UE | |
| 7 | 315-UF | |
| 8 | 315-UG | |
| 9 | 315-UH | |
| 10 | 315-UI | |
| 12 | 315-UK | |
| 13 | 315-UL | |
| 14 | 315-UM | |
| 15 | 315-UN | |
| 16 | 315-UO | |
| 17 | 315-UP | |
| 18 | 315-UQ | |
| 19 | 315-UR | |
| 20 | 315-US | |
| 21 | 315-UT | |
| 23 | 315-UV | |
| 24 | 315-UW | |
| 25 | 315-UX | |
| 26 | 315-UY | |
| 27 | 315-UZ | |
| 28 | 315-VA | |
| 29 | 315-VB | |
| 30 | 315-VC | |
| 31 | 315-VD | |
| 32 | 315-VE | |
| 33 | 315-VF | |
| 34 | 315-VG | |
| 35 | 315-VH | |
| 36 | 315-VI | |
| 37 | 315-VJ | |
| 38 | 315-VK | |
| 39 | 315-VL | |
| 40 | 315-VM | |
| 41 | 315-VN | |
| 42 | 315-VO | |
| 43 | 315-VP | |
| 44 | 315-VQ | |
| 45 | 315-VR | |
| 46 | 315-VS | |
| 47 | 315-VT | |
| 48 | 315-VU | |
| 49 | 315-VV | |
| 50 | 315-VW | |
| 52 | 315-VX | |
| 53 | 315-VY | |
| 54 | 315-VZ | |
| 56 | 315-WA | |
| 57 | F-ZVLB | |
| 61 | 315-WD | |
| 62 | 315-WE | |
| 63 | 315-WF | |
| 64 | 315-WG | |
| 65 | 315-WH | |
| 66 | 315-WI | |
| 67 | 315-WJ | |
| 68 | 315-WK | |
| 69 | 315-WL | |
| 70 | 315-WM | |
| 72 | 315-WO | |
| 73 | 315-WP | |
| 74 | 315-WQ | |
| 75 | 315-WR | |
| 76 | 315-WS | |
| 77 | 315-WT | |
| 78 | 315-WU | |
| 79 | 315-WV | |
| 80 | 315-WW | |
| 81 | 315-WX | |
| 82 | 315-WY | |
| 83 | 315-WZ | |
| 84 | 315-XA | |
| 85 | 315-XB | |
| 86 | 315-XC | |
| 87 | 315-XD | |
| 88 | 315-XE | |
| 89 | 315-XF | |
| 90 | 315-XG | |
| 91 | 315-XH | |
| 92 | F-SEXI [1]* | |
| 93 | 315-XJ | |
| 94 | 315-XK | |
| 95 | 315-XL | |
| 96 | 315-XM | |
| 97 | 315-XN | |
| 98 | 315-XO | |
| 99 | 315-XP | |
| 100 | F-SEXQ [2]* | |
| 101 | 315-XR | |
| 102 | 315-XS | |

| | |
|---|---|
| 103 | 315-XT |
| 104 | 315-XU |
| 105 | F-SEXV [4]* |
| 106 | 315-XW |
| 107 | 315-XX |
| 108 | 315-XY |
| 109 | 315-XZ |
| 110 | 315-YA |
| 111 | 315-YB |
| 112 | 315-YC |
| 113 | 315-YD |
| 114 | 315-YE |
| 115 | 315-YF |
| 116 | 315-YG |
| 117 | F-SEYH [3]* |
| 118 | 315-YI |
| 119 | 315-YJ |
| 120 | 315-YK |
| 121 | 315-YL |
| 122 | 315-YM |
| 123 | 315-YN |
| 124 | 315-YO |
| 125 | 315-YP |
| 126 | 315-YQ |
| 127 | 315-YR |
| 128 | 315-YS |
| 129 | 315-YT |
| 130 | 315-YU |
| 131 | 315-YV |
| 132 | 315-YW |
| 133 | 315-YX |
| 134 | 315-YY |
| 135 | 315-YZ |
| 136 | 315-ZA |
| 137 | 315-ZB |
| 138 | 315-ZC |
| 139 | 315-ZD |
| 140 | 315-ZE |
| 141 | 315-ZF |
| 142 | 315-ZG |
| 143 | 315-ZH |
| 144 | 315-ZI |
| 145 | 315-ZJ |
| 146 | 315-ZK |
| 149 | 315-ZM |
| 150 | 315-ZN |
| 152 | 315-ZO |
| 153 | 315-ZP |
| 154 | 315-ZQ |
| 155 | 315-ZR |
| 158 | 315-ZS |
| 159 | 315-ZT |

**Airbus A.300B2-103**
CEV, Bretigny

| | |
|---|---|
| 03 | (F-BUAD) |

**Airbus A.310-304**
ET 03.060 *Esterel*,
Paris/Charles de Gaulle

| | |
|---|---|
| 421 | F-RADA |
| 422 | F-RADB |

**Airtech CN-235M-100/-200***
ETL 01.062 *Vercours*, Creil;
ETOM 00.052 *La Tontouta*, Noumea;
ETOM 00.082 *Maine*, Faaa-Tahiti

| | | |
|---|---|---|
| 043* | 62-IA | 01.062 |
| 045 | 62-IB | 01.062 |
| 065 | 82-IC | 00.082 |
| 066 | 52-ID | 00.052 |
| 071 | 62-IE | 01.062 |
| 072 | 82-IF | 00.082 |
| 105 | 62-IG | 01.062 |
| 107 | 52-IH | 00.052 |
| 111* | 62-II | 01.062 |
| 114 | 62-IJ | 01.062 |
| 128 | 62-IK | 01.062 |
| 129 | 62-IL | 01.062 |

**Boeing C-135 Stratotanker**
ERV 00.093 *Bretagne*, Istres

| | | |
|---|---|---|
| 470 | C-135FR | 93-CA |
| 471 | C-135FR | 93-CB |
| 472 | C-135FR | 93-CC |
| 474 | C-135FR | 93-CE |
| 475 | C-135FR | 93-CF |
| 497 | KC-135R | 93-CM |
| 525 | KC-135R | 93-CN |
| 574 | KC-135R | 93-CP |
| 735 | C-135FR | 93-CG |
| 736 | C-135FR | 93-CH |
| 737 | C-135FR | 93-CI |
| 738 | C-135FR | 93-CJ |
| 739 | C-135FR | 93-CK |
| 740 | C-135FR | 93-CL |

**Boeing E-3F Sentry**
EDCA 00.036, Avord

| | |
|---|---|
| 201 | 36-CA |
| 202 | 36-CB |
| 203 | 36-CC |
| 204 | 36-CD |

**CASA 212-300 Aviocar**
CEV, Bretigny

| | |
|---|---|
| 377 | MO |
| 378 | MP |
| 386 | MQ |
| 387 | MR |
| 388 | MS |

**Cessna 310**
CEV, Bretigny, Cazaux, Istres & Melun

| | | |
|---|---|---|
| 046 | 310L | AV |
| 185 | 310N | AU |
| 187 | 310N | BJ |
| 188 | 310N | BK |
| 190 | 310N | BL |
| 192 | 310N | BM |
| 193 | 310N | BG |
| 194 | 310N | BH |
| 242 | 310K | AW |
| 244 | 310K | AX |
| 513 | 310N | BE |
| 693 | 310N | BI |
| 820 | 310Q | CL |
| 981 | 310Q | BF |

**D-BD Alpha Jet**
AMD-BA, Istres;
CEV, Bretigny;
EAC 00.314, Tours;
EC 01.002 *Cicogne*, Dijon;
EC 02.007 *Argonne*, St Dizier
ERS 01.091 *Gascogne*, Mont-de-Marsan;
ETO 01.008 *Saintonge* & ETO 02.008 *Nice*, Cazaux;
CEAM (EC 05.330), Mont-de-Marsan;
EPNER, Istres;
*Patrouille de France (PDF)* (EPAA 20.300), Salon de Provence

| | | |
|---|---|---|
| 01 | F-ZJTS | CEV |
| E1 | CEV | |
| E3 | 314-LV | 00.314 |
| E4 | CEV | |
| E5 | 7-PE | 02.007 |
| E7 | 314-LJ | 00.314 |
| E8 | CEV | |
| E9 | 8-MJ | 01.008 |
| E10 | | |
| E11 | 8-MW | 01.008 |
| E12 | CEV | |
| E13 | 8-NM | 02.008 |
| E14 | | |
| E15 | 8-NO | 02.008 |
| E17 | 8-NK | 02.008 |
| E18 | 8-MD | 01.008 |
| E19 | 330-AL | CEAM |
| E20 | 2-EF | 01.002 |
| E21 | 314-UB | 00.314 |
| E22 | 314-TG | 00.314 |
| E23 | 8-MQ | 01.008 |
| E24 | 314-TW | 00.314 |
| E25 | 314-UK | 00.314 |
| E26 | F-TERO | *PDF* [4] |
| E28 | 8-MI | 01.008 |
| E29 | 314-TM | 00.314 |
| E30 | 8-NR | 02.008 |
| E31 | | |
| E32 | 8-NQ | 02.008 |
| E33 | 8-NN | 02.008 |
| E34 | 8-MF | 01.008 |
| E35 | 314-UF | 00.314 |
| E36 | 314-LT | 00.314 |
| E37 | 8-NI | 02.008 |
| E38 | 314-TY | 00.314 |
| E41 | 314-TR | 00.314 |
| E42 | 7-PX | 02.007 |
| E43 | 2-EI | 01.002 |
| E44 | CEV | |
| E45 | 330-AK | CEAM |
| E46 | CEV | |
| E47 | 7-PJ | 02.007 |
| E48 | 314-TD | 00.314 |
| E49 | 314-TA | 00.314 |
| E51 | 314-TH | 00.314 |
| E52 | | |
| E53 | | |
| E55 | 314-UC | 00.314 |
| E58 | 314-LF | 00.314 |
| E59 | 314-LY | 00.314 |
| E60 | EPNER | |
| E61 | | |
| E63 | 314-LN | 00.314 |
| E64 | 314-TL | 00.314 |
| E65 | 8-MU | 01.008 |
| E66 | 8-ME | 01.008 |
| E67 | 314-TB | 00.314 |
| E68 | 2-EL | 01.002 |
| E69 | 8-NX | 02.008 |
| E72 | 314-LA | 00.314 |
| E73 | 314-TV | 00.314 |
| E74 | 8-MS | 01.008 |
| E75 | 2-EM | 01.002 |
| E76 | 7-PW | 02.007 |
| E79 | | |
| E80 | CEV | |
| E81 | F-TERI | *PDF* [8] |
| E82 | 8-NB | 02.008 |
| E83 | | |
| E84 | 8-MH | 01.008 |
| E85 | 330-AL | CEAM |
| E86 | 8-NS | 02.008 |

| | | |
|---|---|---|
| E87 | 314-LU | 00.314 |
| E88 | 314-TF | 00.314 |
| E89 | 314-TQ | 00.314 |
| E90 | | |
| E91 | 8-NL | 02.008 |
| E92 | 314-UE | 00.314 |
| E93 | 314-LD | 00.314 |
| E94 | 314-TE | 00.314 |
| E95 | | |
| E96 | 8-MT | 01 008 |
| E97 | 314-UN | 00.314 |
| E98 | 314-TT | 00.314 |
| E99 | 314-LW | 00.314 |
| E100 | | EPNER |
| E101 | 314-LX | 00.314 |
| E102 | | |
| E103 | | |
| E104 | F-TERB | *PDF* [6] |
| E105 | 314-LE | 00.314 |
| E106 | 314-UL | 00.314 |
| E107 | 8-NA | 02.008 |
| E108 | 8-NF | 02.008 |
| E109 | 8-NJ | 02.008 |
| E110 | 8-NG | 02.008 |
| E112 | DA | 01.091 |
| E113 | 314-LK | 00.314 |
| E114 | 314-TU | 00.314 |
| E115 | 8-NW | 02.008 |
| E116 | 8-MG | 01.008 |
| E117 | | |
| E118 | 314-LM | 00.314 |
| E119 | 7-PZ | 02.007 |
| E120 | F-TERG | *PDF* [9] |
| E121 | F-TERK | *PDF* [3] |
| E122 | | |
| E123 | 8-ML | 01.008 |
| E124 | | |
| E125 | 314-LP | 00.314 |
| E126 | 314-LI | 00.314 |
| E127 | 8-MB | 01.008 |
| E128 | F-TERN | *PDF* [9] |
| E129 | 314-TO | 00.314 |
| E130 | 314-LQ | 00.314 |
| E131 | 314-UD | 00.314 |
| E132 | 314-UJ | 00.314 |
| E133 | 8-NE | 02.008 |
| E134 | | |
| E135 | 8-ND | 02.008 |
| E136 | 314-TN | 00.314 |
| E137 | 314-LB | 00.314 |
| E138 | F-TERM | *PDF* [0] |
| E139 | 330-AH | CEAM |
| E140 | 314-UH | 00.314 |
| E141 | F-TERA | *PDF* [5] |
| E142 | 8-NV | 02.008 |
| E143 | 8-MM | 01.008 |
| E144 | | |
| E145 | 314-LZ | 00.314 |
| E146 | 8-MC | 01.008 |
| E147 | 8-NH | 02.008 |
| E148 | 8-NP | 02.008 |
| E149 | 8-MO | 01.008 |
| E150 | 8-NC | 02.008 |
| E151 | F-TERJ | *PDF* [7] |
| E152 | 8-MP | 01.008 |
| E153 | F-TERH | *PDF* [1] |
| E154 | 8-NT | 02.008 |
| E155 | 314-TP | 00.314 |
| E156 | 314-TI | 00.314 |
| E157 | 314-LG | 00.314 |
| E158 | F-TERG | *PDF* [2] |
| E159 | 7-PP | 02.007 |
| E160 | | |
| E161 | 8-MK | 01.008 |
| E162 | 314-TZ | 00.314 |
| E163 | 314-UM | 00.314 |
| E164 | | |
| E165 | | |
| E166 | 314-TX | 00.314 |
| E167 | 314-LL | 00.314 |
| E168 | | |
| E169 | F-TERQ | *PDF* |
| E170 | 2-EO | 01.002 |
| E171 | 314-TR | 00.314 |
| E173 | 314-LH | 00.314 |
| E175 | F-TERL | *PDF* |
| E176 | 8-MA | 01.008 |

**Dassault Falcon 20**
CEV, Bretigny[1], Cazaux[2], Istres[3] & Melun[4];
CITac 00.339 *Aquitaine*, Luxeuil;
EAM 09.120, Cazaux;
ETEC 00.065, Villacoublay

| | | |
|---|---|---|
| 22 | CS | CEV[3] |
| 49 | 120-FA | 98.120 |
| 79 | CT | CEV[1] |
| 86 | CG | CEV[2] |
| 93 | F-RAED | 00.065 |
| 96 | CB | CEV[1] |
| 104 | CW | CEV[1] |
| 115 | 339-JG | 00.339 |
| 124 | CC | CEV[1] |
| 131 | CD | CEV[1] |
| 138 | CR | CEV[2] |
| 145 | CU | CEV[1] |
| 182 | 339-JA | 00.339 |
| 188 | CX | CEV[4] |
| 238 | F-RAEE | 00.065 |
| 252 | CA | CEV[1] |
| 260 | F-RAEA | 00.065 |
| 263 | CY | CEV[1] |
| 268 | F-RAEF | 00.065 |
| 288 | CV | CEV[1] |
| 291 | 65-EG | 00.065 |
| 342 | F-RAEC | 00.065 |
| 375 | CZ | CEV[1] |
| 422 | 65-EH | 00.065 |
| 451 | 339-JC | 00.339 |
| 483 | 339-JI | 00.339 |

**Dassault Falcon 50**
ETEC 00.065, Villacoublay

| | |
|---|---|
| 5 | F-RAFI |
| 27 | (F-RAFK) |
| 34 | (F-RAFL) |
| 78 | F-RAFJ |

**Dassault Falcon 900**
ETEC 00.065, Villacoublay

| | |
|---|---|
| 2 | (F-RAFP) |
| 4 | (F-RAFQ) |

**Dassault Mirage IVP**
ERS 01.091 *Gascogne*, Mont-de-Marsan

| | |
|---|---|
| 11 | AJ |
| 23 | AV |
| 24 | AX |
| 36 | BI |
| 53 | BZ |
| 59 | CF |
| 61 | CH |
| 62 | CI |

**Dassault Mirage F.1**
CEAM (EC 05.330), Mont-de-Marsan;
CEV, Bretigny & Istres;
EC 01.030 *Alsace* & EC 02.030 *Normandie Niemen*, Colmar;
ER 01.033 *Belfort*,
ER 02.033 *Savoie*
EC 03.033 *Lorraine*, Reims;
EC 04.033 *Vexin*, Djibouti

**Mirage F.1C/F.1CT***

| | | |
|---|---|---|
| 5 | 33-FV | 03.033 |
| 15 | 33-FJ | 03.033 |
| 24 | 33-FC | 03.033 |
| 31 | 330-AC | CEAM |
| 32 | 33-FR | 03.033 |
| 33 | | |
| 52 | 33-FK | 03.033 |
| 62 | 33-FD | 03.033 |
| 64 | | |
| 74 | | |
| 76 | 33-FQ | 03.033 |
| 80 | | |
| 81 | | |
| 82 | 33-FO | 03.033 |
| 83 | 33-LI | 04.033 |
| 84 | | |
| 85 | | |
| 87 | 33-FS | 03.033 |
| 90 | | |
| 100 | 33-FN | 03.033 |
| 103 | 33-FU | 03.033 |
| 201 | 33-FW | 03.033 |
| 202 | 33-LG | 04.033 |
| 203 | 33-FE | 03.033 |
| 205 | | |
| 206 | 33-LA | 04.033 |
| 207* | 330-AO | CEAM |
| 210 | 33-LC | 04.033 |
| 211 | 33-LH | 04.033 |
| 213 | 33-LF | 04.033 |
| 214 | | |
| 218 | 33-FP | 03.033 |
| 219* | 30-SF | 01.030 |
| 220* | 30-QM | 02.030 |
| 221* | 30-SY | 01.030 |
| 223* | | |
| 224 | 33-FT | 03.033 |
| 225* | 30-QE | 02.030 |
| 226* | 30-QU | 02.030 |
| 227* | 330-AP | CEAM |
| 228* | 30-SN | 01.030 |
| 229* | 30-QC | 02.030 |
| 230* | 30-SP | 01.030 |
| 231* | 30-SA | 01.030 |
| 232* | 30-QW | 02.030 |
| 233* | 30-QG | 02.030 |
| 234* | 30-SI | 01.030 |
| 235* | 30-QS | 02.030 |
| 236* | 30-SB | 01.030 |
| 237* | 30-SM | 01.030 |
| 238* | 30-QN | 02.030 |
| 239* | 30-QD | 02.030 |
| 241* | | |
| 242* | 30-SG | 01.030 |
| 243* | 30-QJ | 02.030 |
| 244* | 30-QH | 02.030 |
| 245* | 30-SX | 01.030 |
| 246* | | |
| 247* | 30-QP | 02.030 |
| 248* | 30-SQ | 01.030 |
| 251* | 330-AI | CEAM |
| 252* | 30-QO | 02.030 |

253*
254* 30-QV 02.030
255* 30-QI 02.030
256* 30-QK 02.030
257* 30-SD 01.030
258* 30-SZ 01.030
259*
260* 330-AJ CEAM
261* 30-SL 01.030
262* 30-SE 01.030
264* 30-SW 01.030
265* 30-SH 01.030
267* 30-QB 02.030
268* 30-SR 01.030
271* 30-QQ 02.030
272*
273* 30-QL 02.030
274* 30-QT 02.030
275*
278* 30-QA 02.030
279* 30-SC 01.030
280*
281* 30-QF 02.030
283* 30-SV 01.030

**Mirage F.1B**

501
502 330-AD CEAM
503 33-FG 03.033
504 33-FB 03.033
505
507 33-FA 03.033
509 33-FX 03.033
510 33-FI 03.033
511
512 33-FL 03.033
513 33-FY 03.033
514 33-FZ 03.033
516
517 33-FH 03.033
518 33-FF 03.033
519 33-FM 03.033
520

**Mirage F.1CR**

602 CEV
603 33-CB 01.033
604 33-CF 01.033
605 33-NS 02.033
606 33-NP 02.033
607 33-CE 01.033
608 33-NG 02.033
610 33-NQ 02.033
611 33-NN 02.033
612 33-NJ 02.033
613 33-NK 02.033
614 33-NF 02.033
615 33-CU 01.033
616 33-NM 02.033
617 33-NO 02.033
620 33-CT 01.033
622 33-NH 02.033
623 33-CM 01.033
624
627 33-NI 02.033
628
629 33-CG 01.033
630 33-NL 02.033
631 33-CR 01.033
632 33-NE 02.033
634 33-CK 01.033
635
636 33-NZ 02.033
637 33-CP 01.033
638 33-CI 01.033
640 33-CH 01.033
641 33-CD 01.033
642 33-NC 02.033
643 33-NR 02.033
645 33-CC 01.033
646 33-NW 02.033
647 33-NX 02.033
648 33-NT 02.033
649 33-CZ 01.033
650 33-CJ 01.033
651 33-NB 02.033
653 33-NV 02.033
654 33-CL 01.033
655 330-AT CEAM
656 33-CS 01.033
657 33-CV 01.033
658 33-CW 01.033
659 33-CA 01.033
660 33-CY 01.033
661 33-CX 01.033
662 33-NA 02.033

**Dassault Mirage 2000B/2000-5***

AMD-BA, Istres;
CEV, Bretigny;
EC 02.002 *Côte d'Or*, Dijon;
EC 01.005 *Vendée* &
EC 02.005 *Ile de France*, Orange;
EC 01.012 *Cambrésis* &
EC 02.012 *Picardie*, Cambrai

501* (BX1) CEV
502 5-OH 02.005
504* BOB CEV
505 5-NW 01.005
506 5-OY 02.005
507 5-OX 02.005
508 5-OT 02.005
509 5-OP 02.005
510 5-OQ 02.005
511 5-OR 02.005
512 5-OU 02.005
513 5-OI 02.005
514 5-OE 02.005
515 5-OG 02.005
516 5-OL 02.005
518 5-OM 02.005
519 5-OW 02.005
520 5-OS 02.005
521 5-ON 02.005
522 5-OV 02.005
523 12-YS 01.012
524 330-AZ CEAM
525 2-FV 02.002
526 12-KM 02.012
527 12-KJ 02.012
528 330-AN CEAM
529 2-FS 02.002
530 12-YA 01.012

**Dassault Mirage 2000C/2000-5***

CEAM (EC 05.330), Mont-de-Marsan;
CEV, Istres;
EC 01.002 *Cicogne* &
EC 02.002 *Côte d'Or*, Dijon;
EC 01.005 *Vendée* &
EC 02.005 *Ile de France*, Orange;
EC 01.012 *Cambrésis* &
EC 02.012 *Picardie*, Cambrai

1
2 CEV
3 5-NP 01.005
4 5-OD 02.005
5 5-NC 01.005
8 5-OA 02.005
9 5-OJ 02.005
11 5-NJ 01.005
12 5-NN 01.005
13 5-NM 01.005
14 5-NK 01.005
15 5-NA 01.005
16 5-NE 01.005
17 5-NR 01.005
18 5-OF 02.005
19 5-NS 01.005
20 5-NB 01.005
21 5-NG 01.005
22 5-ND 01.005
25 5-NU 01.005
27 5-NT 01.005
28 5-OK 02.005
29 5-NO 01.005
30 5-NV 01.005
32 5-NQ 01.005
34 5-NH 01.005
35 5-NL 01.005
36 5-OC 02.005
37 5-NF 01.005
38* 2-EU 01.002
40 5-NI 01.005
41* 2-EJ 01.002
42
43
44
45* 2-ES 01.002
46* 2-EN 01.002
47* 2-EP 01.002
48* 2-ER 01.002
49* 2-FF 02.002
51* 330-AS CEAM
52* 2-FC 02.002
53
54* 2-GA 01.002
55* 2-FW 02.002
56* 2-FK 02.002
57
58
59
61
62
63
64 330-AQ CEAM
65* 2-EC 01.002
66* 2-FN 02.002
67* 2-ED 01.002
68
69* 2-EG 01.002
70* 2-FD 02.002
71* 2-EH 01.002
72* 2-FR 02.002
73* 2-EB 01.002
74
76* 2-EK 01.002
77* 330-AX CEAM
78* 2-FS 02.002
79
80 2-FD 02.002
81 12-YI 01.012
82 12-KQ 02.012
83
84
85 12-YE 01.012

| | | |
|---|---|---|
| 86 | 12-KH | 02.012 |
| 87 | 12-YQ | 01.012 |
| 88 | 12-YR | 01.012 |
| 89 | 2-FL | 02.002 |
| 90 | 12-KO | 02.012 |
| 91 | 12-YO | 01.012 |
| 92 | 330-AW | CEAM |
| 93 | 12-KF | 02.012 |
| 94 | 12-KA | 02.012 |
| 95 | 12-YF | 01.012 |
| 96 | 12-KK | 02.012 |
| 97 | 12-KP | 02.012 |
| 98 | 12-YB | 01.012 |
| 99 | 2-FM | 02.002 |
| 100 | 2-FZ | 02.002 |
| 101 | 2-FB | 02.002 |
| 102 | 2-FE | 02.002 |
| 103 | 12-YN | 01.012 |
| 104 | 12-YK | 01.012 |
| 105 | 12-YL | 01.012 |
| 106 | 2-FP | 02.002 |
| 107 | | |
| 108 | 12-KE | 02.012 |
| 109 | 2-FF | 02.002 |
| 111 | 12-KI | 02.012 |
| 112 | 12-YC | 01.012 |
| 113 | 12-KN | 02.012 |
| 114 | 12-KS | 02.012 |
| 115 | 12-KC | 02.012 |
| 116 | 12-KG | 02.012 |
| 117 | 12-YD | 01.012 |
| 118 | 12-YG | 01.012 |
| 119 | 12-KD | 02.012 |
| 120 | 12-YM | 01.012 |
| 121 | 2-FG | 02.002 |
| 122 | 12-YU | 01.012 |
| 123 | 12-KR | 02.012 |
| 124 | 12-KB | 02.012 |

**Dassault Mirage 2000D**
AMD-BA, Istres;
CEAM (EC 05.330), Mont-de-Marsan;
CEV, Istres;
EC 01.003 *Navarre*, EC 02.003 *Champagne* & EC 03.003 *Ardennes*, Nancy

| | | |
|---|---|---|
| 601 | 3-IA | 01.003 |
| 602 | 3-JR | 02.003 |
| 603 | 3-IC | 01.003 |
| 604 | 3-XK | 03.003 |
| 605 | 3-IE | 01.003 |
| 606 | 3-XL | 03.003 |
| 607 | | CEV |
| 609 | 3-XD | 03.003 |
| 610 | 3-II | 01.003 |
| 611 | 3-XS | 03.003 |
| 612 | 3-IL | 01.003 |
| 613 | 3-IF | 01.003 |
| 614 | 330-A. | CEAM |
| 615 | 3-JA | 02.003 |
| 616 | 3-IJ | 01.003 |
| 617 | 3-XA | 03.003 |
| 618 | 3-IG | 01.003 |
| 619 | 3-JE | 02.003 |
| 620 | 3-IM | 01.003 |
| 621 | 3-XC | 03.003 |
| 622 | 3-JF | 02.003 |
| 623 | 3-IB | 01.003 |
| 624 | 3-XF | 03.003 |
| 625 | 3-IK | 01.003 |
| 626 | 3-XH | 03.003 |
| 627 | 3-JG | 02.003 |
| 628 | 330-AE | CEAM |
| 629 | 3-XJ | 03.003 |
| 630 | 3-JI | 02.003 |
| 631 | 3-XI | 03.003 |
| 632 | 3-XM | 03.003 |
| 633 | 3-JT | 02.003 |
| 634 | 3-ID | 01.003 |
| 635 | 3-XP | 03.003 |
| 636 | 3-JJ | 02.003 |
| 637 | 3-JH | 02.003 |
| 638 | 3-IQ | 01.003 |
| 639 | 3-XQ | 03.003 |
| 640 | 3-IR | 01.003 |
| 641 | 3-XG | 03.003 |
| 642 | 3-JB | 02.003 |
| 643 | 3-JC | 02.003 |
| 644 | 3-JD | 02.003 |
| 645 | 3-JO | 02.003 |
| 646 | 3-JP | 02.003 |
| 647 | 330-A. | CEAM |
| 648 | 3-XT | 03.003 |
| 649 | 3-IS | 01.003 |
| 650 | 3-IN | 01.003 |
| 651 | 3-IH | 01.003 |
| 652 | 3-XN | 03.003 |
| 653 | 3-JK | 02.003 |
| 654 | 3-IT | 01.003 |
| 655 | 3-XE | 03.003 |
| 656 | 3-JL | 02.003 |
| 657 | 3-JM | 02.003 |
| 658 | 3-JN | 02.003 |
| 659 | 3-XR | 03.003 |
| 660 | 3-IO | 01.003 |
| 661 | 3-JS | 02.003 |
| 662 | 3-XU | 03.003 |
| 663 | 3-IP | 01.003 |
| 664 | 3-JU | 02.003 |
| 665 | 3-XV | 03.003 |
| 666 | | |
| 667 | 3-JX | 02.003 |
| 668 | | |
| 669 | | |
| 670 | | |
| 671 | | |
| 672 | | |
| 673 | | |
| 674 | | |
| 675 | | |
| 676 | | |
| 677 | | |
| 678 | | |
| 679 | | |
| 680 | | |
| 681 | | |
| 682 | | |
| 683 | | |
| 684 | | |
| 685 | | |
| 686 | | |

**Dassault Mirage 2000N**
CEAM (EC 05.330), Mont-de-Marsan;
CEV, Istres;
EC 01.004 *Dauphiné* & EC 02.004 *Lafayette*, Luxeuil;
EC 03.004 *Limousin*, Istres

| | | |
|---|---|---|
| 301 | | CEV |
| 303 | | CEV |
| 304 | | |
| 305 | 4-CS | 03.004 |
| 306 | 4-CQ | 03.004 |
| 307 | 4-CC | 03.004 |
| 309 | 4-AO | 01.004 |
| 310 | 4-CE | 03.004 |
| 311 | 4-CA | 03.004 |
| 312 | 4-CF | 03.004 |
| 313 | 4-CV | 03.004 |
| 314 | 4-CG | 03.004 |
| 315 | 4-CD | 03.004 |
| 316 | 4-CH | 03.004 |
| 317 | 4-CR | 03.004 |
| 318 | 4-BP | 02.004 |
| 319 | 4-AC | 01.004 |
| 320 | 4-CK | 03.004 |
| 322 | 4-CL | 03.004 |
| 323 | 4-CJ | 03.004 |
| 325 | | |
| 326 | 4-CM | 03.004 |
| 327 | | |
| 329 | 4-CN | 03.004 |
| 330 | 4-CO | 03.004 |
| 331 | 4-BT | 02.004 |
| 332 | 4-BN | 02.004 |
| 333 | 4-AB | 01.004 |
| 334 | 330-AV | CEAM |
| 335 | 4-BJ | 02.004 |
| 336 | | |
| 337 | 4-CB | 03.004 |
| 338 | 4-CI | 03.004 |
| 339 | 4-AD | 01.004 |
| 340 | 4-AA | 01.004 |
| 341 | 4-AF | 01.004 |
| 342 | 4-AG | 01.004 |
| 343 | 4-AH | 01.004 |
| 344 | 4-AJ | 01.004 |
| 345 | 4-AK | 01.004 |
| 348 | 4-AL | 01.004 |
| 349 | 4-BA | 02.004 |
| 350 | 4-CU | 03.004 |
| 351 | 4-AQ | 01.004 |
| 353 | 4-BL | 02.004 |
| 354 | 4-BF | 02.004 |
| 355 | 4-AE | 01.004 |
| 356 | 4-AI | 01.004 |
| 357 | 4-BD | 02.004 |
| 358 | 4-AM | 01.004 |
| 359 | 4-BG | 02.004 |
| 360 | 4-AI | 01.004 |
| 361 | | |
| 362 | 4-BM | 02.004 |
| 363 | 4-BK | 02.004 |
| 364 | 4-BB | 02.004 |
| 365 | 4-BE | 02.004 |
| 366 | 4-BO | 02.004 |
| 367 | 4-AS | 01.004 |
| 368 | 4-AR | 01.004 |
| 369 | 4-BQ | 02.004 |
| 370 | 4-AT | 01.004 |
| 371 | 4-AV | 01.004 |
| 372 | 4-BR | 02.004 |
| 373 | 4-BH | 02.004 |
| 374 | 4-BS | 02.004 |
| 375 | 4-BC | 02.004 |

**Dassault Rafale-B**
AMD-BA, Istres

| | |
|---|---|
| B01 | AMD-BA |
| B1 | AMD-BA |
| 301 | AMD-BA |

**Dassault Rafale-C**
AMD-BA, Istres

| | |
|---|---|
| C01 | AMD-BA |

**DHC-6 Twin Otter 200/300***
CEAM (EET 06.330), Mont-de-Marsan;
ET 00.042 *Ventoux*, Mont-de-Marsan;
GAM 00.056 *Vaucluse*, Evreux

| | | |
|---|---|---|
| 292 | CC | 00.056 |
| 298 | CD | 00.056 |
| 300 | CE | 00.056 |
| 730* | CA | 00.042 |
| 742* | IA | CEAM |
| 745* | IB | CEAM |
| 786* | CT | 00.042 |
| 790* | CW | 00.042 |

**Douglas DC-8-53/72CF***
CEV, Istres;
EE 00.051 *Aubrac*, Evreux;
ET 03.060 *Esterel*, Paris/Charles de Gaulle

| | | |
|---|---|---|
| 45570 | F-ZVMT | 00.051 |
| 46013* | F-RAFG | 03.060 |
| 46043* | F-ZWMT | CEV |
| 46130* | F-RAFF | 03.060 |

**Embraer EMB.121AA/AN* Xingu**
EAT 00.319, Avord

| | |
|---|---|
| 054 | YX |
| 055* | |
| 064 | YY |
| 066* | |
| 069* | |
| 070* | |
| 072 | YA |
| 073 | YB |
| 075 | YC |
| 076 | YD |
| 077* | |
| 078 | YE |
| 080 | YF |
| 082 | YG |
| 083* | ZE |
| 084 | YH |
| 086 | YI |
| 089 | YJ |
| 090* | ZF |
| 091 | YK |
| 092 | YL |
| 095 | YM |
| 096 | YN |
| 098 | YO |
| 099 | YP |
| 101 | YR |
| 102 | YS |
| 103 | YT |
| 105 | YU |
| 107 | YV |
| 108 | YW |
| 111 | YQ |

**Embraer EMB.312F Tucano**
GI 00.312, Salon de Provence

| | |
|---|---|
| 438 | 312-UW |
| 439 | 312-UX |
| 456 | 312-JA |
| 457 | 312-JB |
| 458 | 312-JC |
| 459 | 312-JD |
| 460 | 312-JE |
| 461 | 312-JF |
| 462 | 312-JG |
| 463 | 312-JH |
| 464 | 312-JI |
| 466 | 312-JK |
| 467 | 312-JL |
| 468 | 312-JM |
| 469 | 312-JN |
| 470 | 312-JO |
| 471 | 312-JP |
| 472 | 312-JQ |
| 473 | 312-JR |
| 474 | 312-JS |
| 475 | 312-JT |
| 477 | 312-JU |
| 478 | 312-JV |
| 479 | 312-JX |
| 480 | 312-JY |
| 481 | 312-JZ |
| 483 | 312-UB |
| 484 | 312-UC |
| 485 | 312-UD |
| 486 | 312-UE |
| 487 | 312-UF |
| 488 | 312-UG |
| 489 | 312-UH |
| 490 | 312-UI |
| 491 | 312-UJ |
| 492 | 312-UK |
| 493 | 312-UL |
| 494 | 312-UM |
| 495 | 312-UN |
| 496 | 312-UO |
| 497 | 312-UP |
| 498 | 312-UQ |
| 499 | 312-UR |
| 500 | 312-US |
| 501 | 312-UT |
| 502 | 312-UU |
| 503 | 312-UV |
| 504 | 312-UX |

**Eurocopter AS.332 Super Puma/AS.532 Cougar**
EH 03.067 *Parisis*, Villacoublay;
ETOM 00.082 *Maine*, Faaa-Tahiti;
GAM 00.056 *Vaucluse*, Evreux

| | | | |
|---|---|---|---|
| 2014 | AS.332C | | |
| 2057 | AS.332C | 82-PO | 00.082 |
| 2093 | AS.332C | 82-PP | 00.082 |
| 2233 | AS.332M | 67-FY | 03.067 |
| 2235 | AS.332M | 67-FZ | 03.067 |
| 2244 | AS.332C | 82-PM | 00.082 |
| 2337 | AS.532UL | | 03.067 |
| 2342 | AS.532M1 | FX | 00.056 |
| 2369 | AS.532M1 | FW | 00.056 |
| 2375 | AS.532M1 | FV | 00.056 |
| 2377 | AS.532M | 67-FU | 03.067 |

**Lockheed C-130H/ C-130H-30* Hercules**
ET 02.061 *Franche-Comté*, Orléans

| | |
|---|---|
| 4588 | 61-PM |
| 4589 | 61-PN |
| 5114 | 61-PA |
| 5116 | 61-PB |
| 5119 | 61-PC |
| 5140 | 61-PE |
| 5144* | 61-PF |
| 5150* | 61-PG |
| 5151* | 61-PH |
| 5152* | 61-PI |
| 5153* | 61-PJ |
| 5226* | 61-PK |
| 5227* | 61-PL |

**Morane Saulnier MS.760 Paris**
CEV, Bretigny & Istres;
EAC 00.314, Tours;
EAM 09.115 Orange
EAM 09.116, Luxeuil;
EAM 09.128, Metz;
EAM 09.132, Colmar;
ENOSA 00.316, Toulouse

| | | |
|---|---|---|
| 27 | 316-DQ | 00.316 |
| 30 | 116-CB | 09.116 |
| 34 | 316-DR | 00.316 |
| 54 | 115-MG | 09.115 |
| 57 | 316-DJ | 00.316 |
| 59 | 316-DP | 00.316 |
| 61 | 316-DI | 00.316 |
| 65 | 314-DD | 00.314 |
| 68 | NB | CEV |
| 71 | 316-DO | 00.316 |
| 83 | NC | CEV |
| 91 | 316-DM | 00.316 |
| 93 | 132-CN | 09.132 |
| 94 | 115-MF | 09.115 |
| 115 | OV | CEV |
| 116 | ON | CEV |
| 118 | NQ | CEV |
| 119 | NL | CEV |

**Nord 262A^A/262D^D/ 262D-AEN^N Frégate**
CEV, Istres;
ENOSA 00.316, Toulouse;
EPNER, Istres;
ETE 00.041 *Verdun*, Metz;
ET 00.042 *Ventoux*, Mont-de-Marsan;
ETE 00.043 *Médoc*, Bordeaux;
ETE 00.044 *Mistral*, Salon de Provence;
ETEC 00.065, Villacoublay

| | | |
|---|---|---|
| 58^A | MJ | EPNER |
| 64^D | AA | 00.065 |
| 66^D | AB | 00.065 |
| 67^A | MI | CEV |
| 68^D | AC | 00.065 |
| 76^N | 316-DA | 00.316 |
| 77^D | AK | 00.044 |
| 78^D | AF | 00.065 |
| 80^D | AW | 00.065 |
| 81^D | AH | 00.041 |
| 83^N | 316-DB | 00.316 |
| 86^N | 316-DD | 00.316 |
| 87^N | 316-DC | 00.316 |
| 88^D | AL | 00.044 |
| 89^D | AZ | 00.041 |
| 91^D | AT | 00.065 |
| 92^N | 316-DE | 00.316 |
| 93^D | AP | 00.065 |
| 94^D | AU | 00.065 |
| 95^D | AR | 00.065 |

| | | |
|---|---|---|
| 105[D] | AE | 00.065 |
| 106[D] | AY | 00.041 |
| 107[D] | AX | 00.065 |
| 108[D] | AG | 00.041 |
| 109[D] | AM | 00.043 |
| 110[D] | AS | 00.041 |

**SEPECAT Jaguar**

CEV, Bretigny & Istres;
CEAM (EC 05.330), Mont-de-Marsan;
CITac 00.339 *Aquitaine*, Luxeuil;
EC 01.007 *Provence*,
EC 02.007 *Argonne* & EC 03.007 *Languedoc*, St Dizier

**Jaguar A**

| | | |
|---|---|---|
| A1 | | |
| A17 | 7-HN | 01.007 |
| A25 | | |
| A28 | | |
| A34 | 7-PC | 02.007 |
| A35 | | |
| A43 | | |
| A47 | | |
| A53 | 7-PB | 02.007 |
| A55 | 7-PA | 02.007 |
| A58 | 7-HE | 01.007 |
| A61 | 7-IQ | 03.007 |
| A64 | | |
| A66 | | |
| A67 | 7-PV | 02.007 |
| A75 | 7-HM | 01.007 |
| A84 | 7-PY | 02.007 |
| A87 | 7-PF | 02.007 |
| A88 | 7-PR | 02.007 |
| A89 | 7-HF | 01.007 |
| A90 | 7-HL | 01.007 |
| A92 | 7-PT | 02.007 |
| A93 | 7-PN | 02.007 |
| A94 | 7-IG | 03.007 |
| A96 | 7-HD | 01.007 |
| A98 | | |
| A99 | | |
| A100 | 7-HR | 01.007 |
| A101 | 7-HB | 01.007 |
| A103 | 7-IE | 03.007 |
| A107 | 7-HC | 01.007 |
| A108 | 7-HQ | 01.007 |
| A112 | 7-HS | 01.007 |
| A113 | 7-II | 03.007 |
| A117 | 7-HA | 01.007 |
| A120 | 7-IJ | 03.007 |
| A122 | 7-IM | 03.007 |
| A123 | 7-IO | 03.007 |
| A124 | 7-IN | 03.007 |
| A126 | 7-HJ | 01.007 |
| A127 | 7-IP | 03.007 |
| A128 | 7-IC | 03.007 |
| A129 | 7-IL | 03.007 |
| A130 | 7-HU | 01.007 |
| A133 | 7-HK | 01.007 |
| A135 | 7-IU | 03.007 |
| A137 | 7-HG | 01.007 |
| A138 | 7-HV | 01.007 |
| A139 | | |
| A140 | 7-HI | 01.007 |
| A141 | 7-IB | 03.007 |
| A144 | 7-IF | 03.007 |
| A145 | | |
| A148 | 7-IK | 03.007 |
| A149 | 7-HP | 01.007 |
| A150 | 7-IT | 03.007 |
| A151 | 7-HH | 01.007 |
| A153 | 7-ID | 03.007 |
| A154 | 7-IS | 03.007 |
| A157 | | |
| A158 | 7-HK | 01.007 |
| A159 | 7-HO | 01.007 |
| A160 | 7-IH | 03.007 |

**Jaguar E**

| | | |
|---|---|---|
| E2 | 339-WM | 00.339 |
| E3 | 339-WF | 00.339 |
| E4 | 7-PG | 02.007 |
| E5 | 339-WH | 00.339 |
| E6 | | |
| E7 | 7-PL | 02.007 |
| E8 | 7-PQ | 02.007 |
| E9 | | |
| E10 | 339-WL | 00.339 |
| E12 | 339-WI | 00.339 |
| E15 | | |
| E18 | | |
| E19 | 339-WG | 00.339 |
| E20 | 7-PM | 02.007 |
| E21 | | |
| E22 | 7-PU | 02.007 |
| E23 | | |
| E24 | 7-PH | 02.007 |
| E25 | | |
| E27 | | |
| E28 | 7-PS | 02.007 |
| E29 | 339-WJ | 00.339 |
| E30 | | |
| E32 | 7-PD | 02.007 |
| E35 | 7-PU | 02.007 |
| E36 | 7-PK | 02.007 |
| E37 | 7-PQ | 02.007 |
| E39 | 339-WN | 00.339 |
| E40 | 7-PI | 02.007 |

**SOCATA TBM 700**

CEV, Bordeaux;
ETE 00.041 *Verdun*, Metz;
ETE 00.043 *Médoc*, Bordeaux;
ETE 00.044 *Mistral*, Salon de Provence;
ETEC 00.065, Villacoublay;
EdC 00.070, Chateaudun

| | | |
|---|---|---|
| 33 | 43-XA | 00.043 |
| 35 | 65-XB | 00.065 |
| 70 | 43-XC | 00.043 |
| 77 | 65-XD | 00.065 |
| 78 | 65-XE | 00.044 |
| 80 | 41-XF | 00.041 |
| 93 | 43-XL | 00.043 |
| 94 | 65-XG | 00.070 |
| 95 | 65-XH | 00.065 |
| 103 | 41-XI | 00.041 |
| 104 | XJ | 00.070 |
| 105 | 65-XK | 00.065 |
| 106 | MN | CEV |
| 110 | XP | 00.041 |
| 111 | 65-XM | 00.065 |
| 117 | 65-XN | 00.065 |
| 125 | 65-XO | 00.065 |
| 131 | XQ | |
| 146 | XR | 00.065 |
| 147 | XS | 00.041 |

**Transall C-160A/C-160F/ C-160H/C-160NG/C-160NG GABRIEL*/C-160R**

CEAM (EET 06.330), Mont-de-Marsan;
CEV, Bretigny;
EET 01.054 *Dunkerque*, Metz;
ET 01.061 *Touraine* & ET 03.061 *Poitou*, Orléans;
ET 01.064 *Bearn* & ET 02.064 *Anjou*, Evreux;
ETOM 00.050 *Réunion*, St Denis;
ETOM 00.055 *Ouessant*, Dakar;
ETOM 00.058 *Guadeloupe*, Pointe-à-Pitre;
ETOM 00.088 *Larzac*, Djibouti

| | | | |
|---|---|---|---|
| RA02 | C-160R | 61-MI | 01.061 |
| RA04 | C-160R | 61-MS | 01.061 |
| RA06 | C-160R | 61-ZB | 03.061 |
| R1 | C-160R | 61-MA | 01.061 |
| R2 | C-160R | 61-MB | 01.061 |
| R3 | C-160R | 61-MC | 00.058 |
| R4 | C-160R | 61-MD | 01.061 |
| R5 | C-160R | 61-ME | 01.061 |
| R11 | C-160R | 61-MF | 01.061 |
| R12 | C-160R | 61-MG | 01.061 |
| R13 | C-160R | 61-MH | 00.050 |
| R15 | C-160R | 61-MJ | 01.061 |
| R17 | C-160R | 61-ML | 01.061 |
| R18 | C-160R | 61-MM | 01.061 |
| R42 | C-160R | 61-MN | 01.061 |
| R43 | C-160R | 61-MO | 01.061 |
| R44 | C-160R | 61-MP | 01.061 |
| R45 | C-160R | 61-MQ | 01.061 |
| R46 | C-160R | 61-MR | 01.061 |
| R48 | C-160R | 61-MT | 01.061 |
| R49 | C-160R | 59-MU | CEV |
| R51 | C-160R | 61-MW | 01.061 |
| R52 | C-160R | 61-MX | 01.061 |
| R53 | C-160R | 61-MY | 01.061 |
| R54 | C-160R | 61-MZ | 01.061 |
| R55 | C-160R | 61-ZC | 03.061 |
| R86 | C-160R | 61-ZD | 03.061 |
| R87 | C-160R | 61-ZE | 00.050 |
| R88 | C-160R | 61-ZF | 03.061 |

R89 C-160R 61-ZG 03.061
R90 C-160R 61-ZH 03.061
R91 C-160R 61-ZI 03.061
R92 C-160R 61-ZJ 03.061
R93 C-160R 61-ZK 03.061
R94 C-160R 61-ZL 03.061
R95 C-160R 61-ZM 00.088
R96 C-160R 61-ZN 03.061
R97 C-160R 61-ZO 03.061
R98 C-160R 61-ZP 03.061
R99 C-160R 61-ZQ 03.061
F100 C-160F 61-ZR 03.061
R153 C-160R 61-ZS 03.061
R154 C-160R 61-ZT 03.061
R157 C-160R 61-ZW 03.061
R158 C-160R 61-ZX 03.061
R159 C-160R 61-ZY 03.061
R160 C-160R 61-ZZ 03.061
F201 C-160NG 64-GA 01.064
R202 C-160R 64-GB 02.064
R203 C-160R 64-GC 01.064
R204 C-160R 64-GD 02.064
R205 C-160R 64-GE 01.064
R206 C-160R 64-GF 02.064
R207 C-160R 64-GG 01.064
R208 C-160R 64-GH 02.064
F210 C-160NG 64-GJ 02.064
R211 C-160R 64-GK 01.064
R212 C-160R 64-GL 02.064
R213 C-160R 64-GM 01.064
R214 C-160R 64-GN 02.064
F215 C-160NG 64-GO 01.064
F216 C-160NG* 54-GT 01.054
F217 C-160NG 64-GQ 01.064
F218 C-160NG 64-GR 02.064
F221 C-160NG* 54-GS 01.054
F223 C-160NG 64-GW 01.064
F224 C-160NG 64-GX 02.064
R225 C-160R 64-GY 01.064
R226 C-160R 64-GZ 02.064
H01 C-160H
H02 C-160H
H03 C-160H
H04 C-160H

**Aéronavale/Marine**

**Aérospatiale SA.321G Super Frelon**
32 Flotille, Lanvéoc/Poulmic;
35 Flotille, St Mandrier
101 32F
102 32F
106 32F
118
120 32F
134 32F
137 32F
144 32F
148 32F
150 32F
160 35F
162 32F
163 35F
164 32F
165

**Breguet Br 1050M Alizé**
6 Flotille, Nimes/Garons
22
47
49
50
52
53
55
56
59

**Dassault-Breguet Atlantique 2**
21 Flotille, Nimes/Garons;
23 Flotille, Lorient/ Lann Bihoué
1 21F
2 23F
3 23F
4 21F
5 21F
6 21F
7 23F
8 21F
9 23F
10 23F
11 23F
12 21F
13 21F
14 21F
15 23F
16 21F
17 21F
18 23F
19 23F
20 23F
21 21F
22 23F
23 21F
24 21F
25 21F
26 23F
27 21F
28 23F
29
30

**Dassault Etendard IVPM**
16 Flotille, Landivisiau
107
109
115
118
153

**Dassault Falcon 10(MER)**
ES 57, Landivisiau
32
101
129
133
143
185

**Dassault Falcon 20G Guardian**
ES 9 Tontouta;
ES 12 Papeete
48 12S
65 9S
72 12S
77 9S
80

**Dassault Falcon 50 SURMAR**
24 Flotille, Lorient/ Lann Bihoué
30 F-ZVMB
36 F-ZJTL

**Dassault Rafale-M**
M01 AMD-BA
M02 AMD-BA
1 CEV

**Dassault Super Etendard**
11 Flotille, Landivisiau;
17 Flotille, Landivisiau;
CEV, Bretigny & Istres
1 11F
2 11F
3 17F
4
6 11F
8 11F
10 11F
11 17F
12 17F
13 11F
14 11F
15
16 11F
17 11F
18 11F
19 11F
23 11F
24 11F
25 17F
26 17F
28 17F
30 11F
31 11F
32 11F
33 17F

| | |
|---|---|
| 35 | CEV |
| 37 | 11F |
| 38 | 11F |
| 39 | 11F |
| 41 | 11F |
| 43 | 11F |
| 44 | 17F |
| 45 | 11F |
| 46 | 11F |
| 47 | 17F |
| 48 | 17F |
| 49 | 11F |
| 50 | 17F |
| 51 | 17F |
| 52 | 11F |
| 55 | 17F |
| 57 | 11F |
| 59 | 11F |
| 60 | 11F |
| 61 | 17F |
| 62 | 11F |
| 64 | 11F |
| 65 | 11F |
| 66 | 11F |
| 68 | CEV |
| 69 | 17F |
| 71 | 17F |

**Embraer**
**EMB.121AN Xingu**
28 Flotille, Hyères;
ES 2, Lorient/Lann Bihoué

| | |
|---|---|
| 30 | 2S |
| 47 | 2S |
| 65 | 2S |
| 67 | 2S |
| 68 | 2S |
| 71 | 28F |
| 74 | 2S |
| 79 | 2S |
| 81 | 2S |
| 85 | 2S |
| 87 | 28F |

**Eurocopter**
**SA.365/AS.565 Panther**
32 Flotille, Lanvéoc/Poulmic (with detachments at Cherbourg, La Rochelle & Le Touquet)
35 Flotille, St Mandrier;
36 Flotille, St Mandrier

| | | |
|---|---|---|
| 17 | SA.365N | 32F |
| 19 | SA.365N | 32F |
| 24 | SA.365N | 32F |
| 81 | SA.365N | 32F |
| 91 | SA.365N | 32F |
| 313 | SA.365F1 | 35F |
| 316 | AS.565MA | 35F |
| 318 | SA.365F1 | 35F |
| 319 | AS.565MA | 32F |
| 322 | SA.365F1 | 35F |
| 355 | AS.565MA | 36F |
| 362 | AS.565MA | 32F |
| 436 | AS.565MA | 36F |
| 452 | AS.565MA | 36F |
| 453 | AS.565MA | 32F |
| 466 | AS.565MA | 36F |
| 482 | AS.565MA | 32F |
| 486 | AS.565SA | 36F |
| 503 | AS.565MA | 36F |
| 505 | AS.565MA | 35F |
| 506 | AS.565MA | 36F |
| 507 | AS.565SA | 36F |
| 511 | AS.565SA | |
| 519 | AS.565SA | 36F |
| 522 | AS.565SA | 36F |

**Nord 262E Frégate**
28 Flotille, Hyères;
ERC,Hyères;
ES 2, Lorient/Lann Bihoué;
ES 55, Aspretto;
ES 56, Nimes/Garons

| | |
|---|---|
| 45 | 56S |
| 46 | 56S |
| 51 | 2S |
| 52 | 56S |
| 53 | 56S |
| 60 | |
| 63 | 56S |
| 69 | 56S |
| 70 | 56S |
| 71 | 56S |
| 72 | 28F |
| 73 | 56S |
| 75 | 56S |
| 79 | 28F |
| 100 | 2S |

**Northrop Grumman**
**E-2C Hawkeye**
4 Flotille, Lorient/Lann Bihoué

| | |
|---|---|
| 1 | (165455) |
| 2 | (165456) |

**Westland**
**Lynx HAS2(FN) HAS4(FN)***
31 Flotille, St Mandrier;
34 Flotille, Lanvéoc/Poulmic

| | |
|---|---|
| 260 | |
| 262 | 34F |
| 263 | 31F |
| 264 | 34F |
| 265 | 34F |
| 266 | 34F |
| 267 | 31F |
| 268 | |
| 269 | 31F |
| 270 | 31F |
| 271 | 34F |
| 272 | 31F |
| 273 | |
| 274 | 34F |
| 275 | 31F |
| 276 | 34F |
| 620 | 34F |
| 621 | 34F |
| 622 | 34F |
| 623 | 34F |
| 624 | 31F |
| 625 | 34F |
| 627 | 34F |
| 801* | 34F |
| 802* | 34F |
| 803* | 31F |
| 804* | 34F |
| 806* | 34F |
| 807* | 34F |
| 808* | 34F |
| 810* | 34F |
| 811* | 34F |
| 812* | 31F |
| 813* | 34F |
| 814* | 31F |

**Aviation Legére de l'Armée de Terre (ALAT)**
**Cessna F.406 Caravan II**
EMAT, Rennes

| | |
|---|---|
| 0008 | ABM |
| 0010 | ABN |

**SOCATA TBM 700**
EMAT, Rennes

| | |
|---|---|
| 99 | ABO |
| 100 | ABP |
| 115 | ABQ |
| 136 | ABR |
| 139 | ABS |

**French Govt**
**Aérospatiale AS.355F-1 Twin Ecureuil**
Douanes Françaises

| | |
|---|---|
| F-ZBAC | (5026) |
| F-ZBEF | (5236) |
| F-ZBEJ | (5003) |
| F-ZBEK | (5298) |
| F-ZBEL | (5299) |

**Aérospatiale ATR-42-320**
CNET, Rennes

| | |
|---|---|
| F-SEBK | (264) |

**Cessna 404 Titan**
Douanes Francaises

| | |
|---|---|
| F-ZBDY | (0815) |

**Cessna F.406 Caravan II**
Douanes Francaises

| | |
|---|---|
| F-ZBAB | (0025) |
| F-ZBBB | (0039) |
| F-ZBCE | (0042) |
| F-ZBCF | (0077) |
| F-ZBCG | (0066) |
| F-ZBCH | (0075) |
| F-ZBCI | (0070) |
| F-ZBCJ | (0074) |
| F-ZBEP | (0006) |
| F-ZBES | (0017) |
| F-ZBFA | (0001) |
| F-ZBGA | (0086) |

**Dassault Falcon 20**
AVDEF, Nimes/Garons

| | |
|---|---|
| F-GPAA | Falcon 20ECM |
| F-GPAB | Falcon 20E |

## GERMANY

**Luftwaffe, Marineflieger**
**Airbus A.310-304/MRTT***
1/FBS, Köln-Bonn

10+21
10+22
10+23
10+24*
10+25*
10+26*
10+27*

**Canadair**
**CL601-1A Challenger**
1/FBS, Köln-Bonn

12+01
12+02
12+03
12+04
12+05

12+06
12+07

**Mikoyan MiG-29G/MiG-29GT***
JG-73 *'Steinhoff'*, Laage
29+01
29+02
29+03
29+04
29+05
29+06
29+07
29+08
29+10
29+11
29+12
29+14
29+15
29+16
29+17
29+18
29+19
29+20
29+21
29+22*
29+23*
29+24*
29+25*

**McD F-4F Phantom**
JG-71 *Richthoven*, Wittmundhaven;
JG-72 *Westfalen*, Hopsten;
JG-73 *SteinhoffF* Laage;
JG-74 *Molders* Neuburg/Donau;
TsLw-1, Kaufbeuren;
WTD-61, Ingolstadt
37+01 JG-72
37+03 JG-71
37+04 TsLw-1
37+06 JG-72
37+07 JG-72
37+08 JG-74
37+09 JG-72
37+10 JG-72
37+11 JG-73
37+12 JG-72
37+13 JG-74
37+14 TsLw-1
37+15 WTD-61
37+16 WTD-61
37+17 JG-74
37+22 JG-71
37+26 JG-73
37+28 JG-71
37+29 JG-72
37+31 JG-72
37+32 JG-71
37+33 JG-72
37+34 JG-72
37+35 JG-72
37+36 JG-72
37+37 JG-72
37+38 JG-72
37+39 JG-71
37+42 JG-72
37+43 JG-72
37+44 JG-72
37+45 JG-72
37+47 JG-72
37+48 JG-74
37+49 JG-71
37+52 JG-72
37+54 JG-74
37+55 JG-71
37+58 JG-72
37+61 JG-74
37+63 JG-71
37+64 JG-72
37+65 JG-71
37+66 JG-71
37+67 JG-74
37+71 JG-74
37+75 JG-73
37+76 JG-71
37+77 JG-74
37+78 JG-71
37+79 JG-71
37+81 JG-72
37+82 JG-71
37+83 JG-71
37+84 JG-74
37+85 JG-71
37+86 JG-71
37+88 JG-74
37+89 JG-73
37+92 JG-74
37+93 JG-72
37+94 JG-74
37+96 JG-72
37+97 JG-74
37+98 JG-71
38+00 JG-74
38+01 JG-73
38+02 JG-73
38+03 JG-72
38+04 JG-72
38+05 JG-73
38+06 JG-74
38+07 JG-71
38+09 JG-74
38+10 JG-74
38+12 JG-71
38+13 WTD-61
38+14 JG-71
38+16 JG-74
38+17 JG-74
38+18 JG-74
38+20 JG-72
38+24 JG-74
38+25 JG-74
38+26 JG-74
38+27 JG-71
38+28 JG-74
38+29 JG-74
38+30 JG-71
38+31 JG-72
38+32 JG-71
38+33 JG-73
38+34 JG-72
38+36 JG-71
38+37 JG-72
38+39 JG-74
38+40 JG-71
38+42 JG-71
38+43 JG-72
38+44 JG-71
38+45 JG-71
38+46 JG-71
38+48 JG-74
38+49 JG-71
38+50 JG-72
38+53 JG-74
38+54 JG-73
38+55 JG-71
38+56 JG-73
38+57 JG-74
38+58 JG-73
38+60 JG-74
38+61 JG-72
38+62 JG-72
38+64 JG-72
38+66 JG-73
38+67 JG-73
38+68 JG-74
38+69 JG-74
38+70 JG-74
38+73 JG-72
38+74 JG-74
38+75 JG-71
99+91 WTD-61

**Panavia Tornado Strike/Trainer[1]/ECR[2]**
AkG-51 *'mmelmann*, Schleswig/Jagel;
JbG-31 *Boelcke*, Nörvenich;
JbG-32, Lechfeld;
JbG-33, Büchel;
JbG-34*Algau*, Memmingen;
JbG-38 *Ostfriesland*, Jever;
MFG-2, Eggebek;
TsLw-1, Kaufbeuren;
WTD-61, Ingolstadt
43+01[1] DASA
43+02[1] DASA
43+03[1] DASA
43+04[1] JbG-33
43+05[1] DASA
43+06[1] JbG-38
43+07[1] DASA
43+08[1] JbG-32
43+09[1] DASA
43+10[1] JbG-38
43+11[1] DASA
43+13 DASA
43+15[1] DASA
43+16[1] DASA
43+17[1] DASA
43+18 JbG-31
43+20 JbG-34
43+22[1] JbG-38
43+23[1] JbG-38
43+25 DASA
43+27 JbG-34
43+29[1] JbG-31
43+30 JbG-38
43+31[1] JbG-31
43+32 DASA
43+33[1] JbG-38
43+34 TsLw-1
43+35[1] JbG-38
43+37[1] JbG-38
43+38 JbG-33
43+40 JbG-33
43+41 JbG-31
43+42[1] DASA
43+43[1] JbG-38
43+46 AkG-51
43+47 AkG-51
43+48 AkG-51
43+50 AkG-51
43+52 JbG-38
43+53 JbG-34
43+54 JbG-34
43+55 MFG-2
43+58 JbG-34
43+59 JbG-38
43+60 JbG-34
43+61 TsLw-1

| | |
|---|---|
| 43+62 | JbG-34 |
| 43+63 | JbG-34 |
| 43+64 | JbG-38 |
| 43+65 | JbG-38 |
| 43+67 | JbG-34 |
| 43+68 | JbG-34 |
| 43+69 | JbG-38 |
| 43+70 | JbG-38 |
| 43+71 | JbG-38 |
| 43+72 | JbG-38 |
| 43+73 | AkG-51 |
| 43+75 | DASA |
| 43+76 | JbG-38 |
| 43+77 | JbG-34 |
| 43+78 | JbG-34 |
| 43+79 | AkG-51 |
| 43+80 | AkG-51 |
| 43+81 | AkG-51 |
| 43+82 | AkG-51 |
| 43+85 | JbG-38 |
| 43+86 | JbG-34 |
| 43+87 | MFG-2 |
| 43+90[1] | JbG-38 |
| 43+92[1] | JbG-31 |
| 43+94[1] | JbG-38 |
| 43+96 | AkG-51 |
| 43+98 | AkG-51 |
| 44+00 | JbG-31 |
| 44+02 | JbG-31 |
| 44+04 | AkG-51 |
| 44+05[1] | AkG-51 |
| 44+06 | JbG-34 |
| 44+07 | JbG-31 |
| 44+08 | JbG-38 |
| 44+09 | JbG-33 |
| 44+10[1] | JbG-38 |
| 44+11 | JbG-34 |
| 44+13 | TsLw-1 |
| 44+14 | JbG-31 |
| 44+15 | JbG-38 |
| 44+16[1] | JbG-31 |
| 44+17 | AkG-51 |
| 44+19 | JbG-31 |
| 44+21 | JbG-31 |
| 44+22 | JbG-31 |
| 44+23 | JbG-33 |
| 44+24 | AkG-51 |
| 44+25[1] | JbG-38 |
| 44+26 | JbG-31 |
| 44+27 | JbG-33 |
| 44+29 | JbG-31 |
| 44+30 | JbG-31 |
| 44+31 | JbG-31 |
| 44+32 | JbG-38 |
| 44+33 | JbG-33 |
| 44+34 | JbG-33 |
| 44+35 | JbG-31 |
| 44+37[1] | JbG-38 |
| 44+40 | JbG-33 |
| 44+41 | JbG-31 |
| 44+42 | AkG-51 |
| 44+43 | JbG-34 |
| 44+44 | JbG-31 |
| 44+46 | JbG-34 |
| 44+48 | JbG-33 |
| 44+49 | JbG-31 |
| 44+50 | AkG-51 |
| 44+51 | JbG-31 |
| 44+52 | JbG-34 |
| 44+53 | AkG-51 |
| 44+54 | JbG-33 |
| 44+55 | JbG-38 |
| 44+56 | JbG-34 |
| 44+57 | JbG-31 |
| 44+58 | JbG-31 |
| 44+61 | AkG-51 |
| 44+62 | JbG-33 |
| 44+63 | JbG-33 |
| 44+64 | AkG-51 |
| 44+65 | AkG-51 |
| 44+66 | JbG-31 |
| 44+68 | AkG-51 |
| 44+69 | AkG-51 |
| 44+70 | JbG-31 |
| 44+71 | JbG-31 |
| 44+72[1] | JbG-33 |
| 44+75[1] | JbG-33 |
| 44+76 | JbG-34 |
| 44+78 | JbG-31 |
| 44+79 | JbG-33 |
| 44+80 | JbG-33 |
| 44+83 | JbG-33 |
| 44+84 | JbG-33 |
| 44+85 | JbG-33 |
| 44+86 | AkG-51 |
| 44+87 | AkG-51 |
| 44+88 | AkG-51 |
| 44+89 | JbG-33 |
| 44+90 | JbG-33 |
| 44+91 | JbG-33 |
| 44+92 | JbG-38 |
| 44+94 | JbG-33 |
| 44+95 | JbG-38 |
| 44+96 | JbG-31 |
| 44+97 | JbG-38 |
| 44+98 | JbG-34 |
| 45+00 | JbG-33 |
| 45+01 | JbG-34 |
| 45+02 | JbG-34 |
| 45+03 | JbG-34 |
| 45+04 | JbG-33 |
| 45+06 | AkG-51 |
| 45+07 | JbG-33 |
| 45+08 | JbG-33 |
| 45+10 | JbG-31 |
| 45+12[1] | MFG-2 |
| 45+13[1] | MFG-2 |
| 45+14[1] | JbG-38 |
| 45+15[1] | MFG-2 |
| 45+16[1] | MFG-2 |
| 45+17 | JbG-33 |
| 45+18 | JbG-33 |
| 45+19 | JbG-33 |
| 45+20 | AkG-51 |
| 45+21 | JbG-33 |
| 45+22 | JbG-33 |
| 45+23 | JbG-31 |
| 45+24 | JbG-33 |
| 45+25 | AkG-51 |
| 45+27 | MFG-2 |
| 45+28 | MFG-2 |
| 45+29 | WTD-61 |
| 45+30 | MFG-2 |
| 45+31 | MFG-2 |
| 45+33 | MFG-2 |
| 45+34 | MFG-2 |
| 45+35 | MFG-2 |
| 45+36 | MFG-2 |
| 45+37 | MFG-2 |
| 45+38 | MFG-2 |
| 45+39 | MFG-2 |
| 45+40 | MFG-2 |
| 45+41 | MFG-2 |
| 45+42 | MFG-2 |
| 45+43 | MFG-2 |
| 45+44 | MFG-2 |
| 45+45 | MFG-2 |
| 45+46 | MFG-2 |
| 45+47 | MFG-2 |
| 45+49 | MFG-2 |
| 45+50 | MFG-2 |
| 45+51 | AkG-51 |
| 45+52 | MFG-2 |
| 45+53 | MFG-2 |
| 45+54 | MFG-2 |
| 45+55 | MFG-2 |
| 45+56 | MFG-2 |
| 45+57 | JbG-34 |
| 45+59 | MFG-2 |
| 45+64 | TsLw-1 |
| 45+66 | MFG-2 |
| 45+67 | AkG-51 |
| 45+68 | MFG-2 |
| 45+69 | MFG-2 |
| 45+70[1] | JbG-33 |
| 45+71 | MFG-2 |
| 45+72 | MFG-2 |
| 45+73[1] | JbG-31 |
| 45+74 | MFG-2 |
| 45+76 | JbG-38 |
| 45+77[1] | JbG-33 |
| 45+78 | JbG-33 |
| 45+79 | JbG-31 |
| 45+81 | JbG-34 |
| 45+82 | JbG-31 |
| 45+84 | AkG-51 |
| 45+85 | AkG-51 |
| 45+86 | JbG-33 |
| 45+87 | JbG-34 |
| 45+88 | JbG-33 |
| 45+89 | JbG-34 |
| 45+90 | JbG-31 |
| 45+91 | AkG-51 |
| 45+93 | AkG-51 |
| 45+94 | JbG-33 |
| 45+95 | JbG-34 |
| 45+98 | AkG-51 |
| 45+99[1] | AkG-51 |
| 46+00 | JbG-34 |
| 46+01 | JbG-34 |
| 46+02 | JbG-33 |
| 46+04[1] | JbG-38 |
| 46+05[1] | MFG-2 |
| 46+07[1] | JbG-34 |
| 46+08[1] | JbG-38 |
| 46+09[1] | JbG-34 |
| 46+10 | WTD-61 |
| 46+11 | MFG-2 |
| 46+12 | MFG-2 |
| 46+13 | JbG-34 |
| 46+14 | JbG-34 |
| 46+15 | MFG-2 |
| 46+18 | MFG-2 |
| 46+19 | MFG-2 |
| 46+20 | MFG-2 |
| 46+21 | MFG-2 |
| 46+22 | MFG-2 |
| 46+23[2] | JbG-32 |
| 46+24[2] | JbG-32 |
| 46+25[2] | JbG-32 |
| 46+26[2] | JbG-32 |
| 46+27[2] | JbG-32 |
| 46+28[2] | JbG-32 |
| 46+29[2] | JbG-32 |
| 46+30[2] | JbG-32 |
| 46+31[2] | JbG-32 |
| 46+32[2] | JbG-32 |
| 46+33[2] | JbG-32 |
| 46+34[2] | JbG-32 |
| 46+35[2] | JbG-32 |
| 46+36[2] | JbG-32 |
| 46+37[2] | JbG-32 |

46+38[2] JbG-32
46+39[2] JbG-32
46+40[2] JbG-32
46+41[2] JbG-32
46+42[2] JbG-32
46+43[2] JbG-32
46+44[2] JbG-32
46+45[2] JbG-32
46+46[2] JbG-32
46+47[2] JbG-32
46+48[2] JbG-32
46+49[2] JbG-32
46+50[2] JbG-32
46+51[2] JbG-32
46+52[2] JbG-32
46+53[2] JbG-32
46+54[2] JbG-32
46+55[2] JbG-32
46+56[2] JbG-32
46+57[2] JbG-32
98+03[2] WTD-61
98+59 WTD-61
98+60 WTD-61
98+79[2] WTD-61

**Transall C-160D**
LTG-61, Landsberg;
LTG-62, Wunstorf;
LTG-63, Hohn;
WTD-61, Ingolstadt
50+06 LTG-63
50+07 LTG-61
50+08 LTG-61
50+09 LTG-62
50+10 LTG-62
50+17 LTG-62
50+29 LTG-62
50+33 LTG-62
50+34 LTG-63
50+35 LTG-62
50+36 LTG-63
50+37 LTG-62
50+38 LTG-62
50+40 LTG-61
50+41 LTG-62
50+42 LTG-63
50+44 LTG-61
50+45 LTG-63
50+46 LTG-62
50+47 LTG-61
50+48 LTG-61
50+49 LTG-63
50+50 LTG-62
50+51 LTG-61
50+52 LTG-62
50+53 LTG-62
50+54 LTG-63
50+55 LTG-62
50+56 LTG-63
50+57 WTD-61
50+58 LTG-62
50+59 LTG-63
50+60 LTG-62
50+61 LTG-63
50+62 LTG-62
50+64 LTG-61
50+65 LTG-62
50+66 LTG-61
50+67 LTG-63
50+68 LTG-61
50+69 LTG-63
50+70 LTG-62
50+71 LTG-63
50+72 LTG-63
50+73 LTG-63
50+74 LTG-61
50+75 LTG-63
50+76 LTG-63
50+77 LTG-63
50+78 LTG-62
50+79 LTG-63
50+81 LTG-62
50+82 LTG-63
50+83 LTG-62
50+84 LTG-61
50+85 LTG-63
50+86 LTG-61
50+87 LTG-63
50+88 LTG-61
50+89 LTG-62
50+90 LTG-62
50+91 LTG-62
50+92 LTG-61
50+93 LTG-61
50+94 LTG-63
50+95 LTG-63
50+96 LTG-61
50+97 LTG-62
50+98 LTG-63
50+99 LTG-61
51+00 LTG-62
51+01 LTG-62
51+02 LTG-63
51+03 LTG-62
51+04 LTG-61
51+05 LTG-62
51+06 LTG-61
51+07 LTG-62
51+08 WTD-61
51+09 LTG-63
51+10 LTG-61
51+11 LTG-62
51+12 LTG-62
51+13 LTG-61
51+14 LTG-63
51+15 LTG-61

**LET L-410UVP-S**
3/FBS, Berlin-Tegel
53+09
53+10
53+11
53+12

**Dornier Do.228/Do.228LM***
MFG-3, Nordholz;
WTD-61, Ingolstadt
57+01 MFG-3
57+02* MFG-3
57+03 MFG-3
57+04* MFG-3
98+78 WTD-61

**Breguet Br.1151 Atlantic**
**Elint*
MFG-3, Nordholz
61+03*
61+04
61+05
61+06*
61+08
61+09
61+10
61+11
61+12
61+13
61+14
61+15
61+16
61+17
61+18*
61+19*
61+20

**Eurocopter AS.532U2 Cougar**
3/FBS, Berlin/Tegel
82+01
82+02
82+03

**Westland Lynx Mk88/ Super Lynx Mk88A***
MFG-3, Nordholz
83+02
83+03
83+04
83+05
83+06
83+07
83+09
83+10
83+11
83+12
83+13
83+14
83+15
83+17
83+18
83+19
83+20*
83+21*
83+22*
83+23*
83+24*
83+25*
83+26*

**Westland Sea King HAS41**
MFG-5, Kiel-Holtenau
89+50
89+51
89+52
89+53
89+54
89+55
89+56
89+57
89+58
89+50
89+60
89+61
89+62
89+63
89+64
89+65
89+66
89+67
89+68
89+69
89+70
89+71

**Eurofighter Typhoon**
WTD-61, Ingolstadt
98+29 WTD-61
98+30 WTD-61

**Heeresfliegertruppe**

**Eurocopter EC.135**

HFWS, Bückeburg
82+51
82+52
82+53
82+54
82+55
82+56
82+57
82+58
82+59
82+60
82+61
82+62
82+63
82+64
82+65

**MBB Bo.105**

HFlgRgt-15, Rheine-Bentlage;
HFlgRgt-16, Celle;
HFlgRgt-25, Laupheim;
HFlgRgt-26, Roth;
HFlgRgt-35, Mendig;
HFlgRgt-36, Fritzlar;
HFS-400, Cottbus;
HFVS-910, Bückeburg;
HFWS, Bückeburg;
TsLw-3, Fassberg;
WTD-61, Ingolstadt

80+01 Bo.105M HFR-35
80+02 Bo.105M HFWS
80+03 Bo.105M HFWS
80+04 Bo.105M TsLw-3
80+05 Bo.105M HFR-35
80+06 Bo.105M HFWS
80+07 Bo.105M HFWS
80+08 Bo.105M HFR-25
80+09 Bo.105M HFR-35
80+10 Bo.105M HFR-25
80+11 Bo.105M HFWS
80+12 Bo.105M HFWS
80+13 Bo.105M HFR-15
80+14 Bo.105M TsLw-3
80+15 Bo.105M HFR-15
80+16 Bo.105M HFR-15
80+17 Bo.105M HFS-400
80+18 Bo.105M HFR-15
80+19 Bo.105M HFR-15
80+20 Bo.105M HFS-400
80+21 Bo.105M HFR-15
80+22 Bo.105M HFS-400
80+23 Bo.105M HFR-15
80+24 Bo.105M HFR-15
80+25 Bo.105M HFR-25
80+26 Bo.105M HFR-35
80+27 Bo.105M HFR-35
80+28 Bo.105M TsLw-3
80+29 Bo.105M HFR-35
80+30 Bo.105M HFR-35
80+31 Bo.105M HFR-35
80+32 Bo.105M HFR-35
80+33 Bo.105M HFR-35
80+34 Bo.105M HFR-25
80+35 Bo.105M HFS-400
80+36 Bo.105M HFR-25
80+37 Bo.105M HFS-400
80+38 Bo.105M HFR-25
80+39 Bo.105M HFR-25
80+40 Bo.105M HFR-26
80+41 Bo.105M HFR-25
80+42 Bo.105M HFR-25
80+43 Bo.105M HFR-25
80+44 Bo.105M HFR-25
80+46 Bo.105M TsLw-3
80+47 Bo.105M HFR-25
80+48 Bo.105M HFR-25
80+49 Bo.105M HFS-400
80+50 Bo.105M HFS-400
80+51 Bo.105M HFR-15
80+52 Bo.105M HFR-15
80+53 Bo.105M HFS-400
80+54 Bo.105M HFR-15
80+55 Bo.105M HFS-400
80+56 Bo.105M HFS-400
80+57 Bo.105M HFR-35
80+58 Bo.105M HFR-35
80+59 Bo.105M HFR-35
80+60 Bo.105M HFR-35
80+61 Bo.105M HFS-400
80+62 Bo.105M HFR-35
80+64 Bo.105M HFR-35
80+65 Bo.105M HFR-15
80+66 Bo.105M HFR-15
80+67 Bo.105M HFR-15
80+68 Bo.105M HFR-15
80+69 Bo.105M HFR-15
80+70 Bo.105M HFR-15
80+71 Bo.105M HFR-15
80+72 Bo.105M HFR-15
80+73 Bo.105M HFR-15
80+74 Bo.105M HFR-15
80+76 Bo.105M HFR-15
80+77 Bo.105M HFR-35
80+78 Bo.105M HFR-35
80+79 Bo.105M HFR-35
80+80 Bo.105M HFR-35
80+81 Bo.105M HFR-25
80+82 Bo.105M HFR-25
80+83 Bo.105M HFR-25
80+84 Bo.105M HFR-25
80+85 Bo.105M HFR-25
80+86 Bo.105M HFS-400
80+87 Bo.105M HFR-25
80+88 Bo.105M HFS-400
80+89 Bo.105M HFS-400
80+90 Bo.105M HFS-400
80+91 Bo.105M HFR-35
80+92 Bo.105M HFR-35
80+93 Bo.105M HFS-400
80+94 Bo.105M HFR-25
80+95 Bo.105M HFS-400
80+96 Bo.105M HFR-25
80+97 Bo.105M HFR-35
80+98 Bo.105M HFR-25
80+99 Bo.105M HFR-26
81+00 Bo.105M HFR-25
86+01 Bo.105P HFWS
86+02 Bo.105P HFWS
86+03 Bo.105P HFWS
86+04 Bo.105P HFR-36
86+05 Bo.105P HFWS
86+06 Bo.105P HFWS
86+07 Bo.105P HFWS
86+08 Bo.105P HFWS
86+09 Bo.105P HFWS
86+10 Bo.105P HFR-16
86+11 Bo.105P HFWS
86+12 Bo.105P HFWS
86+13 Bo.105P HFWS
86+14 Bo.105P HFR-16
86+15 Bo.105P HFR-16
86+16 Bo.105P HFWS
86+17 Bo.105P HFVS-910
86+18 Bo.105P HFR-26
86+19 Bo.105P HFR-26
86+20 Bo.105P HFWS
86+21 Bo.105P HFR-36
86+22 Bo.105P HFWS
86+23 Bo.105P HFWS
86+24 Bo.105P HFVS-910
86+25 Bo.105P HFR-16
86+26 Bo.105P HFR-36
86+27 Bo.105P HFR-26
86+28 Bo.105P HFR-16
86+29 Bo.105P HFR-16
86+30 Bo.105P HFR-26
86+31 Bo.105P HFR-16
86+32 Bo.105P HFR-26
86+33 Bo.105P HFR-26
86+34 Bo.105P HFR-26
86+35 Bo.105P HFR-26
86+36 Bo.105P HFR-36
86+37 Bo.105P HFR-16
86+38 Bo.105P HFR-36
86+39 Bo.105P HFR-16
86+41 Bo.105P HFR-16
86+42 Bo.105P HFR-26
86+43 Bo.105P HFR-16
86+44 Bo.105P HFR-26
86+45 Bo.105P HFR-26
86+46 Bo.105P HFR-26
86+47 Bo.105P HFR-16
86+48 Bo.105P HFR-16
86+49 Bo.105P HFR-26
86+50 Bo.105P HFR-16
86+51 Bo.105P HFR-36
86+52 Bo.105P HFR-16
86+53 Bo.105P HFR-26
86+54 Bo.105P HFR-16
86+55 Bo.105P HFR-16
86+56 Bo.105P HFR-36
86+57 Bo.105P HFR-16
86+58 Bo.105P HFR-36
86+59 Bo.105P HFR-16
86+60 Bo.105P HFR-16
86+61 Bo.105P HFR-26
86+62 Bo.105P HFVS-910
86+63 Bo.105P HFR-26
86+64 Bo.105P HFR-26
86+65 Bo.105P HFR-26
86+66 Bo.105P HFVS-910
86+67 Bo.105P HFR-26
86+68 Bo.105P HFR-36
86+69 Bo.105P HFR-26
86+70 Bo.105P HFR-16
86+71 Bo.105P HFR-36
86+72 Bo.105P HFR-36
86+73 Bo.105P HFWS
86+74 Bo.105P HFR-16
86+75 Bo.105P HFR-36
86+76 Bo.105P HFR-26
86+77 Bo.105P HFR-16
86+78 Bo.105P HFR-26
86+80 Bo.105P HFR-16
86+81 Bo.105P HFR-16
86+83 Bo.105P HFR-16
86+84 Bo.105P HFR-16
86+85 Bo.105P HFR-16
86+86 Bo.105P HFR-16
86+87 Bo.105P HFR-16
86+88 Bo.105P HFR-16
86+89 Bo.105P TsLw-3
86+90 Bo.105P HFR-26
86+91 Bo.105P HFR-26
86+92 Bo.105P HFR-36
86+93 Bo.105P HFVS-910
86+94 Bo.105P HFWS
86+95 Bo.105P HFR-16
86+96 Bo.105P HFR-26

| | | |
|---|---|---|
| 86+97 | Bo.105P | HFR-36 |
| 86+98 | Bo.105P | HFR-16 |
| 86+99 | Bo.105P | HFR-26 |
| 87+00 | Bo.105P | HFR-26 |
| 87+01 | Bo.105P | HFR-26 |
| 87+02 | Bo.105P | HFR-26 |
| 87+03 | Bo.105P | HFR-26 |
| 87+04 | Bo.105P | HFR-26 |
| 87+05 | Bo.105P | HFR-26 |
| 87+06 | Bo.105P | HFR-36 |
| 87+07 | Bo.105P | HFR-26 |
| 87+08 | Bo.105P | HFR-16 |
| 87+09 | Bo.105P | HFR-36 |
| 87+10 | Bo.105P | HFR-26 |
| 87+11 | Bo.105P | HFR-36 |
| 87+12 | Bo.105P | HFR-36 |
| 87+13 | Bo.105P | HFR-36 |
| 87+14 | Bo.105P | HFR-36 |
| 87+15 | Bo.105P | HFR-36 |
| 87+16 | Bo.105P | HFR-36 |
| 87+17 | Bo.105P | HFR-26 |
| 87+18 | Bo.105P | HFR-36 |
| 87+19 | Bo.105P | HFR-36 |
| 87+20 | Bo.105P | HFR-26 |
| 87+21 | Bo.105P | HFWS |
| 87+22 | Bo.105P | HFR-16 |
| 87+23 | Bo.105P | HFWS |
| 87+24 | Bo.105P | HFR-16 |
| 87+25 | Bo.105P | HFR-26 |
| 87+26 | Bo.105P | HFR-16 |
| 87+27 | Bo.105P | HFR-16 |
| 87+28 | Bo.105P | HFR-16 |
| 87+29 | Bo.105P | HFR-26 |
| 87+30 | Bo.105P | TsLw-3 |
| 87+31 | Bo.105P | HFR-16 |
| 87+32 | Bo.105P | HFVS-910 |
| 87+33 | Bo.105P | HFR-26 |
| 87+34 | Bo.105P | HFR-26 |
| 87+35 | Bo.105P | HFR-26 |
| 87+36 | Bo.105P | HFR-26 |
| 87+37 | Bo.105P | HFR-26 |
| 87+38 | Bo.105P | HFR-36 |
| 87+39 | Bo.105P | HFR-36 |
| 87+41 | Bo.105P | HFR-16 |
| 87+42 | Bo.105P | HFR-36 |
| 87+43 | Bo.105P | HFR-36 |
| 87+44 | Bo.105P | HFR-36 |
| 87+45 | Bo.105P | TsLw-3 |
| 87+46 | Bo.105P | HFR-16 |
| 87+47 | Bo.105P | HFR-16 |
| 87+48 | Bo.105P | HFR-16 |
| 87+49 | Bo.105P | HFR-16 |
| 87+50 | Bo.105P | HFR-26 |
| 87+51 | Bo.105P | HFR-16 |
| 87+52 | Bo.105P | HFR-16 |
| 87+53 | Bo.105P | HFR-26 |
| 87+55 | Bo.105P | HFVS-910 |
| 87+56 | Bo.105P | HFR-26 |
| 87+57 | Bo.105P | HFR-26 |
| 87+58 | Bo.105P | HFR-26 |
| 87+59 | Bo.105P | HFR-36 |
| 87+60 | Bo.105P | HFR-36 |
| 87+61 | Bo.105P | HFR-35 |
| 87+62 | Bo.105P | HFR-36 |
| 87+63 | Bo.105P | TsLw-3 |
| 87+64 | Bo.105P | HFR-36 |
| 87+65 | Bo.105P | HFR-36 |
| 87+66 | Bo.105P | TsLw-3 |
| 87+67 | Bo.105P | HFWS |
| 87+68 | Bo.105P | HFR-16 |
| 87+69 | Bo.105P | HFR-26 |
| 87+70 | Bo.105P | HFR-16 |
| 87+71 | Bo.105P | HFR-26 |
| 87+72 | Bo.105P | HFR-16 |
| 87+73 | Bo.105P | HFR-16 |
| 87+74 | Bo.105P | HFVS-910 |
| 87+75 | Bo.105P | HFR-16 |
| 87+76 | Bo.105P | HFR-16 |
| 87+77 | Bo.105P | HFR-16 |
| 87+78 | Bo.105P | HFR-16 |
| 87+79 | Bo.105P | HFR-16 |
| 87+80 | Bo.105P | HFR-16 |
| 87+81 | Bo.105P | HFR-16 |
| 87+82 | Bo.105P | HFR-16 |
| 87+83 | Bo.105P | HFR-16 |
| 87+84 | Bo.105P | HFVS-910 |
| 87+85 | Bo.105P | HFR-26 |
| 87+86 | Bo.105P | HFR-26 |
| 87+87 | Bo.105P | HFVS-910 |
| 87+88 | Bo.105P | HFR-26 |
| 87+89 | Bo.105P | HFR-26 |
| 87+90 | Bo.105P | HFWS |
| 87+91 | Bo.105P | HFR-26 |
| 87+92 | Bo.105P | HFR-26 |
| 87+93 | Bo.105P | HFR-26 |
| 87+94 | Bo.105P | HFR-26 |
| 87+95 | Bo.105P | HFR-26 |
| 87+96 | Bo.105P | HFR-26 |
| 87+97 | Bo.105P | HFR-26 |
| 87+98 | Bo.105P | HFR-26 |
| 87+99 | Bo.105P | HFR-36 |
| 88+01 | Bo.105P | HFR-26 |
| 88+02 | Bo.105P | HFR-36 |
| 88+03 | Bo.105P | HFR-36 |
| 88+04 | Bo.105P | HFR-16 |
| 88+05 | Bo.105P | HFVS-910 |
| 88+06 | Bo.105P | HFR-36 |
| 88+07 | Bo.105P | HFR-36 |
| 88+08 | Bo.105P | HFR-36 |
| 88+09 | Bo.105P | HFR-36 |
| 88+10 | Bo.105P | HFVS-910 |
| 88+11 | Bo.105P | HFR-36 |
| 88+12 | Bo.105P | HFR-36 |
| 98+21 | Bo.105C | WTD-61 |
| 98+28 | Bo.105C | WTD-61 |

**Sikorsky/VFW CH-53G**

HFlgRgt-15, Rheine-Bentlage;
HFlgRgt-25, Laupheim;
HFlgRgt-35, Mendig;
HFWS, Bückeburg;
TsLw-3, Fassberg;
WTD-61, Ingolstadt

| | |
|---|---|
| 84+01 | WTD-61 |
| 84+02 | WTD-61 |
| 84+03 | HFR-15 |
| 84+04 | HFWS |
| 84+05 | HFR-35 |
| 84+06 | HFR-15 |
| 84+07 | HFWS |
| 84+08 | HFWS |
| 84+09 | HFR-25 |
| 84+10 | HFWS |
| 84+11 | HFWS |
| 84+12 | HFR-15 |
| 84+13 | HFWS |
| 84+14 | HFWS |
| 84+15 | HFR-25 |
| 84+16 | HFWS |
| 84+17 | HFR-25 |
| 84+18 | HFWS |
| 84+19 | HFWS |
| 84+20 | HFR-35 |
| 84+21 | HFWS |
| 84+22 | HFR-15 |
| 84+23 | HFR-35 |
| 84+24 | HFR-35 |
| 84+25 | HFR-35 |
| 84+26 | HFR-35 |
| 84+27 | HFR-35 |
| 84+28 | HFR-25 |
| 84+29 | HFR-35 |
| 84+30 | HFR-35 |
| 84+31 | HFR-35 |
| 84+32 | HFR-35 |
| 84+33 | HFR-35 |
| 84+34 | HFR-35 |
| 84+35 | HFR-35 |
| 84+36 | HFR-35 |
| 84+37 | HFR-35 |
| 84+38 | HFR-35 |
| 84+39 | HFR-35 |
| 84+40 | HFR-25 |
| 84+41 | HFWS |
| 84+42 | HFR-25 |
| 84+43 | HFR-25 |
| 84+44 | HFR-25 |
| 84+45 | HFR-25 |
| 84+46 | HFR-35 |
| 84+47 | HFR-25 |
| 84+48 | HFR-25 |
| 84+49 | HFWS |
| 84+50 | HFR-25 |
| 84+51 | HFR-25 |
| 84+52 | HFR-25 |
| 84+53 | HFR-25 |
| 84+54 | HFR-25 |
| 84+55 | HFR-25 |
| 84+56 | HFR-35 |
| 84+57 | HFR-25 |
| 84+58 | HFR-25 |
| 84+59 | HFR-25 |
| 84+60 | HFR-25 |
| 84+62 | HFR-25 |
| 84+63 | HFR-25 |
| 84+64 | HFR-35 |
| 84+65 | HFR-35 |
| 84+66 | HFR-35 |
| 84+67 | HFR-35 |
| 84+68 | HFR-15 |
| 84+69 | HFR-15 |
| 84+70 | HFR-15 |
| 84+71 | HFR-15 |
| 84+72 | HFR-15 |
| 84+73 | HFR-15 |
| 84+74 | HFR-15 |
| 84+75 | HFR-15 |
| 84+76 | HFR-15 |
| 84+77 | HFR-15 |
| 84+78 | HFR-15 |
| 84+79 | HFR-15 |
| 84+80 | HFR-15 |
| 84+82 | HFR-35 |
| 84+83 | HFR-15 |
| 84+84 | TsLw-3 |
| 84+85 | HFR-15 |
| 84+86 | HFR-15 |
| 84+87 | HFR-15 |
| 84+88 | HFR-15 |
| 84+89 | HFR-15 |
| 84+90 | HFR-15 |
| 84+91 | HFR-15 |
| 84+92 | HFR-35 |
| 84+93 | HFR-35 |
| 84+94 | HFR-35 |
| 84+95 | HFR-25 |
| 84+96 | HFR-25 |
| 84+97 | HFR-25 |
| 84+98 | HFR-15 |
| 84+99 | HFR-15 |
| 85+00 | WTD-61 |
| 85+01 | HFR-35 |

85+02 HFR-35
85+03 HFR-35
85+04 HFR-25
85+05 HFR-25
85+06 HFR-25
85+07 HFR-15
85+08 HFR-15
85+09 HFR-15
85+10 HFR-35
85+11 HFR-25
85+12 HFR-15

**Eurocopter AS.665 Tiger**
WTD-61, Ingolstadt
98+23
98+25

**GHANA**
**Ghana Air Force**
**Fokker F-28 Fellowship 3000**
VIP Flight, Accra
G-530

**Grumman G.1159A Gulfstream III**
VIP Flight, Accra
G-540

**GREECE**
**Ellinikí Polemiki Aeroporía**
**Lockheed C-130H Hercules**
356 MTM/112 PM, Elefsís
**ECM*
741*
742
743
744
745
746
747*
749
751
752

**Lockheed Martin F-16CF-16D* Fighting Falcon**
330 Mira/111 PM, Nea Ankhialos;
341 Mira/111 PM, Nea Ankhialos;
346 MAPK/110 PM, Larissa;
347 Mira/111 PM, Nea Ankhialos
045
046
047 341 Mira
048 341 Mira
049
050
051
052
053
054 341 Mira
055
056
057
058
059 347 Mira
060
061
062 341 Mira
063
064
065
066
067
068
069
070
071
072 341 Mira
073
074
075
076
077*
078* 341 Mira
079* 341 Mira
080*
081* 347 Mira
082*
083* 347 Mira
084*
110 346 MAPK
111 330 Mira
112 346 MAPK
113 330 Mira
114 346 MAPK
115 330 Mira
116 346 MAPK
117 330 Mira
118 346 MAPK
119 330 Mira
120 346 MAPK
121 330 Mira
122 346 MAPK
123 330 Mira
124 346 MAPK
125 330 Mira
126 346 MAPK
127 330 Mira
128 346 MAPK
129 330 Mira
130 346 MAPK
132 346 MAPK
133 330 Mira
134 346 MAPK
136 346 MAPK
138 346 MAPK
139 330 Mira
140 346 MAPK
141 330 Mira
143 330 Mira
144* 330 Mira
145* 330 Mira
146* 346 MAPK
147* 330 Mira
148* 346 MAPK
149* 330 Mira

**Greek Govt**
**Dassault Falcon 900**
Greek Govt/Olympic Airways, Athens
SX-ECH

**HUNGARY**
**Magyar Honvédseg Repülö Csapatai**
**Antonov An-26**
89 VSD, Szolnok
203 (02203)
204 (02204)
208 (02208)
209 (02209)
405 (03405)
406 (03406)
407 (03407)
603 (03603)

**ISRAEL**
**Heyl ha'Avir**
**Boeing 707**
120 Sqn Tel Aviv
120 RC-707
128 RC-707
137 RC-707
140 KC-707
242 VC-707
248 KC-707
250 KC-707
255 EC-707
258 EC-707
260 KC-707
264 VO-707
272 VC-707

**Lockheed C-130 Hercules**
103 Sqn & 131 Sqn, Tel Aviv
102 C-130H
106 C-130H
302 C-130E
304 C-130E
305 C-130E
307 C-130E
309 C-130H
310 C-130E
311 C-130E
312 C-130E
313 C-130E
314 C-130E
316 C-130E
318 C-130E
420 C-130H
423 C-130H
427 C-130H
428 C-130H
435 C-130H
436 KC-130H
448 C-130H
522 KC-130H
545 KC-130H

**Israel Government**
**Hawker 800XP**
Israeli Govt, Tel Aviv
4X-COV

**ITALY**
**Aeronautica Militare Italiana**
**Aeritalia G222**
9ª Brigata Aerea, Pratica di Mare: 8° Gruppo & 71° Gruppo;
46ª Brigata Aerea, Pisa: 2° Gruppo & 98° Gruppo;
RSV, Pratica di Mare
**G222TCM**
MM62101
MM62102 46-20 2
MM62104 46-91 98
MM62105 46-82 98
MM62109 46-96 98
MM62111 46-83 98
MM62114 46-80 98
MM62115 46-22 2
MM62117 46-25 2
MM62119 46-21 2
MM62120 46-90 98
MM62122 46-23 2

| | | |
|---|---|---|
| MM62123 | 46-28 | 2 |
| MM62124 | 46-88 | 98 |
| MM62125 | 14-24 | 8 |
| MM62126 | 46-26 | 2 |
| MM62130 | 46-31 | 2 |
| MM62133 | 46-93 | 98 |
| MM62134 | 46-33 | 2 |
| MM62135 | 46-94 | 98 |
| MM62136 | 46-97 | 98 |
| MM62137 | 46-95 | 98 |
| MM62143 | 46-36 | 2 |
| MM62144 | 46-98 | 98 |
| MM62152 | RS-45 | RSV |
| MM62153 | RS-46 | RSV |

**G222VS**

| | | |
|---|---|---|
| MM62107 | | 71 |
| MM62138 | | 71 |

**G222RM**

| | | |
|---|---|---|
| MM62139 | 14-20 | 8 |
| MM62140 | 14-21 | 8 |
| MM62141 | 14-22 | 8 |
| MM62142 | 14-23 | 8 |

**G222PROCIV**

| | | |
|---|---|---|
| MM62145 | 46-50 | 2 |
| MM62146 | 46-51 | 2 |
| MM62147 | 46-52 | 2 |
| MM62154 | 46-54 | 2 |
| MM62155 | 46-53 | 2 |

**Aeritalia-EMB AMX/AMX-T***

2° Stormo, Rivolto:
14° Gruppo;
32° Stormo, Amendola:
13° Gruppo &
101° Gruppo;
51° Stormo, Istrana:
103° Gruppo &
132° Gruppo;
RSV, Pratica di Mare

| | | |
|---|---|---|
| MMX595 | Alenia | |
| MMX596 | Alenia | |
| MMX597 | Alenia | |
| MMX599 | Alenia | |
| MM7089 | | |
| MM7090 | 2-14 | 14 |
| MM7091 | 32-64 | 101 |
| MM7092 | RS-14 | RSV |
| MM7093 | | |
| MM7094 | 3-37 | |
| MM7095 | | 103 |
| MM7096 | | |
| MM7097 | 3-36 | |
| MM7098 | 3-35 | |
| MM7099 | | |
| MM7100 | 32-66 | 101 |
| MM7101 | 51-31 | 132 |
| MM7102 | 2-03 | 14 |
| MM7103 | | |
| MM7104 | | |
| MM7105 | 32-20 | 13 |
| MM7106 | 3-25 | |
| MM7107 | | |
| MM7110 | | |
| MM7111 | 3-23 | |
| MM7112 | | |
| MM7114 | 32-15 | 13 |
| MM7115 | 2-12 | 14 |
| MM7116 | 32-11 | 13 |
| MM7117 | 3-34 | |
| MM7118 | 2-11 | 14 |
| MM7119 | | |
| MM7120 | 51-52 | 132 |
| MM7122 | 3-32 | |
| MM7123 | | |
| MM7124 | 3-28 | |
| MM7125 | RS-11 | RSV |
| MM7126 | 32-12 | 13 |
| MM7127 | 3-24 | |
| MM7128 | | |
| MM7129 | | |
| MM7130 | 32-02 | 13 |
| MM7131 | | |
| MM7132 | | |
| MM7133 | | |
| MM7134 | 51-15 | 103 |
| MM7135 | | |
| MM7138 | | |
| MM7139 | 51-16 | 103 |
| MM7140 | | |
| MM7141 | 51-41 | 132 |
| MM7142 | 51-37 | 132 |
| MM7143 | | 103 |
| MM7144 | 51-41 | 132 |
| MM7145 | 3-22 | |
| MM7146 | 51-42 | 132 |
| MM7147 | 32-04 | 13 |
| MM7148 | 51-46 | 132 |
| MM7149 | | |
| MM7150 | 32-65 | 101 |
| MM7151 | 51-52 | 132 |
| MM7152 | 51-53 | 132 |
| MM7153 | 32-60 | 101 |
| MM7154 | 51-54 | 132 |
| MM7155 | 32-05 | 13 |
| MM7156 | 32-10 | 13 |
| MM7157 | 32-06 | 13 |
| CMX7158 | RS-12 | RSV |
| MM7159 | | |
| MM7160 | 32-14 | 13 |
| MM7161 | 2-21 | 14 |
| MM7162 | 51-01 | 103 |
| MM7163 | 51-63 | 132 |
| MM7164 | 3-08 | |
| MM7165 | 51-31 | 132 |
| MM7166 | 51-34 | 132 |
| MM7167 | 2-01 | 14 |
| MM7168 | 2-04 | 14 |
| MM7169 | 3-12 | |
| MM7170 | 2-23 | 14 |
| MM7171 | 2-15 | 14 |
| MM7172 | 2-07 | 14 |
| MM7173 | 2-16 | 14 |
| MM7174 | | |
| MM7175 | 51-43 | 132 |
| MM7176 | 2-20 | 14 |
| MM7177 | 2-22 | 14 |
| MM7178 | 2-24 | 14 |
| MM7179 | 2-02 | 14 |
| MM7180 | | |
| MM7181 | 51-32 | 132 |
| MM7182 | | |
| MM7183 | 32-01 | 13 |
| MM7184 | 51-33 | 132 |
| MM7185 | 51-35 | 132 |
| MM7186 | 51-05 | 103 |
| MM7187 | 32-16 | 13 |
| MM7188 | 51-36 | 132 |
| MM7189 | 51-03 | 103 |
| MM7190 | 32-17 | 13 |
| MM7191 | | |
| MM7192 | 51-50 | 132 |
| MM7193 | 51-07 | 103 |
| MM7194 | 32-07 | 13 |
| MM7195 | 3-10 | |
| MM7196 | 32-13 | 13 |
| MM7197 | 32-21 | 13 |
| MM7198 | 32-03 | 13 |
| MM55024* | 15 | RSV |
| MM55025* | RS-16 | RSV |
| MM55026* | 32-43 | 101 |
| MM55027* | | |
| MM55028* | 3-26 | |
| MM55029* | 3-55 | |
| MM55030* | 32-41 | 101 |
| MM55031* | 32-40 | 101 |
| MM55034* | 18 | RSV |
| MM55035* | 32-50 | 101 |
| MM55036* | 32-51 | 101 |
| MM55037* | 51-55 | 132 |
| MM55038* | 32-53 | 101 |
| MM55039* | 32-54 | 101 |
| MM55040* | 32-52 | 101 |
| MM55041* | 32-55 | 101 |
| MM55042* | 32-56 | 101 |
| MM55043* | 51-10 | 103 |
| MM55044* | 32-57 | 101 |
| MM55045* | 2-10 | 14 |
| MM55046* | 32-47 | 101 |
| MM55047* | 32-45 | 101 |
| MM55048* | 32-44 | 101 |
| MM55049* | 32-46 | 101 |
| MM55050* | | |
| MM55051* | 32-42 | 101 |

**Aermacchi MB339A/MB339CD***

61° Stormo, Lecce:
212° Gruppo &
213° Gruppo
Aermacchi,Venegono;
*Frecce Tricolori* [FT]
(MB339A/PAN)
(313° Gruppo), Rivolto;
RSV, Pratica di Mare

| | | |
|---|---|---|
| MMX606* | | RSV |
| MM54438 | 61-93 | |
| MM54439 | | [FT] |
| MM54440 | 61-00 | |
| MM54441 | RS-28 | RSV |
| MM54442 | 61-95 | |
| MM54443 | 61-50 | |
| MM54445 | 61-25 | |
| MM54446 | 61-01 | |
| MM54447 | 61-02 | |
| MM54449 | 61-04 | |
| MM54450 | 61-94 | |
| MM54451 | 61-86 | |
| MM54452 | | |
| MM54453 | 61-05 | |
| MM54454 | 61-06 | |
| MM54455 | 61-07 | |
| MM54456 | 61-10 | |
| MM54457 | 61-11 | |
| MM54458 | 61-12 | |
| MM54459 | 61-13 | |
| MM54460 | 61-14 | |
| MM54461 | | |
| MM54462 | 61-16 | |
| MM54463 | 61-17 | |
| MM54467 | 61-23 | |
| MM54468 | 61-24 | |
| MM54471 | 61-27 | |
| MM54472 | 61-30 | |
| MM54473 | 8 | [FT] |
| MM54475 | 1 | [FT] |
| MM54477 | 11 | [FT] |
| MM54478 | | [FT] |
| MM54479 | 12 | [FT] |
| MM54480 | 7 | [FT] |
| MM54482 | | [FT] |
| MM54483 | | [FT] |
| MM54484 | | [FT] |

MM54485 9 [FT]
MM54486 6 [FT]
MM54487 61-31
MM54488 61-32
MM54489 61-33
MM54490 61-34
MM54491 61-35
MM54492 61-36
MM54493 61-37
MM54494 61-40
MM54496 61-42
MM54497 61-43
MM54498 61-44
MM54499 61-45
MM54500 4 [FT]
MM54503 61-51
MM54504 61-52
MM54505 61-53
MM54506 61-54
MM54507 61-55
MM54508 61-56
MM54509 61-57
MM54510 61-60
MM54511 61-61
MM54512 61-62
MM54513 61-63
MM54514 61-64
MM54515 61-65
MM54516 61-66
MM54517 3 [FT]
MM54518 61-70
MM54532 61-71
MM54533 61-72
MM54534 61-73
MM54535 61-74
MM54536 5 [FT]
MM54537
MM54538 61-75
MM54539 61-76
MM54541 61-80
MM54542 10 [FT]
MM54543 61-82
MM54544* (Aermacchi)
MM54545 61-84
MM54546 61-85
MM54547 0 [FT]
MM54548 61-90
MM54549 61-107
MM54550 61-110
MM54551 2 [FT]
MM55052 61-96
MM55053 61-97
MM55054 61-15
MM55055 61-20
MM55058 61-41
MM55059 61-26
MM55062* RS-26 RSV
MM55063* RS-27 RSV
MM55064* 61-130
MM55065* 61-131
MM55066* 61-132
MM55067* 61-133
MM55068* 61-134
MM55069* 61-135
MM55070* 61-136
MM55072* 61-140
MM55073* 61-141
MM55074* 61-142
MM55075* 61-143
MM55076* 61-144

**Airbus A.319CJ-115**
31° Stormo, Roma-
Ciampino 93° Gruppo
MM62173
MM62174

**Boeing 707-328B/-3F5C***
9ª Brigata Aerea, Pratica di
Mare: 8° Gruppo;
MM62148 14-01
MM62149 14-02
MM62150* 14-03
MM62151* 14-04

**Breguet Br.1150 Atlantic**
30° Stormo, Cagliari:
86° Gruppo;
41° Stormo, Catania:
88° Gruppo
MM40108 41-70
MM40109 30-71
MM40110 41-72
MM40111 41-73
MM40112 30-74
MM40113 30-75
MM40114 41-76
MM40115 41-77
MM40116 30-01
MM40117 41-02
MM40118 30-03
MM40119 30-04
MM40120 41-05
MM40121 41-06
MM40122 30-07
MM40123 30-10
MM40124 41-11
MM40125 30-12

**Dassault Falcon 50**
31° Stormo, Roma-
Ciampino: 93° Gruppo
MM62020
MM62021
MM62026
MM62029

**Dassault Falcon 900EX**
31° Stormo, Roma-
Ciampino: 93° Gruppo
MM62171
MM62172

**Eurofighter Typhoon**
Aeritalia, Torino/Caselle;
RSV, Pratica di Mare
MMX602 RS-01 RSV
MMX603 Aeritalia

**Grumman**
**G.1159A Gulfstream III**
31° Stormo, Roma-
Ciampino: 306° Gruppo
MM62022
MM62025

**Lockheed F-104 Starfighter**
4° Stormo, Grosseto:
9° Gruppo & 20° Gruppo;
5° Stormo, Cervia:
23° Gruppo;
9° Stormo, Grazzanise:
10° Gruppo;
37° Stormo, Trapani:
18° Gruppo;
RSV, Pratica di Mare

**F-104S-ASA/F104ASA-M***
CMX611* RS-06 RSV
MM6701 4-16 9
MM6704 4-7 9
MM6705 4-5 9
MM6710
MM6713 4-2 9
MM6714 4-11 9
MM6716* 9-31 10
MM6717* 5-41 23
MM6719* 9-52 10
MM6720* 9-51 10
MM6721 4-12 9
MM6722 37-30 18
MM6726 4-6 9
MM6731* 37-03 18
MM6732* 37-04 18
MM6733
MM6734* 5-37 23
MM6735* 9-50 10
MM6736
MM6737* 5-46 23
MM6739* 5-47 23
MM6740* 37-31 18
MM6744 5-07
MM6748
MM6756* 5-42 23
MM6759* 37-20 18
MM6760
MM6761
MM6762* 37-02 18
MM6763
MM6764*
MM6767 37-05 18
MM6768
MM6769 4-53 20
MM6770* 5-31 23
MM6771 22
MM6772 37-11 18
MM6773
MM6774 4-1 9
MM6775
MM6776* 9-46 10
MM6781
MM6785 5-25
MM6786
MM6787* 9-32 10
MM6788 5-01
MM6789
MM6795 4-56 20
MM6796
MM6797
MM6805 4-10 9
MM6807
MM6809
MM6810
MM6812 9-41 10
MM6816 9-40 10
MM6817 4-55 20
MM6818
MM6821
MM6822 4-51 20
MM6823
MM6824 4-3 9
MM6825 37-10 18
MM6826
MM6827 RSV
MM6830 4-42 20
MM6831 4-22 20
MM6833 5-22
MM6836 5-10
MM6838
MM6839
MM6840

| | | |
|---|---|---|
| MM6841 | | |
| MM6842 | 4-54 | 20 |
| MM6845 | 5-11 | |
| MM6847 | | |
| MM6848* | | |
| MM6849* | 5-32 | 23 |
| MM6850 | | |
| MM6870* | 5-45 | 23 |
| MM6872* | 37-23 | 18 |
| MM6873 | 4-52 | 20 |
| MM6875 | 4-14 | 9 |
| MM6876* | 37-21 | 18 |
| MM6879 | 4-15 | 9 |
| MM6880* | | |
| MM6881 | | |
| MM6886 | 5-02 | |
| MM6887* | 5-33 | 23 |
| MM6909 | | |
| MM6912 | | |
| MM6913 | | |
| MM6914* | 37-01 | 18 |
| MM6915 | 5-15 | |
| MM6918 | | |
| MM6920 | | |
| MM6921 | 9-52 | 10 |
| MM6922 | 9-35 | 10 |
| MM6923 | | |
| MM6924 | | |
| MM6925 | | |
| MM6926 | | |
| MM6929* | 9-43 | 10 |
| MM6932 | | |
| MM6934 | RS-07 | RSV |
| MM6935* | 5-30 | 23 |
| MM6936 | 5-36 | 23 |
| MM6937 | 9-42 | 10 |
| MM6939* | 37-22 | 18 |
| MM6940 | 4-50 | 20 |
| MM6941 | 4-4 | 9 |
| MM6942 | | |
| MM6943 | 4-20 | 9 |
| MM6944 | | |
| MM6946 | 37-06 | 18 |

**TF-104G/TF-104G-M***

| | | |
|---|---|---|
| MM54226* | 4-23 | 20 |
| MM54228 | 4-26 | 20 |
| MM54232 | 4-29 | 20 |
| MM54237* | 4-32 | 20 |
| MM54250 | 4-33 | 20 |
| MM54251* | 4-34 | 20 |
| MM54253 | 4-35 | 20 |
| MM54254 | 4-36 | 20 |
| MM54255 | 4-37 | 20 |
| MM54256 | 4-38 | 20 |
| MM54258 | 4-40 | 20 |
| MM54260 | 4-41 | 20 |
| MM54261* | 4-42 | 20 |
| MM54553 | 4-44 | 20 |
| MM54554 | 4-48 | 20 |
| MM54555* | 4-45 | 20 |
| MM54556 | 4-47 | 20 |
| MM54558 | 4-46 | 20 |

**Lockheed C-130H Hercules**

46ª Brigata Aerea, Pisa:
50° Gruppo

| | |
|---|---|
| MM61988 | 46-02 |
| MM61989 | 46-03 |
| MM61990 | 46-04 |
| MM61991 | 46-05 |
| MM61992 | 46-06 |
| MM61993 | 46-07 |
| MM61994 | 46-08 |
| MM61995 | 46-09 |
| MM61997 | 46-11 |
| MM61998 | 46-12 |
| MM61999 | 46-13 |
| MM62001 | 46-15 |

**McDonnell Douglas DC-9-32**

31° Stormo, Roma-Ciampino:
306° Gruppo

MM62012
MM62013

**Panavia Tornado ADV/Trainer[1]**

36° Stormo, Gioia del Colle:
12° Gruppo

| | | |
|---|---|---|
| MM7202 | | (ZE832) |
| MM7203 | 36-02 | (ZE761) |
| MM7204 | 36-05 | (ZE730) |
| MM7205 | 36-06 | (ZE787) |
| MM7206 | 53-05 | (ZE760) |
| MM7207 | 53-10 | (ZE762) |
| MM7208 | 53-16 | (ZE811) |
| MM7209 | 53-07 | (ZE835) |
| MM7210 | 36-14 | (ZE836) |
| MM7211 | 36-16 | (ZE792) |
| MM7225 | 36-04 | (ZE252) |
| MM7226 | 36-21 | (ZE911) |
| MM7227 | 36-22 | (ZG732) |
| MM7228 | 53-03 | (ZG733) |
| MM7229 | 53-06 | (ZG728) |
| MM7230 | 36-11 | (ZG730) |
| MM7231 | 53-11 | (ZG734) |
| MM7232 | 36-10 | (ZG735) |
| MM7233 | 53-04 | (ZG768) |
| MM7234 | 53-14 | (ZE167) |
| MM55056[1] | 36-01 | (ZE202) |
| MM55057[1] | 36-03 | (ZE837) |
| MM55060[1] | 53-01 | (ZE208) |
| MM55061[1] | 53-12 | (ZE205) |

**Panavia Tornado Strike/ Trainer[1]/ECR[2]**

6° Stormo, Ghedi:
102° Gruppo & 154° Gruppo;
50° Stormo, Piacenza:
155° Gruppo;
156° Gruppo Autonomo,
Gioia del Colle;
RSV, Pratica di Mare

| | | |
|---|---|---|
| MM7002 | 6-10 | 154 |
| MM7003 | | |
| MM7004 | 50-52 | 155 |
| MM7005 | 6-05 | 154 |
| MM7006 | 6-16 | 154 |
| MM7007 | 36-37 | 156 |
| MM7008 | | |
| MM7009 | 50-45 | 155 |
| MM7010 | 6-33 | 156 |
| MM7011 | 6-33 | 102 |
| MM7013 | 36-40 | 156 |
| MM7014 | 50-43 | 155 |
| MM7015 | 50-53 | 155 |
| MM7016 | RS-01 | RSV |
| MM7018 | 6-18 | 154 |
| MM7019[2] | 50-05 | 155 |
| MM7020[2] | 50-41 | 155 |
| MM7021[2] | 50-01 | 155 |
| MM7022 | 6-22 | 154 |
| MM7023 | 36-31 | 156 |
| MM7025 | 6-43 | 102 |
| MM7026 | 6-26 | 154 |
| MM7027 | 6-47 | 102 |
| MM7028 | 6-18 | 154 |
| MM7029 | 6-19 | 154 |
| MM7030 | | |
| MM7031 | | |
| MM7033 | 6-11 | 154 |
| MM7034 | 6-30 | 154 |
| MM7035 | 36-47 | 156 |
| MM7036 | 6-36 | 102 |
| MM7037 | 6-07 | 154 |
| MM7038 | 36-41 | 156 |
| MM7039 | 50-03 | 155 |
| CMX7040 | 36-35 | 156 |
| MM7041 | 6-21 | 154 |
| MM7042 | 6-31 | 102 |
| MM7043 | 6-13 | 154 |
| MM7044 | 6-20 | 154 |
| MM7046[2] | 50-46 | 155 |
| MM7047 | 36-36 | 156 |
| MM7048 | 36-54 | Alenia |
| MM7049 | 6-34 | 102 |
| MM7050 | 36-44 | 156 |
| MM7051 | | |
| MM7052 | | |
| MM7053[2] | 50-07 | 155 |
| MM7054[2] | | Alenia |
| MM7055 | 36-33 | 156 |
| MM7056 | | |
| MM7057 | 6-12 | 154 |
| MM7058 | | |
| MM7059 | | |
| MM7060 | 6-32 | 102 |
| MM7061 | 6-01 | 154 |
| MM7062[2] | 50-44 | 155 |
| MM7063 | 36-42 | 156 |
| MM7064 | 6-24 | 154 |
| MM7065 | 6-25 | 154 |
| MM7066 | 6-44 | 102 |
| MM7067 | 67 | 156 |
| MM7068[2] | | Alenia |
| MM7070 | | |
| MM7071 | 6-35 | 102 |
| MM7072 | 6-36 | 102 |
| MM7073 | 36-43 | 156 |
| MM7075 | 50-04 | 155 |
| MM7078 | 50-02 | 155 |
| CMX7079[2] | | Alenia |
| MM7080 | 6-41 | 102 |
| MM7081 | 6-02 | 154 |
| MM7082[2] | 6-14 | 154 |
| MM7083 | 6-37 | 102 |
| MM7084 | | |
| CMX7085 | 36-50 | Alenia |
| MM7086 | 6-04 | 154 |
| MM7087 | 36-35 | 156 |
| MM7088 | 6-18 | 154 |
| MM55000[1] | | |
| MM55001[1] | | |
| MM55002[1] | | |
| MM55003[1] | | |
| MM55004[1] | 6-15 | 154 |
| MM55005[1] | 6-40 | 102 |
| MM55006[1] | 6-44 | 102 |
| MM55007[1] | 50-51 | 155 |
| MM55008[1] | 6-45 | 102 |
| MM55009[1] | 36-56 | 156 |
| MM55010[1] | 6-42 | 102 |
| MM55011[1] | 50-50 | 155 |

**Piaggio P-180AM Avanti**

14° Stormo, Guidonia:
303° Gruppo;
36° Stormo, Gioia del Colle:
636ª SC;
53° Stormo, Cameri:
653ª SC;

RSV, Pratica di Mare
MM62159 636
MM62160 54 RSV
MM62161 653
MM62162 303
MM62163 303
MM62164 RSV

**Piaggio-Douglas PD-808-GE/ PD-808-RM/PD-808-TA**
9ª Brigata Aerea, Pratica di Mare:
8° Gruppo & 71° Gruppo;
RSV, Pratica di Mare
MM61950 TA 71
MM61952 GE 71
MM61954 TA 71
MM61955 GE 71
MM61960 GE 71
MM61961 GE 71
MM61962 GE 71
MM62014 RM 8

**Guardia di Finanza**
**Aérospatiale ATR.42-400MP**
2° Gruppo EM, Pratica di Mare
MM62165 GF-13
CMX62166 GF-14

**Marina Militare Italiana**
**McDonnell Douglas AV-8B/TAV-8B Harrier II+**
Gruppo Aerei Imbarcarti, Taranto/Grottaglie
**AV-8B**
MM7199 1-03
MM7200 1-04
MM7201 1-05
MM7212 1-06
MM7213 1-07
MM7214 1-08
MM7215 1-09
MM7216 1-10
MM7217 1-11
MM7218 1-12
MM7219 1-13
MM7220 1-14
MM7221 1-15
MM7222 1-16
MM7223 1-17
MM7224 1-18
**TAV-8B**
MM55032 1-01
MM55033 1-02

**Italian Govt**
**Dassault Falcon 50**
Italian Govt/Soc. CAI, Roma/Ciampino
I-SAME

**Dassault Falcon 200**
Italian Govt/Soc. CAI, Roma/Ciampino
I-CNEF
I-SOBE

**Dassault Falcon 900**
Italian Govt/Soc. CAI, Roma/Ciampino
I-DIES
I-FICV
I-NUMI

**IVORY COAST**
**Fokker 100**
Ivory Coast Govt, Abidjan
TU-VAA

**JAPAN**
**Japan Air Self Defence Force**
**Boeing 747-47C**
701st Flight Sqn, Chitose
20-1101
20-1102

**JORDAN**
**Al Quwwat al Jawwiya al Malakiya al Urduniya**
**Extra EA-300S**
*Royal Jordanian Falcons*, Amman
JY-RNA
JY-RNC
JY-RND
JY-RNE
JY-RNG

**Lockheed C-130H Hercules**
3 Sqn, Al Matar AB/Amman
344
345
346
347
348

**Jordanian Govt**
**Grumman G.1159C Gulfstream IVSP**
Jordanian Govt, Amman
JY-RAY

**Lockheed L.1011 TriStar 500**
Jordanian Govt, Amman
JY-HKJ

**KAZAKHSTAN**
**Boeing 757-2M6**
Govt of Kazakhstan, Almaty
P4-NSN

**KENYA**
**Kenyan Air Force**
**Fokker 70ER**
308

**KUWAIT**
**Al Quwwat al Jawwiya al Kuwaitiya**
**Lockheed L100-30 Hercules**
41 Sqn, Kuwait International
KAF 323
KAF 324
KAF 325

**Kuwaiti Govt**
**Airbus A.310-308**
Kuwaiti Govt, Safat
9K-ALD

**Grumman G.1159C Gulfstream IV**
Kuwaiti Govt/Kuwait Airways, Safat
9K-AJA
9K-AJB
9K-AJC

**McDonnell Douglas MD-83**
Kuwaiti Govt, Safat
9K-AGC

**KYRGYZSTAN**
**Tupolev Tu-134A-3**
Govt of Kyrgyzstan, Bishkek
EX-65119

**Tupolev Tu-154B/Tu-154M**
Govt of Kyrgyzstan, Bishkek
EX-85294 Tu-154B
EX-85718 Tu-154M
EX-85762 Tu-154M

**LITHUANIA**
**Karines Oro Pajegos**
**Let 410 Turbolet**
I Transporto Eskadrile, Zokniai
01
02

**Lithuanian Govt**
**Lockheed L.1329 Jetstar 731**
Lithuanian Govt, Vilnius
LY-AMB

**LUXEMBOURG**
**NATO**
**Boeing 707-307C/329C***
NAEWF, Geilenkirchen
LX-N19996*
LX-N19997
LX-N19999
LX-N20000
LX-N20198*
LX-N20199*

**Boeing E-3A**
NAEWF, Geilenkirchen
LX-N90442
LX-N90443
LX-N90444
LX-N90445
LX-N90446
LX-N90447
LX-N90448
LX-N90449
LX-N90450
LX-N90451
LX-N90452
LX-N90453
LX-N90454
LX-N90455
LX-N90456
LX-N90458
LX-N90459

**MALAYSIA**
**Royal Malaysian Air Force/ Tentera Udara Diraja Malaysia**
**Lockheed C-130 Hercules**
14 Sqn, Labuan;

20 Sqn, Subang

| | | |
|---|---|---|
| M30-01 | C-130H | 14 Sqn |
| M30-02 | C-130H | 14 Sqn |
| M30-03 | C-130H | 14 Sqn |
| M30-04 | C-130H | 14 Sqn |
| M30-05 | C-130H | 14 Sqn |
| M30-06 | C-130H | 14 Sqn |
| M30-07 | C-130T | 20 Sqn |
| M30-08 | C-130H(MP) | 20 Sqn |
| M30-09 | C-130H(MP) | 20 Sqn |
| M30-10 | C-130H-30 | 20 Sqn |
| M30-11 | C-130H-30 | 20 Sqn |
| M30-12 | C-130H-30 | 20 Sqn |
| M30-13 | C-130H-30 | 20 Sqn |
| M30-14 | C-130H-30 | 20 Sqn |
| M30-15 | C-130H-30 | 20 Sqn |
| M30-16 | C-130H-30 | 20 Sqn |

## MEXICO

**Fuerza Aérea Mexicana**

**Boeing 757-225**

8º Grupo Aéreo, Mexico City

TP-01 (XC-UJM)

## MOROCCO

**Force Aérienne Royaume Marocaine/ Al Quwwat al Jawwiya al Malakiya Marakishiya**

**Airtech CN.235M-100**

Escadrille de Transport, Rabat

| | |
|---|---|
| 023 | CNA-MA |
| 024 | CNA-MB |
| 025 | CNA-MC |
| 026 | CNA-MD |
| 027 | CNA-ME |
| 028 | CNA-MF |
| 031 | CNA-MG |

**CAP-230**

*Marche Verte*

| | |
|---|---|
| 04 | CN-ABD |
| 05 | CN-ABF |
| 06 | CN-ABI |
| 07 | CN-ABJ |
| 08 | CN-ABK |
| 09 | CN-ABL |
| 22 | CN-ABM |
| 23 | CN-ABN |
| 24 | CN-ABO |

**Lockheed C-130H Hercules**

Escadrille de Transport, Rabat

| | |
|---|---|
| 4535 | CN-AOA |
| 4551 | CN-AOC |
| 4575 | CN-AOD |
| 4581 | CN-AOE |
| 4583 | CN-AOF |
| 4713 | CN-AOG |
| 4717 | CN-AOH |
| 4733 | CN-AOI |
| 4738 | CN-AOJ |
| 4739 | CN-AOK |
| 4742 | CN-AOL |
| 4875 | CN-AOM |
| 4876 | CN-AON |
| 4877 | CN-AOO |
| 4888 | CN-AOP |
| 4892 | CN-AOQ |
| 4907 | CN-AOR |
| 4909 | CN-AOS |
| 4940 | CN-AOT |

**Govt of Morocco**

**Boeing 707-138B**

Govt of Morocco, Rabat

CNA-NS

**Dassault Falcon 100**

Govt of Morocco, Rabat

CN-TNA

**Grumman G.1159 Gulfstream IITT/ G.1159A Gulfstream III**

Govt of Morocco, Rabat

| | |
|---|---|
| CNA-NL | Gulfstream IITT |
| CNA-NU | Gulfstream III |
| CNA-NV | Gulfstream III |

## NAMIBIA

**Dassault Falcon 900B**

Namibian Govt, Windhoek

V5-NAM

## NETHERLANDS

**Koninklijke Luchtmacht**

**Agusta-Bell AB.412SP**

303 Sqn, Leeuwarden

R-01
R-02
R-03

**Boeing-Vertol CH-47D Chinook**

298 Sqn, Soesterberg

D-101
D-102
D-103
D-104
D-105
D-106
D-661
D-662
D-663
D-664
D-665
D-666
D-667

**Eurocopter AS.532U2 Cougar**

300 Sqn, Gilze-Rijen

S-400
S-419
S-433
S-438
S-440
S-441
S-442
S-444
S-445
S-447
S-450
S-453
S-454
S-456
S-457
S-458
S-459

**Fokker F-27-200MPA**

336 Sqn, Hato, Antilles

M-1
M-2

**Fokker 50**

334 Sqn, Eindhoven

U-05
U-06

**Fokker 60UTA-N**

334 Sqn, Eindhoven

U-01
U-02
U-03
U-04

**General Dynamics F-16**

(MLU aircraft are marked with a *)

TGp/306/311/312 Sqns, Volkel;
313/315 Sqns, Twenthe;
322/323 Sqns, Leeuwarden

| | | |
|---|---|---|
| J-001 | F-16A* | 322 Sqn |
| J-002 | F-16A* | 323 Sqn |
| J-003 | F-16A* | 322 Sqn |
| J-004 | F-16A* | 322 Sqn |
| J-005 | F-16A* | 322 Sqn |
| J-006 | F-16A* | 322 Sqn |
| J-008 | F-16A* | 322 Sqn |
| J-009 | F-16A* | 322 Sqn |
| J-010 | F-16A* | 323 Sqn |
| J-011 | F-16A* | 322 Sqn |
| J-013 | F-16A* | 322 Sqn |
| J-014 | F-16A* | 313 Sqn |
| J-015 | F-16A* | 312 Sqn |
| J-016 | F-16A* | 323 Sqn |
| J-017 | F-16A | 312 Sqn |
| J-018 | F-16A* | 322 Sqn |
| J-019 | F-16A* | 323 Sqn |
| J-020 | F-16A* | 315 Sqn |
| J-021 | F-16A* | 312 Sqn |
| J-055 | F-16A* | 322 Sqn |
| J-057 | F-16A* | 323 Sqn |
| J-058 | F-16A* | 315 Sqn |
| J-060 | F-16A* | 315 Sqn |
| J-061 | F-16A* | 322 Sqn |
| J-062 | F-16A* | 322 Sqn |
| J-063 | F-16A* | 322 Sqn |
| J-064 | F-16B* | 322 Sqn |
| J-065 | F-16B* | 313 Sqn |
| J-066 | F-16B* | 323 Sqn |
| J-067 | F-16B* | 313 Sqn |
| J-068 | F-16B* | 322 Sqn |
| J-135 | F-16A* | 323 Sqn |
| J-136 | F-16A* | 315 Sqn |
| J-137 | F-16A* | 322 Sqn |
| J-138 | F-16A* | 315 Sqn |
| J-139 | F-16A | 311 Sqn |
| J-141 | F-16A* | 315 Sqn |
| J-142 | F-16A* | 323 Sqn |
| J-143 | F-16A* | 315 Sqn |
| J-144 | F-16A* | 312 Sqn |
| J-145 | F-16A* | 315 Sqn |
| J-146 | F-16A* | 323 Sqn |
| J-192 | F-16A | 312 Sqn |
| J-193 | F-16A | 312 Sqn |
| J-194 | F-16A | 311 Sqn |
| J-196 | F-16A | 311 Sqn |
| J-197 | F-16A | 311 Sqn |
| J-198 | F-16A | 311 Sqn |
| J-199 | F-16A | 306 Sqn |
| J-201 | F-16A | 312 Sqn |
| J-202 | F-16A | 315 Sqn |
| J-203 | F-16A* | 311 Sqn |
| J-204 | F-16A* | 323 Sqn |
| J-205 | F-16A* | 323 Sqn |
| J-206 | F-16A* | 312 Sqn |

| | | |
|---|---|---|
| J-207 | F-16A | 311 Sqn |
| J-208 | F-16B* | 312 Sqn |
| J-209 | F-16B* | 315 Sqn |
| J-210 | F-16B* | 312 Sqn |
| J-211 | F-16B* | 322 Sqn |
| J-220 | F-16A | 311 Sqn |
| J-230 | F-16A | 312 Sqn |
| J-231 | F-16A | 312 Sqn |
| J-232 | F-16A | 312 Sqn |
| J-235 | F-16A | 312 Sqn |
| J-236 | F-16A | 312 Sqn |
| J-241 | F-16A | 311 Sqn |
| J-243 | F-16A | 311 Sqn |
| J-246 | F-16A | 313 Sqn |
| J-248 | F-16A | 312 Sqn |
| J-249 | F-16A | 311 Sqn |
| J-250 | F-16A | 311 Sqn |
| J-251 | F-16A* | 313 Sqn |
| J-253 | F-16A | 312 Sqn |
| J-254 | F-16A* | 312 Sqn |
| J-255 | F-16A | 312 Sqn |
| J-256 | F-16A | 311 Sqn |
| J-257 | F-16A | 312 Sqn |
| J-261 | F-16B | 312 Sqn |
| J-264 | F-16B | 313 Sqn |
| J-265 | F-16B | 313 Sqn |
| J-266 | F-16B | 311 Sqn |
| J-267 | F-16B* | 313 Sqn |
| J-268 | F-16B | 313 Sqn |
| J-269 | F-16B | 306 Sqn |
| J-270 | F-16B | 312 Sqn |
| J-360 | F-16A* | 313 Sqn |
| J-362 | F-16A* | 315 Sqn |
| J-363 | F-16A* | 323 Sqn |
| J-364 | F-16A | 311 Sqn |
| J-365 | F-16A* | 315 Sqn |
| J-366 | F-16A* | 315 Sqn |
| J-367 | F-16A* | 313 Sqn |
| J-368 | F-16B | 306 Sqn |
| J-369 | F-16B* | 315 Sqn |
| J-508 | F-16A* | 315 Sqn |
| J-509 | F-16A* | 315 Sqn |
| J-510 | F-16A* | 323 Sqn |
| J-511 | F-16A* | 315 Sqn |
| J-512 | F-16A* | 313 Sqn |
| J-513 | F-16A* | 323 Sqn |
| J-514 | F-16A* | 315 Sqn |
| J-515 | F-16A* | 323 Sqn |
| J-516 | F-16A* | 312 Sqn |
| J-616 | F-16A | 311 Sqn |
| J-617 | F-16A | 311 Sqn |
| J-619 | F-16A | 311 Sqn |
| J-620 | F-16A* | 312 Sqn |
| J-622 | F-16A* | 311 Sqn |
| J-623 | F-16A | 306 Sqn |
| J-624 | F-16A* | 313 Sqn |
| J-627 | F-16A(R) | 306 Sqn |
| J-628 | F-16A(R) | 306 Sqn |
| J-630 | F-16A(R) | 306 Sqn |
| J-631 | F-16A(R) | 306 Sqn |
| J-632 | F-16A(R) | 306 Sqn |
| J-633 | F-16A(R) | 306 Sqn |
| J-635 | F-16A(R)* | 306 Sqn |
| J-636 | F-16A(R) | 306 Sqn |
| J-637 | F-16A(R) | 306 Sqn |
| J-638 | F-16A(R) | 306 Sqn |
| J-640 | F-16A(R) | 306 Sqn |
| J-641 | F-16A(R) | 306 Sqn |
| J-642 | F-16A(R) | 306 Sqn |
| J-643 | F-16A(R) | 306 Sqn |
| J-644 | F-16A(R) | 306 Sqn |
| J-646 | F-16A(R)* | 306 Sqn |
| J-647 | F-16A(R)* | 306 Sqn |
| J-648 | F-16A(R)* | 306 Sqn |
| J-649 | F-16B | 311 Sqn |
| J-650 | F-16B* | 313 Sqn |
| J-651 | F-16B | 306 Sqn |
| J-652 | F-16B* | 323 Sqn |
| J-653 | F-16B | TGp |
| J-654 | F-16B* | 311 Sqn |
| J-655 | F-16B | 306 Sqn |
| J-656 | F-16B* | 313 Sqn |
| J-657 | F-16B* | 313 Sqn |
| J-864 | F-16A(R) | 306 Sqn |
| J-866 | F-16A(R) | 306 Sqn |
| J-867 | F-16A(R) | 306 Sqn |
| J-868 | F-16A | 311 Sqn |
| J-869 | F-16A | 312 Sqn |
| J-870 | F-16A | 311 Sqn |
| J-871 | F-16A | 312 Sqn |
| J-872 | F-16A | 312 Sqn |
| J-873 | F-16A | 312 Sqn |
| J-874 | F-16A | 312 Sqn |
| J-875 | F-16A* | 311 Sqn |
| J-876 | F-16A | 312 Sqn |
| J-877 | F-16A | 311 Sqn |
| J-878 | F-16A | 312 Sqn |
| J-879 | F-16A* | 313 Sqn |
| J-881 | F-16A* | 323 Sqn |
| J-882 | F-16B | 311 Sqn |
| J-884 | F-16B | 306 Sqn |
| J-885 | F-16B* | 323 Sqn |

**Grumman G-1159C Gulfstream IV**
334 Sqn, Eindhoven
V-11

**Lockheed C-130H-30 Hercules**
334 Sqn, Eindhoven
G-273
G-275

**MBB Bo.105CB/ Bo.105CB-4***
299 Sqn, Gilze-Rijen
B-37*
B-38
B-39*
B-40*
B-41*
B-42
B-43
B-44
B-47
B-48
B-63
B-64
B-66
B-67
B-68
B-69
B-70
B-71
B-72
B-74
B-75
B-76
B-77
B-78*
B-79
B-80
B-83

**MDH AH-64A Apache/ NAH-64D Longbow Apache**
**AH-64A**
301 Sqn, Gilze-Rijen;
302 Sqn, Gilze-Rijen

| | |
|---|---|
| 25430 | 301 Sqn |
| 25465 | 301 Sqn |
| 25471 | 301 Sqn |
| 25472 | 301 Sqn |
| 25474 | 301 Sqn |
| 25480 | 301 Sqn |
| 25482 | 301 Sqn |
| 25485 | 301 Sqn |
| 68970 | 301 Sqn |
| 68983 | 301 Sqn |
| 69029 | 301 Sqn |
| 69033 | 301 Sqn |

**NAH-64D**

| | |
|---|---|
| Q-01 | 302 Sqn |
| Q-02 | 302 Sqn |
| Q-03 | 302 Sqn |
| Q-04 | 302 Sqn |
| Q-05 | 302 Sqn |
| Q-06 | 302 Sqn |
| Q-07 | 302 Sqn |
| Q-08 | 302 Sqn |
| Q-09 | 302 Sqn |
| Q-10 | 302 Sqn |

**McDonnell Douglas KDC-10**
334 Sqn, Eindhoven
T-235
T-264

**Pilatus PC-7**
131 EMVO Sqn, Woensdrecht
L-01
L-02
L-03
L-04
L-05
L-06
L-07
L-08
L-09
L-10
L-11
L-12
L-13

**Sud Alouette III**
300 Sqn, Soesterberg
A-247
A-253
A-275
A-292
A-301

**Marine Luchtvaart Dienst**

**Beechcraft Super King Air 200**
2 MOTU, Maastricht
PH-SBK

**Lockheed P-3C Orion**
MARPAT (320 Sqn & 321 Sqn), Valkenburg and Keflavik
300
301
302
303

304
305
306
307
308
309
310
311

**Westland SH-14D Lynx**
HELIGRP (7 Sqn & 860 Sqn), De Kooij
(7 Sqn operates 860 Sqn aircraft on loan)
260
261
262
264
265
266
267
268
269
270
271
272
273
274
276
277
278
279
280
281
283

**Netherlands Govt**
**Fokker 70**
Dutch Royal Flight, Schiphol
PH-KBX

**NEW ZEALAND**
**Royal New Zealand Air Force**
**Boeing 727-22C**
40 Sqn, Whenuapai
NZ7271
NZ7272

**Lockheed C-130H Hercules**
40 Sqn, Whenuapai
NZ7001
NZ7002
NZ7003
NZ7004
NZ7005

**Lockheed P-3K Orion**
5 Sqn, Whenuapai
NZ4201
NZ4202
NZ4203
NZ4204
NZ4205
NZ4206

**NIGERIA**
**Federal Nigerian Air Force**
**Lockheed C-130H Hercules**
Lagos
NAF-910
NAF-912
NAF-913
NAF-914
NAF-915
NAF-916
NAF-917
NAF-918

**Nigerian Govt**
**Dassault Falcon 900**
Federal Govt of Nigeria, Lagos
5N-FGE
5N-FGO

**Grumman G.1159 Gulfstream II/ G.1159A Gulfstream III**
Federal Govt of Nigeria, Lagos
5N-AGV Gulfstream II
5N-FGP Gulfstream III

**NORWAY**
**Kongelige Norske Luftforsvaret**
**Bell 412SP**
339 Skv, Bardufoss;
720 Skv, Rygge
139 339 Skv
140 720 Skv
141 720 Skv
142 339 Skv
143 339 Skv
144 339 Skv
145 720 Skv
146 339 Skv
147 720 Skv
148 339 Skv
149 339 Skv
161 339 Skv
162 339 Skv
163 720 Skv
164 720 Skv
165 720 Skv
166 720 Skv
167 720 Skv
194 720 Skv

**Dassault Falcon 20 ECM**
717 Skv, Rygge
041
053
0125

**DHC-6 Twin Otter**
719 Skv, Bodø
057
184
7062

**General Dynamics F-16**
(MLU aircraft are marked with a *)
331 Skv, Bodø (*r/w/bl*);
332 Skv, Rygge (*y/bk*);
334 Skv, Bodø (*r/w*);
338 Skv, Ørland
272 F-16A 332 Skv
273 F-16A 338 Skv
275 F-16A 332 Skv
276 F-16A 338 Skv
277 F-16A 332 Skv
279 F-16A 338 Skv
281 F-16A 332 Skv
282 F-16A 338 Skv
284 F-16A 332 Skv
285 F-16A 338 Skv
286 F-16A 338 Skv
288 F-16A 338 Skv
289 F-16A 338 Skv
291 F-16A 338 Skv
292 F-16A 338 Skv
293 F-16A 338 Skv
295 F-16A 338 Skv
297 F-16A* 332 Skv
298 F-16A 338 Skv
299 F-16A* 338 Skv
302 F-16B 338 Skv
304 F-16B 334 Skv
305 F-16B 332 Skv
306 F-16B* 332 Skv
658 F-16A 334 Skv
659 F-16A 334 Skv
660 F-16A 334 Skv
661 F-16A 334 Skv
662 F-16A 334 Skv
663 F-16A 334 Skv
664 F-16A 331 Skv
665 F-16A 334 Skv
666 F-16A 334 Skv
667 F-16A 334 Skv
668 F-16A 334 Skv
669 F-16A 334 Skv
670 F-16A 332 Skv
671 F-16A 334 Skv
672 F-16A 331 Skv
673 F-16A 332 Skv
674 F-16A 332 Skv
675 F-16A 331 Skv
677 F-16A 331 Skv
678 F-16A 334 Skv
680 F-16A* 338 Skv
681 F-16A 331 Skv
682 F-16A 331 Skv
683 F-16A 334 Skv
686 F-16A 331 Skv
687 F-16A 338 Skv
688 F-16A 331 Skv
689 F-16B 338 Skv
690 F-16B 338 Skv
691 F-16B 338 Skv
692 F-16B 334 Skv
693 F-16B 338 Skv
711 F-16B* 332 Skv
712 F-16B 331 Skv

**Lockheed C-130H Hercules**
335 Skv, Gardermoen
952
953
954
955
956
957

**Lockheed P-3C Orion**
333 Skv, Andøya
3296
3297
3298
3299

**Lockheed P-3N Orion**
333 Skv, Andøya
4576
6603

**Northrop F-5A**
336 Skv, Rygge
128
130

131
133
134
896
902

**Northrop F-5B**
336 Skv, Rygge
136
243
244
387
906
907
908
909

**Westland Sea King Mk 43/Mk43A/Mk43B**
330 Skv:
A Flt, Bodø;
B Flt, Banak;
C Flt, Ørland;
D Flt, Sola

| | |
|---|---|
| 060 | Mk 43 |
| 062 | Mk43 |
| 066 | Mk 43 |
| 069 | Mk 43 |
| 070 | Mk 43 |
| 071 | Mk 43B |
| 072 | Mk 43 |
| 073 | Mk 43 |
| 074 | Mk 43 |
| 189 | Mk 43A |
| 322 | Mk 43B |
| 329 | Mk 43B |
| 330 | Mk 43B |

**Kystvakt (Coast Guard)**
**Westland Lynx Mk86**
337 Skv, Bardufoss
207
216
228
232
237
350

## OMAN
**Royal Air Force of Oman**
**BAC 1-11/485GD**
4 Sqn, Seeb
551
552
553

**Lockheed C-130H Hercules**
4 Sqn, Seeb
501
502
503

**Short Skyvan 3M/Seavan 3M***
2 Sqn, Seeb
902
903
904
905
907
908
910*
911
912
914
915*
916*

**Omani Govt**
**Boeing 747SP-27**
Govt of Oman, Seeb
A4O-SO
A4O-SP

**Grumman G.1159C Gulfstream IV**
Govt of Oman, Seeb
A4O-AB
A4O-AC

## PAKISTAN
**Pakistan Fiza'ya**
**Boeing 707-340C**

| | |
|---|---|
| 68-19866 | 12 Sqn |
| 69-19635 | 12 Sqn |

**Pakistani Govt**
**Boeing 737-33A**
Govt of Pakistan, Karachi
AP-BEH

## PERU
**Fuerza Aérea Peruana**
**Douglas DC-8-62AF**

| | |
|---|---|
| 370 | (OB-1372) |
| 371 | (OB-1373) |

## POLAND
**Polskie Wojska Lotnicze**
**Antonov An-26**
13 PLT, Krakow/Balice
1307
1310
1402
1403
1406
1407
1508
1509
1602
1603
1604

**Mikoyan MiG-29A/UB***
1 PLM, Minsk/Mazowiecki
15*
28*
29
38
40
42*
54
56
59
64*
65
66
67
70
77
83
89
92
105
108
111
114
115

**Tupolev Tu-134A**
36 SPLT, Warszawa
102

**Tupolev Tu-154M**
36 SPLT, Warszawa
101
102

**Yakovlev Yak-40**
36 SPLT, Warszawa
032
034
036
037
038
039
040
041
042
043
044
045
047
048

## PORTUGAL
**Força Aérea Portuguesa**
**Aérospatiale SA.330C Puma**
Esq 751, Montijo;
Esq 752, Lajes

| | |
|---|---|
| 19502 | Esq 751 |
| 19503 | Esq 751 |
| 19504 | Esq 751 |
| 19505 | Esq 751 |
| 19506 | Esq 752 |
| 19508 | Esq 751 |
| 19509 | Esq 751 |
| 19511 | Esq 752 |
| 19512 | Esq 751 |
| 19513 | Esq 752 |

**CASA 212A/212ECM*Aviocar**
Esq 401, Sintra;
Esq 501, Sintra;
Esq 502, Sintra;
Esq 503, Lajes

| | |
|---|---|
| 16501* | Esq 501 |
| 16502* | Esq 501 |
| 16503 | Esq 501 |
| 16504 | Esq 501 |
| 16505 | Esq 502 |
| 16506 | Esq 502 |
| 16507 | Esq 502 |
| 16508 | Esq 502 |
| 16509 | Esq 501 |
| 16510 | Esq 401 |
| 16511 | Esq 502 |
| 16512 | Esq 401 |
| 16513 | Esq 503 |
| 16514 | Esq 503 |
| 16515 | Esq 503 |
| 16517 | Esq 503 |
| 16519 | Esq 401 |
| 16520 | Esq 503 |
| 16521* | Esq 401 |
| 16522* | Esq 401 |
| 16523* | Esq 401 |
| 16524* | Esq 401 |

**CASA 212-300 Aviocar**
Esq 401, Sintra
17201
17202

**D-BD Alpha Jet**
Esq 103, Beja;
Esq 301, Beja
15201
15202
15204
15205
15206
15208
15209
15210
15211
15213
15214
15215
15216
15217
15218
15219
15220
15221
15222
15223
15224
15225
15226
15227
15228
15229
15230
15231
15232
15233
15234
15235
15236
15237
15238
15239
15240
15241
15242
15243
15244
15246
15247
15248
15249
15250

**Dassault Falcon 20DC**
Esq 504, Lisbon/Montijo
17103

**Dassault Falcon 50**
Esq 504, Lisbon/Montijo
17401
17402
17403

**Lockheed C-130H/ C-130H-30* Hercules**
Esq 501, Lisbon/Montijo
16801*
16802*
16803
16804
16805
16806*

**Lockheed Martin (GD) F-16A/F-16B***
Esq 201, Monte Real
15101
15102
15103
15104
15105
15106
15107
15108
15109
15110
15111
15112
15113
15114
15115
15116
15117
15118*
15119*
15120*

**Lockheed P-3P Orion**
Esq 601, Lisbon/Montijo
14801
14802
14803
14804
14805
14806

**Marinha**

**Westland Super Lynx Mk 95**
Esq de Helicopteros, Lisbon/Montijo
19201
19202
19203
19204
19205

**QATAR**

**Airbus A.310-304**
Qatari Govt, Doha
A7-AAF

**Airbus A.340-211**
Qatari Govt, Doha
A7-HHK

**Dassault Falcon 900**
Qatari Govt, Doha
A7-AAD
A7-AAE

**ROMANIA**

**Fortele Aeriene Romania**

**Lockheed C-130B Hercules**
19 FMT, Bucharest/Otapeni
5927
6150
6166

**RUSSIA**

**Voenno-Vozdushniye Sily Rossioki Federatsii (Russian Air Force)**

**Sukhoi Su-27**
TsAGI, Gromov Flight Institute, Zhukhovsky
595 Su-27P
597 Su-30
598 Su-27P

**Russian Govt**

**Ilyushin Il-62M**
Russian Govt, Moscow
RA-86466
RA-86467
RA-86468
RA-86536
RA-86537
RA-86540
RA-86553
RA-86554
RA-86559
RA-86561
RA-86710
RA-86711
RA-86712

**Ilyushin Il-96-300**
Russian Govt, Moscow
RA-96012

**Tupolev Tu-134A**
Russian Govt, Moscow
RA-65904

**Tupolev Tu-154M**
Russian Govt, Moscow
RA-85629
RA-85630
RA-85631
RA-85645
RA-85651
RA-85653
RA-85658
RA-85659
RA-85666
RA-85675
RA-85676

**SAUDI ARABIA**

**Al Quwwat al Jawwiya as Sa'udiya**

**BAe 125-800/-800B***
1 Sqn, Riyadh
HZ-105
HZ-109*
110*

**Boeing E-3A/KE-3A* Sentry**
18 Sqn, Riyadh
1801
1802
1803
1804
1805
1811*
1812*
1813*
1814*
1815*
1816*
1817*
1818*

**Grumman G.1159A Gulfstream III G.1159C Gulfstream IV**
1 Sqn, Riyadh
HZ-103 Gulfstream IV
HZ-108 Gulfstream III

**Lockheed**
**C-130/ L.100 Hercules**
1 Sqn, Riyadh;
4 Sqn, Jeddah;
16 Sqn, Jeddah;
32 Sqn, Jeddah

| | | |
|---|---|---|
| 111 | VC-130H | 1 Sqn |
| 112 | VC-130H | 1 Sqn |
| 451 | C-130E | 4 Sqn |
| 452 | C-130H | 4 Sqn |
| 455 | C-130E | 4 Sqn |
| 461 | C-130H | 4 Sqn |
| 462 | C-130H | 4 Sqn |
| 463 | C-130H | 4 Sqn |
| 464 | C-130H | 4 Sqn |
| 465 | C-130H | 4 Sqn |
| 466 | C-130H | 4 Sqn |
| 467 | C-130H | 4 Sqn |
| 468 | C-130H | 4 Sqn |
| 471 | C-130H-30 | 4 Sqn |
| 472 | C-130H | 4 Sqn |
| 473 | C-130H | 4 Sqn |
| 474 | C-130H | 4 Sqn |
| 475 | C-130H | 4 Sqn |
| 476 | C-130H | 4 Sqn |
| 477 | C-130H | 4 Sqn |
| 478 | C-130H | 4 Sqn |
| 479 | C-130H | 4 Sqn |
| 1601 | C-130H | 16 Sqn |
| 1602 | C-130H | 16 Sqn |
| 1603 | C-130H | 16 Sqn |
| 1604 | C-130H | 16 Sqn |
| 1605 | C-130H | 16 Sqn |
| 1606 | C-130E | 16 Sqn |
| 1607 | C-130E | 16 Sqn |
| 1608 | C-130E | 16 Sqn |
| 1609 | C-130E | 16 Sqn |
| 1610 | C-130E | 16 Sqn |
| 1611 | C-130E | 16 Sqn |
| 1612 | C-130H | 16 Sqn |
| 1613 | C-130H | 16 Sqn |
| 1614 | C-130H | 16 Sqn |
| 1615 | C-130H | 16 Sqn |
| 1618 | C-130H | 16 Sqn |
| 1619 | C-130H | 16 Sqn |
| 1622 | C-130H-30 | 16 Sqn |
| 1623 | C-130H-30 | 16 Sqn |
| 1624 | C-130H | 16 Sqn |
| 1625 | C-130H | 16 Sqn |
| 1626 | C-130H | 16 Sqn |
| 1627 | C-130H | 16 Sqn |
| 1628 | C-130H | 16 Sqn |
| 3201 | KC-130H | 32 Sqn |
| 3202 | KC-130H | 32 Sqn |
| 3203 | KC-130H | 32 Sqn |
| 3204 | KC-130H | 32 Sqn |
| 3205 | KC-130H | 32 Sqn |
| 3206 | KC-130H | 32 Sqn |
| 3207 | KC-130H | 32 Sqn |
| 3208 | KC-130H | 32 Sqn |
| HZ-114 | VC-130H | 1 Sqn |
| HZ-115 | VC-130H | 1 Sqn |
| HZ-116 | VC-130H | 1 Sqn |
| HZ-117 | L.100-30 | 1 Sqn |
| HZ-128 | L.100-30 | 1 Sqn |
| HZ-129 | L.100-30 | 1 Sqn |

**Saudi Govt**

**Airbus A.340-211**
Royal Embassy of Saudi Arabia, Riyadh
HZ-124

**Boeing 737-268**
Saudi Royal Flight, Jeddah
HZ-HM4

**Boeing 747-3G1**
Saudi Royal Flight, Jeddah
HZ-HM1A

**Boeing 747SP-68**
Saudi Govt, Jeddah;
Saudi Royal Flight, Jeddah

| | |
|---|---|
| HZ-AIF | Govt |
| HZ-AIJ | Royal Flight |
| HZ-HM1B | Royal Flight |

**Boeing MD-11**
Saudi Royal Flight, Jeddah
HZ-HM7
HZ-HM8

**Canadair CL.604 Challenger**
Saudi Royal Flight, Jeddah
HZ-AFA2

**Dassault Falcon 900**
Saudi Govt, Jeddah
HZ-AFT
HZ-AFZ

**Grumman G.1159A Gulfstream III**
Armed Forces Medical Services, Riyadh;
Saudi Govt, Jeddah

| | |
|---|---|
| HZ-AFN | Govt |
| HZ-AFR | Govt |
| HZ-MS3 | AFMS |
| HZ-MS4 | AFMS |
| HZ-MSD | AFMS |

**Grumman G.1159C Gulfstream IV**
Saudi Govt, Jeddah
HZ-AFU
HZ-AFV
HZ-AFW
HZ-AFX
HZ-AFY

**Lockheed C-130H/L.100 Hercules**
Armed Forces Medical Services, Riyadh

| | |
|---|---|
| HZ-MS6 | L.100-30 |
| HZ-MS7 | C-130H |
| HZ-MS8 | C-130H-30 |
| HZ-MS09 | L.100-30 |
| HZ-MS019 | C-130H |

**Lockheed L.1011 TriStar 500**
Saudi Royal Flight, Jeddah
HZ-HM5
HZ-HM6

## SINGAPORE

**Republic of Singapore Air Force**

**Lockheed C-130 Hercules**
122 Sqn, Paya Labar

| | |
|---|---|
| 720 | KC-130B |
| 721 | KC-130B |
| 724 | KC-130B |
| 725 | KC-130B |
| 730 | C-130H |
| 731 | C-130H |
| 732 | C-130H |
| 733 | C-130H |
| 734 | KC-130H |
| 735 | C-130H |

## SLOVAKIA

**Slovenské Vojenske Letectvo**

**Aero L-39/L-59 (L-39MS) Albatros**
31 SLK/3 Letka, Sliač [SL];
VSL, Košice;
*White Albatroses, Košice (WA)*

| | | |
|---|---|---|
| 0002 | L-39MS | VSL |
| 0003 | L-39MS | VSL |
| 0101 | L-39C | *WA* [4] |
| 0102 | L-39C | *WA* [6] |
| 0103 | L-39C | VSL |
| 0111 | L-39C | *WA* [5] |
| 0112 | L-39C | *WA* [1] |
| 0442 | L-39C | *WA* [2] |
| 0443 | L-39C | *WA* [7] |
| 0730 | L-39V | VSL |
| 0745 | L-39V | VSL |
| 1701 | L-39ZA | 31 SLK |
| 1725 | L-39ZA | 31 SLK |
| 1730 | L-39ZA | 31 SLK |
| 3905 | L-39ZA | 31 SLK |
| 4355 | L-39C | *WA* [3] |
| 4701 | L-39ZA | 31 SLK |
| 4703 | L-39ZA | 31 SLK |
| 4705 | L-39ZA | 31 SLK |
| 4707 | L-39ZA | 31 SLK |
| 4711 | L-39ZA | 31 SLK |

**Antonov An-24V**
32 ZmDK/1 Letka, Pieštany
2903
5605

**Antonov An-26**
32 ZmDK/1 Letka, Pieštany
2506
3208

**Let 410 Turbolet**
31 SLK/4 Letka, Sliač; [SL];
32 ZmDK/1 Letka, Pieštany;
VSL, Košice

| | | |
|---|---|---|
| 0730 | L-410UVP | 32 ZmDK |
| 0927 | L-410T | 31 SLK |
| 0930 | L-410T | 32 ZmDK |
| 1133 | L-410T | VSL |
| 1203 | L-410FG | 32 ZmDK |
| 1521 | L-410FG | 32 ZmDK |
| 2311 | L-410UVP | 32 ZmDK |

**Mikoyan MiG-29A/UB***
31 SLK/1 & 2 Letka, Sliač [SL]
0619
0820
0921
1303*
2022
2123
3709
3911
4401*
5113
5304*

5515
5817
6124
6425
6526
6627
6728
6829
6930
7501
8003
8605
9308

**Sukhoi Su-25K/UBK***
33 SBoLK/2 Letka, Malacky
1006
1007
1008
1027
3237*
5033
5036
6017
6018
8072
8073
8074
8075

**Slovak Govt**
**Tupolev Tu-154M**
Slovak Govt,
Bratislava/Ivanka
OM-BYO
OM-BYR

**Yakovlev Yak-40**
Slovak Govt,
Bratislava/Ivanka
OM-BYE
OM-BYL

**SLOVENIA**
**Slovene Army**
**Let 410UVP-E**
15 Brigada, Ljubljana
L4-01

**Pilatus PC-9**
15 Brigada, Ljubljana
L9-51
L9-52
L9-53
L9-54
L9-55
L9-56
L9-57
L9-58
L9-59
L9-60
L9-61
L9-62
L9-63
L9-64
L9-65
L9-66
L9-67
L9-68
L9-69

**Slovenian Govt**
**Gates LearJet**
Slovenian Govt, Ljubljana
S5-BAA LearJet 35A
S5-BAB LearJet 24D

**SOUTH AFRICA**
**South African Air Force/**
**Suid Afrikaanse Lugmag**
**Boeing 707**
60 Sqn, Waterkloof
1415 328C
1417 328C
1419 328C
1423 344C

**Dassault Falcon 900**
21 Sqn, Waterkloof
ZS-NAN

**Lockheed**
**C-130B Hercules**
28 Sqn, Waterkloof
401
402
403
404
405
406
407
408
409

**SPAIN**
**Ejército del Aire**
**Airtech**
**CN.235M-10 (T.19A)/**
**CN.235M-100 (T.19B)**
Ala 35, Getafe

| | |
|---|---|
| T.19A-01 | 35-60 |
| T.19A-02 | 35-61 |
| T.19B-03 | 35-21 |
| T.19B-04 | 35-22 |
| T.19B-05 | 35-23 |
| T.19B-06 | 35-24 |
| T.19B-07 | 35-25 |
| T.19B-08 | 35-26 |
| T.19B-09 | 35-27 |
| T.19B-10 | 35-28 |
| T.19B-11 | 35-29 |
| T.19B-12 | 35-30 |
| T.19B-13 | 35-31 |
| T.19B-14 | 35-32 |
| T.19B-15 | 35-33 |
| T.19B-16 | 35-34 |
| T.19B-17 | 35-35 |
| T.19B-18 | 35-36 |
| T.19B-19 | 35-37 |
| T.19B-20 | 35-38 |

**Boeing 707**
408 Esc, Torrejón;
Grupo 45, Torrejón

| | | |
|---|---|---|
| T.17-1 | 331B | 45-10 |
| T.17-2 | 331B | 45-11 |
| T.17-3 | 368C | 45-12 |
| TM.17-4 | 351C | 408-21 |

**CASA 101EB Aviojet**
Grupo 54, Torrejón;
Grupo de Escuelas de
Matacán (74);
AGA, San Javier (79);
*Patrulla Aguila*, San Javier*

| | | |
|---|---|---|
| E.25-01 | 79-01 | |
| E.25-05 | 79-05 | |
| E.25-06 | 79-06 | [6]* |
| E.25-07 | 79-07 | |
| E.25-08 | 79-08 | |
| E.25-09 | 79-09 | |
| E.25-10 | 79-10 | |
| E.25-11 | 79-11 | |
| E.25-12 | 79-12 | |
| E.25-13 | 79-13 | |
| E.25-14 | 79-14 | [8]* |
| E.25-15 | 79-15 | |
| E.25-16 | 79-16 | |
| E.25-17 | 74-40 | |
| E.25-18 | 74-42 | |
| E.25-19 | 79-19 | |
| E.25-20 | 79-20 | |
| E.25-21 | 79-21 | [1]* |
| E.25-22 | 79-22 | [5]* |
| E.25-23 | 74-02 | |
| E.25-24 | 79-24 | |
| E.25-25 | 79-25 | [3]* |
| E.25-26 | 79-26 | |
| E.25-27 | 79-27 | |
| E.25-28 | 79-28 | [2]* |
| E.25-29 | | |
| E.25-31 | 79-31 | |
| E.25-33 | 74-02 | |
| E.25-34 | 79-34 | |
| E.25-35 | 79-35 | |
| E.25-37 | 74-04 | |
| E.25-38 | 79-38 | |
| E.25-40 | 79-40 | [7]* |
| E.25-41 | 74-41 | |
| E.25-43 | 74-43 | |
| E.25-44 | 79-44 | |
| E.25-45 | 79-45 | |
| E.25-46 | 79-46 | |
| E.25-47 | 79-47 | |
| E.25-48 | 79-48 | |
| E.25-49 | 79-49 | |
| E.25-50 | 79-33 | |
| E.25-51 | 74-07 | |
| E.25-52 | 79-34 | [4]* |
| E.25-53 | 411-07 | |
| E.25-54 | 79-35 | |
| E.25-55 | 44-05 | |
| E.25-56 | 74-11 | |
| E.25-57 | 74-12 | |
| E.25-59 | 74-13 | |
| E.25-61 | 54-22 | |
| E.25-62 | 74-16 | |
| E.25-63 | 74-17 | |
| E.25-64 | 74-18 | |
| E.25-65 | 79-95 | |
| E.25-66 | 74-20 | |
| E.25-67 | 74-21 | |
| E.25-68 | 74-22 | |
| E.25-69 | 79-97 | |
| E.25-71 | 74-25 | |
| E.25-72 | 74-26 | |
| E.25-73 | 79-98 | |
| E.25-74 | 74-28 | |
| E.25-75 | 74-29 | |
| E.25-76 | 74-30 | |
| E.25-78 | 79-02 | |
| E.25-79 | 74-32 | |
| E.25-80 | 79-03 | |
| E.25-81 | 74-34 | |
| E.25-83 | 74-35 | |
| E.25-84 | 79-04 | |
| E.25-86 | 79-32 | |
| E.25-87 | 79-29 | |
| E.25-88 | 74-39 | |

**CASA 212 Aviocar 212 (XT.12)/212A (T.12B)/ 212B (TR.12A)/212D (TE.12B)/212DE (TM.12D)/212E (T.12C)/ 212S (D.3A)/212S1 (D.3B)/ 212-200 (T.12D)/. 212-200 (TR.12D)**

Ala 22, Morón;
Ala 37, Villanubla;
Ala 46, Gando, Las Palmas;
CLAEX, Torrejón (54);
Grupo 72, Alcantarilla;
Grupo Esc, Matacán (74);
AGA (Ala 79), San Javier;
403 Esc, Getafe;
408 Esc, Torrejón;
721 Esc, Alcantarilla;
801 Esc, Palma/Son San Juan;
803 Esc, Cuatro Vientos;
INTA,Torrejón

| | |
|---|---|
| D.3A-1 | (801 Esc) |
| D.3A-2 | (803 Esc) |
| D.3B-3 | (803 Esc) |
| D.3B-4 | (801 Esc) |
| D.3B-5 | (801 Esc) |
| D.3B-6 | (801 Esc) |
| D.3B-7 | (803 Esc) |
| D.3B-8 | (801 Esc) |
| XT.12A-1 | 54-10 |
| TR.12A-4 | 403-02 |
| TR.12A-5 | 403-03 |
| TR.12A-6 | 403-04 |
| TR.12A-8 | 403-06 |
| T.12B-9 | 74-83 |
| TE.12B-10 | 79-92 |
| T.12B-12 | 74-82 |
| T.12B-13 | 74-70 |
| T.12B-14 | 37-01 |
| T.12B-15 | 37-02 |
| T.12B-16 | 74-71 |
| T.12B-17 | 37-03 |
| T.12B-18 | 46-31 |
| T.12B-19 | 46-32 |
| T.12B-20 | 37-04 |
| T.12B-21 | 37-05 |
| T.12B-22 | 37-06 |
| T.12B-23 | 72-01 |
| T.12B-24 | 37-07 |
| T.12B-25 | 74-72 |
| T.12B-26 | 72-02 |
| T.12B-27 | 46-33 |
| T.12B-28 | 72-03 |
| T.12B-29 | 37-08 |
| T.12B-30 | 74-73 |
| T.12B-31 | 46-34 |
| T.12B-33 | 72-04 |
| T.12B-34 | 74-74 |
| T.12B-35 | 37-09 |
| T.12B-36 | 37-10 |
| T.12B-37 | 72-05 |
| T.12B-39 | 74-75 |
| TE.12B-40 | 79-93 |
| TE.12B-41 | 79-94 |
| T.12C-43 | 46-50 |
| T.12C-44 | 37-50 |
| T.12B-46 | 74-76 |
| T.12B-47 | 72-06 |
| T.12B-48 | 37-11 |
| T.12B-49 | 72-07 |
| T.12B-50 | 74-77 |
| T.12B-51 | 74-78 |
| T.12B-52 | 46-35 |
| T.12B-53 | 46-36 |
| T.12B-54 | 46-37 |
| T.12B-55 | 46-38 |
| T.12B-56 | 74-79 |
| T.12B-57 | 72-08 |
| T.12B-58 | 46-39 |
| T.12C-59 | 37-51 |
| T.12C-60 | 37-52 |
| T.12C-61 | 37-53 |
| T.12B-63 | 37-14 |
| T.12B-64 | 46-40 |
| T.12B-65 | 74-80 |
| T.12B-66 | 72-09 |
| T.12B-67 | 74-81 |
| T.12B-68 | 37-15 |
| T.12B-69 | 37-16 |
| T.12B-70 | 37-17 |
| T.12B-71 | 37-18 |
| TM.12D-72 | 408-01 |
| TM.12D-73 | 408-02 |
| TM.12D-74 | 54-11 |
| T.12D-75 | 403-07 |
| TR.12D-76 | 37-60 |
| TR.12D-77 | 37-61 |
| TR.12D-78 | 37-62 |
| TR.12D-79 | 37-63 |
| TR.12D-80 | 37-64 |
| TR.12D-81 | 37-65 |

**Cessna 560 Citation VI**

403 Esc, Getafe

| | |
|---|---|
| TR.20-01 | 403-11 |
| TR.20-02 | 403-12 |
| TR.20-03 | 403-13 |

**Dassault Falcon 20D/E/F**

Grupo 45, Torrejón;
408 Esc, Torrejón

| | | |
|---|---|---|
| T.11-1 | 20E | 45-02 |
| TM.11-2 | 20D | 45-03 |
| TM.11-3 | 20D | 408-11 |
| TM.11-4 | 20E | 408-12 |
| T.11-5 | 20F | 45-05 |

**Dassault Falcon 50**

Grupo 45, Torrejón

| | |
|---|---|
| T.16-1 | 45-20 |

**Dassault Falcon 900**

Grupo 45, Torrejón

| | |
|---|---|
| T.18-1 | 45-40 |
| T.18-2 | 45-41 |

**Eurofighter Typhoon**

CASA, Getafe
XCE.16-01

**Fokker F.27M Friendship 400MPA**

802 Esc, Gando, Las Palmas

| | |
|---|---|
| D.2-01 | 802-10 |
| D.2-02 | 802-11 |
| D.2-03 | 802-12 |

**Lockheed C-130H/C-130H-30/KC-130H Hercules**

311 Esc/312 Esc (Ala 31), Zaragoza

| | | |
|---|---|---|
| TL.10-01 | C-130H-30 | 31-01 |
| T.10-02 | C-130H | 31-02 |
| T.10-03 | C-130H | 31-03 |
| T.10-04 | C-130H | 31-04 |
| TK.10-5 | KC-130H | 31-50 |
| TK.10-6 | KC-130H | 31-51 |
| TK.10-7 | KC-130H | 31-52 |
| T.10-8 | C-130H | 31-05 |
| T.10-9 | C-130H | 31-06 |
| T.10-10 | C-130H | 31-07 |
| TK.10-11 | KC-130H | 31-53 |
| TK.10-12 | KC-130H | 31-54 |

**Lockheed P-3A/P-3B* Orion**

Grupo 22, Morón

| | |
|---|---|
| P.3-01 | 22-21 |
| P.3-03 | 22-22 |
| P.3-08 | 22-31* |
| P.3-09 | 22-32* |
| P.3-10 | 22-33* |
| P.3-11 | 22-34* |
| P.3-12 | 22-35* |

**McDonnell Douglas F-18 Hornet**

Ala 12, Torrejón;
Grupo 15, Zaragoza;
Grupo 21, Morón

**EF-18A/EF-18B* Hornet**

| | |
|---|---|
| CE.15-1 | 15-70* |
| CE.15-2 | 15-71* |
| CE.15-3 | 15-72* |
| CE.15-4 | 15-73* |
| CE.15-5 | 15-74* |
| CE.15-6 | 15-75* |
| CE.15-7 | 15-76* |
| CE.15-8 | 12-71* |
| CE.15-9 | 15-77* |
| CE.15-10 | 12-73* |
| CE.15-11 | 12-74* |
| CE.15-12 | 12-75* |
| C.15-13 | 12-01 |
| C.15-14 | 15-01 |
| C.15-15 | 15-02 |
| C.15-16 | 15-03 |
| C.15-18 | 15-05 |
| C.15-20 | 15-07 |
| C.15-21 | 15-08 |
| C.15-22 | 15-09 |
| C.15-23 | 15-10 |
| C.15-24 | 15-11 |
| C.15-25 | 15-12 |
| C.15-26 | 15-13 |
| C.15-27 | 15-14 |
| C.15-28 | 15-15 |
| C.15-29 | 15-16 |
| C.15-30 | 15-17 |
| C.15-31 | 15-18 |
| C.15-32 | 15-19 |
| C.15-33 | 15-20 |
| C.15-34 | 15-21 |
| C.15-35 | 15-22 |
| C.15-36 | 15-23 |
| C.15-37 | 15-24 |
| C.15-38 | 15-25 |
| C.15-39 | 15-26 |
| C.15-40 | 15-27 |
| C.15-41 | 15-28 |
| C.15-42 | 15-29 |
| C.15-43 | 15-30 |
| C.15-44 | 12-02 |
| C.15-45 | 12-03 |
| C.15-46 | 12-04 |
| C.15-47 | 15-31 |
| C.15-48 | 12-06 |
| C.15-49 | 12-07 |
| C.15-50 | 12-08 |
| C.15-51 | 12-09 |

| | |
|---|---|
| C.15-52 | 12-10 |
| C.15-53 | 12-11 |
| C.15-54 | 12-12 |
| C.15-55 | 12-13 |
| C.15-56 | 12-14 |
| C.15-57 | 12-15 |
| C.15-58 | 12-16 |
| C.15-59 | 12-17 |
| C.15-60 | 12-18 |
| C.15-61 | 12-19 |
| C.15-62 | 12-20 |
| C.15-63 | 15-32 |
| C.15-64 | 12-22 |
| C.15-65 | 12-23 |
| C.15-66 | 12-24 |
| C.15-67 | 15-33 |
| C.15-68 | 12-26 |
| C.15-69 | 12-27 |
| C.15-70 | 12-28 |
| C.15-72 | 12-30 |

**F/A-18A Hornet**

| | |
|---|---|
| C.15-73 | 21-01 |
| C.15-74 | 21-02 |
| C.15-75 | 21-03 |
| C.15-76 | 21-04 |
| C.15-77 | 21-05 |
| C.15-78 | 21-06 |
| C.15-79 | 21-07 |
| C.15-80 | 21-08 |
| C.15-81 | 21-09 |
| C.15-82 | 21-10 |
| C.15-83 | 21-11 |
| C.15-84 | 21-12 |
| C.15-85 | 21-13 |
| C.15-86 | 21-14 |
| C.15-87 | 21-15 |
| C.15-88 | 21-16 |
| C.15-89 | 21-17 |
| C.15-90 | 21-18 |
| C.15-91 | 21-19 |
| C.15-92 | 21-20 |
| C.15-93 | 21-21 |
| C.15-94 | 21-22 |
| C.15-95 | 21-23 |
| C.15-96 | 21-24 |

**Arma Aérea de l'Armada Española**

**BAe/McDonnell Douglas EAV-8B/EAV-8B+/ TAV-8B+ Harrier II**

Esc 009, Rota

**EAV-8B**

| | |
|---|---|
| VA.2-3 | 01-903 |
| VA.2-4 | 01-904 |
| VA.2-5 | 01-905 |
| VA.2-6 | 01-906 |
| VA.2-7 | 01-907 |
| VA.2-9 | 01-909 |
| VA.2-10 | 01-910 |
| VA.2-11 | 01-911 |
| VA.2-12 | 01-912 |

**EAV-8B+**

| | |
|---|---|
| VA.2-14 | 01-914 |
| VA.2-15 | 01-915 |
| VA.2-16 | 01-916 |
| VA.2-17 | 01-917 |
| VA.2-18 | 01-918 |
| VA.2-19 | 01-919 |
| VA.2-20 | 01-920 |
| VA.2-21 | 01-921 |
| VA.2-22 | 01-922 |

**TAV-8B+**

| | |
|---|---|
| VA.2-23 | 01-923 |

**Cessna 550 Citation 2**

Esc 004, Rota

| | |
|---|---|
| U.20-1 | 01-405 |
| U.20-2 | 01-406 |
| U.20-3 | 01-407 |

## SUDAN

**Silakh al Jawwiya as'Sudaniya**

**Lockheed C-130H Hercules**

1100
1101
1102
1103
1104
1105

## SWEDEN

**Svenska Flygvapnet**

**Aerospatiale AS.332M-1 Super Puma (Hkp.10)**

Flottiljer 7, Såtenäs;
Flottiljer 17, Ronneby/ Kallinge;
Flottiljer 21, Luleå/Kallax

| | | |
|---|---|---|
| 10401 | 91 | F7 |
| 10402 | 92 | F7 |
| 10403 | 93 | F21 |
| 10404 | 94 | F21 |
| 10405 | 95 | |
| 10406 | 96 | |
| 10407 | 97 | F17 |
| 10408 | 98 | |
| 10409 | 99 | F17 |
| 10410 | 90 | F17 |
| 10411 | 88 | F21 |
| 10412 | 89 | |

**Beechcraft Super King Air (Tp.101)**

Flottiljer 7, Såtenäs;
Flottiljer 17, Ronneby/ Kallinge;
Flottiljer 21, Luleå/Kallax

| | | |
|---|---|---|
| 101002 | 012 | F21 |
| 101003 | 013 | F17 |
| 101004 | 014 | F7 |

**Cessna 550 Citation 2 (Tp.103)**

Flottiljer 16, Uppsala

103001

**Grumman G.1159C Gulfstream 4 (Tp.102A/S.102B Korpen*)**

Flottiljer 16, Uppsala;
Flottiljer 16M, Malmslätt

| | | |
|---|---|---|
| 102001 | 021 | F16 |
| 102002* | 022 | F16M |
| 102003* | 023 | F16M |

**Lockheed C-130 Hercules (Tp.84)**

Flottiljer 7, Såtenäs

| | | |
|---|---|---|
| 84001 | 841 | C-130E |
| 84002 | 842 | C-130E |
| 84003 | 843 | C-130H |
| 84004 | 844 | C-130H |
| 84005 | 845 | C-130H |
| 84006 | 846 | C-130H |
| 84007 | 847 | C-130H |
| 84008 | 848 | C-130H |

**Rockwell Sabreliner-40 (Tp.86)**

FMV, Malmslätt

| | |
|---|---|
| 86001 | 861 |
| 86002 | 862 |

**SAAB JAS 39 Gripen**

Flottiljer 7, Såtenäs [G];
Flottiljer 10, Angelholm;
FMV, Malmslätt

**JAS 39 A**

| | | |
|---|---|---|
| 39-2 | 52 | FMV |
| 39-3 | 53 | FMV |
| 39-4 | 54 | SAAB |
| 39-5 | 55 | SAAB |
| 39101 | 51 | FMV |
| 39103 | 03 | F7 |
| 39104 | 04 | F7 |
| 39105 | 05 | F7 |
| 39106 | 06 | F7 |
| 39107 | 07 | F7 |
| 39108 | 08 | F7 |
| 39109 | 09 | F7 |
| 39110 | 10 | F7 |
| 39111 | 11 | F7 |
| 39112 | 12 | F7 |
| 39113 | 13 | F7 |
| 39114 | 14 | F7 |
| 39115 | 15 | F7 |
| 39116 | 16 | F7 |
| 39117 | 17 | F7 |
| 39118 | 18 | SAAB |
| 39119 | 19 | F7 |
| 39120 | 20 | F7 |
| 39121 | 21 | F7 |
| 39122 | 22 | F7 |
| 39123 | 23 | F7 |
| 39124 | 24 | F7 |
| 39125 | 25 | F7 |
| 39126 | 26 | F7 |
| 39127 | 27 | F7 |
| 39128 | 28 | F7 |
| 39129 | 29 | F7 |
| 39130 | 30 | F7 |
| 39131 | 31 | F7 |
| 39132 | 32 | F7 |
| 39133 | 33 | F7 |
| 39134 | 34 | F10 |
| 39135 | 35 | F7 |
| 39136 | 36 | F7 |
| 39137 | 37 | F7 |
| 39138 | 38 | F7 |
| 39139 | 39 | F7 |
| 39140 | 40 | F7 |
| 39141 | 41 | F7 |
| 39142 | 42 | F7 |
| 39143 | 43 | F10 |
| 39144 | 44 | F7 |
| 39145 | 45 | F7 |
| 39146 | 46 | F7 |
| 39147 | 47 | F7 |
| 39148 | 48 | F7 |
| 39149 | 49 | F7 |
| 39150 | 50 | F7 |
| 39151 | 51 | F7 |
| 39152 | 52 | F7 |
| 39153 | 53 | F7 |
| 39154 | 54 | F7 |
| 39155 | 55 | F7 |
| 39157 | 57 | F7 |
| 39158 | 58 | F7 |

39159
39160
39161 61 F7
39162 62 F7
39163 63 F7
39164 64 F10
39165 65 F10
39166 66 F7
39167 67 F10
39168 168 F10
39169 169 F10
39170 170 F-10
39171 171 F-10
39172

**JAS 39 B**

39800 58 FMV
39801 70 F7
39802 802 FMV
39803 72 F7
39804 73 F7
39805 74 F7
39806 74 F7
39807 74 F7

**SAAB SF.340B (Tp.100A)/ SF.340AEW&C (S.100B) Argus***

Flottiljer 16M, Malmslätt

100001 001
100002* 002
100003* 003
100004* 004
100005* 005
100006* 006
100007* 007

**Marine Flygtjänst**

**Vertol 107-II-15 (Hkp.4B)**

11 Hkp Div, Berga

04061 61
04063 63
04064 64

**Kawasaki-Vertol KV.107-II-16 (Hkp.4C)**

11 Hkp Div, Berga;
12 Hkp Div, Säve;
13 Hkp Div, Ronneby/ Kallinge;
FMV, Malmslätt

04065 65 12 Hkp Div
04067 67 12 Hkp Div
04068 68 12 Hkp Div
04069 69 11 Hkp Div
04070 70 11 Hkp Div
04071 71 12 Hkp Div
04072 72 FMV

**Vertol 107-II-15 (Hkp.4A)**

11 Hkp Div, Berga;
12 Hkp Div, Säve;
13 Hkp Div, Ronneby/ Kallinge;

04073 73 11 Hkp Div
04074 74 13 Hkp Div
04075 75 13 Hkp Div
04076 76 13 Hkp Div

**Armen**

**Agusta-Bell AB.412 (Hkp.11)**

Armeflyget 1 (AF1), Boden

11331 31
11332 32
11333 33
11334 34
11335 35
11336 36
11337 37
11338 38
11339 39
11340 40
11341 41
11342 42

**MBB Bo.105CB (Hkp.9B)**

Armeflyget 1 (AF1), Boden;
Armeflyget 2 (AF2), Malmslätt;
FMV, Malmslätt

09201 01 AF2
09202 02 AF1
09203 03 AF2
09204 04 AF2
09205 05 AF1
09206 06 AF1
09207 07 AF1
09208 08 AF1
09209 09 AF2
09210 10 AF1
09211 11 AF1
09212 12 AF1
09213 13 AF2
09214 14 AF2
09215 15 AF2
09216 16 AF2
09217 17 AF2
09218 18 AF1
09219 19 AF1
09220 20 AF2
09221 90 FMV

## SWITZERLAND

**Schweizerische Flugwaffe**

(Most aircraft are pooled centrally. Some carry unit badges but these rarely indicate actual operators.)

**Aérospatiale AS.532 Super Puma**

Leichte Flieger Staffel 5 (LtSt 5), Interlaken;
Leichte Flieger Staffel 6 (LtSt 6), Alpnach;
Leichte Flieger Staffel 8 (LtSt 8), Ulrichen
Detachments at Alpnach, Emmen, Meiringen, Payerne & Sion

T-311
T-312
T-313
T-314
T-315
T-316
T-317
T-318
T-319
T-320
T-321
T-322
T-323
T-324
T-325

**Beechcraft Super King Air 350C**

Flugswaffenbrigade 31, Dübendorf

HB-GII

**Dassault Falcon 50**

VIP Flight, Dübendorf

T-783

**Dassault Mirage III**

Flieger Staffel 3 (FlSt 3), Sion;
Flieger Staffel 4 (FlSt 4), Payerne;
Flieger Staffel 10 (FlSt 10), Buochs;
Gruppe fur Rustunggdienste (GRD), Emmen;
Instrumentation Flieger Staffel 14 (InstruFlSt 14), Payerne

**Mirage IIIBS**

J-2001 InstruFlSt 14

**Mirage IIIUDS**

J-2011 InstruFlSt 14
J-2012 InstruFlSt 14

**Mirage IIIRS**

R-2102
R-2103
R-2104
R-2105
R-2106
R-2107
R-2108
R-2109
R-2110
R-2111
R-2112
R-2113
R-2114
R-2115
R-2116
R-2117
R-2118

**Mirage IIIBS**

U-2004 InstruFlSt 14

**Gates Learjet 35A**

VIP Flight, Dübendorf

T-781

**McDonnell Douglas F/A-18 Hornet**

Flieger Staffel 11 (FlSt 11), Meiringen;
Flieger Staffel 17 (FlSt 17), Payerne;
Flieger Staffel 18 (FlSt 18), Payerne

**F/A-18C**

J-5001
J-5002
J-5003
J-5004
J-5005
J-5006
J-5007
J-5008
J-5009
J-5010
J-5011
J-5012
J-5013

J-5014
J-5015
J-5016
J-5017
J-5018
J-5019
J-5020
J-5021
J-5022
J-5023
J-5024
J-5025
J-5026

**F/A-18D**

J-5232
J-5233
J-5234
J-5235
J-5236
J-5237
J-5238

**Northrop F-5 Tiger II**

Flieger Staffel 1 (FlSt 1), Turtman;
Flieger Staffel 6 (FlSt 6), Sion;
Flieger Staffel 8 (FlSt 8), Meiringen;
Flieger Staffel 11 (FlSt 11), Meiringen;
Flieger Staffel 13 (FlSt 13), Meiringen;
Flieger Staffel 18 (FlSt 18), Payerne;
Flieger Staffel 19 (FlSt 19), Mollis;
Gruppe fur Rustunggdienste (GRD), Emmen;
Instrumentation Flieger Staffel 14 (InstruFlSt 14), Dübendorf;
Patrouille Suisse, Emmen (P. Suisse)

**F-5E**

J-3001
J-3002
J-3003
J-3004
J-3005
J-3006
J-3007
J-3008 InstruFlSt 14
J-3009
J-3010
J-3011
J-3012
J-3014
J-3015
J-3016
J-3019
J-3020
J-3021
J-3022
J-3023
J-3024
J-3025
J-3026
J-3027
J-3029
J-3030
J-3031
J-3032
J-3033
J-3034
J-3035
J-3036
J-3037
J-3038
J-3039
J-3040
J-3041
J-3043
J-3044
J-3045
J-3046
J-3047
J-3049
J-3050
J-3051
J-3052
J-3053
J-3054
J-3055
J-3056
J-3057
J-3058
J-3060
J-3061
J-3062
J-3063
J-3064
J-3065
J-3066
J-3067
J-3068
J-3069
J-3070
J-3072
J-3073
J-3074
J-3075
J-3076
J-3077
J-3079
J-3080
J-3081 P. Suisse
J-3082
J-3083 P. Suisse
J-3084 P. Suisse [4]
J-3085 P. Suisse [3]
J-3086 P. Suisse [6]
J-3087 P. Suisse
J-3088 P. Suisse [5]
J-3089
J-3090 P. Suisse [2]
J-3091 P. Suisse [1]
J-3092
J-3093
J-3094
J-3095
J-3096
J-3097 GRD
J-3098

**F-5F**

J-3201
J-3202
J-3203
J-3204 GRD
J-3205
J-3206
J-3207
J-3208
J-3209
J-3210
J-3211
J-3212

## SYRIA

**Tupolev Tu-134A**

Govt of Syria, Damascus
YK-AYA

## TURKEY

**Türk Hava Kuvvetleri**

**Boeing KC-135R Stratotanker**

101 Filo, Incirlik
00325
00326
23539
23563
23567
72609
80110

**Cessna 650 Citation VII**

224 Filo, Ankara/Etimesğut
93-7024 ETI-024
93-7026 ETI-026

**Grumman G.1159C Gulfstream 4**

224 Filo, Ankara/Etimesğut
003

**Lockheed C-130B Hercules**

222 Filo, Erkilet
3496 (23496)
10960
10963
70527
80736
91527

**Lockheed C-130E Hercules**

222 Filo, Erkilet
00991
01468 12-468
01947
13186 12-186
13187 12-187
13188
13189

**Transall C-160D**

221 Filo, Erkilet
019
020
021
022
023
024
025 12-025
026
027
69-028 12-028
029
031
032
033
034
035
036
037 12-037
038
039
040 12-040

**TUSAS-GD F-16C/F-16D***
**Fighting Falcon**
4 AJÜ, Mürted:
141 Filo & Öncel Filo;
5 AJÜ, Merzifon:
151 Filo & 152 Filo;
6 AJÜ, Bandirma:
161 Filo & 162 Filo;
8 AJÜ, Diyarbakir:
181 Filo & 182 Filo;
9 AJÜ, Balikesir:
191 Filo & 192 Filo

| | |
|---|---|
| 86-0066 | Öncel Filo |
| 86-0068 | Öncel Filo |
| 86-0069 | Öncel Filo |
| 86-0070 | Öncel Filo |
| 86-0071 | Öncel Filo |
| 86-0072 | Öncel Filo |
| 86-0191* | Öncel Filo |
| 86-0192* | Öncel Filo |
| 86-0193* | Öncel Filo |
| 86-0194* | Öncel Filo |
| 86-0195* | Öncel Filo |
| 86-0196* | Öncel Filo |
| 87-0002* | Öncel Filo |
| 87-0003* | Öncel Filo |
| 87-0009 | Öncel Filo |
| 87-0010 | Öncel Filo |
| 87-0011 | Öncel Filo |
| 87-0013 | Öncel Filo |
| 87-0014 | Öncel Filo |
| 87-0015 | Öncel Filo |
| 87-0016 | Öncel Filo |
| 87-0017 | Öncel Filo |
| 87-0018 | Öncel Filo |
| 87-0019 | Öncel Filo |
| 87-0020 | Öncel Filo |
| 87-0021 | Öncel Filo |
| 88-0013* | Öncel Filo |
| 88-0014* | 141 Filo |
| 88-0015* | 141 Filo |
| 88-0019 | Öncel Filo |
| 88-0020 | Öncel Filo |
| 88-0021 | Öncel Filo |
| 88-0024 | Öncel Filo |
| 88-0025 | 141 Filo |
| 88-0026 | Öncel Filo |
| 88-0027 | Öncel Filo |
| 88-0028 | 191 Filo |
| 88-0029 | Öncel Filo |
| 88-0030 | 191 Filo |
| 88-0031 | Öncel Filo |
| 88-0032 | Öncel Filo |
| 88-0033 | 141 Filo |
| 88-0034 | 141 Filo |
| 88-0035 | 141 Filo |
| 88-0036 | 141 Filo |
| 88-0037 | 141 Filo |
| 89-0022 | 141 Filo |
| 89-0023 | 141 Filo |
| 89-0024 | 141 Filo |
| 89-0025 | 141 Filo |
| 89-0026 | 141 Filo |
| 89-0027 | 141 Filo |
| 89-0028 | 141 Filo |
| 89-0030 | 141 Filo |
| 89-0031 | 141 Filo |
| 89-0032 | 141 Filo |
| 89-0034 | 162 Filo |
| 89-0035 | 162 Filo |
| 89-0036 | 162 Filo |
| 89-0037 | 162 Filo |
| 89-0038 | 162 Filo |
| 89-0039 | 162 Filo |
| 89-0040 | 162 Filo |
| 89-0041 | 162 Filo |
| 89-0042* | 141 Filo |
| 89-0043* | 162 Filo |
| 89-0044* | 162 Filo |
| 89-0045* | 141 Filo |
| 90-0001 | 162 Filo |
| 90-0004 | 162 Filo |
| 90-0005 | 162 Filo |
| 90-0006 | 162 Filo |
| 90-0007 | 162 Filo |
| 90-0008 | 162 Filo |
| 90-0009 | 162 Filo |
| 90-0010 | 162 Filo |
| 90-0011 | 162 Filo |
| 90-0012 | 161 Filo |
| 90-0013 | 161 Filo |
| 90-0014 | 161 Filo |
| 90-0015 | 161 Filo |
| 90-0016 | 161 Filo |
| 90-0017 | 161 Filo |
| 90-0018 | 161 Filo |
| 90-0019 | 161 Filo |
| 90-0020 | 162 Filo |
| 90-0021 | 161 Filo |
| 90-0022* | 161 Filo |
| 90-0023* | 161 Filo |
| 90-0024* | 161 Filo |
| 91-0001 | 161 Filo |
| 91-0002 | 161 Filo |
| 91-0003 | 161 Filo |
| 91-0004 | 161 Filo |
| 91-0005 | 162 Filo |
| 91-0006 | 161 Filo |
| 91-0007 | 161 Filo |
| 91-0008 | 141 Filo |
| 91-0010 | 141 Filo |
| 91-0011 | 141 Filo |
| 91-0012 | 141 Filo |
| 91-0013 | 192 Filo |
| 91-0014 | 141 Filo |
| 91-0015 | 192 Filo |
| 91-0016 | 192 Filo |
| 91-0017 | 182 Filo |
| 91-0018 | 182 Filo |
| 91-0019 | 192 Filo |
| 91-0020 | 182 Filo |
| 91-0022* | 141 Filo |
| 91-0024* | 141 Filo |
| 92-0001 | 191 Filo |
| 92-0002 | 192 Filo |
| 92-0003 | 182 Filo |
| 92-0004 | 191 Filo |
| 92-0005 | 182 Filo |
| 92-0006 | 182 Filo |
| 92-0007 | 182 Filo |
| 92-0008 | 182 Filo |
| 92-0009 | 191 Filo |
| 92-0010 | |
| 92-0011 | 182 Filo |
| 92-0012 | 191 Filo |
| 92-0013 | 191 Filo |
| 92-0014 | 191 Filo |
| 92-0015 | 182 Filo |
| 92-0016 | 191 Filo |
| 92-0017 | 191 Filo |
| 92-0018 | 191 Filo |
| 92-0019 | |
| 92-0020 | |
| 92-0021 | 181 Filo |
| 92-0022* | 181 Filo |
| 92-0023* | 191 Filo |
| 92-0024* | 161 Filo |
| 93-0001 | 181 Filo |
| 93-0002 | 181 Filo |
| 93-0003 | 181 Filo |
| 93-0004 | 181 Filo |
| 93-0005 | 181 Filo |
| 93-0006 | 181 Filo |
| 93-0007 | |
| 93-0008 | 181 Filo |
| 93-0009 | 182 Filo |
| 93-0010 | 181 Filo |
| 93-0011 | 182 Filo |
| 93-0012 | 181 Filo |
| 93-0013 | 182 Filo |
| 93-0014 | 181 Filo |
| 93-0657 | 141 Filo |
| 93-0658 | |
| 93-0659 | |
| 93-0660 | 152 Filo |
| 93-0661 | |
| 93-0662 | |
| 93-0663 | |
| 93-0664 | |
| 93-0665 | |
| 93-0666 | |
| 93-0667 | |
| 93-0668 | |
| 93-0669 | 152 Filo |
| 93-0670 | |
| 93-0671 | |
| 93-0672 | 152 Filo |
| 93-0673 | Öncel Filo |
| 93-0674 | 192 Filo |
| 93-0675 | 192 Filo |
| 93-0676 | 192 Filo |
| 93-0677 | 192 Filo |
| 93-0678 | 192 Filo |
| 93-0679 | 192 Filo |
| 93-0680 | 192 Filo |
| 93-0681 | |
| 93-0682 | |
| 93-0683 | 192 Filo |
| 93-0684 | 192 Filo |
| 93-0685 | |
| 93-0686 | 192 Filo |
| 93-0687 | Öncel Filo |
| 93-0688 | Öncel Filo |
| 93-0689 | Öncel Filo |
| 93-0690 | 192 Filo |
| 93-0691* | |
| 93-0692* | 152 Filo |
| 93-0693* | Öncel Filo |
| 93-0694* | |
| 93-0695* | 192 Filo |
| 93-0696* | Öncel Filo |
| 94-0071 | 192 Filo |
| 94-0072 | 192 Filo |
| 94-0073 | |
| 94-0074 | |
| 94-0075 | |
| 94-0076 | |
| 94-0077 | |
| 94-0078 | |
| 94-0079 | |
| 94-0080 | |
| 94-0081 | |
| 94-0082 | |
| 94-0083 | |
| 94-0084 | |
| 94-0085 | |
| 94-0086 | |
| 94-0087 | |
| 94-0088 | |
| 94-0089 | |
| 94-0090 | |
| 94-0091 | |

94-0092
94-0093
94-0094 Öncel Filo
94-0095
94-0096
94-0105* 191 Filo
94-0106* 191 Filo
94-0107* Öncel Filo
94-0108*
94-0109*
94-0110*
94-1557*
94-1558* Öncel Filo
94-1559*
94-1560*
94-1561*
94-1562*
94-1563*
94-1564*

**Turkish Govt**
**Grumman**
**G.1159C Gulfstream IV**
Govt of Turkey, Istanbul
TC-ATA
TC-GAP

**TURKMENISTAN**
**BAe 1000B**
Govt of Turkmenistan, Ashkhabad
EZ-B021

**UGANDA**
**Grumman**
**G.1159A Gulfstream III**
Govt of Uganda, Entebbe
5X-UOI

**UKRAINE**
**Ukrainian Air Force**
**Ilyushin Il-76MD**
321 TAP, Uzin
UR-76413
UR-76537
UR-76624
UR-76677
UR-76687
UR-76697
UR-78820

**UNITED ARAB EMIRATES**
**United Arab Emirates Air Force**
*Abu Dhabi*
**Lockheed C-130H Hercules**
1211
1212
1213
1214

*Dubai*
**Lockheed L.100-30 Hercules**
311
312

**UAE Govt**
**Airbus A.300B4-620**
Govt of Abu Dhabi
A6-PFD
A6-SHZ

**Boeing 737-2W8**
Govt of Sharjah
A6-ESH

**Boeing 737-7F0**
Govt of Dubai
A6-HRJ

**Boeing**
**747SP-31/ 747SP-Z5***
Govt of Dubai
A6-SMM
A6-SMR
A6-ZSN*

**Dassault Falcon 900**
Govt of Abu Dhabi
A6-AUH
A6-UAE
A6-ZKM

**Grumman**
**G.1159C Gulfstream IV**
Dubai Air Wing
A6-HHH

**YUGOSLAVIA**
**Dassault Falcon 50**
Govt of Yugoslavia, Belgrade
YU-BNA (72102)
YU-BPZ (72101)

**Gates**
**LearJet 25B/**
**LearJet 25D***
Govt of Yugoslavia, Belgrade
YU-BJG
YU-BKR*

Colourful Alpha Jet E of 7/11 Sm at Bevekom, was the Belgium Air Force solo display aircraft in 1999.
*PRM*

French Air Force Dassault Mirage 2000C No 18 of EC02.005 *Ile de France* based at Orange. *PRM*

A German Army CH-53G operated by HFR-15 from Rheine-Benklage. *PRM*

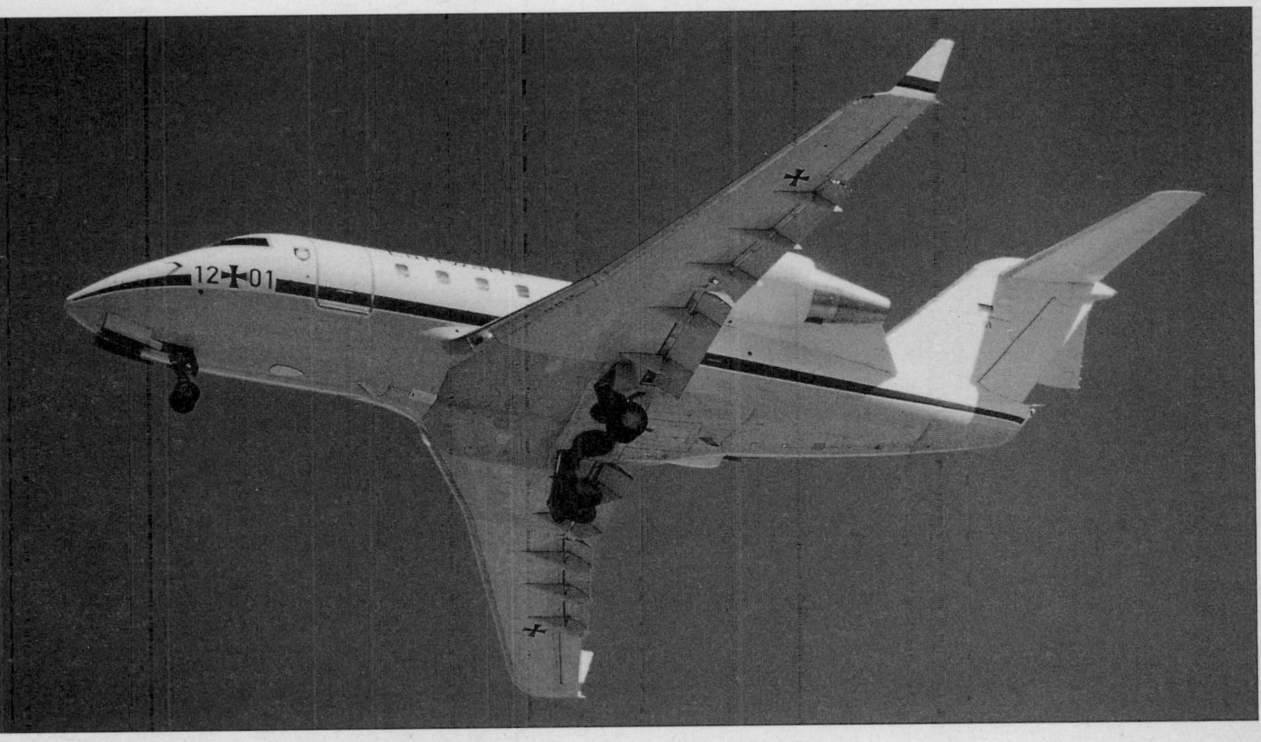


German Air Force VIP CL601-1A Challenger of 1/FBS at Köln-Bonn. *PRM*

With extra aerials and equipment this Israeli Boeing EC-707 255 is operated by 120 Squadron at Tel Aviv for ELINT duties. *PRM*

Piaggio P-180AM Avanti MM62162 used by the Italian Air Force as a VIP transport. *Daniel. March*

# US Military Aircraft Markings

All USAF aircraft have been allocated a fiscal year (FY) number since 1921. Individual aircraft are given a serial according to the fiscal year in which they are ordered. The numbers commence at 0001 and are prefixed with the year of allocation. For example F-15C Eagle 84-001 (84-0001) was the first aircraft ordered in 1984. The fiscal year (FY) serial is carried on the technical data block which is usually stencilled on the left-hand side of the aircraft just below the cockpit. The number displayed on the fin is a corruption of the FY serial. Most tactical aircraft carry the fiscal year in small figures followed by the last three or four digits of the serial in large figures. For example Aviano-based F-16C Fighting Falcon 89-2009 carries 89-009/AV on its tail. Large transport and tanker aircraft such as C-130s and KC-135s sometimes display a five-figure number commencing with the last digit of the appropriate fiscal year and four figures of the production number. An example of this is KC-135R 58-0128 which displays 80128 on its fin.

USN serials follow a straightforward numerical sequence which commenced, for the present series, with the allocation of 00001 to an SB2C Helldiver by the Bureau of Aeronautics in 1940. Numbers in the 165000 series are presently being issued. They are usually carried in full on the rear fuselage of the aircraft.

# UK-based USAF Aircraft

The following aircraft are normally based in the UK. They are listed in numerical order of type with individual aircraft in serial number order, as depicted on the aircraft. The number in brackets is either the alternative presentation of the five-figure number commencing with the last digit of the fiscal year, or the fiscal year where a five-figure serial is presented on the aircraft. Where it is possible to identify the allocation of aircraft to individual squadrons by means of colours carried on fin or cockpit edge, this is also provided.

| *Notes* | *Type* |
|---|---|
| | **McDonnell Douglas F-15C Eagle/ F-15D Eagle/F-15E Strike Eagle** |
| | **LN**: 48th FW, RAF Lakenheath: |
| | 492nd FS *bl*ue/white |
| | 493rd FS black/*y*ellow |
| | 494th FS *r*ed/white |
| | 84-0001 (84-0001) F-15C *y* |
| | 84-0009 (84-0009) F-15C *y* |
| | 84-0010 (84-0010) F-15C *y* |
| | 84-0014 (84-0014) F-15C *y* |
| | 84-0015 (84-0015) F-15C *y* |
| | 84-0019 (84-0019) F-15C *y* |
| | 84-0044 (84-0044) F-15D *y* |
| | 86-0147 (86-0147) F-15C *y* |
| | 86-0154 (86-0154) F-15C *y* |
| | 86-0156 (86-0156) F-15C *y* |
| | 86-0159 (86-0159) F-15C *y* |
| | 86-0160 (86-0160) F-15C *y* |
| | 86-0163 (86-0163) F-15C *y* |
| | 86-0164 (86-0164) F-15C *y* [493rd FS] |
| | 86-0165 (86-0165) F-15C *y* |
| | 86-0166 (86-0166) F-15C *y* |
| | 86-0167 (86-0167) F-15C *y* |
| | 86-0169 (86-0169) F-15C *y* |
| | 86-0171 (86-0171) F-15C *y* |
| | 86-0172 (86-0172) F-15C *y* |
| | 86-0173 (86-0173) F-15C *y* |
| | 86-0174 (86-0174) F-15C *y* |
| | 86-0175 (86-0175) F-15C *y* |
| | 86-0176 (86-0176) F-15C *y* |
| | 86-0178 (86-0178) F-15C *y* |
| | 86-0180 (86-0180) F-15C *y* [48th OG] |
| | 86-0182 (86-0182) F-15D *y* |
| | 90-0248 (90-0248) F-15E *m* [48th FW] |
| | 90-0255 (90-0255) F-15E *bl* |
| | 90-0257 (90-0257) F-15E *bl* |
| | 90-0259 (90-0259) F-15E *bl* |
| | 90-0262 (90-0262) F-15E *bl* [48th OG] |
| | 91-0300 (91-0300) F-15E *bl* |
| | 91-0301 (91-0301) F-15E *bl* |
| | 91-0302 (91-0302) F-15E *bl* |
| | 91-0303 (91-0303) F-15E *bl* |
| | 91-0304 (91-0304) F-15E *bl* |
| | 91-0305 (91-0305) F-15E *bl* |
| | 91-0306 (91-0306) F-15E *r* |
| | 91-0307 (91-0307) F-15E *bl* |
| | 91-0308 (91-0308) F-15E *bl* |
| | 91-0309 (91-0309) F-15E *bl* |
| | 91-0310 (91-0310) F-15E *bl* |
| | 91-0311 (91-0311) F-15E *bl* |
| | 91-0312 (91-0312) F-15E *bl* |
| | 91-0313 (91-0313) F-15E *m* [3rd AF] |
| | 91-0314 (91-0314) F-15E *r* [494th FS] |
| | 91-0315 (91-0315) F-15E *r* |
| | 91-0316 (91-0316) F-15E *r* |
| | 91-0317 (91-0317) F-15E *r* |
| | 91-0318 (91-0318) F-15E *r* |
| | 91-0319 (91-0319) F-15E *r* |

| Type | Notes |
|---|---|
| 91-0320 (91-0320) F-15E *r* | |
| 91-0321 (91-0321) F-15E *r* | |
| 91-0322 (91-0322) F-15E *r* | |
| 91-0323 (91-0323) F-15E *r* | |
| 91-0324 (91-0324) F-15E *r* | |
| 91-0325 (91-0325) F-15E *bl* | |
| 91-0326 (91-0326) F-15E *bl* | |
| 91-0328 (91-0328) F-15E *r* | |
| 91-0329 (91-0329) F-15E *bl* | |
| 91-0330 (91-0330) F-15E *r* | |
| 91-0331 (91-0331) F-15E *r* | |
| 91-0332 (91-0332) F-15E *bl* | |
| 91-0333 (91-0333) F-15E *r* | |
| 91-0334 (91-0334) F-15E *r* | |
| 91-0335 (91-0335) F-15E *r* | |
| 91-0601 (91-0601) F-15E *r* | |
| 91-0602 (91-0602) F-15E *r* | |
| 91-0603 (91-0603) F-15E *r* | |
| 91-0604 (91-0604) F-15E *r* | |
| 91-0605 (91-0605) F-15E *r* | |
| 92-0364 (92-0364) F-15E *r* | |
| 96-0201 (96-0201) F-15E *bl* | |
| 96-0202 (96-0202) F-15E *bl* | |
| 96-0203 (96-0203) F-15E *bl* | |
| 96-0204 (96-0204) F-15E *bl* | |
| 96-0205 (96-0205) F-15E *bl* | |
| 97-0217 (97-0217) F-15E *bl* | |
| 97-0218 (97-0218) F-15E *m* [48th FW] | |
| 97-0219 (97-0219) F-15E | |
| 97-0220 (97-0220) F-15E *bl* | |
| 97-0221 (97-0221) F-15E *bl* | |

**Sikorsky MH-53J/MH-53M***
21st SOS/352nd SOG,
RAF Mildenhall

| Type | Notes |
|---|---|
| 01630 (FY70)* | |
| 14994 (FY67)* | |
| 31648 (FY73) | |
| 31649 (FY73)* | |
| 31652 (FY73)* | |
| 95795 (FY69)* | |
| 95796 (FY69)* | |

**Lockheed C-130 Hercules**
352nd SOG, RAF Mildenhall:
7th SOS* & 67th SOS,

| Type | Notes |
|---|---|
| 37814 (FY63) C-130E | |
| 40476 (FY84) MC-130H* | |
| 61699 (FY86) MC-130H* | |
| 70023 (FY87) MC-130H* | |
| 80193 (FY88) MC-130H* | |
| 80194 (FY88) MC-130H* | |
| 95820 (FY69) MC-130P | |
| 95823 (FY69) MC-130P | |
| 95826 (FY69) MC-130P | |
| 95828 (FY69) MC-130P | |
| 95831 (FY69) MC-130P | |

**Boeing KC-135R Stratotanker**
351st ARS/100th ARW,
RAF Mildenhall [D] (*r/w/bl*)

| Type | Notes |
|---|---|
| 10267 (FY61) | |
| 10284 (FY61) | |
| 10288 (FY61) | |
| 10312 (FY61) | |
| 23498 (FY62) | |
| 23517 (FY62) | |
| 23528 (FY62) | |
| 23533 (FY62) | |
| 23538 (FY62) | |
| 23561 (FY62) | |
| 23564 (FY62) | |
| 23578 (FY62) | |
| 37979 (FY63) | |
| 38017 (FY63) | |
| 71474 (FY57) | |

# UK-based US Navy Aircraft

**Beech UC-12M Super King Air**
Naval Air Facility, Mildenhall [8G]
3840 (163840)
3843 (163843)

# European-based USAF Aircraft

These aircraft are normally based in Western Europe with the USAFE. They are shown in numerical order of type designation, with individual aircraft in serial number order as carried on the aircraft. An alternative five-figure presentation of the serial is shown in brackets where appropriate. Fiscal year (FY) details are also provided if necessary. The unit allocation and operating bases are given for most aircraft.

*Notes* *Type*

**Lockheed U-2S**
OL-FR/9th RW, Istres, France [BB]
01081 (FY80)
01082 (FY80)
01083 (FY80)

**McDonnell Douglas**
**C-9A Nightingale**
86th AW, Ramstein, Germany:
75th AS & 76th AS[1];
Det 1, 86th OG/SHAPE, Chievres, Belgium[2]
*FY71*
10876[2] (VIP)
10879
10880[1] (VIP)
10881
10882
*FY67*
22585

**Fairchild**
**A-10A Thunderbolt II**
**SP:** 52nd FW, Spangdahlem, Germany:
81st FS *black*

| | | | |
|---|---|---|---|
| 81-951 | (81-0951) | *bk* | |
| 81-952 | (81-0952) | *m* | [52nd FW] |
| 81-954 | (81-0954) | *bk* | |
| 81-956 | (81-0956) | *bk* | |
| 81-962 | (81-0962) | *bk* | |
| 81-963 | (81-0963) | *bk* | |
| 81-966 | (81-0966) | *bk* | |
| 81-976 | (81-0976) | *bk* | |
| 81-978 | (81-0978) | *bk* | |
| 81-980 | (81-0980) | *bk* | |
| 81-983 | (81-0983) | *bk* | |
| 81-984 | (81-0984) | *bk* | |
| 81-985 | (81-0985) | *bk* | |
| 81-988 | (81-0988) | *bk* | |
| 81-991 | (81-0991) | *bk* | |
| 81-992 | (81-0992) | *bk* | |
| 82-649 | (82-0649) | *bk* | |
| 82-650 | (82-0650) | *bk* | |
| 82-654 | (82-0654) | *bk* | |
| 82-655 | (82-0655) | *bk* | [81st FS] |
| 82-656 | (82-0656) | *bk* | |

**Beech C-12C/C-12D/C-12F**
JUSMG, Ankara, Turkey;
US Embassy Flight, Athens, Greece;
US Embassy Flight, Budapest, Hungary

| | | |
|---|---|---|
| *FY83* | | |
| 30495 | C-12D | Budapest |
| *FY73* | | |
| 31206 | C-12C | Ankara |
| 31216 | C-12C | Ankara |
| 31218 | C-12C | Athens |
| *FY76* | | |
| 60171 | C-12C | Ankara |
| 60173 | C-12C | Ankara |

**Lockheed Martin (GD) F-16C/F-16D***
**AV:** 31st FW, Aviano, Italy:
510th FS *pu*rple/white
555th FS *gree*n/yellow
**SP:** 52nd FW, Spangdahlem, Germany:
22nd FS *r*ed/white
23rd FS *bl*ue/white

| | | | |
|---|---|---|---|
| 87-350 | (87-0350) | AV *gn* | |
| 87-351 | (87-0351) | AV *gn* | |
| 87-355 | (87-0355) | AV *pr* | |
| 87-359 | (87-0359) | AV *gn* | |
| 88-413 | (88-0413) | AV *pr* | [510th FS] |
| 88-425 | (88-0425) | AV *gn* | |
| 88-435 | (88-0435) | AV *gn* | |
| 88-443 | (88-0443) | AV *pr* | |
| 88-444 | (88-0444) | AV *pr* | |
| 88-446 | (88-0446) | AV *pr* | |
| 88-491 | (88-0491) | AV *pr* | |
| 88-525 | (88-0525) | AV *pr* | |
| 88-526 | (88-0526) | AV *gn* | |
| 88-529 | (88-0529) | AV *pr* | |
| 88-532 | (88-0532) | AV *gn* | [31st OG] |
| 88-535 | (88-0535) | AV *gn* | |
| 88-541 | (88-0541) | AV *pr* | |
| 89-001 | (89-2001) | AV *m* | [31st FW] |
| 89-009 | (89-2009) | AV *pr* | |
| 89-011 | (89-2011) | AV *pr* | |
| 89-016 | (89-2016) | AV *gn* | [16th AF] |
| 89-018 | (89-2018) | AV *gn* | |
| 89-023 | (89-2023) | AV *gn* | |
| 89-024 | (89-2024) | AV *gn* | |
| 89-026 | (89-2026) | AV *pr* | |
| 89-029 | (89-2029) | AV *pr* | |
| 89-030 | (89-2030) | AV *pr* | |
| 89-035 | (89-2035) | AV *gn* | [555th FS] |
| 89-038 | (89-2038) | AV *gn* | |
| 89-039 | (89-2039) | AV *gn* | |
| 89-044 | (89-2044) | AV *gn* | |
| 89-046 | (89-2046) | AV *pr* | |
| 89-047 | (89-2047) | AV *pr* | |
| 89-049 | (89-2049) | AV *pr* | |
| 89-050 | (89-2050) | AV *pr* | |
| 89-057 | (89-2057) | AV *gn* | |
| 89-137 | (89-2137) | AV *pr* | |
| 89-178 | (89-2178)* | AV *pr* | |
| 90-709 | (90-0709) | AV *pr* | |
| 90-795 | (90-0795)* | AV *gn* | |
| 90-796 | (90-0796)* | AV *pr* | |
| 90-800 | (90-0800)* | AV *gn* | |
| 90-813 | (90-0813) | SP *r* | |
| 90-818 | (90-0818) | SP *r* | |
| 90-827 | (90-0827) | SP *r* | |
| 90-828 | (90-0828) | SP *r* | |
| 90-829 | (90-0829) | SP *r* | [22nd FS] |

| Type | Notes |
|---|---|
| 90-831 (90-0831) SP *r* | |
| 90-833 (90-0833) SP *r* | |
| 90-843 (90-0843)* SP *r* | |
| 90-846 (90-0846)* SP *bl* | |
| 91-336 (91-0336) SP *r* | |
| 91-337 (91-0337) SP *r* | |
| 91-338 (91-0338) SP *r* | |
| 91-339 (91-0339) SP *r* [22nd FS] | |
| 91-340 (91-0340) SP *r* | |
| 91-341 (91-0341) SP *r* | |
| 91-342 (91-0342) SP *r* | |
| 91-343 (91-0343) SP *r* | |
| 91-344 (91-0344) SP *r* | |
| 91-351 (91-0351) SP *r* | |
| 91-352 (91-0352) SP *m* [52nd FW] | |
| 91-402 (91-0402) SP *bl* | |
| 91-403 (91-0403) SP *bl* [23rd FS] | |
| 91-405 (91-0405) SP *bl* | |
| 91-406 (91-0406) SP *bl* [23rd FS] | |
| 91-407 (91-0407) SP *bl* | |
| 91-408 (91-0408) SP *bl* | |
| 91-409 (91-0409) SP *bl* | |
| 91-410 (91-0410) SP *bl* | |
| 91-412 (91-0412) SP *bl* | |
| 91-414 (91-0414) SP *bl* | |
| 91-415 (91-0415) SP *bl* | |
| 91-416 (91-0416) SP *bl* | |
| 91-417 (91-0417) SP *bl* | |
| 91-418 (91-0418) SP *bl* | |
| 91-419 (91-0419) SP *bl* | |
| 91-420 (91-0420) SP *bl* | |
| 91-421 (91-0421) SP *bl* | |
| 91-464 (91-0464)* SP *r* | |
| 91-472 (91-0472)* SP *bl* | |
| 91-474 (91-0474)* SP *bl* | |
| 92-915 (92-3915) SP *bl* | |
| 92-918 (92-3918) SP *r* | |
| 96-080 (96-0080) SP *bl* [23rd FS] | |
| 96-081 (96-0081) SP *bl* | |
| 96-082 (96-0082) SP *bl* | |
| 96-083 (96-0083) SP *bl* | |

**Grumman C-20A Gulfstream III**
76th AS/86th AW, Ramstein, Germany
*FY83*
30500
30501
30502

**Grumman C-20H Gulfstream IV**
Det 1, 86th OG/SHAPE, Chievres, Belgium
*FY92*
20375

**Gates C-21A Learjet**
76th AS/86th AW, Ramstein, Germany
*7005th ABS/HQ USEUCOM, Stuttgart, Germany
*FY84*
40068*
40081*
40082*
40083*
40084
40085
40086
40087
40108
40109
40110
40111
40112

**Sikorsky HH-60G Blackhawk**
56th RQS/85th Wing, Keflavik, Iceland [IS]
26109 (FY88)
26205 (FY89)
26206 (FY89)
26208 (FY89)
26212 (FY89)

**Lockheed C-130E Hercules**
37th AS/86th AW, Ramstein, Germany [RS] (*bl/w*)
01260 (FY70)
01264 (FY70) [86th AW]
01271 (FY70)
01274 (FY70)
10935 (FY68)
10938 (FY68)
10943 (FY68) [86th OG]
10947 (FY68)
17681 (FY64)
18240 (FY64)
37885 (FY63)
37887 (FY63)
40502 (FY64)
40527 (FY64)
40533 (FY64)
40550 (FY64)
96566 (FY69) [37th AS]
96582 (FY69)
96583 (FY69)

# European-based US Navy Aircraft

| Notes | Type |
|---|---|

**Lockheed P-3 Orion**
CinCUSNAVFOREUR,
NAF Sigonella, Italy;
NAF Keflavik, Iceland;
VQ-2, NAF Rota, Spain

| | | | |
|---|---|---|---|
| 150495 | | UP-3A | NAF Keflavik |
| 150511 | | VP-3A | CinCUSNAVFOREUR |
| 156519 | [21] | EP-3E | VQ-2 |
| 156520 | [10] | P-3C | VQ-2 |
| 156525 | [11] | P-3C | VQ-2 |
| 156529 | [24] | EP-3E | VQ-2 |
| 157316 | [23] | EP-3E | VQ-2 |
| 157325 | [25] | EP-3E | VQ-2 |
| 157326 | [22] | EP-3E | VQ-2 |
| 161414 | [14] | P-3C | VQ-2 |

**Beech UC-12M Super King Air**
NAF Rota, Spain;
NAF Naples, Italy

| | | |
|---|---|---|
| 3839 | (163839) | Rota |
| 3842 | (163842) | Rota |
| 3844 | (163844) | Naples |

**Fairchild C-26D**
NAF Naples, Italy;
NAF Sigonella, Italy

| | |
|---|---|
| 900528 | Sigonella |
| 900530 | Sigonella |
| 900531 | Naples |
| 910502 | Naples |

**Sikorsky MH-53E Sea Stallion**
HC-4, NAF Sigonella, Italy

| | |
|---|---|
| 162505 | [HC-47] |
| 162506 | [HC-48] |
| 162509 | [HC-49] |
| 162516 | [HC-46] |
| 163053 | [HC-44] |
| 163055 | [HC-45] |
| 163057 | [HC-41] |
| 163065 | [HC-43] |
| 163068 | [HC-42] |

# European-based US Army Aircraft

| Notes | Type |
|---|---|

**Bell UH-1H Iroquois**
LANDSOUTHEAST, Cigli, Turkey;
'B' Co, 2nd Btn, 502nd Avn Reg't, Coleman Barracks;
7th Army Training Center, Grafenwöhr;
Combat Manoeuvre Training Centre, Hohenfels;
HQ/USEUCOM, Stuttgart;
6th Avn Co, Vicenza, Italy

| | |
|---|---|
| *FY69* | |
| 15605 | HQ/USEUCOM |
| 15606 | HQ/USEUCOM |
| *FY68* | |
| 16341 | LANDSOUTHEAST |
| 16662 | LANDSOUTHEAST |
| *FY72* | |
| 21569 | CMTC |
| 21632 | CMTC |
| 21636 | CMTC |
| *FY73* | |
| 21668 | CMTC |
| 21786 | CMTC |
| 21806 | LANDSOUTHEAST |
| 21824 | 7th ATC |
| 22127 | B/2-502nd Avn |
| *FY74* | |
| 22303 | CMTC |
| 22318 | 6th Avn Co |
| 22330 | CMTC |
| 22347 | CMTC |
| 22355 | CMTC |
| 22368 | HQ/USEUCOM |
| 22370 | CMTC |
| 22410 | CMTC |
| 22448 | CMTC |
| 22465 | CMTC |
| 22504 | 7th ATC |
| 22513 | HQ/USEUCOM |
| 22514 | HQ/USEUCOM |

**Beech C-12 Super King Air**
214th Avn, Heidelberg;
'A' Co, 2nd Btn, 228th Avn Reg't, Heidelberg;
LANDSOUTHEAST, Izmir, Turkey;
HQ/USEUCOM, Stuttgart;
6th Avn Co, Vicenza, Italy;
1st Military Intelligence Btn, Wiesbaden

| | | |
|---|---|---|
| *FY84* | | |
| 40144 | C-12F | 214th Avn |
| 40152 | C-12F | 214th Avn |
| 40153 | C-12F | 1st MIB |
| 40155 | C-12F | 214th Avn |
| 40156 | C-12F | 214th Avn |
| 40157 | C-12F | 214th Avn |
| 40158 | C-12F | HQ/USEUCOM |
| 40160 | C-12F | HQ/USEUCOM |
| 40161 | C-12F | 6th Avn Co |
| 40162 | C-12F | 6th Avn Co |
| 40164 | C-12F | LANDSOUTHEAST |
| 40165 | C-12F | LANDSOUTHEAST |
| *FY94* | | |
| 40315 | C-12R | A/2-228th Avn |
| 40316 | C-12R | A/2-228th Avn |
| 40317 | C-12R | A/2-228th Avn |
| 40318 | C-12R | A/2-228th Avn |
| 40319 | C-12R | A/2-228th Avn |
| *FY95* | | |
| 50088 | C-12R | A/2-228th Avn |
| *FY85* | | |
| 50147 | RC-12K | 1st MIB |
| 50148 | RC-12K | 1st MIB |
| 50150 | RC-12K | 1st MIB |
| 50152 | RC-12K | 1st MIB |
| 50153 | RC-12K | 1st MIB |

| Type | | Notes |
|---|---|---|
| 50154 | RC-12K 1st MIB | |
| 50155 | RC-12K 1st MIB | |

**Beech C-12J**
HQ/USEUCOM, Stuttgart
*FY86*
60079

**Cessna UC-35A Citation V**
214th Avn, Heidelberg
*FY95*
50123
50124
*FY97*
70101
70102

**Boeing-Vertol CH-47D Chinook**
'F' Co, 159th Avn Reg't Giebelstadt
*FY87*
70072
70073
*FY88*
80098
80099
80100
80101
80102
80103
80104
80106
*FY89*
90138
90139
90140
90141
90142
90143
90144
90145

**Bell OH-58D(I) Kiowa Warrior**
1st Btn, 1st Cavalry Reg't, Budingen;
1st Btn, 4th Cavalry Reg't, Schweinfurt
*FY90*
00348 1-1st Cav
00371 1-1st Cav
00373 1-4th Cav
*FY91*
10540 1-1st Cav
10544 1-1st Cav
10564 1-1st Cav
*FY92*
20520 1-1st Cav
20529 1-1st Cav
20545 1-1st Cav
*FY93*
30971 1-4th Cav
30996 1-4th Cav
30998 1-4th Cav
31002 1-4th Cav
31005 1-4th Cav
31006 1-4th Cav
31007 1-4th Cav
31008 1-4th Cav
*FY94*
40149 1-4th Cav
40150 1-4th Cav
40151 1-4th Cav
40152 1-1st Cav
40153 1-4th Cav
40154 1-4th Cav
40174 1-4th Cav
40175 1-1st Cav
40176 1-4th Cav
40178 1-1st Cav
40179 1-1st Cav
40180 1-1st Cav
*FY89*
90114 1-1st Cav
90116 1-1st Cav
90117 1-1st Cav

**Sikorsky H-60 Black Hawk**
2nd Btn, 1st Avn Reg't, Ansbach;
45th Medical Co, Ansbach;
'B' Co, 5th Btn, 158th Avn Reg't, Aviano;
'A' Co, 127th Divisional Avn Support Btn, Bad Kreuznach;
357th Avn Det/SHAPE, Chievres;
'B' Co, 70th Transportation Reg't, Coleman Barracks;
'C' Co, 158th Avn Reg't, Giebelstadt;
'D' Co, 158th Avn Reg't, Giebelstadt;
2nd Btn, 501st Avn Reg't, Hanau;
214th Avn, Heidelberg;
'B' Co, 7th Btn, 159th AVIM, Illesheim;
236th Medical Co (HA), Landstuhl;
6th Avn Co, Vicenza, Italy;
'A' Co, 5th Btn, 158th Avn Reg't, Wiesbaden;
'C' Co, 5th Btn, 158th Avn Reg't, Wiesbaden;
159th Medical Co, Wiesbaden
*FY82*
23660 UH-60A C/158th Avn
23675 UH-60A 45th Med Co
23685 UH-60A 159th Med Co
23692 UH-60A C/158th Avn
23693 UH-60A 45th Med Co
23727 UH-60A 159th Med Co
23729 UH-60A 45th Med Co
23735 UH-60A 236th Med Co
23736 UH-60A 236th Med Co
23737 UH-60A 236th Med Co
23738 UH-60A 159th Med Co
23745 UH-60A 236th Med Co
23749 UH-60A 236th Med Co
23750 UH-60A 159th Med Co
23752 UH-60A 236th Med Co
23753 UH-60A 159th Med Co
23754 UH-60A 45th Med Co
23755 UH-60A 45th Med Co
23756 UH-60A 236th Med Co
23757 UH-60A 214th Avn
23761 UH-60A 2-501st Avn
*FY83*
23854 UH-60A 357th Avn Det
23855 UH-60A 214th Avn
23868 UH-60A 214th Avn
23869 UH-60A 214th Avn
*FY84*
23951 UH-60A 45th Med Co
23970 UH-60A C/5158th Avn
23975 UH-60A C/5158th Avn
24019 EH-60A
*FY85*
24391 UH-60A 45th Med Co
24467 EH-60A 2-1st Avn
24475 EH-60A 2-1st Avn
24478 EH-60A 2-1st Avn
*FY86*
24498 UH-60A 2-501st Avn
24530 UH-60A 2-501st Avn
24531 UH-60A 45th Med Co

# US Army Europe

| Notes | Type | | |
|---|---|---|---|
| | 24532 | UH-60A | 45th Med Co |
| | 24538 | UH-60A | 214th Avn |
| | 24550 | UH-60A | 236th Med Co |
| | 24551 | UH-60A | 236th Med Co |
| | 24552 | UH-60A | 159th Med Co |
| | 24554 | UH-60A | C/5-158th Avn |
| | 24555 | UH-60A | 159th Med Co |
| | 24566 | EH-60C | 2-501st Avn |
| | *FY87* | | |
| | 24579 | UH-60A | A/5-158th Avn |
| | 24581 | UH-60A | 159th Med Co |
| | 24583 | UH-60A | 357th Avn Det |
| | 24584 | UH-60A | 357th Avn Det |
| | 24589 | UH-60A | 214th Avn |
| | 24621 | UH-60A | 214th Avn |
| | 24628 | UH-60A | 2-1st Avn |
| | 24634 | UH-60A | 159th Med Co |
| | 24642 | UH-60A | 214th Avn |
| | 24643 | UH-60A | 2-1st Avn |
| | 24644 | UH-60A | 45th Med Co |
| | 24645 | UH-60A | 236th Med Co |
| | 24646 | UH-60A | 2-1st Avn |
| | 24647 | UH-60A | 214th Avn |
| | 24650 | UH-60A | 159th Med Co |
| | 24656 | UH-60A | 159th Med Co |
| | 24660 | EH-60C | 2-501st Avn |
| | 24664 | EH-60A | 2-501st Avn |
| | 24667 | EH-60A | 2-501st Avn |
| | 26001 | UH-60A | 45th Med Co |
| | 26002 | UH-60A | 159th Med Co |
| | 26003 | UH-60A | B/5-158th Avn |
| | 26004 | UH-60A | 2-1st Avn |
| | *FY88* | | |
| | 26019 | UH-60A | 214th Avn |
| | 26020 | UH-60A | 236th Med Co |
| | 26021 | UH-60A | A/5-158th Avn |
| | 26023 | UH-60A | 236th Med Co |
| | 26025 | UH-60A | 214th Avn |
| | 26026 | UH-60A | B/5-158th Avn |
| | 26027 | UH-60A | 214th Avn |
| | 26028 | UH-60A | B/7-159th AVIM |
| | 26031 | UH-60A | 2-1st Avn |
| | 26034 | UH-60A | 236th Med Co |
| | 26037 | UH-60A | B/7-159th AVIM |
| | 26038 | UH-60A | A/5-158th Avn |
| | 26039 | UH-60A | 45th Med Co |
| | 26040 | UH-60A | 2-1st Avn |
| | 26041 | UH-60A | A/5-158th Avn |
| | 26042 | UH-60A | A/5-158th Avn |
| | 26045 | UH-60A | 45th Med Co |
| | 26050 | UH-60A | 127th ASB |
| | 26051 | UH-60A | A/5-158th Avn |
| | 26052 | UH-60A | B/5-158th Avn |
| | 26053 | UH-60A | A/5-158th Avn |
| | 26054 | UH-60A | 236th Med Co |
| | 26055 | UH-60A | 236th Med Co |
| | 26056 | UH-60A | A/5-158th Avn |
| | 26058 | UH-60A | 159th Med Co |
| | 26063 | UH-60A | B/5-158th Avn |
| | 26067 | UH-60A | B/5-158th Avn |
| | 26068 | UH-60A | 2-501st Avn |
| | 26071 | UH-60A | 2-501st Avn |
| | 26072 | UH-60A | 236th Med Co |
| | 26075 | UH-60A | 2-501st Avn |
| | 26077 | UH-60A | C/5-158th Avn |
| | 26080 | UH-60A | 236th Med Co |
| | 26083 | UH-60A | B/5-158th Avn |
| | 26085 | UH-60A | 2-501st Avn |
| | 26086 | UH-60A | 2-501st Avn |
| | *FY89* | | |
| | 26138 | UH-60A | 2-1st Avn |
| | 26142 | UH-60A | B/5-158th Avn |
| | 26145 | UH-60A | B/5-158th Avn |

| Notes | Type | | |
|---|---|---|---|
| | 26146 | UH-60A | 159th Med Co |
| | 26151 | UH-60A | 159th Med Co |
| | 26153 | UH-60A | B/5-158th Avn |
| | 26155 | UH-60A | 2-1st Avn |
| | 26164 | UH-60A | C/5-158th Avn |
| | 26165 | UH-60A | 214th Avn |
| | *FY95* | | |
| | 26621 | UH-60L | 2-1st Avn |
| | 26628 | UH-60L | 2-1st Avn |
| | 26629 | UH-60L | 2-1st Avn |
| | 26630 | UH-60L | 2-1st Avn |
| | 26631 | UH-60L | 2-1st Avn |
| | 26632 | UH-60L | 2-1st Avn |
| | 26633 | UH-60L | 2-1st Avn |
| | 26635 | UH-60L | 2-1st Avn |
| | 26636 | UH-60L | 2-1st Avn |
| | 26637 | UH-60L | 2-1st Avn |
| | 26638 | UH-60L | 2-1st Avn |
| | 26639 | UH-60L | 2-1st Avn |
| | 26640 | UH-60L | 2-1st Avn |
| | 26641 | UH-60L | D/158th Avn |
| | 26642 | UH-60L | D/158th Avn |
| | 26643 | UH-60L | D/158th Avn |
| | 26644 | UH-60L | 2-1st Avn |
| | 26645 | UH-60L | D/158th Avn |
| | 26646 | UH-60L | 2-1st Avn |
| | 26647 | UH-60L | 2-1st Avn |
| | 26648 | UH-60L | 2-1st Avn |
| | 26649 | UH-60L | D/158th Avn |
| | 26650 | UH-60L | D/158th Avn |
| | 26651 | UH-60L | C/158th Avn |
| | 26652 | UH-60L | C/158th Avn |
| | 26653 | UH-60L | C/158th Avn |
| | 26654 | UH-60L | C/158th Avn |
| | 26655 | UH-60L | C/158th Avn |
| | *FY96* | | |
| | 26674 | UH-60L | D/158th Avn |
| | 26675 | UH-60L | D/158th Avn |
| | 26676 | UH-60L | D/158th Avn |
| | 26677 | UH-60L | D/158th Avn |
| | 26678 | UH-60L | D/158th Avn |
| | 26679 | UH-60L | D/158th Avn |
| | 26680 | UH-60L | D/158th Avn |
| | 26681 | UH-60L | D/158th Avn |
| | 26682 | UH-60L | D/158th Avn |
| | 26683 | UH-60L | C/158th Avn |
| | 26684 | UH-60L | C/158th Avn |
| | 26685 | UH-60L | C/158th Avn |
| | 26686 | UH-60L | C/158th Avn |
| | 26687 | UH-60L | C/158th Avn |
| | 26688 | UH-60L | C/158th Avn |
| | 26689 | UH-60L | C/158th Avn |
| | 26690 | UH-60L | C/158th Avn |
| | 26691 | UH-60L | C/158th Avn |
| | 26692 | UH-60L | C/158th Avn |
| | *FY97* | | |
| | 26762 | UH-60L | 2-501st Avn |
| | 26763 | UH-60L | 2-501st Avn |
| | 26764 | UH-60L | 2-501st Avn |
| | 26765 | UH-60L | 2-501st Avn |
| | 26766 | UH-60L | 2-501st Avn |
| | 26767 | UH-60L | 2-501st Avn |
| | *FY98* | | |
| | 26795 | UH-60L | 2-501st Avn |
| | 26796 | UH-60L | 2-501st Avn |
| | 26797 | UH-60L | 2-501st Avn |
| | 26798 | UH-60L | 2-501st Avn |
| | 26799 | UH-60L | 2-501st Avn |
| | 26800 | UH-60L | 2-501st Avn |
| | 26801 | UH-60L | 2-501st Avn |
| | 26802 | UH-60L | 2-501st Avn |
| | 26813 | UH-60L | 2-501st Avn |
| | 26814 | UH-60L | 2-501st Avn |

| Type | | Notes |
|---|---|---|
| **MDH AH-64A Apache** | | |
| 1st Btn, 1st Avn Reg't, Ansbach; | | |
| 127th ASB, Hanau; | | |
| 1st Btn, 501st Avn Reg't, Hanau; | | |
| 2nd Btn, 6th Cavalry Reg't, Illesheim; | | |
| 6th Btn, 6th Cavalry Reg't, Illesheim; | | |
| 'A' Co, 7th Btn, 159th Avn Reg't, Illesheim | | |
| *FY85* | | |
| 25357 | 127th ASB | |
| 25460 | A/7-159th Avn | |
| 25473 | 1-501st Avn | |
| *FY86* | 2-6th Cav | |
| 68941 | 6-6th Cav | |
| 68942 | 2-6th Cav | |
| 68943 | 2-6th Cav | |
| 68946 | 2-6th Cav | |
| 68947 | 6-6th Cav | |
| 68948 | 2-6th Cav | |
| 68949 | 2-6th Cav | |
| 68950 | 6-6th Cav | |
| 68951 | 2-6th Cav | |
| 68952 | 2-6th Cav | |
| 68955 | 2-6th Cav | |
| 68956 | 2-6th Cav | |
| 68957 | 2-6th Cav | |
| 68959 | 2-6th Cav | |
| 68960 | 2-6th Cav | |
| 68961 | 2-6th Cav | |
| 68981 | 2-6th Cav | |
| 69010 | 2-6th Cav | |
| 69011 | 2-6th Cav | |
| 69019 | 2-6th Cav | |
| 69026 | 2-6th Cav | |
| 69030 | 2-6th Cav | |
| 69032 | 2-6th Cav | |
| 69037 | 2-6th Cav | |
| 69039 | 2-6th Cav | |
| 69041 | 1-501st Avn | |
| 69048 | 2-6th Cav | |
| *FY87* | | |
| 70409 | 1-1st Avn | |
| 70410 | 1-501st Avn | |
| 70411 | 6-6th Cav | |
| 70412 | 1-1st Avn | |
| 70413 | 1-1st Avn | |
| 70415 | 1-501st Avn | |
| 70417 | 1-1st Avn | |
| 70418 | 1-501st Avn | |
| 70420 | 1-1st Avn | |
| 70428 | 2-6th Cav | |

| Type | | Notes |
|---|---|---|
| 70435 | 1-501st Avn | |
| 70436 | 1-1st Avn | |
| 70437 | 1-1st Avn | |
| 70438 | 1-501st Avn | |
| 70439 | 1-1st Avn | |
| 70440 | 1-501st Avn | |
| 70441 | 2-6th Cav | |
| 70442 | 1-1st Avn | |
| 70443 | 2-6th Cav | |
| 70444 | 1-501st Avn | |
| 70445 | 1-501st Avn | |
| 70446 | 1-501st Avn | |
| 70447 | 1-501st Avn | |
| 70449 | 1-501st Avn | |
| 70451 | 1-501st Avn | |
| 70455 | 1-501st Avn | |
| 70457 | 1-1st Avn | |
| 70470 | 1-1st Avn | |
| 70471 | 1-1st Avn | |
| 70474 | 1-1st Avn | |
| 70475 | 1-1st Avn | |
| 70476 | 1-1st Avn | |
| 70477 | 1-1st Avn | |
| 70478 | 1-1st Avn | |
| 70481 | 1-1st Avn | |
| 70487 | 1-501st Avn | |
| 70496 | 1-501st Avn | |
| 70503 | 1-501st Avn | |
| 70504 | 1-501st Avn | |
| 70505 | 1-501st Avn | |
| 70506 | 1-501st Avn | |
| *FY88* | | |
| 80197 | 1-501st Avn | |
| 80198 | 1-501st Avn | |
| 80203 | 6-6th Cav | |
| 80212 | 6-6th Cav | |
| 80213 | 6-6th Cav | |
| 80214 | 6-6th Cav | |
| 80215 | 6-6th Cav | |
| 80216 | 6-6th Cav | |
| 80217 | 6-6th Cav | |
| 80219 | 6-6th Cav | |
| 80222 | 6-6th Cav | |
| 80225 | 6-6th Cav | |
| 80229 | 6-6th Cav | |
| 80232 | 6-6th Cav | |
| 80233 | 6-6th Cav | |
| 80234 | 6-6th Cav | |
| 80236 | 6-6th Cav | |
| 80243 | 6-6th Cav | |
| 80246 | 6-6th Cav | |

# US-based USAF Aircraft

The following aircraft are normally based in the USA but are likely to be seen visiting the UK from time to time. The presentation is in numerical order of the type, commencing with the B-**1B** and concluding with the C-**141**. The aircraft are listed in numerical progression by the serial actually carried externally. Fiscal year information is provided, together with details of mark variations and in some cases operating units. Where base-code letter information is carried on the aircrafts' tails, this is detailed with the squadron/base data; for example the 7th Wing's B-1B 30069 carries the letters DY on its tail, thus identifying the Wing's home base as Dyess AFB, Texas.

*Notes* *Type*

**Rockwell B-1B Lancer**

7th BW, Dyess AFB, Texas [DY]:
9th BS (*bk*) & 28th BS (*bl/w*);
28th BW, Ellsworth AFB,
South Dakota [EL]:
13th BS (*bl/br*), 37th BS (*bk/y*)
& 77th BS (*bl*);
127th BS/184th BW, Kansas ANG,
McConnell AFB, Kansas (*r/w*);
128th BS/116th BW, Georgia ANG,
Robins AFB, Georgia [GA];
34th BS/366th Wg, Mountain Home
AFB, Idaho [MO] (*r/bk*);
419th FLTS/412th TW, Edwards AFB,
California [ED]

| Serial | Unit | Marks |
|---|---|---|
| *FY83* | | |
| 30065 | 7th BW | *bk* |
| 30066 | 7th BW | *bl/w* |
| 30067 | 7th BW | *bk* |
| 30068 | 7th BW | *bl/w* |
| 30069 | 7th BW | *bl/w* |
| 30070 | 7th BW | *bl/w* |
| 30071 | 7th BW | *bk* |
| *FY84* | | |
| 40049 | 412th TW | |
| 40050 | 127th BS | *r/w* |
| 40051 | 7th BW | *bk* |
| 40053 | 7th BW | *bl/w* |
| 40054 | 7th BW | *bk* |
| 40055 | 7th BW | *bl/w* |
| 40056 | 7th BW | *bl/w* |
| 40058 | 7th BW | *bk* |
| *FY85* | | |
| 50059 | 128th BS | |
| 50060 | 127th BS | *r/w* |
| 50061 | 128th BS | |
| 50062 | 7th BW | *bl/w* |
| 50064 | 127th BS | *r/w* |
| 50065 | 7th BW | |
| 50066 | 28th BW | *bk/y* |
| 50067 | 7th BW | *bl/w* |
| 50068 | 412th TW | |
| 50069 | 127th BS | *r/w* |
| 50070 | 127th BS | *r/w* |
| 50071 | 128th BS | |
| 50072 | 28th BW | *bk* |
| 50073 | 28th BW | *bk/y* |
| 50074 | 28th BW | |
| 50075 | 28th BW | *bk/y* |
| 50077 | 28th BW | *bk/y* |
| 50079 | 28th BW | *bk/y* |
| 50080 | 127th BS | *r/w* |
| 50081 | 127th BS | *r/w* |
| 50082 | 412th TW | |
| 50083 | 28th BW | *bl* |
| 50084 | 28th BW | *bk/y* |
| 50085 | 28th BW | *bk/y* |
| 50086 | 28th BW | *bk/y* |
| 50087 | 28th BW | *bl/br* |
| 50088 | 127th BS | *r/w* |
| 50089 | 128th BS | |
| 50090 | 28th BW | *bk/y* |
| 50091 | 28th BW | *bl* |
| 50092 | 128th BS | |
| *FY86* | | |
| 60093 | 28th BW | *bk/y* |
| 60094 | 28th BW | *bk/y* |
| 60095 | 127th BS | *r/w* |
| 60096 | 28th BW | *bk/y* |
| 60097 | 28th BW | |
| 60098 | 128th BS | |
| 60099 | 28th BW | *bk/y* |
| 60100 | 7th BW | *bl/w* |
| 60101 | 7th BW | *bl/w* |
| 60102 | 28th BW | *bk/y* |
| 60103 | 7th BW | *bk* |
| 60104 | 28th BW | *bk/y* |
| 60105 | 7th BW | *bl/w* |
| 60107 | 128th BS | |
| 60108 | 7th BW | *bl/w* |
| 60109 | 7th BW | *bl/w* |
| 60110 | 7th BW | *bl/w* |
| 60111 | 28th BW | *bk/y* |
| 60112 | 7th BW | *bk* |
| 60113 | 28th BW | *bk/y* |
| 60114 | 28th BW | *bk/y* |
| 60115 | 127th BS | *r/w* |
| 60116 | 366th Wg | *r/bk* |
| 60117 | 7th BW | *bl/w* |
| 60118 | 366th Wg | *r/bk* |
| 60119 | 7th BW | *bl/w* |
| 60120 | 7th BW | *bk* |
| 60121 | 366th Wg | *r/bk* |
| 60122 | 7th BW | *bl/w* |
| 60123 | 7th BW | *bk* |
| 60124 | 128th BS | |
| 60125 | 366th Wg | *r/bk* |
| 60126 | 127th BS | *r/w* |
| 60127 | 128th BS | |
| 60129 | 28th BW | *bk/y* |
| 60130 | 7th BW | *bl/w* |
| 60131 | 366th Wg | *r/bk* |
| 60132 | 7th BW | *bl/w* |
| 60133 | 128th BS | |
| 60134 | 366th Wg | *r/bk* |
| 60135 | 7th BW | *bk* |
| 60136 | 127th BS | *r/w* |
| 60137 | 7th BW | *bl/w* |

Type | Notes

60138 366th Wg *r/bk*
60139 366th Wg *r/bk*
60140 7th BW *bk*

**Northrop B-2 Spirit**
419th FLTS/412th TW, Edwards AFB, California [ED];
509th BW, Whiteman AFB, Missouri WM]:
325th BS, 393rd BS & 715th BS
(Names are given where known. Each begins *Spirit of . . .*)
*FY90*
00040 509th BW *Alaska*
00041 509th BW *Hawaii*
*FY92*
20700 509th BW *Florida*
*FY82*
21066 Northrop
21067 509th BW *Arizona*
21068 412th TW *New York*
21069 509th BW *Indiana*
21070 Northrop *Ohio*
21071 509th BW *Mississippi*
*FY93*
31085 509th BW *Oklahoma*
31086 509th BW *Kitty Hawk*
31087 509th BW *Pennsylvania*
31088 509th BW *Louisiana*
*FY88*
80328 509th BW *Texas*
80329 509th BW *Missouri*
80330 509th BW *California*
80331 509th BW *South Carolina*
80332 509th BW *Washington*
*FY89*
90127 509th BW *Kansas*
90128 509th BW *Nebraska*
90129 509th BW *Georgia*

**Boeing E-3 Sentry**
552nd ACW, Tinker AFB, Oklahoma [OK]:
963rd AACS (*bk*), 964th AACS (*r*), 965th AACS (*y*), 966th AACS (*bl*)
961st AACS/18th Wg, Kadena AB, Japan [ZZ] (*or*);
962nd AACS/3rd Wg, Elmendorf AFB, Alaska [AK] (*gn*);
*FY80*
00137 E-3C *bk*
00138 E-3C *y*
00139 E-3C *bl*
*FY81*
10004 E-3C *bk*
10005 E-3C *bk*
*FY71*
11407 E-3B *bl*
11408 E-3B *bk*
*FY82*
20006 E-3C *y*
20007 E-3C *m*
*FY83*
30008 E-3C *or*
30009 E-3C *bk*
*FY73*
31674 JE-3C Boeing
31675 E-3B *bl*
*FY75*
50556 E-3B *r*
50557 E-3B *gn*
50558 E-3B *y*
50559 E-3B *m*
50560 E-3B *bk*
*FY76*
61604 E-3B *gn*
61605 E-3B *or*
61606 E-3B *r*
61607 E-3B *bl*
*FY77*
70351 E-3B *y*
70352 E-3B *r*
70353 E-3B *y*
70355 E-3B *r*
70356 E-3B *y*
*FY78*
80576 E-3B *bk*
80577 E-3B *r*
80578 E-3B *gn*
*FY79*
90001 E-3B *r*
90002 E-3B *or*
90003 E-3B *bl*

**Boeing E-4B**
1st ACCS/55th Wg, Offutt AFB, Nebraska [OF]
31676 (FY73)
31677 (FY73)
40787 (FY74)
50125 (FY75)

**Lockheed C-5 Galaxy**
60th AMW, Travis AFB, California: 21st AS (*bk/gd*) & 22nd AS (*bk/bl*);
56th AS/97th AMW, Altus AFB, Oklahoma (*r/y*);
137th AS/105th AW, Stewart AFB, New York (*bl*);
68th AS/433rd AW AFRC, Kelly AFB, Texas;
436th AW, Dover AFB, Delaware: 3rd AS & 9th AS (*y/r & y/bl*);
337th AS/439th AW AFRC, Westover ARB, Massachusetts (*bl/r*)
*FY70*
00445 C-5A 433rd AW
00446 C-5A 433rd AW
00447 C-5A 436th AW *y/r*
00448 C-5A 439th AW *bl/r*
00449 C-5A 60th AMW *bk/gd*
00450 C-5A 97th AMW *r/y*
00451 C-5A 97th AMW *r/y*
00452 C-5A 97th AMW *r/y*
00453 C-5A 436th AW
00454 C-5A 97th AMW *r/y*
00455 C-5A 97th AMW *r/y*
00456 C-5A 60th AMW *bk/gd*
00457 C-5A 60th AMW *bk/gd*
00458 C-5A 433rd AW
00459 C-5A 60th AMW *bk/gd*
00460 C-5A 105th AW *bl*
00461 C-5A 436th AW *y/r*
00462 C-5A 60th AMW
00463 C-5A 436th AW *y/bl*
00464 C-5A 60th AMW *bk/bl*
00465 C-5A 436th AW *y/r*
00466 C-5A 97th AMW *r/y*
00467 C-5A 97th AMW *r/y*
*FY83*
31285 C-5B 436th AW *y/r*
*FY84*
40059 C-5B 436th AW *y/r*
40060 C-5B 60th AMW *bk/bl*
40061 C-5B 436th AW *y/r*

| Notes | Type | | | |
|---|---|---|---|---|
| | 40062 | C-5B | 60th AMW | *bk/gd* |
| | *FY85* | | | |
| | 50001 | C-5B | 436th AW | *m* |
| | 50002 | C-5B | 60th AMW | *bk/bl* |
| | 50003 | C-5B | 436th AW | *y/bl* |
| | 50004 | C-5B | 60th AMW | *bk/bl* |
| | 50005 | C-5B | 436th AW | *y/bl* |
| | 50006 | C-5B | 60th AMW | *bk/gd* |
| | 50007 | C-5B | 436th AW | *y/bl* |
| | 50008 | C-5B | 60th AMW | *bk/gd* |
| | 50009 | C-5B | 436th AW | *y/r* |
| | 50010 | C-5B | 60th AMW | *bk/gd* |
| | *FY86* | | | |
| | 60011 | C-5B | 436th AW | *y/bl* |
| | 60012 | C-5B | 60th AMW | *bk/bl* |
| | 60013 | C-5B | 436th AW | *y/bl* |
| | 60014 | C-5B | 60th AMW | *bk/bl* |
| | 60015 | C-5B | 436th AW | *y/r* |
| | 60016 | C-5B | 60th AMW | *bk/bl* |
| | 60017 | C-5B | 436th AW | *y/bl* |
| | 60018 | C-5B | 60th AMW | *bk/gd* |
| | 60019 | C-5B | 436th AW | *y/r* |
| | 60020 | C-5B | 436th AW | *y/bl* |
| | 60021 | C-5B | 60th AMW | *bk/gd* |
| | 60022 | C-5B | 60th AMW | *bk/bl* |
| | 60023 | C-5B | 436th AW | *y/bl* |
| | 60024 | C-5B | 60th AMW | *bk/bl* |
| | 60025 | C-5B | 436th AW | *y/bl* |
| | 60026 | C-5B | 60th AMW | *bk/gd* |
| | *FY66* | | | |
| | 68304 | C-5A | 439th AW | *bl/r* |
| | 68305 | C-5A | 433rd AW | |
| | 68306 | C-5A | 433rd AW | |
| | 68307 | C-5A | 433rd AW | |
| | *FY87* | | | |
| | 70027 | C-5B | 436th AW | *y/bl* |
| | 70028 | C-5B | 60th AMW | *bk/bl* |
| | 70029 | C-5B | 436th AW | *y/r* |
| | 70030 | C-5B | 60th AMW | *bk/bl* |
| | 70031 | C-5B | 436th AW | *y/r* |
| | 70032 | C-5B | 60th AMW | *bk/bl* |
| | 70033 | C-5B | 436th AW | *y/r* |
| | 70034 | C-5B | 60th AMW | *bk/gd* |
| | 70035 | C-5B | 436th AW | *y/bl* |
| | 70036 | C-5B | 60th AMW | *bk/gd* |
| | 70037 | C-5B | 436th AW | *y/r* |
| | 70038 | C-5B | 60th AMW | *bk/bl* |
| | 70039 | C-5B | 436th AW | *y/r* |
| | 70040 | C-5B | 60th AMW | *bk/gd* |
| | 70041 | C-5B | 436th AW | *y/bl* |
| | 70042 | C-5B | 60th AMW | *bk/gd* |
| | 70043 | C-5B | 436th AW | *y/bl* |
| | 70044 | C-5B | 60th AMW | *bk/gd* |
| | 70045 | C-5B | 436th AW | *y/r* |
| | *FY67* | | | |
| | 70167 | C-5A | 439th AW | *bl/r* |
| | 70168 | C-5A | 433rd AW | |
| | 70169 | C-5A | 105th AW | *bl* |
| | 70170 | C-5A | 105th AW | *bl* |
| | 70171 | C-5A | 433rd AW | |
| | 70173 | C-5A | 105th AW | *bl* |
| | 70174 | C-5A | 105th AW | *bl* |
| | *FY68* | | | |
| | 80211 | C-5A | 439th AW | *bl/r* |
| | 80212 | C-5A | 105th AW | *bl* |
| | 80213 | C-5C | 60th AMW | *bk/bl* |
| | 80214 | C-5A | 436th AW | *y/r* |
| | 80215 | C-5A | 439th AW | *bl/r* |
| | 80216 | C-5C | 60th AMW | *bk/bl* |
| | 80217 | C-5A | 97th AMW | *r/y* |
| | 80219 | C-5A | 439th AW | *bl/r* |
| | 80220 | C-5A | 433rd AW | |
| | 80221 | C-5A | 433rd AW | |

| Notes | Type | | | |
|---|---|---|---|---|
| | 80222 | C-5A | 439th AW | *bl/r* |
| | 80223 | C-5A | 433rd AW | |
| | 80224 | C-5A | 105th AW | *bl* |
| | 80225 | C-5A | 439th AW | *bl/w* |
| | 80226 | C-5A | 105th AW | *bl* |
| | *FY69* | | | |
| | 90001 | C-5A | 97th AMW | *r/y* |
| | 90002 | C-5A | 433rd AW | |
| | 90003 | C-5A | 439th AW | *bl/r* |
| | 90004 | C-5A | 433rd AW | |
| | 90005 | C-5A | 439th AW | *bl/r* |
| | 90006 | C-5A | 433rd AW | |
| | 90007 | C-5A | 433rd AW | |
| | 90008 | C-5A | 105th AW | *bl* |
| | 90009 | C-5A | 105th AW | *bl* |
| | 90010 | C-5A | 60th AMW | *bk/gd* |
| | 90011 | C-5A | 439th AW | *bl/r* |
| | 90012 | C-5A | 105th AW | *bl* |
| | 90013 | C-5A | 439th AW | *bl/r* |
| | 90014 | C-5A | 97th AMW | *r/y* |
| | 90015 | C-5A | 105th AW | *bl* |
| | 90016 | C-5A | 433rd AW | |
| | 90017 | C-5A | 439th AW | *bl/r* |
| | 90018 | C-5A | 97th AMW | *r/y* |
| | 90019 | C-5A | 439th AW | *bl/r* |
| | 90020 | C-5A | 439th AW | *bl/r* |
| | 90021 | C-5A | 105th AW | *bl* |
| | 90022 | C-5A | 439th AW | *bl/r* |
| | 90023 | C-5A | 60th AMW | *bk/bl* |
| | 90024 | C-5A | 97th AMW | *r/y* |
| | 90025 | C-5A | 60th AMW | *bk/gd* |
| | 90026 | C-5A | 60th AMW | *bk/gd* |
| | 90027 | C-5A | 436th AW | *y/bl* |

**Boeing E-8 J-STARS**

Grumman, Melbourne, Florida;
12th ACCS/93rd ACW, Robins AFB, Georgia [WR] (*gn*)

| | | |
|---|---|---|
| *FY90* | | |
| 00175 | E-8A | Grumman |
| *FY92* | | |
| 23289 | E-8C | 93rd ACW |
| 23290 | E-8C | 93rd ACW |
| *FY93* | | |
| 30597 | E-8C | 93rd ACW |
| 30598 | E-8C | |
| 31097 | E-8C | 93rd ACW |
| *FY94* | | |
| 40284 | E-8C | 93rd ACW |
| 40285 | E-8C | |
| *FY95* | | |
| 50121 | E-8C | |
| 50122 | E-8C | |
| 50123 | E-8C | |
| *FY86* | | |
| 60416 | E-8A | 93rd ACW |
| 60417 | TE-8A | 93rd ACW |

**McDonnell Douglas C-9 Nightingale**

86th AW, Ramstein, Germany: 75th AS & 76th AS;
Det 1, 86th OG/SHAPE, Chievres, Belgium;
99th AS/89th AW, Andrews AFB, Maryland;
30th AS/374th AW, Yokota AB, Japan;
11th AS/375th AW, Scott AFB, Illinois

| | | | |
|---|---|---|---|
| *FY71* | | | |
| 10874 | C-9A | 374th AW | |
| 10875 | C-9A | 374th AW | |
| 10876 | C-9A | 86th OG | (VIP) |
| 10877 | C-9A | 374th AW | |

| Type | | | | Notes |
|---|---|---|---|---|
| 10878 | C-9A | 375th AW | | |
| 10879 | C-9A | 75th AS | | |
| 10880 | C-9A | 76th AS | (VIP) | |
| 10881 | C-9A | 75th AS | | |
| 10882 | C-9A | 75th AS | | |
| *FY68* | | | | |
| 10958 | C-9A | 375th AW | | |
| 10959 | C-9A | 375th AW | | |
| 10960 | C-9A | 375th AW | | |
| 10961 | C-9A | 375th AW | | |
| *FY67* | | | | |
| 22583 | C-9A | 374th AW | | |
| 22584 | C-9A | 375th AW | | |
| 22585 | C-9A | 75th AS | | |
| *FY73* | | | | |
| 31681 | C-9C | 89th AW | | |
| 31682 | C-9C | 89th AW | | |
| 31683 | C-9C | 89th AW | | |
| *FY68* | | | | |
| 88932 | C-9A | 375th AW | | |
| 88933 | C-9A | 375th AW | | |
| 88934 | C-9A | 375th AW | | |
| 88935 | C-9A | 375th AW | | |

**McDonnell Douglas**
**KC-10A Extender**

60th AMW, Travis AFB, California:
6th ARS (*bk/r*) & 9th ARS (*bk/bl*);
305th AMW, McGuire AFB,
New Jersey:
2nd ARS (*bl/r*) & 32nd ARS (*bl*)

| Type | | | Notes |
|---|---|---|---|
| *FY82* | | | |
| 20191 | 60th AMW | *bk/bl* | |
| 20192 | 60th AMW | *bk/r* | |
| 20193 | 60th AMW | *bk/bl* | |
| *FY83* | | | |
| 30075 | 60th AMW | | |
| 30076 | 60th AMW | *bk/bl* | |
| 30077 | 60th AMW | *bk/r* | |
| 30078 | 60th AMW | *bk/bl* | |
| 30079 | 305th AMW | *bl/r* | |
| 30080 | 60th AMW | *bk/bl* | |
| 30081 | 305th AMW | *bl/bk* | |
| 30082 | 305th AMW | *bl* | |
| *FY84* | | | |
| 40185 | 60th AMW | *bk/bl* | |
| 40186 | 305th AMW | *bl/r* | |
| 40187 | 60th AMW | *bk/bl* | |
| 40188 | 305th AMW | *bl/r* | |
| 40189 | 305th AMW | *bl* | |
| 40190 | 305th AMW | *bl/r* | |
| 40191 | 60th AMW | *bk/bl* | |
| 40192 | 305th AMW | *bl/r* | |
| *FY85* | | | |
| 50027 | 305th AMW | *bl/r* | |
| 50028 | 305th AMW | *bl/r* | |
| 50029 | 60th AMW | *bk/r* | |
| 50030 | 305th AMW | *bl* | |
| 50031 | 305th AMW | *bl/r* | |
| 50032 | 305th AMW | *bl* | |
| 50033 | 305th AMW | *bl* | |
| 50034 | 305th AMW | *bl/r* | |
| *FY86* | | | |
| 60027 | 305th AMW | *bl* | |
| 60028 | 305th AMW | *bl/r* | |
| 60029 | 60th AMW | *bk/r* | |
| 60030 | 305th AMW | *bl/r* | |
| 60031 | 60th AMW | *bk/r* | |
| 60032 | 60th AMW | *bk/r* | |
| 60033 | 60th AMW | *bk/r* | |
| 60034 | 60th AMW | *bk/r* | |
| 60035 | 305th AMW | *bl* | |
| 60036 | 305th AMW | *bl* | |
| 60037 | 60th AMW | *bk/r* | |
| 60038 | 60th AMW | *bk/r* | |
| *FY87* | | | |
| 70117 | 60th AMW | *bk/r* | |
| 70118 | 60th AMW | *bk/bl* | |
| 70119 | 60th AMW | *bk/r* | |
| 70120 | 305th AMW | *bl* | |
| 70121 | 305th AMW | *bl* | |
| 70122 | 305th AMW | *bl/r* | |
| 70123 | 305th AMW | *bl* | |
| 70124 | 305th AMW | *bl/r* | |
| *FY79* | | | |
| 90433 | 305th AMW | *bl* | |
| 90434 | 305th AMW | *bl/r* | |
| 91710 | 305th AMW | *bl/r* | |
| 91711 | 305th AMW | *bl/r* | |
| 91712 | 305th AMW | *bl/r* | |
| 91713 | 305th AMW | *bl* | |
| 91946 | 60th AMW | *bk/r* | |
| 91947 | 305th AMW | *bl* | |
| 91948 | 60th AMW | *bk/bl* | |
| 91949 | 305th AMW | *bl/r* | |
| 91950 | 60th AMW | *bk/bl* | |
| 91951 | 60th AMW | *bk/bl* | |

**McDonnell Douglas**
**C-17 Globemaster III**

7th AS/62nd AW, McChord AFB,
Washington;
58th AS/97th AMW, Altus AFB,
Oklahoma (*r/y*);
417th FLTS/412th TW, Edwards AFB,
California [ED];
437th AW, Charleston AFB,
South Carolina:
14th AS, 15th AS & 17th AS (*y/bl*)

| Type | | | | Notes |
|---|---|---|---|---|
| *FY00* | | | | |
| 00071 | C-17A | | | |
| 00072 | C-17A | | | |
| 00073 | C-17A | | | |
| 00074 | C-17A | | | |
| 00075 | C-17A | | | |
| 00076 | C-17A | | | |
| 00077 | C-17A | | | |
| 00078 | C-17A | | | |
| 00079 | C-17A | | | |
| 00080 | C-17A | | | |
| 00081 | C-17A | | | |
| 00082 | C-17A | | | |
| 00083 | C-17A | | | |
| 00084 | C-17A | | | |
| 00085 | C-17A | | | |
| *FY90* | | | | |
| 00532 | C-17A | 437th AW | *y/bl* | |
| 00533 | C-17A | 97th AMW | *r/y* | |
| 00534 | C-17A | 437th AW | *y/bl* | |
| 00535 | C-17A | 437th AW | *y/bl* | |
| *FY92* | | | | |
| 23291 | C-17A | 437th AW | *y/bl* | |
| 23292 | C-17A | 437th AW | *y/bl* | |
| 23293 | C-17A | 437th AW | *y/bl* | |
| 23294 | C-17A | 437th AW | *y/bl* | |
| *FY93* | | | | |
| 30599 | C-17A | 437th AW | *y/bl* | |
| 30600 | C-17A | 437th AW | *y/bl* | |
| 30601 | C-17A | 437th AW | *y/bl* | |
| 30602 | C-17A | 97th AMW | *r/y* | |
| 30603 | C-17A | 437th AW | *y/bl* | |
| 30604 | C-17A | 437th AW | *y/bl* | |
| *FY94* | | | | |
| 40065 | C-17A | 437th AW | *y/bl* | |
| 40066 | C-17A | 437th AW | *y/bl* | |
| 40067 | C-17A | 437th AW | *y/bl* | |

| Notes | Type | | | |
|---|---|---|---|---|
| | 40068 | C-17A | 437th AW | *y/bl* |
| | 40069 | C-17A | 437th AW | *y/bl* |
| | 40070 | C-17A | 97th AMW | *r/y* |
| | *FY95* | | | |
| | 50102 | C-17A | 97th AMW | *r/y* |
| | 50103 | C-17A | 97th AMW | *r/y* |
| | 50104 | C-17A | 437th AW | *y/bl* |
| | 50105 | C-17A | 437th AW | *y/bl* |
| | 50106 | C-17A | 437th AW | *y/bl* |
| | 50107 | C-17A | 437th AW | *y/bl* |
| | *FY96* | | | |
| | 60001 | C-17A | 437th AW | *y/bl* |
| | 60002 | C-17A | 437th AW | *y/bl* |
| | 60003 | C-17A | 437th AW | *y/bl* |
| | 60004 | C-17A | 437th AW | *y/bl* |
| | 60005 | C-17A | 437th AW | *y/bl* |
| | 60006 | C-17A | 437th AW | *y/bl* |
| | 60007 | C-17A | 437th AW | *y/bl* |
| | 60008 | C-17A | 437th AW | *y/bl* |
| | *FY87* | | | |
| | 70025 | C-17A | 412th TW | |
| | *FY97* | | | |
| | 70041 | C-17A | 437th AW | *y/bl* |
| | 70042 | C-17A | 437th AW | *y/bl* |
| | 70043 | C-17A | 437th AW | *y/bl* |
| | 70044 | C-17A | 437th AW | *y/bl* |
| | 70045 | C-17A | 437th AW | *y/bl* |
| | 70046 | C-17A | 437th AW | *y/bl* |
| | 70047 | C-17A | 437th AW | *y/bl* |
| | 70048 | C-17A | 437th AW | *y/bl* |
| | *FY98* | | | |
| | 80049 | C-17A | 437th AW | *y/bl* |
| | 80050 | C-17A | 437th AW | *y/bl* |
| | 80051 | C-17A | 62nd AW | |
| | 80052 | C-17A | 62nd AW | |
| | 80053 | C-17A | 62nd AW | |
| | 80054 | C-17A | 62nd AW | |
| | 80055 | C-17A | 62nd AW | |
| | 80056 | C-17A | 62nd AW | |
| | 80057 | C-17A | 62nd AW | |
| | *FY88* | | | |
| | 80265 | C-17A | 437th AW | *y/bl* |
| | 80266 | C-17A | 97th AMW | *r/y* |
| | *FY99* | | | |
| | 90058 | C-17A | | |
| | 90059 | C-17A | | |
| | 90060 | C-17A | | |
| | 90061 | C-17A | | |
| | 90062 | C-17A | | |
| | 90063 | C-17A | | |
| | 90064 | C-17A | | |
| | 90065 | C-17A | | |
| | 90066 | C-17A | | |
| | 90067 | C-17A | | |
| | 90068 | C-17A | | |
| | 90069 | C-17A | | |
| | 90070 | C-17A | | |
| | *FY89* | | | |
| | 91189 | C-17A | 97th AMW | *r/y* |
| | 91190 | C-17A | 437th AW | *y/bl* |
| | 91191 | C-17A | 437th AW | *y/bl* |
| | 91192 | C-17A | 437th AW | *y/bl* |

**Boeing EC-18B**
12th ACCS/93rd ACW, Robins AFB, Georgia [WR] (*gn*);
452nd FLTS/412th TW, Edwards AFB, California [ED];

| | |
|---|---|
| *FY81* | |
| 10891 | 412th TW |
| 10892 | 412th TW |
| 10893 | 93rd ACW |
| 10894 | 412th TW |

**Grumman C-20 Gulfstream III/IV**
99th AS/89th AW, Andrews AFB, Maryland;
OSAC/PAT, US Army, Andrews AFB, Maryland;
Pacific Flight Detachment, Hickam AFB, Hawaii

| | |
|---|---|
| **C-20B Gulfstream III** | |
| *FY86* | |
| 60201 | 89th AW |
| 60202 | 89th AW |
| 60203 | 89th AW |
| 60204 | 89th AW |
| 60206 | 89th AW |
| 60403 | 89th AW |
| **C-20C Gulfstream III** | |
| *FY85* | |
| 50049 | 89th AW |
| 50050 | 89th AW |
| **C-20E Gulfstream III** | |
| *FY87* | |
| 70139 | Pacific Flt Det |
| 70140 | OSAC/PAT |
| **C-20F Gulfstream IV** | |
| *FY91* | |
| 10108 | OSAC/PAT |
| **C-20H Gulfstream IV** | |
| *FY90* | |
| 00300 | 89th AW |

**Boeing C-22B/C-22C***
88th ABW, Wright-Patterson AFB, Ohio;
201st AS/113th FW DC ANG, Andrews AFB, Maryland

| | |
|---|---|
| *FY83* | |
| 34610 | 201st AS |
| 34615 | 201st AS |
| 34616 | 201st AS |
| 34618* | 88th ABW |

**Boeing VC-25A**
89th AW, Andrews AFB, Maryland
*FY82*
28000
*FY92*
29000

**Boeing C-32A**
1st AS/89th AW, Andrews AFB, Maryland
*FY98*
80001
80002
*FY99*
90003
90004

**Gulfstream Aerospace C-37A Gulfstream V**
99th AS/89th AW, Andrews AFB, Maryland
*FY97*
70400
70401

**IAI C-38A Astra**
201st AS/113th FW DC ANG, Andrews AFB, Maryland
*FY94*
41569
41570

| Type | | | Notes |
|---|---|---|---|

**Boeing T-43A/CT-43A***
562nd FTS/12th FTW, Randolph AFB, Texas [RA] (*bk/y*);
201st AS/113th FW DC ANG, Andrews AFB, Maryland;
CinC CentCom 6th ARW, MacDill AFB, Florida

| | | | |
|---|---|---|---|
| *FY71* | | | |
| 11403 | 12th FTW | *bk/y* | |
| 11404 | 12th FTW | *bk/y* | |
| 11405 | 12th FTW | *bk/y* | |
| *FY72* | | | |
| 20283* | 6th ARW | | |
| 20288 | 12th FTW | *bk/y* | |
| *FY73* | | | |
| 31150 | 12th FTW | *bk/y* | |
| 31151 | 12th FTW | *bk/y* | |
| 31152 | 12th FTW | *bk/y* | |
| 31153 | 12th FTW | *bk/y* | |
| 31154 | 201st AS | | |
| 31156 | 12th FTW | *bk/y* | |

**Boeing B-52H Stratofortress**
2nd BW, Barksdale AFB, Louisiana [LA]:
1th BS (*gd*), 20th BS (*bl*) & 96th BS (*r*);
23rd BS/5th BW, Minot AFB, North Dakota [MT] (*r/y*);
93rd BS/917th Wg AFRC, Barksdale AFB, Louisiana [BD] (*y/bl*);
419th FLTS/412th TW Edwards AFB, California [ED]

| | | | |
|---|---|---|---|
| *FY60* | | | |
| 00001 | 2nd BW | *bl* | |
| 00002 | 2nd BW | *gd* | |
| 00003 | 93rd BS | *y/bl* | |
| 00004 | 5th BW | *r/y* | |
| 00005 | 5th BW | *r/y* | |
| 00007 | 5th BW | *r/y* | |
| 00008 | 2nd BW | *r* | |
| 00009 | 5th BW | *r/y* | |
| 00010 | 2nd BW | *r* | |
| 00011 | 2nd BW | *gd* | |
| 00012 | 2nd BW | *bl* | |
| 00013 | 2nd BW | *r* | |
| 00014 | 2nd BW | *bl* | |
| 00015 | 5th BW | *r/y* | |
| 00016 | 2nd BW | *r* | |
| 00017 | 2nd BW | *gd* | |
| 00018 | 5th BW | *r/y* | |
| 00019 | 2nd BW | *r* | |
| 00020 | 2nd BW | *bl* | |
| 00022 | 2nd BW | *r* | |
| 00023 | 5th BW | *r/y* | |
| 00024 | 5th BW | *r/y* | |
| 00025 | 2nd BW | *bl* | |
| 00026 | 5th BW | *r/y* | |
| 00028 | 2nd BW | *r* | |
| 00029 | 5th BW | *r/y* | |
| 00030 | 2nd BW | *bl* | |
| 00031 | 2nd BW | *bl* | |
| 00032 | 2nd BW | *gd* | |
| 00033 | 5th BW | *r/y* | |
| 00034 | 5th BW | *r/y* | |
| 00035 | 2nd BW | *gd* | |
| 00036 | 5th BW | *r/y* | |
| 00037 | 2nd BW | *r* | |
| 00038 | 2nd BW | *gd* | |
| 00041 | 93rd BS | *y/bl* | |
| 00042 | 93rd BS | *r/y* | |
| 00043 | 2nd BW | *bl* | |
| 00044 | 5th BW | *r/y* | |
| 00045 | 93rd BS | *y/bl* | |
| 00046 | 2nd BW | *bl* | |
| 00048 | 2nd BW | *gd* | |
| 00049 | 2nd BW | *bl* | |
| 00050 | 412th TW | | |
| 00051 | 5th BW | *r/y* | |
| 00052 | 2nd BW | *r* | |
| 00053 | 2nd BW | *r* | |
| 00054 | 2nd BW | *r* | |
| 00055 | 5th BW | *r/y* | |
| 00056 | 2nd BW | *r/y* | |
| 00057 | 2nd BW | *bl* | |
| 00058 | 2nd BW | *gd* | |
| 00059 | 2nd BW | *r* | |
| 00060 | 5th BW | *r/y* | |
| 00061 | 2nd BW | *gd* | |
| 00062 | 2nd BW | *bl* | |
| *FY61* | | | |
| 10001 | 5th BW | *r/y* | |
| 10002 | 2nd BW | *gd* | |
| 10003 | 2nd BW | *gd* | |
| 10004 | 2nd BW | *bl* | |
| 10005 | 5th BW | *r/y* | |
| 10006 | 2nd BW | *gd* | |
| 10007 | 5th BW | *r/y* | |
| 10008 | 93rd BS | *y/bl* | |
| 10009 | 2nd BW | *r* | |
| 10010 | 2nd BW | *bl* | |
| 10011 | 2nd BW | *gd* | |
| 10012 | 2nd BW | *gd* | |
| 10013 | 2nd BW | *r* | |
| 10014 | 5th BW | *r/y* | |
| 10015 | 2nd BW | *gd* | |
| 10016 | 2nd BW | *gd* | |
| 10017 | 93rd BS | *y/bl* | |
| 10018 | 5th BW | *r/y* | |
| 10019 | 2nd BW | *r* | |
| 10020 | 2nd BW | *r* | |
| 10021 | 93rd BS | *y/bl* | |
| 10022 | 93rd BS | *y/bl* | |
| 10023 | 2nd BW | *bl* | |
| 10024 | 2nd BW | *r* | |
| 10025 | 2nd BW | *gd* | |
| 10027 | 5th BW | *r/y* | |
| 10028 | 2nd BW | *gd* | |
| 10029 | 93rd BS | *y/bl* | |
| 10031 | 2nd BW | *gd* | |
| 10032 | 93rd BS | *y/bl* | |
| 10034 | 5th BW | *r/y* | |
| 10035 | 5th BW | *r/y* | |
| 10036 | 5th BW | *r/y* | |
| 10038 | 2nd BW | *gd* | |
| 10039 | 2nd BW | *gd* | |
| 10040 | 5th BW | *r/y* | |

**Lockheed F-117A Nighthawk**
49th FW, Holloman AFB, New Mexico [HO]: 7th FS (*si*), 8th FS (*y*) & 9th FS (*r*)
53rd Wg, Nellis AFB, Nevada [OT] (*gy/w*);
445th FLTS/412th TW, Edwards AFB, California [ED]

| | | | | |
|---|---|---|---|---|
| 79-783 | (79-10783) | ED | | |
| 79-784 | (79-10784) | ED | | |
| 80-786 | (80-0786) | HO | *r* | |
| 80-787 | (80-0787) | HO | *si* | |
| 80-788 | (80-0788) | HO | *si* | |
| 80-789 | (80-0789) | HO | *r* | |
| 80-790 | (80-0790) | HO | *r* | |
| 80-791 | (80-0791) | HO | *y* | |
| 81-794 | (81-10794) | HO | *r* | |
| 81-795 | (81-10795) | HO | *y* | |
| 81-796 | (81-10796) | HO | *si* | |

| Notes | Type |
|---|---|
| | 81-797 (81-10797) HO *r* |
| | 81-798 (81-10798) HO *y* |
| | 82-799 (82-0799) HO *y* |
| | 82-800 (82-0800) HO *y* |
| | 82-801 (82-0801) HO |
| | 82-802 (82-0802) HO *y* |
| | 82-803 (82-0803) HO *y* |
| | 82-804 (82-0804) HO *si* [7th FS] |
| | 82-805 (82-0805) HO *si* |
| | 83-807 (83-0807) HO *r* |
| | 83-808 (83-0808) HO *si* |
| | 84-809 (84-0809) HO *r* [9th FS] |
| | 84-810 (84-0810) HO *r* |
| | 84-811 (84-0811) HO *si* |
| | 84-812 (84-0812) HO *r* [49th OG] |
| | 84-824 (84-0824) HO *r* |
| | 84-826 (84-0826) HO *r* |
| | 84-827 (84-0827) HO *y* |
| | 84-828 (84-0828) HO *si* [7th FS] |
| | 85-813 (85-0813) HO |
| | 85-814 (85-0814) HO *y* |
| | 85-816 (85-0816) HO *y* [49th FW] |
| | 85-817 (85-0817) HO *y* |
| | 85-818 (85-0818) HO *y* |
| | 85-819 (85-0819) HO *y* [8th FS] |
| | 85-820 (85-0820) HO *r* |
| | 85-829 (85-0829) HO *y* |
| | 85-830 (85-0830) HO *r* |
| | 85-831 (85-0831) ED |
| | 85-832 (85-0832) HO *y* |
| | 85-833 (85-0833) HO *si* [49th OG] |
| | 85-834 (85-0834) HO *y* |
| | 85-835 (85-0835) HO *r* |
| | 85-836 (85-0836) HO *r* |
| | 86-821 (86-0821) HO *r* |
| | 86-822 (86-0822) HO |
| | 86-823 (86-0823) HO *r* |
| | 86-837 (86-0837) OT *gy/w* |
| | 86-838 (86-0838) HO *y* [8th FS] |
| | 86-839 (86-0839) HO *r* |
| | 86-840 (86-0840) HO *si* |
| | 88-841 (88-0841) HO |
| | 88-842 (88-0842) HO *y* |
| | 88-843 (88-0843) HO *si* [49th FW] |

**Lockheed C-130 Hercules**

1st SOS/353rd SOG, Kadena AB, Japan;
517th AS/3rd Wg, Elmendorf AFB, Alaska [AK] (*w*);
4th SOS/16th SOW, Hurlburt Field, Florida;
7th SOS/352nd SOG, RAF Mildenhall, UK;
8th SOS/16th SOW, Duke Field, Florida;
9th SOS/16th OG, Eglin AFB, Florida;
15th SOS/16th SOW, Hurlburt Field, Florida;
16th SOS/16th SOW, Hurlburt Field, Florida;
17th SOS/353rd SOG, Kadena AB, Japan;
37th AS/86th AW, Ramstein AB, Germany [RS] (*bl/w*);
39th RQS/939th RQW AFRC, Patrick AFB, Florida [FL];
41st ECS/355th Wg, Davis-Monthan AFB, Arizona [DM] (*bl*);
42nd ACCS/355th Wg, Davis-Monthan AFB, Arizona [DM] (*w*);
43rd AW, Pope AFB, North Carolina [FT]: 2nd AS (*bl/y*) & 41st AS (*gn/or*);
43rd ECS/355th Wg, Davis-Monthan AFB, Arizona [DM] (*r*);
53rd WRS/403rd AW AFRC, Keesler AFB, Missouri;
550th SOS/58th SOW, Kirtland AFB, New Mexico;
67th SOS/352nd SOG, RAF Mildenhall, UK;
71st RQS/347th Wg, Moody AFB, Georgia [MY] (*bl*);
95th AS/440th AW AFRC, Genera Mitchell ARS, Wisconsin (*w/r*);
96th AS/934th AW AFRC, Minneapolis/St Paul, Minnesota (*pr*);
102nd RQS/106th RQW, Suffolk Field, New York ANG [LI];
105th AS/118th AW, Nashville, Tennessee ANG (*r*);
109th AS/133rd AW, Minneapolis/ St Paul, Minnesota ANG [MN] (*gn/bl*);
115th AS/146th AW, Channel Island ANGS, California ANG [CI] (*gn*);
122nd FS/159th FW, NAS New Orleans, Louisiana ANG [JZ];
129th RQS/129th RQW, Moffet Field, California ANG [CA] (*bl*);
130th AS/130th AW, Yeager Int'l Airport, Charleston, West Virginia ANG [WV] (*bl/y*);
135th AS/135th AW, Martin State Airport, Maryland ANG [MD] (*bk/y*);
139th AS/109th AW, Schenectady, New York ANG [NY];
142nd AS/166th AW, New Castle County Airport, Delaware ANG [DE] (*bl*);
143rd AS/143rd AW, Quonset, Rhode Island ANG [RI] (*r*);
144th AS/176th CW, Kulis ANGB, Alaska ANG (*bk/y*);
154th TS/189th AW, Little Rock, Arkansas ANG (*r*);
156th AS/145th AW, Charlotte, North Carolina ANG [NC] (*bl*);
157th FS/169th FW, McEntire ANGS, South Carolina ANG [SC];
158th AS/165th AW, Savannah, Georgia ANG (*r*);
164th AS/179th AW, Mansfield, Ohio ANG [OH] (*bl*);
165th AS/123rd AW, Standiford Field, Kentucky ANG [KY];
167th AS/167th AW, Martinsburg, West Virginia ANG [WV] (*r*);
169th AS/182nd AW, Peoria, Illinois ANG [IL];
171st AS/191st AW, Selfridge ANGB, Michigan ANG (*y/bk*);
180th AS/139th AW, Rosencrans Memorial Airport, Missouri ANG [XP];
181st AS/136th AW, NAS Dallas, Texas ANG (*bl/w*);
185th AS/137th AW, Will Rogers World Airport, Oklahoma ANG [OK] (*bl*);
187th AS/153rd AW, Cheyenne, Wyoming ANG [WY];
189th AS/124th Wg, Boise, Idaho ANG [ID];
192nd AS/152nd AW, Reno, Nevada ANG [NV] (*w*);

*Type* *Notes*

193rd SOS/193rd SOW, Harrisburg, Pennsylvania ANG [PA];
198th AS/156th AW, San Juan, Puerto Rico ANG;
204th AS/154th Wg, Hickam AFB, Hawaii ANG;
210th RQS/176th CW, Kulis ANGB, Alaska ANG [AK];
303rd RQS/939th RQW AFRC, Portland, Oregon [PD] (*y*);
314th AW, Little Rock AFB, Arkansas: 53rd AS (*bk*) & 62nd AS (*bl*);
317th AG, Dyess AFB, Texas: 39th AS (*r*) & 40th AS (*bl*);
327th AS/913th AW AFRC, NAS Willow Grove, Pennsylvania (*bk*);
328th AS/914th AW AFRC, Niagara Falls, New York [NF] (*bl*);
357th AS/908th AW AFRC, Maxwell AFB, Alabama (*bl*);
36th AS/374th AW, Yokota AB, Japan [YJ] (*r*);
418th FLTS/412th TW Edwards AFB, California [ED];
463rd AG Little Rock AFB, Arkansas [LK]: 50th AS (*r*) & 61st AS (*gn*);
645th Materiel Sqn, Palmdale, California [D4];
700th AS/94th AW AFRC, Dobbins ARB, Georgia [DB] (*bl*);
711th SOS/919th SOW AFRC, Duke Field, Florida;
731st AS/302nd AW AFRC, Peterson AFB, Colorado (*bl/w*);
757th AS/910th AW AFRC, Youngstown ARS, Ohio [YO] (*bl*);
758th AS/911th AW AFRC, Pittsburgh ARS, Pennsylvania [PI] (*bk/y*);
773rd AS/910th AW AFRC, Youngstown ARS, Ohio [YO] (*r*);
815th AS/403rd AW AFRC, Keesler AFB, Missouri [KT] (*r*)

| | | | |
|---|---|---|---|
| *FY90* | | | |
| 00161 | MC-130H | 15th SOS | |
| 00162 | MC-130H | 15th SOS | |
| 00163 | AC-130U | 4th SOS | |
| 00164 | AC-130U | 4th SOS | |
| 00165 | AC-130U | 4th SOS | |
| 00166 | AC-130U | 4th SOS | |
| 00167 | AC-130U | 4th SOS | |
| *FY80* | | | |
| 00320 | C-130H | 158th AS | *r* |
| 00321 | C-30H | 158th AS | *r* |
| 00322 | C-130H | 158th AS | *r* |
| 00323 | C-130H | 158th AS | *r* |
| 00324 | C-130H | 158th AS | *r* |
| 00325 | C-130H | 158th AS | *r* |
| 00326 | C-130H | 158th AS | *r* |
| 00332 | C-130H | 158th AS | *r* |
| *FY90* | | | |
| 01057 | C-130H | 181st AS | *bl/w* |
| 01058 | C-130H | 130th AS | *bl/y* |
| *FY70* | | | |
| 01259 | C-130E | 43rd AW | *gn/or* |
| 01260 | C-130E | 37th AS | *bl/w* |
| 01261 | C-130E | 43rd AW | *bl/y* |
| 01262 | C-130E | 43rd AW | *gn/or* |
| 01263 | C-130E | 43rd AW | |
| *gn/or* | | | |
| 01264 | C-130E | 37th AS | *bl/w* |
| 01265 | C-130E | 43rd AW | *bl/y* |
| 01266 | C-130E | 43rd AW | *gn/or* |
| 01267 | C-130E | 43rd AW | *gn/or* |
| 01268 | C-130E | 43rd AW | *bl/y* |
| 01270 | C-130E | 43rd AW | *gn/or* |
| 01271 | C-130E | 37th AS | *bl/w* |
| 01272 | C-130E | 43rd AW | *bl/y* |
| 01273 | C-130E | 43rd AW | *gn/or* |
| 01274 | C-130E | 37th AS | *bl/w* |
| 01275 | C-130E | 43rd AW | *bl/y* |
| 01276 | C-130E | 43rd AW | *gn/or* |
| *FY90* | | | |
| 01791 | C-130H | 164th AS | *bl* |
| 01792 | C-130H | 164th AS | *bl* |
| 01793 | C-130H | 164th AS | *bl* |
| 01794 | C-130H | 164th AS | *bl* |
| 01795 | C-130H | 164th AS | *bl* |
| 01796 | C-130H | 164th AS | *bl* |
| 01797 | C-130H | 164th AS | *bl* |
| 01798 | C-130H | 164th AS | *bl* |
| 02103 | HC-130N | 210th RQS | |
| 09107 | C-130H | 757th AS | *bl* |
| 09108 | C-130H | 757th AS | *bl* |
| *FY81* | | | |
| 10626 | C-130H | 700th AS | *bl* |
| 10627 | C-130H | 700th AS | *bl* |
| 10628 | C-130H | 700th AS | *bl* |
| 10629 | C-130H | 700th AS | *bl* |
| 10630 | C-130H | 700th AS | *bl* |
| 10631 | C-130H | 700th AS | *bl* |
| *FY68* | | | |
| 10934 | C-130E | 43rd AW | *bl/y* |
| 10935 | C-130E | 37th AS | *bl/w* |
| 10937 | C-130E | 43rd AW | *gn/or* |
| 10938 | C-130E | 37th AS | *bl/w* |
| 10939 | C-130E | 43rd AW | *gn/or* |
| 10940 | C-130E | 43rd AW | *gn/or* |
| 10941 | C-130E | 43rd AW | *bl/y* |
| 10942 | C-130E | 43rd AW | *bl/y* |
| 10943 | C-130E | 37th AS | *bl/w* |
| 10947 | C-130E | 37th AS | *bl/w* |
| 10948 | C-130E | 463rd AG | *gn* |
| *FY91* | | | |
| 11231 | C-130H | 165th AS | |
| 11232 | C-130H | 165th AS | |
| 11233 | C-130H | 165th AS | |
| 11234 | C-130H | 165th AS | |
| 11235 | C-130H | 165th AS | |
| 11236 | C-130H | 165th AS | |
| 11237 | C-130H | 165th AS | |
| 11238 | C-130H | 165th AS | |
| 11239 | C-130H | 165th AS | |
| 11651 | C-130H | 165th AS | |
| 11652 | C-130H | 165th AS | |
| 11653 | C-130H | 165th AS | |
| *FY61* | | | |
| 12358 | C-130E | 171st AS | *y/bk* |
| 12359 | C-130E | 115th AS | *gn* |
| 12361 | C-130E | 192nd AS | *w* |
| 12367 | C-130E | 115th AS | *gn* |
| 12369 | C-130E | 198th AS | |
| 12370 | C-130E | 171st AS | *y/bk* |
| 12371 | C-130E | 171st AS | *y/bk* |
| 12372 | C-130E | 115th AS | *gn* |
| *FY64* | | | |
| 14852 | HC-130P | 71st RQS | *bl* |
| 14853 | HC-130P | 71st RQS | *bl* |
| 14854 | MC-130P | 9th SOS | |
| 14855 | HC-130P | 303rd RQS | *y* |
| 14858 | MC-130P | 58th SOW | |
| 14859 | C-130E | 711th SOS | |
| 14860 | HC-130P | 303rd RQS | *y* |
| 14861 | WC-130H | 53rd WRS | |
| 14862 | EC-130H | 645th MS | |
| 14863 | HC-130P | 71st RQS | *bl* |
| 14864 | HC-130P | 39th RQS | |

| Notes | Type | | | |
|---|---|---|---|---|
| | 14865 | HC-130P | 71st RQS | *bl* |
| | 14866 | WC-130H | 53rd WRS | |
| | 17680 | C-130E | 314th AW | *bk* |
| | 17681 | C-130E | 37th AS | *bl/w* |
| | 18240 | C-130E | 37th AS | *bl/w* |
| | *FY91* | | | |
| | 19141 | C-130H | 773rd AS | *r* |
| | 19142 | C-130H | 773rd AS | *r* |
| | 19143 | C-130H | 773rd AS | *r* |
| | 19144 | C-130H | 773rd AS | *r* |
| | *FY82* | | | |
| | 20054 | C-130H | 144th AS | *bk/y* |
| | 20055 | C-130H | 144th AS | *bk/y* |
| | 20056 | C-130H | 144th AS | *bk/y* |
| | 20057 | C-130H | 144th AS | *bk/y* |
| | 20058 | C-130H | 144th AS | *bk/y* |
| | 20059 | C-130H | 144th AS | *bk/y* |
| | 20060 | C-130H | 144th AS | *bk/y* |
| | 20061 | C-130H | 144th AS | *bk/y* |
| | *FY92* | | | |
| | 20253 | AC-130U | 4th SOS | |
| | 20547 | C-130H | 463rd AG | *r* |
| | 20548 | C-130H | 463rd AG | *r* |
| | 20549 | C-130H | 463rd AG | *r* |
| | 20550 | C-130H | 463rd AG | *r* |
| | 20551 | C-130H | 463rd AG | *r* |
| | 20552 | C-130H | 463rd AG | *r* |
| | 20553 | C-130H | 463rd AG | *r* |
| | 20554 | C-130H | 463rd AG | *r* |
| | 21094 | LC-130H | 139th AS | |
| | 21095 | LC-130H | 139th AS | |
| | *FY72* | | | |
| | 21288 | C-130E | 374th AW | *r* |
| | 21289 | C-130E | 374th AW | *r* |
| | 21290 | C-130E | 374th AW | *r* |
| | 21291 | C-130E | 314th AW | *bk* |
| | 21292 | C-130E | 463rd AG | *gn* |
| | 21293 | C-130E | 463rd AG | *gn* |
| | 21294 | C-130E | 463rd AG | *gn* |
| | 21295 | C-130E | 314th AW | *bl* |
| | 21296 | C-130E | 314th AW | *bk* |
| | 21298 | C-130E | 374th AW | *r* |
| | 21299 | C-130E | 374th AW | *r* |
| | *FY92* | | | |
| | 21451 | C-130H | 156th AS | *bl* |
| | 21452 | C-130H | 156th AS | *bl* |
| | 21453 | C-130H | 156th AS | *bl* |
| | 21454 | C-130H | 156th AS | *bl* |
| | 21531 | C-130H | 187th AS | |
| | 21532 | C-130H | 187th AS | |
| | 21533 | C-130H | 187th AS | |
| | 21534 | C-130H | 187th AS | |
| | 21535 | C-130H | 187th AS | |
| | 21536 | C-130H | 187th AS | |
| | 21537 | C-130H | 187th AS | |
| | 21538 | C-130H | 187th AS | |
| | *FY62* | | | |
| | 21784 | C-130E | 154th TS | *r* |
| | 21786 | C-130E | 189th AS | |
| | 21787 | C-130E | 154th TS | *r* |
| | 21788 | C-130E | 154th TS | *r* |
| | 21789 | C-130E | 314th AW | *bk* |
| | 21790 | C-130E | 154th TS | *r* |
| | 21791 | EC-130E | 42nd ACCS | *w* |
| | 21792 | C-130E | 463rd AG | *gn* |
| | 21793 | C-130E | 463rd AG | *gn* |
| | 21795 | C-130E | 154th TS | *r* |
| | 21798 | C-130E | 314th AW | *bk* |
| | 21799 | C-130E | 115th AS | *gn* |
| | 21801 | C-130E | 115th AS | *gn* |
| | 21804 | C-130E | 154th TS | *r* |
| | 21806 | C-130E | 96th AS | *pr* |
| | 21808 | C-130E | 314th AW | *bk* |

| Notes | Type | | | |
|---|---|---|---|---|
| | 21810 | C-130E | 314th AW | *bl* |
| | 21811 | C-130E | 115th AS | *gn* |
| | 21812 | C-130E | 192nd AS | *w* |
| | 21816 | C-130E | 314th AW | *bl* |
| | 21817 | C-130E | 189th AS | |
| | 21818 | EC-130E | 42nd ACCS | *w* |
| | 21820 | C-130E | 171st AS | *y/bk* |
| | 21823 | C-130E | 96th AS | *pr* |
| | 21824 | C-130E | 154th TS | *r* |
| | 21825 | EC-130E | 42nd ACCS | *w* |
| | 21826 | C-130E | 115th AS | *gn* |
| | 21829 | C-130E | 192nd AS | *w* |
| | 21832 | EC-130E | 42nd ACCS | *w* |
| | 21833 | C-130E | 115th AS | *gn* |
| | 21834 | C-130E | 374th AW | *r* |
| | 21835 | C-130E | 96th AS | *pr* |
| | 21836 | EC-130E | 42nd ACCS | *w* |
| | 21837 | C-130E | 189th AS | |
| | 21839 | C-130E | 96th AS | *pr* |
| | 21842 | C-130E | 171st AS | *y/bk* |
| | 21843 | MC-130E | 711th SOS | |
| | 21844 | C-130E | 96th AS | *pr* |
| | 21846 | C-130E | 189th AS | |
| | 21847 | C-130E | 96th AS | *pr* |
| | 21848 | C-130E | 96th AS | *pr* |
| | 21849 | C-130E | 815th AS | *r* |
| | 21850 | C-130E | 314th AW | *bk* |
| | 21851 | C-130E | 115th AS | *gn* |
| | 21852 | C-130E | 96th AS | *pr* |
| | 21855 | MC-130E | 8th SOS | |
| | 21856 | C-130E | 143rd AS | *r* |
| | 21857 | EC-130E | 42nd ACCS | *w* |
| | 21858 | C-130E | 192nd AS | *w* |
| | 21859 | C-130E | 192nd AS | *w* |
| | 21862 | C-130E | 115th AS | *gn* |
| | 21863 | EC-130E | 42nd ACCS | *gy* |
| | 21864 | C-130E | 189th AS | |
| | 21866 | C-130E | 314th AW | *bk* |
| | *FY92* | | | |
| | 23021 | C-130H | 773rd AS | *r* |
| | 23022 | C-130H | 773rd AS | *r* |
| | 23023 | C-130H | 773rd AS | *r* |
| | 23024 | C-130H | 773rd AS | *r* |
| | 23281 | C-130H | 328th AS | *bl* |
| | 23282 | C-130H | 328th AS | *bl* |
| | 23283 | C-130H | 328th AS | *bl* |
| | 23284 | C-130H | 328th AS | *bl* |
| | 23285 | C-130H | 328th AS | *bl* |
| | 23286 | C-130H | 328th AS | *bl* |
| | 23287 | C-130H | 328th AS | *bl* |
| | 23288 | C-130H | 328th AS | *bl* |
| | *FY83* | | | |
| | 30486 | C-130H | 139th AS | |
| | 30487 | C-130H | 139th AS | |
| | 30488 | C-130H | 139th AS | |
| | 30489 | C-130H | 139th AS | |
| | 30490 | LC-130H | 139th AS | |
| | 30491 | LC-130H | 139th AS | |
| | 30492 | LC-130H | 139th AS | |
| | 30493 | LC-130H | 139th AS | |
| | *FY93* | | | |
| | 31036 | C-130H | 463rd AG | *r* |
| | 31037 | C-130H | 463rd AG | *r* |
| | 31038 | C-130H | 463rd AG | *r* |
| | 31039 | C-130H | 463rd AG | *r* |
| | 31040 | C-130H | 463rd AG | *r* |
| | 31041 | C-130H | 463rd AG | *r* |
| | 31096 | LC-130H | 139th AS | |
| | *FY83* | | | |
| | 31212 | MC-130H | 15th SOS | |
| | *FY93* | | | |
| | 31455 | C-130H | 156th AS | *bl* |
| | 31456 | C-130H | 156th AS | *bl* |

| Type | | | | Notes |
|---|---|---|---|---|
| 31457 | C-130H | 156th AS | *bl* | |
| 31458 | C-130H | 156th AS | *bl* | |
| 31459 | C-130H | 156th AS | *bl* | |
| 31561 | C-130H | 156th AS | *bl* | |
| 31562 | C-130H | 156th AS | *bl* | |
| 31563 | C-130H | 156th AS | *bl* | |
| *FY73* | | | | |
| 31580 | EC-130H | 43rd ECS | *r* | |
| 31581 | EC-130H | 43rd ECS | *r* | |
| 31582 | C-130H | 317th AG | | |
| 31583 | EC-130H | 43rd ECS | *r* | |
| 31584 | EC-130H | 43rd ECS | *r* | |
| 31585 | EC-130H | 41st ECS | *bl* | |
| 31586 | EC-130H | 41st ECS | *bl* | |
| 31587 | EC-130H | 41st ECS | *bl* | |
| 31588 | EC-130H | 41st ECS | *bl* | |
| 31590 | EC-130H | 43rd ECS | *r* | |
| 31592 | EC-130H | 41st ECS | *bl* | |
| 31594 | EC-130H | 41st ECS | *bl* | |
| 31595 | EC-130H | 43rd ECS | *r* | |
| 31597 | C-130H | 317th AG | *bl* | |
| 31598 | C-130H | 317th AG | *r* | |
| *FY93* | | | | |
| 32041 | C-130H | 204th AS | | |
| 32042 | C-130H | 204th AS | | |
| 32104 | HC-130N | 210th RQS | | |
| 32105 | HC-130N | 210th RQS | | |
| 32106 | HC-130N | 210th RQS | | |
| 37311 | C-130H | 731st AS | *bl/w* | |
| 37312 | C-130H | 731st AS | *bl/w* | |
| 37313 | C-130H | 731st AS | *bl/w* | |
| 37314 | C-130H | 731st AS | *bl/w* | |
| *FY63* | | | | |
| 37764 | C-130E | 815th AS | *r* | |
| 37765 | C-130E | 314th AW | *bl* | |
| 37767 | C-130E | 314th AW | *bl* | |
| 37768 | C-130E | 314th AW | *bl* | |
| 37769 | C-130E | 327th AS | *bk* | |
| 37770 | C-130E | 815th AS | *r* | |
| 37773 | EC-130E | 193rd SOS | | |
| 37776 | C-130E | 327th AS | *bk* | |
| 37777 | C-130E | 192nd AS | *w* | |
| 37778 | C-130E | 314th AW | *bk* | |
| 37781 | C-130E | 463rd AG | *gn* | |
| 37782 | C-130E | 143rd AS | *r* | |
| 37783 | EC-130E | 193rd SOS | | |
| 37784 | C-130E | 314th AW | *bl* | |
| 37785 | MC-130E | 711th SOS | | |
| 37786 | C-130E | 171st AS | *y/bk* | |
| 37788 | C-130E | 143rd AS | *r* | |
| 37790 | C-130E | 374th AW | *r* | |
| 37791 | C-130E | 314th AW | *bl* | |
| 37792 | C-130E | 169th AS | | |
| 37796 | C-130E | 314th AW | *bk* | |
| 37799 | C-130E | 314th AW | *bl* | |
| 37800 | C-130E | 169th AS | | |
| 37804 | C-130E | 314th AW | *bl* | |
| 37805 | C-130E | 815th AS | *r* | |
| 37808 | C-130E | 463rd AG | *gn* | |
| 37809 | C-130E | 463rd AG | *gn* | |
| 37811 | C-130E | 143rd AS | *r* | |
| 37812 | C-130E | 169th AS | | |
| 37813 | C-130E | 314th AW | *bl* | |
| 37814 | C-130E | 67th SOS | | |
| 37815 | C-130E | 193rd SOS | | |
| 37816 | C-130E | 193rd SOS | | |
| 37817 | C-130E | 815th AS | *r* | |
| 37818 | C-130E | 169th AS | | |
| 37819 | C-130E | 374th AW | *r* | |
| 37821 | C-130E | 374th AW | *r* | |
| 37822 | C-130E | 815th AS | *r* | |
| 37823 | C-130E | 327th AS | *bk* | |
| 37824 | C-130E | 143rd AS | *r* | |

| Type | | | | Notes |
|---|---|---|---|---|
| 37825 | C-130E | 135th AS | *bk/y* | |
| 37826 | C-130E | 327th AS | *bk* | |
| 37828 | EC-130E | 193rd SOS | | |
| 37829 | C-130E | 463rd AG | *gn* | |
| 37830 | C-130E | 314th AW | *bk* | |
| 37831 | C-130E | 135th AS | *bk/y* | |
| 37832 | C-130E | 327th AS | *bk* | |
| 37833 | C-130E | 327th AS | *bk* | |
| 37834 | C-130E | 327th AS | *bk* | |
| 37835 | C-130E | 314th AW | *bk* | |
| 37837 | C-130E | 374th AW | *r* | |
| 37838 | C-130E | 314th AW | *bl* | |
| 37839 | C-130E | 463rd AG | *gn* | |
| 37840 | C-130E | 143rd AS | *r* | |
| 37841 | C-130E | 198th AS | | |
| 37842 | C-130E | 1st SOS | | |
| 37845 | C-130E | 463rd AG | | |
| 37846 | C-130E | 314th AW | | |
| 37847 | C-130E | 154th TS | *r* | |
| 37848 | C-130E | 327th AS | *bk* | |
| 37849 | C-130E | 314th AW | *bl* | |
| 37850 | C-130E | 374th AW | *r* | |
| 37851 | C-130E | 192nd AS | *w* | |
| 37852 | C-130E | 815th AS | *r* | |
| 37853 | C-130E | 327th AS | *bk* | |
| 37854 | C-130E | 463rd AG | *gn* | |
| 37856 | C-130E | 815th AS | *r* | |
| 37857 | C-130E | 463rd AG | *gn* | |
| 37858 | C-130E | 169th AS | | |
| 37859 | C-130E | 143rd AS | *r* | |
| 37860 | C-130E | 314th AW | *bl* | |
| 37861 | C-130E | 192nd AS | *w* | |
| 37864 | C-130E | 314th AW | *bl* | |
| 37865 | C-130E | 374th AW | *r* | |
| 37866 | C-130E | 314th AW | *bk* | |
| 37867 | C-130E | 327th AS | *bk* | |
| 37868 | C-130E | 143rd AS | *r* | |
| 37869 | EC-130E | 193rd SOS | | |
| 37871 | C-130E | 374th AW | *r* | |
| 37872 | C-130E | 169th AS | | |
| 37874 | C-130E | 314th AW | *bk* | |
| 37876 | C-130E | 463rd AG | *gn* | |
| 37877 | C-130E | 169th AS | | |
| 37879 | C-130E | 374th AW | *r* | |
| 37880 | C-130E | 314th AW | *bl* | |
| 37882 | C-130E | 314th AW | *bk* | |
| 37883 | C-130E | 327th AS | *bk* | |
| 37884 | C-130E | 463rd AG | *gn* | |
| 37885 | C-130E | 37th AS | *bl/w* | |
| 37887 | C-130E | 37th AS | *bl/w* | |
| 37888 | C-130E | 463rd AG | *gn* | |
| 37889 | C-130E | 143rd AS | *r* | |
| 37890 | C-130E | 314th AW | *bl* | |
| 37892 | C-130E | 327th AS | *bk* | |
| 37893 | C-130E | 314th AW | *bk* | |
| 37894 | C-130E | 463rd AG | *gn* | |
| 37895 | C-130E | 171st AS | *y/bk* | |
| 37896 | C-130E | 463rd AG | *gn* | |
| 37897 | C-130E | 169th AS | | |
| 37898 | C-130E | 8th SOS | | |
| 37899 | C-130E | 314th AW | *bl* | |
| 39810 | C-130E | 71st RQS | *bl* | |
| 39812 | C-130E | 314th AW | *bk* | |
| 39813 | C-130E | 171st AS | *y/bk* | |
| 39814 | C-130E | 314th AW | *bl* | |
| 39815 | C-130E | 171st AS | *y/bk* | |
| 39816 | EC-130E | 193rd SOS | | |
| 39817 | EC-130E | 193rd SOS | | |
| *FY84* | | | | |
| 40204 | C-130H | 700th AS | *bl* | |
| 40205 | C-130H | 700th AS | *bl* | |
| 40206 | C-130H | 142nd AS | *bl* | |
| 40207 | C-130H | 142nd AS | *bl* | |

| Notes | Type | | | |
|---|---|---|---|---|
| | 40208 | C-130H | 142nd AS | bl |
| | 40209 | C-130H | 142nd AS | bl |
| | 40210 | C-130H | 142nd AS | bl |
| | 40211 | C-130H | 142nd AS | bl |
| | 40212 | C-130H | 142nd AS | bl |
| | 40213 | C-130H | 142nd AS | bl |
| | 40475 | MC-130H | 15th SOS | |
| | 40476 | MC-130H | 7th SOS | |
| | *FY64* | | | |
| | 40495 | C-130E | 43rd AW | gn/or |
| | 40496 | C-130E | 43rd AW | bl/y |
| | 40498 | C-130E | 43rd AW | bl/y |
| | 40499 | C-130E | 43rd AW | bl/y |
| | 40500 | NC-130E | 645th MS | |
| | 40502 | C-130E | 37th AS | bl/w |
| | 40504 | C-130E | 43rd AW | bl/y |
| | 40510 | C-130E | 198th AS | |
| | 40512 | C-130E | 154th TS | r |
| | 40514 | C-130E | 135th AS | bk/y |
| | 40515 | C-130E | 135th AS | bk/y |
| | 40517 | C-130E | 43rd AW | gn/or |
| | 40518 | C-130E | 463rd AG | gn |
| | 40519 | C-130E | 314th AW | bl |
| | 40520 | C-130E | 135th AS | bk/y |
| | 40521 | C-130E | 135th AS | bk/y |
| | 40523 | MC-130E | 8th SOS | |
| | 40525 | C-130E | 43rd AW | gn/or |
| | 40526 | C-130E | 135th AS | bk/y |
| | 40527 | C-130E | 37th AS | bl/w |
| | 40529 | C-130E | 43rd AW | gn/or |
| | 40531 | C-130E | 43rd AW | bl/y |
| | 40533 | C-130E | 37th AS | bl/w |
| | 40535 | C-130E | 314th AW | bl |
| | 40537 | C-130E | 43rd AW | gn/or |
| | 40538 | C-130E | 314th AW | bk |
| | 40539 | C-130E | 43rd AW | gn/or |
| | 40540 | C-130E | 43rd AW | bl/y |
| | 40541 | C-130E | 314th AW | bk |
| | 40542 | C-130E | 314th AW | bk |
| | 40544 | C-130E | 135th AS | bk/y |
| | 40550 | C-130E | 37th AS | bl/w |
| | 40551 | MC-130E | 711th SOS | |
| | 40555 | MC-130E | 8th SOS | |
| | 40557 | C-130E | 314th AW | bl |
| | 40559 | MC-130E | 8th SOS | |
| | 40561 | MC-130E | 711th SOS | |
| | 40562 | MC-130E | 711th SOS | |
| | 40565 | MC-130E | 711th SOS | |
| | 40566 | MC-130E | 8th SOS | |
| | 40567 | MC-130E | 8th SOS | |
| | 40568 | MC-130E | 8th SOS | |
| | 40569 | C-130E | 314th AW | bl |
| | 40570 | C-130E | 43rd AW | gn/or |
| | 40571 | MC-130E | 711th SOS | |
| | 40572 | MC-130E | 711th SOS | |
| | *FY74* | | | |
| | 41658 | C-130H | 3rd Wg | w |
| | 41659 | C-130H | 3rd Wg | w |
| | 41660 | C-130H | 3rd Wg | w |
| | 41661 | C-130H | 3rd Wg | w |
| | 41663 | C-130H | 317th AG | bl |
| | 41664 | C-130H | 3rd Wg | w |
| | 41665 | C-130H | 317th AG | bl |
| | 41666 | C-130H | 317th AG | bl |
| | 41667 | C-130H | 317th AG | r |
| | 41668 | C-130H | 3rd Wg | w |
| | 41669 | C-130H | 317th AG | r |
| | 41670 | C-130H | 317th AG | r |
| | 41671 | C-130H | 317th AG | bl |
| | 41673 | C-130H | 317th AG | bl |
| | 41674 | C-130H | 317th AG | r |
| | 41675 | C-130H | 317th AG | r |
| | 41676 | C-130H | 3rd Wg | m |

| Notes | Type | | | |
|---|---|---|---|---|
| | 41677 | C-130H | 317th AG | bl |
| | 41679 | C-130H | 317th AG | bl |
| | 41680 | C-130H | 317th AG | r |
| | 41682 | C-130H | 3rd Wg | w |
| | 41684 | C-130H | 3rd Wg | w |
| | 41685 | C-130H | 3rd Wg | w |
| | 41687 | C-130H | 317th AG | r |
| | 41688 | C-130H | 317th AG | bl |
| | 41689 | C-130H | 317th AG | bl |
| | 41690 | C-130H | 3rd Wg | w |
| | 41691 | C-130H | 317th AG | r |
| | 41692 | C-130H | 3rd Wg | w |
| | 42061 | C-130H | 317th AG | r |
| | 42062 | C-130H | 3rd Wg | w |
| | 42063 | C-130H | 317th AG | bl |
| | 42065 | C-130H | 317th AG | bl |
| | 42066 | C-130H | 3rd Wg | w |
| | 42067 | C-130H | 317th AG | r |
| | 42069 | C-130H | 317th AG | r |
| | 42070 | C-130H | 3rd Wg | w |
| | 42071 | C-130H | 3rd Wg | w |
| | 42072 | C-130H | 317th AG | bl |
| | 42130 | C-130H | 317th AG | r |
| | 42131 | C-130H | 3rd Wg | w |
| | 42132 | C-130H | 317th AG | r |
| | 42133 | C-130H | 3rd Wg | w |
| | 42134 | C-130H | 317th AG | r |
| | *FY94* | | | |
| | 46701 | C-130H | 167th AS | r |
| | 46702 | C-130H | 167th AS | r |
| | 46703 | C-130H | 167th AS | r |
| | 46704 | C-130H | 167th AS | r |
| | 46705 | C-130H | 167th AS | r |
| | 46706 | C-130H | 167th AS | r |
| | 46707 | C-130H | 167th AS | r |
| | 46708 | C-130H | 167th AS | r |
| | 47310 | C-130H | 731st AS | bl/w |
| | 47315 | C-130H | 731st AS | bl/w |
| | 47316 | C-130H | 731st AS | bl/w |
| | 47317 | C-130H | 731st AS | bl/w |
| | 47318 | C-130H | 731st AS | bl/w |
| | 47319 | C-130H | 731st AS | bl/w |
| | 47320 | C-130H | 731st AS | bl/w |
| | 47321 | C-130H | 731st AS | bl/w |
| | 48151 | C-130J | LMTAS | |
| | 48152 | C-130J | 412th TW | |
| | *FY85* | | | |
| | 50011 | MC-130H | 58th SOW | |
| | 50012 | MC-130H | 15th SOS | |
| | 50035 | C-130H | 357th AS | bl |
| | 50036 | C-130H | 357th AS | bl |
| | 50037 | C-130H | 357th AS | bl |
| | 50038 | C-130H | 357th AS | bl |
| | 50039 | C-130H | 357th AS | bl |
| | 50040 | C-130H | 357th AS | bl |
| | 50041 | C-130H | 357th AS | bl |
| | 50042 | C-130H | 357th AS | bl |
| | *FY65* | | | |
| | 50962 | EC-130H | 42nd ACCS | w |
| | 50963 | WC-130H | 53rd WRS | |
| | 50964 | C-130E | 39th RQS | |
| | 50966 | WC-130H | 53rd WRS | |
| | 50967 | WC-130H | 53rd WRS | |
| | 50968 | WC-130H | 53rd WRS | |
| | 50969 | C-130E | 711th SOS | |
| | 50970 | HC-130P | 303rd RQS | y |
| | 50971 | MC-130P | 5th SOS | |
| | 50973 | HC-130P | 71st RQS | bl |
| | 50974 | HC-130P | 102nd RQS | |
| | 50975 | MC-130P | 58th SOW | |
| | 50976 | HC-130P | 303rd RQS | y |
| | 50977 | WC-130H | 53rd WRS | |
| | 50978 | HC-130P | 102nd RQS | |

| Type | | | Notes |
|---|---|---|---|
| 50979 | NC-130H | 412th TW | |
| 50980 | WC-130H | 53rd WRS | |
| 50981 | HC-130P | 129th RQS | *bl* |
| 50982 | HC-130P | 71st RQS | *bl* |
| 50983 | HC-130H | 129th RQS | *bl* |
| 50984 | WC-130H | 53rd WRS | |
| 50985 | WC-130H | 53rd WRS | |
| 50986 | HC-130P | 71st RQS | *bl* |
| 50987 | HC-130P | 71st RQS | *bl* |
| 50988 | HC-130P | 71st RQS | *bl* |
| 50989 | EC-130H | 41st ECS | *bl* |
| 50991 | MC-130P | 9th SOS | |
| 50992 | MC-130P | 17th SOS | |
| 50993 | MC-130P | 17th SOS | |
| 50994 | MC-130P | 17th SOS | |
| *FY95* | | | |
| 51001 | C-130H | 109th AS | *gn/bl* |
| 51002 | C-130H | 109th AS | *gn/bl* |
| *FY85* | | | |
| 51361 | C-130H | 181st AS | *bl/w* |
| 51362 | C-130H | 181st AS | *bl/w* |
| 51363 | C-130H | 181st AS | *bl/w* |
| 51364 | C-130H | 181st AS | *bl/w* |
| 51365 | C-130H | 181st AS | *bl/w* |
| 51366 | C-130H | 181st AS | *bl/w* |
| 51367 | C-130H | 181st AS | *bl/w* |
| 51368 | C-130H | 181st AS | *bl/w* |
| *FY95* | | | |
| 56709 | C-130H | 167th AS | *r* |
| 56710 | C-130H | 167th AS | *r* |
| 56711 | C-130H | 167th AS | *r* |
| 56712 | C-130H | 167th AS | *r* |
| *FY66* | | | |
| 60212 | MC-130P | 58th SOW | |
| 60213 | MC-130P | 9th SOS | |
| 60215 | MC-130P | 17th SOS | |
| 60216 | MC-130P | | |
| 60217 | MC-130P | 9th SOS | |
| 60219 | MC-130P | | |
| 60220 | MC-130P | 9th SOS | |
| 60221 | HC-130P | 129th RQS | *bl* |
| 60222 | HC-130P | 102nd RQS | |
| 60223 | MC-130P | 9th SOS | |
| 60224 | HC-130P | 129th RQS | *bl* |
| 60225 | MC-130P | 9th SOS | |
| *FY86* | | | |
| 60410 | C-130H | 758th AS | *bk/y* |
| 60411 | C-130H | 758th AS | *bk/y* |
| 60412 | C-130H | 758th AS | *bk/y* |
| 60413 | C-130H | 758th AS | *bk/y* |
| 60414 | C-130H | 758th AS | *bk/y* |
| 60415 | C-130H | 758th AS | *bk/y* |
| 60418 | C-130H | 758th AS | *bk/y* |
| 60419 | C-130H | 758th AS | *bk/y* |
| *FY96* | | | |
| 61003 | C-130H | 109th AS | *gn/bl* |
| 61004 | C-130H | 109th AS | *gn/bl* |
| 61005 | C-130H | 109th AS | *gn/bl* |
| 61006 | C-130H | 109th AS | *gn/bl* |
| 61007 | C-130H | 109th AS | *gn/bl* |
| 61008 | C-130H | 109th AS | *gn/bl* |
| *FY86* | | | |
| 61391 | C-130H | 180th AS | |
| 61392 | C-130H | 180th AS | |
| 61393 | C-130H | 180th AS | |
| 61394 | C-130H | 180th AS | |
| 61395 | C-130H | 180th AS | |
| 61396 | C-130H | 180th AS | |
| 61397 | C-130H | 180th AS | |
| 61398 | C-130H | 180th AS | |
| 61699 | MC-130H | 7th SOS | |
| *FY96* | | | |
| 65300 | WC-130J | 53rd WRS | |
| 65301 | WC-130J | 53rd WRS | |
| 65302 | WC-130J | 53rd WRS | |
| 67322 | C-130H | 731st AS | *bl/w* |
| 67323 | C-130H | 731st AS | *bl/w* |
| 67324 | C-130H | 731st AS | *bl/w* |
| 67325 | C-130H | 731st AS | *bl/w* |
| 68153 | C-130J | 815th AS | *r* |
| 68154 | C-130J | 815th AS | *r* |
| *FY87* | | | |
| 70023 | MC-130H | 7th SOS | |
| 70024 | MC-130H | 15th SOS | |
| 70125 | MC-130H | 58th SOW | |
| 70126 | MC-130H | 58th SOW | |
| 70127 | MC-130H | 58th SOW | |
| 70128 | AC-130U | 4th SOS | |
| *FY97* | | | |
| 71351 | C-130J | 135th AS | *bk/y* |
| 71352 | C-130J | 135th AS | *bk/y* |
| 71353 | C-130J | 135th AS | *bk/y* |
| 71354 | C-130J | 135th AS | *bk/y* |
| 71931 | EC-130J | LMTAS | |
| 75303 | WC-130J | 53rd WRS | |
| 75304 | WC-130J | 53rd WRS | |
| 75305 | WC-130J | 53rd WRS | |
| 75306 | WC-130J | 53rd WRS | |
| *FY87* | | | |
| 79281 | C-130H | 95th AS | *w/r* |
| 79282 | C-130H | 95th AS | *w/r* |
| 79283 | C-130H | 95th AS | *w/r* |
| 79284 | C-130H | 700th AS | *bl* |
| 79285 | C-130H | 95th AS | *w/r* |
| 79286 | C-130H | 357th AS | *bl* |
| 79287 | C-130H | 95th AS | *w/r* |
| 79288 | C-130H | 758th AS | *bk/y* |
| *FY88* | | | |
| 80191 | MC-130H | 1st SOS | |
| 80192 | MC-130H | 1st SOS | |
| 80193 | MC-130H | 7th SOS | |
| 80194 | MC-130H | 7th SOS | |
| 80195 | MC-130H | 1st SOS | |
| 80264 | MC-130H | 1st SOS | |
| *FY78* | | | |
| 80806 | C-130H | 185th AS | *bl* |
| 80807 | C-130H | 185th AS | *bl* |
| 80808 | C-130H | 185th AS | *bl* |
| 80809 | C-130H | 185th AS | *bl* |
| 80810 | C-130H | 185th AS | *bl* |
| 80811 | C-130H | 185th AS | *bl* |
| 80812 | C-130H | 185th AS | *bl* |
| 80813 | C-130H | 185th AS | *bl* |
| *FY88* | | | |
| 81301 | C-130H | 130th AS | *bl/y* |
| 81302 | C-130H | 130th AS | *bl/y* |
| 81303 | C-130H | 130th AS | *bl/y* |
| 81304 | C-130H | 130th AS | *bl/y* |
| 81305 | C-130H | 130th AS | *bl/y* |
| 81306 | C-130H | 130th AS | *bl/y* |
| 81307 | C-130H | 130th AS | *bl/y* |
| 81308 | C-130H | 130th AS | *bl/y* |
| 81803 | MC-130H | 1st SOS | |
| 82101 | HC-130N | 102nd RQS | |
| 82102 | HC-130N | 102nd RQS | |
| 84401 | C-130H | 95th AS | *w/r* |
| 84402 | C-130H | 95th AS | *w/r* |
| 84403 | C-130H | 95th AS | *w/r* |
| 84404 | C-130H | 95th AS | *w/r* |
| 84405 | C-130H | 95th AS | *w/r* |
| 84406 | C-130H | 95th AS | *w/r* |
| 84407 | C-130H | 95th AS | *w/r* |
| *FY98* | | | |
| 85307 | WC-130J | 53rd WRS | |
| *FY89* | | | |
| 90280 | MC-130H | 15th SOS | |

| Notes | Type | | | |
|---|---|---|---|---|
| | 90281 | MC-130H | 15th SOS | |
| | 90282 | MC-130H | 15th SOS | |
| | 90283 | MC-130H | 15th SOS | |
| | *FY79* | | | |
| | 90473 | C-130H | 144th AS | *bk/y* |
| | 90474 | C-130H | 185th AS | *bl* |
| | 90475 | C-130H | 204th AS | |
| | 90476 | C-130H | 157th FS | |
| | 90477 | C-130H | 158th AS | *r* |
| | 90478 | C-130H | 204th AS | |
| | 90479 | C-130H | 204th AS | |
| | 90480 | C-130H | 122nd FS | |
| | *FY89* | | | |
| | 90509 | AC-130U | 4th SOS | |
| | 90510 | AC-130U | 4th SOS | |
| | 90511 | AC-130U | 4th SOS | |
| | 90512 | AC-130U | 4th SOS | |
| | 90513 | AC-130U | 4th SOS | |
| | 90514 | AC-130U | 4th SOS | |
| | 91051 | C-130H | 105th AS | *r* |
| | 91052 | C-130H | 105th AS | *r* |
| | 91053 | C-130H | 105th AS | *r* |
| | 91054 | C-130H | 105th AS | *r* |
| | 91055 | C-130H | 142nd AS | *bl* |
| | 91056 | C-130H | 180th AS | |
| | 91181 | C-130H | 105th AS | *r* |
| | 91182 | C-130H | 105th AS | *r* |
| | 91183 | C-130H | 105th AS | *r* |
| | 91184 | C-130H | 105th AS | *r* |
| | 91185 | C-130H | 105th AS | *r* |
| | 91186 | C-130H | 105th AS | *r* |
| | 91187 | C-130H | 105th AS | *r* |
| | 91188 | C-130H | 105th AS | *r* |
| | *FY69* | | | |
| | 95819 | MC-130P | 9th SOS | |
| | 95820 | MC-130P | 67th SOS | |
| | 95821 | MC-130P | 58th SOW | |
| | 95822 | MC-130P | 9th SOS | |
| | 95823 | MC-130P | 67th SOS | |
| | 95824 | HC-130N | 39th RQS | |
| | 95825 | MC-130P | | |
| | 95826 | MC-130P | 67th SOS | |
| | 95827 | MC-130P | | |
| | 95828 | MC-130P | 67th SOS | |
| | 95829 | HC-130N | 39th RQS | |
| | 95830 | HC-130N | 39th RQS | |
| | 95831 | MC-130P | 67th SOS | |
| | 95832 | MC-130P | 9th SOS | |
| | 95833 | HC-130N | 39th RQS | |
| | 96566 | C-130E | 37th AS | *bl/w* |
| | 96568 | AC-130H | 16th SOS | |
| | 96569 | AC-130H | 16th SOS | |
| | 96570 | AC-130H | 16th SOS | |
| | 96572 | AC-130H | 16th SOS | |
| | 96573 | AC-130H | 16th SOS | |
| | 96574 | AC-130H | 16th SOS | |
| | 96575 | AC-130H | 16th SOS | |
| | 96577 | AC-130H | 16th SOS | |
| | 96580 | C-130E | 43rd AW | *gn/or* |
| | 96582 | C-130E | 37th AS | *bl/w* |
| | 96583 | C-130E | 37th AS | *bl/w* |
| | *FY89* | | | |
| | 99101 | C-130H | 757th AS | *bl* |
| | 99102 | C-130H | 757th AS | *bl* |
| | 99103 | C-130H | 757th AS | *bl* |
| | 99104 | C-130H | 757th AS | *bl* |
| | 99105 | C-130H | 757th AS | *bl* |
| | 99106 | C-130H | 757th AS | *bl* |

**Boeing C-135/C-137**

91st ARS/6th ARW, MacDill AFB, Florida (*y/bl*);
65th AS/15th ABW, Hickam AFB, Hawaii;
909th ARS/18th Wg, Kadena AB, Japan [ZZ] (*w*);
99th ARS/19th ARG, Robins AFB, Georgia (*y/bl*);
22nd ARW, McConnell AFB, Kansas: 344th ARS (*y/bk*), 349th ARS (*y/bl*) 350th ARS (*y/r*) & 384th ARS (*y/pr*);
55th Wg, Offutt AFB, Nebraska [OF]: 38th RS (*gn*) & 45th RS (*bk*);
88th ABW, Wright-Patterson AFB, Ohio;
1st AS/89th AW, Andrews AFB, Maryland;
92nd ARW, Fairchild AFB, Washington: 92nd ARS (*bk*), 93rd ARS (*bl*), 96th ARS (*gn*), 97th ARS (*y*) & 98th ARS (*r*);
55th ARS/97th AMW, Altus AFB, Oklahoma (*y/r*);
351st ARS/100th ARW, RAF Mildenhall, UK [D] (*r/w/bl*);
132nd ARS/101st ARW, Bangor, Maine ANG (*w/gn*);
136th ARS/107th ARW, Niagara Falls, New York ANG (*bl*);
108th ARW, McGuire AFB, New Jersey ANG: 141st ARS (*bk/y*) & 150th ARS (*bl*);
106th ARS/117th ARW, Birmingham, Alabama ANG (*w/r*);
121st ARW, Rickenbacker ANGB, Ohio ANG: 145th ARS & 166th ARS (*bl*);
108th ARS/126th ARW, Scott AFB, Illinois ANG (*w/bl*);
126th ARS/128th ARW, Mitchell Field, Wisconsin ANG (*w/bl*);
151st ARS/134th ARW, Knoxville, Tennessee ANG (*w/or*);
116th ARS/141st ARW, Fairchild AFB, Washington ANG (*gn/w*);
191st ARS/151st ARW, Salt Lake City, Utah ANG (*bl/bk*);
203rd ARS/154th Wg, Hickam AFB, Hawaii ANG (*y/bk*);
173rd ARS/155th ARW, Lincoln, Nebraska ANG (*r/w*);
133rd ARS/157th ARW, Pease ANGB, New Hampshire ANG (*bl*);
197th ARS/161st ARW, Phoenix, Arizona ANG;
196th ARS/163rd ARW, March ARB, California ANG (*bl/w*);
168th ARS/168th ARW, Eielson AFB, Alaska ANG (*bl/y*);
171st ARW, Greater Pittsburgh, Pennsylvania ANG: 146th ARS (*y/bk*)/47th ARS (*bk/y*);
153rd ARS/186th ARW, Meridian, Mississippi ANG (*bk/gd*);
117th ARS/190th ARW, Forbes Field, Kansas ANG (*bl/y*);
319th ARW, Grand Forks AFB, North Dakota: 905th ARS (*bl*), 906th ARS (*y*), 911th ARS (*r*) & 912th ARS (*w*);
22nd ARS/366th Wg, Mountain Home AFB, Idaho [MO] (*y/gn*);
452nd FLTS/412th TW, Edwards AFB, California [ED] (*bl*);
434th ARW AFRC, Grissom AFB, Indiana: 72nd ARS (*bl*) & 74th ARS (*r/w*);

Type Notes

336th ARS/452nd AMW AFRC, March ARB, California (*y*);
465th ARS/507th ARW AFRC, Tinker AFB, Oklahoma (*bl/y*);
645th Materiel Sqn, Greenville, Texas;
77th ARS/916th ARW AFRC, Seymour Johnson AFB, North Carolina (*gn);*
63rd ARS/927th ARW AFRC, Selfridge ANGB,Michigan (*pr/w*);
314th ARS/940th ARW AFRC, McClellan AFB, California (*or/bk*);
CinC CentCom (CinC CC)/6th ARW, MacDill AFB, Florida

*FY60*

00313 KC-135R 22nd ARW
00314 KC-135R 434th ARW *r/w*
00315 KC-135R 128th ARW *w/bl*
00316 KC-135E 141st ARW *gn/w*
00318 KC-135R 154th Wg *y/bk*
00319 KC-135R 319th ARW
00320 KC-135R 319th ARW *w*
00321 KC-135R 97th AMW *y/r*
00322 KC-135R 434th ARW *bl*
00323 KC-135R 154th Wg *y/bk*
00324 KC-135R 18th Wg *w*
00327 KC-135E 151st ARW *bl/bk*
00328 KC-135R 18th Wg *w*
00329 KC-135R 154th Wg *y/bk*
00331 KC-135R 97th AMW *y/r*
00332 KC-135R 6th ARW *y/bl*
00333 KC-135R 97th AMW *y/r*
00334 KC-135R 168th ARW *bl/y*
00335 KC-135T 22nd ARW *y/r*
00336 KC-135T 92nd ARW *gn*
00337 KC-135T 92nd ARW *m*
00339 KC-135T 92nd ARW *bl*
00341 KC-135R 121st ARW *bl*
00342 KC-135T 319th ARW *y*
00343 KC-135T 319th ARW *w*
00344 KC-135T 22nd ARW *y/bk*
00345 KC-135T 92nd ARW *y*
00346 KC-135T 92nd ARW *bk*
00347 KC-135R 121st ARW *bl*
00348 KC-135R 319th ARW *r*
00349 KC-135R 916th ARW *gn*
00350 KC-135R 22nd ARW *y/bk*
00351 KC-135R 18th Wg *w*
00353 KC-135R 319th ARW *y*
00355 KC-135R 319th ARW *y*
00356 KC-135R 22nd ARW *y/bl*
00357 KC-135R 22nd ARW *y/bk*
00358 KC-135R 107th ARW *bl*
00359 KC-135R 434th ARW *r/w*
00360 KC-135R 319th ARW *r*
00362 KC-135R 22nd ARW *y/r*
00363 KC-135R 916th ARW *gn*
00364 KC-135R 434th ARW *r/w*
00365 KC-135R 19th ARG *y/bl*
00366 KC-135R 19th ARG *y/bl*
00367 KC-135R 121st ARW *bl*
00372 C-135E 412th TW *bl*
00374 EC-135E 412th TW *bl*
00375 C-135E 412th TW *bl*
00376 C-135E 15th ABW

*FY61*

10264 KC-135R 121st ARW *bl*
10266 KC-135R 155th ARW *r/w*
10267 KC-135R 100th ARW
*r/w/bl*
10268 KC-135E 940th ARW
*or/bk*
10270 KC-135E 927th ARW *pr/w*
10271 KC-135E 927th ARW *pr/w*
10272 KC-135R 434th ARW *r/w*
10275 KC-135R 6th ARW *y/bl*
10276 KC-135R 155th ARW *r/w*
10277 KC-135R 366th Wg *y/gn*
10280 KC-135E 452nd AMW *y*
10281 KC-135E 161st ARW
10284 KC-135R 100th ARW *r/w/bl*
10288 KC-135R 100th ARW *r/w/bl*
10290 KC-135R 154th Wg *y/bk*
10292 KC-135R 22nd ARW *y/pr*
10293 KC-135R 22nd ARW *y/r*
10294 KC-135R 92nd ARW *bk*
10295 KC-135R 319th ARW *bl*
10298 KC-135R 128th ARW *w/bl*
10299 KC-135R 6th ARW *y/bl*
10300 KC-135R 19th ARG *y/bl*
10302 KC-135R 97th AMW *y/r*
10303 KC-135E 452nd AMW *y*
10304 KC-135R 22nd ARW
10305 KC-135R 18th Wg *w*
10306 KC-135R 18th Wg *w*
10307 KC-135R 434th ARW *r/w*
10308 KC-135R 97th AMW *y/r*
10309 KC-135R 128th ARW *w/bl*
10310 KC-135R 157th ARW *bl*
10311 KC-135R 22nd ARW *y/r*
10312 KC-135R 100th ARW *r/w/bl*
10313 KC-135R 916th ARW *gn*
10314 KC-135R 97th AMW *y/r*
10315 KC-135R 97th AMW *y/r*
10317 KC-135R 18th Wg *w*
10318 KC-135R 6th ARW *y/bl*
10320 KC-135R 412th TW
10321 KC-135R 92nd ARW *bl*
10323 KC-135R 6th ARW *y/bl*
10324 KC-135R 452nd AMW *y*
10327 EC-135N CinC CC
10330 EC-135E 412th TW *bl*
12662 RC-135S 55th Wg *bk*
12663 RC-135S 55th Wg *bk*
12666 WC-135W 645th MS
12669 C-135C 412th TW *bl*
12670 OC-135B 55th Wg *bl*
12672 OC-135B 55th Wg *bl*

*FY64*

14828 KC-135R 22nd ARW *y/pr*
14829 KC-135R 319th ARW *r*
14830 KC-135R 6th ARW *y/bl*
14831 KC-135R 18th Wg *w*
14832 KC-135R 154th Wg *y/bk*
14833 KC-135R 6th ARW *y/bl*
14834 KC-135R 434th ARW *r/w*
14835 KC-135R 22nd ARW *y/bk*
14836 KC-135R 319th ARW *r*
14837 KC-135R 92nd ARW *y*
14838 KC-135R 6th ARW *y/bl*
14839 KC-135R 107th ARW *bl*
14840 KC-135R 121st ARW *bl*
14841 RC-135V 55th Wg *gn*
14842 RC-135V 55th Wg *gn*
14843 RC-135V 55th Wg *gn*
14844 RC-135V 55th Wg *gn*
14845 RC-135V 55th Wg *gn*
14846 RC-135V 55th Wg *gn*
14847 RC-135U 55th Wg *gn*
14848 RC-135V 55th Wg *gn*
14849 RC-135U 55th Wg *gn*

*FY67*

19417 EC-137D 6th ARW

*FY62*

23498 KC-135R 100th ARW *r/w/bl*
23499 KC-135R 22nd ARW *y/pr*

| Notes | Type | | | |
|---|---|---|---|---|
| | 23500 | KC-135R | 128th ARW | *w/bl* |
| | 23502 | KC-135R | 319th ARW | *y* |
| | 23503 | KC-135R | 319th ARW | *r* |
| | 23504 | KC-135R | 319th ARW | *bl* |
| | 23505 | KC-135R | 6th ARW | *y/bl* |
| | 23506 | KC-135R | 157th ARW | *bl* |
| | 23507 | KC-135R | 22nd ARW | |
| | 23508 | KC-135R | 19th ARG | *y/bl* |
| | 23509 | KC-135R | 916th ARW | *gn* |
| | 23510 | KC-135R | 434th ARW | *r/w* |
| | 23511 | KC-135R | 121st ARW | *bl* |
| | 23512 | KC-135R | 128th ARW | *w/bl* |
| | 23513 | KC-135R | 366th Wg | *y/gn* |
| | 23514 | KC-135R | 154th Wg | *y/bk* |
| | 23515 | KC-135R | 157th ARW | *bl* |
| | 23516 | KC-135R | 22nd ARW | |
| | 23517 | KC-135R | 100th ARW | *r/w/bl* |
| | 23518 | KC-135R | 434th ARW | *bl* |
| | 23519 | KC-135R | 319th ARW | *r* |
| | 23520 | KC-135R | 319th ARW | *w* |
| | 23521 | KC-135R | 434th ARW | *r/w* |
| | 23523 | KC-135R | 19th ARG | *y/bl* |
| | 23524 | KC-135R | 117th ARW | *w/r* |
| | 23526 | KC-135R | 155th ARW | *r/w* |
| | 23527 | KC-135E | 108th ARW | *bl* |
| | 23528 | KC-135R | 100th ARW | *r/w/bl* |
| | 23529 | KC-135R | 97th AMW | *y/r* |
| | 23530 | KC-135R | 434th ARW | *bl* |
| | 23531 | KC-135R | 121st ARW | *bl* |
| | 23533 | KC-135R | 100th ARW | *r/w/bl* |
| | 23534 | KC-135R | 22nd ARW | *y/pr* |
| | 23537 | KC-135R | 18th Wg | *w* |
| | 23538 | KC-135R | 100th ARW | *r/w/bl* |
| | 23540 | KC-135R | 92nd ARW | *gn* |
| | 23541 | KC-135R | 22nd ARW | |
| | 23542 | KC-135R | 916th ARW | *gn* |
| | 23543 | KC-135R | 434th ARW | *bl* |
| | 23544 | KC-135R | 19th ARG | *y/bl* |
| | 23545 | KC-135R | 319th ARW | *r* |
| | 23546 | KC-135R | 97th AMW | *y/r* |
| | 23547 | KC-135R | 157th ARW | *bl* |
| | 23548 | KC-135R | 22nd ARW | *y/r* |
| | 23549 | KC-135R | 97th AMW | *y/r* |
| | 23550 | KC-135R | 97th AMW | *y/r* |
| | 23551 | KC-135R | 97th AMW | *y/r* |
| | 23552 | KC-135R | 6th ARW | *y/bl* |
| | 23553 | KC-135R | 22nd ARW | |
| | 23554 | KC-135R | 19th ARG | *y/bl* |
| | 23556 | KC-135R | 916th ARW | *gn* |
| | 23557 | KC-135R | 18th Wg | *w* |
| | 23558 | KC-135R | 22nd ARW | *y/bk* |
| | 23559 | KC-135R | 22nd ARW | *y/pr* |
| | 23561 | KC-135R | 100th ARW | *r/w/bl* |
| | 23562 | KC-135R | 319th ARW | *w* |
| | 23564 | KC-135R | 100th ARW | *r/w/bl* |
| | 23565 | KC-135R | 97th AMW | *y/r* |
| | 23566 | KC-135E | 101st ARW | *w/gn* |
| | 23568 | KC-135R | 319th ARW | *w* |
| | 23569 | KC-135R | 19th ARG | *y/bl* |
| | 23571 | KC-135R | 168th ARW | *bl/y* |
| | 23572 | KC-135R | 366th Wg | *y/gn* |
| | 23573 | KC-135R | 22nd ARW | |
| | 23575 | KC-135R | 22nd ARW | |
| | 23576 | KC-135R | 157th ARW | *bl* |
| | 23577 | KC-135R | 916th ARW | *gn* |
| | 23578 | KC-135R | 100th ARW | *r/w/bl* |
| | 23580 | KC-135R | 97th AMW | *y/r* |
| | 23582 | WC-135C | 55th Wg | *bk* |
| | 24125 | RC-135W | 55th Wg | |
| | 24126 | C-135B | 108th ARW | *bk/y* |
| | 24127 | RC-135W | 55th Wg | |
| | 24128 | RC-135S | 55th Wg | |
| | 24129 | TC-135W | 55th Wg | *gn* |

| Notes | Type | | | |
|---|---|---|---|---|
| | 24130 | RC-135W | 55th Wg | |
| | 24131 | RC-135W | 55th Wg | *gn* |
| | 24132 | RC-135W | 55th Wg | *gn* |
| | 24133 | TC-135S | 55th Wg | *bk* |
| | 24134 | RC-135W | 55th Wg | *gn* |
| | 24135 | RC-135W | 55th Wg | *gn* |
| | 24138 | RC-135W | 55th Wg | *gn* |
| | 24139 | RC-135W | 55th Wg | *gn* |
| | *FY72* | | | |
| | 27000 | C-137C | 89th AW | |
| | *FY63* | | | |
| | 37976 | KC-135R | 319th ARW | *bl* |
| | 37977 | KC-135R | 319th ARW | *bl* |
| | 37978 | KC-135R | 22nd ARW | |
| | 37979 | KC-135R | 100th ARW | *r/w/bl* |
| | 37980 | KC-135R | 97th AMW | *y/r* |
| | 37981 | KC-135R | 107th ARW | *bl* |
| | 37982 | KC-135R | 319th ARW | *y* |
| | 37984 | KC-135R | 117th ARW | *w/r* |
| | 37985 | KC-135R | 507th ARW | *bl/y* |
| | 37987 | KC-135R | 319th ARW | *bl* |
| | 37988 | KC-135R | 155th ARW | *r/w* |
| | 37991 | KC-135R | 155th ARW | *r/w* |
| | 37992 | KC-135R | 121st ARW | *bl* |
| | 37993 | KC-135R | 121st ARW | *m* |
| | 37995 | KC-135R | 22nd ARW | |
| | 37996 | KC-135R | 434th ARW | *bl* |
| | 37997 | KC-135R | 19th ARG | *y/bl* |
| | 37999 | KC-135R | 97th AMW | *y/r* |
| | 38000 | KC-135R | 19th ARG | *y/bl* |
| | 38002 | KC-135R | 22nd ARW | |
| | 38003 | KC-135R | 22nd ARW | *y/r* |
| | 38004 | KC-135R | 366th Wg | *y/gn* |
| | 38006 | KC-135R | 19th ARG | *y/bl* |
| | 38007 | KC-135R | 117th ARW | *w/r* |
| | 38008 | KC-135R | 22nd ARW | *y/r* |
| | 38011 | KC-135R | 92nd ARW | *bk* |
| | 38012 | KC-135R | 319th ARW | *bl* |
| | 38013 | KC-135R | 121st ARW | *bl* |
| | 38014 | KC-135R | 92nd ARW | *bl* |
| | 38015 | KC-135R | 168th ARW | *bl/y* |
| | 38017 | KC-135R | 100th ARW | *r/w/bl* |
| | 38018 | KC-135R | 155th ARW | *r/w* |
| | 38019 | KC-135R | 22nd ARW | *y/pr* |
| | 38020 | KC-135R | 97th AMW | *y/r* |
| | 38021 | KC-135R | 319th ARW | *bl* |
| | 38022 | KC-135R | 22nd ARW | *m* |
| | 38023 | KC-135R | 97th AMW | *y/r* |
| | 38024 | KC-135R | 452nd AMW | *y* |
| | 38025 | KC-135R | 319th ARW | *bl* |
| | 38026 | KC-135R | 319th ARW | *y* |
| | 38027 | KC-135R | 92nd ARW | *gn* |
| | 38028 | KC-135R | 168th ARW | *bl/y* |
| | 38029 | KC-135R | 128th ARW | *w/bl* |
| | 38030 | KC-135R | 154th Wg | *y/bk* |
| | 38031 | KC-135R | 19th ARG | *y/bl* |
| | 38032 | KC-135R | 434th ARW | *bl* |
| | 38033 | KC-135R | 92nd ARW | *bl* |
| | 38034 | KC-135R | 97th AMW | *y/r* |
| | 38035 | KC-135R | 117th ARW | *w/r* |
| | 38036 | KC-135R | 107th ARW | *bl* |
| | 38037 | KC-135R | 97th AMW | *y/r* |
| | 38038 | KC-135R | 157th ARW | *bl* |
| | 38039 | KC-135R | 507th ARW | *bl/y* |
| | 38040 | KC-135R | 18th Wg | *w* |
| | 38041 | KC-135R | 434th ARW | *bl* |
| | 38043 | KC-135R | 168th ARW | *bl/y* |
| | 38044 | KC-135R | 319th ARW | *y* |
| | 38045 | KC-135R | 97th AMW | *y/r* |
| | 38050 | NKC-135B | 412th TW | *bl* |
| | 38058 | KC-135D | 190th ARW | *bl/y* |
| | 38059 | KC-135D | 190th ARW | *bl/y* |
| | 38060 | KC-135D | 190th ARW | *bl/y* |

| Type | | | | Notes |
|---|---|---|---|---|
| 38061 | KC-135D | 190th ARW | *bl/y* | |
| 38871 | KC-135R | 18th Wg | *w* | |
| 38872 | KC-135R | 107th ARW | *bl* | |
| 38873 | KC-135R | 6th ARW | *y/bl* | |
| 38874 | KC-135R | 319th ARW | *w* | |
| 38875 | KC-135R | 366th Wg | *y/gn* | |
| 38876 | KC-135R | 168th ARW | *bl/y* | |
| 38877 | KC-135R | 18th Wg | *w* | |
| 38878 | KC-135R | 97th AMW | *y/r* | |
| 38879 | KC-135R | 319th ARW | *bk* | |
| 38880 | KC-135R | 507th ARW | *bl/y* | |
| 38881 | KC-135R | 97th AMW | *y/r* | |
| 38883 | KC-135R | 319th ARW | *w* | |
| 38884 | KC-135R | 22nd ARW | *y/r* | |
| 38885 | KC-135R | 319th ARW | *y* | |
| 38886 | KC-135R | 97th AMW | *y/r* | |
| 38887 | KC-135R | 97th AMW | *y/r* | |
| 38888 | KC-135R | 319th ARW | *bl* | |
| 39792 | RC-135V | 55th Wg | *gn* | |
| *FY55* | | | | |
| 53132 | NKC-135E | 412th TW | *bl* | |
| 53135 | NKC-135E | 412th TW | *bl* | |
| 53141 | KC-135E | 141st ARW | *gn/w* | |
| 53143 | KC-135E | 161st ARW | | |
| 53145 | KC-135E | 940th ARW | *or/bk* | |
| 53146 | KC-135E | 108th ARW | *bk/y* | |
| *FY85* | | | | |
| 56973 | C-137C | 89th AW | | |
| *FY56* | | | | |
| 63593 | KC-135E | 108th ARW | *bk/y* | |
| 63604 | KC-135E | 108th ARW | *bk/y* | |
| 63606 | KC-135E | 101st ARW | *w/gn* | |
| 63607 | KC-135E | 134th ARW | *w/or* | |
| 63609 | KC-135E | 134th ARW | *w/or* | |
| 63611 | KC-135E | 171st ARW | *y/bk* | |
| 63612 | KC-135E | 171st ARW | *y/bk* | |
| 63622 | KC-135E | 101st ARW | *w/gn* | |
| 63626 | KC-135E | 171st ARW | *y/bk* | |
| 63630 | KC-135E | 171st ARW | *y/bk* | |
| 63631 | KC-135E | 151st ARW | *bl/bk* | |
| 63638 | KC-135E | 161st ARW | | |
| 63640 | KC-135E | 101st ARW | *w/gn* | |
| 63641 | KC-135E | 190th ARW | *bl/y* | |
| 63643 | KC-135E | 134th ARW | *w/or* | |
| 63648 | KC-135E | 171st ARW | *y/bk* | |
| 63650 | KC-135E | 141st ARW | *gn/w* | |
| 63654 | KC-135E | 101st ARW | *w/gn* | |
| 63658 | KC-135E | 190th ARW | *bl/y* | |
| *FY57* | | | | |
| 71418 | KC-135R | 186th ARW | *bk/gd* | |
| 71419 | KC-135R | 18th Wg | *w* | |
| 71421 | KC-135E | 141st ARW | *gn/w* | |
| 71422 | KC-135E | 927th ARW | *pr/w* | |
| 71423 | KC-135E | 171st ARW | *bk/y* | |
| 71425 | KC-135E | 134th ARW | *w/or* | |
| 71426 | KC-135E | 161st ARW | | |
| 71427 | KC-135R | 121st ARW | *bl* | |
| 71428 | KC-135R | 163rd ARW | *bl/w* | |
| 71429 | KC-135E | 190th ARW | *bl/y* | |
| 71430 | KC-135R | 157th ARW | *bl* | |
| 71431 | KC-135E | 108th ARW | *bk/y* | |
| 71432 | KC-135R | 117th ARW | *w/r* | |
| 71433 | KC-135E | 161st ARW | | |
| 71434 | KC-135E | 141st ARW | *gn/w* | |
| 71435 | KC-135R | 22nd ARW | *y/r* | |
| 71436 | KC-135R | 163rd ARW | *bl/w* | |
| 71437 | KC-135R | 916th ARW | *gn* | |
| 71438 | KC-135E | 927th ARW | *pr/w* | |
| 71439 | KC-135R | 92nd ARW | *y* | |
| 71440 | KC-135R | 18th Wg | *w* | |
| 71441 | KC-135E | 126th ARW | *w/bl* | |
| 71443 | KC-135E | 101st ARW | *w/gn* | |
| 71445 | KC-135E | 108th ARW | *bk/y* | |

| Type | | | | Notes |
|---|---|---|---|---|
| 71447 | KC-135E | 171st ARW | *y/bk* | |
| 71448 | KC-135E | 101st ARW | *w/gn* | |
| 71450 | KC-135E | 101st ARW | *w/gn* | |
| 71451 | KC-135E | 141st ARW | *gn/w* | |
| 71452 | KC-135E | 161st ARW | | |
| 71453 | KC-135R | 117th ARW | *w/r* | |
| 71454 | KC-135R | 319th ARW | *y* | |
| 71455 | KC-135E | 134th ARW | *w/or* | |
| 71456 | KC-135R | | | |
| 71458 | KC-135E | 126th ARW | *w/bl* | |
| 71459 | KC-135R | 163rd ARW | *bl/w* | |
| 71460 | KC-135E | 190th ARW | *bl/y* | |
| 71461 | KC-135R | 155th ARW | *r/w* | |
| 71462 | KC-135R | 121st ARW | *bl* | |
| 71463 | KC-135E | 190th ARW | *bl/y* | |
| 71464 | KC-135E | 108th ARW | *bk/y* | |
| 71465 | KC-135E | 134th ARW | *w/or* | |
| 71468 | KC-135E | 452nd AMW | *y* | |
| 71469 | KC-135R | 121st ARW | *bl* | |
| 71471 | KC-135E | 101st ARW | *w/gn* | |
| 71472 | KC-135R | 434th ARW | *bl* | |
| 71473 | KC-135R | 319th ARW | | |
| 71474 | KC-135R | 100th ARW | *r/w/bl* | |
| 71475 | KC-135E | 161st ARW | | |
| 71479 | KC-135E | 452nd AMW | *y* | |
| 71480 | KC-135E | 126th ARW | *w/bl* | |
| 71482 | KC-135E | 190th ARW | *bl/y* | |
| 71483 | KC-135R | 92nd ARW | *gn* | |
| 71484 | KC-135E | 161st ARW | | |
| 71485 | KC-135E | 134th ARW | *w/or* | |
| 71486 | KC-135R | 92nd ARW | *r* | |
| 71487 | KC-135R | 434th ARW | *bl* | |
| 71488 | KC-135R | 319th ARW | *w* | |
| 71491 | KC-135E | 101st ARW | *w/gn* | |
| 71492 | KC-135E | 134th ARW | *w/or* | |
| 71493 | KC-135R | 6th ARW | *y/bl* | |
| 71494 | KC-135E | 126th ARW | *w/bl* | |
| 71495 | KC-135E | 161st ARW | | |
| 71496 | KC-135E | 161st ARW | | |
| 71497 | KC-135E | 151st ARW | *bl/bk* | |
| 71499 | KC-135R | 92nd ARW | *gn* | |
| 71501 | KC-135E | 141st ARW | *gn/w* | |
| 71502 | KC-135R | 97th AMW | *y/r* | |
| 71503 | KC-135E | 134th ARW | *w/or* | |
| 71504 | KC-135E | 927th ARW | *pr/w* | |
| 71505 | KC-135E | 101st ARW | *w/gn* | |
| 71506 | KC-135R | 319th ARW | *w* | |
| 71507 | KC-135E | 108th ARW | *bk/y* | |
| 71508 | KC-135R | 154th Wg | *y/bk* | |
| 71509 | KC-135E | 171st ARW | *bk/y* | |
| 71510 | KC-135E | 151st ARW | *bl/bk* | |
| 71511 | KC-135E | 940th ARW | *or/bk* | |
| 71512 | KC-135R | 452nd AMW | *y* | |
| 71514 | KC-135R | 128th ARW | *w/bl* | |
| 72589 | KC-135E | 15th ABW | | |
| 72593 | KC-135R | 121st ARW | *bl* | |
| 72594 | KC-135E | 126th ARW | *w/bl* | |
| 72595 | KC-135E | 171st ARW | *bk/y* | |
| 72597 | KC-135R | 186th ARW | *bk/gd* | |
| 72598 | KC-135R | 452nd AMW | *y* | |
| 72599 | KC-135R | 916th ARW | *gn* | |
| 72600 | KC-135E | 141st ARW | *gn/w* | |
| 72601 | KC-135E | 134th ARW | *w/or* | |
| 72602 | KC-135E | 108th ARW | *bl* | |
| 72603 | KC-135E | 927th ARW | *pr/w* | |
| 72604 | KC-135E | 171st ARW | *y/bk* | |
| 72605 | KC-135R | 6th ARW | *y/bl* | |
| 72606 | KC-135E | 108th ARW | *bl* | |
| 72607 | KC-135E | 171st ARW | *bk/y* | |
| 72608 | KC-135E | 171st ARW | *bk/y* | |
| *FY58* | | | | |
| 80001 | KC-135R | 22nd ARW | | |
| 80003 | KC-135E | 126th ARW | *w/bl* | |

| Notes | Type | | | |
|---|---|---|---|---|
| | 80004 | KC-135R | 186th ARW | *bk/gd* |
| | 80005 | KC-135E | 190th ARW | *bl/y* |
| | 80006 | KC-135E | 151st ARW | *bl/bk* |
| | 80008 | KC-135R | 157th ARW | *bl* |
| | 80009 | KC-135R | 128th ARW | *w/bl* |
| | 80010 | KC-135R | 186th ARW | *bk/gd* |
| | 80011 | KC-135R | 22nd ARW | *y/bl* |
| | 80012 | KC-135E | 151st ARW | *bl/bk* |
| | 80013 | KC-135E | 927th ARW | *pr/w* |
| | 80014 | KC-135E | 126th ARW | *w/bl* |
| | 80015 | KC-135R | 434th ARW | *r/w* |
| | 80016 | KC-135R | 18th Wg | *w* |
| | 80017 | KC-135E | 171st ARW | *y/bk* |
| | 80018 | KC-135R | 22nd ARW | *y/pr* |
| | 80020 | KC-135E | 141st ARW | *gn/w* |
| | 80021 | KC-135R | 128th ARW | *w/bl* |
| | 80023 | KC-135R | 107th ARW | *bl* |
| | 80024 | KC-135E | 171st ARW | *y/bk* |
| | 80027 | KC-135R | 22nd ARW | *y/bl* |
| | 80030 | KC-135R | 117th ARW | *w/r* |
| | 80032 | KC-135E | 108th ARW | *bl* |
| | 80034 | KC-135R | 97th AMW | *y/r* |
| | 80035 | KC-135R | 22nd ARW | *y/bl* |
| | 80036 | KC-135R | 18th Wg | *w* |
| | 80037 | KC-135E | 171st ARW | *bk/y* |
| | 80038 | KC-135R | 916th ARW | *gn* |
| | 80040 | KC-135E | 108th ARW | *bl* |
| | 80041 | KC-135E | 927th ARW | *pr/w* |
| | 80042 | KC-135T | 319th ARW | *y* |
| | 80043 | KC-135E | 151st ARW | *bl/bk* |
| | 80044 | KC-135E | 108th ARW | *bk/y* |
| | 80045 | KC-135T | 92nd ARW | *bl* |
| | 80046 | KC-135T | 92nd ARW | *r* |
| | 80047 | KC-135T | 319th ARW | *w* |
| | 80049 | KC-135T | 92nd ARW | *y* |
| | 80050 | KC-135T | 92nd ARW | *bk* |
| | 80051 | KC-135R | 507th ARW | *bl/y* |
| | 80052 | KC-135E | 452nd AMW | *y* |
| | 80053 | KC-135E | 940th ARW | *or/bk* |
| | 80054 | KC-135T | 92nd ARW | *gn* |
| | 80055 | KC-135T | 92nd ARW | *y* |
| | 80056 | KC-135R | 186th ARW | *bk/gd* |
| | 80057 | KC-135E | 126th ARW | *w/bl* |
| | 80058 | KC-135E | 940th ARW | *or/bk* |
| | 80059 | KC-135R | 186th ARW | *bk/gd* |
| | 80060 | KC-135T | 92nd ARW | *bl* |
| | 80061 | KC-135T | 319th ARW | *r* |
| | 80062 | KC-135T | 92nd ARW | *gn* |
| | 80063 | KC-135R | 507th ARW | *bl/y* |
| | 80064 | KC-135E | 940th ARW | *or/bk* |
| | 80065 | KC-135T | 319th ARW | *bl* |
| | 80066 | KC-135R | 507th ARW | *bl/y* |
| | 80067 | KC-135E | 126th ARW | *w/bl* |
| | 80068 | KC-135E | 126th ARW | *w/bl* |
| | 80069 | KC-135T | 92nd ARW | *y* |
| | 80071 | KC-135T | 22nd ARW | *y/bk* |
| | 80072 | KC-135T | 92nd ARW | *gn* |
| | 80073 | KC-135R | 117th ARW | *w/r* |
| | 80074 | KC-135T | 92nd ARW | *r* |
| | 80075 | KC-135R | 434th ARW | *bl* |
| | 80076 | KC-135R | 434th ARW | *r/w* |
| | 80077 | KC-135T | 92nd ARW | *bk* |
| | 80078 | KC-135E | 108th ARW | *bl* |
| | 80079 | KC-135R | 507th ARW | *bl/y* |
| | 80080 | KC-135E | 151st ARW | *bl/bk* |
| | 80082 | KC-135E | 141st ARW | *gn/w* |
| | 80083 | KC-135R | 121st ARW | *bl* |
| | 80084 | KC-135T | 92nd ARW | *r* |
| | 80085 | KC-135E | 452nd AMW | *y* |
| | 80086 | KC-135T | 92nd ARW | *gn* |
| | 80087 | KC-135E | 108th ARW | *bl* |
| | 80088 | KC-135T | 22nd ARW | *y/bk* |
| | 80089 | KC-135T | 22nd ARW | *y/bk* |
| | 80090 | KC-135E | 940th ARW | *or/bk* |
| | 80092 | KC-135R | 157th ARW | *bl* |
| | 80093 | KC-135R | 319th ARW | *r* |
| | 80094 | KC-135T | 92nd ARW | *bk* |
| | 80095 | KC-135T | 22nd ARW | *y/bk* |
| | 80096 | KC-135E | 940th ARW | *or/bk* |
| | 80098 | KC-135R | 157th ARW | *bl* |
| | 80099 | KC-135T | 92nd ARW | *bl* |
| | 80100 | KC-135R | 22nd ARW | |
| | 80102 | KC-135R | 434th ARW | *r/w* |
| | 80103 | KC-135T | 92nd ARW | *gn* |
| | 80104 | KC-135R | 107th ARW | *bl* |
| | 80106 | KC-135R | 117th ARW | *w/r* |
| | 80107 | KC-135E | 151st ARW | *bl/bk* |
| | 80108 | KC-135E | 940th ARW | *or/bk* |
| | 80109 | KC-135R | 186th ARW | *bk/gd* |
| | 80111 | KC-135E | 108th ARW | *bk/y* |
| | 80112 | KC-135T | 92nd ARW | *bl* |
| | 80113 | KC-135R | 18th Wg | *w* |
| | 80114 | KC-135R | 319th ARW | *r* |
| | 80115 | KC-135E | 108th ARW | *bl* |
| | 80116 | KC-135E | 161st ARW | |
| | 80117 | KC-135T | 92nd ARW | *r* |
| | 80118 | KC-135R | 18th Wg | *w* |
| | 80119 | KC-135R | 319th ARW | *bl* |
| | 80120 | KC-135R | 97th AMW | *y/r* |
| | 80121 | KC-135R | 507th ARW | *bl/y* |
| | 80122 | KC-135R | 168th ARW | *bl/y* |
| | 80123 | KC-135R | 22nd ARW | |
| | 80124 | KC-135R | 22nd ARW | *y/bl* |
| | 80125 | KC-135T | 92nd ARW | *y* |
| | 80126 | KC-135R | 22nd ARW | *y/bl* |
| | 80128 | KC-135R | 6th ARW | *y/bl* |
| | 80129 | KC-135T | 92nd ARW | *bl* |
| | 80130 | KC-135R | 128th ARW | *w/bl* |
| | *FY88* | | | |
| | 86005 | EC-137D | 88th ABW | |
| | *FY59* | | | |
| | 91444 | KC-135R | 121st ARW | *bl* |
| | 91445 | KC-135E | 141st ARW | *gn/w* |
| | 91446 | KC-135R | 186th ARW | *bk/gd* |
| | 91447 | KC-135E | 927th ARW | *pr/w* |
| | 91448 | KC-135R | 163rd ARW | *bl/w* |
| | 91450 | KC-135R | 163rd ARW | *bl/w* |
| | 91451 | KC-135E | 927th ARW | *pr/w* |
| | 91453 | KC-135R | 121st ARW | *bl* |
| | 91455 | KC-135R | 186th ARW | *bk/gd* |
| | 91456 | KC-135E | 108th ARW | *bk/y* |
| | 91457 | KC-135E | 171st ARW | *bk/y* |
| | 91458 | KC-135R | 121st ARW | *bl* |
| | 91459 | KC-135R | 97th AMW | *y/r* |
| | 91460 | KC-135T | 92nd ARW | *bk* |
| | 91461 | KC-135R | 168th ARW | *bl/y* |
| | 91462 | KC-135T | 22nd ARW | *y/bl* |
| | 91463 | KC-135R | 155th ARW | *r/w* |
| | 91464 | KC-135T | 92nd ARW | *bk* |
| | 91466 | KC-135R | 107th ARW | *bl* |
| | 91467 | KC-135T | 92nd ARW | *bl* |
| | 91468 | KC-135T | 92nd ARW | *bl* |
| | 91469 | KC-135R | 916th ARW | *gn* |
| | 91470 | KC-135T | 92nd ARW | *bl* |
| | 91471 | KC-135T | 92nd ARW | *r* |
| | 91472 | KC-135R | 154th Wg | *y/bk* |
| | 91473 | KC-135E | 151st ARW | *bl/bk* |
| | 91474 | KC-135T | 92nd ARW | *y* |
| | 91475 | KC-135R | 319th ARW | *y* |
| | 91476 | KC-135R | 97th AMW | *y/r* |
| | 91477 | KC-135E | 927th ARW | *pr/w* |
| | 91478 | KC-135R | 186th ARW | *bk/gd* |
| | 91479 | KC-135E | 171st ARW | *y/bk* |
| | 91480 | KC-135T | 92nd ARW | *y* |
| | 91482 | KC-135R | 319th ARW | *bl* |
| | 91483 | KC-135R | 121st ARW | *bl* |

| Type | | | | Notes |
|---|---|---|---|---|
| 91484 | KC-135E | 171st ARW | *bk/y* | |
| 91485 | KC-135E | 108th ARW | *bl* | |
| 91486 | KC-135R | 22nd ARW | *y/bl* | |
| 91487 | KC-135E | 126th ARW | *w/bl* | |
| 91488 | KC-135R | 22nd ARW | *y/r* | |
| 91489 | KC-135E | 151st ARW | *bl/bk* | |
| 91490 | KC-135T | 92nd ARW | *bk* | |
| 91492 | KC-135R | 18th Wg | *w* | |
| 91493 | KC-135E | 101st ARW | *w/gn* | |
| 91495 | KC-135R | 155th ARW | *r/w* | |
| 91496 | KC-135E | 171st ARW | *y/bk* | |
| 91497 | KC-135E | 108th ARW | *bl* | |
| 91498 | KC-135R | 366th Wg | *y/gn* | |
| 91499 | KC-135R | 163rd ARW | *bl/w* | |
| 91500 | KC-135R | 19th ARG | *y/bl* | |
| 91501 | KC-135R | 319th ARW | | |
| 91502 | KC-135R | 6th ARW | *y/bl* | |
| 91503 | KC-135E | 108th ARW | *bk/y* | |
| 91504 | KC-135T | 92nd ARW | *y* | |
| 91505 | KC-135R | 163rd ARW | *bl/w* | |
| 91506 | KC-135E | 171st ARW | *bk/y* | |
| 91507 | KC-135R | 22nd ARW | *y/bl* | |
| 91508 | KC-135R | 319th ARW | *r* | |
| 91509 | KC-135R | 163rd ARW | *bl/w* | |
| 91510 | KC-135T | 22nd ARW | *y/bk* | |
| 91511 | KC-135R | 319th ARW | *w* | |
| 91512 | KC-135T | 92nd ARW | *gn* | |
| 91513 | KC-135T | 92nd ARW | *bl* | |
| 91515 | KC-135R | 18th Wg | *w* | |
| 91516 | KC-135R | 163rd ARW | *bl/w* | |
| 91517 | KC-135R | 97th AMW | *y/r* | |
| 91518 | C-135K | 15th ABW | | |
| 91519 | KC-135E | 171st ARW | *y/bk* | |
| 91520 | KC-135T | 92nd ARW | *bl* | |
| 91521 | KC-135R | 168th ARW | *bl/y* | |
| 91522 | KC-135R | 107th ARW | *bl* | |
| 91523 | KC-135T | 92nd ARW | *bk* | |

**Lockheed C-141 Starlifter**

62nd AW, McChord AFB, Washington: 4th AS (*gn/r*) & 8th AS (*gn/si*);
155th AS/164th AW, Memphis, Tennessee ANG (*r*);
183rd AS/172nd AW, Jackson Int'l Airport, Mississippi ANG (*bl*);
305th AMW, McGuire AFB, New Jersey: 6th AS, 13th AS & 18th AS (*bl*);
445th AW AFRC, Wright-Patterson AFB, Ohio: 89th AS & 356th AS (*si*);
452nd AMW AFRC, March ARB, California: 729th AS & 730th AS (*r/y*);
756th AS/459th AW, AFRC, Andrews AFB, Maryland (*y/bk*)

**C-141B/C-141C***

| Type | | | Notes |
|---|---|---|---|
| *FY61* | | | |
| 12778* | 164th AW | *r* | |
| *FY63* | | | |
| 38076 | 62nd AW | *gn/r* | |
| 38080* | 164th AW | *r* | |
| 38081 | 62nd AW | *gn/si* | |
| 38082 | 62nd AW | *gn* | |
| 38084* | 452nd AMW | *r/y* | |
| 38085* | 452nd AMW | *r/y* | |
| 38088 | | | |
| *FY64* | | | |
| 40611 | 62nd AW | *gn/r* | |
| 40612 | | | |
| 40614 | 172nd AW | *bl* | |
| 40615 | 62nd AW | *gn/si* | |
| 40616 | 305th AMW | *bl* | |
| 40618 | | | |
| 40619 | 305th AMW | *bl* | |
| 40620 | 459th AW | *y/bk* | |
| 40621 | | | |
| 40622 | 172nd AW | *bl* | |
| 40627* | 164th AW | *r* | |
| 40628 | | | |
| 40630 | 305th AMW | *bl* | |
| 40631 | 62nd AW | *gn* | |
| 40632 | 172nd AW | *bl* | |
| 40633 | 62nd AW | *gn/si* | |
| 40637 | 459th AW | *y/bk* | |
| 40638 | 305th AMW | *bl* | |
| 40640 | 172nd AW | *bl* | |
| 40643 | 62nd AW | *gn/r* | |
| 40645 | 459th AW | *y/bk* | |
| 40646 | 305th AMW | *bl* | |
| 40649 | 305th AMW | *bl* | |
| *FY65* | | | |
| 50216* | 459th AW | *y/bk* | |
| 50217 | | | |
| 50218 | 62nd AW | *gn/r* | |
| 50219 | | | |
| 50220 | 305th AMW | *bl* | |
| 50221 | 305th AMW | *bl* | |
| 50222* | 164th AW | *r* | |
| 50224 | 305th AMW | *bl* | |
| 50225* | 452nd AMW | *r/y* | |
| 50226 | 459th AW | *y/bk* | |
| 50229* | 452nd AMW | *r/y* | |
| 50230 | 62nd AW | *gn/r* | |
| 50231 | 62nd AW | *gn* | |
| 50232* | 445th AW | *si* | |
| 50235 | 62nd AW | *gn/si* | |
| 50237 | 445th AW | *si* | |
| 50238 | 62nd AW | *gn/si* | |
| 50239 | 62nd AW | *gn/r* | |
| 50240 | 62nd AW | *gn* | |
| 50241 | 62nd AW | *gn/r* | |
| 50244 | 62nd AW | *gn/si* | |
| 50245* | 452nd AMW | *r/y* | |
| 50248* | 452nd AMW | *r/y* | |
| 50249* | 445th AW | *si* | |
| 50250 | 445th AW | *si* | |
| 50251 | 62nd AW | *gn/si* | |
| 50254 | 62nd AW | | |
| 50256* | 445th AW | *si* | |
| 50257* | 452nd AMW | *r/y* | |
| 50258 | 445th AW | *si* | |
| 50259 | 62nd AW | *gn/si* | |
| 50261* | 445th AW | *si* | |
| 50266 | 305th AMW | *bl* | |
| 50267 | 62nd AW | *gn/r* | |
| 50269 | | | |
| 50271* | 459th AW | *y/bk* | |
| 50273 | 305th AMW | *bl* | |
| 50276 | | | |
| 50279 | 305th AMW | *bl* | |
| 50280 | 305th AMW | *bl* | |
| 59401 | 305th AMW | *bl* | |
| 59403 | 62nd AW | *gn/si* | |
| 59408 | 305th AMW | *bl* | |
| 59409* | 445th AW | *si* | |
| 59411 | 305th AMW | *bl* | |
| 59412* | 445th AW | *si* | |
| 59413 | 305th AMW | *bl* | |
| 59414* | 452nd AMW | *r/y* | |
| *FY66* | | | |
| 60130 | 172nd AW | *bl* | |
| 60131 | 305th AMW | *bl* | |
| 60132 | 445th AW | *si* | |
| 60133 | 305th AMW | *bl* | |

| Notes | Type | | |
|---|---|---|---|
| | 60134* | 445th AW | *si* |
| | 60136* | 452nd AMW | *r/y* |
| | 60137 | 62nd AW | *m* |
| | 60139* | 164th AW | *r* |
| | 60140 | 62nd AW | *gn* |
| | 60144 | 62nd AW | |
| | 60146 | | |
| | 60147 | 62nd AW | |
| | 60148* | 445th AW | *si* |
| | 60149 | 62nd AW | *gn/r* |
| | 60151* | 452nd AMW | *r/y* |
| | 60152* | 452nd AMW | *r/y* |
| | 60153 | 459th AW | *y/bk* |
| | 60155 | 305th AMW | *bl* |
| | 60156 | | |
| | 60157* | 164th AW | *r* |
| | 60158 | 62nd AW | *gn/r* |
| | 60160 | 62nd AW | *gn/r* |
| | 60161 | | |
| | 60162 | 305th AMW | *bl* |
| | 60163 | 305th AMW | *bl* |
| | 60164* | 172nd AW | *bl* |
| | 60165 | 62nd AW | *gn/r* |
| | 60166 | 305th AMW | *bl* |
| | 60167* | 452nd AMW | *r/y* |
| | 60168 | 305th AMW | *bl* |
| | 60169 | 305th AMW | *bl* |
| | 60171 | 62nd AW | *gn/r* |
| | 60174 | 459th AW | *y/bk* |
| | 60175 | 62nd AW | *gn/si* |
| | 60177* | 445th AW | *si* |
| | 60181* | 452nd AMW | *r/y* |
| | 60182* | 452nd AMW | *r/y* |
| | 60183 | 62nd AW | *gn/r* |
| | 60184 | 62nd AW | *gn* |
| | 60185 | 172nd AW | *bl* |
| | 60187 | | |
| | 60190 | 172nd AW | *bl* |
| | 60191* | 172nd AW | *bl* |
| | 60192 | | |
| | 60193* | 445th AW | *si* |
| | 60194 | 305th AMW | *bl* |

| Notes | Type | | |
|---|---|---|---|
| | 60195 | 62nd AW | *gn/r* |
| | 60196 | 305th AMW | *bl* |
| | 60197 | 62nd AW | *gn/r* |
| | 60199 | 445th AW | *si* |
| | 60201 | 452nd AMW | *r/y* |
| | 60202 | 305th AMW | *bl* |
| | 60206 | 62nd AW | *gn/si* |
| | 60209 | 62nd AW | *gn/si* |
| | 67944 | 62nd AW | *gn/r* |
| | 67947 | | |
| | 67948 | 305th AMW | *bl* |
| | 67950* | 445th AW | *si* |
| | 67952* | 452nd AMW | *r/y* |
| | 67953 | 445th AW | *si* |
| | 67954* | 445th AW | *si* |
| | 67955 | 62nd AW | *gn/si* |
| | 67956 | 62nd AW | *gn/bl* |
| | 67957* | 452nd AMW | *r/y* |
| | 67959 | 445th AW | *si* |
| | *FY67* | | |
| | 70002 | 62nd AW | *gn* |
| | 70003 | 305th AMW | *bl* |
| | 70004 | 305th AMW | *bl* |
| | 70010 | 305th AMW | *bl* |
| | 70011 | 305th AMW | *bl* |
| | 70012 | 305th AMW | *bl* |
| | 70013 | 305th AMW | *bl* |
| | 70014 | 305th AMW | *bl* |
| | 70015* | 452nd AMW | *r/y* |
| | 70016 | 305th AMW | *bl* |
| | 70018 | 62nd AW | *gn* |
| | 70019 | 305th AMW | *bl* |
| | 70020 | 305th AMW | *bl* |
| | 70021 | 164th AW | *r* |
| | 70022 | | |
| | 70024* | 164th AW | *r* |
| | 70027* | 459th AW | *y/bk* |
| | 70028 | 62nd AW | *gn/si* |
| | 70029* | 164th AW | *r* |
| | 70031* | 445th AW | *si* |
| | 70165 | | |
| | 70166 | 305th AMW (VIP) | |

Carrying the name *Spirit of Indiana* on its undercarriage doors, this Northrop B-2 Spirit (21069) is flown by crews from the 509th BW at Whiteman AFB, MI. *PRM*

# US-based USN/USMC Aircraft

**Lockheed P-3 Orion**
CinCLANT/VP-30, NAS Jacksonville, Florida;
CinCPAC/ETD, MCBH Kaneohe Bay, Hawaii;
CinCUSNAVFOREUR, NAF Sigonella, Italy;
CNO/VP-30, NAS Jacksonville, Florida;
NAF Keflavik, Iceland;
NASC-FS, Point Mugu, California;
NAWC 23, Dallas/Love Field, Texas;
Navy Research Lab, Patuxent River, Maryland;
NFATS, Patuxent River, Maryland;
NWTSPM, NAS Point Mugu, California;
USNTPS, NAS Point Mugu, California;
VP-1, NAS Whidbey Island, Washington [YB];
VP-4, MCBH Kaneohe Bay, Hawaii [YD];
VP-5, NAS Jacksonville, Florida [LA];
VP-8, NAS Brunswick, Maine [LC];
VP-9, MCBH Kaneohe Bay, Hawaii [PD];
VP-10, NAS Brunswick, Maine [LD];
VP-16, NAS Jacksonville, Florida [LF];
VP-26, NAS Brunswick, Maine [LK];
VP-30, NAS Jacksonville, Florida [LL];
VP-40, NAS Whidbey Island, Washington [QE];
VP-45, NAS Jacksonville, Florida [LN];
VP-46, NAS Whidbey Island, Washington [RC];
VP-47, MCBH Kaneohe Bay, Hawaii [RD];
VP-62, NAS Jacksonville, Florida [LT];
VP-64, NAS Willow Grove, Pennsylvania [LU];
VP-65, NAS Point Mugu, California [PG];
VP-66, NAS Willow Grove, Pennsylvania [LV];
VP-69, NAS Whidbey Island, Washington [PJ];
VP-92, NAS Brunswick, Maine [LY];
VP-94, NAS New Orleans, Louisiana [PZ];
VPU-1, NAS Brunswick, Maine;
VPU-2, MCBH Kaneohe Bay, Hawaii;
VQ-1, NAS Whidbey Island, Washington [PR];
VQ-2, NAF Rota, Spain;
VQ-11, NAS Brunswick, Maine [LP];
VX-1, NAS Patuxent River, Maryland

| | | | |
|---|---|---|---|
| 148883 | | NP-3D | NFATS |
| 148889 | | UP-3A | VPU-2 |
| 149674 | | NP-3D | NRL |
| 149675 | | VP-3A | CinCPAC |
| 149676 | | VP-3A | CNO |
| 150495 | | UP-3A | NAF Keflavik |
| 150496 | | VP-3A | CinCLANT |
| 150499 | [337] | NP-3D | NWTSPM |
| 150511 | | VP-3A | CinCUSNAV FOREUR |
| 150515 | | VP-3A | VP-30 |
| 150521 | [341] | NP-3D | NWTSPM |
| 150522 | [340] | NP-3D | NWTSPM |
| 150524 | [335] | NP-3D | NWTSPM |
| 150525 | [336] | NP-3D | NWTSPM |
| 150526 | | UP-3A | |
| 151392 | | TP-3A | VP-47 |
| 152150 | | NP-3D | NFATS |
| 152739 | | NP-3B | NASC-FS |
| 153442 | | NP-3D | NRL |
| 153443 | | NP-3D | USNTPS |
| 154587 | | NP-3D | NRL |
| 154589 | | NP-3D | NRL |
| 156507 | [PR-31] | EP-3E | VQ-1 |
| 156509 | | P-3C | VP-8 |
| 156510 | [LL-44] | P-3C | VP-30 |
| 156511 | [PR-32] | EP-3E | VQ-1 |
| 156514 | [PR-33] | EP-3E | VQ-1 |
| 156515 | [LY-515] | P-3C | VP-92 |
| 156516 | [LL-38] | P-3C | VP-30 |
| 156517 | [PR-34] | EP-3E | VQ-1 |
| 156518 | [LL-49] | P-3C | VP-30 |
| 156519 | [21] | EP-3E | VQ-2 |
| 156520 | [10] | P-3C | VQ-2 |
| 156521 | [LY-521] | P-3C | VP-92 |
| 156522 | [LL-46] | P-3C | VP-30 |
| 156523 | [LL-39] | P-3C | VP-30 |
| 156525 | [11] | P-3C | VQ-2 |
| 156527 | | P-3C | |
| 156528 | [PR-36] | EP-3E | VQ-1 |
| 156529 | [24] | EP-3E | VQ-2 |
| 156530 | [LL-45] | P-3C | VP-30 |
| 157310 | [LL-473] | P-3C | VP-16 |
| 157311 | | P-3C | VP-45 |
| 157312 | | P-3C | |
| 157313 | [LD-313] | P-3C | VP-10 |
| 157314 | [LK-314] | P-3C | VP-26 |
| 157315 | | P-3C | VP-16 |
| 157316 | [23] | EP-3E | VQ-2 |
| 157317 | | P-3C | VP-1 |
| 157318 | [PR-35] | EP-3E | VQ-1 |
| 157319 | [LF-319] | P-3C | VP-16 |
| 157321 | [LK-321] | P-3C | VP-26 |
| 157322 | [322] | P-3C | VP-1 |
| 157323 | | P-3C | VP-62 |
| 157324 | [PD-324] | P-3C | VP-9 |
| 157325 | [25] | EP-3E | VQ-2 |
| 157326 | [22] | EP-3E | VQ-2 |
| 157327 | [LK-327] | P-3C | VP-26 |
| 157328 | [LL-42] | P-3C | VP-30 |
| 157329 | [RD-329] | P-3C | VP-47 |
| 157330 | [LC-330] | P-3C | VP-8 |
| 157331 | [LL-47] | P-3C | VP-30 |
| 158204 | [204] | P-3C | NFATS |
| 158205 | [QE-205] | P-3C | VP-40 |
| 158206 | [JA-03] | P-3C | VX-1 |
| 158207 | [LC-207] | P-3C | VP-8 |
| 158208 | [RD-208] | P-3C | VP-47 |
| 158209 | [QE-209] | P-3C | VP-40 |
| 158210 | [210] | P-3C | VP-8 |
| 158211 | [211] | P-3C | VP-1 |
| 158212 | [QE-212] | P-3C | VP-40 |
| 158214 | [LL-48] | P-3C | VP-30 |
| 158215 | [YD-215] | P-3C | VP-4 |
| 158216 | | P-3C | |
| 158218 | [RD-218] | P-3C | VP-47 |
| 158219 | [LN-219] | P-3C | VP-45 |
| 158220 | | P-3C | VP-47 |
| 158221 | [RC-221] | P-3C | VP-46 |
| 158222 | [QE-222] | P-3C | VP-40 |
| 158223 | [PD-223] | P-3C | VP-9 |
| 158224 | [LK-224] | P-3C | VP-26 |
| 158225 | [RD-225] | P-3C | VP-47 |
| 158226 | [226] | P-3C | VP-47 |
| 158227 | [227] | NP-3D | NRL |
| 158563 | [LD-563] | P-3C | VP-10 |
| 158564 | [LK-564] | P-3C | VP-26 |
| 158565 | [LK-565] | P-3C | VP-26 |
| 158566 | [LN-566] | P-3C | VP-45 |
| 158567 | [LF-567] | P-3C | VP-16 |
| 158568 | [LC-568] | P-3C | VP-8 |
| 158569 | [569] | P-3C | VP-16 |
| 158570 | [LN-570] | P-3C | VP-45 |
| 158571 | [LA-571] | P-3C | VP-5 |
| 158572 | [LA-572] | P-3C | VP-5 |
| 158573 | [LD-573] | P-3C | VP-10 |
| 158574 | | P-3C | NASC-FS |
| 158912 | | P-3C | NFATS |
| 158913 | [QE-913] | P-3C | VP-40 |
| 158914 | [RC-914] | P-3C | VP-46 |
| 158915 | [915] | P-3C | VP-40 |
| 158916 | [LL-30] | P-3C | VP-30 |

| | | | |
|---|---|---|---|
| 158917 | [LC-917] | P-3C | VP-8 |
| 158918 | [YD-918] | P-3C | VP-4 |
| 158919 | [LD-919] | P-3C | VP-10 |
| 158920 | [LF-920] | P-3C | VP-16 |
| 158921 | [YD-921] | P-3C | VP-4 |
| 158922 | [RD-922] | P-3C | VP-47 |
| 158923 | [923] | P-3C | VP-4 |
| 158924 | [LF-924] | P-3C | VP-16 |
| 158925 | [LD-925] | P-3C | VP-10 |
| 158926 | [LD-926] | P-3C | VP-10 |
| 158927 | [927] | P-3C | VP-5 |
| 158929 | [LD-929] | P-3C | VP-10 |
| 158931 | [LN-931] | P-3C | VP-45 |
| 158932 | [LN-932] | P-3C | VP-45 |
| 158933 | [933] | P-3C | VP-45 |
| 158934 | [QE-934] | P-3C | VP-40 |
| 158935 | [LL-43] | P-3C | VP-30 |
| 159318 | [YD-318] | P-3C | VP-4 |
| 159319 | [LK-319] | P-3C | VP-26 |
| 159320 | [320] | P-3C | VP-10 |
| 159321 | [RC-321] | P-3C | VP-46 |
| 159322 | [LD-322] | P-3C | VP-10 |
| 159323 | [RC-323] | P-3C | VP-46 |
| 159324 | [YD-324] | P-3C | VP-4 |
| 159326 | [326] | P-3C | VP-1 |
| 159327 | [PD-327] | P-3C | VP-9 |
| 159328 | [RC-328] | P-3C | VP-46 |
| 159329 | [329] | P-3C | VP-1 |
| 159503 | [LC-503] | P-3C | VP-8 |
| 159504 | | P-3C | VPU-2 |
| 159506 | [568] | P-3C | VPU-1 |
| 159507 | [507] | P-3C | VP-47 |
| 159512 | [LL-16] | P-3C | VP-30 |
| 159513 | [LL-18] | P-3C | VP-30 |
| 159514 | [LL-19] | P-3C | VP-30 |
| 159884 | [LL-14] | P-3C | VP-30 |
| 159885 | [PD-885] | P-3C | VP-9 |
| 159886 | [LL-15] | P-3C | VP-30 |
| 159887 | | P-3C | NASC-FS |
| 159889 | [889] | P-3C | VX-1 |
| 159891 | [LN-891] | P-3C | VP-45 |
| 159894 | [LL-40] | P-3C | VP-30 |
| 160283 | [YB-283] | P-3C | VP-1 |
| 160284 | [LL-17] | P-3C | VP-30 |
| 160286 | [286] | P-3C | VP-26 |
| 160287 | [LK-287] | P-3C | VP-26 |
| 160288 | | P-3C | NASC-FS |
| 160290 | [290] | P-3C | NFATS |
| 160291 | [JA-05] | P-3C | VX-1 |
| 160292 | | P-3C | VPU-2 |
| 160293 | [293] | P-3C | VPU-2 |
| 160610 | [RC-610] | P-3C | VP-46 |
| 160611 | [LU-611] | P-3C | VP-64 |
| 160612 | [LV-612] | P-3C | VP-66 |
| 160761 | [LU-761] | P-3C | VP-64 |
| 160762 | [LV-762] | P-3C | VP-66 |
| 160763 | [LV-763] | P-3C | VP-66 |
| 160764 | [764] | P-3C | NRL |
| 160765 | [LC-765] | P-3C | VP-8 |
| 160766 | [RD-766] | P-3C | VP-47 |
| 160767 | [767] | P-3C | VP-66 |
| 160768 | | P-3C | VQ-1 |
| 160769 | [LK-769] | P-3C | VP-26 |
| 160770 | | P-3C | VP-8 |
| 160999 | [LP-999] | P-3C | VQ-11 |
| 161000 | [LF-000] | P-3C | VP-16 |
| 161001 | [LU-001] | P-3C | VP-64 |
| 161002 | [002] | P-3C | VP-16 |
| 161003 | [003] | P-3C | VP-9 |
| 161004 | [004] | P-3C | VP-8 |
| 161005 | [LU-005] | P-3C | VP-64 |
| 161006 | [006] | P-3C | VP-45 |
| 161007 | [LU-007] | P-3C | VP-64 |
| 161008 | | P-3C | VP-30 |
| 161009 | [LL-50] | P-3C | VP-30 |
| 161010 | [010] | P-3C | VP-8 |
| 161011 | [LK-011] | P-3C | VP-26 |
| 161012 | [YD-012] | P-3C | VP-4 |
| 161013 | [LV-013] | P-3C | VP-66 |
| 161014 | [LV-014] | P-3C | VP-66 |
| 161121 | [LT-121] | P-3C | VP-69 |
| 161122 | [224] | P-3C | VPU-1 |
| 161123 | [LU-123] | P-3C | VP-64 |
| 161124 | [LA-124] | P-3C | VP-5 |
| 161125 | [LV-125] | P-3C | VP-66 |
| 161126 | [PR-50] | P-3C | VQ-1 |
| 161127 | [127] | P-3C | VP-62 |
| 161128 | [128] | P-3C | VP-5 |
| 161129 | [LV-129] | P-3C | VP-66 |
| 161130 | [130] | P-3C | VP-1 |
| 161131 | [LU-131] | P-3C | VP-64 |
| 161132 | [QE-132] | P-3C | VP-40 |
| 161329 | [PG-329] | P-3C | VP-65 |
| 161330 | [YB-330] | P-3C | VP-1 |
| 161331 | [LU-331] | P-3C | VP-64 |
| 161332 | [PG-332] | P-3C | VP-65 |
| 161333 | [PG-333] | P-3C | VP-65 |
| 161334 | [PG-334] | P-3C | VP-65 |
| 161335 | [PZ-335] | P-3C | VP-94 |
| 161336 | | P-3C | VQ-11 |
| 161337 | [PG-337] | P-3C | VP-65 |
| 161338 | | P-3C | VP-16 |
| 161339 | [RD-339] | P-3C | VP-47 |
| 161340 | [LN-340] | P-3C | VP-45 |
| 161404 | | P-3C | VP-30 |
| 161405 | [RD-405] | P-3C | VP-47 |
| 161406 | [PG-406] | P-3C | VP-65 |
| 161407 | [PG-407] | P-3C | VP-65 |
| 161408 | [PZ-408] | P-3C | VP-94 |
| 161409 | [PZ-409] | P-3C | VP-94 |
| 161410 | | P-3C | NAWC 23 |
| 161411 | [LL-3] | P-3C | VP-30 |
| 161412 | [PG-412] | P-3C | VP-65 |
| 161413 | [LL-39] | P-3C | VP-30 |
| 161414 | [14] | P-3C | VQ-2 |
| 161415 | | P-3C | VP-30 |
| 161585 | [LY-585] | P-3C | VP-92 |
| 161586 | | P-3C | VP-30 |
| 161587 | [YD-587] | P-3C | VP-4 |
| 161588 | | P-3C | VP-30 |
| 161589 | [589] | P-3C | VP-9 |
| 161590 | | P-3C | VP-30 |
| 161591 | [PZ-591] | P-3C | VP-94 |
| 161592 | [PZ-592] | P-3C | VP-94 |
| 161593 | | P-3C | VP-30 |
| 161594 | | P-3C | VP-30 |
| 161595 | [PZ-595] | P-3C | VP-94 |
| 161596 | | P-3C | VP-30 |
| 161763 | [PD-763] | P-3C | VP-9 |
| 161764 | [YD-764] | P-3C | VP-4 |
| 161765 | [PJ-765] | P-3C | VP-69 |
| 161766 | [PJ-766] | P-3C | VP-69 |
| 161767 | [PD-767] | P-3C | VP-9 |
| 162314 | [LY-314] | P-3C | VP-92 |
| 162315 | [YD-315] | P-3C | VP-1 |
| 162316 | | P-3C | VP-92 |
| 162317 | [YD-317] | P-3C | VP-4 |
| 162318 | [PJ-318] | P-3C | VP-69 |
| 162770 | | P-3C | NFATS |
| 162771 | [YD-771] | P-3C | VP-4 |
| 162772 | [772] | P-3C | VP-1 |
| 162773 | [773] | P-3C | VP-40 |
| 162774 | [RD-04] | P-3C | NFATS |
| 162775 | [QE-775] | P-3C | VP-40 |
| 162776 | [LN-776] | P-3C | VP-45 |
| 162777 | [RD-777] | P-3C | VP-47 |

| | | | |
|---|---|---|---|
| 162778 | [LL-31] | P-3C | VP-30 |
| 162998 | [RD-998] | P-3C | VP-47 |
| 162999 | [PJ-999] | P-3C | VP-69 |
| 163000 | [PJ-000] | P-3C | VP-69 |
| 163001 | [LT-001] | P-3C | VP-62 |
| 163002 | [LT-002] | P-3C | VP-62 |
| 163003 | [PJ-003] | P-3C | VP-69 |
| 163004 | [LT-004] | P-3C | VP-62 |
| 163005 | [LT-005] | P-3C | VP-62 |
| 163006 | [JA-06] | P-3C | VX-1 |
| 163289 | [LT-289] | P-3C | VP-62 |
| 163290 | [PJ-290] | P-3C | VP-69 |
| 163291 | [LT-291] | P-3C | VP-62 |
| 163292 | [LF-292] | P-3C | VP-16 |
| 163293 | [LA-293] | P-3C | VP-5 |
| 163294 | [LY-294] | P-3C | VP-92 |
| 163295 | [LY-295] | P-3C | VP-92 |

**Boeing E-6 Mercury**
Boeing, McConnell AFB, Kansas;
VQ-3 & VQ-4, SCW-1, Tinker AFB, Oklahoma

| | | |
|---|---|---|
| 162782 | E-6B | VQ-3 |
| 162783 | E-6B | VQ-3 |
| 162784 | E-6B | VQ-3 |
| 163918 | E-6B | VQ-3 |
| 163919 | E-6B | VQ-3 |
| 163920 | E-6B | VQ-3 |
| 164386 | E-6A | VQ-3 |
| 164387 | E-6B | VQ-3 |
| 164388 | E-6A | VQ-4 |
| 164404 | E-6A | VQ-4 |
| 164405 | E-6A | VQ-4 |
| 164406 | E-6B | Boeing |
| 164407 | E-6A | VQ-4 |
| 164408 | E-6A | VQ-4 |
| 164409 | E-6B | VQ-4 |
| 164410 | E-6A | VQ-4 |

**McDonnell Douglas C-9B Skytrain II/DC-9-32***
VMR-1, Cherry Point MCAS, North Carolina;
VR-46, Atlanta, Georgia [JS];
VR-52, Willow Grove NAS, Pennsylvania [JT];
VR-56, Norfolk NAS, Virginia [JU];
VR-57, North Island NAS, California [RX];
VR-58, Jacksonville NAS, Florida [JV];
VR-59, NAS Fort Worth JRB, Texas [RY];
VR-61, Whidbey Island NAS, Washington [RS];

| | | |
|---|---|---|
| 159113 | [RX] | VR-57 |
| 159114 | [JS] | VR-46 |
| 159115 | [RX] | VR-57 |
| 159116 | [RX] | VR-57 |
| 159117 | [JU] | VR-56 |
| 159118 | [JU] | VR-56 |
| 159119 | [JU] | VR-56 |
| 159120 | [JU] | VR-56 |
| 160046 | | VMR-1 |
| 160047 | | VMR-1 |
| 160048 | [JV] | VR-58 |
| 160049 | [JV] | VR-58 |
| 160050 | [JV] | VR-58 |
| 160051 | [JV] | VR-58 |
| 161266 | [RY] | VR-59 |
| 161529 | [RY] | VR-59 |
| 161530 | [RY] | VR-59 |
| 162753 | [JT] | VR-52 |
| 162754 | [JT] | VR-52 |
| 163036* | [JT] | VR-52 |
| 163037* | [JT] | VR-52 |
| 163208* | [RY] | VR-59 |
| 163511* | [JS] | VR-46 |
| 163512* | [RX] | VR-57 |
| 163513* | [JV] | VR-58 |
| 164605* | [RS | VR-61 |
| 164606* | [RS] | VR-61 |
| 164607* | [RS] | VR-61 |
| 164608* | [RS] | VR-61 |

**Boeing TC-18F**
SCW-1, Tinker AFB, Oklahoma
165342
165343

**Grumman C-20D Gulfstream III/**
**C-20G Gulfstream IV***
VR-1, NAF Washington, Maryland;
VR-48, NAF Washington, Maryland [JR];
VR-51, MCBH Kaneohe Bay, Hawaii [RG]

| | | |
|---|---|---|
| 163691 | | VR-1 |
| 163692 | | VR-1 |
| 165093* | [JR] | VR-48 |
| 165094* | [JR] | VR-48 |
| 165151* | [RG] | VR-51 |
| 165152* | [RG] | VR-51 |
| 165153* | | |

**Lockheed C-130 Hercules**
NAWC-AD, NAS Patuxtent River, Maryland;
VR-53, NAF Washington, Maryland [WV];
VR-54, New Orleans NAS, Louisiana [CW];
VR-55, Moffett Field NAS, California [RU];
VR-62, Brunswick NAS,Maine [JW];
VMGR-152, Futenma MOAS, Japan [QD];
VMGR-234, NAS Fort Worth,Texas [QH];
VMGR-252, Cherry Point MCAS, North Carolina [BH];
VMGRT-253, Cherry Point MCAS,
North Carolina [GR];
VMGR-352, MCAS Miramar, California [QB];
VMGR-452, Stewart Field, New York [NY]

| | | | |
|---|---|---|---|
| 147572 | [QB] | KC-130F | VMGR-352 |
| 147573 | [QD] | KC-130F | VMGR-152 |
| 148246 | [GR] | KC-130F | VMGRT-253 |
| 148247 | [QD] | KC-130F | VMGR-152 |
| 148248 | [QD] | KC-130F | VMGR-152 |
| 148249 | [GR] | KC-130F | VMGRT-253 |
| 148890 | [GR] | KC-130F | VMGRT-253 |
| 148891 | [BH] | KC-130F | VMGR-252 |
| 148893 | [QD] | KC-130F | VMGR-152 |
| 148894 | [BH] | KC-130F | VMGR-252 |
| 148895 | [BH] | KC-130F | VMGR-252 |
| 148896 | [BH] | KC-130F | VMGR-252 |
| 148897 | [BH] | KC-130F | VMGR-252 |
| 148898 | [BH] | KC-130F | VMGR-252 |
| 148899 | [BH] | KC-130F | VMGR-252 |
| 149788 | [BH] | KC-130F | VMGR-252 |
| 149789 | [BH] | KC-130F | VMGR-252 |
| 149791 | [QB] | KC-130F | VMGR-352 |
| 149792 | [QB] | KC-130F | VMGR-352 |
| 149795 | [QB] | KC-130F | VMGR-352 |
| 149796 | [QB] | KC-130F | VMGR-352 |
| 149798 | [QB] | KC-130F | VMGR-352 |
| 149799 | [QD] | KC-130F | VMGR-152 |
| 149800 | [QB] | KC-130F | VMGR-352 |
| 149803 | [GR] | KC-130F | VMGRT-253 |
| 149804 | [GR] | KC-130F | VMGRT-253 |
| 149806 | | KC-130F | NAWC-AD |
| 149807 | [QD] | KC-130F | VMGR-152 |
| 149808 | [BH] | KC-130F | VMGR-252 |
| 149811 | [GR] | KC-130F | VMGRT-253 |
| 149812 | [QD] | KC-130F | VMGR-152 |
| 149815 | [QB] | KC-130F | VMGR-352 |
| 149816 | [QD] | KC-130F | VMGR-152 |
| 150684 | [GR] | KC-130F | VMGRT-253 |
| 150686 | [BH] | KC-130F | VMGR-252 |
| 150687 | [GR] | KC-130F | VMGRT-253 |
| 150688 | [GR] | KC-130F | VMGRT-253 |
| 150689 | [QB] | KC-130F | VMGR-352 |

| | | | |
|---|---|---|---|
| 150690 | [QD] | KC-130F | VMGR-152 |
| 151891 | | TC-130G | *Blue Angels* |
| 160013 | [QD] | KC-130R | VMGR-152 |
| 160014 | [QD] | KC-130R | VMGR-152 |
| 160015 | [QB] | KC-130R | VMGR-352 |
| 160016 | [QB] | KC-130R | VMGR-352 |
| 160017 | [QB] | KC-130R | VMGR-352 |
| 160018 | [QD] | KC-130R | VMGR-152 |
| 160019 | [QD] | KC-130R | VMGR-152 |
| 160020 | [QD] | KC-130R | VMGR-152 |
| 160021 | [QB] | KC-130R | VMGR-352 |
| 160022 | [QB] | KC-130R | VMGR-352 |
| 160240 | [QB] | KC-130R | VMGR-352 |
| 160625 | [BH] | KC-130R | VMGR-252 |
| 160626 | [BH] | KC-130R | VMGR-252 |
| 160627 | [BH] | KC-130R | VMGR-252 |
| 160628 | [BH] | KC-130R | VMGR-252 |
| 162308 | [QH] | KC-130T | VMGR-234 |
| 162309 | [QH] | KC-130T | VMGR-234 |
| 162310 | [QH] | KC-130T | VMGR-234 |
| 162311 | [QH] | KC-130T | VMGR-234 |
| 162785 | [QH] | KC-130T | VMGR-234 |
| 162786 | [QH] | KC-130T | VMGR-234 |
| 163022 | [QH] | KC-130T | VMGR-234 |
| 163023 | [QH] | KC-130T | VMGR-234 |
| 163310 | [QH] | KC-130T | VMGR-234 |
| 163311 | [NY] | KC-130T | VMGR-452 |
| 163591 | [NY] | KC-130T | VMGR-452 |
| 163592 | [NY] | KC-130T | VMGR-452 |
| 164105 | [NY] | KC-130T | VMGR-452 |
| 164106 | [NY] | KC-130T | VMGR-452 |
| 164180 | [NY] | KC-130T | VMGR-452 |
| 164181 | [NY] | KC-130T | VMGR-452 |
| 164441 | [QH] | KC-130T | VMGR-234 |
| 164442 | [NY] | KC-130T | VMGR-452 |
| 164597 | [NY] | KC-130T-30 | VMGR-452 |
| 164598 | [QH] | KC-130T-30 | VMGR-234 |
| 164762 | | C-130T | NAWC-AD |
| 164763 | | C-130T | NAWC-AD |
| 164993 | [CW] | C-130T | VR-54 |
| 164994 | [WV] | C-130T | VR-53 |
| 164995 | [CW] | C-130T | VR-54 |
| 164996 | [WV] | C-130T | VR-53 |
| 164997 | [WV] | C-130T | VR-53 |
| 164998 | [WV] | C-130T | VR-53 |
| 164999 | [QH] | KC-130T | VMGR-234 |
| 165000 | [QH] | KC-130T | VMGR-234 |
| 165158 | [CW] | C-130T | VR-54 |
| 165159 | [CW] | C-130T | VR-54 |
| 165160 | [CW] | C-130T | VR-54 |
| 165161 | [RU] | C-130T | VR-55 |
| 165162 | [QH] | KC-130T | VMGR-234 |
| 165163 | [QH] | KC-130T | VMGR-234 |
| 165313 | [JW] | C-130T | VR-62 |
| 165314 | [JW] | C-130T | VR-62 |
| 165315 | [NY] | KC-130T | VMGR-452 |
| 165316 | [NY] | KC-130T | VMGR-452 |
| 165348 | [JW] | C-130T | VR-62 |
| 165349 | [JW] | C-130T | VR-62 |
| 165350 | [RU] | C-130T | VR-55 |
| 165351 | [RU] | C-130T | VR-55 |
| 165352 | [NY] | KC-130T | VMGR-452 |
| 165353 | [NY] | KC-130T | VMGR-452 |
| 165378 | [RU] | C-130T | VR-55 |
| 165379 | [RU] | C-130T | VR-55 |
| 165735 | [BH] | KC-130J | VMGR-252 |
| 165736 | [BH] | KC-130J | VMGR-252 |
| 165737 | | KC-130J | |
| 165738 | | KC-130J | |
| 165739 | | KC-130J | |

# US based US Coast Guard Aircraft

**Grumman C-20B Gulfstream III**
USCG, Washington DC
01

**Lockheed HC-130H Hercules**
USCGS Barbers Point, Hawaii;
USCGS Clearwater, Florida;
USCGS Elizabeth City, North Carolina;
USCGS Kodiak, Alaska;
USCGS Sacramento, California

| | |
|---|---|
| 1500 | Elizabeth City |
| 1501 | Elizabeth City |
| 1502 | Elizabeth City |
| 1503 | Elizabeth City |
| 1504 | Elizabeth City |
| 1601 | Sacramento |
| 1602 | Barbers Point |
| 1603 | Sacramento |
| 1700 | Kodiak |
| 1701 | Barbers Point |
| 1702 | Barbers Point |
| 1703 | Sacramento |
| 1704 | Barbers Point |
| 1705 | Sacramento |
| 1706 | Kodiak |
| 1707 | Kodiak |
| 1708 | Kodiak |
| 1709 | Kodiak |
| 1710 | Kodiak |
| 1711 | Barbers Point |
| 1712 | Clearwater |
| 1713 | Clearwater |
| 1714 | Barbers Point |
| 1715 | Clearwater |
| 1716 | Clearwater |
| 1717 | Clearwater |
| 1718 | Clearwater |
| 1719 | Clearwater |
| 1720 | Clearwater |
| 1790 | Sacramento |

# US Government Aircraft

**BAe 125-800A (C-29A)**
Federal Aviation Administration, Oklahoma

| | |
|---|---|
| N94 | (88-0269) |
| N95 | (88-0270) |
| N96 | (88-0271) |
| N97 | (88-0272) |
| N98 | (88-0273) |
| N99 | (88-0274) |

**Gates LearJet 35A**
Phoenix Aviation/Flight International/
US Navy, Naples
N20DK
N50FN
N88JA

# Military Aviation Sites on the Internet

The list below is not intended to be a complete list of military aviation sites on the Internet. The sites listed cover Museums, Locations, Air Forces, Companies and Organisations that are mentioned elsewhere in 'Military Aircraft Markings'. Sites listed are in English or contain sufficient English to be understood reasonably well. Each site address is believed to be correct at the time of going to press. Please send any additional information or amendments by e-mail to HJCurtis@cwcom.net or prmavia@aol.com.

| *Name of site* | *Internet Dial (all prefixed 'http://')* |
|---|---|
| **MILITARY SITES-UK** | |
| No 8 Sqn | www.users.globalnet.co.uk/~8sqnwad/ |
| No 23 Sqn | www.users.globalnet.co.uk/~23sqnwad/ |
| No 30 Sqn | www.raf-lyneham.org.uk/page24.html |
| No 31 Sqn | members.xoom.com/kariba/31main.htm |
| No 42(R) Sqn | www.kinloss.raf.mod.uk/42rsqn.htm |
| No 47 Sqn | www.secant.co.uk/47sqn/ |
| No 56 Sqn | www.56firebirds.raf.mod.uk/ |
| No 101 Sqn | www.users.globalnet.co.uk/~roxburgh/ |
| No 120 Sqn | www.kinloss.raf.mod.uk/120sqn.htm |
| No 201 Sqn | www.kinloss.raf.mod.uk/201sqn.htm |
| No 206 Sqn | www.kinloss.raf.mod.uk/206sqn.htm |
| Blue Eagles Home Page | www.deltaweb.co.uk/eagles/ |
| DERA | www.dera.gov.uk/dera.htm |
| Fleet Air Arm | www.royal-navy.mod.uk/today/faa.htm |
| Ministry of Defence | www.mod.uk/ |
| RAF College Cranwell | www.cranwell.raf.mod.uk/ |
| RAF Cosford | www.raf.mod.uk/cosford/ |
| RAF Kinloss | www.kinloss.raf.mod.uk/ |
| RAF Lossiemouth | fly.to/raflossie/ |
| RAF Lyneham | www.lyneham.raf.mod.uk/ |
| RAF Marham | www.rafmarham.co.uk |
| RAF Northolt | www.northolt.com/ |
| RAF Northolt (unofficial) | www.fly.to/Northolt/ |
| RAF St Athan | ourworld.compuserve.com/homepages/st_athan/ |
| RAF Valley | www.ecafe.org/~paul/valley.htm |
| RAF Waddington | www.sandygordon.freeserve.co.uk/frames.htm |
| Red Arrows | www.deltaweb.co.uk/reds/redhome.htm |
| Royal Air Force | www.raf.mod.uk/ |
| Royal Air Force Recruitment | www.raf-careers.raf.mod.uk/ |
| Royal Auxiliary Air Force | www.rauxaf.mod.uk/ |
| University of London Air Sqn | www.raf.mod.uk/ulas |
| **MILITARY SITES – US** | |
| 86th AW Home Page | www.usafe.af.mil/bases/ramstein/ramstein.htm |
| 106th Rescue Wing, New York ANG | www.infoshop.com/106rescue/ |
| Air Combat Command | www.acc.af.mil/ |
| Air Force Flight Test Center (Edwards AFB) | www.edwards.af.mil/ |
| Air Force Reserve Command | www.afrc.af.mil/ |
| Air National Guard | www.ang.af.mil/ |
| AMARC - up to date list of aircraft | www.dm.af.mil/amarc/inventory.htm |
| Aviano Air Base | www.aviano.af.mil/ |
| Holloman Air Force Base | www.holloman.af.mil/ |
| Hurricane Hunters Home Page (53rd WRS) | www.hurricanehunters.com/ |
| Liberty Wing Home Page (48th FW) | www.lakenheath.af.mil/ |
| NASA | www.nasa.gov/ |
| Nellis Air Force Base | www.nellis.af.mil/ |
| RAF Mildenhall | www.mildenhall.af.mil/ |
| Spangdahlem Air Base | www.spangdahlem.af.mil/ |
| Travis Air Force Base | www.travis.af.mil/ |
| The Thunderbirds | www.nellis.af.mil/thunderbirds/ |
| USAF | www.af.mil/ |
| USAF Europe | www.usafe.af.mil/ |
| USAF World Wide Web Sites | www.af.mil/sites/ |
| US Army | www.army.mil/ |
| US Marine Corps | www.usmc.mil/ |
| US Navy | www.navy.mil/ |
| US Navy Patrol Squadrons (unofficial) | www.vpnavy.com/ |
| Whiteman Air Force Base | www.whiteman.af.mil/ |

## Military Aviation Internet

| *Name of site* | *Internet Dial (all prefixed 'http://')* |
|---|---|
| **MILITARY SITES – ELSEWHERE** | |
| 8 Wing Trenton (Canadian Forces) | www.8wing.trenton.dnd.ca/ |
| 301 Sqn Klu | www.301sqn.com/ |
| 315 Sqn Klu | www.geocities.com/Pentagon/Quarters/8440/ |
| Armée de l'Air | www.defense.gouv.fr/air/ |
| Armée de l'Air (unofficial) | www.mygale.org/06/airmil/index.shtml |
| Aeronautica Militare | www.aero-mil.difesa.it/ |
| Austrian Armed Forces (in German) | www.bmlv.gv.at/ |
| Belgian Air Force | www.mil.be/luchtmacht/baf/homeuk.htm |
| Brazilian Air Force | www.mat.ufrgs.br/~rudnei/FAB/english.html |
| Canadian Forces | www.achq.dnd.ca/ |
| East European Air Forces (unofficial) | mm.iit.uni-miskolc.hu/Data/Winx/ |
| Finnish Defence Force | www.mil.fi/english/ |
| Forca Aerea Portuguesa | www.emfa.pt/ |
| Frecce Tricolori | users.iol.it/gromeo/ |
| Hellenic Army Aviation | www.evansb.gr/haa/ |
| Indian Air Force | www.bharat-rakshak.com/IAF/ |
| Israeli Defence Force/Air Force | www.idf.il/ |
| Japan Air Self Defence Force | www.jda.go.jp/jasdf/indexE.htm |
| JbG-38 (in German) | members.xoom.com/jabog38/homepage.htm |
| Luftforsvaret | www.mil.no/luftforsvaret/ |
| Luftwaffe | www.bundeswehr.de/bundeswehr/streitkraefte/luftwaffe/luftwaffe.htm |
| NATO | www.nato.int |
| Royal Australian Air Force | www.adfa.oz.au/DOD/RAAF/ |
| Royal Danish Air Force (in Danish) | www.ftk.dk/hovedsid.htm |
| Royal Netherlands AF (unofficial) | web.inter.NL.net/hcc/D.vanDolderen/ |
| Royal New Zealand AF | www.airforce.mil.nz/ |
| Royal Thai Air Force | www.rtaf.mi.th |
| Singapore Air Force | www.mindef.gov.sg/rsaf/ |
| South African AF Site (unofficial) | www.geocities.com/CapeCanaveral/Lab/2789/saaf.htm |
| Spanish Air Force (unofficial) | www.geocities.com/Pentagon/2112/ |
| Swedish Air Force | www.mil.se/FM/flyg/index_e.html |
| Swedish Military Aviation (unofficial) | www.canit.se/%7Egriffon/aviation/ |
| Swiss Air Force (Unofficial) | www.airpic.ch/ |
| Swiss Armed Forces | www.vbs.admin.ch/internet/e/armee/ |
| Turkish General Staff (Armed Forces) | www.tsk.mil.tr/ |
| **AIRCRAFT & AERO ENGINE MANUFACTURERS** | |
| Aérospatiale | www.aerospatiale.fr/ |
| Aero Vodochody Ltd | www.ctx.cz/aero/ |
| Allison Engine Company | www.allison.com/ |
| BAE Systems | www.BAe.co.uk/ |
| Bell Helicopter Textron | www.bellhelicopter.textron.com/index.html |
| Boeing | www.boeing.com/ |
| Bombardier | www.bombardier.com/ |
| CFM International | www.cfm56.com/ |
| Daimler-Benz Aerospace AG | www.dasa.com/ |
| Dassault | www.dassault-aviation.com/ |
| Embraer | www.embraer.com/ |
| Fairchild Dornier | www.fairchilddornier.com/ |
| Fokker | www.fokker.com/ |
| General Electric | www.ge.com/ |
| GKN Westland | www.gkn-whl.co.uk/ |
| Gulfstream Aerospace | www.gulfstreamaircraft.com/ |
| Kaman Aerospace | www.kaman.com/ |
| LET | www.let.cz/ |
| Lockheed Martin | www.lmco.com/ |
| Lockheed Martin Skunk Works | www.skunkworks.net/ |
| Pilatus Britten-Norman | www.britten-norman.com/ |
| Raytheon (Beech, Hawker) | www.raytheon.com/rac/ |
| Rolls-Royce | www.rolls-royce.com/ |
| SAAB | www.saab.se/ |
| Sikorsky | www.sikorsky.com/ |
| **UK AVIATION MUSEUMS** | |
| Aviation Museums in Great Britain | www.rdg.ac.uk/AcaDepts/sn/wsn1/dept/av/gb.html |
| Bournemouth Aviation Museum | www.aviation-museum.co.uk/ |
| Brooklands Museum | www.motor-software.co.uk/brooklands/ |
| Caernarfon Air World | www.users.globalnet.co.uk/~airworld/caernarfonaw.htm |

| *Name of site* | *Internet Dial (all prefixed 'http://')* |
|---|---|
| City of Norwich Aviation Museum | www.mth.uea.ac.uk/~h720/aviation/conam.html |
| De Havilland Heritage Museum | www.netlink.co.uk/users/aeroflt/mus/mosqmus.htm |
| Flambards Village Theme Park | www.flambards.co.uk/ |
| Fly-In Guide to Aviation Museums in the UK | www.avnet.co.uk/greenawa/museums.html |
| Gatwick Aviation Museum | hometown.aol.com/pgvallance/ |
| The Helicopter Museum | www.Geocities.com/CapeCanaveral/Cockpit/2996/ |
| Imperial War Museum, Duxford | www.iwm.org.uk/duxford.htm |
| Imperial War Museum, Duxford (unofficial) | dspace.dial.pipex.com/town/square/rcy85/ |
| The Jet Age Museum | gac.future.easyspace.com/gac.htm |
| Lincs Aviation Heritage Centre | freespace.virgin.net/nick.tasker/ekirkby.htm |
| Midland Air Museum | fly.to/midlandairmuseum/ |
| Museum of Berkshire Aviation | fly.to/MuseumofBerkshireAviation/ |
| Museum of Flight, East Fortune | www.nms.ac.uk/flight/main.htm |
| Museum of Science & Industry, Manchester | www.msim.org.uk/ |
| Newark Air Museum | www.emnet.co.uk/Museums/NewarkAir/ |
| North East Aircraft Museum | members.tripod.com/~BDaugherty/neam.html |
| RAF Manston Spitfire & Hurricane Memorial | www.spitfire-museum.com/ |
| RAF Museum, Cosford | www.rafmuseum.org.uk/flat/cosford/ |
| RAF Museum, Hendon | www.rafmuseum.org.uk/ |
| Science Museum, South Kensington | www.nmsi.ac.uk/on-line/flight/ |
| Yorkshire Air Museum, Elvington | www.yorksairmuseum.freeserve.co.uk/ |
| **AVIATION SOCIETIES** | |
| Air Britain | www.air-britain.com/ |
| Air Britain Merseyside | members.xoom.com/ABM/ |
| Air North | www.airnorth.demon.co.uk/ |
| Cleveland Tailwatchers | members.aol.com/philc2/ctwhome.html |
| East London Aviation Society | dspace.dial.pipex.com/westrowops/ |
| Friends of Leeming Aviation Group | www.crakehal.demon.co.uk/aviation/flag.htm |
| Gatwick Aviation Society | www.totavia.com/hawkeye/ |
| Gilze-Rijen Aviation Society | fly.to/GRAS/ |
| Royal Aeronautical Society | www.raes.org.uk/ |
| St Athan Aviation group | dspace.dial.pipex.com/westrowops/stamu.htm |
| Scramble (Dutch Aviation Society) | www.scramble.nl/ |
| Solent Aviation Society | freespace.virgin.net/anthony.gordon/ |
| South Berkshire Aviation Society | www.sbas.ndirect.co.uk/ |
| Spitfire Society | www.ncl.ac.uk/~nsgg/s_soc1.htm |
| Turnhouse Aviation Group | wkweb1.cableinet.co.uk/j.woodrow/turnhouse/ |
| Ulster Aviation Society | www.d-n-a.net/users/dnetrAzQ/ |
| **OPERATORS OF HISTORIC AIRCRAFT** | |
| B-17 Preservation Ltd | www.deltaweb.co.uk/sallyb/ |
| Battle of Britain Memorial Flight | www.raf.mod.uk/on_display/bbmf.html |
| Catalina Online | www.users.dircon.co.uk/~catalina/ |
| Classic Jet Aircraft Company | www.cjac.flyer.co.uk/ |
| De Havilland Aviation | www.inter-plane.com/dehavilland/ |
| Eastern Stearman | www.swanton-morley.co.uk/ |
| Intrepid Aviation | www.deltaweb.co.uk/intrepid/ |
| Old Flying Machine Company | www.evoke.co.uk/ofmc/ |
| The Fighter Collection | www.avnet.co.uk/tfc/ |
| The Vulcan Operating Company | www.tvoc.co.uk/ |
| **SITES RELATING TO SPECIFIC TYPES OF MILITARY AIRCRAFT** | |
| The 655 Maintenance & Preservation Society | www.jetman.dircon.co.uk/xm655/ |
| The Avro Shackleton Page | www.home.aone.net.au/shack_one/ |
| B-24 Liberator | www.b24bestweb.com/ |
| B-52 Stratofortress Association | www.stratofortress.org/ |
| Blackburn Buccaneer | ourworld.compuserve.com/homepages/andrewbrooks1/ |
| Dassault Mirages | www.decollage.org/mirage/mirages.htm |
| EE Canberra | www.netcomuk.co.uk/~lesb/canberra.html |
| EE Lightning | homepages.enterprise.net/garry/light.html |
| The Eurofighter site | www.eurofighter.org/ |
| The ex FRADU Canberra Site | www.fraduhunters.flyer.co.uk/canberra/ |
| The ex FRADU Hunter Site | www.fraduhunters.flyer.co.uk/ |
| F-4 Phantom II Society | www.f4phantom.org/ |
| F-16: The Complete Reference | www.f-16.net/ |
| F-86 Web Page | www.geocities.com/CapeCanaveral/Launchpad/8608/ |
| F-105 Thunderchief | www.geocities.com/Pentagon/7002/ |
| The Gripen | www.gripen.saab.se/ |
| The Harrier | members.aol.com/stonker/harrier/harrier1.htm |

## Military Aviation Internet

| *Name of site* | *Internet Dial (all prefixed 'http://')* |
|---|---|
| International F-104 Society | detroit.freenet.org/~at892/ |
| Lockheed C-130 Hercules | www.spectrumwd.com/c130/ |
| Lockheed SR-71 Blackbird | www.wvi.com/~lelandh/sr-71~1.htm |
| The MiG-21 Page | www.topedge.com/panels/aircraft/sites/kraft/mig.htm |
| P-3 Orion Research Group | home.wxs.nl/~p3orin/ |
| P-51 Mustang | www.p51mustang.com/ |
| Swiss F-18 Hornet site (unofficial) | www.geocities.com/CapeCanaveral/Lab/6063/ |
| Thunder & Lightnings (Postwar British Aircraft) | www.totavia.com/jetman/ |
| Vulcan 558 Club | www.vulcan558club.demon.co.uk/ |
| Vulcan Restoration Trust | www.XL426.com |
| **MISCELLANEOUS** | |
| Aerodata | dspace.dial.pipex.com/aerodata/ |
| Aeroflight | www.netlink.co.uk/users/aeroflt/ |
| The 'AirNet' Links Site | fly.to/AirNet/ |
| The 'AirNet' Links Site (AOL) | members.aol.com/HJCurtis/ |
| AirSpeed | www.airspeed.ndirect.co.uk/ |
| The Aviator's Network | www.aviators.net/ |
| British Aviation Information Forum | www.comet3.demon.co.uk/baif/ |
| Chinese Military Aviation | www.concentric.net/~Jetfight/ |
| David Hastings' Military Aviation Page | users.ox.ac.uk/~daveh/Military/ |
| f4Aviation | www.f4aviation.co.uk |
| Farnborough Movements & Photographs | www.geocities.com/CapeCanaveral/hangar/1937/ |
| Military Aircraft Database | www.csd.uwo.ca/~pettypi/elevon/gustin_military/ |
| Military Aviation | www.crakehal.demon.co.uk/aviation/aviation.htm |
| Military Aviation Review/MAP | www.mar.co.uk/ |
| Polish Aviation Site | aviation.pol.pl/ |
| Scramble on the Web - Air Show Reports | www.scramble.nl/airshows.htm |
| The Spotter's Nest | www.spotters.it/ |
| UK Military Spotting | www.totavia.com/jetman/spotting/ |

A Pilatus PC-9 (L9-66) of 15 Brigada, Slovenian Army, landing at RAF Fairford in July 1999 for RIAT. *PRM*

Omani Government Boeing 747SP A40-SP, one of two that regularly visits the UK. *PRM*

Royal Netherlands Air Force Fokker 50 U-05. *Daniel March*

USAF/AMC C-17A Globemaster III flies out of Charleston AFB, SC, with the 437th AW. *PRM*

A very anonymous looking US Army AH-64A Apache based in Germany with the 6th Cavalry Regiment. *PRM*

Colourful Portuguese Air Force markings on Yeovilton-based Chipmunk 22. *Daniel March*

Fennec N°119 carries the former US serial 51-7545. *PRM*